Theory and Problems *of* Adolescent Development

DAVID P. AUSUBEL, M.D., Ph.D.

Bureau of Educational Research
University of Illinois, Champaign

GRUNE & STRATTON • New York 1954

Library of Congress Catalog Card Number 54-5776

By the same author:

EGO DEVELOPMENT AND THE
PERSONALITY DISORDERS
A Developmental Approach
to Psychopathology

Copyright © 1954
GRUNE & STRATTON, INC.
381 Park Avenue South
New York 16, New York

First printing - February 1954
Second printing - November 1957
Third printing - December 1958
Fourth printing - September 1960
Fifth printing - September 1962
PRINTED AND BOUND IN THE UNITED STATES OF AMERICA   (B)

Contents

PREFACE xii

PART ONE. INTRODUCTION

1. ADOLESCENCE: A STAGE IN PERSONALITY DEVELOPMENT............ 3
   The Field of Adolescent Psychology...................... 3
      What Justification for a Psychology of Adolescence...... 4
      The Place of Adolescent Psychology in Understanding
         Human Behavior 7
   Approaches to the Study of Adolescence.................. 8
      Biological Approaches to Adolescent Psychology........ 10
      Social Approaches to Adolescent Psychology........... 13
      Adolescence as a Stage of Personality Development..... 22
   The Problem of Evidence................................ 30
      Methods of Obtaining Developmental Data............ 31
      Conclusion 36

2. PROBLEMS OF ADOLESCENT DEVELOPMENT...................... 39
   Classification of Problems of Adolescent Development...... 39
      Psychobiological Problems 40
      Psychosocial Problems 44
   Continuity of Adolescence with Other Periods of Develop-
      ment 46
   The Chief Developmental Tasks of Adolescence........... 48

PART 2. PSYCHOBIOLOGICAL PROBLEMS

3. PROBLEMS OF PSYCHOLOGICAL TRANSITION..................... 53
   The Meaning of Psychological Transition.................. 55
   Transitional Anxiety 56
   Temporal Factors Influencing the Difficulty of Psychological
      Transition 57
      Abruptness of Onset............................... 57
      The Duration of Adolescence........................ 59
      Discrepancies in Rate of Growth.................... 61
   What Precipitates Psychological Transition............... 65
      The Prevention of Developmental Regression.......... 69
   Stages of Adolescence.................................. 70

4. PHYSIOLOGICAL ASPECTS OF PUBESCENCE...................... 73
    The Nature of Pubescence............................. 73
        Genetic Considerations 73
        Pubescence as a Psychobiological Problem............. 75
        Types of Pubescent Changes........................ 76
    The Initiation of Pubescence: Hormonal Changes.......... 78
    Primary Sex Characteristics............................. 81
    Secondary Sex Characteristics........................... 85
        Development of Breasts............................. 86
        Body Build 87
        Hair 88
        Sweat and Sebaceous Glands........................ 90
        Voice 91
    Temporal Aspects of Pubescence........................ 92
        Age Range for Onset of Pubescence.................. 92
        Criteria of Pubescence............................. 93
        Sequence of Pubescent Changes..................... 94
    Other Physiological Changes in Pubescence.............. 95
        Types of Physiological Changes..................... 95
    Health and Disease in Adolescence...................... 99
        Mortality and Morbidity Rates...................... 100
        Common Medical Problems of Adolescence............ 101

5. PHYSICAL GROWTH AND MOTOR DEVELOPMENT................. 108
    Factors Determining Skeletal Growth.................... 108
    Qualitative Changes in Skeletal Tissue.................. 109
    The Adolescent Growth Spurt.......................... 111
        Age of Pubescence in Relation to Adult Height........ 113
        Endocrine Aspects of the Adolescent Growth Spurt..... 114
    Changes in Body Weight............................... 116
    Changes in Body Proportions........................... 117
    Growth in Strength.................................... 118
    Motor Development during Adolescence.................. 119
        Gross Motor Skills................................. 121
        Mechanical Abilities 122
        Interest in Physical Activities...................... 124
        Adolescent Awkwardness 126
        Motor Ability and Personal-Social Adjustment........ 127

6. PSYCHOLOGICAL ACCOMPANIMENTS OF BODILY CHANGE............ 133
    Changes in Interests.................................. 134
    Recasting the Body Image............................. 135

Sex Drive and Sex Awareness............................. 136
    Preadolescent Sex Interests and Activities.............. 136
    The Relationship between Sex Hormones and Sex
        Drives 138
    Psychophysiological and Psychoaffectional Sex Patterns.. 141
Formulating a Biological Sex Role........................ 142
    Sex Role in Preadolescence........................... 142
    Facilitating Factors in Adolescence.................... 143
    Retarding Factors in Adolescence..................... 144
Changes in Emotional Expression......................... 145
    Nonspecific Changes in Emotional Reactivity........... 145
    Changes in Specific Emotions......................... 147
Problems Referable to Early or Late Maturation............ 148
Adjusting to Normal Somatic Changes..................... 150
    Interest in Grooming and Adornment................. 150
    Reaction to Normal Somatic Changes................. 151
Adjusting to Somatic Deviations.......................... 153
    Psychological Concomitants of Somatic Defects........ 154
Somatic Concomitants of Psychological Stress.............. 156
Types and Frequency of Somatic Deviations................ 157
    Primary Sex Characteristics.......................... 158
    Body Build 159
Why Somatic Deviations Are Important during Adolescence.. 160
Factors Determining the Seriousness of Outcome............ 162

7. PERSONALITY MATURATION DURING ADOLESCENCE................ 167
    Childhood as a Period of Dependency.................... 167
        Why Personality Structure Must Be Reorganized....... 174
    Attributes of Adolescent Personality Maturation.......... 175
        The Centrality of Self during Adolescence............ 176
        Adolescent Personality Compared to Infancy and Child-
            hood 177
    Continuity in Personality Development................... 180
        Psychological Bases of Consistency in Personality Develop-
            ment 182
    Preparatory Aspects of Personality Maturation.............. 185
        Factors Bringing About Preparatory Maturation........ 186
    Pubescence: Consummatory Factor in Personality Maturation 192
    Mechanisms of Desatellization........................... 194
        Desatellization through Resatellization............... 194
        Desatellization through the Achievement of Primary
            Status 197

Desatellization through the Exploratory Orientation.... 199
Facilitating and Retarding Factors in Maturation........... 200
  Familial Factors 200
  Cultural Factors 205
Personality Maturation in Non-Satellizers.................. 208
  Later Impact of Non-Satellization on Maturation....... 209

8. PARENT-CHILD RELATIONSHIPS IN ADOLESCENCE.................. 217
The Meaning of Emancipation.......................... 217
Factors Influencing the Nature and Attainment of Emancipa-
  tion 217
  Age Trends 217
  Mechanisms of Emancipation....................... 219
  Facilitating and Retarding Influences.................. 222
  The Unevenness of Emancipation.................... 223
Parent-Youth Conflict in Adolescence.................... 224
  Age Trends 224
  Overt Issues 225
  Underlying Causes 226
  Displacement of Conflict............................ 231
  The Prognosis of Parent-Youth Conflict.............. 232
Discipline in Adolescence.............................. 235
  The Need for Changed Methods of Control.......... 235
  The Need for Discipline in Adolescence.............. 237
Maturational Failure Attributable to Faulty Child Rearing
  Practices 238
  "Developmental" Failure 239
  "Reactive" Failure 241

9. MORAL AND RELIGIOUS DEVELOPMENT........................ 246
General Developmental Changes During Adolescence........ 246
  Greater Independence in Assimilation of Values........ 247
  Values Acquire a Wider Social Base.................. 249
  Changes Reflective of Intellectual Maturation.......... 249
  Decline in Moral Absolutism........................ 250
  Increased Reciprocity of Moral Obligation............ 251
  Greater Expediency in Moral Standards.............. 252
  Guilt Feelings in Relation to Age-Mate Socialization.... 253
Factors Influencing Individual Differences in Adolescent
  Moral Development 255
  Personality Type 255
  Socioeconomic Factors 259

The Moral Reputation of Adolescents..................... 262
The Moral Beliefs of Adolescents........................ 263
    General Characteristics 264
    Beliefs, Knowledge and Intelligence.................. 265
    Beliefs, Character and Conduct....................... 265
    Specific Beliefs and Attitudes........................ 266
Status of Religion during Adolescence.................... 268
    Acceptance or Rejection............................. 268
    Religious Observances 269
    Religious Beliefs 269
    Religious Doubts and Conflicts....................... 270
    The Impact of Adolescence on Religion............... 270
    The Impact of Religion on Personality................ 272

10. INTELLECTUAL GROWTH AND INTEREST PATTERNS................. 276
    Growth Characteristics of General Intelligence during Ado-
        lescence 276
        Effect of Pubescence on Intellectual Growth........... 277
        Stability of General Intelligence during Adolescence.... 279
        Distribution of Adolescent Intelligence............... 279
    Differential Aspects of Growth of Intelligence during Ado-
        lescence 280
        Sex Differences 280
        Impact of Socioeconomic Status..................... 280
        Growth Differences between Bright and Dull Adolescents 282
        Growth Differences among Separate Intellectual Abilities 283
        Differentiation of Intellectual Ability in Adolescence.... 284
    Other Aspects of Intellectual Growth during Adolescence... 285
    Interaction between Intellectual Growth and Personality.... 286
        Intelligence and Personality........................ 287
        Intelligence and Interest Patterns................... 288
        Intelligence and Adjustment........................ 289
        Impact of Personality Trait Development on Cognitive
            Organization 291
    The Nature of Adolescent Interests...................... 292
        The Meaning and Importance of Interests............. 292
        General Characteristics of Adolescent Interests......... 294
        Determinants of Adolescent Interests................. 295
    Recreational Interests 299
        Reading 300
        Mass Media 300
        Hobbies 301

PART THREE. PSYCHOSOCIAL PROBLEMS

11. ADOLESCENTS AND THE WIDER COMMUNITY...................... 311
    The Nature of Psychosocial Problems...................... 311
    Relationship of Adolescents to the Wider Community...... 313
        Increased Contact with and Awareness of the Social
            Order 313
        Acquisition of Adult Status in Modern Society.......... 315
        Estrangement between the Adolescent and Adult Society 316
    Prolongation of Adolescence in Modern Society............ 319
        Causes of Prolongation.............................. 319
        Effects of Prolongation.............................. 324
    Differentiation of the Social Environment................. 327
        Social Class Structure in the United States.............. 327
        Impact of Social Stratification on Adolescent Develop-
            ment 331
        Interaction between Social Classes..................... 333
    Transmission of Social Class Values and Aspirations........ 335
    Impact of Social Change on Adolescent Development....... 336

12. THE ADOLESCENT PEER CULTURE............................. 341
    Importance of Social Relationships during Adolescence...... 342
    The Adolescent Peer Group in Relation to the Wider Com-
        munity 343
    General Characteristics of Adolescent Group Life........... 345
        Greater Emphasis upon Subjective Experience.......... 345
        More Group Consciousness........................... 346
        Greater Stratification along Social Class Lines.......... 346
        Heterosexual Basis of Organization.................... 347
        Changes during the Course of Adolescence............. 348
    Structural Characteristics of Adolescent Peer Groups........ 348
        Origins of the Adolescent Peer Group................. 349
        Differentiation into Cliques.......................... 350
        Conformity Aspects of the Peer Culture............... 353
        Impact of Group Structural Needs on Adolescent Values 358
    Interpersonal Relationships within the Peer Group......... 359
        Individual Approaches to Group Experience........... 359
        Bases for Relative Status and Prestige in the Group.... 362
    Perception of Status in the Group........................ 366
    Adolescent Friendships with Age-Mates of the Same Sex..... 366
        Bases for the Selection of Friends..................... 367

The Stability of Adolescent Friendships............... 368
Sex Differences 369
Leadership in Adolescence............................ 369
   How Leadership Is Achieved and Maintained.......... 370
   Characteristics of Adolescent Leaders................. 372
   Stability of Leadership............................. 372
The Socially Rejected or Deviant Adolescent.............. 372
   Characteristics of Socially Rejected Adolescents........ 373
   Evaluation of Social Rejection...................... 374
   Helping the Socially Rejected Individual............. 375
   Prognosis of Deviancy............................. 376
Adolescent Gangs 376
   Varieties of Deviant Peer Groups.................... 376
   Street-Corner Gangs 377
Summary: Functions of Adolescent Peer Culture........... 382

13. SEXUAL BEHAVIOR IN ADOLESCENCE........................... 390
Psychosocial Aspects of Sexuality........................ 390
   Different Cultural Orientations Toward Sexuality..... 391
   Cultural Patterns of Regulating Adolescent Sex Activity.. 394
The Nature and Cultural Modifiability of Sex Behavior..... 396
   Preadolescent versus Adolescent Sexuality............ 397
   The Repressibility of Sex Urges...................... 398
   Detrimental Effects of Sex Repression................ 399
The Importance of Sexuality in Adolescent Development and
   Adjustment 401
   Relationships between Sexuality and Adolescent Person-
      ality Maturation 401
   Sexuality and Adolescent Adjustment................. 402
Varieties of Adolescent Sexual Expression in Our Culture... 405
   Frequency and Types of Sex Outlets in Boys.......... 405
   Social Class Differences............................ 407
   Sex Expression in Adolescent Girls.................. 409
   Evaluation of the Major Sex Outlets................. 412
Differentiation of Social Sex Roles....................... 414
   Components of Social Sex Role...................... 414
   The Impact of Pubescence on Social Sex Role......... 415
   The Transitional Social Sex Role of Adolescence....... 417
   Sex Differences in the Acquisition of Social Sex Role.... 418
   Biological or Social Determination of Social Sex Role.... 420
Heterosexual Peer Group and Courting Behavior.......... 421
   Developmental Changes in Heterosexual Relationships.. 422

Dating and Courting Beliefs........................ 425
Courtship Problems and Heterosexual Adjustment..... 426
Sex Education and Guidance.......................... 428
Adolescents' Sources of Sex Information.............. 428
The Need for Sex Education in the Schools........... 428
A Program of General Sex Education................ 429
Sex Guidance 432

14. PROBLEMS OF VOCATIONAL CHOICE IN ADOLESCENCE.............. 437
Developmental Changes in Vocational Choice............ 439
The Stability of Vocational Interests................. 441
Determinants of Vocational Choice....................... 442
Social Sex Role.................................... 443
Family Pressures 444
Social Class Factors and Socioeconomic Conditions..... 445
Individual Differences 448
An Evaluation of the Vocational Choices of Adolescents..... 453
Realistic or Unrealistic?........................... 453
Relationship to Factual Knowledge of Self and Job..... 455
Vocational Guidance 458
The Need for Vocational Guidance.................. 458
Vocational Guidance versus Psychotherapy........... 459
Foci of Concern in Vocational Guidance.............. 460
Work Experience during Adolescence..................... 465
Usefulness for Vocational Planning.................. 465
Other Values of Work Experience.................... 466
The Role of the School............................ 466

15. ADOLESCENTS AND THE SCHOOL.............................. 471
General Functions of the School During Adolescence...... 472
Impact of the School on the Developmental Tasks of Ado-
lescence 473
Emancipation from Parents........................ 473
The Acquisition of Primary Status.................. 474
Acquiring Greater Volitional Independence in Dealing
with Adults 475
Other Developmental Tasks of Adolescence.......... 481
Implications of Adolescent Personality Development for
School Learning 482
Impact of General Personality Changes on Learning
Orientation 483

Importance of Current Concerns.................... 485
Individual Differences 487
Implications of Adolescent Intellectual Development for
    School Practices 491
    The Problem of Meaningfulness...................... 491
    The Extension of Schooling......................... 494
    Grouping versus Individualization.................. 495
Social Stratification in the School........................ 496
    Middle-Class Domination of the High School Peer Group 496
    Favoritism by Teachers............................. 497
    Differential Social Class Motivation in the School Setting 498
    "Drop-Outs" as a Function of Social Class Status...... 498
The Adolescent's Evaluation of the School................ 499
What Can Be Done?............................... 500

PART FOUR. MALADJUSTMENT AND MENTAL HYGIENE

16. BEHAVIOR DISORDERS AND DELINQUENCY IN ADOLESCENCE......... 507
    The Evaluation of Behavior Disorder in Adolescence....... 507
        The Role of Emotional Instability................... 508
        The Importance of Childhood Experience............. 510
        The Role of Adolescence........................... 511
        The Meaning of Frustration........................ 513
    A Classification of Adolescent Behavior Disorders.......... 517
    Delinquency in Adolescence............................. 517
        Incidence 518
        The Problem of Culpability......................... 521
        Differential Diagnosis of Delinquency................ 523
        Etiological Factors 524
        Preventive Measures 532

17. MENTAL HYGIENE AND GUIDANCE............................. 537
    The Importance of Parent-Child Relationships in Preado-
        lescence 537
        The Difficulty of Changing Parent Attitudes.......... 538
    Improving Parent-Youth Relations...................... 539
    The Social Hygiene of Adolescence..................... 541
    Counseling in Adolescence............................. 543
    Some General Principles in Guiding Adolescents.......... 546

INDEX 549

Preface

THE AIM of this book is to organize around a comprehensive and integrated theory of adolescent development the vast quantity of research data that has accumulated over the past fifty years in the field of adolescent psychology. Underlying this effort is a conviction that in relation to a systematic theoretical frame of reference such data become more meaningful than a compilation of discrete findings subsumed under topical chapter headings.

Historically, the precedents for such an undertaking are not too encouraging. Partly as a consequence of the virtual collapse of G. Stanley Hall's elaborate biogenetic theory of psychological recapitulation during the past three decades, theoretic approaches to problems of developmental psychology have fallen into disrepute. This has been especially true in the field of adolescent psychology. Some attempts have been made in a theoretic direction by psychoanalytically oriented psychologists; but these efforts have neither been comprehensive in scope nor systematically related to research data.

Two unfortunate and not unrelated developments followed upon Hall's epochal failure to provide a tenable theoretic substructure for adolescent psychology. The most immediate reaction was the placing of undue emphasis upon the collection of objective data as an end in itself. Every conceivable measurable aspect of adolescence was literally measured to death. And although it is undeniable that any scientific discipline must necessarily be grounded upon empirical data, it is generally accepted today that the mere collection of facts undirected by organizing hypotheses is an unsystematic and uneconomical process leading inevitably to conceptual chaos and unintelligibility.

The other unfortunate development was largely an outgrowth of findings in the area of cultural anthropology which helped demolish Hall's theory by demonstrating the existence of cultural variability in the stressfulness and kinds of problems faced by adolescents. These findings, however, were overgeneralized to support the equally untenable position that no general principles of adolescent development exist, that adolescence is not a distinct stage in personality development but a constellation of problems common to teen-agers growing up under repressive social conditions. This point of view, which, in a sense, is a denial of the possibility of ever formulating a general theory of adolescent development, is the theoretic position most widely held today in conjunction with the empiric approach discussed above.* Most textbooks in the field implicitly accept the notion that adolescent psychology embraces no distinctive developmental principles of its own, but is merely general psychology, i.e., perception, learning, motivation, etc., in which special attention is given to variability in these latter phenomena as a function of adolescent age.

The central idea permeating every chapter of this book is that adolescence is a distinctive stage in personality development precipitated by significant changes in the biosocial status of the child. As a result of these changes, which are discontinuous with preceding biosocial conditions of growth, extensive reorganization of personality structure is required. Our thesis is that this process of reorganization shows certain basic uniformities from one culture to another—despite many specific differences in content and degree of stress—because of various common elements inhering in the general psychology of transition and in the psychological implications of sexual maturity, biological sex role, and the new personality traits associated with adult roles and status in the community. The core principle of this point of view is essentially the position adopted by Sherif and Cantril in their *Psychology of Ego-Involvements*. Starting from this basic premise, a systematic theory of adolescent development has been evolved and related to empirical evidence in the field.

Part One, the *Introduction* is devoted to an historical overview of different approaches to adolescent development and to problems of evidence and classification. A distinction is made between (1) *psychobiological* problems of adolescence, which are reflective of general developmental trends and hence, universal in distribution (despite specific cultural differences in form and content), and (2)

---

* To Sherif and Cantril belongs the credit for first seriously challenging this theoretical orientation (see p. 22 and reference *34* on p. 38).

psychosocial problems of adolescence, which are *wholly* conditioned by specific socio-economic factors and modes of regulation peculiar to our own social order.

Part Two deals with *psychobiological problems,* i.e., the psychology of transition; physiologic and physical growth; personality maturation and parent-child relationships; and intellectual and moral development. In the discussion of these problems, general principles of adolescent development are illustrated by reference to the specific forms they assume in our own culture.

Part Three discusses *psychosocial problems,* i.e., problems faced by adolescents in our culture because of the unique norms, traditions, and regulatory phenomena confronting them (e.g., prolongation of sub-adulthood, peer group socialization, extended schooling and vocational apprenticeship, rapid social change, war, economic depression, etc.). Hence, there are chapters dealing with social stratification, the peer culture, sexual behavior, vocational choice, and the school.

Part Four considers problems of behavior disorder, delinquency, mental hygiene and guidance.

A word about the chapters on physiologic and physical growth is in order. Strictly speaking, much of the detail given in these chapters is not relevant to adolescent psychology as such, but in a broader sense is part of adolescent development. Much effort has been expended in reinterpreting the endocrinologic phenomena of adolescence to make them more intelligible to students who have not been primarily trained in physiology. Special attention is given to the distinction between phylogenetic and familial aspects of genetic regulation, to the genetic and physiologic bases of the chronology and sequence of pubescent changes, to the distinction between genetic and hormonal sources of variability in physiologic and sexual maturation, and to psychological correlates of pubescent phenomena. Such topics, with the possible exception of the last-mentioned, have hitherto not received systematic treatment in text-books on adolescent psychology. A special feature of Chapter 4 is a discussion of the role of the adrenal cortex with respect to various normal and pathological conditions of pubescence. In Chapter 5 concepts of hormonal regulation of skeletal growth are reinterpreted in the light of more recent data.

Although organized under separate chapter headings, the book is more of a continuous essay than a series of discrete chapters. All of the specific problems of adolescence are related to the general theoretic orientation, and old materials are constantly reintroduced in new contexts. Extensive cross-referencing is made use of to add unity to related materials separated in the text, but repetition has not been shunned if thought necessary for purposes of clarity.

This approach to the organization of subject matter is based on the premise that learning is primarily a process of progressive differentiation of an uncharted cognitive field. Hence, following a general overview, more specific materials are gradually introduced and related to the original argument. Although this method of presentation undoubtedly does violence to traditional notions of textbook organization, the writer submits that the learning process and the logic of ideas do not necessarily conform to the same principles of organization and development.

The reader might be surprised at the relative absence of tables, figures and graphs in this book. The criterion followed in this matter was that graphic and tabular material would be included only if the concepts to be communicated could *not* be more succinctly and precisely conveyed by words. Only three illustrations and three tables were able to meet this criterion. The resulting space that was saved was used for integrative and interpretative purposes. Case histories were eliminated for similar reasons, and because they are all too frequently accepted as evidence rather than as examples. A genuine effort was also made to avoid including materials that apply to human beings in general rather than specifically to adolescents.

To save space, the characteristics of the populations on which most cited research findings are based are not described in any detail. Interested readers can refer to the original sources which are identified by numbers corresponding to the order in which they are listed in the bibliography following each chapter. In very few of these cases, however, are we dealing with representative samples of adolescents. Hence, it should be borne in mind that unless specifically stated otherwise, findings about adolescents apply only to the populations from which they were derived and not to adolescents in general.* Interpretative comments about adolescent problems are made from the standpoint of the writer's background of experience in medical and psychiatric practice, and research in child and adolescent development.

This book is primarily intended as an advanced textbook in adolescent psychology for graduate students in psychology and education. Since it presupposes a certain amount of psychological and biological sophistication, it is not recommended for any but advanced undergraduates. It is also intended as a reference work for professional workers in child development, clinical psychology, social work, nursing, pediatrics, psychiatry, guidance and education.

My conceptual debt to Sherif and Cantril has already been acknowledged. The inspiration for the title and organization of the book came from Krech and Crutchfield's, *"Theory and Problems of Social Psychology,*† which similarly attempted to provide a theoretical foundation for the interpretation of typical problems in that area of psychology. I am indebted to the National Association of Secondary School Principals for permission to use materials originally presented in an extended article on problems of adolescent adjustment in the January, 1950 issue of *The Bulletin,* and to Grune & Stratton for materials taken from my *Ego Development and the Personality Disorders* (1952). Mrs. Shirley S. Deusch, Miss N. Catherine Hamrick, and Mrs. Irene M. Smith were of invaluable assistance in the preparation of the manuscript.

DAVID P. AUSUBEL

Urbana, Illinois
October, 1953

*This does not mean, of course, that such data are valueless. They provide the kind of preliminary empirical support for hypotheses that is necessary before large-scale, definitive research on more representative populations can be justified. Also, as pointed out on page 36, many research problems in developmental psychology do not require the use of representative populations. The reader is merely cautioned at this point not to generalize findings uncritically from unrepresentative samples of adolescents.

† D. Kretch and R. S. Crutchfield, Theory and Problems of Social Psychology, New York: McGraw-Hill, 1948.

Acknowledgments

The writer wishes to acknowledge the courtesy of the following authors and publishers in permitting quotations from their publications:

American Sociological Review, for excerpts from Talcott Parsons, *Age and Sex in the Social Structure of the United States,* 7:604–616, 1942; and from Allison Davis, *American Status Systems and the Socialization of the Child,* 6:345–354, 1941.

Appleton-Century-Crofts, Inc., for an excerpt from Florence L. Goodenough, *Developmental Psychology,* copyright 1945.

Child Care Publications, for an excerpt from D. E. Partridge, *Guidance of the Adolescent,* in *Handbook of Child Guidance* (E. Harms, ed.), copyright 1947.

Child Development Publications, for excerpts from D. P. Ausubel, *Ego Development and the Learning Process,* Child Development, 20:173–190, 1949; and from Nancy Bayley, *Some Psychological Correlates of Somatic Androgyny.* Child Development, 22:47–60, 1951.

Duke University Press, for excerpts from G. W. Allport, J. S. Bruner, and E. M. Jandorf, *Personality under Social Catastrophe: Ninety Life-Histories of the Nazi Revolution,* Character and Personality, 10:1–22, 1941.

Harvard University Press, for excerpts from Dorothea C. Leighton and Clyde K. M. Kluckhohn, *Children of the People: The Navaho Individual and His Development,* copyright 1947.

Hermitage House, for excerpts from Ruth Benedict, *Continuities and Discontinuities in Cultural Conditioning,* in *A Study of Interpersonal Relations,* (P. Mullahy, ed.), copyright 1949.

International Universities Press, for excerpts from C. M. Fleming, *Adolescence: Its Social Psychology,* copyright 1949.

Journal of Educational Sociology, for excerpts from Margaret Mead, *Social Change and Cultural Surrogates,* 14:92–110, 1940.

National Association for Mental Health, for an excerpt from G. E. Gardner, *The Mental Health of Normal Adolescents,* Mental Hygiene, 31:529–540, 1947.

The National Society for the Study of Education, for excerpts from the 43rd Yearbook, Part I, *Adolescence,* University of Chicago Press, 1947.

The Ronald Press Company, for excerpts from F. A. Beach, *Body Chemistry and Perception,* in *Perception: An Approach to Personality* (R. R. Blake and G. V. Ramsey, eds.), copyright 1951.

W. B. Saunders Company, for excerpts from A. C. Kinsey, W. B. Pomeroy, and C. Martin, *Sexual Behavior in the Human Male,* copyright 1948.

Bureau of Publications, Teachers College, Columbia University, for excerpts from Ruth Cunningham and Associates, *Understanding Group Behavior of Boys and Girls,* copyright 1951; and from A. T. Jersild and Associates, *Child Development and the Curriculum,* copyright 1946.

John Wiley and Sons, for excerpts from *Handbook of Child Psychology* (L. Carmichael, ed.), copyright 1946, as follows: Wayne Dennis, *The Adolescent;* and Kurt Lewin, *Behavior and Development as a Function of the Total Situation;* also for excerpts from Muzafer Sherif and Hadley Cantril, *The Psychology of Ego-Involvements,* copyright 1947; and from R. J. Havighurst and Hilda Taba, *Adolescent Character and Personality,* copyright 1949.

To
CARL LEFF

PART ONE

Introduction

CHAPTER 1

Adolescence: A Stage in Personality Development

THE FIELD OF ADOLESCENT PSYCHOLOGY

By what criteria should the various subdivisions of a given science be organized into recognized fields of specialization? This question is no longer regarded improper, except by those who hold that the arrangements defining the present structure of knowledge are inevitable, axiomatically true, and immutable orders rather than functional contrivances designed to serve social needs. Neither is this question any longer merely academic. Today new fields of knowledge are emerging at an ever accelerated rate, countless interdisciplinary ventures are being launched, and research foundations are scrapping long-established boundaries between traditional areas of specialization in an effort to stimulate the formulation of more significant and basic research problems.

Yet an answer framed in terms of abstract logic would be meaningless and unrealistic. Neither a logician nor a research administrator can abolish an existing field that is flourishing, merely on the grounds that the material it encompasses could be more logically considered under different rubrics. The growth and organization of human knowledge has its own logic, as does any developmental or historical process. The pie can be sliced in innumerable ways, more or less rationally, more or less arbitrarily, with greater or lesser precision—but never according to a preconceived plan following the rules of abstract logic.

This does not mean that the development of new areas of knowledge is arbitrary and capricious, that prevailing boundaries cannot be revised, that the direction of growth cannot be given the benefit of deliberate evaluation and planning. It means rather that to the

3

criterion of logic must be added the criteria of availability, convenience, and the satisfaction of practical social needs. Before a new area of specialization can come into being, some accumulation of facts, principles, and techniques of investigation is necessary. Once this precondition is met, the future viability of the field is determined by whether or not the new organization of material is convenient, promotes the understanding and investigation of significant problems in the area it has staked out for itself, and facilitates the solution of problems of practical importance in human affairs. Hence, it is to these general criteria that we shall turn in answering our next question, "What justification exists for the field of adolescent psychology?"

What Justification for a Psychology of Adolescence?

As a result of the critical scrutiny to which the organization of various scientific disciplines has been subjected in recent years, many persons have come to question whether developmental psychology (and more particularly adolescent psychology) constitutes a legitimate field of specialization. The first type of objection runs something like this: The adolescent after all is a human being and is, therefore, subject to the same general laws of behavior governing all human beings regardless of age. Hence, knowledge of the broad functional areas in psychology—the psychology of perception, emotion, motivation, learning, adjustment, group behavior, mental measurement—can be applied directly to the understanding of any psychological phenomenon occurring in adolescence.

There is some truth in this argument, but only in a very limited sense. The laws of behavior that apply with equal validity at *all* age levels apply at such a high degree of abstraction that they are woefully inadequate in illuminating behavior at any particular age level. To know, for example, that motivation is an essential ingredient in the learning process does not tell us anything about the relative contribution of motivation to adolescent learning or about the relative efficacy of different types of motivations during adolescence. Similarly, a general knowledge of the problems of personal adjustment and of the various mechanisms used in coping with them is inadequate equipment for a counselor, psychologist, or psychiatrist whose special responsibility lies in handling the unique adjustive difficulties of adolescents.

A parallel situation exists in medicine. The specialty of pediatrics arose about one hundred years ago as physicians began to realize that children are more than miniature adults and react to disease-producing and therapeutic agents in ways that are qualitatively, as well as quantitatively, different from those of adults. It is true, for example, that children, like adults, are susceptible to scurvy, diabetes, rickets, poliomyelitis, and typhus fever; but in every instance the incidence, the symptoms, the course, and the prognosis are different. Furthermore, there are in children a whole host of diseases that occur rarely or never at all in adults, as well as separate problems of nutrition, immunization, and therapeutic management.

General acceptance of the conditional nature of the application of most psychological principles to the age factor has led to the formulation of another type of argument disputing the claim of developmental psychology to be a legitimate field of specialization in its own right: Granted that age is an important variable in the learning process, in intellectual organization, and in personal adjustment, would it not suffice merely to include a discussion of age trends (as well as of other important conditional variables such as sex, heredity, and socio-economic status) in textbooks dealing with these functional subdivisions of psychology? The answer is that it would undoubtedly suffice for persons whose primary interests lie in one of these fields. But it would not suffice either in providing an integrated picture of how *all* of these functions change with age or in revealing what they look like in a particular age period. For purposes of understanding the psychology of adolescence, it is just as futile to look up the word "adolescence" in textbooks of social, experimental, and abnormal psychology as it would be to look up the word "learning" in textbooks of developmental, differential, and systematic psychology.

One last argument typified by the following quotation from Wayne Dennis' treatise on adolescence remains to be considered:

> We see no more reasonableness in treating separately the psychology of the teen age than we do in considering separately the psychology of the twenties, the psychology of the forties, etc. All such treatments might have essentially the

same table of contents since all, or nearly all, human responses can occur in any decade after the period of early childhood.[10] *

It is true that most of the psychological phenomena occurring during the period of adolescence take place likewise in subsequent decades and that some noteworthy developmental changes also occur later on. However, adolescence is treated as a separate developmental period not because it covers a decade but because it spans an interval in which certain distinctive changes occur in the biosocial status of the human organism. The adolescent years can be grouped together because they possess a certain homogeneity of developmental content. Throughout the entire period the individual is in a transitional stage of personality organization and enjoys a marginal interim status that is neither child's nor adult's. In terms of social expectations, privileges, prerogatives, parent-child relationships, the thirteen-year-old and the seventeen-year-old have much more in common than the former has with the nine-year-old or the latter with the twenty-one-year-old; yet an identical four year interval separates each pair of ages.

Another criterion for setting apart certain developmental periods for separate study—besides the criterion of homogeneity of biosocial status—is the rate at which psychological change occurs. The rate of change during adolescence, for example, is immeasurably greater than in the preadolescent years or in the third, fourth, and fifth decades of life. As a result of this accelerated rate of change, many marked and distinctive alterations of behavior and psychological functioning occur, and many unique problems of adjustment are generated. Hence, many developmental generalizations that held true a short while ago in the preadolescent era have little relevance and applicability to the adolescent period. Contrariwise, the rate of psychological change during the subsequent three decades is slow enough to allow the same set of developmental generalizations, subsumed under the psychology of maturity, adequately to span a thirty instead of a ten year interval; and following the example of medicine with its flourishing new specialty of geriatrics, it is customary to give separate treatment to the psychology of senescence.

We cannot, therefore, concur in Dennis' conclusion that the only

* Superior numbers throughout, refer to bibliographies at the end of each chapter.

proper subject matter for the psychology of adolescence is a consideration of

> the effects of biological adolescence upon the behavior of the individual; [that] its aim is to examine a certain set of mental-physical correlations, not to treat those aspects of behavior which, although present in adolescents, are also present to the same degree in all other biologically defined classes of subjects.[10]

For us the psychology of adolescence shall embrace the changes in personality organization that are generated by the sudden and violent shifts in the adolescent's biosocial status. We shall be concerned with the ways in which his general potentialities for behavior change with the biological, psychological, and social factors that precipitate this new period of personality development, and with the mechanisms through which basic changes in personality structure are effected. We shall focus especially on the unique problems of adjustment posed by the developmental tasks of adolescence and on some of the distinctive adjustive techniques used by adolescents.

The Place of Adolescent Psychology in Understanding Human Behavior

The chief justification for a separate psychology of adolescence lies in its applicability to everyday problems of interpersonal relations. If adolescents as a group tend to feel, learn, think, or act in certain characteristic ways, if they present certain common problems of adjustment simply because they are all passing through the same developmental period, it behooves all persons who have dealings with them to acquire some understanding of the psychology of adolescence.

By this we do not wish to imply that individual differences are no longer important or that an understanding of adolescence automatically confers insight into the problems of any particular adolescent. We simply wish to reiterate the rather widely-accepted psychological principle that in order adequately to understand any behavioral sequence, four types of psychological data are necessary: (1) the characteristics of the immediate situation to which the individual is responding; (2) the cultural setting in which his behavior is taking place; (3) the significant features of his personality structure, which are the result of continuous interaction between inherited predispositions and unique patterns of individual experience; and (4) the particular developmental period through which he is passing.

Knowledge of the psychology of adolescence provides us with only the last-mentioned category of data required for understanding a given adolescent's behavior. But this in no way detracts from its significance, since behavior at any age level cannot be made intelligible until it is placed in its proper developmental setting. Before it can be meaningfully evaluated we need to know something about the characteristic goals and methods of achieving goals, the self-concepts, the ways in which new values are assimilated, the sources and the level of status and emotional instability that relate to a given stage of personality development. Without such specialized knowledge parents and teachers, for example, cannot understand such perplexing adolescent phenomena as adult-youth conflict, negativism, exaggerated conformity to peer-group standards, and resistance to accepting adult-approved values. Similarly, unless counselors, psychiatrists, and clinical psychologists are able to relate the behavior disorders of adolescents to a revised norm of emotional instability that is consonant with the unusual developmental tensions characteristic of the adolescent period, they will be apt to exaggerate the seriousness of such behavior far out of proportion to its actual significance.

It is quite evident, therefore, that no person whose effectiveness in interpersonal relationships depends in part upon his ability to understand the behavior of others can afford to ignore the developmental factors that shape its form and give it special meaning. And because of the abrupt and important developmental changes that take place during adolescence, as well as the protracted length of the adolescent period, this consideration is never more crucial than at this particular stage of growth.

APPROACHES TO THE STUDY OF ADOLESCENCE

Since developmental psychology is largely a natural (ecological) rather than an experimental science, it is hardly surprising that much of the material conventionally included in the psychology of adolescence is based upon observational data. However, from the time of Aristotle until relatively recently, the method of observation has for the most part been applied to the study of adolescent behavior impressionistically and unsystematically. Because of the apparent self-evident nature of this behavior, observers neglected to distinguish precise descriptions of actual behavior from preconceived notions, unsupported opinions, and popularly-held prejudices.

Partly as a reaction to this unsatisfactory state of affairs and partly as a consequence of the phenomenal growth and rapidly increasing prestige of the testing movement in psychology, developmental psychologists began to measure every conceivable aspect of the adolescent—height, weight, ossification, pubic hair, strength of grip, manual dexterity, intelligence, vocational interests, social maturity. This provided a large body of empirical data for a more objective psychology of adolescence. Although this greater objectivity was a valuable corrective to the previous situation, as an end in itself it was equally unsatisfactory. Unrelated to a comprehensive and tenable theoretical frame of reference, this mass of discrete measurements proved unintelligible and chaotic.

The conventional solution to this problem was to *impose* some order on the empirical data by organizing it into formal categories —physical growth, intellectual growth, emotional growth, social growth—which served also as chapter headings for textbooks on adolescent psychology. But in categorizing discrete measurements, the central significance of adolescence as a stage in personality development was obliterated. The adolescent was viewed less as a person than as a summation of functions undergoing compartmentalized change. And since integrative hypotheses about the nature of adolescent development were not available for interpretive purposes, many of the loose, generalized observations were retained and supplemented by theoretical considerations specifically applicable not to adolescents only but to human beings in general. The final result was a curious mixture of questionable platitudes and a bewildering array of anatomical, physiological, and behavioral growth curves, of which the relevance and significance for the understanding of adolescent behavior was often difficult to perceive.

Organized in this way, the subject matter of adolescent psychology could hardly provide much practical assistance to parents, teachers, and clinicians. In their everyday interpersonal relations with teenage boys and girls these persons require some general appreciation of the personality changes and adjustment problems confronting adolescents rather than an encyclopedic compilation of facts related to various discrete aspects of adolescent growth.

It was largely because of these shortcomings in its historical development—insufficient rigorousness in observational method leading to platitudinous generalizations, and lack of an adequate theory of personality development around which to organize the search for empirical data—that adolescent psychology failed to fulfill the promise it showed at the turn of the century. These shortcomings, rather than want of any intrinsic justification, have subjected adolescent psychology as a legitimate field of specialization to critical and unfavorable scrutiny.

Attempts were made to devise a theoretical framework comprehensive enough to embrace the numerous and scattered data relating to adolescent development. G. Stanley Hall, who is generally credited with establishing the field of adolescent psychology in the closing years of the nineteenth century, promulgated a biogenetic theory of psychological recapitulation which among systems of psychology has few rivals in scope and internal consistency. But it was precisely with this theory that the seeds of the subsequent unfortunate series of events were sown. For when Hall's elaborate theory collapsed under the weight of its own logical untenability and the findings of cultural anthropologists, the biological approach to adolescent psychology was largely discredited. With its theoretical scaffolding undermined, the multitude of data organized in relation to the theory of recapitulation fell into hopeless confusion. An equally serious concomitant of this situation, which also discouraged the formulation of new organizing hypotheses on the nature of adolescent development, was the widespread acceptance of certain implications of the "social approach" to adolescence; this held that adolescence was not a distinct period of personality development but an abortive product of restrictive cultural conditions.

Because of their crucial influence on the subsequent development of adolescent psychology we shall examine each of these approaches in greater detail.

Biological Approaches to Adolescent Psychology

In its simplest and most extreme form, the biological approach to adolescence maintains that the behavioral changes that occur during this period of growth are *completely* conditioned by a series of physiological events depending on the function of the glands of internal secretion. Although these endocrine changes are latent for many years they are predetermined by the genetic constitution of the individual, and their psychological effects, it was argued, are inevitable, universal in distribution, and independent of cultural influences. And to the extent that pubescence represents a period of rapid physiological, sexual, and anatomical maturation common to the life cycle of all mammalian species, they steadfastly insisted on regarding it as a phylogenetic phenomenon.

Implicit in the biological approach, therefore, were these assumptions: (1) Physiological factors are *wholly* responsible for the psychological phenomena of adolescence. (2) The genetic determination of these physiological changes necessarily guarantees that their psychological consequences will be uniform. (3) Physiological events operate directly to produce behavioral change rather than indirectly by contributing to the reorganization of personality structure. (4) The similarity between pubescent phenomena in human and infrahuman species points to a type of phylogenetic inheritance. The first three assumptions, as will be shown, were completely untenable. The fourth assumption, although tenable in itself, was unwarrantably extended by Hall to include a fanciful conception of psychological recapitulation of the history of the race in the life history of the individual. (The essential elements of this theory had been promulgated more than a century earlier by Rousseau.)

Hall's theoretical orientation to adolescent psychology, although not coextensive with the biological approach, soon became closely identified with it. First, he stressed the importance of physiological changes at puberty and their relationship to psychological events during adolescence. Second, his theory of recapitulation was biological in form. It assumed that the experiential history of the race is written into the genetic constitution of the individual, whose development, therefore, is predetermined to unfold in parallel sequence. The unique characteristics of psychological development in adolescence, then, depend upon the fact that the adolescent recapitulates a turbulent, transitional period in human evolution.

This theory had fascinating implications and a certain amount of superficial plausibility, partly because of its resemblance to Haeckel's famous proposition that the embryological development of the individual recapitulates the biological history of the race.

Haeckel, however, confined his analogy to the prenatal period, in which empirical evidence is available, and did not project the parallelism beyond the realm of gross anatomical structure. By extending the analogy to include the postnatal behavior of the individual, on the one hand, and the cultural history of the race on the other, Hall was forced to go far beyond the evidence and to rely upon the discredited doctrine of the inheritance of acquired characteristics.

The widespread rejection of this theory tended to create a climate unfavorable to any new general theoretical position on the nature of adolescent development. Adolescence thereafter was typically viewed eclectically, as a constellation of discrete categories of growth and of adjustment problems characteristic of the second decade of life. In most instances both biological and social aspects of adolescence were considered relevant, and although they were not related to a theoretical frame of reference the possibility of so doing was not expressly denied (but in some cases this possibility was explicitly denied). In other instances biological factors were swept aside as inconsequential, and adolescence was regarded as a social phenomenon rather than as a universal stage of personality development with a core of common psychological principles regardless of the culture in which it occurred. Dennis [10] adopted still another position. He confined the field of adolescent psychology to the behavioral consequences of physiological pubescence. This position did not deny the contribution of the social environment to the adolescent's behavior but insisted that this aspect of the problem was outside the proper field of adolescent psychology, belonging instead to the "social psychology of youth."

Unfortunately, Hall's chief theoretical contribution was lost in the heated controversy over the specific merits of his theory of recapitulation. For unlike the advocates of the biological, the social, or the eclectic approaches he was practically alone in maintaining that adolescence is a distinct period of psychological development which can be explained by reference to a set of general theoretical propositions. Although his particular propositions failed to stand the test of time, they were directed toward a unified and integrated conception of adolescence that later investigators unfortunately chose to ignore.

Social Approaches to Adolescent Psychology

G. Stanley Hall and all other early investigators associated with the biological point of view were naturally limited in their cultural perspective and blinded by ethnocentric bias. They worked in an era in which there was little knowledge of the psychology of adolescence in other ethnic and social settings. It is understandable, therefore, that they should have believed that adolescence the world over is characterized by the same degree of "storm and stress" which form so striking a part of adolescent development in modern Western culture. Having no examples to the contrary, it was only natural for them to infer that if the behavior of adolescents is a product of their biological endowment, this behavior would have to be universal in distribution since all ethnic groups share essentially the same physiological make-up.

Underlying this inference, of course, was an assumption basic to the psychological thinking of the period: if behavior is conditioned by a physiological factor which, in turn, is genetically determined, it must inevitably take the same specific form in every social environment. It was not yet appreciated that visceral stimuli of genetic origin lead only to the universal occurrence of very general drives and propensities for behavior and that the specific patterning and content of such behavior can vary enormously depending on the social environment in which it occurs.

The importance of culture in patterning biologically determined drives was nowhere more forcefully illustrated than in the psychology of adolescence. Beginning in 1925 with Margaret Mead's investigation of adolescent behavior in Samoa, a large body of ethnological data dealing with the comparative psychology of adolescence became available.*

A survey of this material indicates that the problems facing the adolescent vary from culture to culture, rendering the transition to adulthood more or less

* The contrast in specific detail between various aspects of adolescence in different cultures or in different subcultures within our own culture will be made in later sections when we will deal more explicitly with specific features of adolescent development. For persons who are especially intrested in the problem of adolescence in different cultural settings the following works are recommended: R. Benedict,[5] A. Davis,[8] A. Davis and J. Dollard,[9] R. S. Lynd and H. M. Lynd,[25] M. Mead,[26] P. Radin,[30, 31] J. W. M. Whiting,[36] and F. E. Williams.[37]

complicated, more or less conflicting, more or less prolonged. Such studies indicate the necessity of using comparative material from different cultures and times, and the necessity of first placing adolescent ego problems in their social settings. For significant variations and factors of social change necessarily reflect themselves in the status problems of adolescents, who are themselves in a critical and unstable stage of transition.[34]

In the face of overwhelming evidence presented by cultural anthropologists, the naive view that biological factors completely or inevitably determine the nature of adolescent development had to be abandoned. It became apparent that certain special features of adolescence in modern Western civilization were not necessarily inevitable; that the *degree* of conflict, stress, and difficulty experienced by adolescents could be related in part to cultural differences in the norms and restrictions regulating their behavior and aspirations for mature status.

The proponents of the new social approach [11, 19, 24] were no better able to avoid overgeneralizing from their findings than were their colleagues of the biological school. They were soon proclaiming that the biological changes of adolescence are unrelated to its psychological characteristics; that there is no distinct transitional stage of personality development that can be localized during the adolescent period; that no universal psychological principles of adolescent development can be formulated; that adolescence is a purely social phenomenon in certain cultures in which restrictive practices prevail.

They went far beyond their evidence also in the conclusions they drew. Because they were able to relate *degrees* of adolescent conflict to cultural conditions, they jumped illogically to the conclusion that the entirety of adolescent psychology could be regarded largely "as the product of norms and restrictions in the child's surroundings which deny, postpone, or regulate sex and other activities of which he is capable as a maturing person." [19] Because they were successful in demonstrating that biological factors could not account for the *specific* content of adolescent behavior, they erroneously concluded that these factors had no *general* influence on behavior or development independent of the cultural setting.* They failed to recognize

---

* It is noteworthy that in spite of the assertion that "adolescence is culturally determined . . . and to only a very small degree a function of biological change within the individual",[19] the author of this statement devotes several chapters of his textbook on adolescence to endocrine, physiological, and anatomical changes,

that the early and mistaken claims for the specific patterning of behavior by physiological variables were in no sense necessary or crucial for the validity of the proposition that biological factors make important contributions to the development of human behavior.

Hence, it is important to appreciate that the same sex hormones may give rise to markedly different patterns of sex behavior in different cultures, and that in different ethnic and social groups tremendous variability in the accepted economic and social roles of adolescents may prevail. But more important than specific cultural differences in the patterning of biological sex drives, or in the social expectations of appropriate status roles for adolescents, is the common fact that in all cultures adolescence is marked by important shifts in the biosocial status of the child, shifts which are sufficiently crucial to precipitate a thoroughgoing reorganization of personality structure. It is in the causes for and the nature of these shifts and in their consequences for personality and behavior that we can expect to find our relevant subject matter for the psychology of adolescence.

The Sex Repression Theory of Adolescent Emotional Instability. The gross oversimplification of the problem of adolescent development by adherents to the social approach is nowhere more vividly illustrated than in the widely-held theory that adolescent emotional instability in our culture is chiefly attributable to culturally determined frustration of physiological sex drives. This theory is advanced by Dollard among others,[11] and is, of course, in line with his frustration-aggression hypothesis. It has also undoubtedly been influenced by psychoanalytic thinking, since Freud[13] taught for many years that anxiety is an inevitable consequence of sex repression. Although this theory is (as will be shown presently) untenable for many reasons, its advocates ironically committed the very same error for which they so severely berated the champions of the biological approach—the error of minimizing the degree to which even basic drives can be altered by cultural influences, as well as the ability

explaining all the while that these "changes have wide repercussions in terms of the social and psychological behavior and the attitudes toward self and environment which they engender." [19]

of human beings to adapt successfully to such extreme variations.

Data on psychosexual development in our own and other cultures support the view that there is no simple relationship between degree of overt freedom in sexual expression and the development of stress in adolescence. This material demonstrates unequivocally that the suppression of physiological sex urges need not be followed inevitably by psychological conflict. It is true that when social sanction exists for the uninhibited gratification of these urges little mental conflict about sex develops. But the same outcome holds true for many other types of cultural patterning of sex behavior.

From the Arapesh, for example, we learn that all sexuality can be successfully placed on an affectional basis, and that physiological sex urges can be so completely subordinated to affectional needs that they have no independent existence.[26] The possibility of a spontaneous sex drive in response to a hormonal stimulus is not recognized, and both men and women find in monogamous marriage the consummation of the ideal sex life. This transformation of hormonally-inspired sex impulses into a type of affection which does not differ qualitatively from the feeling one has for a daughter or sister [26] obviates the possibility of simple physiological gratification. Yet no signs of psychological conflict about sex have been found among Arapesh adolescents.

What shall we say about the more usual type of cultural situation in which sexual needs do not rest exclusively upon an affectional basis, and which when expressed seem to be, at least in part, a response to internal physiological stimuli? Ethnological and clinical evidence indicates that for those persons who practice repression no conflict results as long as the repression is so complete that at the conscious level the existence of sex feelings is not even acknowledged. At least this would appear to be true of the Manus girl, who manifests no signs of acute or chronic emotional conflict over sexuality despite complete suppression of sex cravings.[26] In this respect she does not differ from many puritanically reared girls in our own culture who are able to stifle sex urgings so completely that none ever reaches the threshold of consciousness. Such girls do not suffer from prolonged abstinence, and like their Manus sisters are often incapable of enjoying sex even on an affectional basis. Hence, complete repression (just like the complete "transformation" of the Arapesh) seems to be one of the many cultural alternatives in the patterning of the hormonal sex drive that is entirely compatible with freedom from psychological conflict about sex; and, paradoxically, both possibilities were completely overlooked by socially oriented students of adolescence.

When physiological sex urges are *not* completely repressed and do find representation in consciousness, mental conflict will not develop as long as the adolescent does not attempt to maintain an inconsistent and unrealistic moral position on the legitimacy of their gratification. It seems to matter little whether no restrictions at all are placed upon premarital sexual intercourse as in Samoa, or whether strict and serious prohibitions are applied as among the Mundugumors. As long as these prohibitions are not *internalized* by the adolescent and as long as clandestine opportunities for gratification are available, neither moral conflict nor emotional tension from unsatisfied psychophysiological needs will develop. The lower-class adolescent boy in our culture occupies a position midway between the Mundugumor and the Samoan (social taboos against premarital sexual intimacies are verbally prescribed, but no one seriously expects that they will be honored) and appears to experience little psychological conflict about sex.

The acute emotional disturbance generated by sexual problems in middle-class youths in our society has led so many psychologists to jump to the ethnocentric conclusion that there is an absolute correlation between freedom of sexual expression and absence of emotional instability in adolescence. Actually this is hardly true since, as we have just pointed out, either complete repression or expression unpreceded by the internalization of social prohibitions is unproductive of emotional stress. The middle-class adolescent male experiences so much conflict about sex not because of external restrictions *per se,* but because he is caught in a curious dilemma: the possession of sex desires is normal and proper, but their satisfaction is morally unallowable. This contradictory situation is a product of the fact that his social class, bolstered by the authority of modern biological and psychological opinion, acknowledges the existence of powerful physiological sex urges in adolescent males but at the same time insists, on ethico-religious grounds, that their premarital implementation must not be furthered. It is the internalization of this class moral edict by middle-class adolescents (rather than the efficiency of any system of chaperonage) that enforces the premarital chastity that by and large prevails in this group. These moral reservations about implementation are logically incompatible with the conviction that these very desires when unimplemented are normal, natural, and acceptable. Furthermore, they are also unrealistic; experience has shown that once sex desires become consciously insistent, efforts toward their satisfaction cannot be successfully repressed.[22, 35]

Emotional conflict about sex, therefore, inevitably arises in the middle-class adolescent male for two reasons: (1) the logical impossibility of fusing incompatible norms of feeling and conduct, and (2) the psychological impossibility of following the internalized moral injunction against premarital satisfaction of his sexual needs. However, by refraining from sexual intercourse and thereby preserving the technical virginity upon which his class places so high a premium, he feels that he has minimized the seriousness of his moral transgression.

It cannot be denied, of course, that a possible source of psychological stress lies in the fact that the ultimate goal of physiological sex desire (intravaginal intercourse) remains frustrated under these conditions. But from all indications it would appear that the greater part of the tension from this source is relieved by the ubiquitous practices of masturbation and petting. There is abundant evidence to show that apart from intravaginal intercourse, repression of sexual activity among middle-class adolescent males is virtually non-existent.[22, 23] Hence, emotional strain cannot be attributed to the tension of unsatisfied psychophysiological needs. It must arise instead from feelings of guilt associated with a self-acknowledged violation of an internalized norm of moral conduct. The violation consists both in the overt attempt to find satisfaction of sexual needs in masturbation and petting and in the significance which these activities hold as substitutes for premarital intercourse, the primary taboo.

Apart from the fact that we have been unable to find any simple relationship between the repression of physiological sex impulses and the degree of psychological conflict about sex, the sex repression theory of adolescent emotional instability is untenable for many other reasons. In the first place, it is quite unlikely that the transition between childhood and adult life can even for Samoan boys and girls, whose adolescent sexual activity is completely unrestricted, be accomplished painlessly. With adolescence they face a change in responsibilities, privileges, social status, and relationships with parents and age-mates. Even in the sexual domain all is not without difficulty. Girls have to overcome a preadolescent attitude of hostility toward boys and customarily do not commence sexual relationships with them for the first two years after the onset of pubescence. Boys are vexed by having to court a girl through an intermediary, with the ever-present possibility of losing the coveted prize to that intermediary.

Second, in those primitive societies in which the degree of stress in adolescence is adversely contrasted to the idyllic situation in Samoa, other more compelling reasons for the disparity can be found besides the usually emphasized differences in social restrictions on adolescent sexual activity. The Manus child, for example, who lives in a happy and carefree world of play and easy comradeship, at adolescence is suddenly catapulted into a ruthlessly aggressive and competitive adult society in which only material values are honored. Marriage is a pure business proposition, devoid of any affectional elements, that involves the assumption of onerous financial burdens. The Manus adolescent can expect no genuine assistance from family, friends, or society in getting started in adult life; nor can he join in any communal economic enterprise. He has no choice but to become an independent entrepreneur and to surrender his self-respect by borrowing from "big men" in the village the where-with-all to do so. Release from this humiliating dependence can be accomplished only by emulating the culturally valued traits of unrelenting industry, acquisitiveness, and ruthless unconcern for human values. In this way he may himself become a successful and prosperous man of property on whom others in turn become dependent.

In sexual matters the Manus boy is in much the same position as our middle-class adolescent male. His culture, too, acknowledges the potency and naturalness of the male physiological sex drive and just as inconsistently as ours applies strict taboos that aim seriously at outlawing its extramarital expression. He is able to find some compensation in peer group and homosexual activities since his social life is not as restricted and supervised as the adolescent girl's. Petting, however, is unknown, and we have no information about masturbation. In all probability, therefore, he experiences much the same type of emotional stress about sex as the middle-class adolescent male in our culture. The Manus girl, on the other hand, does not experience any sexual frustration despite the apparent deprivation; in her case, sex desires have never been allowed to develop. Nevertheless, once she is married, her lot is more difficult because she regards intercourse as loathesome, shameful, and repugnant.

It is apparent that although sexual problems undoubtedly add to the difficulty of adolescence for Manus boys and girls, other causes of emotional stress mentioned cannot be ignored—the severe contrast of adolescence to the carefree existence during childhood, the circumscription of the girl's social life and her isolation from her peer group, the ruthless competitiveness of the economic system and the adolescent's marginal, dependent position in it.

The same conclusion holds true also for the Kwoma [36] and Mundugumor [26] cultures, both of which place severe restrictions on premarital sex activity. These restrictions, however, are not internalized by adolescents. Transgressions of the social standard are followed by feelings of insecurity (by the girl lest her marriageability suffer in consequence, and by the boy lest her relatives harm him) rather than by feelings of guilt or self-reproach. But here too other, nonsexual sources of tension are readily apparent. The highly individualistic Mundugumor society places a premium upon the same personality traits that the Manus people value so highly. Status is not something that the culture graciously confers upon the adolescent as a matter of course when he is mature enough to deserve it; it is a prize to be snatched by means of continuous aggression from elders who yield nothing unless they have to. The Kwoma adolescent, similarly, does not attain full adult status at once. As a way of emphasizing his marginal status, he is obliged to postpone for some time certain activities and to show childish deference to certain elders.

If the contrast in the stress of adolescence between primitive societies that are relatively casual, permissive, cooperative, and unconcerned about status differences (Samoan, Arapesh) and those that are relatively aggressive, individualistic, competitive, and worshipful of prestige and material success (Manus, Mundugumor) is so great, what can we expect in comparing adolescence in the former group to adolescence in our own culture? We have seen that these factors (the implications of which reach far beyond the sphere of sexual adjustment) play a crucial role in enhancing the difficulty of adolescent development in the primitive cultures in which maximal social restrictions are also imposed on adolescent sexual activity. How much more important then, must these nonsexual factors be in our own heterogeneous culture, in which matters of status and socioeconomic organization are infinitely more complicated!

Under the worst conditions, adolescence in primitive societies occupies a relatively short time span. Its onset is clearly demarcated by ritual, and its precise nature is not shrouded in ambiguity. Conflicts among an infinite number of vaguely defined occupational choices do not plague the adolescent. He has little cultural confusion about moral values since alternative value systems are not available. Life is ordered and pre-arranged. There are no trying decisions to make. The social order is relatively static and does not require a series of periodic individual readjustments. The acceptable attributes of masculinity and femininity, although differing widely among cultures, are explicitly defined within a single culture. Emancipation from the home is not indefinitely prolonged; and although marital and vocational status may be hedged in by certain limiting conditions, they are attained shortly after the acquisition of physical maturity. For these reasons our four primitive cultures, despite their considerable differences, probably have more in common with each other than any one of them has in common with our culture; hence, the unique degree of difficulty during adolescence in our society.

Finally, to disprove the sex repression theory of adolescent instability, we need not go beyond the borders of our own culture, which is sufficiently heterogeneous to provide abundant examples of variability in degree and kind of sexual expression sanctioned at various subcultural levels. We have noted already that the middle-class adolescent male experiences most and the lower-class adolescent least emotional conflict about sex. Nevertheless, despite his exemption from conflict in this supposedly crucial area, there is nothing to indicate that the lower-class youth escapes the characteristic adolescent tension and turbulence that is typical of the culture as a whole.

Adolescence as a Stage of Personality Development

From our brief ethnological survey of adolescence we have gained social perspective. We have seen that there is wide cultural variability in the form, content, length, difficulty, and stressfulness of adolescence and that no single factor, such as sex repression, can account for as complex a phenomenon as adolescent emotional instability. But the main purpose for gaining perspective from a comparative approach is not merely negative—avoiding generalizations about the basic nature of adolescence that hold true only for a single culture. The more important, positive purpose, which unfortunately has been largely neglected in the fascination over dramatic differences between cultures, is to abstract the common factors that exist in these differences—to formulate general principles of adolescent development that can be validly applied to any cultural environment. Sherif and Cantril state this very well:

> After learning . . . from the ethnologist we can return to our own work as psychologists carrying with us the implications of the lesson learned. We should start our work by reiterating a methodological consideration appropriate in this connection. With variations in the social setting, the transitional period of adolescence may be more or less prolonged, fraught with more or less intense problems. However, the basic psychological principles which operate in all of these social settings should be the same. If we abandon the search for these psychological principles, we will be falling into the tragic blunder committed by the Fascist advocates of basic race differences.[34]

Adolescence in all cultures can be described as a time of transition in the biosocial status of the individual. It is a period during which marked changes occur in duties, responsibilities, privileges, social and economic roles, and relationships with others. It marks the beginning assumption of adult biological and social sex roles and of a cluster of personality traits that the culture deems appropriate for the mature adult of each sex. It includes the individual's reactions to being swept into a transitional period of development and to being confronted with a new set of social demands and expectations. Under such conditions changed attitudes toward self, parents, peers, and elders become inevitable. New aspirations are generated, new standards of behavior are incorporated, and new ways of learning are adopted.

In short, adolescence everywhere is a time of extensive personality reorganization. It could hardly be otherwise, for how could such significant shifts in status transpire without some profound impact on an individual's organization of attitudes, traits, and propensities for behavior, whatever these may be? Certainly there will be differences in the intensity and kinds of responses made to these shifts, depending upon previous personality structure. But in no way can the necessity for some type of basic restructuring be avoided.

In this context a biosocial approach to adolescent development means more than an attempt to relate directly certain biological and social conditions of adolescence to their *separate* psychological outcomes. It implies a more explicit assessment of the component contributions that various biological and social factors make in effecting a transition from childhood to adult personality status. To avoid a mere cataloguing of the psychological events incident to adolescence requires considerable selectivity in the choice of material, since personality is an inclusive term embracing the trivial and peripheral as well as the more central aspects of an individual's psychological organization. To achieve this measure of selectivity we shall be obliged to use some criterion or gradient in relation to which the contents of personality can be ordered in a hierarchy. Any such criterion to be valid would have to operate so that the more stable, recurrent, and critical aspects of personality, which give it continuity and make possible the prediction of significan' behavior, would occupy a central position in the hierarchical arrangement.

The only possible criterion that meets this requirement is a gradient of self-reference or ego-involvement. According to this conception most significant and crucial are those aspects of personality (attitudes, values, motives, characteristic modes of adjustment) that are endowed with the greatest amount of self-implication. We may expect to find ego-related characteristics such as these constituting the core of personality structure: *an individual's conception of his own importance; his aspirations for self-enhancement; the sources*

from which he desires status; the degree of independence character-
izing his decisions; the notions he has about his ability to control
his environment; the degree of dependence-independence character-
izing his relations with others; his methods of assimilating new
values; his concept of his own capacity for doing things for himself;
his self-esteem and feelings of security; his ability to withstand
frustration; his ability to judge himself realistically; his need for
pleasurable and immediate gratification; his sense of moral obliga-
tion and responsibility; the types of defenses he uses when his
security or self-esteem is threatened.

These are the core-aspects of personality structure that have
been developed during childhood. If significant personality changes
will result from the shifts in biosocial status induced by adolescence,
we can confidently expect that they will occur in these areas.

> From the point of view of ego development, a period during which status
> changes in so many important aspects of life should be of crucial significance.
> For shifts in objective status are reflected as ego-shifts in the psychology of the
> individual. Psychologically speaking, it is especially in the ego of the individual
> that any status problem finds its echo.[34]

Psychoanalytic Approach to Adolescence. Psychoanalytic theorists
have not devoted a great deal of systematic attention to the problem
of adolescent development. But because they have stood virtually
alone in attempting to fit the adolescent period into a general theory
of personality development, a consideration of some of their scattered
formulations will probably prove rewarding.

The psychoanalytic theory of adolescence [12, 28, 38] is similar in
many respects to Hall's biogenetic theory of recapitulation. It, too,
conceives of adolescence as a phylogenetically determined period of
personality development. But here the two approaches part ways.
According to the psychoanalytic view, the adolescent does not repeat
in his individual development the cultural history of the race; he
does retrace previous racial experience in psychosexual development. Both theories, however, are obliged to rely on the discredited
doctrine of the inheritance of acquired characteristics (cultural or
psychological experience). In addition, the psychoanalytic approach
postulates the existence of inherited ideational material in the racial
unconscious and of highly specific drives and patterns of interper-

sonal behavior that are transmitted through the genes and unfold in predetermined sequence.

The readiness with which the first proposition has gained acceptance is somewhat surprising when we consider that the doctrine of innate ideas hitherto had not been seriously advanced since the buffeting it received at the hands of Locke. And the second proposition on the instinctual origins of complex behavior patterns harks back to the highly elaborate "instinct" theories of behavior, theories that apparently had been successfully demolished within the past three decades by numerous widely accepted discoveries in cultural anthropology. These findings had conclusively demonstrated that the specific form and content of any drive tends to be culturally determined.

According to Freudian doctrine,[12, 28, 38] the distinguishing feature of adolescence is the re-establishment of sexual interest and activity in the pubescent individual after a prolonged latency period, during which infantile sexual drives have been successfully repressed and "sublimated" into other areas. The infant and child supposedly pass through oral, anal, and genital stages of sexuality in that order, directing their erotic attentions variously toward themselves, the parent of the same sex, and the parent of the opposite sex. In their most advanced infantile form, when the boy is between the ages of three to six, his sexual urges are said to be genital and directed toward the mother. This precipitates the famous Oedipal situation: an unconscious desire for sexual union with the mother and an unconscious recognition of the father as a rival with a concurrent wish for his death. Consciously the boy is unduly desirous of maternal caresses and exhibits hostility and irritability to the father. As a means both of disowning this hostility (which is dangerous because it invites retaliation) and of justifying it, he projects it onto the father whom he now perceives as threatening him with castration because of his incestuous designs on the mother.

The threat of castration aided by a phylogenetic identification with the father brings the Oedipal period to a close. The father's restrictions and taboos on the child's sexual expression are internalized and result in the formation of conscience (superego); sexual feelings toward the mother are sublimated into simple affection and interest in motor, intellectual, social, and imaginative activities. Thus begins the so-called "latency period" in psychosexual development, which is terminated by the onset of pubescence. At this time, sexual and aggressive (id) drives are so greatly enhanced by endocrine influences that repression is no longer possible. Previous stages of infantile sexuality, including Oedipal wishes and homosexual urges, are briefly reactivated; but reinforced by hormonal stimulation in the appropriate direction, heterosexual impulses of a nonincestuous nature soon became dominant [12, 28, 38] and insistently seek gratification.

Freudian literature has been concerned chiefly with three main problems of personality during the adolescent period of psychosexual development: (1) the relationship between sex repression and anxiety and emotional stability; (2) the achievement of a desirable balance between the expression of sex urges and the demands of conscience; and (3) the establishment of heterosexuality. At first, widespread acceptance of Freud's earlier theory of anxiety as a psychophysiological product of sexual repression stimulated concern about the consequences for adolescent emotional stability of culturally induced repression. Freud's later modification of this theory,[13] however, led to a marked change in emphasis: the very existence of these newly intensified sex drives rather than any attempt to repress them was regarded as the main threat and the source of anxiety. The ego was pictured as overwhelmed by their demands and in constant peril of disregarding the ethical considerations of the superego (conscience). Anxiety was evoked not by repression, but because the individual was confronted both by guilt feelings and by social reprisals as the penalties for yielding to his insistent drives. Repression was reinterpreted as a defensive consequence rather than as a cause of anxiety —as a way in which the adolescent protected himself against the dangerous implications of uninhibited sexual expression, as well as against the anxiety that contemplation of such expression induced. Some writers, therefore, have advocated the imposition of unambiguous environmental limits as a means of helping the adolescent effect the necessary degree of repression of id drives [15] and of sublimating them into artistic, social, and athletic channels. However, the dangers of over-repression (as represented by asceticism, excessive intellectualization, and rigidity of personality structure) were also recognized, and the desirability of striking a happy balance between the respective demands of the id and the superego was advocated.[12]

Finally, psychoanalytic theorists have regarded adolescence as a crucial period for the establishment of appropriate patterns of masculinity and femininity and for the achievement of normal heterosexuality in the choice of love-objects. Fixation at any of the infantile levels of psychosexual development and the lack of suitable adult models of the same sex with whom an adolescent can identify have been postulated as two primary reasons for failure in this critical developmental task of adolescence.[28]

A definitive critique of the psychoanalytic theory of psychosexual development would be decidedly out of place in a textbook on adolescence.* We shall comment only on those aspects that are especially relevant to the theory of adolescent personality development. First, the notion of a "latency" period is not in accord with empirical findings on sex behavior during childhood. There is, on the contrary, evidence of considerable interest in and experimentation with sexual matters throughout the entire elementary school period.[22] In lower class families, especially, sexually immature boys and girls not infrequently make attempts at sexual intercourse.[22] Also, there is every reason to believe that adolescent sexuality does not merely begin at the point at which infantile "sexual" activity terminates; it represents, rather, a definite break in the quality and meaning of such activity. Before adolescence it is sporadic and casual, a form of imitative or exploratory play motivated by curiosity or simple sensuality. Afterwards it becomes regular, insistent, and "an end in itself," acquiring new emotional overtones and new status implications. When the individual then for the first time experiences himself in the biological sex role of the mature adult of his species, an entirely new behavioral component must be incorporated into his changing self-portrait.

Second, we cannot concur with the psychoanalytic view that the problems of psychosexual maturation and adjustment during adolescence are coextensive with the general problem of adolescent development. The acquisition of a biological sex role and the need for regulating hormonally reinforced sex drives certainly constitute

* For a critique of the concepts of infantile sexuality and the Oedipal situation see D. P. Ausubel,[4] L. Kanner,[21] G. Murphy,[27] H. Orlansky,[29] and R. R. Sears.[33]

highly significant factors in the shifting biosocial status and personality configuration of the adolescent. But as already pointed out (p. 22), many other status problems emerge at adolescence and many other aspects of personality structure require reorganization as a result of changing status relationships.

Third, the Freudian concept that most adolescent interests and activities are sublimated products of repressed sex drives is neither theoretically nor empirically tenable.

> Human motives are constantly emerging under the impact of new experiences, new social pressures and expectations, new ways of perceiving the same experience. These motives are also outcomes of positive impulses to manipulate and explore the environment as well as adjustive reactions to frustration.[4]

If only in establishing a new social status for himself, the adolescent certainly has sufficient provocation for initiating a whole host of characteristic peer group activities and relationships. Although these new functions might conceivably compensate in part for the frustration induced by the repression of sex needs, it is illogical to think of them as energized by the latter needs when a more plausible autonomous source of motivation is so apparent.

Furthermore, except in cases of complete repression of physiological sex needs, there is little evidence that repression is even possible once sex desires become consciously insistent. Among unmarried, middle-class males in our culture, the existence of an absent or very low sexual outlet is a rarity indeed.[22, 35] When nonmarital intercourse is shunned, compensation is found in other sexual outlets (masturbation, petting) rather than in nonsexual activities. And in cultural and subcultural groups in which no sex repression of any kind is seriously practiced (lower-class youths in our culture), sublimation does not constitute even a relevant possibility of providing the motivation for adolescent behavior.

The literary and artistic activities of adolescents—because they so often contain material illustrative of adolescent personality conflict —are frequently offered as proof of sublimation.[6] And since they are so peculiarly well adapted to serve as vehicles of symbolic emotional expression, these activities would seem to be the most likely to qualify for a sublimative role. However, in the light of the evidence above, the more plausible explanation is that increased emotionality *per se* rather than sex repression helps to instigate the artistic creations of adolescents. If these efforts portray sexual conflicts, it does not mean necessarily that they provide a substitutive outlet for frustrated sex urges. It requires fewer untenable assumptions to postulate that the subject matter of artistic productions expresses merely amorphous and vaguely defined emotional overtones relating to current areas of significant psychological conflict in the life of the artist.

Hence, it is one thing to *articulate* emotional tensions through artistic expression and to find in such activity an *independent* satisfaction, and quite another thing to *gratify* vicariously in this way the frustrated needs that produce the particular emotional tensions. We know now that middle-class adolescent males generally satisfy their psychophysiological sex needs through various forms of sexual activity short of intercourse. Therefore, it would, not be unreasonable to conclude that artistic productions expressive of sexual tension merely portray emotional reactions to the moral conflict generated by sexual problems.

The Rankian Approach to Adolescence. Otto Rank and his followers also have interpreted the phenomena of adolescence in the light of a distinctive theory of personality development. Although originally stemming from the psychoanalytic tradition, this theory does not place major emphasis upon the impact of psychosexual changes on adolescent personality development. It focuses instead on a more general and crucial area of personality development that undergoes radical change during adolescence: the shifting balance between the individual's contrasting needs for dependence and independence.

According to Rankian psychology, these contrasting needs vary in strength and urgency during different periods of development.[32] The adolescent prizes volitional independence inordinately because it is a developmental task, the achievement of which the culture values very highly but simultaneously makes very difficult.[17] Because of this accentuated need for independence, the formation of personal affectional ties is regarded as highly threatening since they tend to limit autonomy. According to Hankins, the adolescent, therefore, resists sexual urges that might lead to genuine love relationships since he does not wish to surrender any of his painfully acquired independence. Hence, both asceticism and sexual promiscuity serve the same function of isolating him from genuine emotional attachments requiring self-subordination.

In stressing the need for reconciling and finding a proper balance between the needs for dependence and independence, the Rankian school has identified a major developmental problem that lies at the very root of the adolescent's relationships with parents, teachers, peer group, and heterosexual companions. We shall return to this theory later to evaluate its adequacy for explaining various aspects of adolescent development. It will suffice now to point out that the issue of dependence-independence, although of crucial significance, is in no sense coextensive with all of the maturational changes and adjustive problems that are characteristic of adolescence.

THE PROBLEM OF EVIDENCE

The problem of evidence and empirical methodology in building an adequate theory of adolescent development is obviously of central importance if this field is to lay any claim to scientific status. Historically, we have already noted considerable confusion and disagreement about this issue. One extreme approach has stressed the primacy of certain sweeping (and logically untenable) theoretical propositions, unsupported in any rigorous fashion by relevant objective evidence. Another, diametrically opposite, approach has concentrated on precise measurements of adolescent development either completely divorced from theoretical considerations or superimposed upon an essentially irrelevant body of nondevelopmental theory drawn from general psychology. Either approach is obviously unsatisfactory. No scientific discipline can legitimately develop a set of general principles that is not or cannot be related to empirical data. And equally important, the aimless collection of facts undirected by a theoretical orientation is a wasteful, unsystematic process that can never be expected to make a highly significant contribution to scientific understanding.

The precise relationship between theory and evidence, however, is largely a function of the reliability, definitiveness, and adequacy of the latter in relation to the problem under investigation. Depending on these stated properties of the data at hand, the types of generalizations that can be drawn must be qualified by the varying degrees of tentativeness characteristic of scientific laws, theories, or hypotheses. For reasons that will be presently elaborated, it is clear that in adolescent psychology we deal at present almost exclusively with the two latter types of generalizations, and most frequently with the last-mentioned.

In the first place, human behavior is so tremendously complex, in terms of the countless number of variables impinging upon it, that even if completely reliable and valid measuring instruments were available, merely identifying, let alone controlling, the relevant variables involved would constitute a highly formidable task. This fact alone should inspire humility in interpreting the results of any psychological investigation. Second, unlike investigators in many other fields of psychology who are concerned only with determining the relationship between various psychological processes, the student of adolescence is interested also in obtaining data that can be generalized to diverse groups of adolescents, data that are characteristic of adolescence as a developmental period and not of a particular group of adolescents. This requires that he study representative groups of adolescents, an undertaking that is usually prohibitive since it demands the expenditure of large sums of money and the cooperation of many research workers over extended periods of time.

And finally, the study of psychological development involves by definition an inquiry into the nature and types of change in potentiality for behavior that occur between stated points in the life cycle of the individual. In reaching such generalizations, it is essential that we study groups of individuals who, apart from a known difference in maturity, are comparable in all other respects. The difficulty of satisfying this criterion will become apparent in the following discussion of cross-sectional and longitudinal methods of obtaining data.

Methods of Obtaining Developmental Data *

Most developmental studies in adolescent psychology have employed a cross-sectional approach in measuring the growth of

* In this section we can only discuss certain general problems related to the collection of data in developmental studies. For a more exhaustive treatment of these problems and also of the specific techniques used in obtaining data, the reader is referred to the following sources: Abt and Bellak,[1] Anderson,[2] Cronbach,[7] Greulich,[14] Havighurst and Taba,[18] Jones,[20] and Wright and Barker.[39]

psychological functions and behavioral capacities. This method, in brief, seeks to chart the growth of a particular function by comparing mean observations or measurements of *different* groups varying in age. In studies of adolescent development, such growth curves are most frequently based on data obtained from a number of different grade levels ranging from junior high-school to college. The attractiveness of this method lies in its relative ease, availability, and inexpensiveness. In large urban centers investigators do not have too much difficulty in obtaining subjects for such purposes provided their procedures are not too time-consuming. No continuity in research personnel is required, as in studies in which data must be obtained periodically from the same subjects over a long span of years; and the publication of results need not be postponed, as in the latter situation, for a decade or more until the growth of the subjects is completed.

Unfortunately, however, the cross-sectional approach presents serious disadvantages in obtaining developmental data from comparable groups. Attempts at matching different groups for even the important identifiable variables can be at best only approximate. Also, in school populations increasing age itself tends to operate selectively in such important variables as intellectual ability and socio-economic status, since those individuals who complete high-school and go on through college tend to be superior in one or both of these attributes. Third, it is inevitable that subjects in the different age groups will differ in their antecedent backgrounds (even if they are comparable in all other respects) simply because of social and historical change. How comparable apart from age are an eleven-year-old and a sixteen-year-old both measured in the year 1952? The former is completely a product of the turbulent war and post-war years, whereas the latter grew up for the first five years in a period with conditions affecting American family life relatively stable.

In a longitudinal study there is no doubt about the comparability of the subjects furnishing data for different age points on the growth curve, since we are dealing with successive measurements made on the *same* individuals at regularly prescribed intervals in their development. With longitudinal data it is also possible to chart growth curves for individuals and to trace the development of special subgroups within the total population, thus pointing up differential trends that would otherwise become obliterated in computing measures of central tendency for the group. It is also possible, of course, to use cross-sectional data in studying the development of subgroups, by first identifying and making comparable in other respects varying age samples of the subgroups, but unless the criteria for identification are relatively unambiguous and homogeneous in nature (race, sex, physical characteristics), such comparisons cannot be relied upon to provide as accurate a picture of differential development as would be possible were data on the *same* group of special individuals available over a period of years. If, for example, we wished to study the social development of adolescents who as children were rejected by their parents, it would not be very satisfactory to obtain our data from different age groups of rejected children. In either instance, however, comparison with a control group would be necessary before a significant differential trend could be concluded.

Even when the criteria for establishing subgroups are comparatively clear-cut, the longitudinal method enjoys certain advantages over the cross-sectional. This can be illustrated by reference to an important problem in the differential psychology of adolescence—the effect of pubescence (sexual maturity) *per se* on various psychological aspects of adolescent development. Working with either cross-sectional or longitudinal data one can divide all of the cases at successive age levels into pubescent and non-pubescent subgroups, and can plot the growth of the function separately for each subgroup (Fig. 1a). The disparity between the growth curves of the two subgroups can then be attributed to the effect of pubescence on the particular psychological function. However, the use of the longitudinal approach enables us to treat the data in a way that the impact of pubescence on the course of development can be rendered comparable regardless of the age at which it occurs. Since the precise age of pubescence is ascertainable for every individual in our longitudinal group, it is possible to express the temporal relationship of any series of measurements to this event in terms of various stated intervals prior to or subsequent to its occurrence (Fig. 1b). Thus, for every subject, regardless of the age at which he reaches sexual maturity, we have available a measure of status in a given aspect of growth two years prior to puberty, one year prior to puberty, one year subsequent to puberty, etc. Not only does this method increase the number of cases entering into the mean value plotted for each age point on the growth curve (thereby enhancing its reliability), but also it provides a more general picture of the

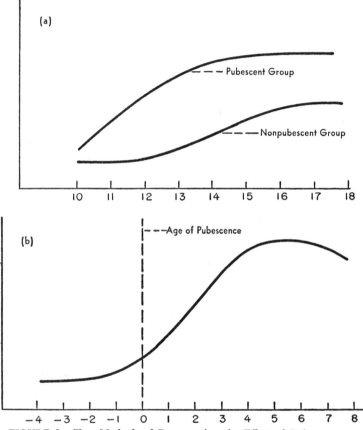

FIGURE 1.—Two Methods of Representing the Effect of Pubescence on the Development of a Given Function during the Adolescent Period.

impact of pubescence on adolescent development by combining comparable data from individuals who become pubescent at different chronological ages.

The longitudinal approach, of course, is not without its methodological disadvantages quite apart from such practical considerations as time, expense, and difficulty. Although comparability of subjects at different age levels is guaranteed, it is difficult to secure a stable population that can and is willing to be measured intensively over a long period of time; and, by definition, any population that meets these requirements of stability must differ in many important respects from a representative group of adolescents. Also, if the span of years covered by a particular longitudinal investigation happens to include or coincide with a period of unusual social or economic stress, it is difficult to determine to what extent the measured change over the years must be attributed to the special influence of the latter phenomenon rather than to the more typical kinds of developmental influences occurring with age.

A variant of the longitudinal approach is the *case-study* method. Here the unit of study is an individual rather than a group; and a much greater quantity of personal data from a wider diversity of sources is assembled for a single case study than ever becomes available for an individual subject in a longitudinal group. From the intimate knowledge thus gained of the interrelationships between significant aspects of an individual's developmental history, personality structure, and overt behavior, it is often possible to acquire valuable insights into the nature of personality development and behavioral adjustment. But apart from their applicability to the individual from whom they are derived, such insights enjoy at best the status of hypotheses which can be tested either by an analysis of a series of case studies or by normative group studies. Although the attempt is frequently made, it should be obvious that no definitive generalizations about human development can be drawn from one individual. There is no possibility of establishing a statistically significant finding or of obtaining any control data for a single case; hence it is impossible to state with any confidence that a given outcome is definitely related to a particular antecedent.

It is also important to remember that unless a case study actually starts in the early childhood of an individual, all retrospective data is subject to errors of forgetting, deliberate distortion, and selective remembering. Even if these factors were not operative, it would still be impossible for an adult to recall childhood events as they *actually* happened and originally appeared to him. In recalling and interpreting the past, it is unavoidable that we use a current frame of reference rather than the apperceptive mass temporally contiguous with the historical event.

Conclusion

Logically prior to obtaining definitive evidence in the field of adolescent psychology is the necessity for relating research efforts to integrative hypotheses derived from a comprehensive theoretical orientation to the nature of adolescent development. Only in this way can we hope to find meaningful answers to crucial questions in this area with a reasonable economy of effort. One of the major purposes of this book, therefore, will be an attempt to formulate a rigorous and systematic theory of adolescence, which lays claim to some logical plausibility, which is consistent with general principles of developmental psychology, and which is in accord with and capable of being tested by empirical findings on adolescents. The fruitfulness of this theoretical approach can then be given a preliminary, experimental test in studies of limited scope which do not aim at representativeness or at charting the course of adolescent development, but seek merely to relate different conditions of adolescent personality and environment to measurable differences in behavior and adjustment. It is premature to project large-scale longitudinal studies in most areas of adolescent development until more systematic attention is given to the elaboration of rigorous theoretical formulations tested and appropriately modified by preliminary experimentation.

Once this point of theoretical sophistication is reached, the acquisition of a significant body of definitive evidence will become a more realistic possibility. This will require the use of more representative experimental populations and the more extensive use of the longitudinal approach in collecting developmental data than has characterized most studies in the field to date. The cross-sectional approach can also provide valid data in many problem areas (when longitudinal researches are unfeasible for practical reasons), providing experimental or statistical controls can be introduced to insure comparability of age groups. Individual case studies are chiefly valuable as a source of fruitful hypotheses; but if the data from a sufficient number of case studies are consolidated and kept free of retrospective error, they can be treated in much the same way as longitudinal data for special subgroups.

REFERENCES AND BIBLIOGRAPHY

1. Abt, L. E. and Bellak, L.: *Projective Psychology*. New York: Knopf, 1950.
2. Anderson, J. E.: "Methods of Child Psychology," in *Manual of Child Psychology* (L. Carmichael, ed.). New York: Wiley, 1946.
3. Ausubel, D. P.: Problems of adolescent adjustment. Bulletin Natl. Assn. Secondary School Principals, *34*:1–84, 1950.
4. Ausubel, D. P.: *Ego Development and the Personality Disorders*. New York: Grune and Stratton, 1952.
5. Benedict, R.: *Patterns of Culture*. Boston: Houghton Mifflin, 1934.
6. Blanchard, P.: "Adolescent Experience in Relation to Personality and Behavior," in *Personality and the Behavior Disorders* (J. McV. Hunt, ed.). Vol. II. New York: Ronald, 1944.
7. Cronbach, L. J.: *Essentials of Psychological Testing*. New York: Harper, 1949.
8. Davis, A. et al.: *Deep South*. Chicago: University of Chicago Press, 1941.
9. Davis, A. and Dollard, J.: *Children of Bondage*. Washington, D. C.: American Council on Education, 1940.
10. Dennis, W.: "The Adolescent," in *Handbook of Child Psychology* (L. Carmichael, ed.). New York: Wiley, 1946.
11. Dollard, J. et al.: *Frustration and Aggression*. New Haven: Yale University Press, 1939.
12. Freud, A.: *The Ego and the Mechanisms of Defence*. London: Hogarth Press, 1937.
13. Freud, S.: *The Problem of Anxiety*. New York: Norton, 1936.
14. Greulich, W. W. et al.: A Handbook of Methods for the Study of Adolescent Children. Monogr. Soc. Res. Child Develpm., Vol. III, No. 2, 1938.
15. Hacker, F. J. and Geleerd, E. R.: Freedom and authority in adolescence. Am. J. Orthopsychiat., *15*:621–630, 1945.
16. Hall, G. S.: *Adolescence*. Vols. I and II. New York: Appleton, 1904.
17. Hankins, D.: The psychology and direct treatment of adolescents. Ment. Hyg., *27*:238–247, 1943.
18. Havighurst, R. J. and Taba, H.: *Adolescent Character and Personality*. New York: Wiley, 1949.
19. Horrocks, J. E.: *The Psychology of Adolescence*. Boston: Houghton Mifflin, 1951.
20. Jones, H. E.: The adolescent growth study: I. Principles and methods. II. Procedures. J. Consult. Psychol., *3*:157–159, 177–180, 1939.
21. Kanner, L.: Infantile sexuality. J. Pediat., *15*:583–608, 1939.
22. Kinsey, A. C. et al.: *Sexual Behavior in the Human Male*. Philadelphia: Saunders, 1948.
23. Kirkendall, L. A.: *Sex Adjustments of Young Men*. New York: Harper, 1940.
24. Klineberg, O.: *Race Differences*. New York: Harper, 1935.

25. Lynd, R. S. and Lynd, H. M.: *Middletown in Transition*. New York: Harcourt, Brace, 1937.
26. Mead, M.: *From the South Seas*. New York: William Morrow, 1939.
27. Murphy, G.: *Personality: A Biosocial Approach to Origins and Structure*. New York: Harper, 1947.
28. Nunberg, H.: *Allgemeine Neurosenlehre auf Psychoanalytischer Grundlage*. Bern: Huber, 1931.
29. Orlansky, H.: Infant Care and Personality. Psychol. Bull., *46*:1–48, 1949.
30. Radin, P.: *Primitive Religion: Its Nature and Origin*. New York: Viking, 1937.
31. Radin, P.: The Autobiography of a Winnebago Indian. University of California Publications in Am. Archaeology and Ethnology, *16*:381–473, 1920.
32. Rank, O.: *Truth and Reality*. New York: Knopf, 1936.
33. Sears, R. R.: *Survey of Objective Studies of Psychoanalytic Concepts*. New York: Social Science Research Council, 1943.
34. Sherif, M. and Cantril, H.: *The Psychology of Ego-Involvements*. New York: Wiley, 1947.
35. Taylor, W. S.: A Critique of Sublimation in Males: A Study of Forty Superior Single Men. Genet. Psychol. Monogr., XIII, No. 1, 1933.
36. Whiting, J. W. M.: *Becoming a Kwoma*. New Haven: Yale University Press, 1941.
37. Williams, F. E.: *Russia, Youth and the Present-Day World*. New York: Rinehart, 1934.
38. Wittels, R.: "The Ego of the Adolescent," in *Searchlights on Delinquency* (K. R. Eissler, ed.). New York: International Univ. Press, 1949.
39. Wright, H. F. and Barker, R. G.: *Methods in Psychological Ecology*. Lawrence, Kansas: University of Kansas, 1950.

CHAPTER 2

Problems of Adolescent Development

IF WE ARE to accept the proposition that the chief significance of adolescence lies in the fact that it constitutes a distinct and crucial stage of personality development, it is essential that we evolve some orderly scheme for categorizing the types of problems it encompasses. To be useful, such classification must be more than a convenient tool for organizing a multiplicity of data in a systematic fashion. It must go beyond a mere arbitrary listing of phenomena which could be ordered just as defensibly in many other equally arbitrary ways. Classification must serve the purpose of abstracting and identifying the most fundamental thread of common factors running through a variety of diverse problems. To serve this function it cannot operate on a *descriptive* level, for to do so would be to give undue weight to superficial resemblances and differences. Only by differentiating between problems in terms of their *origins* is it possible to achieve a grouping that adequately expresses underlying relationships as they actually exist rather than as they appear in their overt manifestations.

The values inherent in adequate classification are of considerable importance here. First, such classification enhances the possibility of gaining meaningful insights into the interrelationships among various aspects of adolescent development. This leads to more fruitful research hypotheses. Furthermore, when intervention is feasible, a more realistic and potentially successful search for facilitative measures can be undertaken if the source from which distressing developmental problems arise can be identified.

CLASSIFICATION OF PROBLEMS OF ADOLESCENT DEVELOPMENT

Acceptance of adolescence as a distinct stage in personality development also predetermines and sets limits to the types of problems that are appropriate for our classification. For by definition we can be concerned only with developmental issues that are uniquely relevant to this period of personality growth. This approach contradicts in no way the well established generalization that developmental continuity must necessarily prevail between adolescence and the age periods that precede and follow it. It simply means that in delimiting our field we shall consider only those aspects of childhood development that impinge directly upon the unique maturational tasks of adolescence or those aspects of adult development that are crucially affected by the outcome of the latter.

Psychobiological Problems

In the present era of psychological sophistication it requires no more than a casual acquaintance with the facts of adolescence to realize that this stage of human development is a biosocial phenomenon. Biologically, it is a period of accelerated physical and sexual maturation that man experiences *in common* with all other mammalian species. Its social foundations, however, are manifested in the *contrast* it presents to pubescence in these other species. For everywhere human adolescence is an institutionalized phenomenon, a socially recognized period of transitional status; and the specific form that it takes varies with differences in culturally-held values. The infrahuman pubescent, on the other hand, unostentatiously assumes an adult role in intra-species life as soon as he is physiologically able, without receiving any explicit group invitation or sanction. There is no formalized period of waiting and no socially prescribed form that his new behavior is required to take. The behavioral concomitants of his physiological maturation are regulated by biogenetic factors that are uniform for all members of a given species.

The terms *psychobiological* and *psychosocial,* however, imply concern with only the psychological or behavioral consequences of the biological and social factors influencing adolescent development rather than with the nature of these factors *per se* or with their other ramifications. And consistent with the theoretical orientation we have adopted toward adolescence, we shall consider psychobiological and psychosocial data not as discrete ends in themselves but only in relation to the respective contributions they make toward reshaping personality structure.

The distinction between *psychobiological* and *psychosocial* insofar as human development is concerned rests with the level of generality of a given phenomenon or principle. When a certain amount of uniformity prevails in the *process* of development (irrespective of specific differences in form, content, or degree attributable to cultural variation), it is meaningful to use the former term. The latter term, on the other hand, refers to those less general aspects of development which reflect the influence of the particular values or social conditions prevailing within a given culture.*

That adolescence should be characterized by a common core of psychobiological problems in a wide diversity of cultural settings is hardly surprising. There are a number of reasons for this. First, there are uniformities that spring from the fact that adolescence is universally a transitional stage in personality development. Transitional periods by their very nature share many properties in common and generate characteristic constellations of psychological problems that inevitably arise when individuals are confronted by radical changes in their biosocial status. For example, the very rapidity of growth during adolescence, its unevenness over various aspects of development, the abruptness of its onset, and the anxiety and disorientation attending any sudden shift in status are bound to constitute a set of developmental common denominators regardless of differences in degree conditioned by cultural factors.

A second source of psychobiological uniformity in the problems of adolescent development is to be found in the common group of physiological and anatomical changes that are everywhere associated with the occurrence of adolescence. These changes give rise to new types of drives, emotions, and states of awareness. Granted that these psychological phenomena will assume different forms and be differently regulated in different cultures, the fact remains that there is a universal need for adolescents to adapt to the very presence of these bodily changes and urges, to overcome feelings of bewilderment and uneasiness at their strangeness, and to subject them to control and direction in ways that are compatible with social expec-

* The use of the term *psychosocial* in this context differs from the more conventional usage in which reference is made only to the psychological accompaniments or consequences of social factors. As used here, social phenomena can give rise to either psychosocial or psychobiological effects depending on the generality (universality) of the developmental process involved.

tations. For the first time since early childhood, potent, emergent drives of organic origin require initial handling and socialization; and like all other drives, the direction of regulation proceeds from the relatively diffuse, experimental, and non-specific mode of gratification to the more highly differentiated condition where to be adequate the form of need-satisfaction must meet increasingly more stringent requirements of specificity.

It might also be noted that the universal occurrence of this highly dramatic event of pubescence gives rise to another type of developmental uniformity. For almost without exception the age of pubescence is culturally recognized as the appropriate time for initiating the changes in personality status that are characteristic of adolescence.

Third, the nature of adolescent development in different cultures will be comparable because certain very important aspects of personality maturation depend upon childhood experience with parent attitudes that are universal in distribution. Despite the presence of a multiplicity of cultural variations in child rearing practices and of clear-cut differences between group norms, the same basic types of parent attitudes can to a greater or lesser extent be demonstrated in all cultural environments. Everywhere we meet parents who are relatively rejecting or accepting, overprotective or underprotective, underdominating or overdominating, although they may express these attitudes in many different and even contradictory ways. The culture cannot completely suppress intimate interpersonal attitudes, such as these which are so completely a product of an individual's personal history, but at best it can influence the mode and intensity of their expression. In all probability greater variability prevails in this respect among individuals within a given cultural group than among different groups.

A fourth source of common psychobiological principles applicable to adolescent development lies in the universality of the various adjustive techniques available to adolescents in meeting the disequilibrium induced by new status problems; repression, aggression, withdrawal, projection, compensation, displacement. Again it is undeniable that the choice, the frequency, and the precise form taken by these mechanisms will vary, depending upon differences in cultural tolerance for different types of defensive behavior. But these reactions are so basic a part of the adaptive repertory of human beings that individual preferences resulting from unique factors of constitution and early background cannot be completely eradicated. Even in the face of serious social disapproval, there is a strong tendency for preferred modes of adjustment (which an individual has found to be successful in overcoming earlier occasions of childhood stress) to recur when he feels himself threatened by adolescent conflict situations.

Finally, a cross-cultural survey of adolescent development reveals that even when marked differences in social environment prevail, there is an unmistakable trend for personality maturation to proceed along roughly parallel lines. This is partly a result of the fact that *certain personality traits* are more appropriate than others for promoting the physical survival of the individual and the group, and of perpetuating the ideals and way of life of a particular culture. Hence, it is understandable that in *these respects* the social ideal of adult maturity will be similar for most cultures, and that social pressure will be exerted on the individual to make him conform to this ideal. For example, most cultures have a vested interest in developing an individual who can manifest independence and responsibility in making decisions and meeting his needs, who can postpone the desire for immediate pleasurable gratification in favor of striving for long-range objectives valued by the group, who is capable of deferring to the moral authority of society.

The course of personality maturation presents certain uniformities also because of a universal tendency toward an increase in the social and economic status of the individual at adolescence. In general he acquires new rights, privileges, and prerogatives and becomes more of an economic asset. This change in status (which is equivalent to the eventual acquisition of full rather than limited membership in the adult community) is everywhere made necessary by the need of parents to be relieved of permanent responsibility for their offspring, and by the need of the culture to equip a new generation to maintain the continuity of the social order. Hence, we can anticipate that this general tendency toward enhancement of the adolescent's socio-economic status will give rise to common inflationary changes in his self-estimate and status aspirations. It will also motivate both parents and social agencies to institute the type of training procedures best calculated to develop the personality traits commensurate with the increased responsibilities of his new status roles.

Central among these traits that home and culture strive to instill in the individual is a desire for status based on his own merit, performance ability, and competence as a person in his own right, rather than for reflected status derived from mere dependent relationship to parents. Internalization of this need by the adolescent motivates him to acquire those supportive attributes of personality structure that will help him realize his newly acquired aspirations.

Thus far, we have presented only general reasons for believing that there must be psychobiological problems of adolescent development. Detailed discussion of these problems will be found in later sections and chapters dealing with psychological transition, physiological changes, physical growth, and personality maturation.

Psychosocial Problems

In the realm of psychosocial problems belong those more specific aspects of adolescent development that are especially conditioned by the special nature of the cultural environment. Here we are concerned with factors accounting for differences rather than for uniformities in the developmental process among cultures. Following the procedure adopted above, we shall examine here only the general sources of such differences, leaving for later chapters detailed treatment of particular psychosocial problems of adolescence with special reference to their manifestations in our own society.

In the first place, although the phenomenon of adolescence receives explicit social recognition in every culture, there are marked differences in the degree of this explicitness in the types of rituals, training measures, and initiation rites, differences in the content, complexity, length, and rigorousness of the latter, and differences in the relative degree of emphasis placed upon maturation of boys as against girls. These differences are closely related to the specific ideals of adult maturity in different social settings; for it stands to reason that the form and content of indoctrination procedures will vary necessarily depending on which adult roles are especially valued (aggressive and competitive exploits, mercantile interests, spiritual devotions, concern for the welfare of others). Every society undertakes in its own way to control and direct the period of adolescence by confronting the pubescent individual with a unique set of social demands and expectations reinforced by appropriate training procedures and institutions. And in every instance it is confidently expected that the graduating adult will embody the particular constellation of traits and virtues that the culture has selected as most befitting the mature members of its community.

Second, as already indicated, cultural differences inevitably arise because of the different ways in which newly emerging drives and emotions of physiological origin are handled and regulated by various ethnic and social groups. Such differences are exemplified in the adequacy of the opportunities afforded for gratification of these needs, the specific kinds of feelings, goal-objects and purposeful behavior with which they may legitimately be identified, the types and stringency of restrictions and taboos that are imposed, and the degree of repression required.

Third, it is apparent that although adolescence manifests many general properties of psychological transition that can be found in any culture, marked individual differences in degree will nevertheless prevail among cultures. This is a result of the fact that the distinguishing features of developmental transition are crucially affected in their *quantitative* aspects by numerous social factors. Hence, the *degree* of abruptness, prolongation, difficulty, and stress of adolescence will vary in accordance with the particular ideals of adult maturity and the particular kinds of training procedures, institutions, and drive-regulating norms that are in force in a given social environment.

Finally,

> In addition to these social phenomena admittedly concerned with the regulation of the adolescent transitional period—whether they consist of primitive initiation ceremonies or complex educational processes—there are other general characteristics of a social order bearing no specific or intended relation to the regulation of adolescence, but which nevertheless affect its development profoundly. For example, what effect do war, depression, rapid social change, conflicting cultural values and restriction of employment opportunities have on the nature of adolescence? [1]

We realize, of course, that problems of adolescent development must necessarily exist which cannot be definitely assigned either to the psychobiological or to the psychosocial categories. This is not a defect of a given classification, but an inevitable limitation which in a sense proves its adequacy, since in nature, contrasting phenomena more usually can be conceptualized as occupying extreme positions on a continuum rather than as genuinely dichotomous. Hence, a fuzzy, indefinite area not infrequently exists on either side of the boundary lines between categories. The value of a particular classification is to be measured not by the tiny-no-man's-land it creates where discriminability breaks down, but by its capacity to differentiate between phenomena on the basis of their underlying essential differences. And as long as differentiating criteria are sharp enough to accomplish this function satisfactorily, a proposed scheme of classification has sufficiently justified its usefulness.

CONTINUITY OF ADOLESCENCE WITH OTHER PERIODS OF DEVELOPMENT

Adolescence is obviously not an isolated island in the total span of development. It is axiomatic that the nature of adolescent development is conditioned by childhood experience and that the years of adult maturity are, in turn, influenced by what transpired during the adolescent period. And just as we must regard much developmental business as already accomplished by the time an individual enters this growth phase, we can anticipate that much still remains to be finished in subsequent years.[5]

For purposes of our classification, however, this statement of the continuity of development is much too general and unprecise. We are concerned in this volume only with those particular problems of adolescents that are specifically relevant to the unique developmental tasks of adolescence. Hence, only to the extent that the mode of accomplishing these tasks and the degree of success attending them is a function of childhood experience can such experience be considered germane to the problems of adolescent development. But the child necessarily brings with him into adolescence the product of his *entire* experiential background, much of which is essentially *unrelated* to the characteristic maturational tasks of this period. The residue of this inapplicable experience cannot, of course, be written off as inconsequential; neither can it be regarded as indigenous to adolescence simply because it exerts an influence on *some* aspect of behavior during the years when adolescent development is taking place.

We are able, in other words, to speak of continuity in development because *all* significant previous experience leaves a functional residue in personality structure. Only part of this residue, however, is relevant to the outcome of the unique developmental tasks characteristic of subsequent age periods. The relevance of prior experience is derived from the fact that it either (1) constitutes in itself a preparatory phase of a continuing developmental sequence, or (2) differentially influences the process whereby later development takes place. For example, the type of training for self-direction and responsibility that a child receives in preadolescence crucially affects the probable success of his subsequent adolescent efforts toward emancipation from the home. Similarly, a previous history of having (or not having) identified with his parents in an emotionally and volitionally dependent sense predetermines in large measure the way in which the adolescent will learn and assimilate the new set of goals and values befitting his enhanced biosocial status.

The remainder of this total residue of antecedent experience, which is carried over into subsequent life periods, is similarly derived from various finished and unfinished developmental tasks of childhood, but it is not intrinsically related to any of the inherently psychobiological phases of later maturation. The residue of *completed* tasks is unobtrusive since it leads to no adjustive difficulties. But in instances in which a child fails to complete the measure of developmental progress that is customarily expected by the close of the childhood era, the resulting residue of retardation is apt to prove troublesome. He carries over into adolescence remnants of earlier personality inadequacies which may become more noticeable and more disabling with age. This is especially true of those defects and insufficiencies that in childhood can be compensated for by special circumstances inherent in the home situation, "and first assume their true pathological significance under the impact of the new adjustive demands made by adolescence." [1] For example,

the shy, bookish, retiring or excessively introverted child who has not learned the elemental techniques for carrying on interpersonal relationships with his [peers], can find solace in parental companionship for his social isolation during childhood. In adolescence, however, because of the pressures that exist for emancipation from the home, this compensation is no longer available at a time when peer relationships become even more important for a successful adjustment.[1]

In terms of our classification, however, the important thing is that difficulties such as these constitute problems of childhood that are merely carried over into and are aggravated by adolescence. They have no special relevance for the unique tasks of adolescent maturation and must be distinguished from aspects of childhood experience that *are* relevant. In this book we shall deal only with the latter component of developmental continuity.

THE CHIEF DEVELOPMENTAL TASKS OF ADOLESCENCE

Thus far we have tried to show that adolescence is a distinctive period of personality development that includes certain unique and universal maturational changes requiring extensive reorganization of personality structure. We have also noted that in the past two decades numerous writers have vehemently denied the fact that the developmental characteristics of adolescence are either unique or universal. In disputing the uniqueness of this period of life they have stressed the continuity of development, the considerable overlapping between adjacent age groups, and the existence of individual differences in the onset and termination of characteristic problems of adolescence. These arguments are logically unsound for several reasons. To prove a developmental period unique one need only show that a distinctive cluster of significant changes (enjoying a specified place in the total developmental cycle) tends to occur consistently within a given age range. It is *not* necessary to prove (1) that developmental and psychological principles applicable to other life periods do *not* apply here as well; (2) that *no* preparatory or consummatory aspects of these changes occur in earlier or later stages of development; or (3) that these changes begin and end at exactly the same point for all individuals. The uniqueness of the period inheres in the nature of the changes it encompasses, not in the age interval it occupies.

In denying the universality of adolescent phenomena, the deniers have pointed to the existence of psychosocial problems, to the presence of cultural differences in the regulation of adolescence. But again it is illogical to conclude that because the nature of adolescence varies from culture to culture in certain of its more specific aspects there can be no common factor in its more general characteristics. The same type of argument has been urged in disputing the stress of adolescence: there are differences among cultures and among individuals in the degree of stress experienced during this age period. And here, too, it hardly seems necessary to point out that a phenomenon does not cease to exist simply because its intensity varies under different conditions. Stress, of course, is a relative term, but it is difficult, if not impossible, to conceive of so many crucial, transitional changes occurring in personality organization without placing considerable strain on the individual's adjustive capacities. We would, however, agree with Kuhlen [6] that it would be desirable to substantiate this logical assumption with empirical evidence.

Surprisingly enough, although most workers have not identified themselves with a general theory of adolescent personality development, there is virtual unanimity on the primary developmental tasks of adolescence [3, 4, 5, 6]—even among those who deny that adolescence is a unique period of growth. These developmental tasks are conceptualized as adjustive difficulties or hurdles that must be surmounted by adolescents before adult status can be realized. They have, in the main, been abstracted from empirical studies in which adolescents were requested through questionnaire, check-list, and interview techniques to indicate their major problems. [2, 7, 8, 10]

Corey's [4] grouping of these problems into five chief categories of developmental tasks is typical of the current thinking. Adolescents, he states, must (1) learn to accept and come to terms with their own bodies; (2) learn an appropriate sex role; (3) establish independence from adult (particularly parental) domination; (4) achieve adult economic status; and (5) develop a system of values. We would not attempt to deny that these are the essential and unavoidable tasks of development that adolescents are required to complete in the course of their transition to adult maturity. We would prefer, however, to relate these developmental tasks to more general maturational changes that are taking place in personality structure (the greater needs for volitional independence and a self-determined status, the devaluation of hedonistic motivation, the increased capacity for sustained striving in relation to long-term goals). Looked at in this way, these developmental tasks constitute the necessary areas of life adjustment in which the gains of adolescent personality maturation must be applied before the various component requirements of adult status can be met. For example, all five developmental tasks can be thought of as different and mutually complementary ways in which the enhanced need for self-assertion can be satisfied. So regarded, they acquire greater generality of meaning in relation to the underlying personality changes of adolescence than when considered merely as separate objectives of adjustment that development during this period should be expected to accomplish.

REFERENCES AND BIBLIOGRAPHY

1. Ausubel, D. P.: Problems of adolescent adjustment. Bulletin Natl. Assn. Secondary School Principals, *34*:1–84, 1950.
2. Bell, H. M.: *Youth Tell Their Story*. Washington, D. C.: American Council on Education, 1940.
3. Cole, L. *Psychology of Adolescence*. New York: Rinehart, 1948.
4. Corey, S. M.: Developmental Tasks of Youth. In John Dewey Society Yearbook. New York: Harper, 1946.
5. Jersild, A. T. et al.: *Child Development and the Curriculum*. New York: Teachers College, Columbia University, 1946.
6. Kuhlen, R. G.: *The Psychology of Adolescent Development*. New York: Harper, 1952.
7. Mooney, R.: Surveying high-school students' problems by means of a problem check list. Educ. Res. Bulletin, *21*:57–69, 1942.
8. Pope, C.: Personal problems of high-school pupils. Sch. & Soc., *57*:443–448, 1943.
9. Sherif, M. and Cantril, H.: The Psychology of Ego-Involvements. New York: Wiley, 1947.
10. Symonds, P. M.: Sex differences in the life problems and interests of adolescents. Sch. & Soc., *43*:751–752, 1936.

PART TWO

Psychobiological Problems

CHAPTER 3

Problems of Psychological Transition

THE MEANING OF PSYCHOLOGICAL TRANSITION

SINCE ALL natural phenomena are in a state of continual flux, we could with justice characterize the whole of development as *transitional*. However, this absolute use of the term would serve no useful purpose in elucidating the nature of change. But inasmuch as there is always marked variability in the rate of development, it is worthwhile and meaningful to distinguish between periods of relative stability and periods of rapid change, between states of being and states of becoming. Change does occur in the former condition but within a framework of qualitative constancy—in quantitative increments or decrements that do not upset the prevailing equilibrium. However, when the rate of change accelerates markedly because of a sudden shift in the direction of development, disequilibrium sets in until the newly evolving form becomes sufficiently consolidated to constitute a relatively stable and permanent state of being. Customarily then, it is to the latter situation that reference is made when the term *transition* is used.

In personality development, periods of transition occur when significant changes take place in the biosocial status of the individual. Such changes generally occur in the interval between infancy and childhood, between childhood and adult life, and between the adult period and senescence. During these transitional periods, the individual is in the marginal position of having lost an established and accustomed status and of not yet having acquired the new status toward which the factors impelling developmental change are driving him. The adolescent, for example, enjoys the status of neither child nor adult. To be sure he is not entirely without any status whatsoever, for that, too, would be impossible; but the status that he does enjoy is vague, ambiguous, and rapidly changing. It is hardly comparable to the relatively permanent and stable type of relationship that prevails between him and his environment in the preceding and succeeding stages of his development; it is primarily a state of becoming rather than a state of being.

Theoretically, there is every reason to believe that transitional periods must necessarily be difficult and productive of stress. If the biosocial status of an individual determines his over-all relationship to his environment, it must by definition provide a comprehensive and stable frame of reference for the organization of his attitudes, values, goals, and behavior. In this framework, which lasts long enough to become both familiar and highly differentiated, he feels oriented and secure in interpreting and reacting to the events that go on around him. He knows what he expects of others and what others expect of him, and he has learned values and roles that are compatible with these expectations. He develops a set of attitudes toward himself as well as a characteristic constellation of motivational traits designed to implement these attitudes. It is hardly conceivable that the impending loss of this status could fail to be anything but disorganizing and traumatic in its effects. Can he reasonably expect to find the same degree of security, and experience similar feelings of confidence and orientation in a new and uncharted psychological field, the landmarks and limits of which are obscure and hazy? On what defensible basis can he learn appropriate new attitudes, goals, values, and roles when he enjoys no clear status against which to measure their suitability? And even if unambiguous criteria were available, would not a tremendous burden of new learning still fall to his lot?

The transitional difficulties of insecurity and disorientation, of having to learn a whole new set of adaptive cues and habits, give rise to a new cause for stress, namely, a growing disinclination for change. This resistance from within to surrendering the security of an established status comes into violent conflict with potent pressures for change that are both internal and external in origin. Hence, arises a conflictful sphere of overlapping needs and loyalties, a psychological marginality of disposition to match the environmental marginality of status. As Lewin puts it:

> Many conflicts in childhood are due to forces corresponding to the various groups to which the child belongs. Such conflicts are particularly important for

children in marginal positions, that is, for children who are standing on the boundary between two groups. One example is the adolescent who no longer wants to belong to the children's group but who is not yet fully accepted by the adults. Uncertainty of the ground on which the child stands leads to an alternation between the values of the one and of the other group, to a state of emotional tension, and to a frequent fluctuation between overaggressiveness and overtimidity. The degree to which such adolescent behavior is shown depends upon the degree to which children and adolescents are treated as separate groups in that culture.[12]

TRANSITIONAL ANXIETY

In addition to feelings of insecurity and disorientation and the sudden need for new adaptive learnings that inevitably accompany the onset of a transitional period in development, still another reason for stress is inherent in psychological transition. The source of this stress is to be found in the relationships that prevail between status, self-esteem, and anxiety.

The *self-esteem* of an individual is largely a reflection of his aspirations for status, and of the discrepancy existing between these aspirations and his actual or potential possession of status. His level of self-esteem tends to be high when the status he enjoys is commensurate with his aspirations, and tends to be low when the opposite condition prevails. Hence, self-esteem will be threatened by situations that either endanger present and potential status, or create aspirations for new status which are disproportionately high in relation to realistic possibilities for succesful attainment.* When the threat to self-esteem becomes sufficiently great to be reacted to emotionally, it evokes a variety of fear response that can be best characterized as a state of anxiety. *Transitional anxiety*, therefore, refers to the fear reactions that are produced by factors inhering in periods of psychological transition that significantly threaten an individual's self-esteem.

During adolescence, for example, there are at least two good

---

* An example of this latter situation occurs in some cultures such as our own where the adolescent fails to appreciate at the outset that the attainment of adult status will not only be delayed for many years, but also will probably not be achieved at the level of social prestige to which he has been encouraged to aspire. However, since this is not a universal consequence of psychological transition, it will be discussed in relation to psychosocial problems of adolescence.

reasons for the generation of transitional anxiety. First, the adolescent is required to repudiate the major source of socially acceptable status that was available to him as a child, the derived status that vicariously accrued to him because of his dependent relationship to his parents. He becomes obliged instead to seek status as a person in his own right, a status based on his own competence in adjusting to the demands of his environment. As a result of this shift there is an immediate loss in current status that threatens his self-esteem and is reacted to with fear.

Second, the culture almost universally creates transitional anxiety for the adolescent by generating an aura of uncertainty about his ultimate attainment of adult status. He is coerced by the relentless pressure of social expectations into internalizing a new set of ego aspirations that are compatible with the status characteristics of adult maturity in his particular social milieu. But the eventual outcome of his strivings is always in doubt until success is finally achieved. The culture is extremely careful always to guarantee nothing from the start, to hold the benefits of future status in abeyance until final discretionary judgment is rendered. In view of the crucial issue at stake—the absolute necessity for achieving adult status and the catastrophic consequences of faliure to do so—the adolescent finds even the slightest uncertainty threatening to his self-esteem and hence productive of anxiety.* He can reduce this anxiety (but never completely eliminate it) by maintaining a high level of striving in relation to the developmental tasks confronting him. Hence, although anxiety in this context is disagreeable for the individual, it undoubtedly serves a "socially-adaptive" function.[6] Regardless whether it is deliberately used as a training device, and quite apart from its implications for mental hygiene, it would be difficult to deny its effectiveness in keeping the course of adolescent maturation moving in the appropriate direction and at the expected rate of progress, whatever these may be in a particular cultural environment.

* Part of the fear response evoked in this situation is precipitated by the individual's anticipation of a threat to his physical safety and biological well-being rather than to his self-esteem. This type of fear can be more appropriately referred to as *insecurity* rather than anxiety.

TEMPORAL FACTORS INFLUENCING THE DIFFICULTY
OF PSYCHOLOGICAL TRANSITION

Three other important characteristics of psychological transition that affect the difficulty of adjusting to it are (1) the abruptness of its onset, (2) discrepancies in the rate of growth of various component functions, and (3) the total length of time it occupies. All three factors define crucial temporal dimensions of transitional periods. In addition, the first two factors, although extremely variable from culture to culture, may be said to be inherent in the very nature of transition. That is, almost by definition, transitional phases of development begin abruptly because of a sudden change in the rate or direction of growth, which is discontinuous with the preceding stage; and when the developmental process is sufficiently complex to encompass several constituent aspects, discrepancies in rate of growth are practically inevitable. The duration of the transitional period, on the other hand, is a completely variable dimension. To be characteristic of psychological transition it need not be either relatively long or relatively short, since either is equally compatible with the essential properties of transitional states. However, the actual length of time involved, as will be shown below, is one of the important variables affecting both the stressfulness of transition and some of its subsidiary properties.

Abruptness of Onset

Abruptness of onset is a characteristic feature of adolescent development in all cultures. This is true despite the fact that many aspects of maturation are inaugurated in the middle years of childhood and undergo preparatory completion during the preadolescent period. Although much variability prevails in this respect, children everywhere follow the general pattern of acquiring greater responsibility and self-sufficiency with age, more responsiveness to social norms, and increased capacity for postponing the gratification of hedonistic needs. In most cultures, also, children have the opportunity of gaining some degree of status in relation to the objective level of their abilities and accomplishments, and sometimes in relation to the actual contributions they are able to make to the economic life of the family or community.

Hence, since the beginnings of most adolescent changes in personality maturation can be traced to earlier periods of development, it is not possible to attribute the abrupt onset of adolescence to a sudden need for incorporating into personality structure a completely alien set of norms for the appropriate characteristics of mature behavior. The abruptness, inheres rather, in the accelerated rate of maturational change and in the sudden shift in context and importance which these developments assume for the total economy of personality organization. Imbedded in a new framework of social expectations for the appropriate content and balance of adult personality structure, the same components of maturation abruptly acquire new meaning and significance. It makes a great deal of difference, for example, whether the *primary* * status one achieves through one's own efforts and competence plays a relatively subsidiary role *vis-a-vis* the *derived* status one receives by virtue of a dependent relationship to parents, or becomes the *major* variety of status which one can legitimately possess; whether the quest for this primary status is undertaken by a sexually immature child volitionally dependent upon his parents and enjoying no recognized position in the adult community, or is undertaken by a biologically mature individual who assumes full responsibility for his own decisions and enjoys complete recognition as a responsible member of the adult social group; whether childish irresponsibility, hedonism, and helplessness are relinquished as a means of placating parents and gaining their approval, or are given up as a necessary adjunctive step in the acquisition of the appurtenances of adult status.

Adolescence, in other words, begins abruptly because adult and childhood personality structure are qualitatively discontinuous in terms of total *Gestalt* rather than in terms of their component constituents. A break with the past is therefore inevitable. It is true, of course, that this break could be made more gradual if the necessary changes in emphasis were introduced less drastically and over a longer period of time. However, the almost invariable relationship between pubescence and the termination of childhood personality

---

* From this point on, the terms *primary* and *derived* status will be used respectively to distinguish between the actual status that an individual earns through his own competencies and efforts as an independent adult, and the status that accrues to him vicariously merely because of a dependent relationship to parents.

status makes this impossible. The dramatic physical and sexual changes of pubescence give impetus to powerful individual and social pressures directed toward the reorganization of personality structure. And, since these biological changes are accomplished within a relatively short space of time, the correlative pressures they generate for personality change are set in motion just as abruptly; for example, parents suddenly withdraw emotional succor and make vastly increased demands for mature behavior. Thus, although the period of adolescent development may, depending on cultural circumstances, be prolonged for a decade or more, its initiation tends to be characteristically abrupt.

Degree of abruptness obviously affects the difficulty of psychological transition by giving rise to more or less disorientation, insecurity, and anxiety, and by providing more or less time and opportunity for the learning of appropriate adaptive responses. It not only differs from culture to culture but also from one transitional period to the next, and accounts in large measure for differences experienced in stressful qualities between both cultures and age periods. The transition between adulthood and senescence (the period of involution) is generally less abrupt than the transition between either infancy and childhood or childhood and adulthood; hence, it is not surprising that for *most* individuals, the involutional period is less turbulent than the two earlier transitional phases of development. We shall also point out later that the almost complete discontinuity between the value systems of children and adults that prevails in our own culture (as well as in certain more primitive cultures such as the Manus) is partly responsible for the unique degree of stress characteristic of adolescent development under such social conditions.

The Duration of Adolescence

The duration of adolescence is not to be confused with the abruptness of its onset. The latter merely refers to the sharpness of the break that is made from childhood status, to the suddenness with which the transitional period is first inaugurated, to the degree of discontinuity that is experienced when the individual is *initially* confronted with the task of personality reorganization. How long before the developmental tasks of adolescent are completed, that is, before adult status is finally attained is an entirely different matter. The difference between the two variables may be made clearer perhaps by reference to a medical analogy. The onset of a disease like pneumonia, for example, is extremely abrupt in comparison with diseases such as cancer or tuberculosis; even a single day before he first reports such violent symptoms as high fever, labored breathing, and severe pain in his chest, the pneumonia patient may experience no noticeable signs of illness. This is in marked contrast to tuberculosis or cancer in which the disease makes its appearance so gradually that several weeks or months may elapse before the patient can definitely report a decided change for the worse in his health. The duration of the disease, on the other hand, refers to the interval between initial establishment of the pathological process and eventual recovery or death. This too is highly variable and fluctuates widely for different diseases.

The duration of adolescence is a highly important dimension of ongoing transitional changes, since it not only influences the degree of adjustive difficulty experienced, but also helps determine significant aspects of the status modifications involved. We have characterized adolescence as a state of becoming rather than as a state of being, as an age period without any definite status features of its own, in which the individual is in the marginal position of having to relinquish his childhood status while still in the process of acquiring adult status. It is now necessary to qualify this generalization. The indefinite and ambiguous no-man's-land of status is tolerable as described only if self-limited in duration, that is, over a period of weeks or months, as in some primitive cultures in which the total length of adolescence is coextensive with the duration of the initiation rites that mark its occurrence. Under these conditions, "no elaborate *interim* arrangements need be made." [2]

But if the transitional period is to cover an interval of several years or a decade, such marginal status is no longer psychologically tenable in terms of the prolonged disorientation, insecurity, and anxiety involved. When society is organized to require an extended period of adolescent transition, it becomes necessary to formalize a definite *interim status*. This status occupies a position intermediate between that of childhood and adult life, but embodies, nevertheless, certain distinctive characteristics which in a limited sense can be considered as ends in themselves. This provides the adolescent with some recognized social standing, an opportunity for acquiring some current self-esteem, and a tangible frame of reference for selectively accepting certain attitudes, values, and goals and rejecting others.

However, no matter how elaborate and seemingly adequate this interim status may become, it still does not suffice to take from adolescence its transitional and marginal character. For concurrently, the individual is still desperately striving to attain the coveted status of an adult, the prerogatives of which society just as carefully keeps beyond his reach. The interim status he enjoys can be no more than a makeshift way-station, a temporary sop to make present deprivation more bearable until the real status he seeks becomes available. Thus, the developmental tasks of adolescence are predicated upon the attainment of the characteristic features of *adult* personality status rather than upon the accomplishment of those transitory intermediate goals that are designed merely to serve a compensatory adjustive function during the bleak, frustration-laden years of transition. In other words, the adolescent individual strives primarily to become an adult and only incidentally to become an adolescent. It is true that in his quest for an interim status he establishes a distinctive subculture of his own. But unlike the other developmental subcultures of infancy, childhood, and adulthood, it lacks true biosocial stability and permanence. It is a creature and special manifestation of prolonged transition rather than a product of developmental equilibrium.

Hence, the prolongation of adolescence cannot do otherwise than add to its stress. Despite the compensations provided by interim status, the major status aspirations of the individual remain unfulfilled; and prolonged status deprivation can only lead to a state of chronic frustration and to a semi-permanent condition of transitional anxiety. Thus, even more than to the exaggeratedly abrupt onset of adolescence, its acute emotional instability in modern Western civilization can be attributed to the unparalleled prolongation of its duration.

Discrepancies in Rate of Growth

Although various component aspects of development are undoubtedly interrelated and frequently exhibit a certain amount of parallelism for a given individual [14] in their relative degrees of maturity, it is apparent that even under optimal conditions, discrepancies in rate of growth are inevitable. "The reasons for this are self-evident. In nature, the characteristics of any growth process are uniquely determined by the special conditions relevant to its development." [2] Hence, it is extremely unlikely that the particular constellation of genetic and environmental factors regulating the development of any given trait or capacity would completely overlap the set of regulatory factors involved in the development of any other trait or capacity.

During transitional periods of development, there are further reasons that serious discrepancies in rate of growth will probably arise. As the tempo of development (or decline) accelerates and as discontinuities in the growth patterns of particular functions occur, greater opportunities prevail for wider disparities to develop between the relative levels of maturity attained by these different functions. It is true that the general tendency toward interdependence in the growth processes of component aspects of development tends to diminish this unevenness as developmental equilibrium is gradually restored. Growth spurts also tend to taper off with age, thereby narrowing the maturational gap between two functions. In the meantime, however, at least initially, glaring discrepancies in rate of growth constitute a characteristic and invariable feature of transitional phases of development.

In adolescence such discrepancies are particularly evident because of the important role of biological factors in precipitating the total complex of changes that arise. To begin with, the determinants of physiological and physical growth are much more constant and invariable than the determinants of intellectual, social, or emotional maturity. The physiological (hormonal) changes of adolescence are chiefly regulated by genetic factors, which by and large follow a phylogenetic timetable that is (as far as we know) completely independent of cultural conditions. All of the other growth functions, however, are largely influenced in their rate of development by the highly variable patterns of stimulation, repression, and expectation that prevail in particular cultural environments. Second, the very fact that the hormonal events of pubescence have important implications for emotional and personality development—both directly by giving rise to new drives, feelings, and states of awareness in the individual, and indirectly by arousing new patterns of expectations in others who customarily influence his behavior—guarantees that a substantial portion of the physiological changes of adolescence, as well as of their more immediate physical consequences, will *precede* growth in these other aspects of development. Hence, the very interrelatedness of the growth process (in the sense that the maturation of one component may serve as the precipitating stimulus for the maturation of another component) insures the existence of an initial discrepancy, although it makes for greater parallelism in the total pattern of growth.

There are innumerable examples of unevenness in adolescent development. When growth in one area is a necessary precondition for or stimulant of growth in another area, a certain amount of lag is inevitable. Thus, muscle strength lags behind the increase in muscle mass,[16] but it precedes the gain in neuromuscular coordination. The growth spurts in social and emotional development necessarily begin *after* the physiological and physical growth spurts which play so important a role in their evolution. In some cases, unevenness in the total growth pattern is caused by the lack of a growth spurt in certain areas. An illustration of this is intellectual development, which is singularly unresponsive to the stimulus of physiological maturation,[9] but may be adversely affected by emotional instability and the sudden influx of competing interests powered by emerging new drives. Body tissues, such as the genital, which have hardly grown since infancy for lack of adequate physiological stimulation suddenly "outstrip [all] other body parts in velocity of growth" [16] as hormonal (gonadal) support is provided; other tissues, such as the lymphoid, decline in growth [8] as their hormonal support (the thymus gland?) is either reduced or more vigorously counteracted (by the adrenal cortex). Another type of "asynchrony of development as between leg length and stem length, hip width and shoulder width . . . is in all probability idiomatic for each individual throughout the whole span of physical growth," but becomes more noticeable when the rate of growth is accelerated.[16]

Discrepancies in rate of growth also occur when biological factors are not involved. In personality development, differences in social attitudes and expectations, in the availability of certain types of status-giving activities, and in the relative flexibility of various social institutions result in marked differences in the maturity levels characterizing the several indices of adult personality status. In our own culture, for example, considerable emancipation from parents' influence on goals, values, and behavior is achieved long before a comparable measure of social and economic recognition is conferred by society at large. Yet even within the home numerous inconsistencies prevail in various aspects of the adolescent's status and independence. Generally speaking, parents are quicker to withdraw emotional support than they are to relinquish the exercise of their traditional authority. They are more intent upon demanding from their children the acquisition of adult responsibility, motivations, and values than they are willing to grant commensurate rewards in increased privileges and prerogatives for appropriate accomplishment.

These growth discrepancies are not without their developmental repercussions. Just as maturation in one area may precipitate or facilitate maturation in another area, the converse holds equally true: relative retardation in a slowly growing function inevitably limits the full expression and complete development of a more rapidly growing function.

> Since in any particular segment of behavior, the adolescent can only function as a total personality, the attainment of adult status must be postponed until all of the major lines of growth are completed. Thus, the first consequence of any growth discrepancy is that earlier-maturing functions, which if considered solely in terms of their own degree of maturity would be ready for earlier use, must still await the maturation of other functions before they can be effectively or fully employed.[2]

Thus, whenever growth in a given function greatly outstrips development in related, supporting functions, only two possibilities of expression exist: The relatively precocious function will (1) be utilized immediately, before the supporting areas are adequately developed, and therefore prematurely; or (2) its utilization will be deferred until related maturational tasks are completed. But regardless of the alternative, the results will prove unsatisfactory. Premature utilization can never be wholly effective or satisfying and often leads to serious dysfunction. For example, complete sexual gratification in our culture cannot be experienced before the attainment of some emotional maturity and socio-economic independence, despite the fact that the physiological apparatus for sexual expression is fully mature in the earliest phase of adolescence; and in addition to its incompleteness, early sexual experience will frequently be characterized by varying degrees of conflict, guilt, and other undesirable emotional consequences associated with promiscuity or various compensatory outlets.

On the other hand, postponement of functional expression until related maturational readiness would lead to emotional tension because of the frustration of current needs, and to developmental retardation resulting from disuse and insufficient role-playing experience. Were the adolescent, for example, to defer his quest for emancipation from the home until he attained economic independence, he would not only be a very unhappy and frustrated individual, but would also be seriously retarded in over-all personality development. Hence, because either alternative presents major difficulties and disadvantages, some form of compromise is usually adopted, depending on the urgency of the needs connected with the early-maturing function and on the severity of the penalties following premature utilization. Thus, the middle-class adolescent male in our society settles for both substitutive sexual outlets and partial emancipation from parents. This compromise avoids completely neither the conflict and the incompleteness of self-expression associated with one alternative, nor the frustrations and retardation of psychosexual and personality development associated with the other alternative. It does, however, spare the adolescent from the more drastic consequences that would follow from the choice of either extreme position.

WHAT PRECIPITATES PSYCHOLOGICAL TRANSITION

A crucial general problem of psychological transition is understanding the conditions that bring it about. When an individual's personality is in a state of developmental equilibrium—true to the principles of homeostasis—it tends to maintain the existing equilibrium until forces sufficiently prepotent to render it untenable intervene. Changes of ordinary magnitude, however, can be easily assimilated within the current framework of personality structure without disrupting homeostatic balance. Thus, the stability and general constancy of personality organization are assured unless the individual is confronted by changes in his biosocial status that are so everwhelming that basic structural reorganization is necessary.

This being true, under what conditions does psychological transition become "a relevant possibility"? What types of changes are likely to be effective in overcoming inertia inherent in this developmental situation? This problem becomes somewhat less formidable if we bear in mind first that the conditions necessary for precipitating a transitional stage of development are *not* necessarily synonymous or coextensive with the conditions required for carrying it forward to a successful conclusion. The circumstances, for example, that make childhood personality status completely untenable and initiate beginning adolescent progress toward adult maturation do not in any sense insure the eventual attainment of adult personality status. Second, under precipitating factors we shall include *both* (1) conditions that are operative for a relatively long period of time, that is, which exert a preparatory or predisposing influence but are inadequate in themselves to effect transition; and (2) factors with a more dramatic and explosive impact that not only supplement and consummate the changes initiated by the predisposing conditions, but also serve as catalysts in accelerating the rate of change to effect the inauguration of psychological transition.

Generally speaking, there are two main *sources* for the changes that compel psychological transition: (a) an urgent need within the culture for a fundamental modification of the social and personality status of an entire group of individuals who are in a given stage of developmental equilibrium; (b) the occurrence of marked changes within the individual, changes in physical make-up, basic drives, competencies, perceptual ability, which are so crucial that present status becomes incompatible with his altered appearance, capacities, needs and perceptions.[2] Both types of precipitating factors are important in adolescence.

The *social* needs for restructuring childhood personality status originate in the unwillingness and inability of parents to assume responsibility indefinitely for their children's economic support, and in society's recognition of the fact that because of the limited duration of life a new generation of individuals must be constantly trained and equipped to take over the task of maintaining and perpetuating the culture. Hence, it becomes a matter of deliberate social policy to develop in adolescents those personality traits that are most important for insuring not only the physical survival of the individual and the group, but also the cultural survival of the particular values and traditions to which the social order subscribes.

Operationally, cultural needs for modifying the direction of personality development are mediated both through specific training institutions and through the more subtle and pervasive device of confronting the individual and everyone responsible for his welfare with a new set of social expectations. Hence, parents of their own volition and under the pressure of new social expectations begin to withdraw derived status from their adolescent children; the adolescents in turn are influenced by the depreciated social value of their derived status in contrast to the increased emphasis placed upon the acquisition of primary status.

The *individual* factors that help precipitate adolescent transition originate less from any startling new advances in intellectual, perceptual, social, or adaptive capacity, than from a cluster of interrelated physiological changes with far-reaching implications for bodily appearance, drives, and emotions. Thus, the combined effect of attaining (a) the outward appearance of adult body form, (b) the reproductive capacity for creating his own family unit, and (c) the biological sex drive and emotional repertory of a mature adult apparently "releases a powerful drive within the individual for establishing himself as a person in his own right." [2] It would be highly unnatural for him to react to his newly acquired physical and biological attributes of adulthood in any way other than by striving for the status prerogatives that they seem to imply. More important, however, than the individual's reaction to his own pubescence is the social response that his sexual maturation elicits; since almost universally, for reasons that are apparently self-evident in the light of its symbolic significance, it constitutes a mandatory and unchallengeable indication for the social termination of childhood personality status.

Two different forces, therefore, converge to precipitate the period of adolescent transition. A long-standing social need is the predisposing condition, whereas the impact of pubescence must be accounted the more crucial precipitating factor. For not only do the physiological changes of pubescence generate important internal needs for reorganizing personality more independently, but they also provide the impetus for releasing latent social pressures directed toward the same end. That is, the conversion of implicit, undirected needs into explicit expectations capable of effecting developmental change is not a spontaneous or self-determined phenomenon, but occurs in response to appropriate and well-defined cues, supplied in this instance by the individual's sexual maturation. Although the interval between the occurrence of pubescence and of cultural recognition of it (in the form of altered social expectations) is generally brief, this is not invariably true. Sometimes, as in Samoa,[13] * several years may elapse before any social notice is taken of what in most other cultures is a highly dramatic event eliciting considerable reaction both from parents and the community.

Hence, although there may be some delay between the attainment of pubescence and the initiation of adolescent transition, the important thing is that the former event always *precedes* and never follows the latter. This is nowhere better illustrated than in those cultural environments in which "economic necessity imposes mature, economic and social tasks upon preadolescent boys and girls." Despite their obligation to assume adult responsibilities and to make adult adjustments in certain areas of life, these individuals still fail to shed their childhood personality status in the eyes of their parents or of society.[15] Thus, although "situations such as these do contribute to the early development and sharpening of the ego,"[15] it is apparent that the inauguration of adolescence only becomes a relevant possibility in a setting of sexual maturity; for only in such a setting does society perceive the individual's strivings for emancipation, volitional independence, equal social membership as having any self-evident legitimacy.

Further proof of the crucial role of pubescence in precipitating adolescent development is the fact that the social needs for altering childhood personality status as well as the important individual preconditions (in terms of social and intellectual maturity) for doing

* It should be realized however that the Samoan situation is the exception to the rule. Many writers, such as Benedict[3] and Kuhlen,[11] have overgeneralized the significance of this fact to mean that puberty institutions are purely social phenomena unrelated to the occurrence of biological pubescence. This view is not supported by the weight of cross-cultural evidence. The *content* of such institutions is socially determined but in the vast majority of cases the precipitating factor impelling cultural recognition is biological.

so have already been operating for several years without effecting psychological transition. Pubescent children do not suddenly become economic burdens, nor do they suddenly loom as potential replacements for dying members of the adult community. Furthermore, their attained level of sheer adaptive ability in relation to the actual amount of intelligence and social skill required for adequate independent adjustment to the physical and cultural environment has long since qualified them for a more mature personality status. The validity of this proposition is substantiated both by the responsible economic tasks successfully managed by children in rural communities and in most primitive cultures, and by the successful adjustments that slightly retarded individuals (who never surpass the preadolescent level of intellectual or social maturity) are able to make even in complex urban environments. Evidently then, in contrast to the situation in other transitional periods of development, we cannot ascribe the onset of adolescence to marked and sudden changes in motor, intellectual, perceptual, or social capacity.

We do not wish to imply by this that the preadolescent gains in biosocial competence have no implications for personality development or receive no recognition from parents or society. The fact is that parents and other social agencies do demand more mature and responsible behavior as children become older; and the latter in turn exercise their newly acquired competencies in acquiring some sources of independent primary status and of mature role-playing experience—whether in school, playground, farm, or newspaper route. As a result of this wider social experience and the independent, non-parental source of ego support that it provides, children view their homes more objectively and begin devaluing their parents. However, until the advent of pubescence these changes take place within the framework of childhood personality status; and in the total economy of ego organization, the parental hearth still remains the major source of current ego status.

The Prevention of Developmental Regression

Once adolescent transition is inaugurated, what prevents a reversal of the change and a restoration of the developmental equilibrium that formerly prevailed? Considering all of the difficulties associated with psychological transition, the adolescent not infrequently—and understandably so—wishes for a return to his childhood personality status. Counteracting this tendency, however, are the very same pressures, social and individual, that precipitated the period of transition. These include the factor of transitional anxiety, which begins to operate as soon as the adolescent loses his former status, internalizes aspirations for a new status and reacts with fear to the uncertainty surrounding the eventual attainment of the latter. This anxiety can be reduced only by making continued progress toward adult personality status. Hence, developmental regression tends to be avoided both because of the high level of striving maintained to minimize anxiety, and because the very contemplation of regression is anxiety-producing.

But again we must emphasize that the pressures that counteract regression—like the factors that precipitate adolescent transition—are not adequate in themselves to result in or insure the attainment of adult personality status. As we shall point out in detail later, the relevant variables affecting the latter outcome are the degree of social recognition as an adult that the adolescent receives, the availability of adult status and role-playing experience, the opportunities for acquiring economic and social independence, the quality of earlier parent-child relationships, and various constitutional factors affecting goal structure. However, the blocking of the road back does guarantee that in the event of maturational failure the individual becomes an unsuccessful, immature adult rather than a re-created, successfully adjusting child.

STAGES OF ADOLESCENCE

It is customary to divide the adolescent period into various stages on the basis of chronological intervals. Thus, Cole [5] distinguishes between "early," "middle," and "late" stages of adolescence, using different age ranges for boys and girls to make allowance for the earlier onset of pubescence in girls. In our opinion, a more defensible and less arbitrary criterion for demarcating stages of adolescence is the degree and type of adjustive stress experienced by the individual during the course of this transitional period. However, regardless of the criterion used, a given classification of stages cannot hold true for all cultures, since the relative length and difficulty of adolescence tends to be socially determined. The following discussion, therefore, will apply only to adolescent development in our own and similar cultures.

For several reasons the initial stage of adolescence presumably involves the greatest amount of stress. First, the individual must contend with the disorientation produced by the abrupt loss of childhood status. Second, in the light of the unrealistic expectations of preadolescents about the status prerogatives enjoyed by adolescents in our culture, the discovery that (despite their close physical resemblance to adults) they are completely rejected by adult society and have almost no opportunities for acquiring adult status comes as a rather rude and traumatic awakening. Third, it takes a certain amount of time for adolescents to anchor themselves in the peer culture that will furnish the major portion of their interim status.

In the second stage of adolescence, therefore, once these initial adaptations are made, there is a substantial decrease in the amount of adjustive stress experienced by the adolescent. As he gradually recovers from the initial shock of disorientation, as he begins to appreciate that his original expectations were unrealistic, and as he becomes reconciled to a prolonged period of interim status, he reacts less acutely to the deprivation of his needs for adult status. In addition, various substitutive satisfactions are available in the peer culture to compensate for the frustration of the adolescent's self-assertive drives. Although the total load of frustration in the second stage of adolescence is reduced by the development of more realistic aspirations and of compensatory sources of status, fluctuations in the level of stressfulness are characteristic. For example, somewhere past the mid-point of this period an accumulation of transitional anxiety and chronic frustration (with no immediate relief forseeable) may give rise to profound feelings of discouragement and despair; whereas only a few years later with the end in sight, the same degree of deprivation can be borne with greater equanimity and cheerfulness.

As already noted, however, we are forced to take exception to the view expressed by Dollard [7] and others that the peer group activities of adolescents represent sublimations (or other types of compensatory derivatives) of frustrated sex drives. We have pointed to evidence [10] that shows that male adolescents in our culture either practice no sex repression at all or, if they do, obtain compensation directly in slightly watered-down forms of sexual expression. The function of the peer culture, therefore, is to provide a source of interim status and an opportunity for adult role-playing experi-

72   THEORY AND PROBLEMS OF ADOLESCENT DEVELOPMENT

ence, and not to compensate for non-existent psychophysiological sex frustration. Furthermore, if such frustration were a prominent feature of adolescence, it would be more logical to conceive of peer group and other interim status activities as autonomously derived from other needs and experiences rather than as direct derivatives of the blocked energies of a single fountain-head of drive.[1] In these circumstances, without in any way meeting the accepted criteria of sublimation, they could still counterbalance the effects of sexual deprivation by providing gratification in other significant areas of personality need.

REFERENCES AND BIBLIOGRAPHY

1. Allport, G. W.: *Personality, A Psychological Interpretation*. New York: Henry Holt, 1937.
2. Ausubel, D. P.: Problems of adolescent adjustment. Bulletin Natl. Assn. Secondary School Principals, *34*:1–84, 1950.
3. Benedict, R.: *Patterns of Culture*. Boston: Houghton Mifflin, 1934.
4. Blos, P.: *The Adolescent Personality*. New York: Appleton-Century, 1941.
5. Cole, L.: *Psychology of Adolescence*. New York: Rinehart, 1948.
6. Davis, A.: "Socialization and Adolescent Personality," in *Adolescence,* 43rd Yearbook, Natl. Soc. Stud. Educ., Part I. Chicago: University of Chicago Press, 1944.
7. Dollard, J. et al.: *Frustration and Aggression*. New Haven: Yale University Press, 1939.
8. Harris, J. A., Jackson, C. M., Paterson, D. G., and Scammon, R. E.: *The Measurement of Man*. Minneapolis: University of Minnesota Press, 1930.
9. Jones, H. E. and Conrad, H. S.: "Mental Development in Adolescence," in *Adolescence,* 43rd Yearbook, Natl. Soc. Stud. Educ., Part I. Chicago: University of Chicago Press, 1944.
10. Kinsey, A. C. et al.: *Sexual Behavior in the Human Male*. Philadelphia: Saunders, 1948.
11. Kuhlen, R. G.: *The Psychology of Adolescent Development*. New York: Harper, 1952.
12. Lewin, K.: "Behavior and Development as a Function of the Total Situation," in *Manual of Child Psychology* (L. Carmichael, ed.). New York: Wiley, 1946.
13. Mead, M.: *From the South Seas*. New York: William Morrow, 1939.
14. Olson, W. C. and Hughes, B. O.: "Growth of the Child as a Whole," in *Child Behavior and Development* (R. G. Barker, J. S. Kounin, and H. F. Wright, eds.). New York: McGraw-Hill, 1943.
15. Sherif, M. and Cantril, H.: *The Psychology of Ego-Involvements*. New York: Wiley, 1947.
16. Stolz, H. R. and Stolz, L. M.: "Adolescent Problems Related to Somatic Variations," in *Adolescence,* 43rd Yearbook, Natl. Soc. Stud. Educ., Part I. Chicago: University of Chicago Press, 1944.

CHAPTER 4

Physiological Aspects of Pubescence

THE NATURE OF PUBESCENCE

PUBESCENCE refers to the characteristic group of bodily changes associated with the sexual maturation of the human individual. As we have already indicated, it covers only a restricted portion of the entire field of adolescent development. *Adolescence,* on the other hand, not only includes the physical phenomena of pubescence, but also all of the behavioral, emotional, social, and personality changes occurring during this developmental period.

Genetic Considerations

In the broader sense of the term, pubescence is a phylogenetic phenomenon. As a result of common racial inheritance, pubescence in man shares all of the major aspects of sexual maturation generally found in mammals. In addition, if we examine the content of these pubescent changes from one individual to the next and the sequence in which they occur, we find a remarkable degree of constancy.

This constancy, not a matter of accident, is determined by the genetic constitution of each individual. Whenever we deal with development that is phylogenetic in nature, that is, common to all members of a biological class of individuals, there are two valid generalizations about the genetic factors involved. (1) *Very little variability between individual members of the species is provided for genetically.* Hence, the course and outcome of development tend to be uniform rather than characterized by a range of individual differences. That is, with relatively few exceptions human infants tend to be born with one head and two eyes, and to creep before they walk, largely because the genes determining these factors are practically identical for all individuals. (2) *The directional influence*

73

exerted by these genetic factors is so potent that it is virtually unmodifiable by environmental conditions. Thus, two individuals exposed to radically different environments, tend to reach practically identical developmental outcomes insofar as the acquisition of phylogenetic traits is concerned. Constancy, therefore, is guaranteed both by the absence of genetic variability and by the neutralization of environmental differences by prepotent genetic influences. We might profitably consider the operation of this latter factor in somewhat greater detail.

It is generally accepted today that heredity *alone* never shapes the ultimate course and outcome of development. From the very moment of conception, when genetic endowment is fixed, its influence on growth is always modified by the environment. This proposition is especially relevant to pubescence in which many years intervene before the effects of hereditary factors are initiated. During the interim, environmental conditions might reasonably be expected to exert considerable unopposed influence on the direction of the development. However, the relative contribution of heredity or environment to the development of a given trait is always proportional to the strength of the influence either factor exerts on the *particular* growth process. Therefore, when genetic factors happen to be prepotent (as they are where phylogenetic development is concerned) environmental differences are for all practical purposes incapable of effecting any variability in developmental outcome.

The same degree of constancy, however, is not to be expected for those aspects of pubescence that are not phylogenetic in nature, such as rapidity and age of onset. The very same genetic considerations as above apply here, but in reverse. Thus, variability between individuals in this instance is predetermined by a certain range of differences in genetic endowment. For example, in a group of girls sharing a relatively homogeneous environment in our culture, the age of first menstruation typically varies between ten and seventeen and tends to be normally distributed.[9, 16, 19] The genetic determination of these individual differences is confirmed by the fact that the daughters of late-maturing mothers tend on the average to experience their first menstruation at a later age than the daughters of early-maturing mothers.[19]

An additional source of variability inheres in the fact that the genetic factors influencing the chronology of pubescence are not sufficiently prepotent to obviate the influence of environmental differences. Thus, possibly because of improved standards of health and nutrition, the age of menarche seems to be lowering in the present generation of girls.[19] Climate is also a factor as shown by the delayed onset of pubescence in northern and tropical climates and its earlier occurrence in temperate areas.[32]

We can, therefore, summarize this discussion of the genetics of pubescence by noting that changing environmental conditions (malnutrition, improved nutrition) modify non-phylogenetic aspects of pubescence such as chronology,* but leave phylogenetic aspects such as sequence unaltered. This difference in susceptibility to environmental influences tends to increase genetically-determined variability in the first (non-phylogenetic) instance, and to maintain genetically-determined invariability in the latter (phylogenetic) instance.

Pubescence as a Psychobiological Problem

The physical changes associated with pubescence result in psychobiological consequences as soon as they affect the emotions, drives, behavior, or personality organization of the pubescent individual. When this point is reached, it becomes appropriate to speak of the entire complex of changes as adolescence. And since the pubescent, infra-human mammal also undergoes psychobiological changes in both his individual and his interpersonal behavior, it is erroneous to restrict the use of the term *adolescence* to the human species. It would be more accurate to state that at the infra-human level adolescence is *purely* a psychobiological phenomenon; that is, the behavioral changes induced by pubescence are not regulated or differentiated by social institutions. Using the same criterion, the frequent statement that individuals in primitive cultures only undergo pubescence and not adolescence (because adult status is achieved so rapidly) is even more erroneous; for in addition to the inevitable psychological reactions to pubescence, there is in every culture, no matter how primitive, some degree of institutionalization of the adolescent period.

---

* At this point it should be noted that culture *per se* does not influence the chronology of pubescence, but only insofar as it is related to such relevant factors as health, nutrition, and climate.

At the human level, pubescence is the cause of psychobiological problems insofar as it has certain general effects on behavior which are universal in distribution and which transcend specific cultural differences in form and content. Some of these common factors include (1) feelings of bewilderment in relation to the strangeness and suddenness of these physical changes, (2) the need for the first time since infancy to socialize new drives and emotions of organic origin, and (3) the direction of regulation from the relatively diffuse to the more highly specific. We have also stated that the occurrence of pubescence is universally a pre-condition for the initiation of adolescent transition and almost invariably is the precipitating factor.

In Chapter 6 we shall discuss in detail the various psychological consequences of pubescence. The task of this chapter and of Chapter 5 will be to describe and explain the physical changes that take place. Underlying this approach (which is traditional for almost all textbooks of adolescent psychology) is the assumption that a proper understanding of the behavioral implications of pubescence depends upon an appreciation of the bodily changes to which they are related. Although in some cases this relationship is clear enough, it must be admitted that most of the physical changes that are usually catalogued have few if any psychological implications, but are merely included to provide a complete picture of adolescent development. In these two chapters, therefore, we shall strive for selectivity rather than for completeness. Even so, the psychological relevance of much explanatory physiological data will be questionable. Nevertheless, they will be included on the theory that even if intrinsically irrelevant for understanding the relationship between physiological events and behavior, they make the former category of events more meaningful, and hence easier to understand and remember.

Types of Pubescent Changes

The physical changes that occur at puberty may be grouped into three levels by the antecedent factors that bring them about. At the *first* level, initiating all of the subsequent changes, is the activation (or increased activity) of the *gonadotropic* and *corticotropic* hormones of the anterior pituitary gland. The antecedent physiological stimulus for this activation is not known at this time but it is undoubtedly regulated in large measure by genetic factors. At the *second* level, we have the immediate consequences of the secretion of these two hormones: (a) the production of mature ova and spermatazoa and the secretion of gonadal hormones as a result of gonadotropic stimulation; and (b) the increased secretion of adrenal cortex hormones as a result of corticotropic stimulation. Both of these latter hormones are responsible for the group of *third* level changes: (a) the development of primary sex characteristics (enlarge-

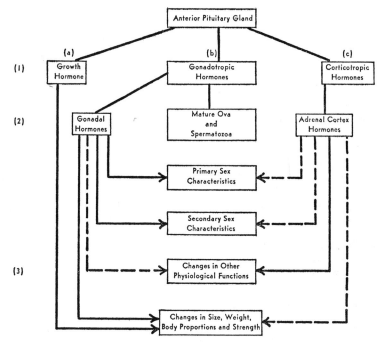

FIGURE 2.—Types of Physical Changes Occurring During Pubescence and their Interrelationships.

ment of penis, testes, uterus); (b) the development of secondary sex characteristics (maturation of breasts, voice changes, growth of pubic hair); (c) changes in other (non-sexual) physiological functions (cardiovascular, respiratory); and (d) changes in size, weight, body proportions, and related changes in strength, coordination, and skill.

Figure 2 represents these different types of physical changes and their interrelationships schematically. The growth hormone of the anterior pituitary gland is included in this diagram because it undoubtedly continues to function and to stimulate skeletal growth during pubescence. However, unlike the gonadotropic hormone, which first becomes functionally active at pubescence, it has been regulating the rate of growth throughout the entire post-natal existence of the individual. The corticotropic hormone, as shown by the growth curve of the adrenal gland,[20] is probably secreted in minimal quantities during childhood, but at pubescence production is markedly increased. In illustrating the effects of the gonadal and adrenal cortex hormones, respectively, a solid line indicates that the gland is chiefly implicated in the particular set of changes shown; a dotted line indicates that in comparison to the other gland it plays only a subsidiary role.

In this chapter it will be convenient to discuss the hormonal changes of pubescence and their effects on sexual maturation (reproductive capacity, primary and secondary sex characteristics) and on other physiological functions. In Chapter 5, the changes in height, weight, body proportions, and strength will be summarized and related to motor development.

THE INITIATION OF PUBESCENCE: HORMONAL CHANGES

The relationship between endocrine factors and the initiation of pubescent phenomena is well established by many parallel and mutually reinforcing lines of evidence. In general such evidence has been obtained in five different ways: [8] (1) experimental extirpation of endocrine glands in animals, or surgical removal in human beings; (2) the injection of hormonal extracts into humans or animals; (3) the determination of the quantity of hormonal substances in the urine of individuals at different age levels—either by chemical analysis or by observing their effects on the sexual maturation of animals; (4) the correlation of precocious puberty with hypertrophy of certain endocrine glands and increased quantities of their hormones in the urine, and the correlation of delayed or absent puberty with destructive lesions of these same glands and diminished hormonal excretion in the urine; and (5) changes with age in the weight and output of endocrine glands, the growth and function of which are known to be regulated by "tropic" hormones. It would serve no useful purpose in a book of this type to present the detailed evidence on which the following outline of the functions of the various hormones in pubescence is based. Nevertheless, the reader should at least be aware of the different methods for ascertaining the function of the glands of internal secretion as they influence pubescent changes.

Although there is an *absolute* difference between pubescent and non-pubescent children in the overt manifestations of pubescence (in the presence of primary and secondary sex characteristics), a corresponding difference in the endocrinological basis of pubescence does not prevail between these two groups. That is, physiologically speaking, prepubescent boys and girls are not asexual. Sex hormones *are* present in the blood stream of these, but in insufficient quantities to give rise to either functional or structural changes; and just as important, no significant difference exists between boys and girls in the ratio of male (androgenic) to female (estrogenic) sex hormones that they produce.[8, 41] The proximate causes responsible for initiating pubescence lie in *critical* changes in the quantitative levels and ratios of these hormones to each other, and in the degree of responsiveness of the tissues they stimulate to their catalytic influence.[41]

The more detailed picture would appear to be something like this: In prepubescent children the adrenal cortex under minimal stimulation from the corticotropic hormone of the anterior pituitary gland secretes whatever androgenic and estrogenic substances are present in the blood stream. These hormones are functionally identical with the estrogens and androgens produced by the gonads (ovaries and testes, respectively).[8] In either sex, the adrenal cortex produces *both* hormones, in each more androgens than estrogens; but the androgenic-estrogenic ratio is only slightly higher in males than in females.[41] The important thing to note, however, is that normally these hormones are not present in sufficient quantities to initiate pubescent changes. But in hypertrophic tumors of either the pituitary cells secreting corticotropic hormone or of the adrenal cortex itself, sufficient amounts of sex hormones are produced to lead to precocious puberty in young children of either sex.[8, 41] In girls, however, pubescence is accompanied and followed by masculinizing changes because of the preponderantly androgenic content of the adrenal cortex hormones.[8, 41]

Biochemically, therefore, prepubescent sexuality seems to be a function of the corticotropic hormone and of the gonadal-like hormones produced by the adrenal cortex. There is no evidence to indicate that the gonads themselves secrete androgens or estrogens before pubescence, and it is definitely established that they do not produce mature sperm or ova. This leads to the conclusion that the gonadotropic hormone that regulates both of these functions is not functionally active before puberty. As a matter of fact, Greulich[18] could find no gonadotropic hormone in the urine of non-pubescent boys; other evidence,[41] however, indicates that despite its absence in the urine, some small quantities are secreted, which (when coupled with the insensitivity of the immature gonads to hormonal stimulation) prove inadequate for any functional gonadal response.

In the normal course of events, two factors change to bring about the structural and overt functional manifestations of sexual maturation: (1) The various genital tissues (penis, uterus, Fallopian tubes) become more sensitive to the stimulation provided by the estrogenic and androgenic hormones of the gonads and adrenal cortex, and these glands, in turn, become more responsive to stimulation by their respective "tropic" hormones secreted by the anterior portion of the pituitary gland. (2) The output of corticotropic and gonadotropic hormones increases markedly. This is shown by the presence of the gonadotropic hormone in the urine for the first time,[18] the phenomenal growth in the size and weight of gonads and adrenals just prior to and during puberty,[20] and by the large increase in the secretion of androgens and estrogens by these glands.[41] Not only do the total quantities of male *and* female sex hormones present in the blood stream increase for *both* sexes (because of increased adrenal cortex output), but the androgenic-estrogenic ratio also rises for boys and falls for girls. This differential secretory pattern for the two sexes is established because the male or female gonad, unlike the adrenal cortex, secretes only *one* kind of sex hormone, the sex-appropriate hormone in each case.

But although the immediate factors (increased secretion by gonadotropic and corticotropic hormones and increased sensitivity of the gonads and adrenal cortex to their stimulation) responsible for initiating the pubescent cycle are fairly well established today, little is known how or why these initiating factors themselves are set in motion. We can only infer that factors known to be correlated with individual differences in age of pubescence, i.e., heredity, climate, nutrition, general health, prepubescent height and weight, are either causally or indirectly related. At any rate, once critical levels of gonadal and adrenal hormone production are reached, primary and secondary sex characteristics appear relatively quickly, as well as physiological changes in other organ systems. Also, unless repressed by cultural influences, psychophysiological sex drives result from the increased presence of estrogenic or androgenic substances in the blood stream. These relationships have been unequivocally confirmed by changes in the expected direction produced by injection of the hormones, surgical castration, and by destructive lesions of the gonads (mumps, tuberculosis) and adrenals (Addison's disease). The production of mature sperm and ova, on the other hand, is not dependent upon hormonal stimulation by the gonads, but is regulated by specific fractions of the gonadotropic hormone.[8]

PRIMARY SEX CHARACTERISTICS

The primary sex characteristics consist of the actual sex organs involved in copulation and reproduction. During the entire period of childhood the growth of these organs lags behind that of all other organ systems.[20] For all practical purposes, such growth is negligible in comparison with the skeletal changes that take place before puberty and the genital growth accompanying pubescence. The reason for this relative stunting has already been made clear. The genital organs grow only in response to an adequate level of gonadal stimulation, an event which does not take place until the age of puberty. Skeletal and visceral growth, on the other hand, is regulated by the growth hormone of the anterior pituitary gland, which is produced in functional amounts even before the birth of the child. As a matter of fact, the genital organs are larger at birth than they are in subsequent years of an infant's life because of the stimulation to which they are subjected by maternal hormones during intra-uterine life.

The growth of the major sex organs of the male is a matter of considerable psychological importance because their location is external; hence, in contrast to those of the female, they afford a basis for comparison with the genitalia of other males. Because of the firmly-rooted belief in our folk-lore that the size of the external genitalia is closely correlated with and symbolic of masculine virility and potency, boys (as well as their parents, teachers, and peers) are deeply concerned with the growth of their external sex organs. Generally speaking, three great sources of variability in the size of the male genitalia exist: (1) individual differences in genetic structural factors limiting the maximal growth attainable regardless of the adequacy of hormonal stimulation; (2) individual differences in androgenic output; and (3) individual differences in the age of pubescence. Unfortunately, however, adolescent boys are bound by the tyranny of the norm and have little regard for individual differences. Their parents and teachers also tend to set unreasonable standards of masculine development.[39, 46] Hence, because textbooks on anatomy and adolescence tend to show a peculiar modesty in treating the growth and dimensions of the male sex organs, these topics, which are of considerable practical importance to parents, teachers, physicians and counselors, will be discussed briefly below. Their psychological implications will be considered in Chapter 6 (see p. 152).

The growth curves for (1) volume of testes, (2) length, and (3) circumference of the fully stretched flaccid penis are practically parallel, although the slope of the last-mentioned is somewhat less steep than that of the first two.[38, 40] (Measurements of the unstretched, flaccid penis are misleading because they correlate poorly with measurements of the erect penis. However, the stretched flaccid penis is about the same length as and 0.77 times the diameter of the erect penis.[38, 40]) Before the age of twelve, growth in all three measurements is negligible. The testes begin to grow first, followed by growth in the length and then in the circumference of the penis. At thirteen the median volume of the testis is 4.8 cubic centimeters (range: 1.5–20), the median length of the fully stretched flaccid penis is 8.8 centimeters (range: 5.5–15.5), and its median circumference is 5.8 centimeters (range: 4.2–9.5). At fifteen, the corresponding measurements for volume of testis are 11.8 (range 2–27), for length of penis 11.8 (range: 6.5–17.5), and for circumference of penis 7.7 (range: 5.5–10.5). At maturity (age 17 to 25) these same measurements are 16 (range: 7–33), 13.5 (range: 8.5–19.5), and 8.5 (range: 6.5–12.5).[38, 40]

In evaluating a case of apparent genital underdevelopment, the three factors making for variability should be kept in mind. The diagnosis of delayed puberty is self-evident (complete absence of primary and secondary sex characteristics), and unless caused by some endocrine disturbance, the condition will eventually right itself; the genitalia will reach their intended size only at a later age. When pubescence is not markedly delayed in onset but appears arrested, underdevelopment of the male sex organs may be due either (1) to genetic factors related to structural limitations, or (2) to insufficient androgenic stimulation referable to gonadal or pituitary insufficiency. In the first situation the small size of the genitalia presents a sharp contrast to the otherwise normal development of expected secondary sex characteristics. In the second, however, retardation in these subsidiary physical indices of masculinity is a distinctive accompaniment of hypogonadism since their development is also dependent upon adequate androgenic stimulation. An example of this condition is provided by Fröhlich's syndrome, which occurs in lesions of the pituitary gland. It is marked by hypogenitalism, adiposity, and female body type.* The crucial distinguishing feature between these two different varieties of hypogenitalism for therapeutic management is the fact that only the type caused by hormonal insufficiency responds to the administration of gonadotropic or androgenic hormones.[8]

In girls, variability in the primary sex characteristics is psychologically unimportant because the major sex organs are internal, and the external genitalia are relatively inconspicuous and hidden from view. Physiologically, however, individual differences are determined by the same three factors making for variability in the size of male genitalia. But even if the female reproductive organs are not open to direct inspection, fairly reliable inferences regarding their relative state of maturity can be drawn from the establishment of the menstrual cycle. Menstruation does not occur in the absence of sexual maturity, and usually the failure to initiate menstruation

* It is important to differentiate this disease from ordinary obesity, in which normally-sized genitalia may appear unduly small as a result of being imbedded in suprapubic fat.

is *prima facie* evidence of sexual immaturity. It may sometimes happen, however, that sexually mature women who have borne several children have never menstruated. Also, although ovulation is usually part of the menstrual cycle, either event (ovulation or menstruation) can occur in the absence of the other. Thus, the establishment of menstruation is not absolutely correlated with reproductive capacity. Menstrual cycles tend to be highly irregular in the beginning but become more regular with increasing age.[16, 21] A period of physiological sterility also exists for one or more years after the occurrence of the first menstruation.[2, 33]

The physiology of menstruation is a highly complex matter, which cannot be entered into fully here. Note, however, that the menstrual cycle involves a series of interrelationships among the gonadotropic hormones, the ovaries, and the uterus. As a result of cyclical gonadotropic stimulation, the ovary produces two kinds of hormones (estrogens and progesterone), which effect hypertropic changes in the internal lining of the uterus. Sometime past the mid-point of the cycle, ovulation occurs. If the ovum is fertilized, the uterine changes that have taken place in the meantime become the maternal contribution to the formation of the placenta, and menstruation does not occur. If fertilization does *not* occur, the preparatory thickening of the inner wall of the uterus becomes superfluous and is sloughed off. The discharge of this necrotic tissue mixed with mucous and blood constitutes the chief overt manifestation of the menstrual cycle.

Hence, the occurrence of the first menstruation is generally accepted as an indication that the primary generative organs of the female have reached functional maturity. It is an event that is comparable in physiological significance to the first ejaculation of semen by the pubescent male except that it is more definite and dramatic; hence, the exact date of its occurrence can be fixed with greater assurance. This definiteness is further highlighted by the fact that menstruation is frequently accompanied by unpleasant physical symptoms such as abdominal cramps, headache, backache, flatulence, nausea, and fatigue. The attention of the pubescent girl may therefore be unduly drawn to this cyclical event, which in her mind becomes symbolic of all the physical changes that have occurred during pubescence. Thus, psychologically speaking, it is more comparable in significance to the enlargement of the male genitalia in the recognition it receives from the individual, her parents, teachers, and contemporaries. It provides a distinct dividing line between girls who are socially accepted as sexually mature and girls who are still regarded as prepubescent.

SECONDARY SEX CHARACTERISTICS

The secondary sex characteristics refer to subsidiary physical features which serve as indices of masculinity and femininity. Since their development is dependent upon stimulation by functional quantities of androgens and estrogens, they do not appear until puberty, overlapping in time of appearance the emergence of the primary sex characters. In terms of significance for heterosexual adjustment, however, they are even more important than the latter. First, they are more readily observable and socially accessible as criteria of sexual maturity and sex-appropriateness, especially to members of the opposite sex. Second, unlike the primary sex organs, they play an important role in determining the physical attractiveness and hence the heterosexual effectiveness of adolescents and adults.

Another important difference between the primary and secondary sex characteristics is the fact that the latter are *not* dichotomous in distribution. That is, in terms of his primary sex organs an individual is *either* male *or* female and not something in-between. Whatever variability exists with respect to the primary sex characteristics must be expressed within the framework of this dichotomy. Hence individual differences are always *intra*-sexual and never *inter*-sexual in nature. The genitalia of a boy may be large or small but under no circumstances can they be placed on the same qualitative scale with female sex organs. Under no circumstances (excluding rare instances of hermaphroditism) can overlapping between the sexes occur.

All of the secondary sex characteristics, on the other hand, are truly continuous in their distribution. No absolute boundary line exists between the two sexes. Male and female can be placed at opposite ends of the same continuum because all differences are quantitative in nature. The same *structures* (breasts, pubic hair, facial hair) are present in both sexes varying only with respect to such factors as size, quantity, extensiveness. Hence, although there is a distinct and unmistakable difference between the mean measurements of boys and girls on any of these variables, overlapping does occur at the center of the distribution. For example, in a late-adolescent group of 77 boys and 79 girls rated by Bayley and Bayer [7] in terms of androgyny (maleness) of body build, the scores of each sex were normally distributed with a large difference betwen the means of each group. However, there was overlapping of scores at the low end of the male distribution and the high end of the female distribution.

As commonality of structure provides the anatomical basis for bisexuality in the secondary sex characteristics, the hormones of the adrenal cortex provide the physiological basis. At puberty the adrenals in both sexes secrete larger quantities of both estrogens and androgens (more of the latter in each sex). However, when the gonads are functioning adequately, the quantity of sex-appropriate hormone they produce tends to overshadow the effect of the opposite sex hormone secreted by the adrenals. In cases of gonadal insufficiency, on the other hand, this effect may be sufficient to result in highly undifferentiated or even inappropriate secondary sex characteristics (e.g., Fröhlich's syndrome).

The appraisal of a given case of sex-inappropriateness of the various physical criteria of masculinity and femininity requires careful consideration of the same three sources of variability listed above for the primary sex characters. The diagnosis of late pubescence presents no difficulty. Cases of hormonal insufficiency will be marked by small genitalia and by a general lack of appropriateness in *all* of the secondary sex characteristics. However, if the primary sex organs are normal in size and only one or two physical traits are inappropriate, the condition may be attributed to specific genetic factors regulating the structural development of the trait.

Development of Breasts

Enlargement of the breasts is the earliest and most important social criterion of sexual maturation in girls. Because of their conspicuousness, which is only slightly affected by clothing, they are even more significant in this respect than the male genitalia. During prepubescence and prior to the first menstruation, the first change that is observable is an elevation of the pigmented area surrounding the nipple (the areola). This is often referred to as the "bud stage." It differs from the characteristic form of the breast in early childhood (after the age of three) in which only the nipple projects above the level of adjacent structures.[17] The next change that occurs, beginning before the menarche and continuing well into adolescence is a gradual enlargement and protrusion of the area surrounding the areola. For the most part, this is caused by the deposition of fat tissue.[17] No striking increase in glandular tissue itself takes place until pregnancy ensues.

The growth of the breasts from rudimentary childhood structures to full-sized adult organs is dependent upon adequate hormonal stimulation from the gonads. It will not take place in girls who suffer from gonadal insufficiency. For the same reason, the breasts of men normally persist as rudimentary organs. Mammary enlargement does occur in newborn male infants because of the stimulation provided by maternal hormones, and sometimes in male adolescents in response to the initial increase in estrogenic production by the adrenals. Also in certain diseases of the liver in which the usual amount of deactivation of estrogens fails to take place, an embarrassing degree of mammary development (gynecomastia) may occur and persist in adolescent boys and men.[8]

Body Build

Characteristic changes in body build take place during pubescence. These changes tend to follow a typical pattern in each sex, thereby giving rise to male and female body types. Standards of maleness and femaleness of body form have been developed for 17- to 18-year olds by Bayley and Bayer [7] from rear-view nude photographs. The distribution of *somatic androgyny* scores based on these standards for a group of adolescents in the California Growth Study has been discussed above. According to Bayley,

> Variations in form are of two principle kinds. There is the *degree* of differentiation ranging from the neutral childhood form . . . to the extreme or exaggerated characteristics of either sex. . . . There is also variation in the extent to which an individual has physical characteristics of the opposite sex. . . . These two variables, of degree and kind of differentiation, seem to be partially independent.[6]

In our classification of sources of variability in secondary sex characteristics (see p. 86), differences in *degree* would be attributable to gonadal functioning, whereas differences in *kind* would more likely be determined by genetic factors relating to structure.

Salient features of masculinity and femininity include flaring and rounding of the hips in girls, and broadening of the shoulders in boys with a concurrent accentuation of muscular development in the shoulder girdle, arms, thighs, and calves. There is also a characteristic sex difference in the distribution of fat. In girls with a feminine body form, fat is generally deposited in the buttocks, thighs and upper arms. In boys who are masculine in body build, the more usual location for the deposition of fat is the anterior abdominal wall.

Hair

Puberal changes in hair occur in both sexes. From the standpoint of microscopic structure, these changes are identical for both boys and girls. And in many parts of the body such as the head and axilla, even the location of these changes and the approximate quantity of hairs involved are similar. However, in other parts of the body such as the pubic region, face, abdomen, arms, legs, and shoulders, characteristic differences between the sexes occur in the location and proportion of the hairs undergoing structural modification from the childhood to the adult type.

Variability betwen individuals in this particular secondary sex characteristic is extremely great, and overlapping between the sexes is not uncommon. Although gonadal insufficiency invariably gives rise to sex-inappropriateness in the distribution of mature hair, there is still considerable room for genetically-determined differences between individuals who are otherwise comparable in sex hormone output as indicated by general degree of sexual maturity.

During infancy and childhood the dominant variety of hair is called *vellus* or down. Microscopic examination shows that it lacks a core (*medulla*) and contains relatively little pigment. Beginning with the hairs on the head, vellus is gradually replaced by *terminal* or adult hair which is longer, thicker, more highly pigmented, and medullated. This replacement occurs at an accelerated rate during puberty in both sexes. But in many parts of the body the rate of replacement is less rapid for girls than boys, and in some parts (for example, the face) does not occur at all.

Pubic and Other Bodily Hair. In girls, because of the inconspicuousness of the external genitalia, the growth of pubic hair is an important social criterion of pubescence. It generally follows the initial changes in breast development but is fairly well established by the time the menarche occurs. In boys, pubic hair first begins to develop after the testes have started to grow. The sequence of changes is the same in both sexes. First, there is an increase in the quantity of unpigmented and straight downy hair. This is followed by an intermediate type of coarse down, which is longer, thicker, more abundant, and slightly pigmented. With age, all of these changes become accentuated, and in addition the hairs become kinky and cover a wider area. In most girls, the area is triangular in shape with the base or upper border formed by a broad horizontal line running the width of the pelvis. In boys, growth continues from this horizontal line in an upward direction, describing another triangle the apex of which is at or above the umbilicus. Thus, the area covered by pubic hair tends to be rhomboidal in men; but exceptions to this rule are numerous and not of great significance.[17]

Axillary hair does not usually appear until the growth of pubic hair is almost complete.[17] By this time the menarche has occured in girls and first ejaculation in boys. Sex differences are not apparent in either quantity, texture, or distribution of axillary hair. However in males, beginning with middle pubescence, pigmented hairs appear on the forearms, arms, legs, and thighs and finally around the areola of the nipple and on the chest.[17] In girls, if terminal hairs grow in these areas at all, the growth tends to be scantier and less pigmented. But individual differences in this respect are marked. It is not unusual to find women who are more "hairy" than the average male.

Facial Hair. Sex differentiation in hair is most marked on the face. Prior to puberty no sex difference whatsoever exists; but the development of the beard is one of the most significant of all the secondary sex characteristics in adolescent boys. It indicates that the period of sexual maturation is finally drawing to a close.

The growth of facial hair follows a characteristic sequence of events.[18] First, a juvenile type of mustache develops from an increase in the length, thickness and pigmentation of the downy hair on the upper lip. These same changes then occur in order on the upper cheeks, lower lip, chin, and mandibular regions of the face, and lastly on the submandibular portions of the neck.[18] When these intermediate hairs are finally replaced by coarser and more highly pigmented terminal hairs, shaving becomes necessary (mean age of 16–17).

General speaking, terminal facial hair does not develop in girls.[18] Sometimes, however, (more frequently in dark-skinned girls) an intermediate type of growth occurs, especially on the upper lip. But unless there are other obvious signs of sex-inappropriateness, hormonal disturbance is not indicated. Slight hirsutism (overgrowth of facial hair in women) is usually an anatomical peculiarity of genetic origin. When it is pronounced, other signs of masculinization are generally present, and further investigation usually leads to the diagnosis of hyperactivity of the adrenal cortex.[8]

Sweat and Sebaceous Glands

In addition to the pubescent changes in the hair follicles, two other important developments take place in the skin: (1) enlargement of the *apocrine* sweat glands and (2) increased activity of the *sebaceous* (oil-producing) glands. These changes are not differentiated according to sex, but are general indices of sexual maturity in either sex. Their chief significance lies in their relation to body odor and to the cosmetic appearance of the skin, both of which are highly important for social and heterosexual adjustment during adolescence.

The growth and activity of the apocrine (in contrast to the *merocrine*) sweat glands are closely related to sexual maturity and functioning. Unlike the merocrine glands which are distributed over the skin of the entire body, the apocrine glands are found only in areas of the skin having special significance for sex functions or development (the armpits, breasts, genital regions). Their enlargement during puberty is responsible for "the characteristic odor of axillary perspiration" which is not observable prior to this time.[18] In sexually mature girls and women the activity of these glands is increased during the premenstrual phase of the menstrual cycle. The function of these glands, therefore, seems to be comparable to that of the scent glands of other mammals,[18] and to bear little relation to the heat-regulating function of the ordinary merocrine sweat glands.

The sebaceous glands enlarge and become more active during puberty, producing increased quantities of their oily secretion. But since the excretory ducts of these glands do not enlarge proportionately to accommodate the increased secretion, drainage is poor. The ducts frequently become blocked with hard plugs of waxy material to which dust particles adhere. These are the familiar "blackheads," which occur most commonly on the sides of the nose, on the chin and forehead. And since the blocked sebaceous glands easily become inflamed and secondarily infected, this condition is frequently associated with acne. Few individuals are fortunate enough to escape completely this common skin disturbance of puberty, which from the standpoint of psychological trauma is one of the most serious of all the somatic complications of adolescent development.

Voice

Voice changes constitute a rather conspicuous feature of pubescence in boys because the suddenness with which they take place frequently causes "cracking" or loss of control. The vocal chords become much longer resulting in a marked lowering of pitch. But since anatomical growth proceeds at a more rapid rate than neuromuscular learning, an embarrassing loss of ability to regulate and maintain constancy of pitch occurs in almost all boys.

This accelerated period of vocal growth is usually a feature of late adolescence (16–18), although the first signs of deepening may generally be noted soon after the appearance of the first pubic hair. In girls, the growth of the vocal chords is both less marked and more gradual. Hence, the lowering of pitch does not proceed as far, and loss of control rarely occurs.

Variability in depth of voice—just like variability in quantity of body hair and density of beard in men—is largely a function of genetic factors regulating the growth of the larynx. Only in extreme cases (male sopranos) does there appear to be a relationship between depth of voice and gonadal insufficiency. Eunuchoidism—produced either by castration or disease—is invariably accompanied by absence of pubescent voice changes. In fact, castration of certain prepubescent males has been practiced by various ethnic groups for just this purpose.

TEMPORAL ASPECTS OF PUBESCENCE

In studying the temporal relations of pubescence it is important to distinguish as we did above between *chronology* and *sequence.* Chronology refers to the *age range* in which pubescence occurs; sequence refers to the *order* in which the component physical changes of puberty take place. Differences in chronology reflect the operation of genetic variability and environmental influences. Sequence, however, as a phylogenetic phenomenon tends to be devoid of individual differences as a consequence of both genetic invariability and lack of sensitivity to relevant environmental factors. Closely related to the problem of chronology is the question of which criterion of pubescence shall be used in establishing the age at which it occurs. And the problem of sequence is complicated by the fact that each component change does not take place instantaneously but over a variable period of time that differs from one physical trait to the next. Thus, change X may *begin* before change Y, but the latter may reach completion first.

Age Range for Onset of Pubescence

The age at which puberty *actually* occurs cannot be determined with any exactitude since it differs when the averages of different groups are taken and also when different criteria of sexual maturity are used. For our purposes, however, only two facts are important: (1) there is a wide range of normal variability within each sex group (10–18 in girls, 12–18 in boys); and (2) it is reasonable to infer that on the average girls reach sexual maturity one to two years before boys.

When the menarche is used as the criterion of sexual maturity in girls, different studies place the mean age of puberty at 12.5,[45] 13.1,[9] 13.2,[43] 13.5,[16] and 13.6.[19] When the criterion of straight, pigmented pubic hair is used for boys, typical averages are 13.1,[14] 13.4,[13] 13.9 [3] and 14.4.[3] Thus if these two different criteria were truly comparable, little difference between the sexes would exist. However, a more comparable criterion (since it can be used for both sexes) is mean age at which the maximum yearly increment in height takes place. Shuttleworth [43] found this to be two years later in boys (14.8) than in girls (12.6).

Hence, for purposes of convenience we may place the average age of pubescence at thirteen for girls and 14.5 for boys, if we realize that these are estimates rather than true values. This sex difference in age of pubescence in favor of girls is confirmed by the greater maturity of girls as judged by their social and heterosexual interests between the ages of twelve and fifteen (see pp. 134–135). However, this does not mean that girls mature earlier than boys in terms of sexual *experience* and *activity*. Kinsey,[26] for example, found that practically all boys experience orgasm by the age of fifteen, whereas fewer than a quarter of girls do (see p. 409). Nevertheless, the earlier sexual maturation of girls (in a physical and social sense) is one of the most important facts of adolescence; and its implications for social and emotional development as well as for education will be fully discussed in later chapters.

Criteria of Pubescence

The choice of an adequate criterion of sexual maturity in determining the age of pubescence is many ways a pseudo-problem. First, pubescence by definition refers to a *constellation* of typical bodily changes associated with sexual maturation, and not to any particular change. The choice of reproductive capacity as the most crucial and representative of the physical changes that take place is purely arbitrary, and is hardly defensible on either biological or behavioral grounds. Second, each of the component bodily changes occurs over a period of time rather than all at once. Hence, when the physical phenomena of pubescence are considered as a whole, it is meaningless to conceive of a definite *age* of puberty. It is more reasonable to think of an *interval* of several years embracing a series of changes that are initiated in characteristic sequence and progress to completion at different rates of development. Only for convenience in research and in the day-to-day handling of boys and girls does it become worthwhile to estimate "when" puberty *really* occurs; and to do this it is necessary to select arbitrarily one or more criteria of pubescence.

Obviously, different criteria will differ in validity, definiteness, convenience, presence in both sexes, and the accuracy with which they can be measured. In girls, the menarche is a convenient index of sexual maturity, the occurrence of which can be definitely and accurately determined providing one does not rely on retrospective memory. But although menstruation is unequivocably indicative of maturity of the primary sex organs, the converse does not necessarily always hold true. Also, as pointed out above, menstruation and ovulation are not absolutely correlated. Another difficulty is the absence of a completely analogous event in boys. The emission of semen is only approximately analogous, and is a poor criterion besides, because the date of initial occurrence is less definite and more subject to retrospective errors of memory.

Pubic hair is a convenient, definite, and accurately measurable bisexual criterion. However, its validity for assessing the pubescent status of a given *individual* is questionable in view of large, individual differences unrelated to sexual maturity. The same holds true for age of maximum growth. But for comparing the pubescent status of different *groups,* (boys *vs.* girls) these individual differences are unimportant if a large enough sample is employed. For research purposes, therefore, both of these criteria are quite serviceable.

In nonresearch settings, parents, teachers, and contemporaries of either sex use whatever combination of criteria are most accessible. Boys, for example, tend to be most influenced by the factor of mammary development in assessing the sexual maturity of girls; whereas girls rely unduly upon such factors as height and facial hair in making comparable judgments of boys. On the other hand, parents, teachers, and peers of the same sex frequently have more complete and valid data (menarche, pubic hair, seminal emissions, enlargement of male genitalia) on which to base an estimate of sexual maturity. At any rate, serious mistakes in assessing pubescent status are rarely made in actual practice regardless of the criterion that is used. But when errors are made, they are usually in the direction of under-estimates because of a tendency to set unreasonably high standards of sex appropriateness.[39]

Sequence of Pubescent Changes

The phylogenetic invariability of the sequence of pubescent changes has been confirmed by several lines of evidence. Different investigators working with different populations report different mean ages for various events, but there is substantial agreement on sequential appearance. Furthermore, in cases of precocious or retarded puberty—whether that within the normal range of differences or that caused by endocrine pathology—the same sequence of changes is followed as in the instances of more typical chronology. Apparently then, there is a genetically determined order (that is the same for all individuals) in which the various body tissues implicated in sexual maturation become sensitive to the influence of estrogenic and androgenic substances. The order in which the changes once initiated reach completion is also predetermined. But since these two varieties of sequence are somewhat independent of each other, considerable overlapping occurs.

By pooling data from the various studies discussed we arrive at the following sequential picture of pubescence: In girls [36, 43] the order of onset is: initial enlargement of the breasts; appearance of straight, pigmented pubic hair; age of maximum growth; appearance of kinky pubic hair; the menarche; and growth of axillary hair. In boys [18, 26, 35, 40, 43] the corresponding order of pubescent phenomena is: beginning growth of the testes, first pubic hair (straight, pigmented), early voice changes, first ejaculation, kinky pubic hair, age of maximum growth, axillary hair, marked voice changes, and development of the beard.

OTHER PHYSIOLOGICAL CHANGES IN PUBESCENCE

In addition to the bodily changes that are integrally related to sexual maturation and functioning (primary and secondary sex characteristics) practically every organ system of the body is affected by the endocrine developments of pubescence. Skeletal and muscular changes will be considered in Chapter 5. In this section we shall consider the changes occurring in all other non sexual organ systems.

Types of Physiological Changes

Two main types of non-sexual physiological change occur during pubescence: (1) the completion of physiological maturity; and (2) the disturbance of physiological equilibrium (as a result of new hormonal activity) and the gradual process of adjustment and establishment of a new equilibrium.

Shock [41] refers to the first type of change as "physiological 'learning.' "

> Just as pediatricians have discovered that the young child is not simply a miniature adult, so students of human development have come to the realization that the adolescent is neither child nor adult in his physiological reactions. In the adolescent many new physiological adjustments are being made which were unnecessary in the young child and which become stabilized in the adult. . . . As an example, the regulation of body temperature may be cited. The rather wide fluctuations in body temperature observed in young children give way to a more stable regulation of temperature by the beginning of the second decade. Thus the growing organism has "learned" to utilize and coordinate the numerous mechanisms involved in temperature control [41] [p. 56; quoted by permission of the Society].

Other examples include the attainment of adult respiratory capacity and the adult pattern of cardiovascular dynamics.

The second kind of change—initial hormonal disequilibrium followed by gradual adaptation and restoration of equilibrium—is reflected in the disturbances of the sebaceous glands referred to above (adolescent acne). Spontaneous recovery from this condition with age is indicative both of tissue adaptation to hormonal imbalance and of eventual stabilization of the total endocrine picture. Its responsiveness to hormonal therapy also adds credence to this interpretation of its etiology.

Other Endocrine Glands. The main endocrine changes related to pubescence occur in the anterior pituitary gland, the gonads, and adrenals. The sudden increased functioning of these glands not only leads to important changes attributable to the effects of their own enhanced output but also to a disturbance of the entire endocrine balance.

The growth of the thymus gland is inversely related to that of adrenals during puberty.[8, 20] Preliminary investigation indicates that the thymus gland inhibits sexual maturation and facilitates skeletal growth, but these results are far from conclusive.[8] It is definitely known, however, that the thymus gland will not shrink in size until the adrenals become more active. In atrophic diseases of the adrenals (Addison's disease), the thymus remains prominent; in hypertrophic tumors of the adrenals, the thymus begins to degenerate

prematurely. The functions of the thymus and adrenals are reciprocally antagonistic, at least in lympathic if not sexual development.
The shift in thymus-adrenal balance is partly responsible for the
decline in lymphoid tissue during puberty and the diminished
lymphatic response to bacterial infection. The thymus gland also
probably exerts an inhibitory influence on muscular tonus, since
hypertrophic tumors of the thymus result in excessive muscular
relaxation and weakness. Hence, the large gain in muscular strength
that occurs with pubescence (see p. 118) may possibly be related in
part to the decline in the size and importance of the thymus gland.

Changes in the thyroid gland are largely mirrored by alterations
in basal metabolic rate (which provides an index of body heat
production in a state of physical, gastro-intestinal, and mental rest).
Although basal metabolic rate (expressed as calories per square
meter of body surface per hour) is largely a function of thyroid
activity, other important variables are also involved. Relatively less
heat, for example, must be produced per pound of body weight if
less heat is lost either through better temperature control or as a
result of the fact that the ratio of body surface area to body weight
is declining. Both of these facts become increasingly true with age
from infancy to adult life. Hence, during adolescence, the thyroid
gland enlarges and more *total* heat is produced by the individual
(because he becomes heavier); but since less heat tends to be lost,
the basal metabolic rate expressed as above declines in both boys
and girls.[41] At all ages, however, basal metabolism is higher in boys
than in girls.

Cardiovascular Changes. During pubescence the cardiovascular
system undergoes tremendous expansion in volume and physiological
capacity. The heart especially increases in size and in the thickness
of its muscular walls.[30] Hence, with each stroke it can pump a much
larger volume of blood through the circulatory system, thereby
increasing systolic blood pressure (the pressure of blood within the
arteries accompanying each heart beat).[37, 41] Diastolic blood pressure,
the blood pressure between heart beats, also rises because of the
heightened resistance to blood flow provided by increased vascular
tonus.[37, 41] Both changes are undoubtedly brought about by

enhanced functioning of the adrenal cortex; but since systolic blood pressure rises more rapidly, "pulse pressure" (the difference between systolic and diastolic pressures) tends to rise during the course of puberty.[37, 41] Also beginning with puberty, systolic blood pressure rises more rapidly in boys than in girls, accounting perhaps for the sex difference in athletic capacity.[41]

An immediate consequence of this increase in cardiac capacity is a drop in pulse rate. Since more blood can be delivered in a single stroke, the heart need not beat as rapidly to pump the same volume of blood through the vessels in the space of a minute. Pulse rate drops "eight to nine beats per minute" for both sexes during adolescence, but at all ages is "two to six beats per minute faster" for girls,[41] the sex difference increasing somewhat with age. This sex difference in pulse rate parallels the sex difference in systolic blood pressure, but naturally is in the opposite direction.

The pattern of circulatory adjustment to maximal physical effort changes in a comparable fashion during pubescence. The increased needs of muscle tissue for oxygen and glucose are met more by a rise in cardiac output (as reflected by systolic blood pressure changes) than by a rise in pulse rate.[41] As one might anticipate, the compensatory increment in blood pressure is greater in boys than in girls, and the sex difference tends to become even greater with age. On the other hand, girls respond to exercise with a greater rise in pulse rate, which also takes a longer time to reach the basal level during the recovery period.

Because of greater cardiac capacity it is apparent that pubescent children are capable of greater physical exertion than non-pubescents. But recovery from exercise (in terms of oxygen consumption) decreases as age increases.[41] However, as Shock [41] points out, the total amount of work done in a period of "all-out" exercise is much greater for older than for younger children; and if this difference were greater than could be accounted for by the corresponding difference in weight, the resulting decline in recovery rate would be spurious. Hence, it is clear that pubescent individuals are physiologically capable of doing a greater amount of work than younger children, but it is not yet clear whether more or less physiological strain (as measured by recovery time) is involved for an equivalent amount of work (an amount of work adjusted for body size).

Respiratory Changes. In terms of absolute units (liters per minute), there is a large increase in respiratory capacity during pubescence.[42] The chest cavity enlarges and the lungs increase in size and weight. The rate of breathing also declines. However, if respiration volume is corrected for body size, it is easily seen that respiratory capacity does not keep pace with general body growth. Throughout the adolescent period there is a steady decline in respiratory volume expressed as liters *per square meter* per minute.[42]

The most significant fact about respiratory changes during adolescence is the huge difference in lung capacity that develops between boys and girls. This is probably both a cause and a consequence of the sex difference in athletic activity and prowess. Prepubescent boys and girls have nearly the same respiratory capacity, but with increasing age the difference becomes increasingly greater in favor of boys.

HEALTH AND DISEASE IN ADOLESCENCE

Health and disease are relevant topics for adolescent development for two main reasons. First, different age periods are marked by characteristic patterns of disease. In terms of both the pathological processes and the kinds of tissues involved, these differential patterns reflect significant changes in physiological status and development. It is not a matter of coincidence, for example, that the site at which rickets occurs changes with age; that certain infectious diseases are most common in childhood; that tuberculosis, endocrine disorders, and acne figure so prominently in adolescence; and that arteriosclerosis and other degenerative diseases occur mostly in middle and old age. The diseases of adolescence mirror the physiological stresses and strains and the disturbances in physiological equilibrium that occur during this particular stage of development.

Second, physical illness and defects become more important for personal adjustment during adolescence. Because of the increased social premium that is placed upon physical attractiveness and conformity to group physical norms, both the individual and his group tend to be more concerned by injury and disfigurement. Disease, therefore, constitutes a much greater hazard to normal personality adjustment during the adolescent period. And since at this time the body also tends to become a more important part of the individual's psychological field, both in terms of its social significance and in terms of his own self-concept, physical disturbances are more likely to arise as complications of emotional disorder.

Mortality and Morbidity Rates

In terms of mortality rate, adolescence marks the beginning of an ascending trend that is maintained for the rest of the life span. The death rate is very high in infants under one year of age; it drops precipitously between the age of one and four and then more gradually until the ages of ten to fourteen.[31] In 1948, mortality rates per 100,000 white males were 61.1 in the age range from ten to fourteen years. But in the age group from fifteen to nineteen, the corresponding rate was almost double (113.0). For white females the comparable figures were 37.3 and 53.1. The hazards to life during adolescence, therefore, are approximately twice as great as during preadolescence, and about twice as severe in males as in females. The greatest single cause for the increased mortality rate is the spectacular rise in the number of fatal accidents. The other major causes of death in this age group are tuberculosis, heart disease, and pneumonia; but these diseases still account for only slightly more than half the number of deaths caused by accidents.[31]

The health picture during adolescence is much brighter if we use morbidity rather than mortality rates as our criterion of freedom from illness. Using such indices of incidence as total number of illnesses, physicians' calls, number of days in bed, number of hospital days,[11] and number of days of absence from school,[1] the adolescent appears to advantage over the preadolescent child. We may conclude that neither the incidence nor the mortality of disease increases during adolescence if we exclude accidents and injuries from consideration. It is in the *kinds* of illness that are most prevalent that the greatest contrast between the two age groups is found. The common childhood diseases, rheumatic fever, and poliomyelitis [12] decline in incidence during adolescence, whereas tuberculosis, endocrine disorders, and acne become increasingly more frequent.

Common Medical Problems of Adolescence

Infectious Diseases. Adolescents are not immune to the common childhood diseases (measles, mumps, etc.). Except for chicken pox, they are just as susceptible to these diseases as younger children, but contract them less frequently merely because these are so contagious that few persons can escape them as children. In fact, a disease such as diphtheria is actually becoming more common in adolescents and adults than in children because the former are less recently immunized against it. Mumps is a much more serious disease in adolescents than in children because of testicular swelling, which occurs in almost one-third of the cases. If bilateral, it may even lead to sterility.

The incidence of new cases of rheumatic fever declines during adolescence but is still quite substantial.[12] In addition, there are the residual cases of heart damage remaining from childhood attacks. The restriction on physical activity which this necessitates creates serious problems of emotional and social adjustment for many boys and girls.[25] Tuberculosis becomes the most frequent cause of death during the age range from fifteen to nineteen, increasing more than threefold over the preceding five year period.[31] Preliminary experimental work with animals in recent years indicates that increased susceptibility to tuberculosis is partly a function of gonadal secretion.[28]

Endocrine Disorders. Disturbances related to the establishment of sex functions naturally first become prominent during the adolescent period. Early or late sexual maturation is usually a function of genetically-determined variability, providing that it occurs between the ages of ten to seventeen. Beyond this normal range, endocrine pathology or nutritional deficiency should be suspected. The most common cause of precocious puberty is overactivity of the adrenal cortex or of the basophilic cells of the anterior pituitary gland which produce gonadotropic and 'corticotropic hormones (Cushing's syndrome).[27] Delayed puberty (including general signs of sex inappropriateness) is induced by atrophic lesions of these same glands (Addison's disease, Fröhlich's syndrome) or of the gonads themselves (tuberculosis, mumps). But regardless of whether puberty is chronologically displaced because of normal genetic variability or because of organic pathology, the same consequences in skeletal growth (see pp. 113–114) and psychological disturbance (see p. 148) take place.

Menstrual irregularities are almost universal during the first year of puberty until normal rhythm is established. The menarche is delayed in instances of late puberty caused by any of the hormonal conditions described above, and sometimes in instances of nutritional deficiency and emotional trauma. But even after menstruation is well established, various difficulties—pain, distress, irregularity, excessive or insufficient flow—are very common. Some of these cases are attributable to gonadal imbalance, liver dysfunction, thyroid or nutritional deficiency, or organic pathology of the uterus, and respond to treatment along these lines. In many other instances, however, minor disturbances are either consciously or "unconsciously" exploited for psychological reasons, for example, to avoid distasteful physical or social activity, to gain sympathy from others, or to rationalize poor performance.

When pregnancy occurs in adolescence, labor is apt to be shorter in duration, cesarean section is less frequently necessary, and infant and maternal mortality are lower.[29] Psychiatric care, however, is extremely important for unwed adolescent mothers because of the shame and fear involved in the experience of childbearing. The greater frequency of toxemia (a complication of pregnancy marked by high blood pressure, convulsions, swelling of the extremities, and other symptoms) among adolescents has been attributed in part to this psychological trauma.

Two other endocrine disturbances are also more common in adolescence than in childhood, diabetes and goiter (enlargement of the thyroid).[34] General hormonal imbalance is probably a factor in both diseases. Diabetes in adolescents is more severe than in adults and much more difficult to keep under control, partly because of its refractoriness to insulin treatment and partly because of the resistance of adolescents to dietary regimentation.[15] A good deal of the thyroid enlargement that occurs in adolescence is probably a reflection of the greater need for iodine in the diet that arises at this time because of increased body heat production. If the iodine

content of the drinking water is barely adequate to supply childhood needs, compensatory enlargement of thyroid takes place. This
is shown by the greater incidence of goiter in the Great Lakes
region where iodine deficiency is much greater than in any other
part of the country.[34]

Although acne is not an endocrine disorder *per se,* its relation
to hormonal imbalance * has already been discussed (see p. 91).
It is, in all probability, the most common disease of adolescence
and by any criterion the most serious in terms of its psychological
consequences. Its chronicity and stubborn refractoriness to treatment
are especially troubling to adolescents with their limited time perspective. In the image that they have of their own bodies, this
defect occupies a very prominent place and is projected almost
indefinitely into the future. Adults tend to minimize the seriousness
of this condition because they prefer to forget the concern that
they manifested over it as adolescents, and because pride makes
their own adolescent children and acquaintances simulate indifference. Time (the regaining of physiological equilibrium) is the most
important therapeutic factor, although scrupulous cleanliness, ultra-
violet treatment, dietary control, and endocrine therapy have all
proven beneficial.

Nutritional Disturbances. The nutritional disorders of adolescence
are a reflection of the unusual needs for proteins and certain vitamins and minerals during this period of development. The requirements of tissue growth demand a protein intake about three times
that of the adult period. Similarly, larger amounts of calcium and
vitamin D are needed for skeletal growth than at any other time of
life with the possible exception of early infancy.[22] The large increase
in blood volume also creates a greater need for iron, especially in
girls, who lose menstrual blood periodically. It is in these requirements that nutrition is most likely to be deficient rather than in
total caloric intake; and experience shows that where these nutritional deficiencies occur, an insufficiency of the B complex vitamins

---

* Androgens are a prerequisite for the development of acne. In adolescent
girls the disease is caused by the increased production of adrenal cortex androgens
which stimulates secretion of the sebaceous glands. Acne does not occur in eunuchs.

is frequently present. Reference has already been made to the increased need for iodine.

The chief cause of nutritional disturbances in adolescence is the lack of knowledge of adolescents and their parents about these special dietary requirements. A contributing cause is indiscriminate dieting by girls intent on losing weight. Less important are the peculiar food habits that are popularly attributed to teen-age boys and girls. Indulgence in soft drinks, candy, and hot dogs is a social rather than a physiological phenomenon of adolescence, and tends to supplement rather than to replace the conventional three meals a day.

Obesity is a common medical problem in adolescence and one with important psychological and social implications. In girls it is a serious handicap to heterosexual relationships, and in boys it frequently gives rise to an apparent underdevelopment of the genitalia (see p. 83). As in other periods of life, the main cause of obesity is overeating and insufficient exercise in persons constitutionally predisposed to gaining weight. Obesity attributable to thyroid deficiency or to adrenal and pituitary disturbances (Fröhlich's syndrome, Cushing's syndrome) is relatively rare. A more important cause of adolescent obesity is compulsive over-eating, which serves as a defense against anxiety or as a compensation for social inadequacy.

Accidents. It has already been noted that accidents constitute the greatest single cause of death in the age group of fifteen to nineteen and account for the greater part of the increase in the mortality rate over the preceding half decade. This rise in the frequency of accidents can be attributed to greater freedom of movement away from the home, to participation in more violent physical activity, to poor judgment and irresponsibility, and to recklessness stemming from aggressive defiance of adult rules and regulations. The major causes of accidental death are automobile mishaps, drowning, falls, and injuries from firearms.[44] As one might easily anticipate, fatal accidents are much more frequent among boys than among girls.

The psychological implications of bodily disease and injury are discussed in Chapter 6 (see pp. 153–164).

REFERENCES AND BIBLIOGRAPHY

1. Altman, I. and Ciocco, A.: School absence due to sickness in the war years. Child Develpm. *16*:189–199, 1945.

2. Ashley-Montagu, M. F.: *Adolescent Sterility*. Springfield, Ill.: C. C. Thomas, 1946.

3. Baldwin, B. T.: "A Measuring Scale for Physical Growth and Physiological Age," in 15th Yearbook, Nat. Soc. Stud. Educ., Part I, 1916.

4. Baldwin, B. T.: *The Physical Growth of Children from Birth to Maturity*. University of Iowa Study in Child Welfare, Vol. 1. Iowa City: University of Iowa, 1921.

5. Barker, R. G., Wright, B. A., and Gonick, M. R.: *Adjustment to Physical Handicap and Illness: A Survey of the Social Psychology of Physique and Disability*. Bulletin No. 55. New York: Social Science Research Council, 1946.

6. Bayley, N.: Some psychological correlates of somatic androgyny. Child Develpm., *22*:47–60, 1951.

7. Bayley, N. and Bayer, L. M.: The assessment of somatic androgyny. Amer. J. Phys. Anthrop., *4*:433–461, 1946.

8. Best, C. H. and Taylor, N. B.: *The Physiological Basis of Medical Practice*. 5th ed. Baltimore: Williams and Wilkins, 1950.

9. Boas, F.: Studies in growth. Hum. Biol., *4*:307–350, 1932.

10. Boyd, W. A.: *Textbook of Pathology*. 5th ed. Philadelphia: Lea and Feibiger, 1947.

11. Collins, S. D.: Sickness and health: Their measurement, distribution and changes. Ann. Amer. Acad. Pol. Sci. *237*:152–163, 1945.

12. Collins, S. D.: The incidence of rheumatic fever as recorded in general morbidity surveys in families. Supplement 198, U. S. Public Health Reports, 1947.

13. Crampton, C. W.: Physiological age—a fundamental principle. Amer. Phys. Educ. Rev., *13*:144–154, 214–227, 268–283, 345–358, 1908.

14. Dimock, H. S.: *Rediscovering the Adolescent*. New York: Association Press, 1937.

15. Dolger, H.: Clinical evaluation of vascular damage in diabetes mellitus. J. A. M. A., *134*:1289–1291, 1947.

16. Engle, E. T. and Shelesnyak, M. C.: First menstruation and subsequent menstrual cycles of pubertal girls. Hum. Biol., *6*:431–453, 1934.

17. Greulich, W. W.: "Physical Changes in Adolescence," in *Adolescence*, 43rd Yearbook, Natl. Soc. Stud. Educ., Part I. Chicago: University of Chicago Press, 1944.

18. Greulich, W. W. et al.: *Somatic and Endocrine Studies of Pubertal and Adolescent Boys*. Monogr. Soc. Res. Child Develpm., VII, No. 3. Washington, D. C.: National Research Council, 1942.

19. Gould, H. N. and Gould, M. R.: Age of first menstruation in mothers and daughters. J. A. M. A., *98*:1349–1352, 1932.

20. Harris, J. A., Jackson, C. M., Paterson, D. G., and Scammon, R. E.: *The Measurement of Man*. Minneapolis: University of Minnesota Press, 1930.

21. Hartman, C. G.: *Time of Ovulation in Women*. Baltimore: Williams and Wilkins, 1936.

22. Johnston, J. A.: Nutritional problems of adolescence. J. A. M. A., *137*:1587–1589, 1948.

23. Jones, H. E.: *Development in Adolescence*. New York: Appleton-Century-Crofts, 1943.

24. Jones, H. E.: Physical ability as a factor in social adjustment in adolescence. J. Educ. Res., *40*:287–301, 1946.

25. Josselyn, I. M.: Emotional implications of rheumatic heart disease in children. Am. J. Orthopsychiat., *19*:87–100, 1949.

26. Kinsey, A. C. et al.: *Sexual Behavior in the Human Male*. Philadelphia: Saunders, 1948.

27. Lowrey, G. H. and Brown, T. G.: Precocious sexual development. J. Pediat., *38*:325–340, 1951.

28. Lurie, M. B. et al.: Constitutional factors in resistance to infection. I. The effect of estrogen and chorionic gonadotropin on the course of tuberculosis in highly inbred rabbits. Am. Rev. Tuberculosis, *59*:168–185, 1949.

29. Marchetti, A. A. and Menaker, J.: Pregnancy and the adolescent. Am. J. Obst. & Gynec., *59*:1013–1020, 1950.

30. Maresh, M. M.: Growth of heart related to bodily growth during adolescence. Pediatrics, *2*:382–404, 1948.

31. Metropolitan Life Insurance Company Statistical Bulletin. *30*:1, 1949.

32. Mills, C. A.: Geographic and time variations in body growth and age at menarche. Hum. Biol., *9*:43–56, 1937.

33. Mills, C. A. and Ogle, C.: Physiological sterility of adolescence. Hum. Biol. *8*:607–615, 1936.

34. Oleson, R.: Endemic goiter in Tennessee. U. S. Public Health Reports, *44*:865–897, 1929.

35. Ramsey, G. V.: The sexual development of boys. Amer. J. Psychol., *56*:217–233, 1943.

36. Reynolds, E. L.: Individual differences in physical changes associated with adolescence in girls. Amer. J. Dis. Child. *75*:329–350, 1948.

37. Richey, H. G.: The blood pressure in boys and girls before and after puberty: Its relation to growth and maturity. Amer. J. Dis. Child., *42*:1281–1330, 1931.

38. Schonfeld, W. A.: Primary and secondary sexual characteristics. Am. J. Dis. Child., *65*:535–549, 1943.

39. Schonfeld, W. A.: Inadequate masculine physique as a factor in personality development of adolescent boys. Psychosom. Med., *12*:49–54, 1950.

40. Schonfeld, W. A. and Beebe, G. W.: Normal growth and variation in the male genitalia from birth to maturity. J. Urology, *48*:759–779, 1942.

41. Shock, N. W.: "Physiological Changes in Adolescence," in *Adolescence*, 43rd Yearbook, Natl. Soc. Stud. Educ., Part I. Chicago: University of Chicago Press, 1944.

42. Shock, N. W.: Some physiological aspects of adolescence. Texas Rep. Biol. Med., *4*:289–310, 1946.

43. Shuttleworth, F. K.: *The Physical and Mental Growth of Boys and Girls Age Six to Nineteen in Relation to Age at Maximum Growth.* Monogr. Soc. Res. Child Develpm., Vol. IV, No. 3, 1939.

44. Shuttleworth, F. K.: *The Adolescent Period: A Pictorial Atlas.* Monogr. Soc. Res. Child Develpm., XIV, No. 2. Evanston, Ill.: Child Development Publications, 1949.

45. Simmons, K. and Greulich, W.: Menarcheal age and the height, weight, and skeletal age of girls age 7 to 17 years. J. Pediat., 22:518–548, 1943.

46. Stolz, H. R. and Stolz, L. M.: "Adolescent Problems Related to Somatic Variations," in *Adolescence,* 43rd Yearbook, Natl. Soc. Stud. Educ., Part I. Chicago: University of Chicago Press, 1944.

47. Stolz, H. R. and Stolz, L. M.: *Somatic Development in Adolescence.* New York: Macmillan, 1951.

48. White House Conference on Child Health and Protection: Growth and Development of the Child, Part II: Anatomy and Physiology. New York: Century Co., 1933.

CHAPTER 5

Physical Growth and Motor Development

MATURATIONAL CHANGES in the skeletal tissue (bone, muscle, and fat) are among the more important physical developments of pubescence. These changes are significant for two main reasons. (1) They alter such crucial aspects of body form and appearance as height, weight, and body proportions which figure so prominently in social and individual concepts of adult physical maturity; and (2) they are crucially related to changes in skeletal mass, strength, and coordination, which have important implications for the development of motor skills.

Skeletal maturation is part of the pubescent cycle because it is intimately related to the endocrine developments that give rise to the primary and secondary sex characteristics and to maturational changes in other organ systems. It consists both of quantitative dimensional changes, such as growth spurts in height and weight, and to qualitative changes in tissue composition and function. Like the secondary sex characteristics, these changes occur in both sexes, differing only in *degree* for boys and girls.

The relationship between the endocrine phenomena of pubescence and the gross as well as the qualitative changes that take place in the skeletal system are exceedingly complex. A discussion of this relationship will be reserved until a more descriptive account of the internal skeletal changes and of the adolescent growth spurt is given.

FACTORS DETERMINING SKELETAL GROWTH

It is important to realize at the outset that pubescence is, relatively speaking, only a minor factor in determining an individual's final *adult* height. The significance of the age of sexual maturation lies chiefly in its relation to *when* the pubescent growth spurt occurs, that is, to the relative height of an individual at various points in his adolescent career. As long as the age of pubescence falls within the normal range of individual differences, postpubescent height can be predicted from prepubescent and even from early childhood height with a reasonable amount of accuracy.[42] Pubescence, in other words, does not significantly affect the ultimate height an individual will eventually attain, provided it does not occur extremely early or unusually late.

Heredity is the principal variable determining skeletal growth. A close relationship exists between the stature of parents and the adult height of their offspring.[22] The influence of genetic factors is mediated through the growth hormone of the anterior pituitary gland and operates with considerable uniformity over the age span from ante-natal existence to maturity. A child who is tall at birth also tends to be tall at the age of six and at the age of nineteen. But since height is an individual rather than a phylogenetic trait,* it is somewhat susceptible to the influence of environmental factors. Nutrition—especially the intake of protein, calcium, and vitamin D—seems to determine whether the individual will attain the maximum height that is possible with his genetic limitations. This is the most plausible explanation we have for the mean increase in stature of approximately three inches that has taken place over the hundred year interval between 1830 and 1930.[10]

QUALITATIVE CHANGES IN SKELETAL TISSUE

An important change that takes place during pubescence is an alteration in the relative proportions of the various skeletal tissues that constitute the total breadth of an extremity. In the calf, for example, there is a sharp rise in the breadth of bone and muscle tissue for both boys and girls, a rise that is greater for boys than for girls. This sex difference is possibly related to the general muscular hypertrophy which androgenic hormones induce in labo-

---

* It is true, of course, that the *range* in which human stature occurs is a species characteristic. Consistent differences are also found between the mean heights of children of different racial stocks growing up in the same environment, e.g., Chinese, Japanese, Hawaiian, South European and North European on the islands of Hawaii.[52] However, considerable overlapping between racial groups makes individual prediction on the basis of these differences practically worthless.

ratory animals.[37] The amount of fat tissue, on the other hand, decreases for boys and increases slightly for girls.[39] That these changes are a function of pubescence rather than of age is shown by the greater growth of all three tissues in early-maturing girls in contrast to late-maturing girls.[38]

More important is the change that takes place in the composition and structure of the bones. As the skeleton becomes increasingly more mature, the proportion of osseous to cartilagenous tissue increases. First, cartilage is replaced by osseous matter; then the process of ossification is completed by the deposition of calcium. Vitamin C is necessary for the first step, and vitamin D is required for the latter step. The "skeletal age" of an individual is an expression indicating the percentage of his total wrist area that is ossified (as determined by X-ray pictures), in relation to the mean values of various age groups. Hence, a child of ten with precocious skeletal maturity may have a skeletal age of twelve. In terms of skeletal age, girls are consistently more mature than boys over the entire age span. At the age of six the difference is only about one year; but at fourteen, girls and boys are two years apart [4, 18, 47] on this index of skeletal maturity, and the gap is not closed until the termination of the adolescent period.

Skeletal age is an extremely useful index of physiological maturity. For one thing, it is closely related to growth in stature. During pubescence final adult height can be predicted more accurately if the individual's skeletal age is known.[6, 42] Second, it is highly correlated with other criteria of sexual maturity [20, 21] and can be used as an objective index of pubescent status.[20] The age of menarche is more closely related to prepubescent skeletal age than to height, weight, or annual increments in height.[43]

In order to appreciate the relationships between bone structure, skeletal maturation, and longitudinal growth, it is necessary to trace the development of a typical long bone such as the femur or tibia of the lower extremity. As illustrated schematically in Figure 3, a long bone consists of a *shaft* containing the bone marrow cavity and a wider portion at either end called the *epiphysis*. At birth the entire bone is composed of cartilage except for small centers of ossification in the epiphyses. During infancy and childhood the epiphyses and the shaft gradually undergo ossification, except for a strip of cartilage situated at their junction known as the *epiphysial cartilage.* It is here that all longitudinal growth of the bone takes place. As long as these cartilage cells remain unossified, they are able to multiply and add length to the bone. The hormonal developments that are responsible for initiating the rapid growth spurt during preadolescence and early adolescence and for terminating

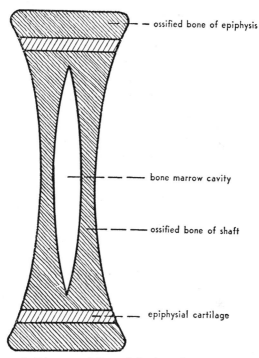

— — ossified bone of epiphysis

— — — bone marrow cavity

— — — ossified bone of shaft

— — — epiphysial cartilage

FIGURE 3.—Schematic Diagram of Frontal Section of a Long Bone of the Lower Extremity during the Pubescent Period.

growth at the end of adolescence (by leading to ossification of the epiphysial cartilage) are extremely complicated and will be discussed in a later section (see pp. 114–116).

THE ADOLESCENT GROWTH SPURT

Skeletal growth takes place over an interval of approximately twenty years. The rate of growth, however, is far from constant. It is marked by two spurts, each of which is succeeded by periods of very slow growth. The first spurt occurs in early infancy and is followed by a long period during which the yearly increments in stature are small and relatively constant. The second growth spurt begins one to two years before pubescence, about the age of eleven in girls and approximately two years later in boys.[42] Shuttleworth found the mean age of maximal growth to be 12.6 in girls and 14.8 in boys.[42] For girls, this is six months [42] to a year [9] before the occurrence of the menarche; for boys, it is slightly more than a year after the appearance of first pubic hair and initial ejaculation of semen. Thereafter, a period of gradual deceleration sets in until the ages of eighteen to twenty when growth ceases completely.

The adolescent growth spurt, although beginning before the onset of other criteria of sexual maturation, is definitely related to the endocrine changes that initiate pubescence.[35] To begin with, the age at which the period of accelerated growth starts is a function of the age of pubescence. The earlier onset of sexual maturation in girls is reflected in the fact that between the ages of eleven and fourteen girls for the first and only time tend to be taller than boys.[3] Second, characteristic differences exist between the growth patterns of

> individuals who show different rates of maturing. For both sexes, the faster maturing children have more intense spurts of rapid growth with the period of acceleration both starting and stopping abruptly, while the late-maturers have less intense periods of acceleration and with a subsequent growth which is longer continued, more even, and gradual [7] [pp. 46, 47; quoted by permission of the Society].

Finally, as shown by the data of Crampton [12] and others, only a very small percentage of prepubescent individuals are as tall as the average postpubescent.

Not only do children who mature sexually at an earlier age undergo the adolescent growth spurt sooner, but also they hold a consistent advantage over late-maturing children in height and weight long before any signs of puberty are evident.[2, 7, 40, 42] That is, early-maturing children are found to be taller and heavier than slow-maturers even at the age of six.[40, 42] In addition, they tend to be "broad-built with relatively wide hips" in contrast to the latter who "are more likely to be long-legged and slender." [7]

Age of Pubescence in Relation to Adult Height

It is clear that early-maturing children are taller at all ages (at least from six onwards), and both enter and complete the adolescent growth spurt at an earlier age than their late-maturing contemporaries. It is less clear, however, whether the age at which pubescence occurs affects an individual's ultimate adult stature. In general, the statement we made earlier holds true: A positive and predictable relationship prevails between prepubescent and postpubescent height providing that sexual maturation does not occur extremely early or extremely late. This means that the age of pubescence (within normal limits) affects only the age at which the growth spurt begins and that at which it terminates and does not affect the individual's ultimate stature. A tall, prepubescent child tends to mature earlier and, therefore, has an earlier occurring growth spurt. But he also becomes a taller adult than the shorter prepubescent child. Hence, early-maturing children tend to develop into taller adults and vice versa.

At the extremes of the distribution—in examples of precocious or retarded puberty—postpubescent height can no longer be predicted from prepubescent height. Here, an inverse relationship prevails between age of sexual maturation and ultimate adult height. If puberty occurs precociously, not only does the growth spurt take place precociously, but it also ceases long before normal adult height is attained, resulting in a form of dwarfism.[19] If, on the other hand, the onset of pubescence is abnormally delayed, growth continues for too long a time and a very tall, long-legged adult develops.[19] The same condition is produced by prepuberal castration.[44]

It is somewhere between these extreme conditions and the more typical ages of sexual maturation that the data are somewhat equivocal, and interpretation is difficult. The situation is somewhat clearer for boys than it is for girls. Various investigators agree that there is either no significant relationship between earliness of pubescence and the terminal adult height of boys [8, 40] or that the relationship is positive.[7, 42] For girls, on the other hand, some workers report no significant relationship [8, 40, 49] whereas others [5, 7, 42] report an *inverse* relationship (early maturers end up shorter and *vice versa*). The latter differences may be a function of just *how* early- or late-maturing these various groups of girls are. For example, Shuttleworth [42] determined the adult height of three groups of girls whose mean ages of maximal growth were 10.5, 12.5, and 14.5 respectively. In order of adult stature at age nineteen, these groups differing in age of sexual maturation ranked as follows: middle, early, and late. It seems possible, therefore, that relatively early (although not precocious) pubescence may limit final height in girls but not in boys. In this connection, Bayley and Tuddenham [7] suggest that "the female sex hormones are more potent than the male sex hormones in terminating physical growth."

Endocrine Aspects of the Adolescent Growth Spurt

We have already shown that the occurrence of the adolescent growth spurt is closely related to the onset of sexual maturation and to structural changes in bones that determine the individual's skeletal age. The formidable task still remains of explaining how the cells of the epiphysial cartilage are stimulated to multiply at this time, and how their multiplication is finally terminated by ossification during the decelerating stage of growth in late adolescence.

The most generally accepted hypothesis is that the prepubescent growth spurt is initiated by a sudden increase in the production of the pituitary growth hormone. The gonadal hormones are believed to account for the decelerating phase and for the eventual termination of growth by causing "a gradual reduction in either the amount or the effectiveness of the growth hormone." [19] As the secretion of gonadal hormone increases, a turning point is reached (age of maximal growth), and thereafter the rate of growth diminishes until it ceases completely. In precocious puberty, growth is stunted because the influence of the growth hormone is prematurely cut short by the abnormally early appearance of the gonadal hormone. If, on the other hand, puberty is delayed, the growth hormone operates unopposed on the expansion of the epiphysial cartilage for too long a period, and a long-legged, eunuchoidal individual results. [19]

This theory accounts satisfactorily for the termination of growth and for the sequence of events in precocious and retarded puberty.

However, it explains less adequately (1) the initiation of puberty, (2) the positive relationship between earliness of sexual maturation and adult height in the normal range of puberal onset, and (3) the demonstrable fact that adrenal cortex and gonadal hormones stimulate bone growth.*

There is no evidence to support the view that the growth hormone becomes more active in prepubescence. Furthermore, if this theory were true (1) why should rapid growth continue into early pubescence when gonadal secretion increases, (2) why should early-maturing individuals grow more rapidly and (except in extreme instances in girls) end up just as tall, and (3) why should injections of gonadal hormones induce skeletal growth as well as sexual maturation? [41]

To overcome these difficulties, the writer is proposing the following alternative hypothesis: Estrogenic and androgenic hormones have two effects on cartilage. (1) Like the growth hormone they stimulate cartilagenous proliferation, but (2) they *also* speed up the process of ossification which terminates bone growth. According to this view, the prepubescent growth spurt would be initiated as increasing amounts of estrogenic or androgenic substances are produced and add to the existing stimulation supplied by the growth hormone. This event would precede the occurrence of other signs of sexual maturation because of the greater sensitivity of cartilage tissue to sex hormone stimulation. Then, as the level of gonadal secretion increases, skeletal growth would reach a maximum and finally begin to decelerate since more and more cartilage would simultaneously be ossified. If puberty were markedly retarded, the growth hormone would have a longer time in which to function before both the adolescent growth spurt and ossification would supervene; and if it took place prematurely, the early ossification would deprive the epiphysial cartilage of the benefit of several years of growth hormone stimulation during the childhood period.

Within the median range of distribution of age of pubescence,

---

* In cases of precocious puberty it is true that the individual does not attain normal adult stature. Nevertheless, he is considerably taller than children of comparable chronological age. And what is more significant, as shown by Greulich's own data,[20] he is far advanced in skeletal changes. This is presumptive evidence that androgenic hormones stimulate cartilagenous growth rather than oppose the action of the growth hormone.

the positive genetically determined relationship between earliness of maturation and terminal skeletal height is not disturbed. As long as the epiphysial cartilage is open for a reasonably long period of time (and hence subject to stimulation by the growth hormone), final adult height is not differentially influenced by the age at which puberty and intense gonadal stimulation commence. The latter factor merely affects the age at which the adolescent growth spurt occurs. Thus, the boy who is tall at six tends to mature earlier than his shorter contemporary, undergoes an earlier growth spurt, and becomes a taller adult. Earliness of pubescence is thus positively correlated with terminal stature because both factors are similarly related to initial height.

Operating antagonistically to this relationship is the inverse relationship between earliness of maturation and ultimate height that prevails when there is a marked increase or reduction in the total length of time during which the epiphysial cartilage is open (retarded or precocious puberty). Somewhere between the extremes and the normal limits of the distribution of age of pubescence, these two factors will counterbalance each other and result in a relationship that follows neither pattern. This point of equilibrium seems to show a sex difference since the inverse relationship sets in earlier in girls,[7] leading to the hypothesis that estrogenic substances surpass male sex hormones in their propensity for stimulating ossification of cartilage.

CHANGES IN BODY WEIGHT

An adolescent spurt in weight is as regular an accompaniment of sexual maturation as a spurt in height. Like the spurt in height, it occurs earlier in children who enter pubescence at a younger age, and tends to precede other signs of sexual maturation. In girls it usually takes place between the ages of ten and fourteen, whereas in boys it occurs two years later.[11, 13] Between the ages of twelve and fifteen girls for the first time become heavier than boys, but thereafter boys regain their superiority.[13] Crampton found no prepubescent boy who was heavier than the mean postpubescent boy in his sample of 361 cases.[12] The heavier child, just like the taller child, tends to become pubescent earlier. We have referred to sex differences in the distribution of fat (see pp. 88 and 104). The best current device available for assessing the adequacy of growth in weight (according to the individual's own idiosyncratic growth pattern) is the Wetzel Grid technique, which rates maturity in terms of "the percentage level reached with respect to ultimate level." [50]

CHANGES IN BODY PROPORTIONS

Concomitantly with the growth spurt, a change in body proportions takes place. The most important change, occurring in both sexes, is a reversal of the ratio of trunk to leg growth, which alters "the proportion of sitting to standing height." [7] In contrast to the preadolescent years, the trunk begins to grow "more rapidly than the legs until the ratio stabilizes as growth is completed." [7] The upper portion of the face, particularly the nose, grows at a faster rate than in childhood giving rise to a marked change in facial appearance. According to Krogman,[32] growth of the face during adolescence occurs primarily in length (depth) and least in height, with growth in width occupying a middle position. This is precisely the opposite of the situation in preadolescence.[32]

The relative growth of various organ systems may be compared in Scammon's grouping of their growth trends under four general types: lymphoid, neural, general, and genital.[22] Genital growth increases most spectacularly during adolescence, and there is a substantial but not as great an increase in general (skeleton, musculature, internal organs) growth. Neural growth tapers off, and lymphoid tissues actually decrease in weight. Growth of the respiratory and vascular organs tends to keep pace with growth in skeletal (bone and muscle) tissue,[34] thereby obviating the possibility of physiological imbalance in meeting the enhanced nutritive needs of an enlarged body frame.

Other changes in adolescent body proportions are either sex linked or related to "velocity of maturation." [7] In girls the most prominent change is a relative widening of the hips, and in boys a corresponding increase in the breadth of the shoulders.[7] These differences, together with characteristic sex differences in muscular development and distribution of fat, constitute the basis for standards of male and female body build (see p. 88). The chronology of their occurrence (as well as the changes in trunk-limb ratio and in facial proportions) is naturally a function of the age of pubescence. In addition, however, characteristic differences exist between early- and late-maturing individuals. Late-maturing boys and girls tend to be relatively long-legged and to have shorter trunks than their more rapidly maturing contemporaries. Early-maturing boys also tend to be relatively broad-hipped and narrow-shouldered in comparison to late-maturing boys.[7]

Stolz and Stolz [45] refer to these shifting patterns in the rate of growth of various body parts as "asynchrony of development" (see p. 63). And since the resulting changes in body proportions take place within a relatively short space of time, they are quite noticeable and call for some form of psychological adjustment (see pp. 135–136).

GROWTH IN STRENGTH

A striking consequence of skeletal maturation during pubescence, with important implications for motor development, is a marked gain in strength. In part, this reflects the increase in the size of long bones, of the shoulder and pelvic girdles, and of the musculature in general. In part, it may reflect an increase in the strength of individual muscle fibers as a result of a shift in the endocrine (thymus-adrenal-gonadal) balance (see p. 97). However, that growth in strength should lag behind growth in muscle mass [45] is not at all surprising since the acquisition of structure generally precedes the acquisition of function. Time is needed before new structural capacities can become functional. A clear illustration of this principle is found in the vocal chords which increase greatly in size during early pubescence but not correspondingly in strength.[23]

When strength of grip is plotted against age, an increase in the rate of growth is noted for both sexes during the years of pubescence.[26] Dimock found that during the four year period from twelve to sixteen, the physical strength of boys increased twofold.[15] That this gain in strength is mostly a function of pubescence rather than a function of age is shown by the significantly greater scores made by pubescent as compared to prepubescent boys and girls.[12, 15, 26, 28, 29] The average pubescent boy exceeds 97 per cent of prepubescent boys in strength.[12] Precocious development of strength is also a characteristic of premature puberty.

More important for their motor and social implications than the gain in strength made by both boys and girls are the differences between the two sexes. In girls, the growth spurt begins earlier, reaches a maximum more quickly, and then begins to taper off about the age of thirteen or fourteen. In boys, the gain in strength does not reach a maximum until age sixteen and tapers off more slowly. Hence, the sex difference in strength tends to be widened during adolescence.

Sex differences in strength are no doubt, at least partly, a function of cultural conditioning. Muscular development depends to a large extent upon opportunity for use and exercise which by virtue of cultural tradition is heavily weighted in favor of boys. However, there are good reasons for believing that anatomical and physiological factors are also involved. Androgens, as already suggested, may exert a differential effect upon muscular development.[37] Because of their greater height and weight, the greater breadth of their shoulders, and the greater length of their bones, boys have a decided advantage in terms of leverage. In locomotor activities boys are also favored by the more advantageous angle that the neck of the femur makes with the pelvis. Physiologically, boys also have greater tolerance for physical exertion because of a greater respiratory volume and a greater ability to compensate for increased work load through a rise in systolic blood pressure (see p. 98).

As Jersild and his associates suggest, the social implications of this sex difference in strength are

> . . . that joint participation by boys and girls in the more robust athletic activities after the age of about fifteen will not function primarily in the nature of a competitive contest between or among equals. Such participation will mainly serve the social purpose of enabling the members of the two sexes to be together.[25]

MOTOR DEVELOPMENT DURING ADOLESCENCE

The subject of motor development during adolescence may be most relevantly considered in relation to the growth in size, strength, and body proportions described in the preceding pages. These events provide the underlying basis for whatever changes take place in physical performance during this period. In personality development, however, such objective shifts in motor capacity are less important in themselves than in relation to the changed biosocial status of the adolescent. Hence, we shall be primarily concerned with the implications of adolescent motor development for social and vocational adjustment.

The motor ability of an individual during adolescence, just as in earlier stages of development, constitutes an important component of his feeling of competence in coping with the environment. It enables him to feel either executively competent and capable of looking after many of his own needs or relatively dependent on the physical assistance of others. In addition, it continues to provide an important source of personal satisfaction, pleasure, relaxation, and leisure time activity. But in many ways it acquires new significance for personal and social adjustment.

First, during adolescence motor competence enters more crucially into the matter of the individual's primary status.* Throughout childhood, the capacity for self-help is something which the individual acquires largely in response to parental pressures and in order to retain parental approval; motor ability serves as a source of primary status chiefly in relation to his peer group. Now, however, it becomes a significant consideration in his quest for primary status in the adult world. For this reason it figures prominently in his deliberations about choice of a vocation.

The second major difference is that the prestige and "social esteem" associated with "competitive athletic skills" becomes for boys a major rather than a secondary source of current status during the adolescent period. This is not to say that physical prowess is socially unesteemed in the age period preceding puberty. In the earlier stage, however, the primary status achieved by the child through his own competence still is subsidiary to the derived status he enjoys at home (see p. 58). Success in competitive physical skills becomes much more eagerly sought after by the adolescent since it constitutes a more crucial determinant of his self-esteem.

Finally, because of the greater significance attached to the body during adolescence (see p. 99), noticeable physical incompetence or awkwardness becomes a more acute source of self-consciousness and embarrassment and of social ridicule. Thus, for this reason

* For the distinction between primary and derived status, see footnote on page 58.

alone motor handicaps are more likely to result in serious damage to the individual's self-concept.

Gross Motor Skills

The developmental picture for dynamic strength (running, jumping, throwing), is similar in some respects to the situation described for static manual strength (strength of grip), and different in others. The two abilities are significantly correlated during the adolescent period.[51] The differences are attributable to the fact that dynamic strength is more closely related to the *functional utilization* of strength as involved in athletic performance. In addition to strength, the factors of speed of movement, coordination, agility, and dexterity are implicated.

The parallel to growth of strength of grip is much greater for boys than for girls. In boys, dynamic, like static, strength is more highly correlated with physiological than with chronological age.* [16] It also grows slowly, reaching a maximum after the age of fifteen; but the gain is relatively less than in static strength.[16] In girls, on the other hand, dynamic strength tends to show an actual *decrease* (rather than merely to decelerate in rate of growth as in strength of grip) in most functions (broad jump, fifty-yard dash) after the age of thirteen.[16] Thus, while sheer strength remains a function of maturational status in girls, cultural factors influencing interest and inclination become more important after this point in determining whether increased strength will be used in the gross motor skills. Hence, during adolescence the divergence between the sexes in these abilities tends to become even greater than in strength. However, overlapping does occur and an occasional girl exceeds the average boy in both respects. Girls who are stronger and more physically fit participate more in physical activities,[48] a fact which demonstrates the interrelationships between strength and skill on the one hand and exercise on the other.

Therefore, to those biological causes of sex differences in strength

* It should be noted, however, that scores on the Brace test of *motor aptitude* (in contrast to dynamic strength as measured by athletic ability) are negatively correlated with pubescent status. Prepubescent boys, in other words make better scores than pubescent boys on this test.[15]

listed above, we must add factors of "cultural expectation . . . motivation and practice" in explaining the ever widening gap between boys and girls in competitive athletic skills after the onset of pubescence.[26] These sex differences are obviously important for their social implications in the peer group. However, in modern industrial society, with the gradual elimination of the need for physical strength and gross motor skill in most occupations, they are becoming increasingly less significant as relevant factors affecting vocational choice and aptitude.

Mechanical Abilities

Fine motor and mechanical abilities follow still another growth pattern than strength and gross motor skills. Involving as they do limited, swift, and precise movements of the small muscles of the hand rather than gross movements of large muscle groups, they are not implicated in the characteristic pubescent changes in muscle mass, strength, and coordination. The aspects of motor development that are most specifically related to sexual maturation involve the long bones and the muscles that are attached to them. Hence, development of fine motor and mechanical abilities pursues its own growth pattern in relation to chronological age, and seems to be relatively independent of the influence that pubescence exerts on other functions.*

In accordance with the principle of "developmental direction" (which states that muscles closer to the midline of the body mature earlier), manual coordination lags behind that of the wrist, elbow, and shoulder in the order stated. Hence, fine motor skills are acquired relatively late in comparison to abilities involving the larger muscle groups. When compared to the growth curve for intelligence, which is similarly unaffected by the physiological events of pubescence, the growth in mechanical ability during the adolescent period is not only less in magnitude but also terminates at any earlier age.

---

* Jones and Seashore in discussing the development of these abilities among subjects in the California growth study report that "there are some indications . . . that the early-maturing boys and girls tend to show somewhat steeper growth curves in early adolescence and tend to reach an earlier plateau. The differences however are smaller and less consistent than in the case of strength and gross motor performance." [30]

Another important difference between gross and fine motor abilities is the greater degree of intercorrelation among the former. The fine motor abilities are much more specialized, so that if an individual is superior in one mechanical ability it is no indication that he is likely to be superior in another. Jones and Seashore conclude:

> We find practically no evidence for . . . a general factor in fine motor skills, but a great deal of evidence for rather narrow group factors, and always for at least some specific factors in each test. . . . The group factors are not only relatively narrow as to the tests included within each group, but they often exclude tests which at first glance seem logically related. Also the group factors are only slightly related among themselves. . . . [Thus] in view of the specific nature of motor skills it is misleading to speak of a "general motor ability" [30] [pp. 133, 136, 137; this and the following quotation are by permission of the Society].

If, as these findings suggest, fine motor abilities are highly specific and there is no such thing as "general mechanical ability," it becomes necessary to re-evaluate the predictive value of various test batteries designed to measure manual dexterity and aptitude. Although it is conceivable that a particular subscore on such a battery may be highly predictive of success in a closely related occupation, the composite score is not likely to be very meaningful. We should also remember that success in any specific mechanical vocation depends upon factors other than mechanical aptitude, such as general intelligence, previous experience, motivation, and technical training.[30] These additional factors may explain

> . . . why highly skilled workers in a mechanical occupation make higher test scores than do lower-skilled workers. . . . The only conclusive evidence for the aptitude nature of a mechanical test is to administer it to a group of subjects before training and to show that the test scores do predict success as measured by rate of learning or by final levels of achievement after considerable experience in practical work [30] [p. 141].

Sex differences in mechanical abilities tend to be inconsistent in direction. Under conditions of relatively equal opportunity for practice, differences are small and in most instances statistically unreliable (for example, reaction time to sound, spatial eye-hand coordination, bimanual coordination, manual steadiness).[30] In "temporal eye-hand coordination," boys are consistently superior to girls whereas the reverse is true in a test "requiring the selection of an appropriate finger movement in response to a series of numbers visually perceived." [30]

In everyday mechanical skills, however, as we might suspect from the specificity of these skills, relative superiority is almost completely a function of differential opportunity for practice. Boys, for example, tend to outdo girls in skills involving the use of carpentry tools, whereas girls show to advantage in skills such as sewing and dress-making.[25] Certainly, a legitimate vocational implication that can be drawn from consideration of these data is "that there can be much more latitude of vocational choice, notably for girls, than conventionally has been allowed." [25] It would seem more reasonable and less wasteful of talent and ability, as Jersild suggests, to relate vocational opportunity to the "actual potentialities" of boys and girls than to purely arbitrary considerations of sex appropriateness dictated by cultural tradition.[25]

Interest in Physical Activities

With adolescence begins the increasing trend toward sedentary habits that is perhaps the most characteristic psychological datum of the aging process. A sharp decline in both interest in and volume of physical activity occurs.[31]

> Children who earlier were on the go much of the time now do more sitting or standing around. There is a decline in participation in vigorous sports and a relative increase in the time spent as a spectator of sports.[25]

This change is much more thoroughgoing and abrupt in girls since, as we have noted, competitive physical activities continue to play an important role in determining the peer group status of adolescent boys. This loss of interest among girls also accounts for the decline in their performance in gross athletic skills (see p. 121). It is largely a response to cultural standards of sex appropriate behavior reinforced by a fear that vigorous physical activity will induce masculine bodily characteristics (for example, bulging muscles). Hence, even the most confirmed preadolescent "tom-boy" generally mends her ways with the advent of puberty.

In both sexes the decline in physical activity is partly a function of the competition offered by new social interests (extracurricular clubs, dancing). To an unknown extent, also, it is probably a normal accompaniment of aging, since as individuals become older there appears to be a noticeable loss of pleasure in sheer exertion and a noticeable increase in their disposition to avoid bodily activity. A related change is

> a decrease in the number of different or separate play activities [which] begins even during elementary years. It occurs, in part, . . . by reason of occupation with more highly organized games which combine many operations into one large activity (a well-organized baseball game, for example, combines running, dodging, chasing, throwing and the like).[25]

The implications of this shift toward a more sedentary existence are uniformly undesirable. It is not only unnecessary in terms of actual physical capacity at this stage of life, but it is also unhygienic. From the standpoint of losing a good source of "pleasure, relaxation, . . . release from boredom" and leisure time activity, it is equally unfortunate.[25] It has also been observed that an adult will seldom pursue as a hobby a motor skill that has not been learned during childhood and early adolescence.[36]

Part of the responsibility for this unsatisfactory state of affairs must be laid to the physical education program of schools, which emphasize varsity sports and the type of athletic team activity that adults can continue only with difficulty after leaving school (football or baseball in contrast to handball, tennis, swimming).[25] The writer can thoroughly endorse the following statement by Jones:

> The student of child development is inclined to believe that in this field our chief objectives should be conceived, not in terms of providing new and larger stadia for champions, but in terms of providing informed guidance and wholesome physical activities for students in general [26] [p. 119; this and the remaining excerpted quotations in this chapter are by permission of the Society].

A special problem of guidance arises for high-school or college athletes who later enter sedentary occupations. During the years of active athletic participation the heart muscle hypertrophies to accommodate the increased needs of the skeletal muscles. If physical activity is abruptly discontinued, a certain portion of the hypertrophied cardiac tissue becomes superfluous and is no longer used; and, as so frequently happens when tissues are no longer functional, "disuse atrophy" sets in. In the heart the most common form of atrophy is fatty degeneration, which leads to impaired cardiac capacity. To avoid this unfortunate sequence of events it is necessary for athletes to undergo a gradual tapering off program when they contemplate retirement from strenuous physical activity.

Adolescent Awkwardness

Much controversy currently rages over the issue of whether or not awkwardness in adolescence is biologically or socially determined. Both Dennis [14] and Kuhlen [33] cite investigations that purport to show that in the Brace test of gross motor aptitude, there is for boys a consistent gain with age over the adolescent period. They attribute the apparent awkwardness to various social factors. These include lack of experience in common social situations (making introductions, applying for a job), "razzing" from others when the adolescent first attempts to exercise such adult functions as dancing, and the replacement of automatic action in gait and posture with embarrassed self-consciousness. Dennis also points to the "size-age illusion" as a contributing cause. The early-maturing child who undergoes an early growth spurt "is perceived as older . . . [and hence] arouses expectations of agility and skill above average for his age." [14]

We will not attempt to deny that these social factors are responsible for much of the awkwardness of adolescence. However, biological variables are also relevant. We have noted from the growth curves for the respective functions that the gain in muscle mass precedes the gain in muscle strength, which in turn precedes the gain in gross motor skill. This is an expression of the familiar biological principle that functional capacity is not attained concomitantly with but subsequent to structural growth. This principle is especially evident in the neuro-muscular system where practice and learning are such important factors. It is also understandable that simple functions such as strength involving a single set of muscles will be acquired before complex functions requiring coordination of several muscle groups either concurrently or in a given temporal sequence.

If structural changes take place gradually, "the young boy or girl can adjust his coordinations to his new bodily dimensions as rapidly as they are achieved." [14] But this does not describe the situation during pubescence when growth in size and strength takes place in spurts and "precipitates too sudden a need for acquiring new patterns of physical coordination consonant with increased physical capacity." [1] "Many of the eye-hand coordinations built up over the years of childhood may be rendered obsolete by these changes." [17] The sudden shift in body proportions contributes still another biological reason for adolescent awkwardness.

During adolescence the growth curves for speed of movements involving the elbow, wrist, and fingers are all *parallel* [30] despite the fact that rate of growth in size and strength in the larger muscle groups is much greater. Also, when the growth curves on the Brace test are plotted *separately* for pubescent and prepubescent boys, the prepubescents are found to be superior [15] in the age range of 12.5 to 14.5. Jones [26] reports that "boys tend to show a lag or even a recession in [motor] growth at around the skeletal age of fourteen years." The argument that mechanical skill and manual dexterity improve during adolescence is not relevant since these functions are not particularly affected by pubescence. The significant skeletal changes of adolescence are principally in the long bones and in the large muscle groups; and it is here that we should look for dispro-portions in the rate of growth to result in dysfunction (defective coordination, awkwardness).

Motor Ability and Personal-Social Adjustment

We have pointed out that an adolescent's motor development cannot be isolated from broader issues of personal and social adjust-ment.

> Particularly among adolescent boys the ability to take part in play-ground games and to play a normally lively role in various physical activities is more often than not an important factor in the development of successful social relationships. . . . With the coming of pubertal changes, girls tend to lose interest in active games and in the display of various forms of athletic prowess. . . . Among boys, however, competitive athletic skills are among the chief sources of social esteem. . . . These relationships would seem to be due not merely to the high premium which adolescents place upon athletic proficiency, but also to the fact that strength and other aspects of physical ability are closely joined to such favorable traits as activity, aggressiveness and leadership [26] [pp. 101, 117, 118].

Jones documents this statement with data from a study by Bower, who showed that in seventh- and ninth-grade boys, "popularity was unrelated to intelligence, height, home ratings, or school adjustment, but was significantly related to strength and to physical ability as measured by a series of track-event tests." [26] Presenting data of his own collected over a period of six to eight years, Jones finds significant differences in personal and social adjustment between boys making high and low scores respectively on tests of strength. The former were superior on ratings of popularity, "emotional buoyancy," social adjustment, and family adjustment, whereas the latter were rated higher on such items as "generalized tensions," "personal inferiority," and "physical symptoms." [27] In general, these differences between the two groups tended to become more marked over a six year period.

Retardation in motor competence is the beginning of a vicious cycle in social maladjustment that is difficult to break. Boys with poor physical ability tend to enjoy low social prestige in the group. They have reason to shun both physical activities and group participation because both are associated with failure.

> The child with negative and withdrawing traits is unfavorably regarded by his classmates; his failure to participate in physical activities increases his poor reputation and at the same time, through lack of practice, he falls further and further behind his classmates in those very characteristics that are needed to maintain status. Moreover, the child who seeks to participate but is unable to do so because of lack of skill may be forced to take refuge in withdrawal as his only defense against conspicuous social rejection [26] [p. 118].

It is possible, of course, that as a consequence of inferiority in physical skills, an individual may be motivated to develop other abilities from which he can derive compensatory satisfaction or prestige. But as Jones points out, "it is a critical question whether in so doing, he will lose contact with his classmates, or, on the other hand, will find a socially adequate use of such favorable traits as he may possess." [26] If the compensatory outlet does not promise to result in social isolation, it may legitimately be encouraged as an activity that possesses as much as or greater intrinsic value than athletic pursuits. In any event, however, the potential adjustive value of direct guidance (individual coaching) in motor skills should not be overlooked. Jack has shown that as a result of such individual guidance socially timid children become more ascendent and self-assertive in their peer relationships. [24]

The feasibility of guidance in physical skills is enhanced by their specificity and their susceptibility to improvement as a result of practice guided by instruction directed toward

... the detection and elimination of the particular difficulties of each individual which constitute his 'bottleneck' toward progress in learning that skill. . . . A person who has a poor initial score in a motor activity is in many cases only temporarily handicapped and if the skill is important to him he can often attain at least normal levels of proficiency by means of remedial training adapted to the nature of his difficulties.

If it is desirable for [the] best performers to receive special coaching in their activities it should be at least equally desirable and perhaps even more important to provide even larger amounts of such coaching for the lower ranking members of the group.

This, of course, does not assume that every person should attempt to develop a high degree of skill in every type of motor activity, but simply that there should be facilities to encourage those who have initial handicaps to develop at least far enough to be able to play a normal role in everyday activities or in informal competition within their groups. Emphasis upon the general principles of good form in an activity can be taught in groups, with special attention to those for whom still more intensive training is necessary [30] [p. 142].

In the case of boys who are temporarily retarded in growth informed guidance implies an understanding of their individual growth patterns and potentialities [26] [p. 119].

REFERENCES AND BIBLIOGRAPHY

1. Ausubel, D. P.: Problems of adolescent adjustment. Bulletin, Natl. Assn. Secondary School Principals, *34*:1–84, 1950.
2. Baldwin, B. T.: *A Measuring Scale for Physical Growth and Physiological Age.* 15th Yearbook, Natl. Soc. Stud. Educ., Part I, 1916.
3. Baldwin, B. T.: *Physical Growth of Children from Birth to Maturity.* University Iowa Stud. Child Welfare, Vol. 1, No. 1, 1921.
4. Baldwin, B. T., Busby, L. M., and Garside, H. V.: *Anatomic Growth of Children: A Study of Some Bones of the Hand, Wrist and Lower Forearm by Means of Roentgenograms.* University of Iowa Stud. Child Welfare, Vol. IV, No. 1, 1928.
5. Barker, R. G. and Stone, C. P.: Physical development in relation to menarcheal age in university women. Hum. Biol. *8*:198–222, 1936.
6. Bayley, N.: Size and body build of adolescents in relation to rate of skeletal maturing. Child Develpm., *14*:51–89, 1943.
7. Bayley, N. and Tuddenham, R. D.: "Adolescent Changes in Body Build," in *Adolescence,* 43rd Yearbook, Natl. Soc. Stud. Educ., Part I. Chicago: University of Chicago Press, 1944.
8. Boas, F.: Observations on the growth of children. Science, *72*:44–48, 1930.
9. Boas, F.: Studies in growth. Hum. Biol. *4*:307–350, 1932.
10. Bowles, G. T.: *New Types of Old Americans at Harvard and at Eastern Women's Colleges.* Cambridge: Harvard University Press, 1932.

11. Collins, S. D. and Clark, T.: Physical measurements of boys and girls of native white stock (third generation native born) in the United States. U. S. Publ. Health Reports, 44:1059–1083, 1929.

12. Crampton, C. W.: Physiological age as a fundamental principle. Child Develpm., 15:1–52, 1944.

13. Davenport, C. B.: Human metamorphosis. Amer. J. Phys. Anthrop., 9:205–232, 1926.

14. Dennis, W.: "The Adolescent," in Manual of Child Psychology (L. Carmichael, ed.). New York: Wiley, 1946.

15. Dimock, H. S.: Rediscovering the Adolescent. New York: Association Press, 1937.

16. Espenschade, A.: Motor Performance in Adolescence. Monogr. Soc. Res. Child Develpm. Vol. V, No. 1. Washington, D. C.: National Research Council, 1940.

17. Frank, L. K.: "Adolescence as a Period of Transition," in Adolescence, 43rd Yearbook, Natl. Soc. Stud. Educ., Part I. Chicago: University of Chicago Press, 1944.

18. Flory, C. D.: Osseus Development in the Hand as an Index of Skeletal Development. Monogr. Soc. Res. Child Develpm., Vol. I, No. 3. Washington, D. C.: National Research Council, 1936.

19. Greulich, W. W.: "Physical Changes in Adolescence," in Adolescence, 43rd Yearbook, Natl. Soc. Stud. Educ., Part I. Chicago: University of Chicago Press, 1944.

20. Greulich, W. W.: The rationale of assessing the developmental status of children from roentgenograms of the hand and wrist. Child Develpm., 21:33–44, 1950.

21. Greulich, W. W. et al.: Somatic and Endocrine Studies of Pubertal and Adolescent Boys. Monogr. Soc. Res. Child Develpm., Vol. VII, No. 3, Washington: National Research Council, 1942.

22. Harris, J. A., Jackson, C. M., Paterson, D. G., and Scammon, R. E.: The Measurement of Man. Minneapolis: University of Minnesota Press, 1930.

23. Howard, F. E.: Child Voice in Singing. New York: Birchard, 1935.

24. Jack, L. M., Manwell, E. M., Mengert, I. G., et al.: Behavior of the Preschool Child. University of Iowa Stud. Child Welfare, Vol. IX, No. 3, 1934.

25. Jersild, A. T. et al. Child Development and the Curriculum. New York: Teachers College, Columbia University, 1946.

26. Jones, H. E.: "The Development of Physical Abilities," in Adolescence, 43rd Yearbook, Natl. Soc. Stud. Educ., Part I. Chicago: University of Chicago Press, 1944.

27. Jones, H. E.: Physical ability as a factor in social adjustment in adolescence. J. Educ. Res., 40:287–301, 1946.

28. Jones, H. E.: Skeletal maturing as related to strength. Child Develpm., 17:173–185, 1946.

29. Jones, H. E.: The sexual maturing of girls as related to growth in strength. Res. Quart., 18:135–143, 1947.

30. Jones, H. E. and Seashore, R. H.: "The Development of Fine Motor and Mechanical Abilities," in *Adolescence*, 43rd Yearbook, Natl. Soc. Stud. Educ., Part I. Chicago: University of Chicago Press, 1944.
31. Jones, M. C.: *ICW Interest Record: Revised Form for Presentation of the Cumulative Record of an Individual with Group Norms by Items for a Seven-Year Period.* Berkeley, Calif.: Institute of Child Welfare, University of California, 1944.
32. Krogman, W. M.: Facing facts of face growth. Amer. J. Orthod. Oral Surg., 25:724–731, 1939.
33. Kuhlen, R. G.: *The Psychology of Adolescent Development.* New York: Harper, 1952.
34. Maresh, M. M.: Growth of the heart related to bodily growth during childhood and adolescence. Pediatrics, 2:382–404, 1948.
35. McCloy, C. H.: Appraising Physical Status: Methods and Norms. University of Iowa Stud. Child Welfare, Vol. XV, No. 2, 1938.
36. Nestrick, W. V.: Constructional Activities of Adult Males. New York: Teachers College, Columbia University, 1939.
37. Papanicolaou, G. N. and Falk, E. A.: General muscular hypertrophy induced by androgenic hormone. Science, 87:239, 1938.
38. Reynolds, E. L.: Sexual maturation and growth of fat, muscle and bone in girls. Child Develpm., 17:121–144, 1946.
39. Reynolds, E. L. and Grote, P.: Sex differences in the distribution of tissue components in the human leg from birth to maturity. Anat. Rec., 102:45–53, 1948.
40. Richey, H. G.: *The Relation of Accelerated, Normal and Retarded Puberty to the Height and Weight of School Children.* Monogr. Soc. Res. Child Develpm., Vol. II, No. 1, 1937.
41. Schonfeld, W. A.: Inadequate masculine physique as a factor in personality development of adolescent boys. Psychosom. Med., 12:49–54, 1950.
42. Shuttleworth, F. K.: *The Physical and Mental Growth of Boys and Girls Age Six to Nineteen in Relation to Age at Maximum Growth.* Monogr. Soc. Res. Child Develpm., Vol. IV, No. 3, 1939.
43. Simmons, K.: *The Brush Foundation Study of Child Growth and Development: II. Physical Growth and Development.* Monogr. Soc. Res. Child Develpm., Vol. IX, No. 1, 1944.
44. Stockard, C. R.: *The Physical Basis of Personality.* New York: Norton, 1931.
45. Stolz, H. R. and Stolz, L. M.: "Adolescent Problems Related to Somatic Variations," in *Adolescence*, 43rd Yearbook, Natl. Soc. Stud. Educ., Part I. Chicago: University of Chicago Press, 1944.
46. Stolz, H. R. and Stolz, L. M.: *Somatic Development in Adolescence.* New York: Macmillan, 1951.
47. Todd, T. W.: *Atlas of Skeletal Maturation.* St. Louis: Mosby, 1937.
48. Van Dalen, D. B.: A differential analysis of the play of junior high school girls. J. Educ. Res., 43:22–31, 1949.

49. Viteles, M. S.: The influence of age of pubescence upon physical and mental status of normal school students. J. Educ., Psychol., *20:*360–368, 1929.
50. Wetzel, N. C.: "Growth," in *Medical Physics* (O. Glaser, ed.). Chicago: Yearbook Publishing Co., 1944.
51. Willgoose, C. E.: The relationship of muscular strength to motor coordination in the adolescent period. J. Educ. Res. *44:*138–142, 1950.
52. Wissler, C.: Growth of children in Hawaii based on observations by Louis R. Sullivan. Memoirs of the Bernice P. Bishop Museum, *11:*109–257, 1930.

CHAPTER 6

Psychological Accompaniments of Bodily Change

CHAPTERS 4 AND 5 reviewed the physiological events of adolescence: the endocrine changes and their consequences for primary and secondary sex characteristics; the physiological changes in other organ systems; and skeletal changes and their implication for height, weight, body proportions, strength, and skill. In this chapter we shall examine the *psychological* phenomena that accompany these physiological changes. But in contrast to the approach in Chapter 3 (when we were concerned with pubescence merely as the major change in the individual's biosocial status responsible for *precipitating* the adolescent reorganization of personality structure), we shall be concerned here with the more *direct* behavioral consequences of physiological happenings.

In addition to the contribution of pubescence to the altered biosocial status of adolescents, there are several other ways in which physical changes influence psychological accompaniments. (1) Endocrine substances and changes in hormonal balance are capable of lowering the general threshold of behavioral reactivity and of altering (in a nonspecific fashion) the intensity and feeling-tones of emotional responses. Through this facilitating effect, general changes in emotional expression, in range, depth, specificity, direction, consistency, and stability, are induced. (2) Hormones are able also to provide a physiological substrate for the generation of more *specific* drives, interests, emotions, and states of awareness. The sex hormones, for example, furnish the nucleus and the raw material from which a large part of the heterosexual feelings, motivations, and interests of adolescents are fashioned. This relationship is exceedingly complex, is by no means inevitable, and depends upon the interaction among physiological events, individual psychological experience, and cultural influences. (3) On a purely perceptual basis, both the individual and the social group observe and react to the bodily changes that have taken place. These changes are perceived not in isolation but in relation to the similarities and differences that arise between one person and the next "by reason of variation in rate and pattern of maturing".[23] The individual is obliged to alter the mental image of his own body form, and various members of the group regard his body in a new light, as an object with a positive rather than neutral sex valence. (4) The individual responds to the social reactions that his own bodily changes elicit. To the social responses of approval or disapproval, admiration or ridicule, acceptance or rejection, he makes corresponding reactions in his own self-estimate and self-defense systems.

CHANGES IN INTERESTS

The influence of pubescence on the interests of adolescents is customarily measured by correlating the maturity level of their interests with various physical indices of sexual maturity. However, even when a positive correlation is found, a direct causal relationship need not necessarily be assumed. It is true that hormonal factors may directly create a differential sensitivity to stimuli of a heterosexual nature. But at the same time, much of the increased interest in heterosexual activities is generated indirectly through a process of social identification; that is, the pubescent individual tends to identify with and be accepted by pubescent elements in the community, and to associate himself with their interests. This latter mechanism is also a more plausible explanation of relationships between physiological maturity and shifts in interests that are either unrelated to sex activities (athletics), or related in only a culturally determined sense (criteria of masculinity and femininity).

When the maturity of boys' interests was expressed in the form of "developmental age",[17] Sollenberger found a moderately high correlation between that index and the quantity of androgens excreted in the urine.[49] Postmenarcheal girls achieve scores indicative of greater maturity on the Pressey Interest Attitude Test[51] and also show more interest than premenarcheal girls in grooming, heterosexual activities, and daydreaming but less interest in athletic activities.[52] Terman and Miles[56] found that early-maturing boys and girls obtained higher masculinity and femininity scores, respectively, than their late-maturing counterparts of corresponding chronological age. The only reliable difference in play interests between pre- and postpubescent boys of similar age is in automobile driving.[12]

RECASTING THE BODY IMAGE

The body image is the mental picture that each individual has of his own appearance in space. It includes such factors as height, weight, body build, facial appearance, the hair, eyes, voice.[41] Ordinarily, during most periods of life, the body image changes imperceptibly because the body itself changes in this way. Especially during the preadolescent years growth is slow and gradual. The small changes in appearance and quantitative increments in height are easily absorbed in the prevailing image the child has of his own body; no radical revisions are necessary.

During adolescence such rapid changes take place in size, body proportions, primary and secondary sex characteristics, facial appearance, that minor adjustments in the body image are no longer sufficient. "The old body-image becomes incompatible with the new perception of the physical appearance and bodily dimensions of self." [1] Nothing less will do than a conscious and wholesale restructuring of the outmoded body image. However, not only is there a drastic change in the structure of the body image, but also in its importance.

> Changes in body contours, new sensory experiences from developing sex organs, the upsurge of energy, new as well as heightened emotional responses —all tend to focus the attention of a boy or girl on his body. . . . This focusing of attention on the body is probably a concomitant of those periods in human life when the velocity of physical change is rapid, as in infancy and adolescence. . . . As changes in growth bring changes in sensations or appearance, interest in the body is renewed and concepts of self undergo revisions. . . .
>
> These bodily experiences are the not-to-be-ignored signs of growing up and become in a certain sense the symbol of emerging manhood or womanhood. The changing body becomes a symbol, not only of being different from last month or last year, but of a new attitude toward self, toward others, toward life [50] [p. 83; quoted by permission of the Society].

The body image, of course, is not of uniform significance and importance to adolescents throughout this entire period of growth. When junior high school students were asked what they liked and did not like about themselves, they mentioned physical characteristics more frequently than they did social relationships or intellectual status.[24] This trend was much less marked in senior high school. In all probability adolescents attach more importance to their own physical shortcomings than their age-mates do, although it must be admitted that this concern has considerable basis in objective fact.

SEX DRIVE AND SEX AWARENESS

The activation of the sex hormones creates an emergent problem of adaptation during pubescence. For the first time since early infancy a powerful, new, organically determined drive appears on the psychological scene, requiring initial regulation, direction, and socialization. In this respect at least, the problem of personality maturation during adolescence is more comparable to that of infancy than of childhood. If at this time the individual is older, more responsive to social norms, and has more compelling reasons to control hedonistic impulses, it is also true that he stands at the threshold of a new era of self-assertion and desire for volitional independence.

Preadolescent Sex Interests and Activities

There is abundant evidence from the behavior of preadolescent subprimates (males only),[15] primates,[15] and humans in our society [9, 10, 14, 20, 27, 31, 63] and in primitive societies [15, 34] to indicate that sex interest, curiosity, and activity prior to puberty are natural and frequently occurring phenomena. Such activities and manifestations of sex interest include masturbation, "peeking," mutual exhibitionism and genital manipulation,[10, 15, 27, 31, 63] interest in obscene talk and pictures, flirtation, and attempts at intercourse.[9, 15, 27] In some cultures, such as our own, preadolescent sex play is frowned upon and suppressed, but nevertheless it is indulged in surreptitiously. In other cultures such as the Alorese, Lepacha, Trobriand, Hopi, and Ifugao, adults take "a completely tolerant and permissive attitude toward sex expression in childhood".[15] Not only do some of these peoples "permit children free sex play . . . [and] also allow them opportunity to observe adult sexual behavior," but they also encourage experimentation in heterosexual intercourse.[15] Ford and Beach conclude:

> After reviewing the cross-species and cross-cultural evidence, we are convinced that tendencies toward sexual behavior before maturity and even before puberty are genetically determined in many primates, including human beings. The degree to which such tendencies find overt expression is in part a function of the rules of the society in which the individual grows up, but some expression is very likely to occur under any circumstances.[15]

But despite this evidence of prepuberal sex activity, there are good reasons—both theoretic and empirical—for believing that postpuberal sex behavior is *qualitatively* different from that which takes place prior to puberty.

> The matter of sexual expression assumes such compelling new urgency and so many rich new feeling-tones during adolescence that qualitatively the problems of control and direction are no longer recognizable as those present during childhood. Hence, it is to be expected that regardless of the various types of outlet (or lack of outlet) provided for this drive in different societies, "the stirring of sexual instincts (resulting from the increased production of sex hormones within the adolescent's own body) will give rise" to universal feelings of uneasiness and bewilderment in relation to the emergent needs for their control and direction. Whether he feels shame or pleasure, guilt or joy, is another matter which is determined by family or cultural conditioning.[1]

Adult (or postpubescent) sexuality can only be conceived of "as a form of self-expression (functionally or historically related to hormonal stimulation) which is related to the individual's experience of himself in a biological sex role".[2] Adolescent sexuality does not begin where childhood sexuality terminates. There is a qualitative difference, a definite break between the two. Childhood sexuality consists primarily of erogenous sensuality, of exploratory and manipulative activity, of curiosity about the anatomy and physiology of sex and reproduction, and of imitative attempts to simulate adult romanticism and sex play. It is "more or less a part of his other play . . . and usually sporadic".[27] After pubescence it becomes "an end in itself, frequent and regular".[27] In at least half of the instances of childhood history of sex activity

> . . . preadolescent play ends well before or with the onset of adolescence, and more adult sexual activities must start from new points, newly won social acquirements, newly learned techniques of physical contact. In many cases, the newly adolescent boy's capacity to ejaculate, his newly acquired physical character-

istics of other sorts do something to him which brings child play to an end and leaves him awkward about further sexual contacts.[27]

Malinowski, after observing the uninhibited sex play (including attempted coitus) of Trobriand Island children, reached the same conclusion as Kinsey:

> As the boy or girl enters upon adolescence, the nature of his or her sexual life becomes more serious. It ceases to be mere child's play and assumes a prominent place among life's interests. What was before an unstable relationship culminating in an exchange of erotic manipulation or an immature sexual act becomes an absorbing passion and a matter for serious endeavor.[34]

The Relationship between Sex Hormones and Sex Drives

Having concluded that sex hormones make for a qualitative difference between pre- and postpubescent sex behavior, we shall examine this relationship in greater detail. Exactly what role does any hormone or organic condition of the body play in generating a drive?

For a long time psychologists have spoken about "primary" or "innate" drives that are organically determined, and "secondary" or "acquired" drives that are developed as a product of experience. However, this distinction is really gratuitous since there are no innate drives; all drives are the outcome of experience. The notion that there exist at birth ready-made and preformed drives capable of energizing behavior is a relic of Hippocratian psychology. It was carried to an extreme by psychoanalytic theorists who attributed to these "innate" drives complex structure and patterning in content, goal-object, and mode of gratification.

It requires fewer untenable assumptions to postulate that man is born neither with drives nor with emotions but with a *capacity* to develop both. There is no storehouse where drives are stored before birth. At birth even a hunger drive does not exist. It develops as a result of the experience of having the stomach empty for approximately three hours so that hunger contractions take place.

Sex hormones are physiological. The sex drive, on the other hand is a psychological state or condition (conscious or "unconscious") that arouses the organism to seek and be selectively receptive to sexual experience. As a result of the facilitating influence that gonadal hormones exert on the nervous system, sex drives may be generated under certain conditions. But the conversion of sex hormones into sex drives is by no means inevitable, and in no way can the former be conceived of as drives * in themselves.

In subprimate mammalian species, the relationship between sex hormones and sex drives seems to be relatively invariable. Experience is still necessary for the one to be translated into the other, but it contributes little more than the necessary opportunity in time. That is, in these species there tends to be relatively little sexual behavior that is independent of hormonal stimulation, especially in females.[15] In the primates, however, sexual behavior to a large extent acquires freedom from hormonal regulation.

> If we turn our attention to monkeys, apes and other animals of higher evolutionary status we find that the . . . relation between sex hormones and sex behavior has become less precise. The full-grown female chimpanzee with constant opportunity for sexual contact displays an obvious cycle of sexual desire that correlates fairly well with the rhythm of ovarian hormone secretion. Nevertheless she may, under certain conditions invite or permit copulation by the male at times when she is not fertile and when the estrogen concentration is low. In contrast to the tendencies of lower mammals the female ape engages in sex play long before the first menstrual cycle or puberty.
>
> For the majority of women the greatest degree of sexual reactivity is experienced just before or just after the period of menstrual flow. . . . In women as in females of other species, the secretion of estrogen is greatest at or about the time of ovulation, that is, somewhere near the midpoint between the two periods of menstrual flow. Yet relatively few women feel their highest sexual drive at this time. Peaks of sexual desire that occur near the time of menstruation cannot be accounted for in terms of high estrogen levels. Factors other than hormonal ones have become maximally important in determining the level of sexual responsiveness in females of the human species.
>
> This conclusion is substantiated by observations to the effect that surgical or natural menopause need not produce a decrease in the sexual activities of healthy, emotionally well-balanced women. Although ovarian hormones are no longer present in the system many individuals continue to experience sexual desires and to participate in sexual relations.[5]

Once sex drives are generated in primate species (after pubescence), it is evident that the presence of sex hormones is no longer required for their continued existence and functioning. Many men castrated after puberty show little loss in sex drive or in copulatory activity.[5, 46] Further proof of the relative lack of dependence of human sex

* It has been customary in the past to define a drive as "a stimulus, usually internal, that arouses persistent mass activity." [43]

behavior on hormonal control is the noteworthy fact that male and female sex hormones do not stimulate masculine or feminine behavior respectively in homosexuals, but will stimulate either pattern depending upon other, psychological factors involved.[15]

But the degree of freedom from hormonal control is far from absolute. Some contact with an adequate level of sex hormone stimulation is necessary for adult sex desires to develop. "Studies on humans surgically deprived of their sex glands have indicated that when the operation is performed prior to puberty, interest in individuals of the opposite sex fails to develop." [46] * Oriental potentates have relied upon this fact for centuries in selecting eununchs to manage their harems. Dennis [11] has presented a summary of the literature about men with retarded sexual development who did not experience sex desire and potency until treated with male sex hormones.

There is no longer any doubt that sex hormones facilitate the generation of sex drive. Besides the evidence from normal pubescence, we have referred to the effect of administering sex hormones to castrated and hypogonadal individuals. A review of cases of precocious puberty also suggests that early "endocrine changes greatly increase the strength of the sexual drive" [11] making it comparable to that found in adults. However, the mechanism whereby "the chemical compound androgen exerts its effect upon behavior" [5] still remains to be identified. Undoubtedly, the nervous system is chiefly implicated, but as Beach has shown, androgens may influence sex behavior in at least one other way. An adequate level of male sex hormone is necessary to prevent deteriorative changes in the skin of the glans penis of the male rat. These changes reduce tactile sensitivity of the glans and probably contribute to the "inhibitory effect upon copulatory performance." [5]

Under favorable psychological conditions the inherent *potential* drive in sex hormones becomes actualized. The most important variable affecting this outcome is cultural tolerance toward the initial sex interest and desire induced by the hormone acting with various perceptual stimuli. Other factors contributing to erotic feelings are tactile sensations from the sex organs and the sight of the

---

* It should be noted, however, that prepuberal castration "does not necessarily prevent the development of strong sexual reactions in male chimpanzees." [5]

primary and secondary sex characteristics of others. Provocative stimuli mentioned by adolescent boys in a questionnaire study were female nudity, daydreaming, obscene pictures, motion pictures, sex conversation, burlesque shows, dancing, and nude art.[39]

However, if the cultural environment *completely* denies the existence of the sex drive, it remains latent and unactualized. Nothing need be repressed because nothing is created. If for thirteen years it is impressed upon a girl that girls do *not* experience sex drives, the facilitating effect of sex hormones on the nervous system comes to naught. No sex feelings enter her psychological field because of the potent negative influence of prestige suggestion. We cannot perceive what we already *know* not to exist. In Chapter I we discussed several examples of this phenomenon. Both Manus girls and Puritanically reared girls in our own culture fail to develop any sex drive. And Arapesh boys and girls both fail to develop sex desires apart from a specific affectional object (see pages 16 and 393).

Once sex drives are generated and enter the psychological field they become too insistent ever to be completely repressed. In instances of apparent complete repression, it is more correct to speak of the drives as never having been formed. We have referred to the definitive evidence obtained by Taylor,[54] Kirkendall[28] and Kinsey[27] showing that middle-class adolescent males in our culture are unable to repress their sex urges successfully (see pp. 17–18).

Psychophysiological and Psychoaffectional Sex Patterns

A qualitative difference between preadolescent and adolescent sex activity has been postulated on the association of adolescent sex activity (functional or historical) with sex hormones. A further distinction remains to be drawn between two different kinds of hormonally inspired sex desire. If sex urges are directed toward a specific affectional object, they may be regarded as *psychoaffectional*. If they exist apart from feelings of love and affection for a given person, they may be termed *psychophysiological*. Any combination of these two components of sex behavior may be found.

In most cultures, including our own, the two patterns exist concomitantly, varying in relative importance at different stages in the life cycle. The psychoaffectional pattern requires greater emotional maturity and generally appears later, especially among boys of the lower educational levels. Indiscriminate sexual promiscuity involving no emotional attachments is a good example of psychophysiological sex activity. The psychoaffectional pattern by itself is more common among women in our culture,* and is the only type of sex activity that is recognized for both men and women in Arapesh society. On the other hand, there are individuals who never develop anything but psychophysiological sex desires, and women in some societies (Manus) repudiate both patterns of sex behavior.

FORMULATING A BIOLOGICAL SEX ROLE

Sexual maturation and the generation of sex drives create another urgent problem for the adolescent: the necessity of accepting a biological sex role. The need is precipitated not only by his reactions to his own changed physical appearance and the intensification of his sex awareness, but also by the reactions of others to him as an adult sex object. Even if he does not become intensely aware of the developing opposite sex, he is obliged to cope with the attention and sex desires of age-mates directed toward his body. When a preadolescent girl undergoes changes in hip and chest contours, older boys look at her with different eyes and she cannot help but notice. Along with this comes a more formal but implicit acceptance of the individual by society at large as a member of an adult sex clan. The insistence of this social expectation cannot be long ignored!

Sex Role in Preadolescence

The preadolescent child undoubtedly identifies strongly with his own sex group and develops intense feelings of loyalty to it. But this identification occurs primarily for purposes of social grouping and play interests; it carries "none of the implications of biological sex role that are associated with membership in an adult sex clan." [1] In our culture, as in many others, the preadolescent peer group is based upon a social segregation of the sexes.

We have already concluded that individuals cannot assume a

---

* In more recent times, as a result of the trend toward equal social rights for women, and of sex and biological education in the schools, "girls [too] are beginning to wonder if they too are endowed with physiological sex urges." [1]

biological sex role until they both (1) become capable of adult sexuality and (2) receive cultural recognition as sexually mature adults. Neither condition can be met prior to pubescence. This does not mean, however, that preliminary experimentation with adult sex roles does not take place in prepubescents. Besides the motivation of curiosity and sensuality, preadolescent sex play is largely motivated by the desire to experiment with biological sex roles. This accounts for much of the imitation of adult romanticism, for the flirtation that occurs with the parent of opposite sex, and even for the attempts at heterosexual intercourse. In addition, the preadolescent assimilates much of the cultural folk-lore (four-letter words, "dirty" stories, and so forth) and moral values about sex: that sex is ugly or natural, that it is to be expressed or repressed, that it is permissible for men but not for women. He elaborates in fantasy many unshared misperceptions and half-truths which remain socially immature because they are not subject to social validation. And in our culture he bears his share of the social guilt surrounding sexuality because of his sexual curiosity, activities, and fantasy.

Facilitating Factors in Adolescence

The incorporation of an appropriate (heterosexual) biological sex role is facilitated by several factors in childhood and adolescent experience: (1) a model of happy marital relationships provided by parents; (2) strong positive identification with the sex role of the like-sexed parent; and (3) favorable initial experience with members of the opposite sex. The hormonal changes of adolescence, do *not* (as was formerly believed) strengthen heterosexual impulses; they merely intensify the expression of the existing sex role (homosexual or heterosexual).[15]

The attitudes of parents can exert a strong facilitating influence. It is helpful if the parent of the opposite sex reacts to his son or daughter as an individual with a biological sex role. This is especially important in preadolescence, since the normal segregation of the sexes precludes a good deal of the potential experimentation that would otherwise take place. "A girl needs her father's overt approval and outspoken admiration of herself as a young woman to help her to clarify and accept the feminine role."[16] Similarly a boy's mother should not make him feel that the "male's interest in sex is repulsive to a woman," [16] or cling to him so that he is prevented from making normal contacts with girls of his own age. If parents are able to accept as normal the adolescent's preoccupation with sexual concerns and fantasies, the latter does not feel nearly so guilty about sex. On the other hand, a parental attitude (implicit or explicit) to the effect that "my daughter is too pure to have such thoughts" interferes with the acceptance of a biological sex role, or, at the very least, induces unnecessary guilt feelings.

Retarding Factors in Adolescence

Hindering the adoption of an appropriate biological sex role is the absence of many of the facilitating factors mentioned above: the lack of a suitable adult model of the same sex with whose sex role the adolescent can identify, unhappy marital relations between his parents, and unfavorable initial experience with the opposite sex. As Frank [16] points out, if the parent of opposite sex deprecates the sex role of his adolescent child, the child finds it extremely difficult to identify with that role. If the father, for example, belittles girls and women, his daughter is more likely to reject the feminine sex role. Many cases of female sex delinquency start precisely in this way. The belittled girl uses sex as a means of obtaining power and revenge from the sex group that wronged her.[16]

Clinically, homosexuality is found most frequently in instances in which the child overidentifies with the sex role of the parent of opposite sex, for example, the boy identifying with his mother's sex role. Another common cause is narcissism, or a superfluity of self-love. Next to loving oneself, loving a person who is like oneself is the best possible substitute.

Hence, the adolescent, depending on the psychological climate, may adopt one of three possible attitudes toward his appropriate biological sex role: (a) accepting, leading to heterosexuality; (b) rejecting, leading to homosexuality or asexuality; and (c) ambivalent, leading to an alternation of attitudes (bisexuality), or to sex delinquency. It should not be thought that rejection of heterosexuality always leads to homosexuality. The more common outcome is either asexuality (a complete renunciation of sex), bisexuality, or sex delinquency.

CHANGES IN EMOTIONAL EXPRESSION

Very little that is definitive is known about the emotional concomitants of pubescence. The empirical data bearing on this subject
are fragmentary, inadequate, contradictory, and equivocal. Also,
as Kuhlen [29] points out, "most of the studies contrast older children
with younger children, but fail to study the situation in the years
following adolescence." However, the lack or unavailability of positive evidence does not enable us to conclude that no relationship
exists between pubescence and emotionality. It means only that the
research designs of previous studies have been inadequate for the
problem under investigation, and that final judgment must be
reserved until truly adequate data are available for evaluation. It
should be evident that more sensitive and subtle instruments than
paper-and-pencil personality tests and questionnaires are needed to
throw light on a matter as complex and resistive to measurement as
emotional expression. More fruitful approaches include extended
longitudinal observations, clinical interviews, projective techniques,
and physiological indicators of emotionality. In the meantime, we
can best rely on theoretical considerations and logical inferences
from related data.

Nonspecific Changes in Emotional Reactivity

The existence of a syndrome of nonspecific behavioral changes
associated with a pattern of emotional instability is a well accepted
principle of modern experimental psychopathology. The medical
evidence for the emotional concomitants of hormonal imbalance
(thyroid dysfunction, hyperinsulinism, the menopausal syndrome) is
unequivocal. From the experimental studies of Pavlov,[37] Masserman,[35] Maier,[33] and Hamilton,[19] there are positive indications that
chronic frustration, states of prolonged confusion, perceptual disorientation, and unresolved conflict lead to a similar condition of
altered emotional reactivity. This consists of the following clearly
defined behavioral syndrome:

> A greater magnitude of response to a smaller stimulus; a response which is
> more generalized, undirected, perseverative, and unadaptive, frequently in
> reaction to a less specific stimulus; sometimes complete blocking of activity;
> aggressive responses; subjective feelings of anxiety, insecurity, inadequacy and
> depression; and finally a facilitation of various compensatory, substitutive, or

indirectly adjustive mechanisms such as withdrawal (flight), rationalization, displacement of affect, regression, etc.[1]

Adolescence is characterized by a host of psychobiological and psychosocial conditions that "make for [just such] a heightened capacity for emotional reactivity":

> . . . the state of physiological flux and disequilibrium, the increased hormon-ally-inspired sex consciousness and sex drive, the lack of experience in con-trolling and directing the latter; . . . the abrupt loss of childhood ego status, the sudden lack of stable ego links and anchorages, discrepancies in rate of growth, transitional anxiety over proving oneself; problems related to somatic variations and to early or late maturation; too sudden needs for revising body image and incorporating biological sex role; and tensions relevant to emancipa-tion and parent-child conflict. . . . The same results may [also] be brought about by a [number] of psychosocial factors: prolonged deprivation of status, confusion concerning socio-economic sex role, inconsistencies and discontinui-ties in the social order, and the pressures that come from living in an aggressive competitive society.[1]

A cross sectional study of Rorschach responses shows that the affec-tive energy available to the child is at a maximum during adoles-cence.[57]

Greater emotional reactivity depends on a general lowering of the threshold for emotion-producing stimuli. As a result, emotional reactions become more intense, and occur in response to a wider range of stimuli, which are more subtle and less specific in nature. Until this new capacity for emotionality is brought under control and appropriately modulated (a task requiring considerable learn-ing experience) inconsistency, flightiness, instability, and lability of mood are inevitable. Moodiness, giggling, exaggerated emotional responses, irritability, indolence, and disorganized desultory activity have been described by both Tryon [59] and Hurlock and Sender [22] in studies based on observation of adolescents. In the study, by Hurlock and Sender, however, we have no comparable data for the preceding or succeeding periods of growth, and are, therefore, unable to relate these behaviors specifically to the adolescent period.

Other less convincing evidence of increased emotional instability in adolescence is found in the greater incidence of fingernail bit-ing; [62] in the higher ratio of unpleasant to pleasant items listed by older children in a twenty minute interval; [58] and in the greater number of themes of anxiety, discouragement, and fear produced by adolescents in response to a series of pictures.[53] As noted, however, other evidence (of a comparable lack of definitiveness) contradicts these findings. One group of investigators found no increase in the incidence of behavior problems in junior high school children.[7] And on a paper-and-pencil inventory of social and emotional adjustment, adolescent children showed no greater percentage of responses indicative of emotional instability.[60]

Several studies seem to agree that girls manifest greater emotional instability than boys during adolescence.[6, 36, 40, 48, 60] This sex difference is in part reflective of greater cultural tolerance for emotional display by the female sex. However, it may also be indicative of actual greater emotional stress during the adolescent period, which is a result of changing norms for biological and social sex roles, greater parental repression of strivings toward independence, and less developmental continuity in the factors accounting for status in the peer group (see pp. 227 and 418–420).

Changes in Specific Emotions

Specific categories of emotion also undergo change during adolescence. This is especially true of the emotions of aggression, affection, and fear. The causes of these changes are partly biological and partly social.

In addition to the cultural expectations leading to greater self-assertiveness in adolescents, hormonal factors also play a role.

Androgen treatment of hypogonadal men often . . . [augments] aggressive tendencies [which] may be expressed in social relations. . . . A similar correlation between androgen and aggressive behavior exists in many animal species. . . . Fighting is increased in fishes, reptiles and birds by androgen administration. Male rats and mice fight less frequently and vigorously after castration, and normal or even hypernormal aggressiveness can be evoked in castrates by administration of large amounts of male hormone. Female mammals and birds become increasingly likely to fight with each other or with males if they are treated with male hormone. . . .

Female chimpanzees that are socially subordinate to their masculine partners often become temporarily dominant during the period of estrus. If two female apes are kept together in the absence of males, a fairly stable dominance pattern emerges; and this is frequently reversed when one or the other animal comes into estrus. Similar reversals can be induced in spayed apes by the injection of ovarian hormone.[5]

Sex hormones also undoubtedly influence the quality and intensity of affectional responses that the adolescent is capable of making. These new feelings enter into the psychoaffectional sex drive. However, the difficulty of obtaining direct empirical evidence on this relationship is practically insurmountable. What evidence we do have is only inferential.* Prolactin, a hormone of the anterior pituitary gland, induces maternal behavior when injected into virgin or male animals.[5] David Levy has brought forth evidence indicating a positive relationship between degree of motherliness and length of menstrual flow.[32]

Hormonal changes at adolescence are probably less influential of fear reactions, although it is well known that the anxiety and depression frequently found in menopausal women are related to a decrease in gonadal hormones and an increase in pituitary gonadotropins.[5] The changes that occur in adolescence, however, seem to be more closely related to social factors and intellectual development. Fear of specific physical hazards declines, but worries associated with social and economic concerns become more prominent. The influence of cultural tradition on this trend can be seen in the fact that girls lose their fear of physical dangers less completely than boys do, acquire worries about social relationships earlier, and develop fewer anxieties about vocational aptitude and opportunity.[60] This is in accord with evidence of a shift in adolescence toward social, intellectual, and religious stimulus words as the chief causes of blocking and muscular tension in word association experiments.[44]

PROBLEMS REFERABLE TO EARLY OR LATE MATURATION

Large differences prevail "in the rate at which different individuals approach maturity" [46] (see pp. 92–93).

There are wide differences in rate of maturation that are still compatible with normality, each individual developing at his own optimal rate of speed.

---

* Postpubescent children react less violently to melodramatic danger scenes but more responsively to movie love scenes (W. S. Dysinger and C. A. Ruckmick, *The Emotional Responses of Children to the Motion Picture Situation.* New York: Macmillan, 1933.)

Unfortunately, however, children and adolescents never seem to adopt this viewpoint spontaneously, and hence, torture themselves and their age-mates over trivial deviations from the norm. . . . This attitude springs largely from the exaggerated need for conformity that is basic to the structure of the adolescent peer group.[1]

The seriousness of this problem depends largely upon the degree and conspicuousness of the difference, that is, the number of years of acceleration or retardation. The slow maturer is perhaps at a greater disadvantage because of the uncertainty of his situation and the limited time perspective characteristic of adolescents. He has no way of knowing when his pubescence will eventually occur. In the meantime, he "begins to wonder if he is a biological anomaly and frequently entertains serious doubts that he will ever mature." [1] He is also at a serious disadvantage socially. In athletics, he is hardly in a position to compete with boys of his own age who are much taller, heavier and stronger. His position on the social dance floor is equally untenable. Ostracism from the peer group, therefore, is not a rare or unlikely occurrence under these circumstances; and it is hardly "surprising that in order to prove himself, he sometimes resorts to behavior which is far from socially acceptable to adults." [46] Self-consciousness about his retarded physical development may also cause him to develop "greater or lesser degrees of shyness or timidity in his behavior." [45] According to Jones, late pubescence may result in a loss of previously held status in the group, and "when the biological innovations of adolescence are at last clearly avowed, a turning point may be reached . . . in social recognition and in feelings of personal security." [25] Such an outcome, of course, presupposes that the individual had not isolated himself completely from group participation during this interval.

Early maturation is much less of a handicap and in a certain sense may even be considered an advantage. Once the initial embarrassment of being a physical misfit is overcome, the early-maturer has all of the advantages of superior height, weight, strength, and heterosexual effectiveness on his side. In addition, as a result of his early maturation he obtains greater opportunity to enact mature roles and acquire mature role-playing experience. On the other hand, he may "find himself embarrassed by the disproportionate expectations of adults." [1] The early-maturing boy also is closer to the girl's body build than the later-maturing boy. Bayley and Tuddenham conclude:

> The poorest adjusted among the four extreme groups [are] the early-maturing girls and the late-maturing boys [since in a] coeducational school in which grade placement [is] largely [determined] by chronological age [these] two groups would stand out in a school room as physically the most different." [3]

We must also consider here the psychological readjustments that are necessary when sudden shifts in relative size, weight, and physical attractiveness are a consequence of early or late maturation. For example, the individual who matures very early stands head and shoulders above his prepubescent age-mates. But by the time he is fifteen or sixteen the reverse situation may prevail. Similarly, the late-maturing individual must adjust to the realignment in physical and social status when his delayed pubescence finally occurs.

ADJUSTING TO NORMAL SOMATIC CHANGES

In addition to the reactions leading to an alteration of the body image, the adolescent displays other perceptual responses to the physical changes of pubescence. Some of these perceptual reactions result in feelings of uneasiness, self-consciousness, and embarrassment. Nevertheless, we must agree with Jersild that

> . . . we should not overdo our compassion. In some accounts of physical development it has been the fashion to paint a highly lugubrious picture. If the child is fat he is miserable; if he is skinny he is sad. If he is tall for his years, he staggers under the responsibilities that fall upon him; if he is short, life is a bitter pill. The woe that goes with a big bosom is equaled only by the misery that comes with a flat chest.
>
> Actually, of course, adolescent growth has both its dark and bright aspects. The changes that mark the transition to adult status not only present problems but also bring occasion for joy and pride.[23]

Interest in Grooming and Adornment

One of the more obvious psychological reactions of adolescents to bodily changes is an increased concern with grooming and personal appearance. This is in marked contrast to the preadolescent indifference to these matters. The preadolescents (notably boys), as a matter of fact, seem to pride themselves on being dirty and slipshod. However, beginning with adolescence there is an abrupt change in attitude. As already noted, Stone and Barker found statistically reliable differences between pre- and postmenarcheal girls in interest in grooming and appearance.[52] Among the concerns are the hair, facial appearance, fingernails, and clothes.

Three kinds of motivations seem to underlie the development of these new interests. (1) The adolescent desires to increase his heterosexual effectiveness without alienating or provoking the criticism of his own sex group.[21] (2) He desires to assert his right to adult status by assuming the prerogatives associated with adult physical appearance. Hence, the desire for long trousers, adult dress styles, rouge, face powder, lipstick. Silverman found that the use of facial cosmetics by girls increases steadily after the age of twelve.[47] (3) A third motivation is the need for conformity to peer group standards. The adolescent peer group desires to establish its unique individuality and its recognizability from adult society. It is able to do this and still mimic adult society by adopting extreme forms of adult dress and grooming (extreme styles, excessive use of cosmetics). When a conflict exists between adult and peer group standards, the adolescent can usually be depended upon to cast his lot with his age mates.

Reaction to Normal Somatic Changes

In contrast to the somatic *deviations* that occur in some adolescent individuals but not in others are a group of bodily changes that constitute a characteristic of pubescence. How does the adolescent react to them?

The mere attainment of adult physical stature is a source of serious misperception by adolescent boys and girls in our culture. Because of it, they feel they are entitled to the rights and privileges which they have always associated with adult physical form. It takes considerable time and many bitter disappointments before they appreciate that the achievement of adult personality status involves more than the acquisition of physical maturity. But if growth in stature is a cause for ego enhancement, the typical history of asynchrony in skeletal development is also a cause for serious concern. Adolescents do not and cannot realize in advance that temporary disproportions in body dimensions will eventually be corrected. Perhaps the most disturbing of all instances of asynchrony is the early and sudden spurt in the growth of the nose. Although the initial prominence of the nose is frequently corrected by corresponding growth in other facial features, its disproportionate size is one of the more common causes of homeliness in both men and women.

The development of primary and secondary sex characteristics is for the most part a source of pride rather than of psychological disturbance. This conclusion can be inferred in part from the fact that lack of normal development of these characteristics is one of the most serious categories of somatic problems mentioned by adolescents.[50] Even the onset of menstruation, a phenomenon associated with considerable shame, embarrassment, secrecy, and dread in our culture, is accepted unemotionally or eagerly by a majority of girls. Because of the relative degree of prominence of the changes, primary sex characteristics are more important for boys, and secondary sex characteristics are more important for girls (see pp. 81–82, 83).

A group of secondary sex characteristcis involving the skin and associated structures elicit particularly strong emotional reactions from adolescent boys and girls. Boys are extremely eager for the dense growth of body and facial hair, whereas girls are equally concerned that these hairs fail to develop. Another skin phenomenon about which adolescents are particularly sensitive is body odor. This sensitivity is a product of cultural factors: the high premium placed on cleanliness in the United States and the influence of commercial advertisements stressing the terrible social consequences of "B.O." or "halitosis." From a purely biological standpoint, there is reason to believe that certain body odors reflect increased sexual functioning and play an important role in arousing the sexual sensibilities of the opposite sex (see pp. 90–91).

The most important and prevalent source of emotional disturbance associated with the somatic changes of adolescence is acne. The seriousness of this problem is generally underestimated by parents, teachers, and counselors because adolescents find it too traumatic to admit their concern. The actual importance of the problem, however, is revealed in the number of hours spent in front of the mirror and in the willingness of adolescents to experiment with every conceivable remedy suggested for the disguise or amelioration of the condition. Although empirical evidence is lacking, many persons who work with adolescents feel that acne is an important determinant of social unpopularity (and even ostracism) during adolescence. The individual's response to this social reaction consists of damage to the self-concept (loss of self-esteem) and withdrawal from social activities. Because of the greater importance of facial beauty in girls, the occurrence of acne in them is probably more traumatic than in boys. However, girls have the advantage of using cosmetics to effect disguise. Also, boys have to contend with the widely accepted popular myth that acne is a consequence of excessive masturbation.

ADJUSTING TO SOMATIC DEVIATIONS

The relationship between physical defect and behavioral maladjustment is two-sided and reciprocal. Either condition almost inevitably gives rise to the other, which in turn reinforces and tends to perpetuate the original state of affairs. A vicious circle is established; and it often becomes difficult indeed to ascertain which component existed first.

In adolescence the psychosomatic (or somatopsychic) relationship is more important than in childhood because of the more significant role played by the body in the individual's social status and self-concept. Physical attractiveness and sex appropriateness become crucial determinants of individual status within the peer group and also of heterosexual effectiveness. Thus, the increased social disadvantage of physical deviancy has important repurcussions on the self-concept of the deviant individual, who becomes predisposed to respond with various manifestations of behavior disorder.

The characteristics of behavior disorder also tend to be more physical during adolescence. Clinical experience with different age groups demonstrates vividly that the area in which behavioral response to frustration is most likely to occur is that region of the psychological field that is most central at a given stage of development. In early infancy when the feeding situation is so crucial to mother and child, interpersonal friction leads to feeding disorders. At a later stage, when the child's conformity to parental training demands becomes the most crucial issue, behavior disorder takes the form of negativism. And in adolescence when bodily changes play so prominent a role in the changing self-concept, it is understandable that the physical components of the emotional and behavioral response to frustration will be correspondingly enhanced.

Psychological Concomitants of Somatic Defects

Physical defects first of all constitute an objective limitation to the individual's capacity to adjust to his environment. Cardiac and orthopedic disabilities restrict participation in athletic and social activities. Sensory (visual and auditory) defects restrict the range of sensitivity and responsiveness to important intellectual and social stimuli. When unsuspected and uncorrected, therefore, they make school learning difficult and simulate mental deficiency. Indirectly, also, they may lead to failure in school by placing too great a strain on the individual's capacity for attentiveness. Rather than contend with the continual burden of this strain and failure, he may prefer to disengage himself from the entire painful situation and develop an attitude of either indifference to or active dislike for the frustrating school environment.

A number of physical conditions also give rise to behavioral disturbance by lowering the general threshold of reactivity. When this happens the individual manifests undue irritability, restlessness, and distractibility, and responds to trifling stimuli with exaggerated, undirected, inappropriate and frequently aggressive responses. Some of the more common causes of this altered state of behavioral reactivity are fatigue, chronic physical strain, pain, hunger, and hormonal imbalance. Hormonal imbalance is characteristic of all adolescents, and chronic strain, pain, and excessive fatigue may be associated with any number of physical and sensory defects that occur during adolescence.

More important than the objective handicap inherent in physical defects, especially during the adolescent period, is the social disadvantage at which they place the deviant individual. Deviancy from group physical norms elicits a highly negative response from his peers, and almost guarantees that he will be treated differently from his fellows. The least common denominators of this differential treatment are devaluation, avoidance, rejection, and accordance of a lower status. Regardless of verbal statements of sympathy or of verbal claims that they are uninfluenced by another's physical disability, the fact remains that adolescents in their *actual* behavior accord highly discriminatory treatment to persons with physical handicaps. These persons tend to enjoy lower status in the group, are frequently ostracised, fail to receive their share of attention from the opposite sex, and are often treated with open contempt and hostility.[25, 26.] It would be an understatement to say that adolescents take competitive advantage of the physical shortcomings of their rivals in the competitive race for status in the group and for favor in the eyes of the opposite sex.

The individual's response to his own physical disability is largely a reflection of the social reaction to it. During adolescence when he is so dependent on the peer group for status he tends to accept as real the value that the group places on him. Because the group's opinion was less important in childhood, on the other hand, it was possible for him to retain a more flattering self-image, provided that he was intrinsically accepted and valued by his parents. Hence, disability in adolescence almost inevitably leads to damaged self-esteem. At the very least, it results in hypersensitivity and self-consciousness about the defect. The individual imagines that the eyes of everyone are focused on his disability and that it constitutes the chief topic of conversation when he is absent. This is especially true of persons with sensory impairment, who normally tend to feel suspicious because so much of what goes on around them must remain a matter of conjecture. Another manifestation of this hypersensitivity to physical defect is the resistance displayed by so many adolescents to physical examination. They are unhappy about revealing their inadequacy or sex inappropriateness to physicians whom they believe to be especially sensitive (by virtue of training) to the slightest degree of abnormality or deviancy.

The situation becomes more serious when ego damage becomes severe enough to lead to a significant withdrawal from social life. Interpersonal relationships acquire a negative valence in the individual's psychological field since they are associated with traumatic ego feelings. Avoiding social interaction thus becomes a self-protective device which may lead to irreversible defects in the socialization process. Deprived of the experience required for learning the elemental techniques of social adjustment, he may incur a developmental deficit that permanently incapacitates him for normal interpersonal relations in adult life. For this reason, any of the compensatory or aggressive forms of ego enhancement are far less serious than withdrawal as a reaction to the ego deflating implications of somatic defect.

Somatic Concomitants of Psychological Stress

For the very same reason that somatic defects are a most important cause of psychological disturbance during adolescence, psychological disturbance, in turn, is more frequently mediated through bodily manifestations. As a more prominent component of the ego, the body becomes more intimately implicated in disturbances involving this core constituent of personality structure. The adolescent individual is more apt to respond to frustration of any kind with physical symptoms and disability.

The simplest variety of psychosomatic manifestation consists of the ordinary physiological (autonomic) accompaniments of emotion or anxiety: sweating, rapid heart beat, vasomotor disturbance, muscular tension, diminished salivation. One of the more common consequences of emotional stress in this category is a subjective feeling of overwhelming fatigue or exhaustion. These symptoms acquire secondary adjustive value when they are used by the individual as justification for failure, poor performance, or avoidance of a disagreeable situation (rationalization). A related adjustive use to which they can be put is to serve as convenient foci for the displacement of anxiety. That is, it appears to the adolescent that the real cause of his anxiety is not concern over his studies, peer group relations, or vocational problems, but some physical condition.[8, 50] This may be an actual somatic defect, such as obesity or acne, rather than a physiological consequence of anxiety. At any rate, it is less anxiety-producing for the individual to believe that the source of the threat to his self-esteem is something tangible and physical, such as obesity, rather than an unflattering personal characteristic, such as low intelligence or lack of social acceptability.

In addition to physiological concomitants of emotion and existing somatic defects of independent origin which are utilized for rationalization, withdrawal, and displacement purposes, there is a type of physical injury that is an indirect consequence of psychological stress. "Accident-proneness" in adolescents is not an uncommon outlet for aggressive proclivities.[13] "As a means of expressing their resentment against parents and elders, [and] of provoking guilt feelings in the latter, adolescents may unconsciously expose themselves to danger." [1]

But regardless of whether disturbance originates in the somatic or in the psychological area, the effects are almost invariably circular and reciprocal. Obesity of physical origin (glandular dysfunction), for example, induces psychological feelings of inferiority, which may, paradoxically enough, worsen the original condition by leading to compensatory overeating. On the other hand, the origin may be in inadequate social adjustment, which leads to an attempt to secure substitutive gratification.

Types and Frequency of Somatic Deviations

By definition somatic deviations consist of departures from culturally established norms of physical appropriateness for men and women. Individuals are generally regarded as ugly or attractive insofar as they conform to or deviate from the median anatomical measurements of their own sex group in a given cultural setting.[38] Because of the multiplicity of factors in the determination of physical attractiveness, few individuals escape deviancy in at least one bodily characteristic. And almost invariably, for reasons to be discussed below, the most serious deviations are those that relate to norms of sex appropriateness, to physical standards of masculinity and femininity. The nicknames resented most by boys are those which make reference to inadequacies in masculine physique.[18]

In the California Growth Study, twenty-nine of ninety-three boys showed evidence of being disturbed by the following physical characteristics [50] [this, and the subsequent table for girls, are from p. 86, quoted by permission of the Society].

Lack of size—particularly height	7
Fatness	7
Poor physique	4
Lack of muscular strength	4
Unusual facial features	4
Unusual development in the nipple area	4
Acne	3
Skin blemishes, scars	2
Bowed legs	2

Obvious scoliosis 2
Lack of shoulder breadth... 1
Unusually small genitalia.. 1
Unusually large genitalia.. 1

Similar data from eighty-three girls yield the following breakdown among the "thirty-eight who gave evidence of being disturbed by their physical characteristics":

Tallness 7
Fatness 7
Facial features 5
General physical appearance.. 5
Tallness and heaviness... 3
Smallness and heaviness.. 3
Eye glasses and strabismus... 2
Thinness and small breasts... 2
Late development 2
Acne 1
Hair 1
Tallness and thinness.. 1
Big legs 1
One short arm... 1
Scar on face.. 1
Brace on back... 1

Primary Sex Characteristics. As noted, deviations in the primary sex characteristics, such as smallness of the external genitalia, are of psychological significance in boys only (see p. 81). But as just for acne, the seriousness of this problem cannot be estimated from the verbal reports supplied by adolescents. Few individuals who are vitally troubled by such actual, or imaginary, defects are willing to undergo the ego trauma involved in even admitting this concern to themselves. And here, because of the vital implications for masculinity, the "tyranny of the norm" is even more unreasonable and inflexible.

The size of the male external genitalia is correlated with psychological aspects of sexuality (sex drive, masculinity) only in unusual cases of insufficiency. The reason for this has been made clear (see pp. 81–82, 83). Genetic variables in structure are more important determinants of variability in size than hormonal stimulation except in extreme cases (hypogonadism or hypergonadism of endocrine origin). Also, psychological experience *per se,* divorced of any connection with either genetic or hormonal influences, is an important factor in psychosexual behavior.

In helping adolescents adjust to this somatic deviation, much can be accomplished by exposition of the relevant facts. Simple assurance from a physician that the range of normal variability is wide, that size is negligibly correlated with drive, that (except in extreme cases) copulation is not seriously affected, and that heterosexual effectiveness is not impaired has a great deal of therapeutic value. In cases of hormonal inadequacy, endocrine therapy is indicated and may effect evident improvement in a matter of weeks.[42] Pseudo-hypogenitalism due to obesity can be cured by correcting the obesity.

Body Build. Shortness of stature is a genuine social handicap in our culture which naturally has its reflections in ego feelings.

> A short boy or man seems to have greater difficulty in commanding the attention of strangers or casual acquaintances; at the level of superficial social reactions we are apt to associate size with masculine dignity. When we look for leaders among a group of boys whom we do not know very well, we tend to try the larger boys. . . . More specifically shortness is a real handicap to a junior or senior high school boy who seeks prestige through athletic prowess in the popular team games. In none of the sports most popular among adolescent boys do short boys succeed in achieving representation proportionate to their incidence.
>
> In following the appropriate adolescent urge to establish satisfying social relations with girls, the short boy often finds his lack of size a handicap. This handicap arises partly from the culturally developed preference of girls for men who are 'tall and handsome', and partly as the result of the special precocity of girls in relation to boys at this particular stage in their development. At a time when girls tend to seek the companionship of boys older than themselves they are most apt to snub the advances of contemporary boy friends who still both look and act like small boys. In social dancing, both girls and boys much prefer a partnership in which the boy is at least as tall as the girl [50] [p. 88; this, and the following five quotations are by permission of the Society].

In girls, precisely the opposite condition prevails. Tallness is not an accepted cultural standard of femininity and represents "a genuine emotional hazard." [50] Shortness in girls or tallness in boys does not become a problem except in extreme divergence from the norm.

Obesity is a very common somatic deviation with wide variability in psychological outcome. Some boys and girls are extremely disturbed by it and are willing to institute strict dieting regimens to ameliorate the condition. Other adolescents seem to be completely unconcerned.

> Comments and humorous allusions to getting fat are so frequent in casual conversation, especially among women, that too much significance must not be attributed to verbal protestations about the matter. Avowed disturbance over slight deviations from the fashionable dress-model figure may serve as convenient conversational camouflage to cover other more important dissatisfactions with self [50] [p. 89].

On the other hand,

> . . . excessive fat is both cumbersome and unsightly at any age. It interferes with graceful and effective performance of any locomotor activity . . . and is, therefore, particularly unwelcome to the adolescent boy who seeks social recognition through athletic achievement. In early adolescence this is to some extent true for girls also, but their disturbance over being fat is more closely connected with the fear of being unattractive in terms of our current cultural ideals. . . .
>
> In any case, the nicknames and thoughtless derogatory comments which, before the adolescent period, may cause the fat boy or girl only rather vague discomfort or no discomfort at all, take on a new penetrating quality for the physically self-conscious and socially sensitive juvenile in the less friendly atmosphere of the junior high school [50] [p. 90].

With respect to "sex-inappropriate physical traits", the adolescent boy is most disturbed by a syndrome consisting of a

> . . . considerable increase of fat around the hips . . . combined with small external genitalia, scanty pubic hair, narrow shoulders and an unusual development of subcutaneous tissue about the nipples. In such a case the feeling of sex inappropriateness arises not merely from a lack of what is considered acceptable male development, but also from the superficial similarity of the whole pattern to that popularly associated with female development. . . .
>
> During the adolescent period girls, also, are sometimes concerned because their bodily size and configuration do not correspond closely enough to their ideals for themselves. . . . Some of the commonly occurring physical traits which in our culture may combine to give adolescent girls a feeling of sex-inappropriateness are: unusual tallness, squattiness, large hands, large feet, clumsy ankles, undeveloped breasts, pigmented facial hair, extreme thinness, moderate or extreme fatness, heaviness of lower jaw, hairiness of arms and legs, general massiveness of body build [50] [pp. 91–92].

Why Somatic Deviations Are Important during Adolescence

Somatic deviations become so crucial during adolescence because of the increased importance of the body in the individual's self-concept.

One obvious reason for this is the enhanced awareness of their bodies which adolescents acquire, partly from the consciousness of their own physical development, and partly from their increasing identification with culturally determined ideals concerning appropriate physical characteristics for men and women. . . . Thus each boy and girl in our culture gradually cumulates into "self" attitudes toward his body a mixture of identification and rejection, of pride and embarrassment, of concern and ignoring. . . . [And since] all human beings are most vulnerable in those areas where lie their strongest drives, it can be assumed that any condition which cuts across vital urges or endangers their fulfillment becomes a hazard for an individual and a potential source of basic frustration [50] [pp. 84, 85, 87].

Concern with cultural standards more specifically entails sensitivity to the norms of the peer group. Since the peer group becomes the chief source of his status and prestige, the adolescent desires to conform to "the specific 'norms of body proportions and growth' prevailing in his own limited circle." [1] Now, for the first time, physical attractiveness becomes a crucial determinant of the girl's sociometric status among her peers of both sexes. In similar fashion, a boy's sociometric status is largely governed by his relative degree of masculinity and athletic prowess.

These same characteristics are also important for heterosexual effectiveness, but more so for boys than for girls. A girl who is unattractive to and unpopular with other girls can still be very attractive to boys. But for boys to be popular with girls, they must first win recognition of superior masculine attributes among their own sex.[61] For this reason somatic deviations are more serious for boys than for girls during adolescence despite the fact that girls "are far more apt to do something to relieve their frustration than boys are. In the improvement of face or figure they are willing to spend time, forego pleasure, withstand the demands of hunger, endure pain and discomfort." [61] However, it seems much more likely that this greater disposition to "do something about it" is more a result of the greater availability of corrective measures and of greater cultural tolerance for such ameliorative procedures than of stronger motivation from greater frustration or ego damage. In adult life, on the other hand, it is clear that the effects of somatic deviation on heterosexual adjustment are much less disastrous for men than for women. Men can always compensate for physical unattractiveness to the opposite sex through vocational success.

"The greater significance which these bodily variations assume at adolescence is partly due to the fact that they are now associated with a sense of finality that was not present during childhood." [1] As the Stolzes so eloquently put it: "In childhood, years of growth stretch indefinitely ahead and growing-up, adequate in every respect, is taken for granted. But during puberty, boys and girls begin to realize that the years of growth are numbered and they are faced with the reality of permanent differences of size in relation to other people." [50] The impact of this sense of finality is compounded by "the notoriously limited time perspective of adolescents . . . since it is imagined that conformity to peer standards will *always* be as important. . . . [Hence] the traumatic effect of somatic variations . . . must be evaluated in terms of the fact that the 'ego lives' less in the future than is customarily its wont." [2]

Factors Determining the Seriousness of Outcome

All adolescents do not react in the same way to somatic deviations.

How serious such problems may become for any boy or girl will depend upon how strong the drive is and how drastically the condition interferes with the satisfaction of his urges. How each person "takes" these frustrations will be determined by previous life experiences and will be modified by the extent to which he is finding genuine satisfactions in other basic areas of life which may lessen the strains in the frustrated areas [50] [p. 85].

It need not be imagined, for example, that self-depreciation is an inevitable accompaniment of organic defects or disabilities. After cataloguing the major somatic deviations of adolescence, Stolz and Stolz conclude, "of all the items mentioned, acne seems to be the only one which almost universally causes emotional difficulties for an adolescent boy or girl." [50]

Numerous other factors affect the seriousness of the problem: the extent of the deviation, both from the norm of the peer group and from the child's ideal; its "probable duration," and its obviousness to others; its relation to other physical defects and to problems of adjustment arising from non-somatic sources; [50] and the attitudes of the individual, his parents, and his peers toward the condition. In most instances the individual tends to magnify the seriousness of his defect out of all proportion to the impression it makes on his associates. Yet in view of the premium that our culture places on beauty, especially in girls, this is hardly surprising. We tend to take for granted that good-looking persons can "get away with murder." It is also important to remember that objective fact is completely irrelevant in such matters. "For the practical purposes of individual guidance, problems of adjustment exist only when an individual says that he is disturbed or acts as though he were disturbed" [50] [p. 97].

"The matter of becoming reconciled to limitations in physical form and appearance thus becomes one of the major adjustment problems of adolescence." [1] It is not "an easy thing to accept an ugly, unattractive body as the final physical representation of self." [2] Hence adolescents in trying to accept

> the reality of their appearance, [strive] to make that reality as pleasant as possible. Not all boys and girls succeed in mastering this developmental task. This is evidenced in everyone's experience by individuals in adult life who continually struggle with their appearance or in some way or another try to compensate for real or imagined defects [61] [p. 223].

The different modes of adjusting to such somatic defects are legion in number. As a last resort ugliness may even be perceived as a virtue.

Many guidance procedures can be used to supplement medical treatment in helping adolescents adjust to somatic variations.

> In one case this may consist of persuading the adolescent that he is exaggerating the differences which are really unimportant. Another adolescent may need assurance that the differences are but a passing phase of normal development. Sometimes a boy or girl can be helped by learning techniques of dress or grooming which render an undesirable physical variation less obvious. Sometimes they need help in developing compensatory assets which will gain for them social acceptance in spite of their physical peculiarities [50] [p. 98; quoted by permission of the Society].

Conditions exist, however, in which there is no possible hope for effecting any physical improvement. In such cases (patients with congenital defects or chronic disabling diseases), adjustment is furthered best by having the individual accept the reality of the poor prognosis as early as possible. A certain amount of stoicism is necessary, after which the building of self-acceptance along other lines can be attempted.[42]

Finally, in evaluating the significance of psychological reactions to bodily disturbance, it is important for the counselor not to be misled as to the *actual* source of the emotional stress in many cases. "Through the common mechanism of displacement of affect, anxieties of entirely different origin may be ascribed to a somatic defect." [1]

REFERENCES AND BIBLIOGRAPHY

1. Ausubel, D. P.: Problems of adolescent adjustment. Bulletin, Natl. Assn Secondary School Principals, *34*:1–84, 1950.
2. Ausubel, D. P.: *Ego Development and the Personality Disorders.* New York: Grune and Stratton, 1952.
3. Bayley, N. and Tuddenham, R.: "Adolescent Changes in Body Build," in *Adolescence*, 43rd Yearbook, Natl. Soc. Stud. Educ., Part I. Chicago: University of Chicago Press, 1944.
4. Beach, F. A.: *Hormones and Behavior.* New York: Paul B. Hoeber, 1948.
5. Beach, F. A.: "Body Chemistry and Perception," in Perception: Approach to Personality (R. R. Blake and G. V. Ramsey, eds.). New York: Ronald, 1951.
6. Bernreuter, R. G.: *The Personality Inventory.* Stanford, Calif.: Stanford Univ. Press, 1935.
7. Blatz, W. E., Chant, S. N. F., and Salter, M.D.: *Emotional Episodes in the Child of School Age.* University of Toronto Stud. Child. Develpm. Series, No. 9, 1937.
8. Blos, P.: *The Adolescent Personality.* New York: Appleton-Century, 1941.
9. Childers, A. T.: Some notes on sex mores among Negro children. Am. J. Orthopsychiat., *6*:442–448, 1938.
10. Davis, K. B.: Sex Factors in the Lives of Twenty-Two Hundred Women. New York: Harper, 1929.
11. Dennis, W.: "The Adolescent," in *Manual of Child Psychology* (L. Carmichael, ed.). New York: Wiley, 1946.
12. Dimock, H. S.: *Rediscovering the Adolescent.* New York: Association Press, 1937.
13. Dunbar, H. F.: *Emotions and Bodily Changes.* New York: Columbia University Press, 1938.
14. Ellis, H.: *Studies in the Psychology of Sex.* New York: Random House, 1936.
15. Ford, C. S. and Beach, F. A.: *Patterns of Sexual Behavior.* New York: Harper and Paul B. Hoeber, 1951.
16. Frank, L. K.: "The Adolescent and the Family," in *Adolescence,* 43rd Yearbook, Natl. Soc. Stud. Educ., Part I. Chicago: University of Chicago Press, 1944.
17. Furfey, P. H.: A revised scale for measuring developmental age in boys. Child Develpm., *2*:102–114, 1931.
18. Habbe, S.: Nicknames of adolescent boys. Amer. J. Orthopsychiat., *7*:371–377, 1937.
19. Hamilton, G. V.: *An Introduction to Objective Psychobiology.* St. Louis: C. V. Mosby, 1925.

20. Hamilton, G. V.: *A Research in Marriage*. New York: Boni, 1929.
21. Hurlock, E. B.: *Motivation in Fashion*. Archives Psychology, No. 111, New York, 1929.
22. Hurlock, E. B. and Sender, S.: The "negative phase" in relation to the behavior of pubescent girls. Child Develpm., *1:*325–340, 1930.
23. Jersild, A. T. et al.: Child Development and the Curriculum. New York: Teachers College, Columbia University, 1946.
24. Jersild, A. T.: *In Search of Self*. New York: Teachers College, Columbia University, 1952.
25. Jones, H. E.: *Development in Adolescence*. New York: Appleton-Century, 1943.
26. Jones, H. E.: Physical ability as a factor in social adjustment in adolescence. J. Educ., Res., *40:*287–301, 1946.
27. Kinsey, A. C. et al.: *Sexual Behavior in the Human Male*. Philadelphia: Saunders, 1948.
28. Kirkendall, L. A.: *Sex Adjustments of Young Men*. New York: Harper, 1940.
29. Kuhlen, R. G.: *The Psychology of Adolescent Development*. New York: Harper, 1952.
30. Landis, C. et al.: *Sex in Development*. New York: Paul B. Hoeber, 1940.
31. Landis, C. and Bolles, M. M.: *Personality and Sexuality of Physically Handicapped Women*. New York: Paul B. Hoeber, 1942.
32. Levy, D. M.: Psychosomatic studies of some aspects of maternal behavior. Psychosom. Med., *4:*223–227, 1942.
33. Maier, N. R. F.: Experimentally induced abnormal behavior. Scientific Monthly, *67:*210–216, 1948.
34. Malinowski, B.: *The Sexual Life of Savages in North-Western Melanesia*. New York: Harcourt, Brace, 1929.
35. Masserman, J. H.: *Principles of Dynamic Psychiatry*. Philadelphia: Saunders, 1946.
36. Mathews, E.: A study of emotional stability in children. J. Delinquency, *8:*1–40, 1923.
37. Pavlov, I. P.: *Conditioned Reflexes*. London: Oxford University Press, 1927.
38. Perrin, F. A.: Physical attractiveness and repulsiveness, J. Exp. Psychol., *4:*203–217, 1921.
39. Ramsey, G. V.: The sexual development of boys. Amer. J. Psychol., *56:*217–233, 1943.
40. Remmers, H. H., Whisler, L., and Durwald, V.: Neurotic indicators at the adolescent level. J. Soc. Psychol., *9:*17–24, 1938.
41. Schilder, P.: *The Image and Appearance of the Human Body*. Psyche Monograph No. 6. London: Kegan, Paul, Trench, Trubner, 1935.
42. Schonfeld, W. A.: Inadequate masculine physique as a factor in personality development of adolescent boys. Psychosom. Med., *12:*49–54, 1950.
43. Shaffer, L. F.: *The Psychology of Adjustment*. Boston: Houghton Mifflin, 1936.
44. Sharp, D. L.: "Group and Individual Profiles in the Association-Motor Test," in *Studies in Emotional Adjustment*, University of Iowa Stud. Child Welfare, Vol. XV, No. 1, 1938.

45. Sherif, M. and Cantril, H.: *The Psychology of Ego-Involvements*. New York: Wiley, 1947.

46. Shock, N. W.: "Physiological Changes in Adolescence," in *Adolescence*, 43rd Yearbook, Natl. Soc. Stud. Educ., Part I. Chicago: University of Chicago Press, 1944.

47. Silverman, S. S.: *Clothing and Appearance: Their Psychological Implications for Teen-Age Girls*. New York: Teachers College, Columbia University, 1945.

48. Smith, H. P.: The relationship between scores on the Bell Adjustment Inventory and participation in extra-curricular activities. J. Educ. Psychol., *54:* 27–71, 1939.

49. Sollenberger, R. T.: Some relationships between the urinary excretion of male hormone by maturing boys and their expressed interests. J. Psychol., *9:*179–189, 1940.

50. Stolz, H. R. and Stolz, L. M.: "Adolescent Problems Related to Somatic Variations," in *Adolescence*, 43rd Yearbook, Natl. Soc. Stud. Educ., Part I. Chicago: University of Chicago Press, 1944.

51. Stone, C. P. and Barker, R. G.: Aspects of personality and intelligence in postmenarcheal and premenarcheal girls of the same chronological age. J. Comp. Psychol., *23:*439–455, 1937.

52. Stone, C. P. and Barker, R. G.: The attitudes and interests of premenarcheal and postmenarcheal girls of the same chronological age. J. Genet. Psychol., *54:*27–71, 1939.

53. Symonds, P. M.: Inventory of themes in adolescent fantasy. Am. J. Orthopsychiat., *15:*318–328, 1945.

54. Taylor, W. S.: *A Critique of Sublimation in Males: A Study of Forty Superior Single Men*. Genet. Psychol. Monogr., XIII, No. 1, 1933.

55. Terman, L. M.: *Psychological Factors in Marital Happiness*. New York: McGraw-Hill, 1938.

56. Terman, L. M. and Miles, C. C.: *Sex and Personality*. New York: McGraw-Hill, 1936.

57. Thetford, W. N., Molish, H. B., and Beck, S. J.: Developmental aspects of personality structure in normal children. J. Proj. Techn., *15:*58–78, 1951.

58. Thompson, G. G. and Kepler, M. O.: A study of the production of pleasant and unpleasant items as related to adolescent development. J. Educ. Psychol., *36:*535–542, 1945.

59. Tryon, C. M.: *Evaluations of Adolescent Personality by Adolescents*. Monogr. Soc. Res. Child Develpm., Vol. IV, No. 4, 1939.

60. Tryon, C. M.: *UC Inventory I, Social and Emotional Adjustment*. Revised Form. Berkeley, California: University of California, 1939.

61. Tryon, C. M.: "The Adolescent Peer Culture," in *Adolescence*, 43rd Yearbook, Natl. Soc. Stud. Educ., Part I. Chicago: University of Chicago Press, 1944.

62. Wechshler, D.: The incidence and significance of fingernail biting. Psychoan. Rev., *18:*201–209, 1931.

63. Willoughby, R. R.: *Sexuality in the Second Decade*. Monogr. Soc. Res. Child Develpm. Vol. II, No. 3, 1937.

CHAPTER 7

Personality Maturation During Adolescence

CHILDHOOD AS A PERIOD OF DEPENDENCY

OUR CROSS-CULTURAL SURVEY of preadolescence has brought us to the conclusion that childhood is inevitably a period of biosocial dependency. The reasons for this inhere partly in the child's relative incompetence in the motor, intellectual, and social skills that are necessary for survival, and partly in the universal cultural tendency to deny equal social membership to sexually immature individuals regardless of their capacity for environmental adaptation.

The actual developmental situation is far more involved than this simple statement of dependency indicates. Three other variables complicate the picture. First, there is never a complete correspondence between objective biosocial realities and parent attitudes. In early infancy, for example, when the child is most helpless and dependent, he is treated with considerable deference by his parents. They make few if any demands upon him and usually accede to his legitimate requirements.

This is true to a greater or lesser degree in most cultures. Infancy is invariably the period of life accorded most indulgence. The Navaho,* for example, are even more extreme in these practices than we are.

> Children are highly valued by the people and are almost invariably wanted. . . . All Navahos make a fuss over babies. They receive from the start a very great amount of attention and a great deal of facial stimulation by touch. . . . The child is nursed whenever he cries. Only occasionally is there any delay. . . . The baby himself determines not merely when he wishes to suck but also when he is finished. . . .
>
> To the Navaho baby . . . other persons must appear warm and dependable, for every time he cries something is done for him. Every step he takes toward

---

* The following description would hold with hardly an exception for the Chamorros of Saipan.[24]

social participation is rewarded. . . . The child runs from person to person and is petted by each in turn or consoled if it has met with some small accident. . . . Older persons are almost always quite tolerant of displays of aggression and little temper tantrums. When a two-year-old has something taken from him or fails to get what he wants, he will scream, arch his back, brace himself, and be quite inconsolable until his elders give in (which they often do) or somehow distract him.

The child is under much less pressure to hurry up and walk than white children, and the Navaho mother counts it no disgrace that the chlid takes his time to grow up. . . . All training in the first two or three years of life is delayed, gradual and gentle. Not until he can talk and understand is pressure put on a child to learn Navaho conventions of excretion. . . . A child at this age is almost never cuffed or even spoken to harshly. . . . The positive side of child training in this period is mainly a matter of constant encouragement in the acquisition of language and other skills.[26] *

Although the infant is *executively* helpless to gratify his own needs, he tends to perceive himself as *volitionally* independent and relatively omnipotent.[5] That is, he perceives his own inability to satisfy his wants, but this dependency is only a small part of the larger *Gestalt* of perceived volitional power characterizing the self. Executive dependence detracts not a whit from the feeling of omnipotence since a volitionally omnipotent individual has no *need* for executive competence as long as others are at his beck and call. In fact, it may even enhance the child's notion of his own power that success in need gratification takes place *despite* the manifest handicap of executive incompetence. He might, therefore, legitimately conclude: "My will must be powerful indeed if a tiny, helpless creature like myself can compel omniscient adults to gratify my desires."

A second complication lies in the discrepancy between objective reality and subjective perceptual content. It is obvious that a large number of environmental and social situations are complex and subtle enough to require considerable experience and sophistication before realistic perception is possible. Maturation of perceptual capacity is a regular feature of psychological development. There is, for example, a steady progression with age in children's ability to

* Reprinted by permission of the publishers from Dorothea Cross Leighton and Clyde Kay Maben Kluckhohn, *Children of the People: The Navaho Individual and his Development.* Cambridge, Mass.: Harvard University Press, Copyright, 1947, by the President and Fellows of Harvard College.

perceive accurately their own and others' sociometric [6] or social class [36] status. The infant possesses sufficient perceptual ability to distinguish between the deferential behavior of his parents and the matter-of-fact or competitive attitudes of his siblings. What he is not mature enough to perceive is the motivation underlying his parents' overt subservience. From this arises the misperception that the parent is *obliged* to defer to his powerful will rather than that the deference is altruistic in the face of his helplessness and limited frustration tolerance. A similar lack of perceptual maturity underlies the expansiveness, negativism, and "out-of-bounds" aspects of four-year-old behavior. The child overestimates his executive competence and believes himself capable of managing his own affairs without direction or supervision.[5]

Finally, the dependency of childhood must be qualified in degree. The neonate can not even perceive that he is executively dependent since a notion of dependency can not arise before he has both a perception of his own helplessness and an appreciation of the causal relationship between the actions of others and the satisfaction of his needs. At first, the parent is merely a conditioned stimulus that happens to be present when his needs are being gratified. Later, as the child becomes mature enough to appreciate that he is dependent upon the parent for physical survival, he concomitantly develops a notion of volitional omnipotence. This phenomenon necessarily awaits the development of a concept of volition, which is an outgrowth of the observation that the unlearned adaptive response of crying (when he is hungry or uncomfortable) is almost *invariably* efficacious in relieving his distress.

The notion of executive dependence becomes but a subsidiary part of the self-concept of volitional omnipotence. It merely imposes qualifying restraints on this independence. That is, omnipotence is perceived as not unlimited but in relation to the availability of a specific executive arm (the parents) subservient to his will and devoted to his interests. Thus, the infant's sense of security—"his level of confidence with respect to the future beneficence of his environment insofar as his safety and the provision of his basic needs are concerned" [5]—becomes a function of his executive dependence. Sudden separation of the nine-month-old infant from his mother leads to strong feelings of insecurity accompanied by severe disturbances of mood and behavior (continuous crying, depression, apathy, loss of weight, eczema).[35] The infant's sense of adequacy, on the other hand—"his feeling of personal worth, importance, and ability to control and manipulate the environment to his own ends" —is derived from a misinterpretation of early parental subservience to his needs and desires as a result of which he vastly exaggerates his volitional power and independence.[5]

This situation usually exists until about the age of two or three. In the meantime, the child acquires more executive competence and becomes more capable of responding to parental direction. The parent, desiring to assume the volitionally ascendent role in the relationship and to train the child in the traditions of the culture, begins to make demands on the child. The environmental supports for the belief in volitional independence now collapse. As perceptual maturity advances, the child begins to perceive that his parents are free agents, not obliged to defer to him; that he is dependent upon them volitionally as well as executively; that he is relatively impotent and dependent upon their good will for the satisfaction of his wishes; that executive incompetence is the basis of his volitional impotence rather than the proof of his omnipotence.

How reminiscent of our own culture, for example, is the situation of the Navaho (also the Chamorro [24]) toddler in contrast to his idyllic infantile existence:

> Except for ill health, the Navaho child's troubles may be said to begin only at the weaning period. . . . [He] comes to learn that the world around him makes demands and imposes restrictions in addition to giving reassurances and rewards. . . .
> The Navaho weaned child must face keenly felt deprivations. . . . Weaning means less and less of the mother's attention. Deprivation of the breast is merely one sign of a general loss. For the weaned child is no longer allowed to sleep every night by the mother's side. His sleeping place is now under the blanket which also covers the two or three other children nearest him in age. The mother surrenders to these older children most of the care of the weaned baby. . . .
> Latterly he had been accustomed to nurse as much for comfort as for nourishment. Now this solace is denied him even when he is tired, angry, cross or frightened. . . . Crying is less immediately responded to and less fully tolerated. A weaned baby who gets in the mother's way may be rather roughly jerked aside. . . .
> Moreover the mother starts to make demands of him. . . . No longer is

everything done for him with hardly any effort on his part; instead he must learn to feed, wash and dress himself. . . . Serious demands for bladder and bowel control usually coincide with weaning or come shortly thereafter. . . . Soon performance of simple chores, such as bringing in sticks of wood for the fire or snow to be melted for water, comes to be expected. Neglect of these, or getting into mischief, will bring a harsh scolding or a cuff or, a little later, a mild switching. . . . The weaned child . . . finds that no longer are almost all his responses rewarded, no longer does his mother devote herself mainly to his pleasure. After the child really begins to talk he finds that all responses and rewards are made much more *selectively* by his elders—he has to do the right thing for attention and praise.[26] *

The crisis in ego development that results requires a complete reorganization of ego structure on a greatly devalued basis. The most acceptable and least traumatic alternative is for the child to adopt the role of a satellite to his parents. By doing this he acquires a *derived* status, which he enjoys vicariously by the mere fact of their accepting and valuing him for himself, regardless of his competence or performance ability. A much more reliable feeling of adequacy can develop from this type of status, conferred by fiat, than from a more *primary* type of status, which he would have to earn by virtue of his own ability to manipulate the environment. At this stage, volitional and executive dependence are not perceived as unrelated phenomena; executive is perceived as a necessary prerequisite of volitional independence. The child is dependent in both aspects and derives from the new satellizing relationship his feelings both of security and of adequacy.

It is apparent that satellizing will not occur in just any type of home environment; it is necessary that the child be accepted and valued for his own sake. Obviously, if derived status is a function of these two conditions, it cannot be acquired in an atmosphere of either rejection or of extrinsic valuation (when the parent values the child as an extension of his own ego, in anticipation of the child's eventually gratifying his own frustrated ambitions). And lacking the advantages of intrinsic security and adequacy that are associated with derived status, the child has little incentive for relinquishing the notions of volitional omnipotence and independ-

* Reprinted by permission of the publishers from Dorothea Cross Leighton and Clyde Kay Maben Kluckhohn, *Children of the People: The Navaho Individual and His Development.* Cambridge, Mass.: Harvard University Press, Copyright, 1947, by the President and Fellows of Harvard College.

ence and of becoming subservient to the will of another. Even when parents accept and intrinsically value, the child finds the crisis of ego devaluation difficult to accept. He submits only after a stage of negativism: the grandiose features of his infantile ego structure are asserted in a last show of defiance before acknowledging that the advantages of derived status offer him a more tenable biosocial position.[5] The modifications in personality development that occur in extrinsically valued or rejected children who are unable to satellize will be described in a later section (see pp. 208–214).

The consequences of satellizing for the future course of personality are profound. Extensive devaluation of the notions of ego importance (the centrality of self in a given interpersonal environment), of omnipotence, and of volitional independence takes place. But to compensate for this, the child acquires a guaranteed source of derived status from which he obtains intrinsic feelings of security and adequacy. In addition, as he accepts a volitionally dependent and subordinate role to his parents, it becomes more and more important for him to obtain and retain their approval; only in this way can he feel sure that the status he enjoys by the fiat of acceptance will continue. Thus, his sense of security and adequacy becomes increasingly dependent upon conformity to parental standards and expectations of more mature and appropriate behavior. In almost all cultures this means that he will acquire greater executive independence, more ability to forego immediate hedonistic satisfactions for the sake of long-range objectives, and a new sense of obligation to abide by internalized parental values.

Finally, as a result of satellization the child acquires a frame of reference for assimilating values and attitudes. He acquires a strong motivational set to perceive the world in the light of the values and expectations of his parents. His security depends on this ability. Later this learning orientation is reinforced by personal loyalty and by the desire to avoid the guilt feelings he knows will ensue if he repudiates parental values. Learning, in other words, is primarily a by-product of identification (satellization) with the person on whom he is dependent; the actual content of the value or goal that is assimilated is of secondary importance. The renunciation of a value so learned is tantamount to an act of personal disloyalty and may, therefore, produce guilt feelings.

However, no sooner is the dependency of satellization achieved than new conditions are created which undermine it and alter the shifting balance of dependence-independence. At the same time that he enjoys the derived status of dependent child in the home, he begins to acquire a primary, performance-based status in the peer group and in school.* Here he is valued not for himself but primarily for what he can do and how well he can perform in comparison with his fellows.† As he makes vast strides in executive competence through expansion of motor, intellectual, and social capacities he begins to perceive himself in a less dependent light. His parents loom less omnipotent and less omniscient in relation to his own abilities. He fancies himself entitled by virtue of his new capacities to greater volitional independence, to greater extrinsic status, to a more responsible role in the social order.

But the extrinsic status of childhood—even if achieved in economically significant activities, as in primitive cultures and rural environments—can constitute only a subsidiary source of status.

* In primitive cultures and rural communities, the dependent child finds his source of primary status in the home more than in school or peer group. Especially in primitive societies, life is usually hard, and "children start working as soon as they are able, helping more and more as they grow older." [26] The *quality* of their performance then becomes a factor in determining whether they are to be rewarded (see p. 171). At nine years of age, Navaho girls are "already capable of taking entire care of the house and younger children in their parent's absence. Their reward would be the approval of their relatives and perhaps a gift of lambs or new clothes from the trading post if the family could afford them." [26]

† This competitive aspect of *primary* status is almost inevitable in our culture, but it is not a necessary component of such status in all cultures. "The Navaho is completely unaccustomed to an explicitly stated hierarchical ranking of persons such as is carried out in the grading system in white schools. At first, at least, being singled out from one's fellows for superior performance is embarrassing or actively disturbing rather than rewarding." [26] The essential feature of primary status is that it is gained through an individual's own efforts, (rather than vicariously by virtue of a dependent relationship to others) and depends upon the quality of his performance. It is always ego-enhancing but not necessarily ego-aggrandizing. That is, the rewards associated with primary status may be the achievement of personal satisfaction, group approval, or feelings of safety and security (as among the Navaho) rather than prestige, "success" or competitive advantage. Paradoxically, therefore, self-enhancing primary status may be best acquired through a good job of self-effacing, self-denying cooperative activity directed toward the welfare of others.

The sexually immature individual can nowhere acquire adult personality status no matter how vital his contribution to the economic life of the home or community. The primary status he enjoys must inevitably play a subordinate role in the larger *Gestalt* of volitional dependency and derived status, which characterize the biosocial position of children the world over.

Why Personality Structure Must Be Reorganized

In terms of the needs arising out of the child's dependent biosocial status, satellization is the most felicitous of all possible solutions to the crisis of ego devaluation. In response to the various pressures at the close of infancy

> . . . it effects a reorganization of infantile ego structure that is more stable and tenable under the changed environmental and perceptual conditions of childhood. However, beginning in later childhood and extending throughout adolescence, a second major shift in biosocial status precipitates a new crisis in ego development, the maturation crisis which demands a reorganization of comparable scope and significance.[5]

With changed conditions confronting him, the child finds the satellizing organization of personality just as untenable and unadaptive as the omnipotent organization was at an earlier date. Thus, whereas satellization may constitute "the surest foundation upon which a healthy personality structure is built, ego maturation represents the essential ingredient of the superstructure which is the immediate functional organ of personality in adult life." [5]

Although a good deal of cultural uniformity characterizes the personality changes of adolescent and adult maturation (see p. 43), different cultures provide diverse varieties of specific content to these changes; even within a given cultural setting parents differ in the precise manner of executing the cultural prescription. Nevertheless, the goals of personality maturation are remarkably similar in all cultures because of the operation of the same principles of individual development and societal organization (the needs of individual and group survival, the necessity for transmitting cultural traditions).

Hence, the concept of maturation can be defined only in terms of a pan-cultural norm indicating

> . . . the direction in which certain aspects of personality structure must change if the [desired goal] of an acceptable adult member of society is to be realized.

This cultural ideal of personality maturity influences in turn prevailing expectations relative to changes in goal structure during adolescence, the latter being inevitably fashioned in terms of enhancing the former.[5]

The essence of this concept of maturation, that is, acquiring the motivation to achieve greater volitional independence and a more primary source of ego status, is obviously incompatible with a relationship of satellization. The satellizing orientation must be weakened before the individual will strive to seek status on the basis of his proficiency in the virtues and competencies valued in his particular culture. This orientation when applied to the learning of goals and values has been called "incorporative." [5]

Once these basic maturational goals are internalized, they can be implemented only if a number of other personality attributes are simultaneously modified in the appropriate direction.

For example the enhancement of extrinsic status requires that an individual pay less attention to the immediate gratification of hedonistic needs and concern himself more with planning for long-range prestige goals; that he acquire greater competence in implementing decisions by himself; and that he at least give the appearance of conforming to the moral standards of his social group. . . .

The adolescent is required to give greater self-reference to considerations involving his own competence and his status in the group. Accordingly he finds it necessary to adopt much more of the incorporative orientation in the learning of more mature goals and values—because only within the framework of this learning orientation can he efficiently enhance the objective of extrinsic status . . . [When related to this goal] the criteria of blind loyalty, personal allegiance and craving for personal approval cannot be very reliable motivations for the acceptance of new values. More efficacious and realistic in this situation are such criteria as expediency and perceived superiority in expediting the gratification of particular status needs. The overt satellizing orientation is also frowned upon socially because it conflicts with the maturational ideal of greater volitional independence which is so crucial for the success of the new approach to status problems.[5]

ATTRIBUTES OF ADOLESCENT PERSONALITY
MATURATION

The typical course of personality development in our culture— and the one least calculated to generate internal stresses leading to neurotic anxiety and its complications (see pp. 208f) or to the consequences of inadequate ego maturation (see pp. 239f)—is a history of childhood satellization followed by desatellization in preadolescence and adolescence. The following list is a summary of the characteristic features of ego maturation that appear in related contexts in preceding or succeeding sections of this volume:

EGO MATURATION TASKS DURING ADOLESCENCE *

A. The Acquisition of Greater Volitional Independence.
   1. Independent planning of goals and reaching of decisions.
   2. Assimilation of new values on the basis of their intrinsic validity or their relation to major goals of the individual, rather than on the basis of loyalty to parents or parent surrogates.
   3. Greater reliance on nonparental (that is, societal) sources of ego support.
   4. Aspiring to more realistic goals and roles—adopting a level of ego aspiration that is more consonant with ability and environmental possibilities.
   5. Increased frustration tolerance, the ability to withstand more intense and prolonged experience with frustration, without marked loss of self-esteem, collapse of aspirational level, or deterioration of performance.
   6. Emergence of an adequate self-critical faculty—the ability to evaluate own performance critically, to perceive deficiencies and inadequacies in this performance, to become cognizant of discrepancies between an objective standard and own efforts to attain it.
   7. Abandonment of special claims on others' indulgence.
B. Reorganization of Goal Structure on a Less Devalued Basis.
   1. Greater need for obtaining primary (as opposed to derived) status.
   2. Heightened level of ego aspiration.
   3. Increased self-valuation.
C. Replacement of Hedonistic Motivation by Long-Range Status Goals.
D. Acquisition of Increased Executive Independence.
E. Acquisition of Moral Responsibility on a Societal Basis.

The Centrality of Self during Adolescence

There are a number of reasons for believing that the self-concept occupies a more prominent place in the individual's psychological field during adolescence, and that considerable upward revision of self-estimate and level of ego aspiration takes place. In contrast to the carefree and extroverted self of later childhood, the adolescent self becomes a more crucial and clearly delineated object of awareness. The adolescent appears concerned with more precise verbalization of his feelings about himself. For all practical purposes, diaries are almost an exclusive adolescent (and feminine) phenomenon.[25] Daydreaming is more common in postpubescent than in prepubes-

* Adapted from D. P. Ausubel, *Ego Development and the Personality Disorders*. New York: Grune and Stratton, 1952.

cent girls of comparable age.[38] Developmental studies of personality structure using the Rorschach Test agree that adolescents are more introspective and given to fantasy, more introverted and concerned with exploring subjective experience than individuals of younger or older age groups.[17, 18, 41] Increased awareness of and interest in other traditional symbols of selfhood such as the body,[21, 37] grooming [34] and one's name [14] are also characteristic of adolescence. Concern with intellectual status and social relations have considerable self-reference and are important sources of self-esteem in the adolescent.[21] Awareness of own sociometric status is enhanced during adolescence.[6] Finally, adolescent preoccupation with sexual matters can be partly explained by the usefulness of the opposite sex as a contrast medium for self-expression and sharper definition of individuality.

Adolescence is a period of inflation of ego aspirations and self-estimate. In contrast to the early crisis of devaluation, it may be regarded as a time of ego revaluation. All of the maturational tasks of adolescence—the acquisition of volitional independence and primary status, emancipation from parents, achievement of economic independence, release from dependence on parents in assimilating values, learning a biological sex role, emphasis upon executive independence and long-range status goals, the acquisition of adult body form—have ego-inflationary implications. This supposition is confirmed by analysis of the content of adolescent fantasy, which casts the ego in heroic and amorous roles [15, 19] with emphasis upon vocational success and material gain.[32, 43] Analysis of the inferred goals of high-school students,[9] and the fact that the vocational goals of adolescents tend to be at a higher level than are justified by a realistic consideration of aptitude and job opportunities [11] lead to the same conclusion.

Adolescent Personality Compared to Infancy and Childhood

The tasks of adolescent personality development overlap sufficiently with those of infancy and childhood to make a more detailed comparison profitable.

To begin with,

. . . the crisis of maturation just like the crisis of devaluation precipitates an extended period of developmental disequilibrium. All of the difficulties attending a transitional stage of ego development must be endured again. A secure and established biosocial status is exchanged for a new status which is unsettled, marginal, conflictful and uncertain of attainment. A highly differentiated and familiar psychological field must be abandoned for one that is uncharted, ambiguous, undifferentiated and fraught with unknown implications. The quest for orientation must be begun anew. It is no wonder then that resistance to change will come from within as well as from without.[5]

Second, adolescence resembles infancy more than childhood in that a new biological drive (sex) must undergo initial socialization. This emergent phenomenon presents a problem that has not arisen since early infancy, and the control of this new source of hedonistic motivation is comparable in many ways to the early regulation of hunger, thirst, and bladder and bowel evacuation.

Third, there is reactivation of the issues of dependence *versus* independence, of self-assertion *versus* subservience, which have lain relatively dormant since the crisis of devaluation.

Again violent fluctuations in these dichotomous needs are the order of the day until a new equilibrium is found. But the general trend of change is in the opposite direction. The pendulum swings closer to the infantile goals of volitional independence and mastery of the environment than to the subservient attitude of childhood. This does not mean that the young adult is back in the same place which he left at the close of infancy; for behind this shift in ego development is considerable growth in perceptual ability and executive capacity, and fundamental changes in social pressures and expectations. Thus, the positions which were abandoned as untenable after the fierce resistance from three to five are given a new basis in reality which turns the tide of battle and enables them to be held permanently following the equally turbulent struggles of adolescence.[5]

Reference has been made to the emphasis that Rank and his followers place upon the shift in the independence-dependence balance during adolescence (see pp. 29–30). This shift, however, is, in and of itself not coextensive with the process of adolescent personality maturation; it is only one component aspect of the more general constellation of changes catalogued in this section, and can not be appreciated properly apart from them. For example, the need for greater volitional independence is accentuated by higher ego aspirations, greater self-valuation, and increased demands for primary status. The adolescent individual who (a) has more modest ego demands, (b) values himself more modestly, and (c) is more content with vicarious status can also tolerate considerably lower levels of volitional independence with much greater equanimity than his more ambitious contemporary with a more grandiose self-concept.

As in the crisis of devaluation, negativism is a prominent aggressive response of the individual to the insecurities and anxieties of the rapid transition in biosocial status. In devaluation, however, the general direction of change is toward a decrease in status, whereas in the new situation the reverse holds true.* More important is the difference in the cause of the disproportion between status and capacity that gives rise to much of the conflict-provoking negativistic behavior. In the earlier period, the two- and three-year-old demands volitional freedom far out of proportion to his executive capacity. The adolescent, on the other hand, receives too little volitional independence in relation to his ability.[3] Status deprivation exists in both instances; in the first case this is attributable to the unrealistic aspirations of the child, but in the second to the inability or unwillingness of parents or social order to provide status commensurate with capacity.

The same difference underlies a general similarity between infancy and adolescence in still two other areas. The adolescent like the presatellizing child is more concerned with achieving primary (in contrast to derived) status, but has a more realistic claim in actual executive competence. Similarly, the adolescent's higher self-valuation is more realistically grounded in environmental supports.

Finally, the adolescent resembles the presatellizing child in owing to personal loyalty relatively little (in comparison with the satellizing child) of his feelings of accountability to parental moral standards. But unlike the situation in infancy, these feelings are based on more abstract propositions, are directed by societal sanctions and guilt feelings, and do not owe their force to more tangible applications of reward and punishment.

On the other hand, adolescence is in several respects more nearly continuous with the direction of personality development during satellization. The childhood trends toward greater executive independence, toward increased reliance on long-range goals, toward

---

* However, the status of the infant is heading toward greater stability and security in childhood, whereas the transition from childhood to adolescence involves a comparable loss in these areas.

greater over-all moral responsibility (despite the shift in the basis for these), and toward greater conformity to societal demands [41] are extended during adolescence. Hedonistic motivation is further attenuated.

> But this time the motivation . . . is different. It reflects a need for attaining recently internalized more mature goals which would be frustrated by pre-occupation with pleasure-seeking activities, rather than a need to gain parental approval.[5]

And although the adolescent shift toward primary status is more reminiscent of infancy, there is continuation of the childhood trend to seek such status on the basis of actual executive competence.

CONTINUITY IN PERSONALITY DEVELOPMENT

In this chapter we are primarily concerned with those aspects of continuity in personality development which have special relevance for the unique maturational tasks of adolescence. However, it is necessary to consider in a more general way the nature of and the factors responsible for longitudinal consistency in the patterning of personality.

In the discussion of the similarities and differences between adolescence and earlier stages of personality development, it became clear that

> . . . as in every evolutionary process, continuity although less striking and dramatic goes hand in hand with modification. The consequences of previous modes of ego organization leave a permanent residue in personality structure which plays an important directional role in future developments.[5]

Numerous evidences of continuity in personality development can be cited. For example, analysis of the life-histories of over ninety anti-Nazi German refugees both prior and subsequent to Hitler's accession to power lead Allport, Bruner, and Jandorf to conclude:

> Very rarely does catastrophic social change produce catastrophic alterations in personality. Neither our cases nor such statistics as are available reflect any such number of regressions, hysterias or other traumatic neuroses as the gravity of the social crisis might lead one to expect. On the contrary, perhaps the most vivid impression gained by our analysts from this case-history material is the extraordinary continuity and sameness in the individual personality. . . . Resistance to social catastrophe is the outstanding characteristic of our cases. . . .

Personalities studied by independent investigators working a full year apart in a period of serious disruption are seen by a new set of judges to be recognizably the same. Where change does take place, it seems invariably to accentuate trends clearly present in the pre-emigration personality. Radical transformations do not occur, selective reinforcement and partial inhibition accounting for what change there is. In no case does the alteration correspond to the complete upset in the life space.[1]

Somewhat closer to the age span immediately relevant to our problem is the evidence that judges were able to match significantly better than chance personality sketches of two-year-old children with sketches of these same children prepared independently fifteen years later.[30] Less definitive because of the cross-sectional nature of the data is Rorschach evidence that "the child's method of approaching the world tends to remain constant."[41]

These data by no means point to the invariability of the personality pattern once it is laid down. As Leighton and Kluckhohn point out,

In spite of the fact that Navaho infants receive a maximum of protection and gratification, when they grow to be adults they are very moody and worry a great deal. . . . The theorists . . . claim too much for the earliest years and do not pay enough attention to later events and to the total situation in which the mature person finds himself. Infantile indulgence probably does constitute the firmest foundation upon which, if later circumstances are reasonably favorable, a secure and confident adult personality can be built. But it affords only a possible basis; it does not, in and of itself promise fulfillment. The high degree of tension observed among adult Navahos may be traced partly to the exceedingly grave pressures to which Navaho society is at present subject, and also to the conflicts caused by weaning, other experiences of later childhood and beliefs about supernatural forces.[26] *

Satellization alone will not predispose toward the attainment of normal adult personality unless it is followed by desatellization in later childhood and adolescence.[5] Favorable infantile experience may be appreciably vitiated by later experience with chronic or crippling disease, later rejection by parents, and by delayed onset of adolescence.[23] Parent attitudes or their perception by the child may undergo drastic change as the child advances in age. The

* Reprinted by permission of the publishers from Dorothea Cross Leighton and Clyde Kay Maben Kluckhohn, *Children of the People: The Navaho Individual and His Development.* Cambridge, Mass.: Harvard University Press, Copyright, 1947, by the President and Fellows of Harvard College.

adolescent child's emergence from either a highly benevolent or a highly rejecting home into a more neutral peer environment may release latent introversive or extroversive trends (previously masked by their respective opposites) which had been more appropriately evoked in the social climate of the home.

Psychological Basis of Consistency in Personality Development

Developmental consistency in personality patterning is a consequence of numerous psychological factors. These factors may be classified roughly as those emanating from (a) the child, (b) the environment, and (c) self-perpetuating psychological mechanisms associated with various dimensions of personality structure.

Persistence in personality patterns undoubtedly inheres partly in certain genetic and constitutional prepotencies. These predispositions may be strong enough to resist intensive training in the opposite direction by parents and teachers.[23, 33, 42] Thus, a large measure of the consistency in the parent-child relationship is a function of the child's constitutional make-up. Differences in this make-up evoke different components of the parent's repertory of possible behaviors. A particular parent will respond differently toward an active or passive, toward a docile or self-assertive child. Likewise, different children, depending on their constitutional predispositions, will behave differently in response to a particular pattern of parental behavior, thereby tending either to change or perpetuate the pattern. Thus, in some instances, dominance in the child may intensify an attitude of rejection in the parent, whereas in other instances may hold it in check.

The child makes a further contribution to the consistency of the parent-child relationship through the phenomenon of "perceptual constancy." By this is meant a tendency to persist in perceiving parental attitudes in the same way despite an *actual* change in the attitudes. Just as in the perception of physical phenomena, well-established conceptual "sets" may exert such a prepotent influence on the resulting perceptual content that the actual properties of the stimulus (parent behavior) may prove all but irrelevant.

The parent adds to the consistency of the child's personality development by providing a continuing environment that tends to remain relatively constant during the important formative years of the child's growth. This constancy, of course, is an expression of the parent's own general consistency in personality structure from year to year. Its effect is enhanced by the necessarily restricted nature of the child's environment during the early years (which isolates him from possible counterbalancing influences outside the home) and by the tremendous power of the parent in regulating the child's life during this accelerated stage of development.

During the periods of middle childhood, preadolescence, and adolescence, the parent continues to provide more or less the same quality of training for personality maturation; but by this time his influence is diluted by other forces in the culture. However, the growing child navigates primarily within the restricting confines of a limited social class environment, which resembles his home in many aspects and which is also characterized by substantial continuity in value systems over a score of years.

Finally, consistency in personality development is a function of both (1) the stability of certain central dimensions of ego structure, and (2) the self-perpetuating nature of some of the mechanisms of personality construction. As a result of characteristic ways of interacting with significant persons in the environment, more or less permanent constellations of ego needs, and habitual modes of self-evaluation arise. Examples of such constellations are differential feelings of security and adequacy, and needs for ego status and independence that emerge in crucial developmental experiences like satellization or failure to undergo devaluation. These constellations give rise to propensities for characteristic modes of learning, aspiring, socialization, ego-defense, and attitudes toward authority and group demands. Such propensities are, with situational factors, the immediate variables in most current behavior. They affect behavior in two ways: (a) as *proximate* determinants entering directly into the formulation of learning and socialization patterns at the level of current biosocial status, and (b) as *substrate* or background factors that contribute more indirectly to the operations of current biosocial status.

The difference between these two types of propensities may be illustrated as follows. An adolescent with a previous history of satellization derives most of his current biosocial status from primary rather than from derived sources. Nevertheless, he continues to display *subsidiary* satellizing patterns in his learning orientation and approach to group functions (see pp. 194–197); these furnish a subsidiary derived source of status. On the other hand, certain residual products of his satellizing history provide a substrate which does not function concurrently as a subsidiary source of derived status, but affects the *major* current type of status (primary status). For example, our ex-satellizing adolescent has residual intrinsic feelings of security and adequacy which permit him to acquire and gain satisfaction much more readily than the non-satellizer (see pp. 208–214). Also, because of this residue the ex-satellizer has less need for, and hence is not as highly motivated to attain high extrinsic status. He can become reconciled more easily to failure and downward revision of his level of ego aspiration (see pp. 210–211).

The consistent development of personality is finally a reflection of certain self-perpetuating mechanisms by which accretions to its structure are ordinarily acquired. Theoretically, a given need can be satisfied in an almost infinite number of ways. However in accordance with Gardner Murphy's concept of canalization,[29]

> . . . whenever a need is initially satisfied by a specific mechanism (i.e., response or goal-object), which is then repeatedly and satisfactorily reinforced by successful repetition of the need-satisfaction sequence, the particular mechanism (which originally was only one of a large number of potentially adequate responses) becomes endowed with the unique property of being the *sole* adequate satisfier of the need in question.[5]

Such habitual mechanisms soon get to be important needs in their own right. *Anybody* can pick up a crying five-month-old infant and soothe him, but at eight months the need for the mother as the uniquely adequate soother is as strong as the need for soothing.

Canalization, therefore, imposes severe limits on the theoretically possible range of behavior, and provides continuity to personality development by insuring to a restricted class of objects and relationships a relatively stable monopoly for satisfying basic needs. Because of their roles as primary and almost exclusive models in the early years of restricted environment, parents enjoy the unique opportunity of selectively determining the initial course of personality development. And by virtue of canalization, this influence extends far beyond the immediate present.

The principle of canalization is supplemented by the phenomenon of reaction-sensitivity. "Habitual modes of reaction" once established "sensitize" the individual

> . . . to certain aspects of his experience and dull him to others. When he enters new surroundings and meets new people, he is more ready to respond in one direction than another, and this readiness itself acts selectively to bring him more of similar kinds of experience. Thus, he develops his basic personality organization by a continuing process, certain behavior trends initiated early in life being reinforced and perpetuated through his similar reactions in related situations later on.[10]

Thus "unless behavior trends in one phase of personality development are modified deliberately or by chance, they are very likely to help determine the direction of development in a succeeding phase." [10] In adolescence this is especially evident despite the apparent disappearance of certain adjustive mechanisms during the elementary school years. As later parent-child conflict is rekindled, earlier modes of successful adjustment to external authority and internal aggressive trends tend to be reactivated before newer techniques are evolved.

PREPARATORY ASPECTS OF PERSONALITY MATURATION

From the standpoint of *ultimate* criteria of maturity, the satellizing era of middle and late childhood is a period of mixed progress. The attenuation of hedonistic motivation, the gain in executive independence, and the enhancement of feelings of moral responsibility are all steps toward adult maturation. But in relation to other, more crucial characteristics of mature personality structure, such as volitional independence and reliance on primary status, satellization constitutes at least a temporary setback. It is true that realistic progress toward these goals also occurs; but as already pointed out, whatever primary status is achieved occupies only a subsidiary position in the total *Gestalt* of biosocial dependency (see pp. 173–174).

Childhood may be regarded as a period of apprenticeship in acquiring the *qualitative* aspects of personality maturity that are necessary for individual and cultural survival. Adolescence, on the other hand, is more a period of apprenticeship in attaining the prerogatives and behavioral capacities associated with volitional independence and primary status. Thus, much of the personality development necessary for maturity is achieved before adolescence or exists at a near-threshold level, and is, therefore, a function of the quality of training for maturation provided during this period.

Factors Bringing About Preparatory Maturation

First among the factors impelling change toward personality maturation is the cumulative impact of progress in perceptual and executive capacities, which in turn induces modification of parental and societal expectations. During the period of middle childhood, there is an unspectacular but steady gain in the child's ability to comprehend abstract relationships, to reason, and to generalize.[8, 20] His level of sophistication in perceiving the attitudes, needs, and feelings of others, the relative status positions of various persons (including his own) in the group,[6, 31] and the distinguishing criteria of social class status [36] is gradually pushed forward. Hence, the first precondition for acquiring more mature behavior patterns, readiness for learning, is satisfied.

But as a result of widespread acceptance of the doctrines of Gesell and of the advocates of ultra-permissive education, it is commonly believed that maturation is solely a spontaneous process, generated from within when the child is ready to move on. The application of external pressures is held to be unnecessary and unwise, and productive of resistiveness. But, although the removal of external coercion will eliminate negativism, it will *also* obviate the possibility of maturation.

> Gains in maturity do not arise spontaneously and automatically out of the needs of the child. They are more than a reflection of increased readiness to undergo training as a result of increased capacity proceeding from growth, although this factor must also not be ignored. Involved in every noteworthy maturational advance relative to ego structure is some change in the expectations of significant persons in the child's environment which is enforced by some coercive form of pressure.[5]

Just as important for maturation as appropriate revisions in expectations is sufficient opportunity for learning mature and responsible behavior. Without the requisite experience and practice, maturation could evolve no more readily in response to altered external expectations alone, than by spontaneous generation from changed conditions of internal readiness.

Parents play a strategic role in the changing environmental expectations inducing personality maturation in the child. The new demands they set reflect their own needs and desires as well as their changed perceptions of the child's growing capacities for responsible behavior. "Also channeled through them are changing cultural expectations of appropriately mature behavior at various stages of development." [5] And in either case it is they who apply whatever coercive measures are required to effect the necessary degree of conformity. The parent is "unwilling to serve indefinitely as the executive arm of his offspring's will. . . . At the termination of infancy he welcomes the increased self-sufficiency of the child since it frees him for other tasks, and approves of the shift in ascendence-submission which gives him greater control and direction of the latter's activities." [5]

To enforce conformity to his new expectations the parent can rely upon reward and punishment, approval and disapproval, prestige authority, and the moral restraints imposed by the child's guilt when he strays from the path of internalized duty. Also at the parent's disposal is the power to extend or withhold the appreciation which chiefly motivates the child's early bids for extrinsic status. Although it is true that external controls and extrinsic considerations (reward and punishment) generally tend to be replaced by some form of self-discipline,

> . . . the process of internalization is a very gradual one and by definition presupposes the original existence of external controls, since obviously nothing can be internalized which does not first possess an external form. . . . [And] even after internalization is fairly well established, the presence of external controls in the background serves a salutory effect.[5]

In the new face he presents to his child, the parent is for the most part playing the role of cultural representative. "Reality training is important . . . among all people who survive" the usual conditions.[26] Under an economy of scarcity, everyone must develop certain minimal skills and a willingness to work. When life is more abundant, the child's actual economic contributions to family survival may be deferred until early adulthood, but in any case he is no longer permitted the self-indulgence and irresponsibility of earlier years. At the very least, a large share of self-help is demanded.

> As in the post-weaning period the [Navaho] child learns that he cannot indefinitely continue to have his way, so between five and eight, he has to acquire a sense of responsibility. Every society has to teach its members that they can not always indulge themselves and that they have duties toward others. The difference lies in when, and how, and by whom the child is disciplined. White society's training in some types of self-restraint . . . comes early. The Navaho child is "beaten down" later after he is sure of the fundamental affection of his relatives.[26] *

The sanctions for appropriate behavior are eventually referred to some social norm. Parents in our culture appeal to children not to shame *them* by their misbehavior in the eyes of the neighborhood, but the Navaho parent says, "If you behave like that people will make fun of *you*."

In contrast to the extreme indulgence with which they are treated in infancy and early childhood, Navaho

> . . . children are severely rebuked and even whipped if they take shelter during a storm while out herding and lose track of the sheep. Neglect or abuse of livestock is the least forgivable of childhood misdemeanors. When children first begin to help with the herding at six or seven, they tend to ride and chase the sheep and goats and otherwise disturb and distract them from feeding. Harsh scoldings break them of these habits quite quickly. . . . The culprit is dressed down properly, and an effort is made to shame him into more responsible conduct. . . .
>
> The growth of a sense of responsibility is facilitated by the custom of setting aside each year a sheep or two which, with their increase, belong to the child himself. The young herder feels, then, that he isn't just doing a job for his father and mother—he is also looking after his own property. His own interests become involved in his learning to care properly for the flocks. . . .
>
> The period from six through the early teens is a time for learning skills as well as for developing responsible behavior. Besides the chores of chopping and bringing in firewood, emptying ashes, hauling water, husking corn, etc., instruction in more specialized tasks begins. From about the age of eight on, children of the two sexes tend to be separated a good deal of the time. Each group is trained in certain skills by their elders of the same sex.[26]

---

* This, and the following quotation, reprinted by permission of the publishers from Dorothea Cross Leighton and Clyde Kay Maben Kluckhohn, *Children of the People: The Navaho Individual and His Development*. Cambridge, Mass.: Harvard University Press, Copyright, 1947, by the President and Fellows of Harvard College.

The culture not only regulates (a) the general direction (see pp. 41, 43–44) of preparatory maturation, which is typical of most human societies, and (b) the more specific aspects that are idiosyncratic to its particular values and traditions, but also places "limits upon the personal punishments and even the scoldings which may be imposed on children." [26] Within this general pattern, however, there is considerable room for individual family differences, both in the emphasis placed upon different goals of maturation and in the type, severity, and feeling tones behind the controls used to effect their realization.

Estrangement of Parent and Child in Urban Cultures. In rural and primitive cultures, the home serves as both the source of subsidiary extrinsic status and the training institution for developing more mature and responsible behavior.

> In modern urban cultures, however, children have little opportunity for exercising independence, responsibility and identification with the world of adult concerns, . . . necessitating a complete separation of the activity and interest systems of child and adult. Such children are given no responsibilities in the work-a-day world of adult concerns, and hence, evolve a complete set of prestige-giving values of their own.[5]

In almost all spheres of life,

> . . . our culture goes to great extremes in emphasizing contrasts between the child and the adult. . . . The child must be protected from the ugly facts of life, the adult must meet them without psychic catastrophe; the child must obey, the adult must command this obedience. These are all dogmas of our culture, dogmas which, in spite of the facts of nature other cultures commonly do not share. . . .
>
> We think of the child as wanting to play and the adult as having to work. . . . But in many societies . . . when the child can run about it accompanies its parents . . . doing tasks which are essential and yet suited to its powers; and its dichotomy between work and play * is not different from that its parents recognize, namely the distinction between the busy day and the free evening. The tasks it is asked to perform are graded to its powers, and its elders wait quietly by, not offering to do the task in the child's place.[7]

---

* The distinction between work and play is also less marked in primitive cultures. Curle [12] suggests that the segmentation of life in modern civilization as a result of rapid social change, the greater availability of leisure time, and the greater freedom of individual choice in heterogeneous societies has brought this about.

This absence of absolute dichotomy between child and adult prevails among the Navaho.

> Children and adults do not belong to two separate worlds. The same set of standards prevails in most things for all ages, from the child (as soon as he can talk) to the very old people. . . . [At the same time] Navaho practice is to expect only so much from children at each age level. The white tendency is to project adult standards down into all except the earliest childhood.[26] *

Ruth Benedict reports essentially the same situation for the Cheyenne Indians:

> The essential point of such child training is that the child is from infancy continuously conditioned to responsible social participation, while at the same time the tasks that are expected of it are adapted to its capacity. The contrast with our society is very great. A child does not make any labor contribution to our industrial society except as it competes with an adult; its work is not measured against its own strength and skill but against high-geared industrial requirements. Even if we praise a child's achievement in the home we are outraged if such praise is interpreted as being of the same order of praise of adults. . . .
>
> At birth the little [Cheyenne] boy was presented with a toy bow, and from the time he could run about serviceable bows suited to his stature were specially made for him by the man of the family. . . . When he finally killed a buffalo, it was only the final step of his childhood conditioning, not a new adult role with which his childhood experience had been at variance.[7]

Among the Canadian Ojibwa,

> . . . the boy accompanies his father [on hunting trips] and brings in his catch to his sister just as his father does to his mother; the girl prepares the meat and skins for him just as his mother does for her husband. . . . The young child is taught consistently that it has only itself to rely upon in life, and this is as true in the dealings it will have with the supernatural as in the business of getting a livelihood. This attitude he will accept as a successful adult just as he accepted it as a child.[7]

Such training in responsibility inevitably brings with it some subsidiary primary status and volitional independence.

> The techniques . . . by which a child is conditioned to a responsible status role . . . depend chiefly upon arousing in the child the desire to share responsibility in adult life. To achieve this, little stress is laid upon obedience,

---

* Reprinted by permission of the publishers from Dorothea Cross Leighton and Clyde Kay Maben Kluckhohn, *Children of the People: The Navaho Individual and his Development.* Cambridge, Mass.: Harvard University Press, Copyright, 1947, by the President and Fellows of Harvard College.

but much stress upon approval and praise. Many American Indian tribes are especially explicit in rejecting . . . any dichotomy according to which an adult expects obedience and a child must accord it. . . . [Maternal uncle] and child share reciprocal privileges and obligations which in our society can only develop between age mates. . . . Such kinship conventions allow the child to put in practice from infancy the same form of behavior it will rely upon as an adult; behavior is not polarized into a general requirement of submission for the child and dominance for the adult.[7] *

In urban societies, on the other hand, the culture is not organized to provide children with many important opportunities for extrinsic status. Mature roles must be learned by a course other than gradual participation in family or communal responsibilities. "Denied a place in adult reality they [children] must find other outlets for the independence and mature interests which personality growth has stimulated."[5] They are obliged to find sources of primary status in peripheral activities (school, peer group athletics) far removed from the main current of status in the adult world. They supplement this with the vicarious status that can be obtained through identification with the glamorous exploits of prominent figures in public life, and with whatever satisfaction can be gained by carrying on covert guerrila warfare with adults and adult standards.

Thus, the child's interests and concerns become "oriented more toward his contemporaries than toward his parents." In his peer group he is given a chance to obtain the mature role-playing experience from which adult society excludes him and which his parents are unable to furnish. Identification with this group also provides a substitute source of derived status, providing him with ego supports that reduce his dependence upon parental approval. And "by attributing the prerogatives of judgment, decision, choice and initiative to a group fashioned in his own image, he . . . effectively demolishes his exclusive association of these powers with parental figures and thus paves the way for eventually assuming them himself."[4]

School serves a very similar function. It provides both a new subsidiary source of primary status based upon academic ability,

* This and the preceding three quotations with citations of reference (7) are from *A Study of Interpersonal Relations*, edited by Patrick Mullahy. New York: Hermitage House, 1949.

and a fresh source of derived status which challenges the parent's monopoly of this commodity and of omniscience as well.

All of these factors—availability of other sources of derived status, reduction of absolute dependency on parents for ego support, need for going beyond the home for extrinsic status, the child's own greater competence, and the emergence of a new authority to challenge his parent's omniscience—tend to break down "the deified picture" he nurtures of his parents. And as the parent's omnipotence declines, his power to confer by fiat an absolute intrinsic value on the child begins to ebb. This stimulates an intensified quest to satisfy status needs beyond the home.

The net effect of this urban displacement of the home as a training institution for personality maturation is threefold. (1) Desatelliza-tion from parents is undoubtedly accelerated by their devaluation, although not until adolescence is over is the child "sufficiently free of the attitude of subservience to evaluate them with critical detach-ment." [5] (2) The lack of actual role-playing experience in the adult world can not be completely compensated for by the various sub-stitutes available in school, peer group, and hero-worship activities. Lacking the stimulation of genuine social expectations of mature behavior in the adult sense, and sufficient opportunity for suitable practice, the individual must inevitably lag in ego maturation. [3] (3) Finally, this situation

> . . . inaugurates a long period of estrangement between children and adults which persists until the former attain adulthood themselves. Insurmountable barriers to commonality of feeling, to mutual understanding and to ease of communication are built up. This alienation is not unaccompanied by resent-ment and bitterness. Although outright resistance to adult authority is usually withheld until adolescence, there is reason to believe that the preadolescent's apparent conformity is only a veneer which hides the smoldering rebellion from view. This is revealed by the often contemptuous and sneering remarks he makes about adults in his own company, and by the studied indifference to adult standards which he professes out of earshot of the latter.[5]

PUBESCENCE: CONSUMMATORY FACTOR IN PERSONALITY MATURATION

The preparatory changes in personality maturation catalogued above, as well as the factors bringing them about, are not to be minimized in evaluating the total maturational change from the close of infancy to the beginning of adult life. Yet the transition can not be consummated merely by the cumulative impact of these same factors: i.e., parental and cultural needs for personality maturation (see pp. 186–188); increased executive competence of the child; new sources of derived status and ego support; the weakening of dependency ties on parents; the deflation of parents and the continued progress toward desatellization; the achievement of an independent, subsidiary source of primary status. This is true even where children are not relegated to a separate and discontinuous world of status opportunity, but contribute to the economic sustenance of the family. The conclusion is inescapable that whatever independence and primary status children can earn before pubescence can occupy only a subsidiary role in the larger *Gestalt* of biosocial dependency. The gains in these areas are primarily a by-product of the training in responsibility and the attenuation of hedonistic impulses that constitute the main maturational business of childhood.

The personality maturity of adolescence and adulthood are *qualitatively* different from the maturity of childhood. In our own culture this qualitative difference is explicitly recognized in the dichotomy characterizing the types of status activities and opportunities for independence available to children and adults respectively. In cultures which do not erect such dichotomies (see pp. 189–191), this qualitative difference prevails nevertheless as a result of a transcendental leap that becomes effective at a crucial transitional point on a continuous quantitative scale. This point is reached when in the total economy of ego organization, primary and derived sources of status exchange positions as subsidiary and dominant (or peripheral and central) figures in the *Gestalt*.

Pubescence plays the role of crucial catalytic agent in shifting the direction of the source of status, and hence in inaugurating the consummatory aspects of personality maturation. It is the cue for reversing social expectations about the major type of status that the child may appropriately seek. Hence in relation to the pubescent individual,

> . . . the social value of derived status depreciates while the corresponding value of extrinsic status increases. The adolescent, thus, not only finds that he is increasingly expected to establish his status through his own efforts, but

also that the latter criterion tends to displace the childhood criterion (i.e., of derived status) as the chief measure by which his social milieu tends to evaluate him. Simultaneously, social pressure is put on the parents to withdraw a large portion of the emotional support which they had hitherto been extending to him by way of conferring intrinsic status.[5]

In addition to the fact that of his own volition and under cultural pressure the parent acts to provide less derived status, his power to do so is also impaired. Continued widening of the child's social horizon tends to effect an increasing devaluation of the parent's stature. This process is accelerated by (1) the now more glaring inability of the parents (in comparison with other cultural agencies) to furnish an extrinsic source of status, and (2) the more critical and objective appraisal the child can make of his parent when he is freed of the bias and "halo effect" implicit in an attitude of subservience.

Pubescence also exerts a catalytic effect on the child's strivings for personality maturation. In the face of the altered cultural expectations that puberty induces, he feels that his aspirations for greater status and independence are more legitimate. But even apart from these social sanctions and pressures, his reactions to his newly attained adult physical form, reproductive power, and biological sex drive cannot do otherwise than generate aspirations for the status with which these attributes are patently associated.

MECHANISMS OF DESATELLIZATION

This discussion obviously relates to children with a history of satellization during the childhood era. The mechanisms whereby non-satellizing individuals undergo personality maturation will be given separate treatment (see pp. 209–214).

Desatellization through Resatellization

Within the satellizing orientation itself we have delineated two different patterns of maturation. The more familiar type is characteristic of modern urban civilization. It involves gradual replacement of parents by age-mates as the essential socializing agent. The age-mates not only supply the child's needs for extrinsic status and the opportunity for mature role-playing experience but also displace the parents as the persons in relation to whom any residual remnants of the satellizing orientation are maintained (resatellization). This pattern, as already pointed out, involves considerable devaluation of and desatellization and alienation from parents, yet also carries with it relatively slow and inefficient maturation during preadolescence and the middle years of childhood. But

> . . . although this substitution of age-groups standards for home standards is often regarded as a phenomenon rooted so deeply in the psychology of maturation as to be inevitable, cross-cultural investigations show this is not so. In Samoa the young boys and girls are given increasing status in the community as they reach and pass adolescence, but there is no period when they rebel against the authority of the head of household and substitute instead a set of counter and antagonistic standards.[27]

Frank makes the same observation: "In a static, tradition bound society, the process of emancipation does not necessarily imply a supplantation of the family as the principal medium through which the culture operates." [16] "Here the family could still serve as the primary source of goals and standards while the adolescent's position in relation [to parents] merely shifts from a dependent to an independent role." [4] "That is, the adolescent could still learn most of what he needs to know as an adult from his parents, but would assimilate this knowledge for use in the role of an independent person in his own right." [5]

In addition to the factors already mentioned as contributing to devaluation of parents and renunciation of their standards (see pp. 173–174) is the fact that the

> . . . role we give to parents that they must pose as better and more complete representatives of their culture than they really are also exposes growing children to almost inevitable disillusion. Furthermore the notion that children are different in kind from adults fosters attitudes in children's and adolescents' groups which are qualitatively different from the attitudes of the adults.[27]

The gap thus created between children and parents under these circumstances is further widened by the rapid rate of social change. Adding to the psychological and social distance already present are the very different worlds in which the two generations grow up, producing an actual discrepancy in the content of the values each accepts. Hence, "the children who continue to adhere to the standards set up by their parents carry the stigma of being 'old-fashioned,' 'out of date,' 'prigs,' 'prudes,' or lacking in social consciousness." [27]

What are some of the outstanding consequences of this substitution of age-mate for parental socialization? Besides inducing more complete devaluation, it also accelerates desatellization. The mere fact that individuals of their own generation assume the function of setting standards, a power that had always been regarded as the prerogative of omniscient elders, serves to devalue parents as suitable foci for satellization, and to sanction the legitimacy of their own assumption of this power. But this very same factor leads also to another quite different result:

> There is a difference in the positive self-valuation of the individual who is attempting to meet standards represented by remote and highly respected persons . . . and the individual who is striving hard to meet the standards of persons who inspire no great respect. . . . The rejection of parental standards in favor of late-recognized and antagonistic age-grade standards results, therefore, in an attenuation of self-respect and a weakening of the internalized standards of behavior upon which the operation of our culture is still postulated.[27]

According to Margaret Mead, age-mate socialization has important reciprocal repercussions on social change. An entire revolution of standards becomes possible merely by appealing to the readiness of youth to reject parental ways in favor of a new set of mores. Such change, however, which is founded on no other basis than the need to conform to group norms, does not necessarily bring progress.

> The quantity of the surrogates replaces their quality, for a single individual or pair of individuals, who are highly respected as different in kind and better than the child, is substituted the *number* of age mates who approve and follow a certain course of behavior.[27]

Thus is lost an important potentiality for social progress inherent in the older system of socialization by parents, namely, the "striving to avoid the self-reproach of failing to realize an unobtainable ideal, the picture of the parent . . . conceived in childhood." [27]

The repudiation of parental standards in favor of less idealistic age-grade norms also makes youth reared on an earlier diet of satellization more susceptible to demagogic influence. As Mead points out, this readiness to accept alien doctrines is not unaccompanied by feelings of *guilt* in rejecting prior loyalties.[27]

And it is this element in their character structure which leaves room for the leader, a parent surrogate who will lift their conformity to the mob on a higher level again and make them feel less guilty of apostasy toward their own infantile acceptance of their parents' dictated systems of morality.[27]

As we shall see later, however (see pp. 335–336), the greater readiness of the adolescent to accept age-grade in preference to parental norms does not necessarily make for a complete overthrow of the standards previously accepted; for the new norms presented by the peer group tend to hew more closely to the values of the social class in which the adolescent claims membership than to the alien values of a different social class. The same values that the child rejects because they are proposed by the parent are eagerly accepted when advocated by the peer group in slightly different form but with essentially the same content.

Desatellization through the Achievement of Primary Status

More important for the outcome of desatellization than the issues of who is the basic socializing agent and who (parents or peer group) becomes the focus of residual satellizing trends is the mode of acquiring primary status. The satellizing orientation is abrogated primarily by the displacement of derived by primary status as the chief source of self-esteem in the adolescent individual. However, the major socializing agent must inevitably constitute the source of the extrinsic status in question. Hence, we find the same split between rural and primitive cultures on the one hand, and urban cultures on the other, in the manner in which extrinsic status is attained.

Generally speaking, adolescence is less prolonged in cultures in which adolescents gain extrinsic status by participating in the same types of economic activities as their parents. But in cultures characterized by age-mate socialization, parental sources of status are not available to adolescents, adolescence is extremely prolonged, and primary status is achieved in peripheral functions far removed from the main economic currents of the social order. We have already referred to the latter situation as *interim* status (see pp. 60–61). Although from a long-range standpoint the goals of this type of status have only temporary "stop-gap" significance, they do constitute distinctive objects of striving in their own right during the adolescent period.

198 THEORY AND PROBLEMS OF ADOLESCENT DEVELOPMENT

Here, arises another source of discontinuity between children and adults. Three discrete value and status systems must be learned before adult life is reached. And during adolescence the individual is obliged simultaneously to satisfy the need for immediate age-mate status while keeping an eye toward the more long-range goals of adult status.

In either setting it is important to realize that primary status does not necessarily mean individual success, prestige, power, or pre-eminence. It may just as well be competence that is not compared with another's, modest security, safety, approval for group-mindedness, maintenance of "face." Thus, among the Navaho,

> . . . the youngster is not urged to strive for individual achievement. There is no promise of personal success for the able and hard-working or the good and righteous. On the other hand, a sense of worthlessness is never drummed into a child so that his whole subsequent life is a struggle to justify himself. . . . To accept authority over his fellows or to take initiative in any obvious fashion has for the Navaho the psychological meaning of separating him from the social group to which he looks for both support and regulation. . . . But a sense of responsibility is none the less real for being divided and shared, for being—to the white person—vague and unfixed. . . . The majority seem to be only interested in safety. . . . They themselves will sometimes say, 'All we want is enough to eat for ourselves and our families'. . . . The predominant drive is for moderate material well-being.[26] *

From this we may conclude (1) that the magnitude of residual intrinsic adequacy feelings available to adolescents and adults is partly a function of a societal norm the mean value of which varies from culture to culture, with considerable room for individual family differences; (2) that the drive for extrinsic status is inversely related to the magnitude of these residual feelings of adequacy; and (3) that the particular orientation of the goals toward which primary status is directed (competitive and individualistic or cooperative and group-related) is conditioned by the prevailing value system of a culture or sub-culture.

In both types of socialization patterns (age-grade and parental) a transitional variety of primary status is evident. That is, the child's

* Reprinted by permission of the publishers from Dorothea Cross Leighton and Clyde Kay Maben Kluckhohn, *Children of the People: The Navaho Individual and His Development.* Cambridge, Mass.: Harvard University Press, Copyright, 1947, by the President and Fellows of Harvard College.

initial quests for extrinsic status are largely bids for parental appro-
bation, and as such must be considered modified manifestations of
satellization. If they elicit appropriate signs of appreciation from
parents, their continuation as ends in themselves is encouraged.

Desatellization through the Exploratory Orientation

Two modes of assimilating values have already been discussed,
the satellizing orientation and the incorporative orientation, as
characteristic of childhood and adulthood respectively (see pp. 172,
175). The incorporative is naturally an accompaniment of the quest
for greater extrinsic status since it utilizes a criterion of ego enhancement as the preparatory set in reacting to new value experience.
The satellizing orientation, on the other hand, is predicated upon
personal loyalty and the need to retain parental approval (or to
avoid the guilt engendered by repudiation of parental standards).
Common to both orientations, however, to a greater or lesser degree,
is a subjective bias favoring the generation and perpetuation of a
given type of status (primary or derived), and a relative indifference
to objective considerations impinging on the empirical or logical
validity of the value in question.

A third type of learning orientation (exploratory) is not status-
oriented in either sense, but is directed toward objective problem
solution regardless of the status implications involved.

> In every person's psychological world there is a . . . sphere of value-laden,
> ego-involved learning experience in which the task itself and not its relation
> to ego status is the primary focus of concern. Where task-oriented goals or
> values are concerned, levels of aspiration operate, success or failure is experi-
> enced, but self-esteem is not necessarily affected since ego status is not at stake.
> The basis of the exploratory [orientation] lies in the active curiosity which is
> manifested by human beings from the earliest days of infancy.[5]

The utilization of the exploratory orientation is obviously limited
during childhood,

> . . . for as soon as the implications of independent objective investigation are
> pursued to their logical conclusion, the danger always exists that they will
> conflict with values tied to primary allegiances, and hence precipitate an
> avalanche of guilt feelings.[5]

But as subservience to parental values wanes, the exploratory orientation can be used more freely and continued use promotes desatel-

lization by de-emphasizing considerations of personal loyalty in value assimilation.

Unfortunately, however, the development of the exploratory orientation is severely curtailed in the course of age-mate socialization. The adolescent's marginal status and his dependence on the peer society for status permits very little deviation from group values, and hence little opportunity for independent exploration. On the other hand, when the adolescent owes his opportunities for extrinsic status to his elders, there are similar pressures to make him adhere to traditional values. In both instances, the exploratory orientation tends to be sacrificed because of the adolescent's need to conform to the standards of the agents who control the sources of his primary status. The very operation of this factor, in other words, is merely another manifestation of the incorporative orientation.

FACILITATING AND RETARDING FACTORS IN MATURATION

Factors that serve either to advance or impede the progress of maturation may be conveniently divided into (1) conditions relating to familial or parent-child relationships, and (2) cultural arrangements impinging on the acquisition of status by adolescents.

Familial Factors

The existence of a general set of cultural imperatives and expectations for the course of personality maturation does not necessarily insure that the maturation will take place as culturally anticipated. For the actual implementation of these policies, the culture must rely on the individual family. And since parents in a given culture differ among themselves, and since different children react in different ways to the same parental practice, maturation depends largely on various dimensions of the parent-child relationship. The parental attitudes or behaviors that are particularly relevant to maturation are (a) degree of protectiveness (care, solicitude), (b) dominance (self-assertiveness or deference to child's will), and (c) appreciation (recognition) of child's competence.

These parental attitudes affect maturation by promoting or discouraging (a) the child's freedom in obtaining extrinsic status or in attempting the incorporative and exploratory orientations in value assimilation; (b) the development of "multiple sources of security and adequacy through satellization with persons and groups outside the home"; and (c) the development of "skills in independent planning and goal-setting by providing opportunities for practice, and appropriate conditions for learning realistic roles and goals, adequate frustration tolerance and realistic self-criticism".[5]

For children to develop "the skills that are necessary for competent exercise of volitional independence," they require "opportunity for exercising choice, making plans and decisions, practicing self-direction, and learning from [their] own mistakes".[5]

> Adequate freedom for exploration, for trial-and-error learning, and for manipulating a variety of social situations is needed. Mature volitional behavior can only be learned [through] actual role-playing experience. Hence, overdominated children whose parents make all their decisions, and overprotected children who are never exposed to the possibility of making an independent decision lest they [injure themselves, experience frustration or] make a fatal error, are inestimably handicapped in the learning of volitional maturity.[5]

A mature capacity for volitional independence is also characterized by a capacity (1) for bearing frustration without unduly abandoning level of aspiration, self-esteem, self-criticism, independence of decision, or performance ability; (2) for setting goals and aspiring to roles that are realistically possible; (3) for acquiring a reasonably accurate estimate of own status, abilities, and performance; and (4) for making demands on others that are legitimate and tolerable. The realization of these goals is largely dependent upon

> . . . direct experience with frustrating and restrictive aspects of [the] environment. It presupposes acceptance of the barriers and limitations imposed upon the free, unhampered exercise of will by the inherent structure of the social order and by the prevailing social expectations and prohibitions surrounding individual behavior. . . . The irreducible condition for achieving these objectives is to confront the child consistently, firmly and unambiguously . . . with the unadorned realities that define his biosocial position at home and in his culture.[5]

There is no other way to learn to handle frustration than to have first-hand experience with it. "Purposeful and persistent avoidance of frustration creates for the child a conception of reality which is so distorted that he becomes exclusively conditioned to living in a hedonistic environment".[4]

> Development of frustration tolerance, therefore, requires that a child be encouraged to solve his own problems . . . that his course through life not be continually smoothed by systematic elimination of the problems which confront him. He must learn to take responsibility for the consequences of his behavior when mistakes are made and failure ensues. Parental "whitewashing" . . . reinforces the immature tendency to cope with failure and misbehavior by rationalization, disclaiming of responsibility, and abandonment of even minimal standards of self-criticism.[5]

The overly permissive parent fails to develop frustration tolerance in the child by acceding to the child's demands for help whenever he encounters difficulty. He fails also to structure realistically the limiting and restrictive aspects of the child's world, thereby making difficult the setting of realistic goals and the accurate perception of self-role.

> The conditions under which self-role can be realistically learned require a clear appreciation of what can be legitimately included within the appropriate age-sex subculture role, and what must perforce be excluded from it. The attitude of unvarying permissiveness fulfills neither condition. By advocating unrestricted freedom for the child in setting his goals, by refusing to impose limitations on behavior which is socially unacceptable, and by denying the legitimacy of status differences between children and adults, the overly permissive parent or teacher makes it impossible for the child to perceive the boundaries of his role. . . .
> Extreme . . . exposure to this variety of child-rearing [may] lead to extreme unrealism regarding the demands which an individual can legitimately make on others. . . . He develops the notion that he is a very precious and priviliged person. His parents *have* to do things for him and have to help him . . . because he has a special claim on their indulgence. [And] eventually this orientation is extended to the world at large.[5]

Desatellization and the utilization of learning orientations other than satellization are also facilitated if the child is accepted unconditionally, that is, if obedience and conformity as ends in themselves are not made the price of acceptance. Navaho parents never demand socially acceptable behavior as the condition of parental love and protection or say to a child, "If you do that, mother won't love you anymore".[26] Hence volitional and moral independence becomes less fraught with dangerous consequences.

Similarly, the more impersonal the basis on which obedience and conformity are required, the less likely is the desire for independence to be inhibited by feelings of personal loyalty and guilt. Navaho parents do not demand obedience as a personal right or regard disobedience as "bad," but point out "the advantages of obedience [and] the value in taking advice and instruction from more experienced persons".[26] Threats are not warnings of personal reprisal for insubordination but objective predictions of disaster for children who fail to heed prudent admonition. The authority for discipline is impersonalized and referred either to supernatural forces or to agencies "outside of the immediate family circle".[26] If a plea for good conduct is made by appealing to shame-avoidance, it is from the child rather than from the parent that the plea for deflection of shame is made.[26] In all of these ways, the overly dependent and personal aspects of satellization are minimized.

The dangers of extreme satellization are also avoided

> ... if the child can find derived status in multiple sources rather than in his parents alone. Under such circumstances the one source is no longer so precious. He need not tread so warily to avoid arousing disapproval. Fortified by the ego support he receives from friends, grandparents, older siblings, teachers, group leaders, etc., he can afford more often to assert his independence and risk arousing parental ire.[5]

The part that the peer group plays in this process in our culture is played by the "extended family" in many cultures like the Navaho, in which the child is reared more by a group of relatives than by parents. This results in an attenuation of attachment and loyalty to a single person or pair of persons. Similarly, the greater diffusion of authority results in fewer manifestations of personal resentment and rebellion.

Even when parents are not overprotective or overdominating, inherent factors in the parent-child relationship make them ambivalent toward the child's emancipation. They tend to fear the loss of love that removal of his dependency creates.[28]

> They have a vested interest to protect—the satisfactions, the ego supports, the feelings of power and importance that go with having another individual dependent upon them for guidance and direction. "Emancipation requires much sacrifice by parents. They must relinquish authority" and "learn the patience and restraint required to develop the capacity for self-direction in

the child." This is naturally a much more difficult task for parents who are exploiting the dependent aspects of the child's attachment for them as a substitute source of status and affection in instances of vocational or marital maladjustment.[5]

Such feelings of ambivalence naturally give rise to parental inconsistencies in behavior and expectations which confuse the child and compound the retarding influence the ambivalence exerts on maturation.

Feelings of rivalry, often only dimly perceived, also complicate the parents' attitudes towards the child's maturation. They cannot help comparing their waning powers and motivations with the child's growing competencies and naively sanguine aspirations. If these are a source of pride, they also represent a threat which, with each passing day, brings the shadow of eventual displacement closer. "Unconsciously," therefore, they may be motivated to slow the progress of maturation. However, the resentment which these attitudes provoke in the child may bring about the opposite effect (desatellization) by deepening the estrangement which already so frequently exists.

Not to be ignored in this picture is the possibility of serious lag between alteration of attitudes and appropriate modification of related behavior. It is a commonplace observation that underlying attitudes may remain unaltered despite formal changes in outward behavior. Less frequently recognized is the equally important tendency for old behavior patterns to persist out of sheer inertia despite modification of the attitudinal substrate. It takes time to learn the appropriate gestures, mannerisms, and inflections of a new role even if one has mastered the required shift in feeling tones. And even then the phenomenon of perceptual constancy in the child may force altered parental behavior into the same perceptual molds because of the prepotency of habitual expectations.

Hence, the child frequently fails to respond appropriately to changes in parental expectations of greater maturity because he cannot reorganize into a new *Gestalt* what to him can only have a fixed and constant perceptual meaning despite manifest changes in stimulus content. He thus withdraws from parents "for no other reason than the fact that they always are the ones to whom he has always *been* a helpless child".[44]

Personality maturation also suffers from ambivalence of the child. He is naturally reluctant to part with the protection and security of dependency and a familiar biosocial role for the anxiety and insecurity inevitably associated with any transition in development (see pp. 55–56). And, "unfortunately, sufficient ambiguity prevails regarding the biosocial role considered appropriate for adolescents, and the period of transition is sufficiently prolonged" to offer considerable support for the yearning to return to the "good old days" of childhood.[5] This regressive alternative has a more powerful attraction for children with strong needs for hedonistic gratification (who find long-range striving difficult), and for sedentary, shy, "thin-skinned," and introverted individuals to whom self-assertion comes painfully.

Desatellization, therefore, is, even under the best of circumstances, "a difficult and inevitably conflictful phase of ego development." The child must contend with ambivalence, rivalry, and the inertia of habitual attitudes and behavior patterns in his parents, and with his own ambivalence and perceptual constancy. If he becomes too independent he provokes parental resistance and internal feelings of guilt. On the other hand, if he remains too dependent and submissive, he "loses face in his own eyes and in the eyes of his peers, feels inadequate for failure to gain extrinsic status, and develops feelings of hostility and resentment toward parents for thwarting his growth".[5]

Cultural Factors

There is no doubt that the cultural availability of extrinsic status is the crucial variable affecting the rate, the duration, and the difficulty of adolescent maturation. Almost all of the distinctive characteristics of adolescent development in Western civilization are derivatives of the fact that pubescent children's greater executive competence can receive no social recognition in terms of adult status-giving activity. On the other hand, in primitive rural cultures such as the Navaho, "there is no period of several years when the individual is neither a child nor an adult as the adolescent in White American society today. The Navaho's physical maturity and social maturity are more nearly coincidental".[26] Our adolescents must customarily look forward to an eight-year period of sub-adulthood that provides a marginal, interim status in peripheral activities, and a good deal of uncertainty regarding the eventual attainment of adult status.

Such a situation is more or less inevitable in any complex culture requiring extended education and apprenticeship. The peer group is obliged, then, to provide compensatory sources of status and to assume responsibility as the major training institution of adolescence. But this dichotomy need not be as absolute as it is presently. With some intelligent social engineering, adolescents even as apprentices could be provided with a good deal of status-giving experience and responsibility in projects involving the community as a whole (see pp. 541–542).

The reasons for the prolonged adolescence in our culture and its grosser behavioral consequences will be discussed at length in Chapter 11 (see pp. 319–327). Here we shall be concerned only with what at first glance seems to be a purely self-evident phenomenon, namely,

> . . . the precise nature of the mechanisms whereby socio-economic conditions necessitating a prolongation of the transitional period of sub-adulthood becomes translated into an actual process of retardation in the sphere of psychological development. The relationship between social status on the one hand and ego valuation on the other is a fundamental problem of ego psychology.[4]

The most important intervening variables in this process of transmutation—"the level of social expectations regarding rate of maturation and the availability of mature role-playing experience"— are intimately related. The former, in fact, is almost completely a function of the latter, which depends upon socio-economic factors influencing the need for adolescent manpower. In accordance with fluctuations in this need, society keeps shifting its view of the urgency with which adolescent maturation should take place.

> This relationship is never a one-to-one affair since a certain minimal level of status change is anticipated on the basis of pubescence alone, and a certain amount of time lag is inevitable between the onset of changed economic conditions and the evolution of new social attitudes. Nevertheless the correspondence is quite close; and in the more usual type of economic situation in our culture, conditions are such that little sense of urgency is felt regarding the rapidity of maturation. Thus, although the adolescent may desire to gain

status more rapidly than he is allowed to, he feels no pressure to do so—at least from the adult segment of society.[5]

Having no other frame of reference as a guide than prevailing social expectations,

> . . . his level of aspiration with respect to the proper rate of maturation generally corresponds to the relative urgency with which society regards the problem. Most adolescents would believe any other course to be virtually impossible, since like children, they tend to believe that prevailing social arrangements are absolutely given and hence immutable.[4]

Why do adolescents base their levels of aspiration regarding maturational progress on cultural expectations? First, as in any unstructured field, these expectations undoubtedly exert considerable influence in the form of prestige suggestion. Second, they have motivational properties emanating from their capacity to generate *transitional anxiety*. The mere existence of these expectations constitutes a threat. Adolescents are expected to mature at a certain rate or else face the possible loss of "status advantages otherwise accruing from successful maturation." The feelings of anxiety and insecurity instigated by this threat can only be reduced by suitable evidences of maturation, thereby giving rise to appropriately pitched motivations (levels of aspiration).[13]

Culturally induced low levels of aspiration for maturational progress actually result in developmental retardation by "making the adolescent disinclined to seek out . . . role-playing experiences propitious for personality development".[5] And the most proximate variable involved in this chain of events, the one directly responsible for the lagging rate of maturation, is deprivation of the necessary experience required for personality growth.

When the cultural unavailability of adult status becomes very extreme, it retards personality maturation even more directly. By ruling out access to needed experience to individuals who would otherwise obtain it by high endogenous motivation (despite social discouragement), it exerts a levelling influence negating motivational variability of other origin.

In addition to status deprivation, other social factors largely idiosyncratic to our culture, such as various types of cultural discontinuities and discrepancies in attaining adult status, also tend to retard adolescent personality maturation. These will be discussed in Chapter 11 (see pp. 320–327).

PERSONALITY MATURATION IN NON-SATELLIZERS

The preceding picture of personality maturation is characteristic of all children who undergo devaluation and subsequent satellization. But not all children present this typical developmental history; and since mode of maturation is largely a function of childhood personality structure, we will have to consider this problem separately for the non-satellizers.

The prerequisite parent attitudes necessary for devaluation and satellization, and the parent attitudes leading to non-satellization (rejection and extrinsic valuation) have already been discussed (see pp. 171–172). It is true that different cultures vary in the degree of socially sanctioned acceptance and intrinsic valuation that parents are expected to extend to children (see p. 174); but familial *intra*-cultural differences are a much more striking source of variance than *inter*-cultural variability in parent attitudes (see p. 42).

The child who fails to satellize also fails to undergo ego devaluation. The infantile personality structure that is not presented with appropriate conditions for reorganization tends to persist despite various changes in the child's biosocial status. Unable to achieve feelings of security and adequacy on a derived basis, he continues to operate on the basis of their extrinsic counterparts. And under these auspices he is not obliged to surrender the volitional independence and the grandiose level of ego aspiration, renunciation of which is implicit in the self-subordination of anyone who satellizes, who derives his status vicariously by the mere fact of relationship to or acceptance by an omnipotent figure.

Reasons other than failure to satellize also tend to prevent devaluation. (1) Reconciliation to a primary status that the child would be realistically entitled to on the basis of actual biosocial competence involves too drastic, abrupt, and traumatic a shift from the previous ego organization to be acceptable. (2) In the absence of any intrinsic source of adequacy, extrinsic status serves a compensatory function; and hence the need for it is greater and less easily relinquished than among satellizers. (3) Other factors in the parent-child relationship operate against devaluation. The rejected child reacts with bitterness and vengeful fantasies to the humiliating depreciation to which his self-esteem is subjected; and implementation of the vengeance and self-vindication he seeks requires the attainment of more than ordinary success. The home environment of the extrinsically valued child, on the other hand, continues to support the grandiose properties of infantile ego organization. The parent intends to aggrandize his own ego through the child's attainments, and hence does all in his power to maintain the fiction of the child's infantile omnipotence by maintaining a worshipful and deferential attitude. It will be convenient, therefore, to refer to the extrinsically valued child as "overvalued."

Hence, during childhood both varieties of non-satellizers remain un-devalued with these main differences between them: The rejected unlike the overvalued child suffers from impaired self-esteem and has no opportunity for the exercise of volitional independence or for the satisfaction of exalted ego needs. The rejected child also is usually overdominated and obliged to adhere to stringent standards of mature behavior, to develop executive independence, capacity for postponing hedonistic gratification, and a sense of responsibility. The overvalued child, on the other hand, is usually underdominated and under less pressure to acquire these attributes of maturity. With either, however, the only basis on which the child accepts the desirability of maturation is not the satellizer's need for retaining derived status, but the perception of mature behavior *from the very beginning* as a necessary precondition for the attainment of primary status in the community; and in rejected children there is the additional consideration of submitting to the exacting demands of persons on whom they are economically dependent for survival.

Later Impact of Non-Satellization on Maturation

Desatellization, as represented by the tasks of acquiring greater volitional independence, primarily striving for extrinsic status, raising the level of ego aspiration, and adopting the incorporative and exploratory learning orientations, is ordinarily the main business of adolescent maturation. Since in non-satellizers these tasks are accomplished in advance, it follows that maturation involves a less comprehensive change and is more likely to be successful. The non-satellizer with his high ego aspirations and his exaggerated needs for primary status has always regarded dependence disdainfully, as symbolic of defeat in his quest for these goals. "Volitional independence had never been really surrendered, and hence does not have to be regained." [5]

Other aspects of maturation take place for the express purpose of implementing the acquisition of primary status—provided there are "no overwhelming contraindications emanating from the non-satellizing situation itself".[5] For example, goal frustration tolerance, self-critical ability, executive independence, and long-range goals are acquired easily enough.

> But the imperious need for superior accomplishment and pre-eminent extrinsic status effectively prevents the setting of realistic goals in many cases. Although level of ego aspiration is uniformly high in non-satellizers and is extremely resistant to lowering in the face of frustration, there is no reason for believing that the distribution of ability in this group is [uniformly high]. . . . Aspirational level will, therefore, be persistently and unrealistically high except in the small minority of individuals whose abilities are commensurate with their ambitions.[5]

It would be reasonable to expect also that the attenuation of immature personality traits on the basis of expediency (ego enhancement) is a much less stable arrangement than attenuation on the basis of satellization. In satellization there is implicit and unquestioning acceptance of the desirability for change. In the former instance, on the other hand, "where changes are made with specific ends in view," (1) abandonment of ends leads to reversal of change, and (2) incompatibility of the change with underlying ends often leads to sabotage of change. Thus, should either the goals of ego enhancement be abandoned (as in periods of severe personality disorganization), or should any of the goals of ego maturation be perceived as in conflict with the ends of ego enhancement, maturational regression could easily take place. The most vulnerable aspect of this type of maturation lies in the durability of feelings of moral accountability under conditions that are prejudicial to personal gain and advantage. Lacking the satellizer's implicit acceptance of the duty to abide by all internalized moral values, the non-satellizer is sorely tempted to let these values "go by the board" if the stakes are sufficiently high and the chances of apprehension and retribution sufficiently low (see pp. 256–258).

If maturation is more often successful in non-satellizers it is also more stressful. The satellizer's extrinsic self-esteem * is damaged by status deprivation during adolescence, but this injury tends to be peripheral because of a residual core of intrinsic self-acceptance. The non-satillizer's self-esteem, on the other hand, is "wholly a creature of the environmental vicissitudes which deny or gratify" the exalted ego aspirations on which he has "staked his value as a human being".[5] Hence, the absence of intrinsic feelings of adequacy makes the damage wrought to the only type of self-esteem he knows (extrinsic) central rather than peripheral. And in addition it is only when intrinsic self-esteem is lacking do threats to extrinsic self-esteem have the power to induce neurotic anxiety.[7]

The destructive impact of status deprivation on self-esteem and potential for anxiety response is greater in non-satellizers for still another reason besides lack of intrinsic adequacy. Because of their exaggerated needs for ego enhancement (which are highly resistant to discouragement), they find the same degree of status deprivation much more deflating to self-esteem. They are denied also the current source of derived status that adolescent ex-satellizers enjoy by maintaining in part a satellizing orientation † toward peer group, teachers, and employers. They are unable to experience the "ego support and 'we feeling' that is derived from the act of dependent identification with and self-subordination to group interests".[5]

Maturation of Rejected Children. Although rejected children find adolescent status deprivation more stressful than do satellizers,

* In this discussion, the term, "feelings of adequacy," is used synonymously with "self-esteem." When "extrinsic," they are referable to *primary* status; when "intrinsic," they are referable to current or residual *derived* status. Anxiety is a tendency to respond with fear to anticipated situations which threaten self-esteem. Neurotic anxiety exists when the basis of this tendency inheres in already impaired self-esteem rather than in an objectively hazardous situation. Neurotic anxiety thus appears to be an "over-response." Clinical observations have led to the conclusion that only persons who lack intrinsic feelings of adequacy are vulnerable to sufficient loss of self-esteem to be subject to neurotic anxiety.[5]

† It might be noted here that non-satellizers also use the incorporative and exploratory orientations exclusively in value assimilation.

adolescence often presents quite a few more opportunities for status than childhood. The decreased importance of the rejecting home in comparison with the importance of school and peer group is in itself an ego inflating factor. The fact of rejection becomes less catastrophic as the importance of the rejecting figures in the psychological world diminishes. Also, in comparison with childhood many new opportunities of achieving extrinsic status present themselves.

Rejected children do have a latent capacity for forming satellizing-like relationships to non-threatening individuals. Their original failure to satellize was due to the absence of suitable parental figures in the home rather than to a disinclination. When removed from the home, the possibility of satellization is increased, although fear of repetition of rejection makes them move cautiously.

Neurotic anxiety is almost invariably present in rejected children from the very beginning. Self-esteem is sufficiently impaired, both by (a) the absence of intrinsic feelings of adequacy and (b) by the catastrophic injury to extrinsic adequacy feelings implicit in the rejecting situation, to constitute the major source of threat in any adjustive situation.

The socialization of the rejected child is made difficult by his inability to assert himself adequately and to protect himself from the aggression of others. This is a consequence of a learning deficit acquired in the course of having to submit so long and helplessly to parental aggression that he cannot master the roles necessary for adult self-assertion. Aggression by others evokes an habitual response of helpless submissiveness.

> What other persons usually fail to recognize, however, is that this aggression and domination are only outwardly accepted; that quite unlike the over-dominated satellizer who genuinely accepts the subservience to which he is subjected, the overdominated non-satellizer gradually accumulates a reservoir of resentment and hostility which eventually overflows with such violence as to rupture existing relationships beyond repair.[5]

Typically, the rejected child tends to be taken advantage of, appears to accept the situation meekly, and then to the amazement of others erupts violently and impulsively. To avoid this sequence of events he prefers to withdraw from conflict situations and to intellectualize his aggression. Either course of action, however, does little to promote effective interpersonal relationships.

Maturation of Overvalued Children. In contrast to its effect on the rejected child, adolescence usually brings a marked *loss* in extrinsic status and self-estimate to the overvalued child. He can hardly expect the same flattery and adulation in school and peer group that he was accustomed to receive at home. In fact, adolescence frequently marks the onset of neurotic anxiety; for only now is the impairment to his extrinsic self-esteem sufficiently catastrophic to predispose him to this personality disorder. But unlike that of the rejected child, his anxiety is not offset by the possibility of obtaining some derived status (and, therefore, some intrinsic self-esteem) through the belated establishment of satellizing-like relationships.* His failure to undergo devaluation and satellization was less a compensatory reaction of self-defence, than an outcome of the parent's active fostering the infantile ego organization. Thus, he tends to find satellization too degrading, and is usually too obnoxiously selfish, self-centered, and narcissistic either to inspire genuine love in others or to be capable of relating himself emotionally to them.[5]

The overvalued child differs from the rejected child also by manifesting no incapacity for self-assertion and aggression. In fact his socialization is hindered by an excess rather than by a deficiency of these qualities. He tends to alienate associates initially by his overbearing, domineering, and importunate behavior.

> But in his case the motivation is available to modify the strategy of his interpersonal relationships and to learn more acceptable social behavior, since he recognizes the importance of good social relations in the struggle for power. Through assiduous study and intelligent application of self-control he is able to acquire an agreeable set of formal manners and a superficial veneer of good fellowship to mask his formerly offensive aggression and self-seeking. . . . Hence . . . he is able to learn a highly effective form of self-assertion in interpersonal relationships.[5]

Last, because of his excessively permissive upbringing, the overvalued child experiences more initial difficulty than the rejected

* Neurotic anxiety may be allayed in the rejected child by his achievement of intrinsic status *per se,* and by the reduction of frustration which this permits through a lowering of level of ego aspirations.

child in acquiring goal frustration tolerance, long-range goals, self-critical ability, and executive independence, and in relinquishing hedonistic motivations. But unlike the underdominated satellizer, his lack of intrinsic self-esteem, and his exaggerated needs for ego enhancement and genuine volitional independence motivate him more strongly eventually to acquire these attributes of maturity.

REFERENCES AND BIBLIOGRAPHY

1. Allport, G. W., Bruner, J. S., and Jandorf, E. M.: Personality under social catastrophe: Ninety life-histories of the Nazi revolution. Character and Personality, *10*:1–22, 1941.
2. Ausubel, D. P.: Ego development and the learning process. Child Develpm., *20*:173–190, 1949.
3. Ausubel, D. P.: Negativism as a phase of ego development. Am. J. Orthopsychiat., *20*:796–805, 1950.
4. Ausubel, D. P.: Problems of adolescent adjustment. Bulletin, Natl. Assn. Secondary School Principals, *34*:1–84, 1950.
5. Ausubel, D. P.: *Ego Development and the Personality Disorders.* New York: Grune and Stratton, 1952.
6. Ausubel, D. P., Schiff, H. M., and Gasser, E. B.: A preliminary study of developmental trends in sociempathy: Accuracy of perception of own and others' sociometric status. Child Developm., *23*:111–128, 1952.
7. Benedict, R.: Continuities and discontinuities in cultural conditioning. Psychiatry, *1*:161–167, 1938.
8. Biber, B. et al.: *Child Life in School.* New York: Dutton, 1942.
9. Brown, M. and Martin, V.: The University High School study of adolescents: Characteristics of high school students. Univ. High School Journal, *19*:177–219, 1941.
10. Cameron, N.: *The Psychology of Behavior Disorders: A Biosocial Interpretation.* Boston: Houghton Mifflin, 1947.
11. Carter, H. D.: "The Development of Interest in Vocations," in *Adolescence,* 43rd Yearbook, Natl. Soc. Stud. Educ. Chicago: University of Chicago Press, 1944.
12. Curle, A.: Incentives to work: An anthropological appraisal. Hum. Relat., *2*:41–47, 1949.
13. Davis, A.: "Socialization and Adolescent Personality," in *Adolescence,* 43rd Yearbook, Natl. Soc. Stud. Educ. Chicago: University of Chicago Press, 1944.
14. Eagleson, O. W.: Students' reactions to their given names. J. Soc. Psychol., *23*:187–195, 1946.
15. Forman, H. J.: *Our Movie-Made Children.* New York: Macmillan, 1935.
16. Frank, L. K.: "The Adolescent and the Family," in *Adolescence,* 43rd Yearbook, Natl. Soc. Stud. Educ. Chicago: University of Chicago Press, 1944.

17. Hertz, M. R. and Baker, E.: Personality patterns in adolescence as portrayed by the Rorschach ink-blot method: II. The color factors. J. Gen. Psycho., 28:3-61, 1943.
18. Hertzman, M. and Margulies, H.: Developmental changes as reflected in Rorschach test responses. J. Genet. Psychol., 62:189-215, 1943.
19. Hollingworth, L. S.: *The Psychology of the Adolescent*. New York: Appleton-Century, 1928.
20. Jersild, A. T.: *Child Psychology*. New York: Prentice-Hall, 1947.
21. Jersild, A. T.: *In Search of Self*. New York: Teachers College, Columbia University, 1952.
22. Jersild, A. T. and Markey, F. V.: *Conflicts Between Preschool Children*. Child Develpm. Monogr. No. 21. New York: Teachers College, Columbia University, 1935.
23. Jones, H. E.: *Development in Adolescence: Approaches to the Study of the Individual*. New York: D. Appleton-Century, 1943.
24. Joseph, A. and Murray, V. F.: *Chamorros and Carolinians of Saipan: Personality Studies*. Cambridge, Mass.: Harvard University Press, 1951.
25. Kuhlen, R. G.: *The Psychology of Adolescent Development*. New York: Harper, 1952.
26. Leighton, D. and Kluckhohn, C.: *Children of the People: The Navaho Individual and his Development*. Cambridge, Mass.: Harvard University Press, 1947.
27. Mead, M.: Social change and cultural surrogates. J. Educ. Sociol., 14:92-110, 1940.
28. Meyers, C. E.: Emancipation of adolescents from parental control. Nervous Child, 5:251-262, 1946.
29. Murphy, G.: *Personality: A Biosocial Approach to Origins and Structure*. New York: Harper, 1947.
30. Neilon, P.: Shirley's babies after fifteen years: A personality study. J. Genet. Psychol., 73:175-186, 1948.
31. Parten, M. B.: Leadership among preschool children. J. Abnorm. & Soc. Psychol., 28:430-440, 1933.
32. Shaffer, L. F.: *The Psychology of Adjustment*. Boston: Houghton Mifflin, 1936.
33. Shirley, M. M.: Impact of mother's personality on the young child. Smith College Stud. Soc. Work, 12:15-64, 1941.
34. Silverman, S. S.: *Clothing and Appearance: Their Psychological Implications for Teen-Age Girls*. New York: Teachers College, Columbia University, 1945.
35. Spitz, R. A.: "Anaclitic Depression," in *Psychoanalytic Study of the Child*, Vol. II. New York: International Universities Press, 1946, pp. 313-342.
36. Stendler, C. B.: *Children of Brasstown*. Urbana, Illinois: University of Illinois Press, 1949.
37. Stolz, H. R. and Stolz, L. M.: "Adolescent Problems Related to Somatic Variations," in *Adolescence*, 43rd Yearbook, Natl. Soc. Stud. Educ. Chicago: University of Chicago Press, 1944.

216   THEORY AND PROBLEMS OF ADOLESCENT DEVELOPMENT

38. Stone, C. P. and Barker, R. G.: The attitudes and interests of premenarcheal and postmenarcheal girls. J. Genet. Psychol., *54*:27–71, 1939.
39. Symonds, P. M.: *The Psychology of Parent-Child Relationships.* New York: D. Appleton-Century, 1939.
40. Symonds, P. M.: *Adolescent Phantasy.* New York: Columbia University Press, 1949.
41. Thetford, W. N., Molish, H. B., and Beck, S. J.: Developmental aspects of personality structure in normal children. J. Proj. Tech., *15*:58–78, 1951.
42. Washburn, R. W.: A Study of the Smiling and Laughing of Infants in the First Year of Life. Genet. Psychol. Monogr., *6*:397–539, 1928.
43. Washburne, J. N.: The impulsions of adolescents as revealed by their written wishes. J. Juv. Res., *16*:193–212, 1932.
44. Zachry, C. B. "Preparing Youth to Be Adults," in *Adolescence,* 43rd Yearbook, Natl. Soc. Stud. Educ. Chicago: University of Chicago Press, 1944.

CHAPTER 8

Parent-Child Relationships in Adolescence

THE MEANING OF EMANCIPATION

"THROUGHOUT THE ENTIRE animal kingdom where parents play an altruistic role in the rearing of their young 'emancipation seems to be quite a natural process'." [1] But neither among animals nor in human societies can emancipation be considered "synonymous with the more general problem of achieving adult personality status. It is merely that component part of the latter which depends upon a readjustment of the parent-child relationship on a basis that is more compatible with the [growing child's] increased capacity to fend for himself". [1] The achievement of full adult personality status requires a degree of social recognition that transcends the mere alteration of intra-familial relationships.

Parents at the infra-human level cease to exercise responsibility for their young even before the young acquire sexual maturity. Animal society, however, does not recognize adult status until the onset of pubescence. Once this point is reached, acceptance as an adult depends only on various interpersonal determinants of intra-group structure, such as sex, strength, number of individuals in the group, relative dominance, newness in the group.

In human societies, total emancipation rarely if ever precedes pubescence; and the interval of time between emancipation and the achievement of adult status is always culturally institutionalized. That is, this achievement is not merely a function of interpersonal relationships within the group, but is a product of social regulation based upon traditions, values, beliefs, and institutions transcending individual differences and the specific population characteristics and dominance hierarchy of a given group. In primitive cultures the time lag between these two phenomena tends to be relatively short. But

. . . in our society a large degree of emancipation is achieved relatively early compared to the delayed acquisition of adult social status. Through emancipa-

217

tion the adolescent establishes himself as a person in his own right, apart from his parents, prepared to strive for adult goals and willing to assume responsibility for the direction of his own affairs. But it is one matter to achieve this preparatory state of resolution and independence in a family setting, and still another to achieve that degree of social recognition as an adult which will afford the necessary experience in playing actual adult roles that is required for the attainment of this new personality status. Also since it is quite impossible even [in a family setting] to conceive of oneself as an independent adult ready for mature tasks and responsibilities in the face of prolonged socioeconomic dependence, adolescents can only achieve a certain limited measure of emancipation until their economic independence is an accomplished fact.[1]

Thus, emancipation is an important aspect both of personality maturation and of the achievement of adult personality status. A very large share of personality maturation is achieved in the home in relation to parents. Although much of this maturational change in the home antecedes pubescence, emancipation remains incomplete without it (see pp. 193–194). The final transition between emancipation and the achievement of adult status, on the other hand, is a function of cultural arrangements that are initiated by pubescence but depend for their consummation on other socioeconomic factors. And, finally, emancipation and the attainment of adult status influence each other reciprocally: An unemancipated individual is inevitably handicapped in the quest for social recognition as an adult; and conversely, deferment of recognition as an adult necessarily delays the completion of emancipation.

The specific developmental tasks implicated in emancipation have already been catalogued (see pp. 175–176). It is the universality of these tasks and of the general direction of personality change in relation to them during adolescence that enables us to regard emancipation as one of the basic psychobiological problems of adolescence.

FACTORS INFLUENCING THE NATURE AND ATTAINMENT OF EMANCIPATION

Age Trends

The course of emancipation in our culture is typically marked by two periods of slow and gradual growth each of which is followed by a period of acceleration. The first period which begins with the child's entrance into school and his absorption into a peer group, is climaxed by a spurt induced by pubescence. Prior to this time any gains in self-help and independence are primarily executive advances and are accompanied by a tightening of parental volitional control (see pp. 185–192). After the initial acceleration of emancipation in response to pubescence, the rate of growth is slow again until adult status is achieved as a result of financial independence, marriage, or induction into military life.

This sequence of events is so self-evident that little attempt has been made to verify it empirically. There is a low but reliable correlation between scores on Dimock's emancipation scale for boys and chronological age, but an even higher correlation between emancipation status and such criteria of pubescence as height, weight, and strength.[10] Havighurst, Robinson, and Dorr [16] found a definite shift away from parents as emulatory models from middle childhood to early adolescence. Other more indirect evidence includes a gradual increase with age in the amount of unsupervised spending money children receive from parents,[22] the increased frequency with which children attend movies unchaperoned by their parents,[9] and the steady decline with age in scores that children make on a test of suggestibility.[28]

Mechanisms of Emancipation

The mechanisms by which emancipation is achieved are no different from those already described for personality maturation (see pp. 194–200). Most important are the distinctions between (a) the characteristic emancipation patterns of satellizing and non-satellizing children respectively, and (b) the differences between parent-directed socialization in more primitive cultures and rural communities, and peer group socialization in urban, industrial centers.

In urban cultures in which the peer group constitutes the chief training institution of adolescence, emancipation

... is largely the outcome of positive changes in the relationships between adolescents and *non-parents,* rather than the result of any positive modification of the parent-child relationship itself. Seldom is there any planned or deliberate determination of policy. There is merely the deterioration of a relationship as it is replaced by new loyalties, new standards, and new sources of status. Parental influence and prestige wane to the point where the peer culture is even obliged to take over the functions of transmitting and enforcing class attitudes, aspirations and standards of behavior.[8]

Thus, desatellization or emancipation from parents is to a large extent a product of resatellization. Values and goals are still acquired by intellectual satellization, that is, as by-products of subservience to others on whom the individual is dependent for derived status; but now personal loyalties have been transferred from parents to age-mates and such other parent surrogates as teachers, adult group-leaders, and representatives of the church.

How the parent is displaced as an emulatory model is revealed by an analysis of children's essays on the theme, "The Kind of Person I Want to Be".[16] In middle childhood the idealized person is almost invariably the parent. In adolescence the parent yields partly to various romantic and glamorous figures; and in late adolescence, the emulated individual is most likely an attractive visible adult or a composite portrait of admired adults in the community.[16] The first displacement is less threatening and uncomplimentary to the parent since it is largely on a fantasy level. But the second displacement (which presupposes sufficient social experience and independence of attitude to warrant an objective evaluation of the parent) reflects an actual devaluation of the deified stature of the parent in favor of *real* persons in the environment.

At the level of daily operations, however, it is the peer group that accomplishes most of the desatellization since it furnishes the only stable frame of reference and the principal source of both primary and derived status available to adolescents. It is in relation to this group that parents seem less and less important. And the main hold that parents still exert on the child who is slowly drifting away is his lingering sense of guilt as he repudiates the values and hence the personal loyalties on which they are founded. It is this sense of guilt that slows down the rate of desatellization and leads in many instances to strong attachments to authoritarian parent substitutes in school and church. But this latter phenomenon is also a form of resatellization that weakens the dependent bond to parents.

The expansion of the child's social horizon during adolescence, as his physical mobility increases, also plays a role in emancipation. The widening of his social contacts makes him realize that his parents' home embodies only one specific representation of the culture, that other and perhaps better patterns of values are possible. For the first time he may gain insight into "the discrepancies between [parental] pretensions and the actual situation".[12] Adolescents may thus

> . . . become concerned about their own families, sensitive and worried about family customs and patterns and ways of living which now appear peculiar, different and embarrassing. . . . The boy or girl especially of foreign-born parents or of some conspicuously minority group may want to conceal his family from his contemporaries as a social liability. . . . [The parents in turn may] find it difficult to understand such apparent disloyalty. . . . [They] cannot see that their adolescent boy acts and speaks in such a manner just because he is so concerned about his family . . . and so eager to have them appear better than they are. It is a reversal of parent-child positions [with respect to the source of pressure for improvement] [12] [pp. 249, 250; quoted by permission of the Society].

However, the impact of increased social awareness on emancipation cannot be attributed solely to the wider knowledge it provides for making invidious comparisons. Equally important is the newly acquired ability to use this information critically in appraising parents, a result of liberation from the unconditional acceptance of parental dicta.

It should be realized that important as these new sources of derived status are in displacing the parent and inducing desatellization via resatellization, their efficacy in emancipation depends largely on their ability to provide *primary* status to the adolescent. And since this status becomes increasingly important with the progress of adolescence, this second mechanism through which allegiance is deflected from parents must be accounted the major emancipating influence of adolescence in urban cultures. In support of this interpretation is the indisputable fact that emancipation is successfully accomplished in rural and primitive cultures in which parents and elders retain control of the socializing process and of the extrinsic status available to adolescents. The only essential factors necessary for emancipation are (a) pubescence, (b) the withdrawal of derived status by the parents, (c) the existence of parental and social expectations that adolescents shall seek primary status, and (d) the availability of adult role-playing experience.

Facilitating and Retarding Influences

In general, the same factors promote and retard emancipation as affect personality maturation in the same ways. The availability of freedom of movement and of adult role-playing experience, sources of security outside the home, unconditional parental acceptance, withdrawal of derived status by parents, and heightened social expectations of achieving adult status all facilitate emancipation. On the other hand, residual habits of parental interference, rivalry, ambivalence about relinquishing control, and lack of appreciation for progress in achieving executive or volitional independence discourage emancipation. Particularly detrimental are overprotective and overdominating parent attitudes which inhibit the learning of self-reliance.[40]

Various factors originating in the child also influence the course of emancipation. We have already mentioned the ambivalent attitude toward the need for personality maturation and the phenomenon of perceptual constancy (see pp. 204–205). The individual's attitude, in childhood, toward authority is also important since it tends to predetermine in large measure what it will be in adolescence: blindly accepting, conditionally accepting, accepting under protest, overtly rebellious, resentful. Extroverts by and large find less difficulty in emancipation since they are less likely to shrink from distasteful conflict and self-assertion, and are more prone to engage in the types of activity that lead to status in adolescence.

Physical maturity is an extremely important determinant of rate of emancipation. Height, weight, and strength are all positively correlated with boys' degree of emancipation from parents as measured by Dimock's scale.[10] The reasons for this are self-evident. Parents and teachers scale their expectations of mature behavior in terms of physical development rather than in terms of chronological age. This fact is strikingly illustrated in a study by Barker, Wright, and Gonick in which expectations of parents and teachers for children of similar chronological age but different physical status were compared.[4]

Evidence from several sources indicates that boys achieve emancipation from parents more rapidly than do girls. Boys, for example, are more frequently permitted to attend movies unaccompanied by their parents.[9] Almost three times as many men as women comprised the "most emancipated" group in Sherman's question-naire study of the emancipation status of college students.[32] The reasons for this sex difference as well as its consequences in parent-youth conflict will be examined in the following section.

Important social factors affecting the rate of emancipation in-clude the availability of extrinsic status for adolescents, and the degree of discreteness characterizing the status roles available to children and adults respectively (see pp. 189–192). The advantage in these respects that children in primitive cultures and rural com-munities enjoy over their urban contemporaries is somewhat offset by the desatellizing influence exerted by alienation from parents and the parents' inability to provide extrinsic status. Rural parents are also less favorably disposed toward granting freedom from super-vision to their adolescent children.[40] But even within urban centers, subcultural differences exist in degree of freedom from parental control. Middle-class parents are slower to relinquish control than their proletarian counterparts, and instigate, therefore, a corre-spondingly greater amount of rebelliousness in their offspring.[19] Other social class differences in the attainment of adult status, as well as the effect of such socioeconomic factors as war and depression, will be discussed in Chapter 11 (see pp. 322–324, 327–333).

The Unevenness of Emancipation

In no other task of adolescence is the characteristic unevenness of growth in a transitional phase more apparent than in the acquisition of emancipation. Parents in our culture are much quicker to with-draw emotional succor than to relinquish their traditional authority, and are more readily disposed to retract derived status than to provide primary status. Their expectations of greater responsibility and maturity of behavior are far in excess of their willingness to grant their adolescent children autonomy of decision and recog-nition as adults. This discrepancy between expectations and de-mands, on the one hand, and prerogatives and privileges on the other, is much greater than the comparable situation confronting the adolescent in the peer group, but is considerably less disconcert-ing than the discrepancy in the culture at large. The lag in attaining emancipation is shorter than the lag in acquiring social status as an adult.

Although the home, like society in general, offers little in the way of status-giving activities, its greater structural flexibility allows for greater modification of [interpersonal] relationships than do other social institutions. Thus, the adolescent can achieve a considerable measure of emancipation from the home in the way of self-assertion and independent activity even though he fails to acquire much status. His changed physical appearance makes complete perpetuation of the old parent-child relationship difficult. Society, on the other hand, is protected from the impact of individual pubescence by buffers of impersonality and emotional distance.[3]

But "since the family unit cannot be set apart or insulated from the larger society of which it is a part, we may expect the process of emancipation to reflect" the major characteristics of the adolescent's position in the culture.[1] Thus, it is inevitable that the "unusual prolongation of adolescence in our society results in an extended period of partial emancipation".[1]

Being supported tends to keep the adolescent a child in his parents' house—a child whose opinions don't count, whose judgments are overriden, who is expected to seek and follow advice. And he is no longer a child. But neither is he grown up enough to comprehend. To him his inability to earn a living and to accept responsibility are a reflection, a sign of inadequacy. He is a failure. If the pressures become too great, the adolescent boy unable to stand the feelings of humiliation and the sense of guilt arising from the unbearable realization that he is a burden on his parents, runs away from home [46] [p. 336; quoted by permission of the Society].

PARENT-YOUTH CONFLICT IN ADOLESCENCE
Age Trends

All available evidence [2, 5, 7, 44] indicates that parent-child relations are more conflictful during pubescence than either before or after this period. Surprisingly enough, however, pubescence *per se* seems to be unrelated to the greater conflict that ensues concomitantly with its onset. Stone and Barker [36] found that the parent-child relations of post-menarcheal girls were no more stressful than those of pre-menarcheal girls of similar chronological age.

Parent-child conflict does not start *de novo* in adolescence but has antecedents in childhood. Retrospectively, as a matter of fact, college men indicate only a very moderate (but statistically significant) deterioration of the parent-child relationship during adolescence; women, on the other hand, indicate a marked increase in conflict coincident with pubescence.[2] After adolescence, most parent-child conflict disappears, but more residual stress remains for women than for men.[2]

Overt Issues

The overt issues that result in disharmonious relationships between parents and adolescents are not necessarily the actual or crucial causes of the conflict. In some instances they do provide a clue to the underlying issues. In others, they are quite trivial in themselves, serving merely as the battleground for hostile feelings engendered by causes quite remote from the points at issue.

A recent questionnaire study conducted in three different universities required young adult students in courses on adolescent psychology to rate (a) the cordiality of relationships with parents, (b) various parental attitudes, and (c) the degree of conflict with parents over specific issues from early childhood to post-adolescence.[2] In this area of investigation retrospective data from young adults are superior to current data from adolescents, since the passage of years permits the individual to evaluate problems (otherwise distorted by the influence of current vivid emotion) with greater perspective and objectivity. As a result of this difference in methodology, certain problems were rated less intensely than in similar studies [5, 26] performed with high school students. Nevertheless there was agreement that little overlap prevails between the types of problems adolescent boys experience with parents and the corresponding kinds of problems experienced by girls.[5]

Retrospectively, boys' problems of emancipation centered around *specific* adolescent privileges of growing up. Girls' problems were more concerned with *broader* issues of independence, self-determination, and sex role.[2] For example, the following twelve problems on the check list loomed important for girls: parental imposition of goals, parental interference in personal affairs, parental interference in choice of friends, late hours, excessive restriction of freedom of movement, spending money, parental violation of privacy, differences about boy-girl relations, parental denial of decision, differences about smoking, differences about clothes, arguments over home chores. Only seven problems were checked as important by boys. Of the six that appear on both lists, all were rated as significantly more severe by girls.* In order of importance they were: late hours, spending money, differences about smoking, differences about boy-girl relations, parental denial of self-decision, excessive restriction of freedom of movement, teasing about boy-girl relations. The last problem seemed to be unique for boys.

The outstanding sex difference, besides the lower intensity of problems for boys, was the fact that four of the five most important girls' problems were related to general rather than specific issues of parental interference and restrictiveness; whereas the situation was precisely reversed for boys. Both boys and girls tended to have reliably more problems with their mothers than with their fathers, girls having more problems than boys with both parents. These findings confirm the results of an earlier study by Stott on adolescents' criticisms of parental behavior.[38]

Underlying Causes

The most important single cause of parent-youth conflict is the perseveration of parents' attitudes that interfere with the adolescent's greatly expanded need for volitional independence. The factors that generally influence parents to retain a restrictive, authoritarian, and interfering role—feelings of ambivalence and rivalry, and the persistence of habits of domination (accentuated by perceptual constancy of the child)—have already been discussed.† Several studies [13, 37, 39] indicate that such restrictive attitudes are widespread at all social levels among parents of adolescents. Parents as a group favor attitudes that are much less conducive to the development of self-reliance in children than do specialists in child development.[30] In addition, certain parents tend to be more overdominating and overprotective than others, rural parents tend to be more restrictive than urban parents,[40] and middle-class parents more authoritarian than working-class parents.[19] Retrospective reports of young adults of both sexes indicate that of the two parents, the mother is more overprotective, domineering, restrictive, and interfering during adolescence, whereas the father is described as more indifferent, neglectful, and preoccupied with himself.[2]

---

* Similar findings are reported by Block,[5] Stott,[38] and Tryon.[44]

† English [11] also attributes the admonishing, criticizing, and scolding attitudes of parents to their fears that the adolescent will not grow up to be a responsible, mature, and respectable individual.

In support of the findings of greater extent and severity of overt manifestations of adolescent-parent conflict in girls is the noteworthy fact that both parents display more restrictive attitudes toward their adolescent daughters than toward their sons.* [2] Parents evidently reconcile themselves to the fact that their sons must undergo emancipation; from childhood, to adolescence, to post-adolescence, there is a steady change in attitudes toward sons that is in line with the requirements of emancipation.[2] On the other hand, they seem unwilling to acknowledge the newly evolving emancipation needs of girls.

> Just as girls are expected to satellize more than boys, they are expected to desatellize less. At the termination of adolescence, parents do not contemplate that their daughters will have severed the ties of dependency.[3]

Hence, parents' attitudes toward their daughters usually remain more consistent from one developmental stage to the next. Instead of gradually relinquishing control during the adolescent period, their approach (as perceived retrospectively by their adult daughters) becomes even more authoritarian. Furthermore, this domineering attitude tends to persist during the post-adolescent period until marriage supervenes.[2]

> This parental attitude is reflective of the more sheltered vocational and sexual position [traditionally] accorded women in our culture. But there are indications that this cultural position has changed more radically in recent years than the supporting attitudes which it supposedly justifies. The net outcome of this attitudinal lag on the part of parents is to prolong the course of desatellization longer than would otherwise follow from the actual social roles played by modern generations of women.[3]

A direct corollary of the overly restrictive attitude of parents that is responsible for much friction during adolescence is the lack of respect they show for their children.

> It is very humiliating for one aspiring to be an adult to be castigated like a child, to be nagged, yelled, and shouted at.[46] But even worse are the scorn, the ridicule and the condescending attitude that greet physical awkwardness, faltering or confused articulation of political views, and clumsy efforts at

---

* Consistent with all of these findings that girls experience a more stressful adolescence than boys insofar as friction with parents is concerned is the fact that they also reveal more maladjustment on the Thurstone Personality Schedule.[31] The problem of sex differences in stressfulness of adolescence is also considered in relation to the differentiation of social sex roles (see pp. 418–420).

heterosexual expression. Even if he cares little about everything else, every adolescent—just because he is first aspiring to adult status—cherishes an ideal about the essential dignity of a human being, which, if respected, would leave him decidedly less provocative and resistive to guidance.[1]

Misunderstandings are also more or less inevitable because parents cannot help but approach the problems of their children in the light of their own conflicts and anxieties at a similar age. They find it difficult to appreciate that "adolescents develop their own standards and codes to guide their behavior, and what is more confusing, these standards shift and change as children mature".[27] And in addition to this cognitive block to understanding caused by projection, the rearousal of forgotten conflicts leads to anxiety that can be most easily allayed by arbitrarily ruling out of bounds for the child the same impulses that in adolescence created difficulty for the parent.

In another sense, however, the memory of parents seems too short rather than too long. Not only do they project their own experiences where these are no longer applicable, but also they fail to profit by experience that is relevant.

> They tend to forget that as adolescents they, too, found it necessary to defy their own parents for just and adequate cause. Hence, it not rarely happens that the parent, who himself was most rebellious as an adolescent in defense of his legitimate rights of self-determination, becomes the most ruthless in suppressing his own children when they demand the same rights.[1]

And, finally, the parent generates conflict not because of what he does or feels, but simply because he is, in the eyes of his child, a representative of the adult society that is denying him status and equal membership. The parent inevitably "becomes the undeserved target for the child's resentment against the deprivations, the frustrations, and the prolonged withholding of adult status to which the latter is subjected".[1]

The adolescent is also largely responsible for the generation of parent-youth conflict. To begin with, he cherishes unrealistic expectations of achieving complete emancipation with the onset of pubescence. Second, as a consequence of his increased emotional instability and precarious lack of status, many conflicts that hitherto remained below threshold level during the more stable period of middle childhood are reactivated. Among these are various temperamental incompatibilities, which had aroused friction in early childhood but had lain dormant during the relatively carefree and extroverted elementary school years. However, it has been suggested that the preadolescent's greater conformity to adult authority is more apparent than real; that conformity may merely be expedient, or reflect a greater capacity for dissimulation [3] (see pp. 191–192).

The most serious cause of parent-youth conflict emanating from the child is the fact that the adolescent cannot escape "challenging parental authority as the price of his own individual maturation and of acceptance in his own age group".[12]

> What actually happens in most cases is that the adolescent mimics the stylized and stereotyped attitude of hostility toward adults that is fashionable in his peer group; and whether he believes in it or not is obliged to act the part, at least in public. Being forced in this way to satisfy at the same time the conflicting norms of home, school, and friends, it is inevitable that loyalty to the home will give way first, since the adolescent derives the least portion of his status from the home situation. This conflict is brought to a head if the parents adopt a hostile, "either-or" attitude toward the values of the peer group.[6] Gardner [14] refers to an "untouchable phase of adolescence in which the adolescent looks for confirmation or denial of his ideas to someone—almost anyone—beyond the home. It is the age of the girl chum or boy pal whose knowledge of facts and values and estimates of worth are inevitably taken to be truer than those of the parents." [1]

The adolescent, therefore, orients himself to a social norm that anticipates and even requires a certain amount of defiance of parents. In the light of these expectations, bravado and hostility, if felt, can more easily be given expression than affection.[6]

An inevitable and ubiquitous cause of parent-youth conflict, one that has always been with us and that probably always will be, is a condition known as "generation conflict." This refers to the misunderstandings, difficulties of communication, and conflict of interests that necessarily arise simply because of the difference in age between individuals of two generations. Merely on the basis of temperamental differences related to developmental status, we would anticipate a certain amount of friction. Those on the ascending limb of life in terms of vigor and level of aspiration tend to have a different outlook on life from those on the descending limb. It is the contrast between the physically active, impulsive, hopeful, and idealistic individual who still has to experience many of the hard realities of life, and the more sedentary, inflexible, cautious, realistic, and perhaps embittered individual whose optimism has been tempered by a wider range of sobering experience.

Illustrative of such differences are the different rank values that eighth-grade children and their parents assign to various types of experiences thought suitable for adolescents. The three most important experiences valued by parents (work at home without pay, work or play with younger children, leadership in the peer group) were ranked ninth, thirty-third, and thirteenth in a list of forty items by the children. The three most important experiences valued by the children (talk with adults doing various kinds of work, work for pay, work or play in a group of four or five people) were ranked ninth, thirty-second and twenty-first by parents.[8]

In addition to differences attributable to developmental status, generation conflict is also induced by differences in the value systems of each age group. The extent of such disparity is obviously a function of the rate of social change. In periods of rapid change, such as that following the introduction of industry into a rural community, it is inevitable that wide discrepancies will exist between the value systems of parents and children. A similar cleavage is commonly seen between immigrant parents and their native-born children.* And since an adult tends to think in terms of the values of his youth and to evaluate the behavior of his children in terms of the norms that prevailed when he was growing up, misunderstandings are not an inexplicable outcome.

Finally, parent-youth conflict is enhanced by any socio-economic event, such as economic depression, which prolongs emancipation and thereby increases both intrafamilial contact and the adolescent's emotional instability. This situation is further aggravated if the father is unemployed. Under such conditions intrafamilial tension is increased by the father's loss of morale and prestige (especially if his children are working) and by his lowered threshold of irritability.[18]

---

* Any type of social mobility, such as from urban to rural living, from a lower to a higher social class, will produce the same result.

Displacement of Conflict

The direct expression of hostile impulses toward the instigating agent or situation is always a function of the strength of the inhibitory forces that are simultaneously brought into play. When parents are the instigating agents of the child's aggression, numerous factors limit the intensity of its direct expression: feelings of affection, guilt, and respect, fear of retaliation, cultural reinforcement of the hallowed role of parenthood. Under such conditions, when specific aggressive impulses must be inhibited, a generalized lowering of all other thresholds of aggressive response occurs. Hostility will be displaced into a related area of low threshold value, which is both available (subject to less inhibition) and compatible with the individual's habitual mode of expressing aggression (physically or intellectually, impersonally or face-to-face, frontally or by innuendo). The following example, illustrating the Navaho child's reaction to weaning, is typical of the mechanism of displaced aggression in parent-youth conflict:

> If the initial experiences with the mother have been good, . . . it seems to be one or more of the older brothers and sisters who bears the brunt of the hostility generated at the period of weaning. Expression of hostility toward the new baby would be an unforgivable sin in a society where children are so highly valued. . . . But the freshly weaned child and the older sister (or brother) who has the care of him and bears much of the disciplinary responsibility for him take out a good deal on each other. Certainly the younger child . . . deflects most of its "meanness" onto one or more older sisters or brothers—especially the one who has him in charge. The older children, in turn, appear sometimes to displace against "run-about" youngsters some of the animosity which they suppressed when a baby actually dethroned them.[21] *

In addition to deflecting hostility to such ready targets as siblings and teachers, adolescents, especially the more intellectual and introverted, find a more indirect and devious outlet in intellectual areas. Several studies (without in any way passing on the validity of radical ideas *per se*) indicate that poor parent-child relations and rejection by parents are more common among radical students of

* Reprinted by permission of the publishers from Dorothea Cross Leighton and Clyde Kay Maben Kluckhohn, *Children of the People: The Navaho Individual and His Development*. Cambridge, Mass.: Harvard University Press, Copyright, 1947, by the President and Fellows of Harvard College.

college age than in a matched group of more conservative students.[20, 34] Aggressive international attitudes of high-school seniors were found to be significantly related to personality measures of "extro-punitive" hostility.[25]

Adolescent aggression is sometimes expressed in a distorted and cynical materialism which denies any possibility of virtue or altruism, such as a crass epicureanism or nihilism. It is noteworthy that the philosophy of existentialism[33] flourishes largely in an adolescent age group. A religious heresy not derived from genuine intellectual conviction is also a familiar adolescent phenomenon. It may be regarded as a substitutive aggression against parents insofar as the church is identified with parental authoritarian values. But the most extreme manifestation of displaced adolescent hostility is a not uncommon variety of juvenile delinquency. Some evidence indicates that the parents of delinquent adolescents are less affectionate, solicitous, and accepting than the parents of non-delinquents.[45, 47]

The Prognosis of Parent-Youth Conflict

Just because parent-child conflict increases during adolescence, we should not exaggerate its significance or ignore the many positive aspects of this relationship.

> Friction in various forms is almost inevitable if the home is peopled by real persons. . . . The normal home has its quota of bickering and disagreement. One of the functions of a good home is to serve as a place where husbands, wives, and children can become annoyed with each other without suffering dire consequences. The more solid the affection between members of the family the more will each feel free to be himself. . . .
>
> While the adolescent is striking off on lines of his own, his parents and his home continue to be of great importance in his life. He needs the anchorage which the home affords. It is important to him to be able to count on his parents as persons who regard him with disinterested affection and in whom he can confide without fear of ridicule or betrayal.
>
> He needs the home as a base of operations that is stable when other things are in flux. He also needs the home as a place where he can relax, let down his hair, so to speak, and give way occasionally to petulance, complaints and childish behavior which he would not allow himself to display in his relations with his peers or with adults outside the home.[17]

Serious parent-youth conflict is not inevitable, even in urban cultures where the peer group is the chief socializing institution. And in rural cultures such as the Navaho,

> . . . the feelings of a child for his parents are much less likely to be seriously mixed than is the case among white people. . . . Instances of open aggression against the mother even in stories and dreams are exceedingly rare. . . . The relationship of children and fathers is also dominantly a warm one. The stereotype of the harsh, tyrannical father is lacking in Navaho culture.[21] *

Although there is a strong positive relationship between the relaxing of parental controls and the attainment of emancipation, the two are not necessarily coextensive. "The absence of parental control [per se] should not be considered an indication of maturity. The task of equipping the child for self-direction is no less formidable than the problem of getting parent and child to let go of each other in a progressive fashion." [10] Many overly permissive parents avoid conflict by abandoning all controls precipitously. In the long run, however, although conflict may be avoided, such emancipation is less complete than instances in which parents take an active part in the upbringing of their adolescent children. Avoiding friction, in other words, is not an end in itself. No genuine progress can be accomplished painlessly.

In most instances, parent-youth conflict is a transitory phenomenon that disappears with the conclusion of the adolescent period. In the retrospective study already discussed (see pp. 225–226), no specific issues of any significance remained for either sex. However, parents still displayed overprotective attitudes toward their daughters. A very small minority reported the continuation of intense conflict with their parents or a complete rupture of relations.[2]

The frequency with which adolescents are brought to guidance centers "because they manifest an exaggerated need for independence, because they delight in being perverse and contrary, and because they defy parental authority" requires that we establish prognostic criteria. Parents are understandably concerned about

---

* Reprinted by permission of the publishers from Dorothea Cross Leighton and Clyde Kay Maben Kluckhohn, *Children of the People: The Navaho Individual and His Development.* Cambridge, Mass.: Harvard University Press, Copyright, 1947, by the President and Fellows of Harvard College.

this situation and want to know how it will turn out. Clinical experience with disturbed adolescents has led the writer to classify all cases of parent-youth conflict into two broad categories: (1) In the prognostically hopeful group, the condition is a transitory phenomenon brought on by factors specific to the developmental problems of adolescence. It

> . . . may be an exaggerated response to status deprivation or to the parents' ambivalent attitude; it may be incited by the militancy of the child's peer group, or it may represent a distorted idea of the very meaning of emancipation in the mind of the adolescent. Under these circumstances the problem can often be quickly solved by interpreting parent to child or *vice versa,* or by favorable manipulation of the environment.[3]

(2) In the prognostically unfavorable group, the disturbed emancipation process is rooted in a fundamental distortion of the parent-child relationship that is in no way specific to the tasks of adolescent maturation. The three most common types of children and the parent-child relationships responsible for their unsatisfactory situation are: (a) the dominant, self-assertive child who has been harshly rejected; (b) the overvalued child who has been rejected in later childhood or adolescence; and (c) the overdominated and overmotivated child who rebels openly against parental domination. "Such conflict may lead to serious consequences, i.e., delinquency, running away from home, impulsive marriage, abrupt withdrawal from school, with the likelihood that the conflict will persist into adult life." [1]

These clinical impressions were tested by comparing from twenty of the most serious cases of parent-youth conflict in the writer's retrospective study[2] ten individuals who showed little residual conflict as adults with ten other individuals who showed considerable residual conflict. Both groups manifested significantly greater conflict with parents during childhood than the population at large, but the non-improving group reported significantly less favorable parental [5] *attitudes* before adolescence than the group that eventually improved. Another significant difference was a change for the better in the parental * attitudes of the improving group in the *post-adolescent* period.[2]

---

* *Parental attitudes* refer to the attitudes of the parents of the subjects in this study and not to the attitudes on parenthood of the subjects themselves.

Parents can, therefore, be "given assurance that if their relationships with their children had been established on a basis of mutual respect and affection, it is reasonably certain that the same relationships will be re-established once the turbulent period of adolescence is over." [1] After the capacity for self-direction is achieved, "the exaggerated tension and conflict existing between parent and child are usually resolved." [1]

His acute sensitivity with respect to self-determination now laid aside, once the question of his adult status is finally settled, the child—now adult—can meet his parents with a new sense of ease. He can afford to listen attentively to their advice, neither accepting nor rejecting it because of its source, but evaluating it on the basis of its intrinsic merits and assuming responsibility himself for making the final decision.[1]

Thus, the products of

. . . the emancipated situation should include a retention of mutual trust between parent and child. It should include a continuation of respect and honor for parents and of genuine devotion and concern by the parents for the offspring.[29]

DISCIPLINE IN ADOLESCENCE
The Need for Changed Methods of Control

It is self-evident that methods of parental control must be adapted to meet changing conditions of personality organization and maturity. Physical restraint, parental approval, uncritical obedience, and personal loyalty are no longer appropriate measures for exacting conformity from the desatellizing individual. New methods must recognize the adolescent's need for greater volitional independence, his greater capacity to respond consistently to more abstract and rational principles of conduct, and the changes in his learning orientation.

Discipline must necessarily be less authoritarian. Obedience can no longer be demanded for its own sake, and once this untenable position is abandoned, many "supposed occasions for punishment melt away." Navaho parents, as already pointed out, never expect this type of obedience. They regard disobedience not as intrinsically "bad," but as dangerous because of its consequences. However, some parents of adolescents in our culture still insist on unquestioned obedience as an inalienable right. They make it clear that they will "stand for no nonsense" and will "put the child in his place." [46]

Such discipline may be temporarily effective and achieve a certain outward conformity to visible authority by employing the repressive measures of fear, pain, ridicule and deprivation.[46] What it fails to achieve, however, is that *inner* control based upon an acceptance of the moral authority of society which underlies adult as contrasted to childhood moral behavior; and in addition it carries the danger of provoking further aggressive defiance and encouraging further sabotage or repudiation of adult goals.[1]

The consequences of over-strict, authoritarian control, which is not genuinely accepted by the adolescent, may extend beyond the parent-child relationship. In the classroom it leads to a loss of volitional independence, passive dependence upon the teacher, and aggressive intra-group behavior.[24] That juvenile delinquency [35, 45] and marital difficulties [43] were found more frequently in children coming from homes in which parents use this type of control is simply another illustration of the phenomenon of displaced hostility. An authoritarian parent does not countenance the direction of any aggression toward himself; hence, if any hostility is to be expressed, other outlets must be found.

Not only the severity, but also the methods of discipline need revision during adolescence. Physical punishment obviously inappropriate, is seldom used.[39] However, a derogatory type of scolding that is the most common form of punishment [39] leads to almost as much resentment. The very nature of adolescence, as a period of emancipation, requires a nondirective type of discipline that relies more on explanation, discussion, and opportunity for individual decision than on appeal to dogmatic sanctions. "Reasons contributed by other people seldom mean a thing to [the adolescent]; he has to be helped to work things out for himself in his own mind."

Several features of Navaho discipline are especially suited to the requirements of adolescence. The Navaho concept of punishment, for example, is less personal and less vindictive. The authority for discipline resides in the group rather than in a single powerful figure.[21] Discipline, therefore, provokes less resentment and rebellion in an individual who is trying to emancipate himself from parental control. Parents in our culture could emulate with profit the Navaho practice of achieving control of the individual by

> . . . "lateral sanctions" rather than by sanctions from above. That is, the Navaho from childhood on is brought into line more by the reactions of all the people around him rather than by orders and threats of punishment from someone who stands above him in a hierarchy. "Shame" is the agony of being found wanting and exposed to the disapproval of others, as opposed to the fear that some single superior person will use his power to deprive one of rewards and privileges if specified tasks are not carried out according to instructions.[21] *

The peer group, as a matter of fact, does achieve this type of control over adolescents in our culture, but parents usually work in opposition to it rather than in collaboration with it.

The Need for Discipline in Adolescence

Advocating changed methods of discipline in adolescence does not mean that *no* discipline is required. As already pointed out, "spontaneous maturation" is a myth in human development, except perhaps in certain physical growth with a strong phylogenetic component. Personality maturation is largely the outcome of responding to a body of very explicit social expectations, reinforced by appropriate sanctions. Unrestricted freedom

> . . . leaves little room for the development of moral responsibility or of respect for the rights of others. Secondly, it frustrates the adolescent's need for definite and unambiguous standards of social reality with the aid of which he can control and orient his new emotional urges and ego demands. It is one of the main functions of both home and school, as representatives of the social order, to make certain very firm, definite and consistent demands on adolescents.[1]

The removal of all pressures for conformity eliminates immediate interpersonal conflict, but also leaves an immature, insecure, and disoriented individual who acquires little frustration tolerance and self-critical ability, and is unable to aspire to realistic roles and goals.

One can control adolescents by relying more heavily on reward

* Reprinted by permission of the publishers from Dorothea Cross Leighton and Clyde Kay Maben Kluckhohn, *Children of the People: The Navaho Individual and His Development.* Cambridge, Mass.: Harvard University Press, Copyright, 1947, by the President and Fellows of Harvard College.

motivation un-reinforced by appropriate punishment than one can with younger children. That is, principles of conduct are now established on a level abstract enough that rewarding the "good" alternative implies simultaneous condemnation of the "bad." But this implication is never completely thorough-going since it requires

> . . . a level of logical consistency that is rare in the typical person's organization of values and attitudes. . . . Hence, consistent and unambiguous discipline requires explicit definition of the limits of unacceptable behavior, reinforced by tangible evidences of disapproval.[3]

Also, even though one can rely more on self-discipline in adolescents, it is still necessary to keep external restraints visible. Such restraints are not the chief support of acceptable conduct, but they are necessary to discourage "the temptation to test the limits of tolerance for unacceptable behavior, i.e., to see how much one can 'get away with' before incurring retribution." Needless to say, tendencies such as these are "present in all of us, irrespective of whether a generally wholesome conscience is operating," and make us thankful for the presence of the policeman on the corner.[3]

MATURATIONAL FAILURE ATTRIBUTABLE TO FAULTY CHILD REARING PRACTICES

Maturity is only a relative term. That is, an individual may be characterized only as *more* or *less* mature, depending on the degree to which he exemplifies the composite virtues of the ideal of maturity in a given subculture. Considering all of the variables that enter into the attainment of maturity (see pp. 200–208), we realize that few persons can expect to reach adult life without incurring one or more maturational defects of varying severity. In this section we shall be concerned only with maturational defects that are both (a) attributable to some serious derangement of the parent-child relationship, and (b) gross and disabling enough to warrant a diagnosis of "maturational failure."

Appraising the seriousness of maturational defects is extremely important in child guidance work. The problem of differential diagnosis is the same as that in evaluating the significance of parent-youth conflict. Parents are rightly concerned when their children present evidence of maturational retardation. They want to know what the prognosis is. Hence, the most useful classification of problems of maturation uses prognosis as the chief nosologic criterion.

Just like parent-youth conflict, maturational retardation may be divided into (1) a transitory, prognostically favorable type that is merely symptomatic of the general stress of adolescent development in our culture; and (2) a more serious, prognostically unfavorable variety (maturational failure) that does not clear up with adolescence and is reflective of deep-seated disturbance of the parent-child relationship. The transitory type is partly an expression of the ambivalent attitude that both parent and child adopt toward maturation (see pp. 203–205). The greater portion of it, however, springs from a reluctance to part with the interim values and status built up so painstakingly in the peer group. This reluctance represents more than the usual resistance to developmental change; it is also a form of group defiance and revenge for the earlier insult of being excluded from the adult orbit of status operations.

The permanent kind of maturational retardation (failure) can be divided into two subcategories: (a) maturational failure in satellizers that is simply an outgrowth of parent attitudes unfavorable for desatellization; and (b) maturational failure, especially in non-satellizers, that is an aggressive, vengeful response to harsh rejecting or overdominating parent attitudes. We will refer to the first type as "developmental," and to the second type as "reactive" failure.

"Developmental" Failure

Maturational failure attributable to inappropriate parental attitudes is the "terminal phase of a progressive developmental condition." [3] It is "a relatively rare extreme form of a phenomenon which in varying degrees of lesser severity is a quite common occurrence." [3] Other variables relating to social conditions and individual personality differences among satellizers (see pp. 200–208) are also contributing factors. In the more complete forms of failure (in overprotected and underdominated children), the major tasks of maturation—acquisition of adult volitional independence, striving for primary status, attenuation of hedonistic motivation, the attainment of increased executive independence and societal moral responsibility—are not accomplished. In overdominated and underappreciated children, the degree of maturational failure is less complete and less severe.

The *overprotected* child (see pp. 201–202) fails to gain volitional and executive independence because he is shielded from necessary experience with mature roles, from choice-making decisions (lest he injure himself by unwise choices), and from frustration of any kind. His parents differentially reward behavior that makes him more dependent upon them, and make no demands that he surrender derived status, seek primary status, or relinquish hedonistic motivations. Peer group socialization, frustration tolerance, and self-critical ability are lacking because of inadequate experience in social situations and in overcoming frustration through his own resources and ingenuity. Concepts of moral responsibility remain tied to specific parental contexts and acquire no social generality; the individual is unable to conceive of himself as an independent entity functioning in a community and therefore responsible to its moral authority.

Underdominated children (see pp. 201–202), on the other hand, have considerable experience in self-assertion and choice-making. But as a result of growing up in an undemanding, indulgent, and unrestricted home, they do not develop those personality attributes that implement volitional independence on an adult level: frustration tolerance, self-critical ability, and capacity for setting realistic goals. They too are under no pressure to relinquish hedonistic motivation, to strive for primary status, or to acquire executive independence. Accustomed to their parents' submission, they are unable to accept authority,[42] make unreasonable demands upon others, and expect special consideration.[23] Not required to curb their hedonistic impulses or to develop any responsibility to the ethical values of their parents, they uncritically accept them as valid, but behave as if they "were exempt from the usual moral restraints governing most people." [3]

> The net result of this curious imbalance in volitional development, in which the desire for volitional independence is totally unmatched by capacity for same, is that the individual *wills* to be dependent on the will of others. . . . As long as the outward appearance of self-assertion is preserved—a need which is too basic to be relinquished—it can actually serve the purpose of establishing and reinforcing a relationship founded on volitional dependency. . . . What he mainly demands from others . . . is that they accept responsibility for planning his future and smoothing his way.[3]

When a parent's *overdomination* is benevolent, consistent, and acceptable to the child, neither rebellion nor complete maturational failure results. "Under the circumstances 'continued acceptance of authority on the child's part' [29] can be maintained even into his old age." [3] The authoritarian parent sets high standards and does not countenance immature behavior. Overdominated children, therefore, are industrious, highly motivated, responsible, and self-critical.[42] What they lack is experience in and opportunity for self-assertion and independent decision-making. They are excessively docile and submissive, and lack spontaneity and self-confidence.[42] Making decisions seems to them a prerogative of parents and those in authority. Also, they acquire moral responsibility on a societal basis with considerable difficulty because their ethical values "are so completely dominated by the personal figures of parents."[3] In extreme examples, incapacity for freeing themselves from parental domination is so marked that marriage even becomes unthinkable.

The *underappreciated* child is discouraged early in life from seeking primary status. As an accepted satellizer, he has no lack of derived status, but he finds that his parents take his accomplishments for granted. He sees little purpose in striving, since regardless of his efforts, the only reward that means anything to him, parental approval, is not forthcoming. Because it is a very unrewarding process maturation is undertaken half-heartedly; and without later motivation provided by the appreciation of parent surrogates, it is very likely to proceed irregularly and terminate at a sub-adult level.[3]

"Reactive" Failure

In "reactive" failure, the necessary conditions for maturation are present, but the child deliberately chooses failure as an instrument for revenge upon parents. Under ordinary circumstances, non-satellizers are strongly motivated to achieve a high degree of maturity since they perceive that it is a precondition for attaining the large-scale ego enhancement they desire. The motive of revenge, when present, is more important to overvalued than to rejected children, since the parents of the rejected child cannot be hurt by the failure of a career about which they are unconcerned.

Maturational failure in overvalued children is precipitated by a sudden replacement (in late childhood or preadolescence) of overvaluing attitudes by authoritarian control. The parent may grow tired of his obsequious and adulatory role, or of the child's arrogance, which he formerly thought "cute" or portentous of future greatness. He may finally perceive that the child will never be a "genius" or even a "great man," or that a younger sibling has greater potentialities. Sometimes, especially with girls, the parent seeks to regain control at adolescence simply because he is concerned about sexual experimentation or aggression. The child, who is completely unprepared for this sudden about-face and is quite incapable of submitting to authoritarian control, becomes understandably resentful and rebellious. His resentment is increased by the fact that his friends are winning greater freedom while his is being curtailed. Hence, despite the tremendous need for ego enhancement

> . . . the desires for achieving absolute independence and for wreaking vengeance on the resented parent become the dominant motives in life. Both aims can be best served simultaneously by adopting an attitude of obstinate perverseness, by repudiating the entire process of adult maturation, and by choosing goals and standards of behavior which are diametrically opposite to those advocated by the parent. . . . Motivational immaturity and childish irresponsibility are combined with inflated ambitions and an exaggerated need for volitional independence (which is often in marked disparity to the individual's actual executive dependence). In extreme cases this pathological need for independence is generalized to include freedom from control of any sort whatsoever. The individual then sets himself up as being above any criticism or moral censure, and acknowledges no responsibility to be bound by the moral authority of society.[1]

The overvalued child may sometimes undergo temporary maturational retardation even in the absence of traumatic reversal of parental attitudes. In spite of high prestige aspirations the overvalued child tends to be hedonistic, self-indulgent, and undisciplined because of parental underdomination (see pp. 213–214). Systematic work outside his immediate realm of interests is distasteful. If, before he is reconciled to the "sacrifices" of mature behavior for long-range ego enhancement, he is confronted with the necessity of conforming to an exacting program of school work, he may reject maturation and choose a less irksome alternative. Instead of overcoming his distaste for systematic application to uninteresting tasks, he may choose always to cast his plans in grandiose terms that stamp him as "being different," but nevertheless fail to provide the sustained effort needed for completion. There is enough ego satisfaction in merely evolving such high-flown plans and in "being different" to gratify his needs for extrinsic status. And he rationalizes his obvious lack of accomplishment: "I'm so superior to ordinary mortals that I don't have to bother following through on my plans."

Rejected children, even the thick-skinned, extroverted, self-assertive ones who rebel against overdomination, are less apt to choose reactive failure as a weapon against parents. To do so would hardly constitute adequate revenge since the parents would not be greatly hurt. In fact, such failure would justify their rejection of him; whereas the child desires to reverse their original judgment that he is not worth bothering with. At the very worst, his exaggerated need to free himself from "hatefully regarded parental authority" leads to extreme parent-youth conflict and to a permanent rupture of relationships with parents.[3] The rejected child also finds the tasks of maturation less onerous than the overvalued child since he has never been conditioned to an excessively permissive environment. He is less likely to balk at the self-discipline that maturation requires or to regress to immaturity when "the going is rough."

Reactive failure sometimes occurs in overdominated satellizers who find themselves eventually unable to tolerate parental authority. This reaction is relatively rare since enough affection for parents is usually generated in a satellizing relationship to preclude the need for such extreme vengeance. It is more likely to occur when the parent's discipline is harsh and inconsistent.[42] Under these circumstances the more self-assertive child may rebel openly and repudiate the goals of maturation. The less aggressive child will more likely sabotage the ambitious goals his parents set for him, and defer outright rejection of maturity until the parents' death.

REFERENCES AND BIBLIOGRAPHY

1. Ausubel, D. P.: Problems of adolescent adjustment. Bulletin Natl. Assn. Secondary School Principals, *34*:1–84, 1950.
2. Ausubel, D. P.: Appraisal of current and residual parent-youth conflict in adolescence. Unpublished manuscript, 1951.
3. Ausubel, D. P.: *Ego Development and the Personality Disorders.* New York: Grune and Stratton, 1952.
4. Barker, R. G., Wright, B. A., and Gonick, M. R.: *Adjustment to Physical Handicap and Illness,* Bulletin No. 55. New York: Social Science Research Council, 1946.

5. Block, V. L.: Conflicts of adolescents with their mothers. J. Abnorm. & Soc. Psychol., *32*:192–206, 1937.
6. Blos, P.: *The Adolescent Personality: A Study of Individual Behavior*. New York: Appleton-Century, 1941.
7. Bühler, C.: "The Social Development of the Child," in *Handbook of Child Psychology* (C. Murchison, ed.). Worcester, Mass.: Clark University Press, 1931.
8. Cunningham, R.: *Understanding Group Behavior of Boys and Girls*. New York: Teachers College, Columbia University, 1951.
9. Dale, E.: *Children's Attendance at Motion Pictures*. New York: Macmillan, 1935.
10. Dimock, H. S.: *Rediscovering the Adolescent*. New York: Association Press, 1937.
11. English, O. S.: Adolescence. Philad. Med., *42*:1025–1026, 1947.
12. Frank, L. K.: "The Adolescent and the Family," in *Adolescence*, 43rd Yearbook, Natl. Soc. Stud. Educ. Chicago: University of Chicago Press, 1944.
13. Gabriel, A.: A study of the attitudes of parents of adolescents. Univ. Iowa Stud. in Child Welfare, *17*:129–156, 1939.
14. Gardner, G. E.: The mental health of normal adolescents. Ment. Hyg., *31*: 529–540, 1947.
15. Hackett, C. G.: An opinion polling technique in a study of parent-child relationships. Purdue Univ. Stud. Higher Educ., No. 75, 1951.
16. Havighurst, R. J., Robinson, M. Z., and Dorr, M.: The development of the ideal self in childhood and adolescence. J. Educ. Res., *40*:241–257, 1946.
17. Jersild, A. T. et al.: *Child Development and the Curriculum*. New York: Teachers College, Columbia University, 1946.
18. Komarovsky, M.: *The Unemployed Man and His Family*. New York: Dryden, 1940.
19. Koskas, R.: L'adolescent et sa famille. Enfance, *2*:68–71, 1949.
20. Krout, M. H. and Stagner, R.: Personality development in radicals. Sociometry, *2*:31–46, 1939.
21. Leighton, D. and Kluckhohn, C.: *Children of the People*. Cambridge, Mass.: Harvard University Press, 1947.
22. Leonard, E. A.: *Concerning Our Girls and What They Tell Us*. New York: Teachers College, Columbia University, 1930.
23. Levy, D. M.: *Maternal Overprotection*. New York: Columbia University Press, 1943.
24. Lewin, K., Lippitt, R., and White, R. K.: Patterns of aggressive behavior in experimentally created "social climates." J. Soc. Psychol., *10*:271–279, 1939.
25. Lucht, K. G.: Relationships among socio-political attitudes of adolescents, socio-political attitudes of their parents, and some measures of adolescent hostility. Microfilm Abst., *11*:743–744, 1951.
26. Lynd, R. S. and Lynd, H. M.: *Middletown*. New York: Harcourt, Brace, 1929.
27. Mackenzie, G. N.: "Implications for Teachers and Counselors," in *Adolescence*, 43rd Yearbook, Natl. Soc. Stud. Educ. Chicago: University of Chicago Press, 1944.

28. Messerschmidt, R.: The suggestibility of boys and girls between the ages of six and sixteen years. J. Genet. Psychol., *43*:422–437, 1933.
29. Meyers, C. E.: Emancipation of adolescents from parental control. Nervous Child, *5*:251–262, 1946.
30. Ojemann, R. H.: The measurement of attitude toward self-reliance. Univ. Iowa Stud. Child Welfare, *10*:101–111, 1934.
31. Remmers, H. H., Whisler, L., and Duwald, V. F.: Neurotic indicators at the adolescent level. J. Soc. Psychol., *9*:17–24, 1938.
32. Sherman, A. W.: Emancipation status of college students. J. Genet. Psychol., *68*:171–180, 1946.
33. Silverman, H. L.: The Philosophy and psychology of existentialism. Psychiat. Quart. Supp. *21*:10–16, 1947.
34. Stagner, R.: Studies of aggressive social attitudes: III. The role of personal and family scores. J. Soc. Psychol., *20*:129–140, 1944.
35. Stevens, G. C.: Autobiographical material concerning the childhood environments and the effects on the after-adjustments of 100 recidivists and 100 college freshmen. Am. J. Orthopsychiat., *2*:279–303, 1932.
36. Stone, C. P. and Barker, R. G.: The attitudes and interests of premenarcheal and postmenarcheal girls. J. Genet. Psychol., *54*:27–71, 1939.
37. Stott, L. H.: Personality Development in Farm, Small-Town and City Children, Res. Bulletin No. 114. Univ. Nebraska Agric. Exper. Station, 1939.
38. Stott, L. H.: Adolescent dislikes regarding parental behavior, and their significance. J. Genet. Psychol., *57*:393–414, 1940.
39. Stott, L. H.: Home punishment of adolescents, J. Genet. Psychol., *57*:415–428, 1940.
40. Stott, L. H.: Parental attitudes of farm, town, and city parents in relation to certain personality adjustments in their children. J. Soc. Psychol., *11*:325–329, 1940.
41. Symonds, P. M.: A study of parental acceptance and rejection. Amer. J. Orthopsychiat., *8*:679–688, 1938.
42. Symonds, P. M.: *The Psychology of Parent-Child Relationships.* New York: Appleton-Century, 1939.
43. Terman, L. M.: *Psychological Factors in Marital Happiness.* New York: McGraw-Hill, 1938.
44. Tryon, C. M.: *U C Inventory I, Social and Emotional Adjustment.* Berkeley, Calif.: University of Calif. Press, 1939.
45. Wittman, M. P. and Huffman, A. V.: A comparative study of developmental, adjustment, and personality characteristics of psychotic, psychoneurotic, delinquent, and normally-adjusted teen-age youths. J. Genet. Psychol., *66*:167–182, 1945.
46. Zachry, C. B.: "Preparing Youth To Be Adults," in *Adolescence,* 43rd Yearbook, Natl. Soc. Stud. Educ. Chicago: University of Chicago Press, 1944.
47. Zucker, H. J.: *Affectional Identification and Delinquency.* New York: Archives of Psychology (Columbia University), 1943.

CHAPTER 9

Moral and Religious Development

PART OF THE PROCESS of personality maturation involves various shifts in the individual's organization of moral (and religious) values and behavior. Our first task in this chapter will be to review certain *general* changes in the nature, organization, and psychological basis of moral values, changes attributable to adolescent development. Second, we shall be concerned with personality and social factors accounting for individual and subcultural differences in moral values. Third, we shall examine some of the determinants and consequences of the social estimate of an adolescent's character, his reputation. Last, we shall make an inventory of some of the specific moral and religious beliefs of adolescents in our culture and of their relationship to behavior.

GENERAL DEVELOPMENTAL CHANGES DURING ADOLESCENCE

The term "conscience" is an abstraction referring to the cognitive-emotional organization of an individual's moral values and to the psychological processes on which that organization is based. Conscience presupposes an internalization of moral values from standards in the social environment, and the acceptance of a sense of obligation * or responsibility to conform to them. Also necessary for the functioning of conscience is the ability to anticipate the

---

* The sense of obligation is itself a moral value, and must undergo internalization in order to be stable and effective in regulating behavior. But it is also the core value of an individual's moral system which not only makes possible the implementation of other values but also gives generality to moral behavior. For example, the disposition to refrain from committing an act of dishonesty depends on more than the strength of the value of honesty in a given context. Equally important is the strength of the moral obligation to abide by *all* internalized values.[2]

consequences of behavior, and to exercise inhibitory control to bring these anticipated consequences into line with perceived obligation. When behavior is not appropriately regulated to conform to moral obligation, a special kind of negative self-evaluation occurs known as *guilt*. Guilt consists of feelings of shame, "self-disgust, self-contempt, remorse, and various characteristic visceral and vasomotor responses." [2] Since guilt is an extremely uncomfortable, self-punishing, and anxiety-producing phenomenon, guilt avoidance is a strong motivating force to keep behavior consistent with moral obligation. However, guilt cannot be experienced in the absence of the capacity for realistically appraising one's intentions and behavior in the light of internalized moral principles. Conscience, therefore, remains at a rudimentary level until the self-critical faculty is developed.

But conscience is no more an inherent given than any other aspect of personality.

> It shifts with changes in the parent-child relationship, in social expectations, perceptual ability and cognitive organization, and with maturational advances in biosocial competence and goal structure; and in turn it has an important influence on all of the latter aspects of ego development.[2]

The nature of conscience necessarily changes with personality development since all of its component psychological processes undergo developmental change. Intellectual growth affects the generality, consistency, and abstract quality of moral values, and sharpens the self-critical faculty. The widening of the social horizon, and various shifts in allegiance and dependency modify values and the basis on which moral obligation is sustained. In this section we shall examine several major developments in the organization of conscience that begin with the onset of desatellization and are consummated during the adolescent period.

Greater Independence in Assimilation of Values

The increased importance of the incorporative and exploratory orientations during adolescence (see pp. 195–199) brings about a change in the basis on which moral values are accepted. Personal loyalty to parents becomes a less impelling motive to accept and abide by moral values than considerations of equity and ego enhancement; and satisfaction of these considerations demands much more critical examination of values and much less reliance on prestige authority. This is reflected in part in the greater liberality, tolerance, and flexibility of moral outlook that takes place during adolescence,[53, 58] indicating some degree of liberation from uncritical acceptance of dogmatic teachings. Fewer adolescents than sixth-graders disapprove of such activities (traditionally regarded as wrong by stern or "old-fashioned" moralists) as smoking, card-playing, and dancing, but more disapprove of such unfavorable personality traits as conceit.[53] Not only does the percentage of individuals using alcoholic beverages increase from age 11 to 24, but the percentage of those who disapprove of drinking also declines—among drinkers and non-drinkers as well.[58]

Essentially, however, there is less rejection of old moral values than a change in the basis on which they are accepted. Adolescence is not a period of moral upheaval. The basic moral values of our culture are inculcated in the early years, and show little variability in degree of acceptance from childhood to adult life.[14, 66] However, adolescents are more likely to give their own rather than conventional reasons for disapproving of such practices as lying and stealing,[14, 61] and place equity in interpersonal relationships above such considerations as fear of "getting caught." [14]

Continuity in moral structure (despite desatellization and shifts in allegiance) is maintained by the tendency of the peer group to adhere closely to the basic values of the social class in which it holds membership.[59] Furthermore, values assimilated on the basis of satellizing loyalties are remarkably durable and resist displacement. To meet the requirements of emancipation it is enough to give acceptable and independent reasons for holding these values rather than to reject them outright. On the basis of free volitional choice alone, for example, it would certainly be difficult to explain why 81 per cent of adolescents join the same church as their parents.[4]

And, finally, the adolescent's real independence in the choice of moral values is highly limited. It is true that he is liberated from slavish conformity to parental standards. But at the same time he gains a new master who demands even greater conformity and has the power to enforce it, the peer group. The difference is that he conforms to peer group expectations because he consciously recognizes the expediency of so doing rather than because he implicitly believes in the validity of the values he espouses.

Values Acquire a Wider Social Base

Concomitant with resatellization (in cultures characterized by age-mate socialization) is a gradual broadening of the source from which values are acquired. Increased exposure to new social environments, coupled with a loss of subservience to parental values, enables the adolescent to perceive the standards of his home as merely special variants of subcultural norms. With increasing age, his values tend to become more typical of the culture at large but less typical of the values held by his parents. Remmers and Weltman found less correspondence between the attitudes of older adolescents and their parents than between younger adolescents and their parents.[56] The degree of resemblance between attitudes of parents and adolescents, however, varies considerably depending on the particular issue involved and on occupational level.[48] In general, parental influence upon attitudes is greater in lower socio-economic groups, and diminishes slightly with increasing age.[48] At the same time the conformity aspects of personality, as measured by Rorschach responses, increase with age,[65] and children's values tend to approximate more closely the adult norm with each developmental level.[14, 53] Also, as already noted, parents decline in popularity as models as children enter adolescence,[23] and other visible adults and historical and public figures are chosen more frequently.[23, 25]

Changes Reflective of Intellectual Maturation

Growth in cognitive capacity alone accounts for several significant changes in character organization during adolescence. For one thing, moral concepts, like all other concepts, become more abstract. This enables moral behavior to acquire greater generality and consistency from situation to situation, since abstraction presupposes the identification of essential common elements. Hartshorne and May, for example, using objective tests of character traits, found a significant trend with increasing age toward greater consistency of moral behavior.[22]

Growth in intellectual ability * also makes possible the more critical, objective, and rational approach to moral values that dis-

---

* This, of course, is only a subsidiary factor. The more crucial variables here are the influences that bring about desatellization.

tinguishes the incorporative and exploratory orientations from the satellizing orientation. And by sharpening the self-critical faculty * (making possible the perception of finer discrepancies between precept and conduct), it leads to over-all strengthening of moral obligation through the guilt-avoidance mechanism. It is obvious, however, that the growth of the self-critical faculty depends on more than intellectual capacity, since the ability to criticize others antecedes the development of self-critical ability. The capacity for judging one's own behavior on the same terms as the behavior of others represents a signal degree of liberation from infantile egocentricity.

Decline in Moral Absolutism

By "moral absolutism," Piaget [51] means the tendency of the young child to accept rules as self-evident, axiomatic givens rather than as human contrivances to facilitate interpersonal relationships. This inherent sacredness of moral standards depends in part upon a perception of parents as infallible and omniscient beings. It begins to break down as parents become devalued, as the child realizes that there are other authorities, various moral alternatives, and different versions of the truth. As he joins older peer groups in which roles and relationships are clearly differentiated and in which he himself takes part in the formulation of rules, a functional rather than a "sacred" concept of moral law emerges. Because the "group is never dignified by the same halo of sanctity surrounding his parents . . . the child can adopt the exploratory orientation in his peer group long before he dares to do so at home." [2]

The extended period of peer group socialization in which the adolescent can experiment with moral law of his own making undoubtedly facilitates the development of a functional morality. However, the elaboration of new standards generally stays within the framework of values of the social class reference groups to which adolescents owe allegience. [59] Furthermore "despite greater flexibility in the group evolution of new values, once these are determined more complete conformity is demanded than in the adult culture." [2]

The development of a functional morality is facilitated also by the availability of alternative moral standards in a heterogeneous

* Dimock [11] found a marked increase in the self-critical attitudes of boys from ages 12 to 16.

society. But this is not an indispensible condition: adolescents in a simple American Indian culture develop a "rational morality based on . . . actual human needs and social relationships."[49] It suffices, therefore,

> to have an exploratory and problem-solving approach unencumbered by rigid adherence to a traditional code which has lost contact with actual needs in interpersonal situations and relies instead upon the self-evident rightness of a sacred authority.[2]

Increased Reciprocity of Moral Obligation

Implicit in the satellizing orientation is the acceptance of unilateral obligation—as proof of personal loyalty—to abide by the values internalized from parents. There is as yet no notion of moral law as a system of reciprocal obligations; this arises as the individual assumes various roles in communal and group enterprises. Piaget[51] found that as children grow older they become increasingly desirous of interpersonal relationships based upon reciprocity. Such relationships can, of course, be established much more easily with peers than with elders.

The principle of reciprocity involves more than an expectation of bilaterality, that others have moral obligations toward oneself and vice versa. The individual must free himself from the egocentricity that does not enable him (a) to criticize himself on the same basis as he criticizes others; (b) to approach questions of equity on a detached, objective, and task-oriented basis; (c) to argue from the standpoint of another, or of an abstract proposition; and (d) to be aware of the needs and interests of others. There is general agreement that these capacities are expanded during the elementary school years and during adolescence, but most American researchers disagree with Piaget's view that older and younger children are qualitatively different in their egocentricity. There is little doubt, however, that "true liberation from egocentricity requires mutual respect and freedom to criticize in a climate of equality."[2]

Once the individual conceives of himself as an independent entity operating in a social community and acquires a sense of reciprocal obligation, he completes the process of transferring "his feeling of moral accountability from parents to the moral authority of society."[2]

Greater Expediency in Moral Standards

When the basis for moral values shifts from personal loyalty to ego enhancement (or the acquisition of primary status), it is inevitable that greater compromise of principle and reliance upon an approach of expediency occur. If conformity to group norms is the price of social acceptance, adherence to absolute standards of morality is extremely unrewarding. If "getting ahead" requires cutting moral corners, most individuals will yield to the pressure and develop a less stringent code of ethics. Two-thirds of junior high school students are willing to condone stealing under certain conditions (for example, from a public utility corporation), and only one-tenth are unqualifiedly opposed to it.[61] From the fifth to the twelfth grade there is a sharp rise in the percentage of children who justify "social lies." [67] The "double standard" of sexual morality was defended by over seventy per cent of college students at Syracuse University.[34] In the adolescent peer culture of Prairie City, Havighurst and Taba found that

> . . . accepting familiar stereotypes is one outstanding characteristic of [most] beliefs. . . . Individual positions deviating from the generally accepted code are feared and shunned. This is shown by hesitancy in expressing opinions contrary to common beliefs, and by approving wrong behavior if most of one's associates are involved in the act. There is a marked tendency to subordinate individually held positions to both adult and peer-group opinion, even when one's own positions are considered morally right.[24]

Despite the general trend toward greater expediency in moral judgments during adolescence, moral perfectionism is a characteristic adolescent phenomenon, especially in ascetic and overintellectual individuals.

> In some cases it is indicative of the naiveté, inexperience and impulsiveness of adolescents, and of the initial reaction to the shock of disenchantment upon being initiated into the corruption existing in certain areas of public life formerly believed to be sacrosanct. In other cases, however, it has the same significance as exaggerated cynicism, namely as a form of aggression against adult society, in which a strong motivational "set" exists to perceive all adult behavior in an unfavorable light. The cynical adolescent then proceeds to emulate and outdo the behavior he purports to perceive in adults, while the perfectionist in an orgy of self-righteousness sets himself up as a champion of truth and virtue against a hopelessly wicked world.[2]

Guilt Feelings in Relation to Age-Mate Socialization

In recent years several cultural anthropologists [38, 42, 43] have advanced the notion that a different type of relatively guiltless conscience operates under conditions in which an omnipotent parent does *not* personally administer the moral sanctions of the culture. Leighton and Kluckhohn,[38] for example, assert that among all Navaho age groups, "sensitivity to shame largely takes the place that remorse and self-punishment have in preventing anti-social conduct in white society." And Mead, in describing the moral behavior of adolescents in our culture who undergo peer-group rather than parent-regulated socialization states: "Shame, the agony of being found wanting and exposed to the disapproval of others, becomes a more prominent sanction behind conduct than guilt, the fear of not measuring up to the high standard which was represented by the parents." [42]

This point of view is based upon the psychoanalytic premise that a guilt-enforced conscience (superego) can only develop under certain specified conditions of the parent-child relationship: that the culture assign *qualitatively* different roles to parent and child, that the parent or parent surrogate *personally* enforce the moral code with appropriate rewards and punishments, and that the parent demand obedience as an inherent right and punish disobedience as morally *wrong* rather than as dangerous or inexpedient. It makes the further assumptions (a) that guilt feelings can *only* arise in response to an acknowledged violation of moral standards developed under the above conditions; (b) that "true" conscience is not operative unless moral behavior is enforced *only* by internal sanctions such as loyalty or fear of guilt; and (c) that guilt and shame are dichotomous.

Our analysis of the development of the satellizing, guilt-centered conscience has shown that only three developmental conditions are absolutely necessary: the internalization of moral values, the internalization of a feeling of obligation to abide by them, and the ability to perceive a discrepancy between one's conduct and one's values. Despite Leighton and Kluckhohn's denial of internalized moral values and obligations among the Navaho, their own descriptions of typical Navaho behavior assume that the individual strongly identifies with the moral code of his culture and recognizes obligations to conform to this code which are not *wholly* dependent upon social sanctions of reward and punishment.

A satellizing bond can also be established in relation to a group (peer group or extended family) as well as to single individuals. Although less intense, such bonds are nevertheless potent enough to induce guilt feelings when recognized moral values and obligations internalized from the group are violated. Neither is it necessary for the child to perceive the parent or the group as *qualitatively* superior or as entitled to implicit obedience, as long as they are endowed with sufficient prestige authority to structure an otherwise undifferentiated moral field. Furthermore, the distinction between quantitative and qualitative superiority is an abstraction devised by cultural anthropologists, the subtlety of which undoubtedly transcends the child's perceptual capacity at the age when his moral development is most influenced by the perception of adult superiority.

As pointed out, at no time are internal sanctions ever unreinforced by external restraints. Throughout life, from early childhood to old age, conscience is buttressed by external controls the importance of which fluctuates from one developmental level to the next. Hence, the assumption that true conscience cannot be operative if such other external sanctions as shame, expediency, ego enhancement, physical punishment, and supernatural retribution are simultaneously present, is purely gratuitous.

Mead's depreciation of the role of guilt in adolescence assumes that guilt feelings can arise only in an omnipotent parent-subservient child type of relationship. She ignores the facts that (a) the satellizing history of the individual is perpetuated by substrate representation in current personality organization (see pp. 183–184); (b) that ex-satellizers continue to form satellizing relationships during and after adolescence; and (c) that guilt can be experienced apart from a satellizing relationship provided genuine moral obligations are internalized.

The claim that shame replaces guilt as the chief moral sanction behind conduct in adolescence is based on the assumption that shame and guilt are mutually incompatible and dichotomous. Actually, shame is part of every guilt reaction although types of shame exist apart from guilt. The shame component of guilt is the negative self-evaluation that arises from an acknowledged violation of internalized moral obligation. Shame, however, can take place under *any* condition involving self-depreciation *vis-a-vis* the group. An individual may experience shame for violating a group norm (although no internalized moral obligations are involved) simply because he is exposed to public scorn and ridicule. But the mere fact that guiltless shame is invoked as a moral sanction does not mean that guilt and the shame of guilt are not also operative in this same situation.

FACTORS INFLUENCING INDIVIDUAL DIFFERENCES IN ADOLESCENT MORAL DEVELOPMENT

The preceding review of changes in moral development in adolescence does not take into account differences among individual adolescents. Despite the developmental pressures being uniform for all individuals sharing a common social environment, "character is formed differently in different personalities." [24] In the first section we shall be concerned mainly with personality differences that influence different types of moral development, and in the following section shall consider some socio-economic factors relevant to the same relationship.

There are no adequate reasons to believe that pubescence per se influences the course of moral development. Stone and Barker did find significant differences in maturity of moral judgments between pre- and postmenarcheal girls; [62] but these differences undoubtedly reflected the spurt in social maturity accompanying pubescence rather than any physiological correlate of pubescence itself. Dimock [11] did not find any correlation between physical maturity and moral knowledge in boys.

Personality Type

"Good character (or bad character) may have a very different meaning in the lives of two individuals when seen in the total configuration of their personalities. . . . It is influenced by a different set of causative factors and by a different set of learning experiences." [24] We may reasonably expect to find important differences in moral development between satellizers and non-satellizers, and between the various subtypes making up each of these primary personality types.

The non-satellizer obviously fails to undergo the various changes in conscience development associated with satellization, and he is similarly spared the changes resulting from desatellization. His moral development, therefore, involves more continuity from one stage to the next. During early and middle childhood,

> instead of a sense of obligation developing in relation to a general attitude of value subservience, loyalty, and need for approval and retention of derived status, the non-satellizer continues to conform to parental standards for the same expediential reasons as during infancy. He is sensitive to prestige suggestion at the hands of parents, but only because he recognizes the latter's objectively greater knowledge and competence—not because he is motivated by a strong need to unconditionally reflect their value judgments. Fear of deprivation and loss of succorance rather than guilt avoidance keep him in line and check the overt expression of his hostility and aggression. Moral obligations are assimilated on a selective basis only, that is, if they are perceived as leading to ego enhancement.[2]

During late childhood, the non-satellizer becomes capable of internalizing moral values and obligations on the basis of the exploratory orientation. Unhampered by satellizing loyalties, he finds it easier to grasp functional concepts of moral law based on equity and reciprocal obligations. In this way, too, he acquires the prerequisites for a guilt-governed conscience. But the stability of moral obligations that circumvent a preliminary history of satellization (prior to assimilation in final adult form) is highly precarious because

> (a) infantile irresponsibility has never been attenuated by strong, emotionally charged feelings of obligation in relation to significant individuals in the child's interpersonal world; and (b) powerful needs for ego enhancement are often in conflict with the content and goals of ethical norms.[2]

Under such conditions, moral obligations are seldom repudiated outright; this would require direct and inexpedient conflict with cultural sanctions. However, two less drastic alternatives are available: (1) indirect evasion of the demands of conscience and of the punishment of guilt when the needs of ego aggrandizement are too strong to be denied; and (2) buttressing conscience by the mechanism of reaction-formation when moral obligations are too solidly entrenched to be circumvented.

Moral obligation may be evaded in two ways: (a) by selectively inhibiting the self-critical faculty so that, when convenient, even glaring discrepancies between precept and practice cannot be perceived; and (b) by claiming superior status so that one is *above* the law for *ordinary* people. This concept has been institutionalized in justifying the exploitation, enslavement, and extermination of "inferior" races.

Reaction-formation rigidly suppresses motives that are at variance with internalized moral obligations and substitutes more acceptable motives in their place. Nevertheless, many loopholes for surreptitious circumvention are still present. Suppression does not imply rejection and can never be wholly complete. Antisocial trends can also be expressed under the guise of lofty ideals. At the very best, the moral behavior of the non-satellizer

> becomes unspontaneous, stereotyped and unduly circumscribed. . . . Awareness of the underlying strength of unacceptable attitudes encourages the erection of exaggerated defenses. Afraid to trust himself at all, iron-clad security is sought in rigid tabus instituted against the undesirable behavior, accompanied by a self-conscious over-emphasis of the antithetical moral trait. Moral judgment passed on others' conduct tends to be formal and absolutistic rather than related to the relevant situational and personality context in which . . . the behavior could be more fairly evaluated for ethical content.[2]

The overvalued child who has never felt much pressure to conform to parental standards frequently regards himself as immune from ordinary moral obligations. The rejected child, on the other hand, is not likely to claim such unique exemptions since he has been subjected to rigorous discipline. In most instances he will acquire a strong rational conscience, buttressed by reaction-formation, and permitting occasional moral lapses through impairment of the self-critical faculty. However, the concomitance of harsh rejection by parents and extreme self-assertiveness in the child may result in the child's repudiating the entire pattern of parental moral values; this type of delinquent child is known as the aggressive antisocial psychopath. When rejection is expressed in parental neglect and self-love, the child displaces the hostility he feels for his parents onto others. Such behavior is reinforced by the parents' tendency to condone it as long as they are not disturbed. Delinquents report more often than normal children that their parents are neglectful and lacking in solicitude and affection.[20]

> On the positive side, however, the rejected child possesses a latent capacity for forming satellizing-like relationships which enable him to experience the type of guilt feelings that occur in normally satellizing children.[2]

Among *satellizers*, aberrations in conscience development are generally less severe. The most serious problem is presented by the underdominated child who has great difficulty acquiring a sense of moral obligation. To begin with, he is not required to inhibit hedonistic motivations or to curb aggressive impulses. The limits of unacceptable behavior are poorly defined and inadequately or inconsistently enforced. Second, like the overvalued child, he is treated as a specially privileged person exempt from the usual responsibilities toward others, and is not encouraged to develop a realistic self-critical faculty. Fortunately, however, unlike the overvalued child, the motivation for immoral behavior is more likely to lie in hedonistic self-indulgence than in unprincipled ego enhancement at the expense of others. Also, there is always the possibility of his forming satellizing relationships to teachers and group leaders who are able to provide greater firmness and consistency of discipline.

The chief difficulty for overprotected and overdominated children, lies in transferring feelings of moral obligation from parents to society (see p. 240) and in arriving at independent value judgments. The situation leads to no serious consequences as long as the parent is alive and does not subscribe to antisocial attitudes. However, if the parent is a moral deviant, uncritical loyalty of the child can lead to delinquent behavior; whereas the death or removal of the parent can create a vacuum in moral responsibility. But again this is not apt to be serious since infantile irresponsibility has been attenuated in satellization, and there is no driving need to further ego enhancement at any price.

Using a case history and clinical conference approach, Havighurst and Taba [24] analyzed character differences corresponding to five different personality types, submissive, adaptive, self-directive, defiant, and unadjusted individuals. The "submissive person," always concerned whether he is conforming to the expectations of authority figures, corresponds to our overdominated satellizer. "Adaptive persons," who "take on the beliefs and principles of their social environment readily without much question and without much inner commitment," appear to be either mild and well-emancipated satellizers, or non-satellizers with a poorly developed rational conscience. They are not troubled by deep-seated loyalties either to persons or to abstract principles. "The self-directive" individual, highly scrupulous, self-critical, and independent in his moral behavior, is generally a non-satellizer who has adopted a strong exploratory approach to moral problems; less frequently he may be an individualistic and highly emancipated satellizer. The "defiant" person, who has "rejected the generally approved moral beliefs and principles," corresponds to the rebellious, overdominated child, to the harshly rejected or neglected self-assertive individual, or to the overvalued child rejected during late childhood.

> In the stable social environment of Prairie City, where middle-class ideals are the accepted pattern, there is not much difference in the moral behavior of the self-directive, the adaptive and the submissive persons. In general they behave honestly, responsibly, and loyally. Their reputations and their characters [are] acceptable for they are reasonably well adjusted to the environment in which they live. Certainly it is to be expected that a large majority of people will show good moral behavior if they live in an environment that rewards conformity.[24]

"But what if these boys and girls are placed in a different social environment? What will be the effect upon moral character?"[24] The self-directive person will continue to rely upon his rational conscience, and the submissive person will either adhere to the primary code of values learned from his parents or attach himself in a subservient role to some new authority. The defiant person remains a social rebel and moral outcast in any environment because of his underlying need for vengeance and the expression of hostility. The adaptive person, on the other hand, having no strong moral commitments and an intense need for either social applause or social approval, alters his moral behavior to meet the changed expectations of the new environment.

Socio-Economic Factors

In addition to differences in character development attributable to personality make-up, individuals differ depending on the "value systems of the social groups" to which they belong or to which they relate themselves positively or negatively.[24]

> The values held by the family, by the dominant groups and institutions in the community, and by persons in positions of authority and high status constitute the "moral climate" in which a young person grows up. These groups and persons are in a position to punish undesirable conduct and to reward desirable conduct, and their expectations have much to do with the standards of behavior developed by the individual.[24]

Within a given social class environment, the attitudes toward sex morality,[35] aggression, honesty, thrift, community responsibility [24, 27] and political philosophy [9] have a certain consistency. But, naturally, complete social class homogeneity in moral belief or behavior never exists. Considerable interaction and diffusion among classes occur, generally proceeding from above downward. Hence, heterogeneity within the lower social classes tends to be greater than in the upper classes.[24, 27]

> Where a single institution such as the high school becomes the common meeting ground of a number of subcultural groups, the moral standards of the resulting peer society reflect the morality of the middle-class which controls it. Adolescents from other social class backgrounds must either adapt to these standards or choose to remain on the periphery of social acceptance.[2]

Some of the seeming homogeneity in moral outlook among different social classes, however, is more apparent than real when one distinguishes "between official and actual" ideologies.[24]

> The differences in moral values among the various social classes are probably greater in practice than in words. People all up and down the social scale in Prairie City tend to agree verbally with an official moral ideology from which their actual moral behavior departs in various ways.[24]

The gap between practice and professed belief is probably smallest in middle-class children since parents, school, church, and community agencies all cooperate in enforcing the official ideology. In lower-class homes, however, parents are more lax in executing the middle-class mores which they incompletely accept but find convenient to profess in public. One outcome of this inconsistency is a more authoritarian and inflexible approach by lower-class children to such moral problems as lying, stealing, and obedience.[21] This indicates, perhaps, that "values which are accepted only half-heartedly and under inconsistent circumstances must be adhered to rigidly if they are to be maintained at all." [2]

The phenomenon of moral confusion is not restricted to any social class, but is a general characteristic of our rapidly changing culture. Genuine concern for traditional moral values is disappearing at an alarming rate as greater cultural emphasis is placed on achieving immediate material advantage. Precept and practice drift farther apart when expediency, opportunism, and conformity become the chief passports to success. Under such circumstances formal appearances become more important than content, and the letter of the law replaces its ostensible intentions. "Anything goes which can be provided with a veneer of legitimacy that protects the individual from legal reprisal." [2]

Why is it that such a "selective morality" [29] (which condemns an unethical practice that is illegal, yet sanctions a very similar practice that violates no existing statute) can be so easily assimilated despite its glaring inconsistencies. Simply because our modern youth has

> . . . developed an extremely high tolerance for moral ambiguity and confusion. Because of the prestige suggestion inherent in the operation of social norms, they are assimilatable . . . in such a way that their incompatibility is never perceived; it is presumed by the perceiver that inconsistency in cultural values is inconceivable, and, therefore, an advance "set" exists to perceive such values as consistent regardless of manifest content—even if logic-tight compartments must be constructed to prevent critical comparisons from being made.[2]

As yet no research has been done on the effect of this type of moral climate on the conscience development of children and adolescents. Enough is known, however, about primitive cultures such as the Dobu,[5] Manus,[41] and Betsileo,[33] in which comparable moral practices have been institutionalized, to predict that human beings can perceive such a state of affairs as perfectly natural and can adapt their value systems to conform to it. But while we are still in the transitional stage of this social revolution in moral values, considerable variability will prevail in the reaction of single individuals depending on their perceptual acuity, their susceptibility to prestige suggestion, their need for ego enhancement, and the strength of their moral convictions.

Many individuals will fail to see that any problem of moral inconsistency exists. Others will be acutely disillusioned, but the degree to which they will adapt to the requirements of the situation will depend on the kind of conscience they possess and on their need for extrinsic status. This type of moral climate is in a sense made to order for the ego needs of the non-satellizer, except when he happens to have a strong rational conscience. The satellizer,* on the other hand, who perceives what is going on

> . . . is unable to make the required adaptations without experiencing feelings of conflict, guilt, self-reproach, and resentment toward a culture that requires such moral compromises for the sake of survival and legitimate ego enhancement. He feels impelled to crush all vestiges of moral feeling in himself because he perceives them as a handicap in a jungle existence. . . . But try as he may he cannot stifle his conscience completely. In desperation he may adopt a double moral code: one for his friends and family, another for his colleagues and competitors. But in any case guilt feelings exercise considerable restraint over his behavior so that his violations of the moral code are generally less flagrant and more defensible than the non-satellizer's. His immorality more usually serves the interests of survival rather than catering to the predatory needs of aggressive ego aggrandizement.[2]

THE MORAL REPUTATION OF ADOLESCENTS

Reputation is the social aspect of character. It reflects a community perception or evaluation of an individual's moral constitution. Hence it bears the same relationship to character that any social perception bears to its evocative stimulus. Such perceptions

> are necessarily subjective, distorted by social class and other types of bias, and vitiated by the distinction between private and public aspects of personality; and since reputation is largely based upon the latter aspects, it mirrors to an unknown extent the ability of an individual to accurately perceive and simulate the behavioral traits expected of him.[2]

As Havighurst and Taba point out, persons with good reputations do not necessarily have good character on an "internal basis," stable character, good motivation for character, or good character without anxiety and worry.[24] Reputation and moral beliefs are not highly correlated.[24]

Nevertheless the significance of reputation is not to be minimized.

* The quoted paragraph applies also to the non-satellizer with a strong rational conscience.

Whereas character may be intrinsically more important in its *actual* impact on interpersonal relationships, reputation is the more proximate variable that enters into group relations. An individual is known not by his character but by his reputation, even though his capacity to influence friends, relatives, associates, and social events is *ultimately* a function of his character. And despite the various biases that enter into the determination of reputation, it enjoys considerable stability through the course of years and a fair amount of generality over observers.[24]

Adolescent reputation is moderately correlated with social class, those in the upper social classes generally enjoying higher reputations than those in the lower social classes.[24] But this relationship is less a function of prevailing stereotypes about the moral character of the various social classes than a function of conformity to school requirements.[24] The correlation between reputation and school achievement is higher than the correlation of either with social class.[24] Thus, individuals who accept the central middle-class value of school achievement enjoy high reputation regardless of their social class membership, although it is true that identification with this value is greater in the upper social classes. For the very same reason, adaptive, submissive, and self-directive persons have high character reputations, whereas defiant and unadjusted persons enjoy poor reputations. Religious observance is also a "good index of middle-class morality" and is positively correlated with character reputation.[24]

THE MORAL BELIEFS OF ADOLESCENTS

Expressed belief is probably a more valid reflection of an individual's moral structure than is reputation. Since expressed beliefs obviously do not correspond completely to actual beliefs because of understandable desires for self-embellishment, there is a widespread tendency to regard them as inferior to conduct as indices of character.

> But are not most persons highly motivated to obtain "good" reputations, which means that they frequently will *behave* in accordance with perceived expectations rather than with their own moral values? As a matter of fact, many individuals will often express their true feelings verbally, whereas in situations calling for translation of same into action they are constrained by fear of reprisal.[2]

General Characteristics

The moral values of our culture are implanted early in life. Hence, studies of developmental changes in beliefs fail to show startling changes as children enter adolescence. When change occurs it is more striking in actual conduct as opposed to mere verbal statement of belief.[58] Traditional beliefs need not be changed when they require no supporting behavior, even if they are not in accord with actual sentiments. But when such beliefs demand self-denial (abstinence from alcohol, church attendance), developmental shifts toward greater liberalism take place.[58]

As could be readily anticipated,

the moral beliefs of adolescents in Prairie City are strongly conditioned by their families, the community mores, religion and peer influence. . . . The influence of the school affects primarily the sense of responsibility and honesty; it is less effective as far as loyalty, moral courage, and friendliness are concerned.[24]

Less easily predictable was the finding that in Prairie City

moral beliefs are formed by accumulating reactions to immediate situations, not by a conscious formulation of a generalized code of conduct. This reflects the fact that the teaching of what is right and wrong is done with reference to isolated, concrete acts of behavior; relatively little effort is made to help young people generalize from these situations or to help them develop a coherent moral philosophy. The development of a personal and rational code, when it does take place, grows out of the accidents of personal make-up and patterns of adjustment.[24]

Thus, although there is a fair amount of generality among moral beliefs ("subjects who are high on one trait tend also to be high on others, and vice versa"), many inconsistencies between beliefs point up the lack of a sufficiently generalized code of ethics.[24]

The trend toward greater conformity to group norms in adolescence is reflected in the tendency to accept "familiar stereotypes . . . requiring little thought or analysis" [24] and to avoid conflict situations. At the age of sixteen

the ability to apply moral beliefs to an increasing range of conflicting life situations is quite undeveloped. . . . These subjects see the more obvious lines of action but seem at a loss whenever a subtle weighing of values is called for. They find conflicts hard to face; they tend to solve conflicts by using slogans rather than by using concepts of the relative significance of values.[24]

Nevertheless, Havighurst and Taba take a hopeful view of adolescent moral behavior:

> Most of these young people seem to be eager to respond to moral values. Even those who rebel against their environment seem to cherish an inward ideal of desirable conduct. It seems, therefore, that rebellion and bad conduct are usually rooted in causes other than rejection of moral values themselves.[24]

Beliefs, Knowledge, and Intelligence

Since values obviously have a cognitive aspect, we could reasonably anticipate that they would be influenced both by intelligence and by moral knowledge. However, these two variables become significantly related to moral beliefs only when they fall below a critical minimal level. Beyond this minimal degree of intellectual ability required for acquiring acceptable values, personality and motivational factors are the truly important variables. Thus, both IQ and school achievement are only poorly correlated with measures of moral belief.[24] Moral knowledge bears a similar relationship to beliefs, and is related to intelligence, socio-economic status, and the moral knowledge scores of associates.[11]

Beliefs, Character, and Conduct

The *actual* moral beliefs of an individual are the truest measures of his character. If they could be validly ascertained it would certainly be found that they are significantly related to conduct. The widespread opinion that belief and conduct are unrelated springs from: (a) the confusion between moral belief and moral knowledge; (b) the confusion between *expressed* and *true* beliefs; and (c) the confusion between deliberate insincerity, on the one hand, and actual lack of discriminative ability, on the other, as a determinant of the discrepancy between belief and conduct.

Moral knowledge involves only the cognitive aspect of belief, and is relatively minor in the total configuration of variables impinging on its evolution. Scores on moral knowledge tests are not highly correlated with conduct as measured by objective performance tests of character,[22] and these tests are unable to differentiate between delinquent and non-delinquent boys.[3] Such scores are also less highly correlated than intelligence test scores with conduct.[22] This would indicate that intelligence influences conduct not only by affecting moral knowledge but also in some extraneous manner, that is, "intelligent children have less reason to cheat in order to do well in school work, and are more apt to perceive the conditions when cheating might prove dangerous." [2]

Another reason for the apparent discrepancy between belief and conduct is that either expressed belief or behavior may be insincere (not reflective of *true* belief) for reasons of justifiable expediency. First, behavior may be congruent with true if not with expressed belief; and second, it may be only phenotypically at variance with true belief under conditions of duress. When the disparity between belief and conduct is not attributable to legitimate expediency, it indicates that the reprehensible behavior reflects the dominant belief that actually exists, regardless of the verbal form it takes.

Lastly, conduct may be inconsistent with belief not because of a deliberate attempt at dissimulation by the individual, but (a) because of cognitive limitations in logic, insufficient generalization of moral values, and inability to apply beliefs to real life problems; and (b) because of institutionalized inconsistencies in cultural values that the individual is either unable to perceive or obliged to accept.

Specific Beliefs and Attitudes

Prejudices. By the time children reach adolescence, racial and ethnic prejudices are well-established. Although it is true that preferences of school children for their own racial and ethnic groups increase from the first to the sixth grade, considerable variability is present.[36, 45, 46] After the sixth grade, however, homogeneity of attitude increases;[36] and by the twelfth grade, preference for own racial group is practically uniform.[36]

The primary effect of adolescence on prejudices is to draw caste and class lines more sharply. Adolescents take on the actual interpersonal attitudes of their class reference groups and *behave* as their elders do. Before this time, a certain amount of adult indulgence is shown toward manifestations of childish tolerance; children are still operating in their own world of values and are not, so to speak, "playing for keeps." Beginning with adolescence, however, they are expected to conform to adult social prejudices and to "watch their step" if they expect to succeed in life. The supporting climate of public opinion is the crucial factor. Northern college students who study in Southern universities gradually become more and more similar to native Southerners in their attitudes toward the Negro.[60] Taboos against intermarriage across religious lines are well-established by high school age and in general reflect social opinion.[15]

In relation to such pressures, considerations of rationality are totally irrelevant. At the same time that prejudicial *behavior* in choice situations increases, the attitudes (intellectual judgments) of white children toward Negroes become more tolerant.[45] Education does not reduce the incidence of anti-Semitic attitudes,[8] but the reasons given for intolerant attitudes toward national groups become more sophisticated and more highly rationalized with increasing age.[44] Interfaith education on an impersonal and intellectual level does not reduce prejudices, but the discussion of personal experiences and attitudes is effective in reducing these.[32]

Superstitions. A diminishing prevalence of superstitious belief from the seventh to the ninth grade,[7] from high school to college,[39] and from one level of college to the next [13, 68] reflects the increased intellectual sophistication accompanying adolescence. The decline in superstitious belief is a function of the general rise in level of intellectual sophistication paralleling school instruction rather than a function of increasing chronological or mental age.[7] Educated adults unschooled in the physical sciences make as many animistic interpretations of natural phenomena as children.[50] High school students who prefer books on science also have fewer superstitions than those who prefer fiction.[40] Significantly, superstitions that are culturally anachronistic (beliefs in luck charms, witchcraft, and evil spirits) are least often believed,[39] whereas others less antagonistic to prevailing thought (animistic, supernatural, and teleological conceptions of causality; astrology; and phrenology) enjoy the greatest degree of acceptance.[39, 64]

Traditional Moral Virtues. Using a questionnaire and a Life Problems test, Havighurst and Taba undertook to ascertain what the concepts of honesty, responsibility, moral courage, loyalty, and friendliness meant to sixteen-year-olds in Prairie City.[24]

The notions of friendliness emphasized amiability, popularity, politeness, willingness to do favors for others, and having many friends. At least on a verbal level, loyalty to friends was subordinated to personal convictions, duty, and honesty.[24]

"Of the five traits, standards of honesty [were] the most widely and unquestioningly accepted." [24] At the core of the concept of honesty was scrupulousness in money matters and in telling the truth. Responsibility was also a highly valued trait, especially in duties toward school, home, and employment. "There [was] great assurance that the first duty of a student [was] toward his own success whether in earning grades or in preparing for life work." [24]

Beliefs about loyalty were especially "confused and uncertain," and particularly in relation to "ideas, principles and values" and "where a conflict of several loyalties or conflict of loyalty with other values were involved." [24] Standards of moral courage were similarly ill-defined except in defending own and others' rights. There was considerable hesitancy in adhering to convictions that alienate persons in authority or jeopardize "popularity with peers." [24]

These findings support the general picture we have drawn of adolescent moral belief. The weakness of the concepts of loyalty and moral courage reflect the widespread moral confusion in our culture as well as the current overvaluation of expediency. On the other hand, concepts of friendliness, honesty, and responsibility are still relatively unambiguous; and by adhering to familiar stereotypes, the adolescent can neatly fit them into the pattern of moral expediency he deems so necessary for achieving all-important success.

STATUS OF RELIGION DURING ADOLESCENCE

Acceptance or Rejection

Just as adolescence brings no great upheaval in moral structure, it effects no revolution in religious belief or activity. Contrary to widespread opinion there is no rampant repudiation of religion during adolescence. A majority of American adolescents belong to a church, usually the same church as their parents,[4] attend church services once a month or more,[4, 52] have a favorable attitude toward the church, rely upon prayer,[52, 55] and believe in a personal, omnipotent, omniscient God who, although bodyless, participated in the writing of the Bible and guides the affairs of men and nations.[13, 19, 47, 55]

This evidence by no means indicates homogeneity in the religious beliefs or practices of adolescents. As a matter of fact significant differences exist between the sexes,[28, 55] among age groups,[37, 55] among religious denominations,[4, 28, 37, 55] between high and low income groups, and between urban and rural adolescents.[55, 57] It does indicate, however, that organized religion as a moral, philosophical, and social institution has not lost its grip on American youth.

Religious Observances

There is a gradual trend toward decreasing church attendance [34, 58] from early to late adolescence, but this does not necessarily reflect diminished religious belief. To some extent it indicates dissatisfaction with church services.[34, 37] Girls attend church more regularly than boys,[54] and Catholics are more assiduous in this respect than either Protestants or Jews.[4]

Religious Beliefs

Changes in religious beliefs during adolescence show the same trends as those of moral values in general. As a result of intellectual maturation, religious beliefs become more abstract and less literal between the ages of twelve and eighteen.[37] God is conceptualized as an omniscient power rather than as a corporeal being. Religious views also become more tolerant and less ritualistic; virtue is identified less with strict observance of specific denominational doctrine.[16, 37]

For most adolescents, prayer serves to request personal benefits or to give thanks; less frequently it is used as a form of communion, to seek guidance or comfort, or to comply with habit.[52] With increasing age fewer adolescents regard prayer as a form of penance, or believe that prayers are answered.[37]

College attendance effects relatively little change in religious belief, but merely accentuates the developmental changes noted above.[6, 12, 19, 30, 34] Atheism is an extremely rare outcome of college education.[34] Changes in religious belief are attributed by college students to teaching in philosophy and science courses, to personal contacts with students and professors, and to general maturation.[34] These changes are usually considered to contribute to a more satisfactory philosophy of life, and only a small minority feel that they represent a loss of something essential.[34]

Religious Doubts and Conflict

A general increase in religious skepticism does not occur during adolescence, but there is less acceptance of the more literal, ritualistic and dogmatic aspects of religious belief—the literal interpretation of the Bible and belief in heaven, hell, and the hereafter.[37] The typical adolescent today admits a certain amount of religious perplexity, especially about beliefs questioned by scientific discoveries, but he seems to accept this situation as more or less normal.[55] For the most part, such doubts are peripheral, and do not seriously undermine the core of religious faith.

Radical views about religion are more common in college men than in college women, and are less frequently held by Catholics than by Protestants.[28] A comparison of religious radicals and conservatives at the University of Iowa showed that the radicals were more intelligent and less suggestible, whereas the conservatives more frequently came from larger, church-going families and had more sympathetic attitudes toward their parents.[28]

The Impact of Adolescence on Religion

Religious Awakening. No evidence supports the prevalent belief that biological changes of pubescence produce an emotional crisis resulting in religious "awakening." Although the typical age range for the occurrence of religious conversions was reported as fifteen to twenty at the turn of the twentieth century, this phenomenon was undoubtedly a product of the unique cultural conditions prevailing at that time. A more recent study in 1928 found the modal age to be twelve, which is somewhat earlier than the usual onset of puberty.[10] It thus seems more likely, as Hollingworth[26] maintains, that any intensification of religious interest or experience coincident with pubescence is attributable to intellectual maturation (which stimulates concern with problems of truth, causality, and the meaning and purpose of life) rather than to pubescence per se.* In support of this position Hollingworth contended that an intensification of religious interest occurs in intellectually gifted children who are only eight years old but have a mental age of twelve.[26]

In any event, the type of religious "awakening" that occurs in

* No difference was found between the religious experiences of pre- and post-menarcheal girls of equivalent chronological age (M. P. Hillery, "The Religious Life of Adolescent Girls," Washington, D. C.: Catholic Univ. of America, 1937.)

most adolescents is gradual rather than characterized by an emotional or crisis experience. Religious crises that do occur take place more frequently among individuals who live in rural areas and belong to churches with a more pietistic and evangelistic theology.[10]

Intellectual Maturation. The cumulative impact of gradual progress toward intellectual maturity is responsible for most of the changes in religious belief occurring during adolescence. Increased ability to generalize results in more abstract religious concepts and less emphasis upon the more literal aspects of religious doctrine. The general broadening of social experience, exposure to different doctrinal beliefs, and awareness of hypocrisy and inconsistencies in religious practice lead to greater tolerance and liberalness in religious outlook. Interest in religious questions is intensified by the newly attained capacity to pursue such abstract problems as the origin and purpose of life, the nature of truth, and the meaning of causality. And last, exposure to scientific teachings creates a certain amount of skepticism toward the literal interpretation of many theological doctrines.

Personality Factors. Part of the shift toward a more liberal and more highly rationalized concept of religion can be ascribed to the operation of the exploratory orientation with its emphasis upon independently discovered reasons and its de-emphasis of personal loyalty as an adequate explanation per se. The residual impact of the satellizing orientation, and the importance of the incorporative orientation (its concern with considerations of extrinsic status) are also evident in the fact that for the most part the essential core of traditional religious belief remains intact through adolescence despite the multiplicity of factors that challenge faith. It strains credulity to believe that if choice of religious faith depended on reason and objective merit alone, 81 per cent of adolescents would choose the denomination of their parents.

We have noted that in certain instances of parent-youth conflict, displaced aggression toward the parent may be directed against the church, resulting in a characteristic type of adolescent heresy. At the other extreme, increased identification with the church may represent (a) a compensation for the loss of security in the weakening of ties with parents, or (b) an anchor in the face of general value disorientation and the marginal status of adolescence. By the degree of resatellization thereby effected, the process of emancipation is furthered; and to the extent that conflicts and anxieties of other origin are displaced to the religious realm (where resolution is more easily accomplished than in reality), preoccupation with religion may be regarded as an adjustive mechanism. Margaret Mead suggests that the adolescent's susceptibility to authoritarian religious influence may represent an expiation for the guilt engendered by repudiation of parental values.[42]

The Impact of Religion on Personality

What influence does religion have on personality development? We know that church membership is important in determining an individual's character *reputation*. "It . . . is one of the things that communities like Prairie City expect of their 'good, respectable people.' . . . Most people who value their status do not treat it lightly." [24] At the same time evidence points to the fact that religious observance is negligibly correlated with moral *conduct*.[22, 63]

Neither type of evidence about religious *observance,* however, sheds much light on the relationship between religious *belief* and moral conduct. On the other hand, it is apparent that in the lives of many individuals religion plays a central role in the formulation of goals and values and in the enforcement of moral obligations. In Prairie City, Lutheran adolescents enjoy extremely high reputations for honesty and responsibility despite the fact that "the Lutheran subjects rank lowest among the four Protestant churches in social status".[24]

Religious orthodoxy may also be significantly related to mode of thinking and value assimilation as shown by its positive correlation with ethnocentrism and anti-Semitism.[1] On a priori grounds alone, one would anticipate that it would lead to avoidance of the exploratory situation and to rigidity of thought. Considerable research is presently going on to test this hypothesis.

REFERENCES AND BIBLIOGRAPHY

1. Adorno, T. W. et al.: *The Authoritarian Personality: Studies in Prejudice Series.* New York: Harper, 1950.
2. Ausubel, D. P.: *Ego Development and the Personality Disorders.* New York: Grune and Stratton, 1952.
3. Bartlett, E. R. and Harris, D. B.: Personality factors in delinquency, Sch. & Soc., *43:*653–656, 1936.

4. Bell, H. M.: *Youth Tell Their Story.* Washington, D. C.: American Council on Education, 1938.
5. Benedict, R.: *Patterns of Culture.* Boston: Houghton Mifflin, 1934.
6. Brown, F. J.: *The Sociology of Childhood.* New York: Prentice-Hall, 1939.
7. Caldwell, O. W. and Lundeen, G. E.: Further study of unfounded beliefs among junior-high-school pupils. Teach. Coll. Rec., *36*:35–52, 1934.
8. Campbell, A. A.: "Factors Associated with Attitudes Toward Jews," in *Readings in Social Psychology* (T. M. Newcomb and E. L. Hartley, eds.). New York: Holt, 1947.
9. Centers, R.: *The Psychology of Social Classes.* Princeton, N. J.: Princeton University Press, 1949.
10. Clark, E. T.: *The Psychology of Religious Awakening.* New York: Macmillan, 1929.
11. Dimock, H. S.: *Rediscovering the Adolescent.* New York: Association Press, 1937.
12. Dudycha, G. J.: Religious beliefs of college students. J. Appl. Psychol., *17:* 585–603, 1933.
13. Dudycha, G. J.: The superstitious beliefs of college students. J. Appl. Psychol., *17:*586–603, 1933.
14. Eberhart, J. C.: Attitudes toward property: A genetic study by the paired-comparison rating of offenses. J. Genet. Psychol., *60:*3–35, 1942.
15. *Fortune* Survey: Youth has its say about itself and the world. Fortune, *26:*8–20, 1942.
16. Franzblau, A. N.: *Religious Belief and Character among Jewish Adolescents.* New York: Teachers College, Columbia University, 1934.
17. Frenkel-Brunswik, E. and Sanford, R. N.: Some personality factors in anti-Semitism. J. Psychol., *20:*271–291, 1945.
18. Frenkel-Brunswik, E., Levinson, D. J., and Sanford, R. N.: "The Anti-democratic Personality," in *Readings in Social Psychology* (T. Newcomb and E. Hartley, eds.). New York: Holt, 1947.
19. Gilliand, A. R.: The attitude of college students toward God and the church. J. Soc. Psychol., *11:*11–18, 1940.
20. Glueck, S. and Glueck, E.: *Unraveling Juvenile Delinquency.* New York: Commonwealth Fund, 1950.
21. Harrower, M. R.: Social status and the moral development of the child. Brit. J. Educ. Psychol., *1:*75–95, 1934.
22. Hartshorne, H., May, M. A., et al.: *Studies in the Nature of Character. I. Studies in Deceit. II. Studies in Self-Control. III. Studies in the Organization of Character.* New York: Macmillan, 1930.
23. Havighurst, R. J., Robinson, M. Z., and Dorr, M.: The development of the ideal self in childhood and adolescence. J. Educ. Res., *40:*241–257, 1946.
24. Havighurst, R. J. and Taba, H.: *Adolescent Character and Personality.* New York: Wiley, 1949.
25. Hill, D. S.: Personification of ideals by urban children. J. Soc. Psychol., *1:* 379–393, 1930.
26. Hollingworth, L. S.: "The Adolescent Child," in *A Handbook of Child Psychology* (C. Murchison, ed.). Worcester, Mass.: Clark University Press, 1933.

27. Hollingshead, A. B.: *Elmtown's Youth.* New York: Wiley, 1949.

28. Howells, T. H.: A Comparative Study of Those Who Accept as against Those Who Reject Religious Authority. Univ. Iowa Stud. Charact. II, No. 2, 1928.

29. Jersild, A. T. et al.: *Child Development and the Curriculum.* New York: Teachers College, Columbia University, 1946.

30. Jones, E. S.: The opinions of college students. J. Appl. Psychol., *10:*427–436, 1926.

31. Jones, V.: "Character Development in Children," in *Manual of Child Psychology* (L. Carmichael, ed.). New York: Wiley, 1946.

32. Kagan, H. E.: *Changing the Attitude of Christian toward Jew: A Psychological Approach through Religion.* New York: Columbia University Press, 1952.

33. Kardiner, A. and Linton, R.: *The Individual and His Society.* New York: Columbia University Press, 1939.

34. Katz, D. and Allport, F. H.: *Students' Attitudes.* Syracuse, N. Y.: Craftsman Press, 1931.

35. Kinsey, A. C. et al.: *Sexual Behavior in the Human Male.* Philadelphia: Saunders, 1948.

36. Koch, H. L.: The social distance between certain racial, nationality, and skin pigmentation groups in selected populations of school children. J. Genet. Psychol., *68:*63–95, 1946.

37. Kuhlen, R. G. and Arnold, M.: Age differences in religious beliefs and problems during adolescence. J. Genet. Psychol., *65:*291–300, 1944.

38. Leighton, D. and Kluckhohn, C.: *Children of the People.* Cambridge, Mass.: Harvard University Press, 1947.

39. Lundeen, G. E. and Caldwell, O. W.: A study of unfounded beliefs among high-school seniors. J. Educ. Res., *22:*257–273, 1930.

40. Maller, J. B. and Lundeen, G. E.: Sources of superstitious beliefs. J. Educ. Res., *26:*321–343, 1933.

41. Mead, M.: *From the South Seas.* New York: William Morrow, 1939.

42. Mead, M.: Social change and cultural surrogates. J. Educ. Sociol., *14:*92–110, 1940.

43. Mead, M.: "Some Anthropological Considerations Concerning Guilt," in Feelings and Emotions (M. L. Reymert, ed.). New York: McGraw-Hill, 1950.

44. Meltzer, H.: The development of children's nationality preferences, concepts and attitudes. J. Psychol., *11:*343–358, 1941.

45. Minard, R. D.: Race attitudes of Iowa children. Univ. Iowa Stud. Charact. IV, No. 2, 1931.

46. Moreno, J. L.: *Who Shall Survive?* Washington, D. C.: Nervous and Mental Disease Publishing Co., 1934.

47. Nelson, E.: Student Attitudes toward Religion. Genet. Psychol. Monogr., No. 22, 324–423, 1940.

48. Newcomb, T. M. and Svehla, G.: Intra-family relationships in attitudes. Sociometry, *1:*180–205, 1937.

49. Nichols, C. A.: *Moral Education Among North American Indians.* New York: Teachers College, Columbia University, 1930.

50. Oakes, M. E.: *Children's Explanations of Natural Phenomena.* New York: Teachers College, Columbia University, 1947.

51. Piaget, J.: *Moral Judgment of the Child.* New York: Harcourt, Brace, 1932.

52. Pixley, E. and Beekman, E.: The faith of youth as shown by a survey in public schools of Los Angeles. Relig. Educ., *44*:336–342, 1949.

53. Pressey, S. L. and Robinson, F. P.: *Psychology and the New Education.* New York: Harper, 1944.

54. Punke, H. H.: Leisure-time attitudes and activities of high-school students. Sch. & Soc., *43*:884–888, 1936.

55. Remmers, H. H., Myers, M. S., and Bennett, E. M.: Some personality aspects and religious values of high school youth. Purdue Opin. Panel, 10, No. 3, 1951.

56. Remmers, H. H. and Weltman, N.: Attitude inter-relationships of youth, their parents and their teachers. J. Soc. Psychol., *26*:61–68, 1947.

57. Rommetveit, R. Tileigning av religiøs tru og åtferd, grandska ut fra socia-psykologisk og laeringspsykologisk synsstad. Nord. Psykol., *3*:157–169, 1951.

58. Rosander, A. C.: Age and sex patterns of social attitudes. J. Educ. Psychol., *30*:481–496, 1939.

59. Sherif, M. and Cantril, H.: *The Psychology of Ego-Involvements.* New York: Wiley, 1947.

60. Sims, V. M. and Patrick, J. R.: Attitude toward the Negro of northern and southern college students. J. Soc. Psychol., *7*:192–204, 1936.

61. Stendler, C. B.: A study of some socio-moral judgments of junior high-school students. Child Develpm., *20*:15–29, 1949.

62. Stone, C. P. and Barker, R. G.: The attitudes and interests of premenarcheal and postmenarcheal girls. J. Genet. Psychol., *54*:27–71, 1939.

63. Strang, R.: Religious activities of adolescent girls. Relig. Educ., *24*:313–321, 1929.

64. Ter Keurst, A. J.: The acceptance of superstitious beliefs among secondary school pupils. J. Educ. Res., *32*:673–685, 1939.

65. Thetford, W. N., Molish, H. B., and Beck, S. J.: Developmental aspects of personality structure in normal children. J. Proj. Tech., *15*:58–78, 1951.

66. Thompson, G. G.: Age trends in social values during the adolescent years. Abstract. Amer. Psychologist, *4*:250, 1949.

67. Tudor-Hart, B. E.: Are there cases in which lies are necessary? J. Genet. Psychol., *33*:586–641, 1926.

68. Valentine, W. L.: Common misconceptions of college students. J. Appl. Psychol., *20*:633–658, 1936.

CHAPTER 10

Intellectual Growth and Interest Patterns

INTELLECTUAL GROWTH is the least typical aspect of adolescent development. In all other components of growth—hormonal, skeletal, motor, personality, moral, and social—there is an accelerated period of transitional development. Intellectual growth, on the other hand, follows a pattern very similar to the development of fine mechanical abilities (see pp. 122–124). Of all the major tissues of the body and segments of the personality it seems that only the small muscles and the intellect remain unaffected by the catalytic impetus to growth supplied by pubescence. The development of these continues to respond to hereditary and environmental influences impinging upon them, just as if pubescence were not taking place. Their growth curves proceed smoothly, unmarked by any discontinuity, to assume the adolescent form that could be projected for them from developmental data of earlier years.

Growth of this kind is not unimportant. In such growth new capacities are attained by the gradual accumulation of small increments of progress rather than by abrupt and discontinuous spurts of development. Cognitively, the adolescent is a different and more mature person than the preadolescent, but not discontinuously so. And the acquisition of these increased cognitive abilities plays an important role in personality, moral, and religious development.

GROWTH CHARACTERISTICS OF GENERAL INTELLIGENCE DURING ADOLESCENCE

The growth curve of general intelligence (computed from either scaled * scores [56, 116] or from scaled scores transformed into per-

* The purpose of scaling is to make raw scores from different tests and from different age groups comparable by expressing them in such a way that at any point of the scale, the distances between units of measurement are equal in difficulty value.

centages of adult performance [27, 112]) shows a fairly steep rise in early adolescence which tapers off in middle adolescence until ultimate capacity is achieved. The tapering off is so gradual that it is difficult to tell when growth actually ceases. The best estimates, based on testing a wide age sample of a relatively homogeneous population,[56] or on retesting the same population at suitable intervals,[37, 108, 111] places the age of terminal growth at eighteen to twenty, or even beyond. This conclusion is at variance with the widely accepted finding by Terman and Merrill that mental age ceases to increase after the age of sixteen on the revised Stanford-Binet test.[103]

Because intellectual growth continues at least until the end of the high school period for all brightness groups, it would seem reasonable to insist on compulsory school attendance until the age of eighteen, which is well above the minimum required in most states.[89] The growth curve for intelligence also indicates that some school subjects, which a particular child may find too difficult at the beginning of adolescence, might easily fall within his capacity several years later. This would be especially true of duller pupils.[54]

The termination of growth in "vertical" capacity also does not mean that all intellectual development ceases. Although beyond this point the individual may be unable to solve more difficult *novel* problems, he continues to grow "in a 'horizontal' direction—in the sense of increased information, knowledge, ability to draw upon past experience, increased ability to make decisions, to form judgments, to exercise common sense, and so forth".[54] And since the majority of problems an individual encounters can hardly be classified as novel, the continuing horizontal growth may be of much greater practical significance than the level of vertical growth already attained.*

Effect of Pubescence on Intellectual Growth

The most striking feature of the growth curve for intelligence during adolescence is the absence of the typical growth spurt we have

* The practical validity of the concept of *general* intelligence in adolescents and adults is open to question. The increasing differentiation of mental abilities with advancing age tends to make any composite score ambiguous in meaning and limited in usefulness for guidance purposes (see pp. 282–283).

seen in other aspects of adolescent development. Although youngsters
suffering from pathologically precocious puberty are considerably
taller and stronger than their fellows, the intellectual tendency, if
any, is for them to be retarded.[60] And

> in the case of intellect and judgment the lack of growth spurt concomitant
> with sexual maturation is even more noticeable than in the case of intelligence;
> since, unlike the latter, not only do these functions exhibit an indefinite period
> of chronological growth, but they may also be adversely affected by the emo-
> tional instability characteristic of adolescence.[7]

It is true, however, that postmenarcheal girls are slightly but significantly superior to premenarcheal girls on group intelligence test
scores [95] and that both early-maturing boys and girls tend to surpass
later-maturing adolescents in intelligence during the age range from
ten to sixteen [3]; but since this superiority is evident before pubescence, it can hardly be attributed to the influence of sexual maturation per se. The most likely explanation is that *both* intelligence
and age of pubescence are positively correlated with socioeconomic
status and so with each other.

The relatively negligible correlation between pubescent status and
intelligence raises the familiar issue of grouping high school students on the basis of physical maturity instead of on the basis of
chronological age. This procedure would necessarily increase the
existing heterogeneity of mental ability in a given grade level even
further. Since intelligence level is more closely related to chronological age than to physical maturity, grouping on the basis of
physical maturity would bring together in the same class younger
individuals (mostly girls) and older individuals (mostly boys) who,
although physically and socially homogeneous, are quite divergent
in intellectual capacity. It becomes a question of which is the greater
evil for purposes of instruction—intellectual or social heterogeneity. Some authorities favor socially homogeneous grouping
modified by individualized guidance and enrichment of the curriculum to adjust for differences in mental ability.[35] This plan is
also advocated as superior to acceleration and demotion in adjusting
to the range of individual differences in intellectual capacity that
normally occurs quite apart from any heterogeneity of chronological age.[35, 89]

What effect does adolescent emotional instability have on the maturation of intellectual ability? Although it seems self-evident that emotional instability would impair the exercise of judgment and the orderly acquisition of subject matter, there is no convincing evidence that it interferes with the growth of intellectual *capacity*. Despert and Pierce [28] did find that fluctuations in the IQ correlated with changes in emotional instability, but these fluctuations were not outside the range of the error of measurement of the test used.[43]

Stability of General Intelligence during Adolescence

When the child is at the age of adolescence, test scores of general intelligence acquire a fair amount of stability. The correlation of scores of intelligence tests given at the onset of adolescence with those given at the close of adolescence is in the neighborhood of .80.[5] From year to year this correspondence is even greater.[108] Thus, while some fluctuation in test score occurs in individual growth curves, most individuals tend to retain the same relative position in the group throughout the adolescent period.[37] In extreme instances, of course, there are large fluctuations in test scores; but these fluctuations tend to be associated with unusual disorganizing factors in life history (illness, for example [48]) rather than with intrinsic irregularity of growth pattern or unreliability of the measuring instrument.

For purposes of *individual* guidance, however, a reliability coefficient of .80 is not too reassuring. In dealing with a *particular* individual it does not suffice to know that a *majority* of individuals at age eighteen will occupy the same relative position in the group in IQ as they did at age thirteen. There is sufficient variability in individual growth patterns to warrant frequent and periodic testing of intelligence if test scores are to be used at all for guidance purposes.

Distribution of Adolescent Intelligence

Intelligence tests continue to yield normal distributions during the course of adolescence.[24, 109] Variability in test scores at any age or grade level is considerable. The distribution of mental ability, for example, among fourteen-year-old students in New York State is represented by a range of mental ages from ten to eighteen with the mode at fourteen.[24]

Surprisingly enough, despite the tremendous increase in high-school enrollment from 1916 to 1940, with a corresponding elimination of the intellectual selectivity that formerly operated when only one-third of the adolescent population attended high-school, there has been no drop in the mean IQ of the high-school population.[34] This phenomenon may perhaps be accounted for by the greater experience that present-day students have with tests, and by the closer correspondence between current methods of school instruction and the types of capacities measured by intelligence tests.

DIFFERENTIAL ASPECTS OF GROWTH OF INTELLIGENCE DURING ADOLESCENCE

Sex Differences

Girls show a slight superiority over boys in general intelligence during early adolescence,[23, 37] which is related to their more precocious sexual maturation. Differences between the sexes are larger and more significant when the comparison is of component subabilities of intelligence tests. Girls are consistently superior on such verbal items as vocabulary,[22, 41, 61] language usage,[61] and analogies,[56] and on memory [41, 61] and clerical ability.[61] Boys are superior in subtests involving spatial relations and mechanical abilities,[61] and in arithmetic (in later adolescence).[41, 56, 61]

Boys exhibit greater variability in IQ than girls, achieving a larger proportion of extreme scores at either end of the distribution.[73] Terman's 25-year, longitudinal study of intellectually gifted children showed that boys more frequently than girls retained their high intellectual status as they advanced in age.[105] Differential factors of motivation and cultural pressure can perhaps explain part of the sex difference at the upper extreme of intelligence, but they cannot very well account for differences at the lower extreme.

Impact of Socioeconomic Status

The influence of environmental stimulation on the development of general intelligence appears to be fairly well established. Significant differences in mean IQ for practically all intelligence tests have been found between various socioeconomic and occupational levels. Part of these differences can be attributed to hereditary factors since (a) it would not be unreasonable to hypothesize some degree of positive relationship between innate ability and occupational level, and (b) heredity has an unquestionable influence on the development of intelligence as shown by the positive correlation between the IQ's of monozygotic twins reared in different environments.[77] It is also undoubtedly true, as Allison Davis [26] claims, that most intelligence tests are so constructed as to favor the types of learning experience provided in middle-class homes. But the very fact that these tests favor such children demonstrates that the environment *can* operate to develop selectively certain aspects of intellectual endowment. This conclusion is compatible with the findings that intelligence becomes more and more differentiated with increasing age,[41, 89] and that sex differences in many specific intellectual functions increase or reverse themselves as children grow older.[61]

But even when considerations of heredity and test bias are taken into account, it appears likely that general level of environmental stimulation affects the growth of intelligence. Children of parents in upper occupational levels maintain a *constant* superiority of about 10 IQ points over children coming from lower-class homes during the age range from eight to eighteen.[92] And in instances of very extreme deprivation (for example, Kentucky and Tennessee mountain children), there is a progressive decline in IQ level as the children advance from middle childhood to adolescence.[6, 117] But although a meager environment may depress intellectual growth, it appears that improvement in the environment will raise intelligence level only in the very young among those who have been seriously deprived.[83]

In conclusion, environment probably affects intellectual development in two important ways: (a) in determining the degree of functional capacity actualized from genetically fixed endowment; and (b) in selectively determining which *particular* abilities will be more or less developed as general intelligence becomes more highly differentiated with increasing age. High socioeconomic status favors the development of verbal aspects of intelligence as shown by the positive correlation of .46 between size of vocabulary and socioeconomic status in ninth-grade children [87] and by positive correlations between socioeconomic status and verbal ability at ages ten and sixteen.[45, 50]

Closely related to socioeconomic differences in intellectual level is the impact of continued schooling on the growth of intelligence. Follow-up studies of children matched for IQ in the eighth grade indicate that even twenty years later reliable differences in intelligence test scores appear in favor of those who attended high-school.[68] Nevertheless, schooling did not appreciably alter the relative positions of the individuals on the original ordering of IQ's determined in the eighth grade. More impressive are the findings that in a number of subtests involving reasoning and abstract ability, improvement continues until the end of the college period.[44, 85, 91, 111] Furthermore, the particular areas in which greatest improvement occurs (for example, verbal or numerical ability) seem to depend on the area of specialization in college.[44] It is therefore difficult to avoid the implication that schooling differentially influences the growth of the more complex components of verbal intelligence.

Freeman, Conrad, and Jones stress two further implications of these data:

> In order to secure the full development of intelligence, either to fit the individual for his highest vocational attainment, or for discharging the responsibilities of citizenship or for realizing the fullest development of personality, it is essential to continue general education beyond the teens. This does not imply full-time schooling for all. For many it means participation in adult education. Many persons can better carry forward the later stages of this intellectual development in association with the prosecution of a vocation rather than as a full-time enterprise.
>
> One of the aims of [mental measurement] . . . has been to find means of measuring *inherent* capacity and growth. So far as the later stages of development of the higher intellectual powers are concerned, this aim seems incapable of realization. Without training, the later stages are not evidenced. . . . It is desirable to free our tests so far as possible from the effects of specific variations in training, but to free them from the general effects of education is probably impossible. To seek to do so is to restrict the tests to the measurement of narrow and perhaps unimportant functions [22] [pp. 178, 179; quoted by permission of the Society].

Growth Differences between Bright and Dull Adolescents

The growth curve for intelligence is not identical for bright and dull individuals. Although the terminal age of intellectual growth is the same for both groups,[22] the bulk of the evidence (based on studies of changes in the variability of the distribution of intelligence test scores with increasing age) indicates that the bright "tend to grow away from the dull".[22, 84, 112] In addition, there are qualitative differences between bright and dull adolescents of comparable mental age in several intellectual sub-abilities tested by various achievement tests. The bright surpass the dull on items requiring abstraction, a large vocabulary, differentiation of subtle shades of meaning, imagination, and generalization.[81]

The implications of these findings are that dull students need not drop out of high-school at the tenth grade as they frequently do at present, but could profit from schooling until at least the age of eighteen. To maximize the benefit that such students can derive from continued instruction, the more difficult subjects could be placed at the end of the high-school curriculum, and abstract materials could be concretized and made more meaningful in terms of life situations.[89] And "in order to recognize their peculiar capacities and help them achieve success rather than failure, the school needs to provide for them a wide variety of learning activities".[89]

Growth Differences Among Separate Intellectual Abilities

Subtest analysis of various tests of intellectual ability shows that several important differences exist in the rate of growth, age of terminal growth, and rate of decline among the component sub-abilities.

Simple rote memory (memory span) reaches an earlier peak of development than either general intelligence,[22] vocabulary, or arithmetical ability [41]; but this is not true of more perceptive and analytical types of memory.[56] During the preadolescent and adolescent periods, vocabulary and ability to dissect sentences grow at a more rapid rate than reasoning ability despite identical rates of growth during early and middle childhood.[22] Ability on the analogies test reaches an earlier terminal growth than on either the completions or opposites tests. On the other hand, decline in ability sets in earlier for such functions as analogies and completions than for vocabulary and general information.[56]

In conclusion, it appears that in general the more complex intellectual abilities have a more gradual rate of growth, reach maturity at a later age, but show evidence of decline earlier in life.

Differentiation of Intellectual Ability in Adolescence

As already suggested, the concept of general intelligence is much less meaningful in adolescence than in childhood because of the increasing differentiation of intellectual ability that takes place. By the time an individual reaches adolescence, differential factors of interest, relative ability, specialization of training, motivation, success and failure experiences, and cultural expectation operate selectively to develop certain abilities and to leave others relatively undeveloped. Thus the intercorrelations among abilities become substantially less with increasing age.[40, 41] An individual's standing in one ability has relatively little predictive value for his standing in another ability; and composite scores on intelligence tests are not very useful for predicting performance in a given school subject. Much more meaningful than a total score, is a profile showing the relative standing of an individual on a wide variety of basic intellectual abilities.

The increased differentiation of intellectual ability during adolescence is a *general* phenomenon but it is also relative to various other differential factors. Segel's evidence shows that differentiation among intellectual traits is greater for bright than for dull adolescents.[89] We have cited evidence of the differentiation of intellectual abilities along social class and sex lines, and as a product of prolonged or specialized education. Especially interesting are data indicating that superiority in a given function reflecting higher *general* ability at a younger age level may undergo reversal during adolescence as a result of differentiation. For example, girls have higher language *and* arithmetical ability than boys at the beginning of adolescence, but boys eventually surpass them in arithmetical ability before the close of adolescence.[61] Children from upper socioeconomic groups are superior to lower-class children on tests of both verbal *and* mechanical ability at age ten, but at age sixteen retain their superiority only on the verbal tests.[45, 50]

This progressive differentiation of mental ability requires a correspondingly increasing differentiation of curricular offerings. As Segel points out, a core curriculum is better suited to the intellectual organization of junior than senior high school students.[89] Another consequence of this increasing differentiation apparent from studies of drop-outs from school is

> that between the ages of ten and fourteen, maladjustment through lack of general mental ability is an item of importance among the factors causing youth to leave school. However, between the ages of fifteen and eighteen such maladjustment does not result in large numbers of youth leaving school.[89]

OTHER ASPECTS OF INTELLECTUAL GROWTH
DURING ADOLESCENCE

Intellectual development during adolescence can be considered from quite another frame of reference than the growth of general intelligence and its component parts. The intellectual life of adolescence is characterized by certain properties that distinguish it phenomenologically from the intellectual life of childhood. But again this is a quantitative rather than a qualitative difference. No new intellectual abilities appear in adolescence. Growth increments are gradual and cumulative; there are no discontinuous spurts. Horizontal growth in intellect (vocabulary, information) and judgment continues long after intelligence ceases to grow—well into middle age, before signs of deterioration are evident.[56]

In comparison with childhood, the cognitive life of adolescence is considerably more dominated by symbolization and abstraction.

> The ability to generalize, to manipulate abstractions, to reason from the standpoint of an abstract proposition is enormously expanded. The direction of thought relating to interpersonal issues is from the specific to the general, from the concrete to the abstract, from the personal to the impersonal.[9]

Many abstract concepts of government, interpersonal relations, characterology, science become clear for the first time for a majority of individuals.[52] Hence more difficult problems of logic and reasoning can be handled.[52] Imagination is more "rational" and symbolic and deals less with manipulation of concrete images, even in such relatively non-abstract areas as spatial relationships.[74] Rorschach responses reveal greater ability to organize meaningful relationships.[106]

> All of these changes lead the child to a clearer and more comprehensive understanding of the nature of the environment in which he lives. He feels less awed by its complexity, and more confident to navigate alone and unguided.[9]

In the formation of judgments (see pp. 249–250), greater objectivity can be brought to the weighing of evidence, and less egocentricity and subjectivity are involved in arguing the validity of an abstract proposition (see p. 251). Both of these developments reflect the growing influence of the exploratory orientation and the sharpening of the self-critical faculty. In moral judgment this aids the development of functional and reciprocal concepts of moral obligation (see pp. 250–251).

Expanded knowledge in many different areas has a noticeable

effect in reducing the prevalence of misconceptions and superstitions (see p. 267). The validity of a perception of causality is largely dependent on the quality of the judgment about the relevance of an antecedent event for a particular consequence.[10] This in turn depends on the individual's experience or sophistication in a given area.[10, 78] Even

> when adults are required to provide explanations for events completely outside their sphere of competence, they tend to give answers that are remarkably similar to those of children.[78] When nón-science teachers were shown some simple demonstrations of principles in physics "there was a marked tendency on the part of these adults to support the views [they had] once stated in the prediction or its explanation, even when these views were in conflict with the observation. There were striking instances of this reluctance to change even when the subject was looking at the phenomenon itself." [10]

Adolescents can make more valid judgments of relevance, and hence of causality, than children, because of their wider knowledge derived from both training and incidental experience. Sixth-graders were found to be superior to third-graders and kindergarten children in "the ability to learn a relevant causal sequence and to inhibit the learning of an irrelevant causal sequence." [10]

On the negative side, however, it is a fair inference that the judgments of adolescents are adversely influenced by their greater affectivity, and by the lability and impulsiveness of their emotional responses.[69, 106]

INTERACTION BETWEEN INTELLECTUAL GROWTH AND PERSONALITY

The impact of intellectual growth on adolescent personality development has been considered in large measure in the preceding three chapters. The acquisition of greater cognitive powers contributes to the need for more volitional independence, sharpens the child's perception of the environment, enables him to formulate more abstract and generalized moral values, and alters cultural expectations of the level of maturity appropriate for him. In all probability, the effects of intellectual growth on personality development are more important than the changes they induce in cognitive organization per se.

Changes in personality organization also bring about marked

changes in learning orientation. These changes in mode of acquiring values are also more significant than the increased capacity to assimilate more objective kinds of cognitive data.

Last, some relationship exists between intelligence and (a) interests, success, and adjustment, and (b) individual personality traits. The former relationship is probably a reflection of the fact that level of intelligence is one of many variables that influence the outcome of these other phenomena. The relationship to individual personality traits, on the other hand, is probably not indicative of any intrinsic association between intelligence and character, but instead reflects the operation of certain relatively extraneous considerations.

Intelligence and Personality

Numerous investigations concur in the finding that various personality traits such as reliability, perseverence, independence, and emotional stability are positively correlated with intelligence.[19, 105] Striking differences between intellectually gifted and average children are found in these character traits. However, there is no reason to believe that the development of character and of intelligence are organically related in terms of the factors that impinge on their respective growth processes. Cattell's summary of the types of personality traits associated with intelligence sheds considerable light on some of the more adventitious reasons responsible for this relationship:

> It looks as if intelligence is directly more associated with character conceived in a narrow, self-conscious sense, and with regard to habits that are acquired later and through conscious ideals, rather than with basic emotional integration and goodness of character in the wider sense as might result from the emotional adjustment derived from the upbringing of the first few years or from relatively constitutional stability.[19]

The following factors probably contribute to the positive relationship between intelligence and some personality traits. (1) Brighter children are better able to perceive the expectations of their culture and to learn appropriate forms of conduct. They can also perceive more accurately which character traits are required for success. (2) The personality traits that correlate most highly with intelligence are also most highly prized by middle-class homes; and, as already pointed out, intelligence test scores are positively related to social class status. (3) The wide variability in the degree to which the academic work output of children is responsive to an incentive of social prestige [8] suggests that this factor may influence in part the extent to which an individual's genetic endowment of verbal intelligence is functionally actualized. Highly motivated children tend to be persistent, stable, and responsible, on the one hand, and to make the most of their intellectual endowment in terms of IQ score.* That more intelligent children seem to be more honest is less a function of superior moral beliefs than of such relatively extraneous factors as less need to cheat to pass examinations, superior ability to avoid detection, and greater astuteness in estimating the chances of "getting caught" (see p. 266).

Intelligence and Interest Patterns

Although intellectual achievement (as measured by subject-matter achievement tests) tends to be unrelated to broad categories of interests (scientific, mechanical, persuasive, clerical) measured by such standard interest inventories as the Kuder and Strong,[113] more subtle qualitative differences between the interest patterns of bright and dull adolescents have been uncovered. As could be reasonably expected, brighter individuals exhibit greater range and variability in their choice of hobbies and activities,[14, 63, 67] participate more frequently in intellectual activities,[64, 101] and are more apt to acquire collections of objects demanding complex schemes of classification.[30] They also show greater interest than their duller contemporaries in solitary pursuits requiring serious cerebration.[63, 64] Throughout adolescence and preadolescence they do much more extracurricular reading, and their reading interests achieve a higher level of maturity.[64, 101, 110]

All of these differences in favor of bright individuals follow directly from their possession of sufficient intellectual capacity to support the interests. Everything else being equal, most persons naturally develop those interests that they can prosecute most successfully. *Within* a given individual quite a high relationship exists

* High motivation could conceivably raise IQ by actually stimulating the development of verbal intelligence and by yielding maximal performance in test situations.[8]

between hierarchies of interests and abilities,[107] which results in mutual reinforcement, and accounts in part for the greater differentiation of ability with increasing age.

Intelligence and Adjustment

Intelligence level is obviously a factor contributing to the individual's ability to adjust to his environment. The brighter person has more resources in solving problems of adaptation, and (other things being equal) is, therefore, less likely to experience frustration and failure. Intellectually gifted children * surpass children of average ability on all measures of adjustment,[101, 105] whereas extremely dull children acquire many typical distortions of behavior that reflect the different ways in which they attempt to compensate for their school failure and social isolation.

Because of the high price that adolescents place upon intelligence, as reflected in the things they mention as increasingly important in their self-estimate [53] and in the attributes desirable in the opposite sex,[72] inferior intellectual ability (just like physical unattractiveness) constitutes a definite handicap to which some adjustment must be made. One of the commonest forms of adjustment is self-delusion or inhibition of the self-critical ability. This is reflected in the fact (a) that high-school students regard "lack of brains" as one of the *least* important causes of school failure [42] and (b) that a larger percentage of students making poorer than better scores on academic aptitude tests are less inclined to believe that the test scores are truly reflective of their actual ability.[93]

Although a larger proportion of the low-scoring individuals are also opposed to reporting test results to students and deny that knowledge of score affects performance,[93] awareness of low standing apparently motivates increased academic efforts.[76, 86] However, with certain individuals who both lack intrinsic feelings of adequacy and entertain high opinions of their mental ability, knowledge of low or average IQ score may have considerable traumatic effect on self-esteem. Because of the almost superstitious awe in which the IQ is frequently held, such reports are sometimes accepted as possessing

* Leta Hollingworth points out, however, that children with *extremely* high IQ's tend to be maladjusted by the social isolation that their intellectual superiority imposes upon them.[47]

the same reliability and catastrophic implications as a diagnosis of cancer or tuberculosis, and therefore precipitate acute anxiety.

Increased intelligence creates as well as helps solve problems. The bright individual is sensitive to many disconcerting and threatening elements in the environment that do not disturb the equanimity of the duller person. The greater complexity of his existence provides an additional source of strain. On the other hand, the destructive potential of strain can only be estimated in terms of the capacity for resistance to stress. The possession of greater resources for coping with the environment offsets much of the strain that increased sensitivity would otherwise create for more able persons. Thus the bright and the dull tend to have distinctive types of adjustment problems [65, 119] which differ both in level of complexity and in the sophistication of the adaptive resources brought to them.

Despite these characteristic differences in degree and quality of adjustment level for individuals *near* but not *at* the very extremes of the distribution of intelligence, there is little relationship between these two variables in the middle range of intelligence which accounts for ninety or more per cent of the population.[22, 54]

> The reason for this is, of course, that the importance of intellectual status is usually relative to what is expected of a person and what he himself wants. ... At least five factors are involved in the relation between intelligence and adjustment. These are the child's absolute level of intelligence; the level of intelligence required in the activities toward which he is being pointed through the ambitions of his family and friends; the social pressures which arise from such ambitions; his own "felt needs" and level of aspiration; and his actual achievement. These factors are interconnected in a variety of ways and a great variety of complex patterns may result [22] [p. 180; quoted by permission of the Society].

The complexity of the relationship between intelligence and adjustment is therefore not to be underestimated. It is apparent that a bright individual may have an overambitious level of aspiration, may be subjected to excessive family or social pressure, may underachieve for a large variety of reasons other than lack of intelligence, and may have little resistance to strain. On the other hand, other things being equal, it is also apparent that by virtue of greater ability such an individual is *less* likely than his less gifted contemporary (a) to aspire to goals far in excess of innate capacity, (b) to experience excessive failure and frustration, and (c) to lack the necessary resources to combat stressful and anxiety-producing situations. For these reasons he does not risk overtaxing his frustration tolerance as readily. Hence, _complete_ lack of relationship between these two variables throughout the middle range of intelligence is somewhat surprising, and suggests that the situation is at least in part a result of the inadequacy and grossness of available measures of adjustment. Given instruments capable of more subtle measurement of adjustment, the low but positive relationship that is theoretically indicated might conceivably emerge.

Another related problem is the relationship between intelligence and success. In academic achievement, success in various subject-matter fields generally correlates near 0.5 with intelligence or academic aptitude test scores. Thus, although the two factors are obviously related, much room is left for the operation of personality variables. Comparison of educationally successful and unsuccessful gifted children reveals that the successful have better study habits, exhibit more "compensatory" as contrasted to "protective" ego mechanisms, have more realistic levels of aspiration, and excel in such personality traits as dependability, self-reliance, ambition, investigativeness, and persistence.[66, 82, 88]

As a group, intellectually superior individuals tend to gravitate toward professional occupations, to be more successful vocationally, and to experience less unemployment.[80, 105] _Within_ a group of gifted children (IQ's over 140), however, Terman and Oden found that the adults successful twenty five years later were as children more integrated in goal structure, more self-confident, and more persevering that the unsuccessful adults, but that the two groups were quite evenly matched in intelligence.[105] We can conclude that better-than-average intelligence is undoubtedly a vocational asset, but that beyond this, unusual success in a vocation is more a function of special talent and of various personality traits than of extremely high general intelligence. There is no evidence that would indicate that creativity and general intelligence are positively related beyond this critical minimal point.

Impact of Personality Trait Development on Cognitive Organization

The selective influence of ego-involvement, ethnocentrism, prejudice on transitory cognitive phenomena in perception, learning, and retention is too well-known to require elaboration.* More relevant to

* For a summary of these findings, see M. Sherif and H. Cantril.[90]

this discussion is a consideration of the effects of basic personality trends, particularly developmental trends, on continuing aspects of cognitive organization. Evidence suggestive of this—the association of orthodoxy, authoritarianism, ethnocentrism, and anti-Semitism,[4] and the negative relationship between intelligence and orthodoxy [36, 49]—has already been cited. At the level of "response set" to learning tasks, it has been found that anxiety predisposes toward rigidity and the avoidance of improvisation in novel, problem-solving situations.[11, 39] The anxiety-ridden individual who suffers from impaired self-esteem over-reacts with fear to novel adjustive situations because of feelings of inadequacy in coping with them. To reduce his anxiety he approaches such situations with an habitual response set of avoiding the need for improvisation by "priming" himself in advance, or by adapting a familiar and stereotyped response pattern to the demands of the new problem.[9, 11]

Somewhat more significant than the influence of personality trends on the learning of objective data is their effect on the assimilation of values. The important shift during adolescence from satellizing to incorporative and exploratory orientations, and the adoption of a generalized anti-parent or anti-adult point of view is illustrative of the relationship between adolescent personality development and value organization. This topic has been given extensive treatment in previous chapters (see pp. 199–200, 172 and 175), and will be considered again in Chapter 15 dealing with the school.

THE NATURE OF ADOLESCENT INTERESTS

The general topic of adolescent interests is introduced in this chapter because these are an important product of the interaction between intellectual growth and personality development. This much was evident in the discussion of the relationship between intelligence and interests (see pp. 288–289). We shall examine here only (a) certain general characteristics of adolescent interests and their determinants, and (b) those recreational interests with strong cognitive or intellectual components. Specific social, vocational, motor, and school interests are considered in appropriate chapters.

The Meaning and Importance of Interests

Interests can be legitimately regarded as motives in the sense that they are selective determinants of behavior and reflect the direction and relative strength of valences associated with different objects and activities in the individual's psychological world. Practically, however, since they only reflect the selective aspect of motivation, it is more convenient to regard them as *organizers* of the psychological field, and to restrict the term *motive* to the discriminable properties of the *goal* attributes of behavior.

Viewed within this conceptual framework then, the psychological field of any individual can be divided into different concentric zones reflecting varying degrees of intensity of ego-involvement. The more central zones are areas of concern and importance to him. He has a vital stake in them. What happens in these areas is a source of pride or shame, of feelings of success or failure. Because of a selective perceptual and cognitive sensitization to these segments of the environment, they acquire a high degree of differentiation. Peripheral zones, on the other hand, are poorly differentiated and are regarded with indifference. Failure in such areas is easily sloughed off, and success does not inspire elation.

But this map identifies only the areas and activities (interests) with which the individual is concerned. It does not make explicit the reasons (motives) for his concern. The motivation for some ego-involved activities may in fact be entirely unrelated to ego enhancement, being energized solely by a need to acquire mastery or to discover a valid solution to a problem (exploratory orientation). The outcome is naturally attended by feelings of success or failure, but self-esteem is not primarily affected. Other interests may be prosecuted as a source of either derived (satellizing orientation) or primary (incorporative orientation) status. In the former instance, the underlying motive is to gain approval or vicarious status from the person with whom the satellizing relationship is established, or to make manifest feelings of personal loyalty to him. In the latter instance, the underlying motive is the acquisition of extrinsic self-esteem by means of superior achievement. Social recognition or applause obviously enhances primary status, but self-enhancement can take place even when achievement is anonymous, through the simple expedient of an individual competing with himself.[8]

In addition to their role as selective organizers of the psychological field, interests are also valuable indices of developmental maturity. In a given cultural environment interest patterns undergo characteristic shifts at different stages of development. Thus, despite considerable variability and overlapping between age groups (which reflect individual differences), fairly regular and predictable developmental changes occur. On the basis of interest patterns it is possible to make a general assessment of maturity that takes into account intellectual, social, and personality growth. This, in fact, is the basis of tests of "developmental age," such as Furfey's for boys [38] and Sullivan's for girls.[99]

The selective process inherent in interests can also be put to another useful diagnostic purpose. Selectivity is never accidental. Particular interests (apart from limitations of capacity and opportunity) always reflect individual personality trends (introversion-extroversion, egocentricity-sociocentricity, subtlety or grossness of perception), and the relationship is invariably a reciprocal one. Participation in certain activities is, therefore, a determinant as well as a reflection of given personality characteristics.

General Characteristics of Adolescent Interests

Compared to preadolescence, interests during adolescence show both continuity and modification. Many of the activities of childhood are continued into adolescence but assume more complex or organized form; e.g., sports, games, reading, interest in mass media.[63] Other activities are continued but for different reasons. Thus, during adolescence, interests become less ends in themselves and more means by which extrinsic status, social prestige, heterosexual effectiveness, or pre-vocational competence are attained. Changes in interest patterns, however, lack the characteristic abruptness of the physical alterations of pubescence since they depend on more complex phenomena than shifts in internal hormonal balance. Even when childhood activities are eventually destined to be discarded (dolls, marbles, tops), this is done gradually.[63]

Although less abrupt in onset than physical changes of adolescence, interest patterns show a similar deceleration in rate of change. This is as true of vocational interests, which become relatively stable by the age of twenty-five,[97, 98] as of the more generalized interests measured by tests of developmental age, which cease to show change at the much earlier age of sixteen.[38] No systematic attention has been given to the stability of the detailed content (as contrasted to general maturity trends) of interests during adolescence. Although it has been established that specific adolescent interests decline with increasing age during later adult life,[15] no empirical studies have tested the widespread impression that these interests reflect short-lived fads and intense but transitory enthusiasms which disappear almost as abruptly as they arise. This impression, however, is consistent with the general picture of adolescent emotional lability.

The total amount of time available for recreation decreases during adolescence because of the encroachment of other responsibilities, such as study, work, and travelling to school or work.[29] More important are changes in the content of recreational activities. Interests that promote social contact with the opposite sex (dancing, dating, parties) are increasingly valued,[12, 63] whereas interests requiring vigorous physical activity decline.[12, 29, 63, 96] The loss of interest in physical activities is quite abrupt among girls,[63, 96] but it is much more gradual among boys. Outdoor sports are still popular with young adolescent boys, but they become more complex and highly organized, and are motivated more by considerations of social prestige with members of both sexes.[12, 29, 63] In later adolescence this motivation still inspires considerable participation in team sports, but the general trend is toward more sedentary and spectator activities.[12, 29, 63]

The number of recreational activities indulged in drops markedly with increasing age.[29, 63] This is in part a reflection of (a) the trend toward increased selectivity, canalization, and differentiation of interests and abilities, and (b) the decreased availabilty of leisure time. In part, however, it is only indicative of the growing complexity and formalization of adolescent activities. Many "kid" games and "gang" activities are abandoned simply because they are too informal, and so seem juvenile. Other simpler single activities, such as running, throwing, dodging, become incorporated into more complex games such as football.[52]

Determinants of Adolescent Interests

The foregoing changes in interest patterns characteristic of the adolescent period are attributable to the two major kinds of variables we have dealt with thus far—psychobiological and psychosocial. In the first category belong factors that are relatively universal in cultural distribution. These factors (pubescence, intellectual maturation) are responsible for the more general changes in direction and content of adolescent interests, namely, their increased reference to social sex themes and to primary status as the underlying motivation, their decelerating rate of change, and their increased complexity and lability. In the second category belong factors that are more specific to a given social environment and account for differences among cultures, subcultures, and social classes. These differences are the product of differential cultural expectations. Sex differences in interest patterns, for example, for the most part reflect institutionalized concepts of social sex role.

In this section we shall also consider determinants of differences between the interest patterns of individuals of comparable developmental status who share the same social environment.

Impact of Pubescence. Pubescence exerts both a direct and an indirect influence upon adolescent interests (see pp. 134–135). Directly—by lowering the threshold of awareness for sexual stimuli and by contributing to the evolution of sexual drives—it is largely responsible for the increased interest in social activities with heterosexual reference.* Indirectly—by modifying cultural expectations of appropriate behavior for children at this stage of development—it leads to the de-emphasis of certain juvenile activities and to the encouragement of more mature interests. This influence is evident in the positive correlation between developmental age (maturity level of interests), on the one hand, and height [38] and androgenic content of boys' urine on the other.[94] Postpubescent boys and girls also achieve higher scores on tests of developmental age than their prepubescent contemporaries,[18, 95] and postmenarcheal girls exceed premenarcheal girls of matched chronological age in their concern with adornment and heterosexual social activities and in their aversion to vigorous physical activity.[96]

That pubescence alone is not responsible for all of the changes in adolescent interest patterns, especially those *not* relating to heterosexual social activities, is evident from the absence of significant

---

* Some of the differences in heterosexual social activities between pre- and postpubescent individuals are less a direct reflection of increased hormonal stimulation than of physical advantages associated therewith (height), which makes such activities as dancing, dating, and automobile driving more feasible and socially acceptable.

differences between the play interests of prepubescent and post-pubescent boys of similar chronological age.[29] Also, although adolescent and preadolescent boys *do* differ in their play interests, the very gradual transition in interest patterns (in contrast to the relative abruptness of physical changes) suggests that other variables are involved in this developmental process. A large number of preadolescent interests that are not obviously inappropriate will survive because of the inertia from canalization (see p. 184). Once the psychological world of the individual is selectively organized into zones of differential ego-involvement, reciprocal channels of reinforcement (see p. 293) increase differentiation in the same direction unless there are compelling forces of an antagonistic nature.

Sex Differences. Differences in adolescent interest patterns of the sexes are influenced chiefly by the different cultural expectations of the appropriate social sex roles of boys and girls. To a lesser extent they reflect differences in age of pubescence and in gross motor skills. Hence, although the general trends in social and physical interests are the same for both sexes, (a) the heterosexual social interests of girls emerge at an earlier age, and (b) the interests of boys in active sports do not begin to wane until middle and late adolescence. The greater concern of girls with matters of personal attractiveness and of boys with vocational and money matters reflect the differential social pressures.[100]

During adolescence, lines defining activities and roles traditionally considered appropriate for a single sex group are more sharply drawn. Prior to this time there is some overlapping despite the increasing segregation of the sexes in middle childhood and preadolescence; and the overlapping more frequently involves an invasion of boys' interests by girls [62, 64] (girls' interest in baseball, rough games, and juvenile books written for boys) than *vice versa*. Few "tomboys," however, carry their revolt into adolescence. At no other period of life is the divergence between the sexes in scores on the Masculinity-Femininity Test as great as during adolescence.[104]

Social Environment. The influence of gross social and cultural factors (differences in national culture, urban-rural differences) on the development of interests is self-evident. Differences in the physical environment, in the availability of recreational materials and participants, and, most important, in the prevailing values, conventions, and expectations of the cultural group impose many specific characteristics on the general developmental picture. Rural children, for example, participate more in solitary, out-of-doors, and collecting activities, and are required by the low density of population to play less organized and less formal games embracing a wider age range of participants.[64, 121]

Social class and race differences in interest patterns reflect discrepancies in purchasing power (purchase of automobile or individual athletic equipment) as well as broader differences in values. Adolescents from upper socioeconomic and educational levels do more reading,[12, 80] read higher quality books and magazines,[80, 115] do less "loafing," [12] and participate more in individual as against team sports.[12] For related reasons, the same differences are found in a comparison of Negro and white youths.[12]

Individual Differences. More important perhaps than differences among contrasting groups (racial, rural-urban, sex, educational, socioeconomic) are differences among individual adolescents with similar group affiliations. Such individual differences reflect variability (a) in the distribution of human abilities (motor, intellectual); (b) in those aspects of personality organization determining selectivity in tastes; (c) in the unique experiential background of every individual (in the types of activities to which he is exposed); and (d) in the types of activities that are encouraged and rewarded by significant persons in each child's familial, school, and peer group environment.

Original proclivities for certain activities (based on differences in ability and personality make-up) perpetuate themselves by leading to successful and satisfying experiences, frequent practice, and, hence, to greater enhancement of the ability or trait. Through canalization, perceptual sensitization, and progressive differentiation of the psychological field, increasing selectivity in ordering ego-involvements becomes a characteristic feature of psychological development. Relative degree of interest in a given activity is most likely a good criterion of level of ability in that activity—but only in the hierarchy of abilities *within* an individual, not *between* a group of individuals.[107] Sometimes, however, such degree of interest more faithfully reflects differences in the hierarchy of rewards associated with different activities.

The relationship between interests and activities is a reciprocal one. Just as interests stimulate related activities, activities undertaken without any special interest may inspire such interest retroactively. Similarly, in the course of involvement, the motivation for an interest may change (the exploratory orientation may supplant or replace the incorporative orientation or vice versa).

During infancy and early childhood, as Jersild [52] points out, what a child does and is interested in doing is almost completely a reflection of what he is *able* to do. Later, opportunity, stimulation, and differential reward become equally important. Thus, the older child exercises only *some* of his potential capacities, and his *expressed* interests can no longer be considered coextensive with the potential range of interests he is capable of developing with appropriate stimulation. For these reasons, the current widespread tendency to regard the expressed interests of the child at any given moment as "sacrosanct" and representative of his "true" needs and capacities is not defensible on logical grounds. Needs and interests do not simply "unfold" during development from the impetus supplied by internal maturational factors. At all times they represent the interaction between genetic predispositions and environmental influences.

The teleological notions that only "endogenously derived" needs are genuine and worth while, and that *only* the child "knows" what is best for him and can suitably select what he truly needs are supported neither by logic nor by facts. They have been uncritically extrapolated from experiments with animals and human infants that indicate that in *certain* instances spontaneously selected foods best meet nutritional requirements.

> Accordingly, an educational policy of utilizing children's interests should be aimed to help children to cultivate and to acquire the most rewarding interests and should not be bound by the particular interests that children happen to have acquired.[52]

RECREATIONAL INTERESTS

Some of the general changes in the interest patterns of adolescents can be illustrated by specific recreational activities that reflect both intellectual growth and characteristic shifts in the relative appeal value of different aspects of the cognitive field.

Reading

The adolescent does more reading than the preadolescent,[55] and reads more discriminately, critically, and purposefully.[63, 102] He reads less "for fun," and more in pursuit of his own specialized interests.[63, 102] His more critical and serious tastes in reading are illustrated by an increasing preference for nonfiction,[32] for informational books dealing with politics and economics,[16] for higher quality magazines,[33] for magazine articles concerning world events and political news,[55, 58] and for the news, editorial, and society sections of the newspaper.[55] At the same time he desires more adult fiction and humor in books and magazines,[16, 33, 59] and his interest in juvenile fiction [16, 59] and in magazine content dealing with westerns, detective stories, and motion picture stars declines.[58] All of these changes reflect (a) increased intellectual maturity, (b) expanding interest in the wider cultural environment embracing real persons and social problems, and (c) growing concern with self-improvement as an instrument for acquiring primary status.

Mass Media

The recreational activities of the modern adolescent are increasingly dominated by the numerous varieties of mass media available.[70] Newspapers, magazines, and the radio receive increased attention during adolescence, whereas movie attendance drops only slightly.[25, 70] Television has begun to supplant radio, reading, and the movies, and to some extent is encroaching upon peer group and play activities.[71]

Changes in movie and radio interests during adolescence closely parallel those for reading. News broadcasts and commentators attract a larger audience of adolescents than preadolescents.[51] During early adolescence increasing preference is shown for more serious and realistic radio drama and for more subtle humor.[51] Concomitantly, interest in children's and mystery programs begins to wane.[17, 20, 21, 114] The greatest change in radio interests, however, is shown in the rather abrupt increase in the popularity of dance music and popular songs.[17, 20, 21, 114] This undoubtedly reflects the more intense absorption with heterosexual social activities.

Movie preferences follow the same pattern. Preference for westerns declines and is partly replaced by increased interest in historical and romantic themes.[75] Romantic movies are especially appealing to girls,[75] but both sexes respond maximally to the erotic stimulation in love scenes from sixteen to eighteen.[31] The gain in critical judgment is reflected (as in reading and radio tastes) in greater insistence on subtlety in humor, and on plausibility, restraint, and ingenuity in the creation of suspense and dramatic plot.[1, 2]

Hobbies

An analysis of the types of collections adolescents make and of the reasons they give for undertaking them gives another good index of the change in adolescent interest patterns. Collecting interests, like reading interests, become noticeably more purposeful and discriminating during adolescence. The number of collections per individual diminished, but those maintained are more related to actual interests and to envisaged needs.[118, 120] No longer are useless articles collected just "for fun."[118] Changes in content are also consistent with the general trend of adolescent interests. Marbles, coins, stamps, and beads give way to letters, photographs, old magazines, and theatre programs.[58, 118]

REFERENCES AND BIBLIOGRAPHY

1. Abbott, M. A.: A sampling of high-school likes and dislikes in motion pictures. Sec. Educ., 6:74–76, 1937.
2. Abbott, M. A.: Children's standards in judging films. Teach. Coll. Rec., 39:55–64, 1937.
3. Abernathy, E. M.: Relationships Between Mental and Physical Growth. Monogr. Soc. Res. Child Develpm., I., No. 7, 1936.
4. Adorno, T. W. et al.: The Authoritarian Personality. New York: Harper, 1950.
5. Anderson, J. E.: "The Prediction of Terminal Intelligence from Infant and Preschool Tests," in Intelligence: Its Nature and Nurture, 39th Yearbook, Natl. Soc. Stud. Educ., Part I. Chicago: University of Chicago Press, 1940.
6. Asher, E. J.: The inadequacy of current intelligence tests for testing Kentucky mountain children. J. Genet. Psychol., 46:480–486, 1935.

7. Ausubel, D. P.: Problems of adolescent adjustment. Bulletin. Natl. Assn. Secondary School Principals, *34*:1–84, 1950.

8. Ausubel, D. P.: Prestige Motivation of Gifted Children. Genet. Psychol. Monogr. *43*:53–117, 1951.

9. Ausubel, D. P.: *Ego Development and the Personality Disorders.* New York: Grune and Stratton, 1952.

10. Ausubel, D. P. and Schiff, H. M.: The effect of incidental and experimentally induced experience in the learning of relevant and irrelevant causal relationships by children. J. Genet. Psychol. In Press.

11. Ausubel, D. P., Schiff, H. M., and Goldman, M.: Qualitative characteristics in the learning process associated with anxiety. J. Abnorm. Soc. Psychol., *48*:537–547, 1953.

12. Bell, H. M.: *Youth Tell Their Story.* Washington, D. C.: American Council on Education, 1938.

13. Biber, B. et al.: *Child Life in School.* New York: Dutton, 1942.

14. Boynton, P. L.: The relationship between children's tested intelligence and their hobby participations. J. Genet. Psychol., *58*:353–362.

15. Briggs, E. S.: How adults in Missouri use their leisure time. Sch. & Soc. *47*:805–808, 1938.

16. Brink, W. G.: Reading interests of high-school pupils. Sch. Rev., *47*:613–621, 1939.

17. Brown, F. J.: *The Sociology of Childhood.* New York: Prentice-Hall, 1939.

18. Carey, T. F.: *The Relation of Physical Growth to Developmental Age in Boys.* Washington, D. C.: Catholic University of America, 1935.

19. Cattell, R. B.: Personality traits associated with abilities. I. With intelligence and drawing abilities. Educ. and Psychol. Measurement, *5*:131–146, 1945.

20. Clark, W. R.: Radio listening activities of children. J. Exper. Educ., *8*:44–48, 1939.

21. Clark, W. R.: Radio listening habits of children. J. Soc. Psychol., *12*:131–149, 1940.

22. Conrad, H. S., Freeman, F. N., and Jones, H. E.: "Differential Mental Growth," in *Adolescence,* 43rd Yearbook, Natl. Soc. Stud. Educ., Part I. Chicago: University of Chicago Press, 1944.

23. Conrad, H. S., Jones, H. E., and Hsaio, H. H.: Sex differences in mental growth and decline. J. Educ. Psychol., *24*:161–169, 1933.

24. Cornell, E. L.: *The Variability of Children of Different Ages and its Relation to School Classification and Grouping.* Albany, N. Y.: University of State of New York, 1936.

25. Dale, E.: *Children's Attendance at Motion Pictures.* New York: Macmillan, 1935.

26. Davis, W. A.: *Social Class Influences upon Learning.* Cambridge, Mass.: Harvard University Press, 1948.

27. Dearborn, W. F., Rothney, J. W. M., et al.: *Predicting the Child's Development.* Cambridge, Mass.: Sci.-Art Publishers, 1940.

28. Despert, J. L. and Pierce, H. O.: The Relation of Emotional Adjustment to Intellectual Function. Genet. Psychol. Monogr., *34*:3–56, 1946.

29. Dimock, H. S.: *Rediscovering the Adolescent*. New York: Association Press, 1937.

30. Durost, W. N.: *Children's Collecting Activity Related to Social Factors*. New York: Teachers College, Columbia University, 1932.

31. Dysinger, W. S. and Ruckmick, C. A.: *The Emotional Responses of Children to the Motion Picture Situation*. New York: Macmillan, 1933.

32. Eberhart, W.: Evaluating the leisure reading of high-school pupils. Sch. Rev., *43*:257–269, 1939.

33. Elder, V. and Carpenter, H. S.: Reading interests of high school children. J. Educ. Res., *19*:276–282, 1929.

34. Finch, F. H.: Enrollment Increases and Changes in the Mental Level of the High-School Population. Appl. Psychol., Monogr., No. 10, 1946.

35. Fleming, C. M.: *Adolescence: Its Social Psychology*. New York: International Universities Press, 1949.

36. Franzblau, A. N.: *Religious Belief and Character among Jewish Adolescents*. New York: Teachers College, Columbia University, 1934.

37. Freeman, F. N. and Flory, C. D.: *Growth in Intellectual Ability as Measured by Repeated Tests*. Monogr. Soc. Res. Child Develpm., II, No. 2. Washington, D. C.: National Research Council, 1937.

38. Furfey, P. H.: A revised scale for measuring developmental age in boys. Child Develpm., *2*:102–114, 1931.

39. Gaier, E. L.: *Selected Personality Variables and the Learning Process*. Psychol. Monogr., Vol. 66, No. 17, 1952.

40. Garrett, H. E: A developmental theory of intelligence. Am. Psychologist, *1*:372–378, 1946.

41. Garrett, H. E., Bryan, A. I., and Perl, R. E.: The Age Factor in Mental Organization. New York: Archives of Psychology (Columbia University), 1935.

42. Gilbert, H. H.: High-school students' opinions on reasons for failure in high-school subjects. J. Educ. Res., *23*:46–49, 1931.

43. Harris, R. E. and Thompson, C. W.: The relation of emotional adjustment to intellectual function: A note. Psychol. Bull., *44*:283–287, 1947.

44. Hartson, L.: Does college training influence test intelligence? J. Educ. Psychol., *27*:481–491, 1936.

45. Havighurst, R. J. and Janke, L. L.: Relations between ability and social status in a mid-Western community. I. Ten-year-old children. J. Educ. Psychol., *35*:357–368, 1944.

46. Hendrickson, G.: Mental development during the preadolescent and the adolescent periods. Rev. Educ. Res., *20*:351–360, 1950.

47. Hollingworth, L. S.: *Children Above 180 I.Q., Stanford-Binet*. Yonkers, N. Y.: World Book Co., 1942.

48. Honzik, M. P., Macfarlane, J. W., and Allen, L.: The stability of mental test performance between two and eighteen years. J. Exper. Educ., *17*:309–324, 1948.

49. Howells, T. H.: Comparative Study of Those who Accept as Against Those who Reject Religious Authority. Univ. Iowa Stud. Charact., II, No. 2, 1928.

50. Janke, L. L. and Havighurst, R. J.: Relations between ability and social status in a mid-Western community. II. Sixteen-year-old boys and girls. J. Educ. Psychol., *36*:499–509, 1945.

51. Jersild, A. T.: "Radio and Motion Pictures," in *Child Development and the Curriculum,* 38th Yearbook, Natl. Soc. Stud. Educ., Part I. Chicago: University of Chicago Press, 1939.

52. Jersild, A. T.: *Child Psychology.* New York: Prentice-Hall, 1947.

53. Jersild, A. T.: *In Search of Self.* New York: Teachers College, Columbia University, 1952.

54. Jersild, A. T. et al.: *Child Development and the Curriculum.* New York: Teachers College, Columbia University, 1946.

55. Johnson, B. L.: Children's reading interests as related to sex and grade in school. Sch. Rev., *40*:257–272, 1932.

56. Jones, H. E. and Conrad, H. S.: *The Growth and Decline of Intelligence: A Study of a Homogeneous Group Between the Ages of Ten and Sixty.* Genet. Psychol. Monogr., XIII, No. 3, 1933.

57. Jones, H. E. and Conrad, H. S.: "Mental Development in Adolescence," in *Adolescence,* 43rd Yearbook, Natl. Soc. Stud. Educ., Part I. Chicago: University of Chicago Press, 1944.

58. Jones, M. C.: *ICW Interest Record.* Berkeley, Calif.: Institute of Child Welfare, University of California, 1944

59. Jordan, A. M.: *Children's Interests in Reading.* New York: Teachers College, Columbia University, 1921.

60. Keene, C. N. and Stone, C. P.: Mental status as related to puberty praecox. Psychol. Bull., *34*:123–133, 1937.

61. Kuhlen, R. G.: *The Psychology of Adolescent Development.* New York: Harper, 1952.

62. Lazar, M.: *Reading Interests, Activities and Opportunities of Bright, Average and Dull Children.* New York: Teachers College, Columbia University, 1937.

63. Lehman, H. C. and Witty, P. A.: *The Psychology of Play Activities.* New York: A. S. Barnes, 1927.

64. Lehman, H. C. and Witty, P. A.: A study of play in relation to intelligence. J. Appl. Psychol., *12*:369–397, 1928.

65. Levy, J.: A quantitative study of the relationship between intelligence and economic status as factors in the etiology of children's behavior problems. Am. J. Orthopsychiat., *1*:152–162, 1931.

66. Lewis, W. D.: A comparative study of the personalities, interests and home backgrounds of gifted children of superior and inferior educational achievement. J. Genet. Psychol., *59*:207–218, 1941.

67. Lewis, W. D. and McGehee, W. A.: A comparison of the interests of mentally superior and retarded children. Sch. & Soc., *52*:597–600, 1940.

68. Lorge, I.: Schooling makes a difference. Teachers College Rec., *46*:483–492, 1945.

69. Lucena, J. et al.: O test de Rorschach en um grupo de adolescentes. Neurobiologia, Pernambuco, *11*:275–344, 1948.

70. Lyness, P. I.: The place of the mass media in the lives of boys and girls. Journalism Quart., 29:43–54, 1952.

71. Maccoby, E. E.: Television: Its impact on school children. Publ. Opin. Quart., 15:421–444, 1951.

72. Mather, W. G. The courtship ideals of high-school youth. Sociol. & Soc. Res., 19:166–172, 1934.

73. McNemar, Q. and Terman, L. M.: Sex Differences in Variational Tendency. Genet. Psychol. Monogr., XVIII, No. 1, 1936.

74. Michaud, S.: L'Interpretation de figures geometriques par l'enfant. J. de Psychol. Normal. et Pathol., 42:295–308, 1949.

75. Mitchell, A. M.: Children and movies. Chicago: University of Chicago Press, 1929.

76. Mitchell, C.: Why do pupils fail? Junior-Senior High School Clearing House, 9:172–176, 1934.

77. Newman, H. H., Freeman, F. N., and Holzinger, K. J.: Twins: A Study of Heredity and Environment. Chicago: University of Chicago Press, 1937.

78. Oakes, M. E.: Children's Explanations of Natural Phenomena. New York: Teachers College, Columbia University, 1947.

79. Pressey, S. L., Janney, J. E., and Kuhlen, R. G.: Life: A Psychological Survey. New York: Harper, 1939.

80. Pressey, S. L. and Robinson, F. P.: Psychology and the New Education. New York: Harper, 1944.

81. Purvis, A. W.: An analysis of the abilities of different intelligence levels of secondary-school pupils. Unpublished Ed.D. thesis, Harvard University, 1938.

82. Regensburg, J.: Studies of Educational Success and Failure in Supernormal Children. New York: Archives of Psychology (Columbia University), 1931.

83. Reymert, M. and Hinton, R., Jr.: "The Effect of a Change to a Relatively Superior Environment upon the I.Q.'s of One Hundred Children," in Intelligence: Its Nature and Nurture, 39th Yearbook, Natl. Soc. Stud. Educ., Part II. Chicago: University of Chicago Press, 1940.

84. Richardson, C. A. and Stokes, C. W.: The Growth and Variability of Intelligence. B. J. Psychol. Monogr. Supplements, XVIII, 1933.

85. Rogers, A. L.: The growth of intelligence at the college level. Sch. & Soc., 31:693–699, 1930.

86. Ross, C. C.: Should low-ranking college freshmen be told their scores on intelligence tests? Sch. & Soc., 47:678–680, 1938.

87. Schulman, M. J. and Havighurst, R. J.: Relations between ability and social status in a mid-Western community. IV. Size of Vocabulary. J. Educ. Psychol., 38:437–442, 1947.

88. Sears, P. S.: Levels of aspiration in academically successful and unsuccessful children. J. Abnorm. & Soc. Psychol., 35:498–536, 1940.

89. Segel, D.: Intellectual Abilities in the Adolescent Period. Washington, D. C.: Federal Security Agency, 1948.

90. Sherif, M. and Cantril, H.: The Psychology of Ego-Involvements. New York: Wiley, 1946.

91. Shuey, A. M.: Improvement in scores on the American Council Psychological Examination from freshman to senior year. J. Educ. Psychol., *39*:417–426, 1948.

92. Shuttleworth, F. K.: "The Cumulative Influence on Intelligence of Socio-Economic Differentials Operating on the Same Children over a Period of Ten Years," in *Intelligence: Its Nature and Nurture*, 39th Yearbook, Natl. Soc. Stud. Educ., Part II. Chicago: University of Chicago Press, 1940.

93. Snyder, T. A.: Reporting intelligence test scores to high-school pupils. Sch. Rev., *45*:105–111, 1937.

94. Sollenberger, R. T.: Some relationships between the urinary excretion of male hormone by maturing boys and their expressed interests. J. Psychol., *9*:179–189, 1940.

95. Stone, C. P. and Barker, R. G.: Aspects of personality and intelligence in postmenarcheal and premenarcheal girls of the same chronological age. J. Comp. Psychol., *23*:439–445, 1937.

96. Stone, C. P. and Barker, R. G.: The attitudes and interests of premenarcheal and postmenarcheal girls. J. Genet. Psychol., *54*:27–71, 1939.

97. Strong, E. K.: Interest maturity. Personnel Journal, *12*:77–90, 1933.

98. Strong, E. K.: *Vocational Interests of Men and Women*. Stanford, Calif.: Stanford Univ. Press, 1943.

99. Sullivan, Sister C.: A Scale for Measuring Developmental Age in Girls. Stud. Psychol. & Psychiat., Catholic University of America, 3, No. 4, 1934.

100. Symonds, P. M.: Sex differences in the life problems and interests of adolescents. Sch. & Soc., *43*:751–752, 1936.

101. Terman, L. M. et al.: Mental and Physical Traits of a Thousand Gifted Children. Stanford, Calif.: Stanford University Press, 1925.

102. Terman, L. M. and Lima, M.: *Children's Reading*. New York: Appleton-Century, 1927.

103. Terman, L. M. and Merrill, M. A.: *Measuring Intelligence*. Boston: Houghton Mifflin, 1937.

104. Terman, L. M. and Miles, C. C.: *Sex and Personality*. New York: McGraw-Hill, 1936.

105. Terman, L. M. and Oden, M.: *The Gifted Child Grows Up: 25 Years' Follow-Up of a Superior Group*. Stanford, Calif.: Stanford University Press, 1949.

106. Thetford, W. N., Molish, H. B., and Beck, S. J.: Developmental aspects of personality structure in normal children. J. Proj. Tech., *15*:58–78, 1951.

107. Thorndike, E. L.: Early interests: Their permanence and relation to abilities. Sch. & Soc., *5*:178–179, 1917.

108. Thorndike, E. L: On the improvement of intelligence scores from thirteen to nineteen. J. Educ. Psychol., *17*:73–76, 1926.

109. Thorndike, E. L. et al.: *The Measurement of Intelligence*. New York: Teachers College, Columbia University, 1927.

110. Thorndike, R. L.: *Children's Reading Interests: A Study Based on a Fictitious Annotated Titles Questionnaire*. New York: Teachers College, Columbia University, 1941.

111. Thorndike, R. L.: Growth of intelligence during adolescence. J. Genet. Psychol., *72*:11–15, 1948.
112. Thurstone, L. L. and Ackerson, L.: The mental growth curve for the Binet Tests. J. Educ. Psychol., *20*:569–583, 1929.
113. Triggs, F. O.: A study of the relation of the Kuder Preference Record scores to other various measures. Educ. and Psychol. Measurement, *6*:3–16, 1946.
114. Tyler, I. K.: Radio studies in Oakland schools. Educ. on the Air, *5*:297–312, 1934.
115. Warner, W. L. and Lunt, P. S.: *The Social Life of a Modern Community.* New Haven: Yale University Press, 1941.
116. Wechsler, D.: *The Measurement of Adult Intelligence.* Baltimore: Williams and Wilkins, 1939.
117. Wheeler, L. R.: The intelligence of east Tennessee mountain children. J. Educ. Psychol., *23*:351–370, 1932.
118. Whitley, M. T.: Children's interest in collecting. J. Educ. Psychol., *20*:249–261, 1929.
119. Wile, I. S. and Davis, R. M.: Behavior differentials of children with I.Q.'s 120 and above, and I.Q.'s 79 and below with some reference to socio-economic status. Am. J. Orthopsychiat., *9*:529–539, 1939.
120. Witty, P. A. and Lehman, H. C.: Further studies of children's interest in collecting. J. Educ. Psychol., *21*:112–127, 1930.
121. Witty, P. A., and Lehman, H. C.: Collecting interests of town children and country children. J. Educ. Psychol., *32*:176–184, 1933.

PART THREE

Psychosocial Problems

CHAPTER 11

Adolescents and the Wider Community

THE NATURE OF PSYCHOSOCIAL PROBLEMS

UNDER THE HEADING of psychosocial problems we shall consider the more specific aspects of adolescent development attributable to the unique social conditions within a given culture. These problems reflect differences rather than uniformities in the developmental process between cultures. The chief sources and categories of psycho-social problems have been catalogued in Chapter 2 (see pp. 44–45). Problems such as these, characteristic of adolescent development in modern Western civilization, were at one time considered inevitable and universal consequences of man's biological heritage. Only recently, since the emergence of cultural anthropology * as a scientific discipline, have we come to regard these problems as "unique by-products of the specific values, socioeconomic conditions, and training institutions presently current in our society." [2] Viewed within the perspective of numerous studies of the comparative ethnology of adolescence the *specific* problems confronting adolescents are apparently to a large extent culturally conditioned.[34]

At this point it might be reasonable to inquire why the problems discussed in the preceding chapters on motor, somatic, personality, moral and intellectual development could not be legitimately characterized as psychosocial. Is it not true, for example, that the very determination of the content as well as the significance of a somatic deviation is socially conditioned; that it is meaningless to consider the problems of emancipation or personality maturation apart from the matrix of social factors in which they are embedded? The answer is that a psychobiological problem is only a classificatory abstraction that has no phenomenological existence. By definition it reflects

---

* For a critique of the social approach to adolescence, the assertion that all problems of adolescence are psychosocial in origin, that no developmental uniformities prevail from one culture to the next, see pp. 14–15.

commonality in process or principle which is universally true only when expressed in such a highly generalized form that it corresponds to no actual situation anywhere. That is, there *are general principles of adolescent development which do transcend cultural boundaries.* But since discussion of such principles in abstract form not only would be artificial, but also would present almost insuperable difficulties to comprehension, it has been convenient to consider them in the setting of present-day American culture. We have so far discussed *universal* problems of adolescent development—problems theoretically rooted in a common culture-free base of physiological, personality, and intellectual change—as manifested in the particular social environment that is most familiar to us.

How do such psychobiological problems differ from genuine psychosocial problems when given social reference? In the concluding seven chapters of this book we shall be concerned with three main categories of psychosocial problems: (a) Problems that possess very little universality because they do not stem from basic features of adolescent development but "owe their origin to the particular way in which a given society undertakes to handle or control the period of adolescence." [2] Such problems, e.g. schooling, vocational, peer group, are, in other words, essentially "handling" rather than growth problems, and are not likely to exhibit any features in common with other dissimilar cultures. Emancipation from parents, on the other hand, is a universal theme of adolescent development with specific variations in every culture. (b) Problems that do arise from universal developmental needs (for example, sexual expression) but depend almost entirely on specific social conditions for their mode of gratification. Apart from the existence of the basic need, there is no developmental uniformity from culture to culture at the level of implementation. (c) In addition to these two types of psychosocial problems, which arise from directed social efforts to regulate the "adolescent transitional period—whether they consist of primitive initiation ceremonies or complex educational processes—there are other general characteristics of a social order bearing no specific or intended relation to the regulation of adolescence, but which nevertheless affect its development profoundly. For example, what effect do war, depression, rapid social change, conflicting cultural values and restriction of employment opportunities have on the nature of adolescence?" [2]

We shall, therefore, be dealing in the following chapters with the *unique* problems of the American adolescent. We will not use his problems to illustrate more universal developmental principles that have widespread generality despite specific cultural patterning. This will be the story of adolescents who are denied membership in adult society, who create an elaborate, semi-independent interim subculture of their own, who undergo prolonged schooling and vocational apprenticeship, who live in a world of rapid social change and of conflicting moral ideologies, and who are required to submit to prolonged sexual control and postponement of marriage.[17] We shall *not* be concerned with general attributes of personality maturation, with level of ego aspiration, with degree of volitional independence, with type of status sought, with the quality of striving, with the mode of assimilating values. Instead we shall try to ascertain *how*, within the framework of American culture, adult goals are differentiated with respect to cultural values and in terms of class and sex roles, because the adolescent strives

> to stabilize his ego values . . . in relation to his reference group, whatever this may be to him in his particular social milieu. He does his level best to incorporate into his ego . . . the norms of the group in his particular social setting.[34]

Since our culture is not a homogeneous one, we will have to give considerable attention to the impact of social stratification on the behavior of the various social groups to which our adolescents owe allegiance. Thus, it might be more accurate to characterize the task of this concluding section as an inquiry into the nature of the psychosocial problems confronting the *several* subcultures of adolescents in the total American population of this age group.

RELATIONSHIP OF ADOLESCENTS TO THE WIDER COMMUNITY

Increased Contact with and Awareness of the Social Order

With adolescence comes an inevitable widening of the child's social horizon. He grows away from the restricting confines of the family and of the neighborhood peer group. Through increased, broadened, and more direct contact with the wider community he acquires more first-hand knowledge of social institutions and of the differences in caste and class mores and values in our mosaic-like culture. This improved perspective of our cultural heterogeneity, however, depends upon more than increased social experience alone. Also implicated are growth in ability to formulate abstractions and to perceive both hierarchical relationships in group structure [4] and the distinguishing symbols of social class status.[36]

The adolescent's enhanced social experience is itself a function of several changed factors. His greater size and appearance of maturity, plus the newly-won emancipated status in the home, increase his physical mobility. He is more free to come and go as he pleases, to participate in activities at a distance from home, and to make friends beyond the radius of the neighborhood. Even overprotective parents must be reconciled to letting him travel to high school or to work. And, apart from the broadening influence of such travel, he is more likely to come into contact with associates drawn from a more diverse social class environment than his neighborhood elementary school.

The adolescent's increased social awareness creates a new and objective basis for evaluating his home and parents (see p. 221). With his liberation from attitudinal and emotional subservience to parental dicta, it helps in his devaluation of parents and in his emancipation from home. At the same time it leads to a certain amount of social disenchantment. Direct and first hand experience with the foibles of authority figures and with the inconsistencies and injustices in many social institutions leads to different and somewhat more tarnished perceptions of the social order than the idealized ones he had naively accepted from Sunday school and textbook descriptions.

Increased awareness of the wider social environment is accompanied by increased interest in current events, politics, and social and economic issues. This is reflected by appropriate shifts in reading and radio listening interests (see pp. 300–301). Growing concern with social problems is shown in the increased percentage of adolescents (as compared to preadolescents) who express humanitarian views,[25] in the large percentage of adolescents who hold very definite opinions on social issues,[5] and in the participation of youth in various social and political movements.*

Acquisition of Adult Status in Modern Society

The determination of when an individual attains adult status can be made only in reference to a social criterion. Among other things such a criterion must include equal membership in a given adult community, the right to assume accepted adult roles, and the privilege of equal access to activities that determine primary status on an adult level. In other words, the individual attains adult status in relation to the wider community and not in relation to the home or his peer group. The partial recognition as an adult that the adolescent receives in a family setting is too limited in scope and generality to confer adult status; and although the peer group offers complete equality of membership and unrestricted access to primary status, it does so only on a "sub-adult" level.

But the adolescent's need for primary status—"sub-adult" or otherwise—is so desperate that he is obliged to seek it wherever it is to be found. Denied membership in the wider adult community he is forced to predicate his status needs upon performance in school and peer groups. And

> the home—once so important for the regulation of the childhood era—is now caught between the vise of these two more important determinants of interim status and becomes reduced to a vestigial role, often serving as a mere boarding house until he can stand on his own two feet.[2]

In most primitive cultures, adult status is attained more directly and expeditiously in relation to the occurrence of pubescence, taking place concurrently with the emancipation from parents. It

> is usually consummated as the result of initiation ceremonies involving various traditional ordeals and rituals. Then once these are successfully completed, the entire, brief transitional period is happily and speedily brought to a close by the conferring of full adult status.[2]
>
> These rites mark definite shifts in the social and economic status of the individual. . . . Psychologically all of these steps, trials—ceremonies and preachings—which achieve the transition of the adolescent to the adult status, mean formation of attitudes related to his new relative role in society, his

---

* Except for the period of years spanned by the economic depression of 1929–1941, the volume of such activities among American youth has been negligible in comparison with that of youth in Europe, Asia, and South America.

conformity in respecting property and sex rights of elders and interest groups, his settling down in the place assigned him by the established authority of his society.[34]

In most instances the puberty rites for boys are more complex than those for girls. In part this may represent an attempt to match the natural drama in the phenomenon of menstruation. In part, however, it may reflect the greater importance attached to the socio-economic role of men in most cultures.[6] This interpretation is strengthened by Radin's observation that the initiation ceremonies for the girl "become progressively more complex and differentiated as her economic functions become more important, after the introduction of agriculture, for instance. Occasionally, as in some West African tribes, puberty rites exist for her only." [32]

Estrangement between the Adolescent and Adult Society

It comes as quite an unpleasant shock to many adolescents that "the achievement of adult status is not a direct consequence of attaining physical maturity. . . . As children they fail to grasp the significant difference in status separating adults from the younger individuals who resemble them in form only." [3] They nurture an idealized conception "of the status, privileges, and prerogatives which are accorded adolescents in our society." [2] Having this naive aspiration of graduating immediately to adult status, they are keenly disappointed to discover "that they still have no standing in the adult world. In fact, in many respects they are still treated exactly as children, but without enjoying the secure, protected status of the latter." [3]

> Considerable time must still elapse before they completely understand the painful fact that adult status will be withheld for many years. They still have to learn that the achievement of adult status in our society is such a protracted process that it cannot be accomplished directly, but requires instead the interposition of a complex interim status.[2]

Because of the almost complete separation of the value and interest systems of child and adult in our culture, adolescents experience considerable discontinuity and hardship in abruptly scrapping the prestige-giving values of childhood and identifying with adult values. This is particularly difficult since "not very long ago they had enjoyed the king-pin status of being the biggest children in the world of play," and had reluctantly relinquished this status "in the process of assimilating adult goals and standards of responsibility." [3] The unexpected rejection only adds insult to injury. For now the adolescent

> must temporarily hold in abeyance and even reject these new value-identifications for those revered in the adolescent peer society. Here he starts once more at the bottom rung of the ladder; and when, towards the close of adolescence, he reaches the top, he is sent hurtling down to the bottom again as a fledgling adult to start climbing yet another ladder of values.[2]

Ruth Benedict has called attention to the fact that in many "age-graded cultures [which] characteristically demand different behavior of the individual at different times of his life," the trauma of discontinuity is softened by the practice of "graduating publicly and with honor from one of these groups to another." [7]

> By this means an individual who at any time takes on a new set of duties and virtues is supported not only by a solid phalanx of age mates but by the traditional prestige of the organized "secret" society into which he has now graduated.[7]

But in our culture,

> children no longer achieve adult status following the attainment of certain well-defined attributes of physical or sexual growth or after proving that they possess certain vocational and physical skills; and society has done away with the rituals and ceremonies which primitive peoples use to mark the accomplishment of various developmental tasks with their concomitant acquisition of more adult privileges and responsibilities. These "rites of passage" formerly gave a certain definiteness and continuity to the business of growing up and becoming adult. Adolescents knew just what was expected of them at each stage of development; and after achieving the expected tasks they were clearly and ceremoniously rewarded with the prerogatives of adulthood. Now, they are not only confused about the goals of maturation at any particular stage of the game, but also never seem to know what is coming next since the sequence of developmental steps is vague and ambiguous and is subject to frequent change and even to individual preference. Deprived of the ceremonies and rituals, adolescents are always left wondering and unassured about what has already been accomplished and what has yet to be done.[2]

Adolescents are alienated from the adult culture by still another discontinuity. This is "caused by the discreteness, the non-interrelatedness of the various institutions and agencies that deal with the child or the group during any one day," [38] the five or six different teachers, the parents, the church, the peer group and the recreational agency.

> All pursue their own aims and methods separately and independently of the others; and the child is left to reconcile their contradictions, to choose from among them, to take sides, and, hence, to provoke conflict and discord.[2]

The extreme heterogeneity of our society places a heavy strain upon the task of identification; in fact, feelings of *complete* membership or belonging are probably no longer possible.[12] And when to this is added the moral confusion and conflict of our society (see pp. 261–262), the resulting disenchantment with the social order makes the prospect of identification with it not too inviting.

The adolescent, therefore, has sufficient reason to feel ambivalent toward the wider community—its unexpected rejection of his bid for membership, its prolonged withholding of status, its failure to provide signposts of progress and recognition, its fragmentation and compartmentalization of the training process, and its heterogeneity and moral confusion, which make identification difficult and unpalatable. He needs time to become reconciled to this state of affairs and to find anchorage in his own peer culture.

> But until these compensatory adjustments are effected and the initial resentment wanes, hostility and aggressive reactions are the most appropriate mechanisms of defense available to the injured and threatened ego. . . . A good part of the adolescent's exaggerated quest for independence and apparent contempt for established values can be attributed to his need for rejecting the norms of the adult culture which denies him membership. He responds with the attitude that what he cannot have is not worth having in the first place. To show just how little he cares about the adult world and his exclusion from it, he joins a peer subculture which strives to make itself as recognizably distinct and separate from adult society as possible; and as a further expression of his hostility he "takes provocative delight in fashioning norms of behavior which are shocking to adult sensibilities." [3]

Even after the bitterness wears off, the estrangement is perpetuated simply because the adolescent is now anchored almost completely in his own distinctive subculture. The goals and values of the interim status that it provides are partly ends in themselves, which are not held in common with the wider community. Nevertheless, throughout this entire period, regardless of how preoccupied he may appear to be with his peer culture, he keeps one eye focused on his future place in adult society. Ambivalence by definition is a two-sided feeling. What he rejects and purports to scorn, he also reveres and aspires to attain. How else could we explain

> his deliberately premature advocacy of certain external prerogatives of adult-hood such as late hours, smoking, automobiles, fur coats, make-up, drinking, etc.? If adults were *really* beneath his contempt would he strive so hard to imitate and distort their behavior, even if the object of his imitation were to express aggression and to arouse anger and grief? [3]

In conclusion, we can summarize the adolescent's relation to the wider community. His contact with the social order is broader and more direct, and his insight into the workings of the culture is more mature and sophisticated. Through firsthand contact—instead of through the buffer relationship provided by the home—he acquires a more representative perception of cultural process than was possible from the biased interpretation by his parents. He also identifies more with broader social groups and becomes more concerned with social problems. But by no stretch of the imagination can the wider community be considered his primary social group. Rejected by the adult society he seeks to enter, he transfers his primary social affiliations from home to peer group. At first, resentment and various discontinuities inherent in this shift, and later, the very separateness of his own subculture contribute to the estrangement between him and the culture at large. Nevertheless, he never loses sight of the interim quality of his peer culture status and is preparing for his eventual entry into the adult world.

PROLONGATION OF ADOLESCENCE IN MODERN SOCIETY

Causes of Prolongation

Generally speaking, the duration of infancy and the length of the dependency of the young on parents are proportional to the length of fetal gestation and of the life span in a given species. This proportionality, however, breaks down for the human species, with its culture.[39] "Culture complicates and extends the process of psychological development." [3] The more complex a given culture, the longer it takes for psychological development to be completed. Evidence in the previous chapter showed that growth in complex intellectual capacities extends into the college years (see pp. 281–

282). But apart from the necessity of continuing training and education to complete psychological development, the training period must be extended to insure the continuity of the social order, which obviously depends upon transmitting cultural values and traditions to the young.[2, 3]

> This at least is the theoretical premise which underlies the modern educational practice of advocating a broad academic background for all children regardless of future vocation or field of specialization. Actually it is just as much of an institutionalized rationalization to "fill in" productively the extended period of adolescence (caused in part by the evaporation of job possibilities for youth) as it is a progressive development in education. This role of education is more transparent to colonial peoples, who witnessing it for the first time are less indoctrinated by our rationalizations. Thus, they are more uninhibited about cursing their schooling when it does not lead to vocational opportunity.[34] It first became apparent to us, when the sudden manpower shortage during the war resulted in a relaxation of minimum schooling laws which had hitherto been uncompromisingly defended as inviolable guardians of our culture.[2]

Although the extension of education for a large percentage of youth may be a very desirable thing in itself, we should remember that the primary motivation has been the inability of society to provide jobs for adolescents. It is mere sophistry to pretend that they are psychologically too immature to find a place in our economy. Although it may be true that intellectual growth can continue past the high-school period, this growth can frequently be fostered most advantageously by extended education that takes place supplementary to rather than in lieu of job placement.

Postponing the vocational problem by continued schooling provides some immediate feelings of status and social acceptance, but does not completely allay anxiety about occupational security. Two-thirds of all youth regard economic security as their main problem.[5] College students are apt to experience (a) feelings of inadequacy and immaturity referable to their dependent status, and (b) considerable apprehensiveness and uncertainty about the outcome of their schooling and the possibility of obtaining the job for which it supposedly prepares them. The youth who forgoes continuing his education for the sake of immediate employment is more likely to regret his choice later in life than during adolescence. Achieving economic independence during adolescence adds greater enhancement to self-esteem than the pursuit of education. In not a few instances, however, college provides a welcome respite, an opportunity of escaping for several more years the frightening prospect of making a vocational choice, relinquishing economic dependence, or competing in the adult world.

Socioeconomic Factors. Adolescence is prolonged in modern society chiefly by the unique economic situation, in which the productive labor of adolescents is not only unnecessary for cultural survival but also represents a threat to the interests of adult workers. In practically all other cultures, adolescents participate vigorously in the economic life of the community or begin to prepare seriously for some occupational pursuit; and in many of the less favored cultures, the economic contribution of the child is demanded even before pubescence.[34] But

> in our industrial society conditions are such as to make it extremely difficult to provide youth with the work experience so essential for normal personality development, and it is even more difficult to open up for youth avenues leading to gainful employment of a kind that gives tone and zest to life. It is a significant fact that for most youth today creative labor must be had in factory, shop, or office instead of in communal family relations. But when youth turn from home and school to find part-time or full-time employment, they are faced by the ominous fact that our economy, in peace time, cannot make full use of their productive energy [18] [p. 190; quoted by permission of the Society].

The availability of gainful employment for adolescents is even less promising for future years because of the "increasing tendency for persons in the middle and older age groups to constitute a greater proportion of the total population." And "so long as full employment is denied older workers, youth will stand at the threshold of occupational life baffled and frustrated."[18] Trade unions understandably cannot tolerate adolescent competition in a labor market that is never fully depleted under normal peacetime conditions.

> It should be noted [however] that whereas humanitarian concern for health and education [has] led to the elimination of abuses in unregulated child labor, society has given little thought to the harmful effects of status deprivation induced by an almost complete removal of opportunity for adolescent work experience.[2]

Although the shrinking availability of work experience for adolescents is a *general* cultural phenomenon, there is considerable
room for individual differences in inclination. Thus,

> many young people in high school and college find ways of earning part or all
> of their own keep. Even during rather hard times enterprising young persons
> find a surprising number of things to do. Others, again, do not choose to seek
> remunerative work, or are urged by parents not to do so, on the ground that
> it is better for them to invest their time in preparing for future work than
> to divert some of their energies into work of a part-time, stop-gap sort. Still
> others, perhaps, hold themselves above the kinds of jobs that are available.[22]

In addition to the scarcity of job opportunities for adolescents,
the available work lacks the qualities that facilitate personality
development. Excessive specialization has made most jobs highly
monotonous and routinized. There is little opportunity for exercising individual initiative or for obtaining the personal satisfaction
that comes "with an integrated view of total accomplishment." [18]
Modern adolescents fail to derive from the employment that is
available

> the same sense of personal importance and social usefulness that comes with
> greater individual participation in the planning and creative aspects of work.[2]

Special Cultural Conditions. Since biosocial status is most fluid
in adolescence, of all the developmental periods, society easily shifts
its expectations of adolescents with the exigencies of the economic
situation.[46] In times of economic distress adolescents' needs are the
last to be considered, but when the need for manpower becomes
suddenly urgent their participation is taken for granted without the
benefit of any advance preparation.

It is not at all unexpected, therefore, that

> the psychological effects of economic depression weigh heaviest of all on
> adolescents. "With their parents suffering, their own future clouded, the
> ordinary roads to success closed, they blindly seek a way out." [34] At such times,
> children must live almost indefinitely with their parents. Full emancipation
> and marriage are postponed nearly beyond the point of tolerance. Education
> is lengthened even further, but is undertaken only half-heartedly, for seem-
> ingly it leads nowhere.[2]

It is "under circumstances such as these that the characteristic
emotional instability of adolescence reaches its maximum intensity"; [2] for it appears to the adolescent as if all "the organized

power of society [were] arrayed against him in his legitimate quest for status." [8]

> Would it be possible to confront an ego already threatened by body changes, developmental tensions and abrupt loss of status with anything more traumatic? Regardless of the basic strength of his intrinsic self-acceptance, there must be considerable ego deflation—at least in his extrinsic notion of ego adequacy (which is ordinarily a reflection of the value society places upon him). Even if he does blame his environment for his misfortunes, he cannot avoid accepting the verdict that he is a stunted, developmental failure, a permanent sub-adult with marginal and indeterminate status.[3]

The situation is precisely reversed, both quantitatively and qualitatively, during time of war. Vocational opportunity is almost unlimited. Numerous highly responsible jobs become available for relatively inexperienced youths when "endurance, speed, agility . . . and boldness" are at a premium in many military and war industry positions. Under such conditions economic independence is quickly acquired; adolescents virtually have "maturity thrust upon them." [15]

This unaccustomed speed in transformation of status generates distinctive problems of its own. The inflationary value placed upon human service—"when adolescents are given jobs, responsibility, and salaries far out of proportion to their capacity for judgment and discretion"—twists "self-appraisal, appraisal of reality, and expectations from life" completely out of focus.

> In the sudden intoxication of independence, increased hostility develops toward adult authority. Youthful arrogance and conceit grow by leaps and bounds; and parent-youth conflict is intensified as parents feel that their children are "acting too big for their breeches." . . . Older workers resent the sudden influx of youngsters and barely tolerate them. . . .
> The worst of it, however, comes with the inevitable deflation of this new status when the nation settles down to a peacetime economy. For then the frustrations and deprivations formerly regarded as the normal heritage of adolescence become greatly magnified against the relatively "plush" background of the wartime era.[2]

Although the general effect of a war economy is to "accelerate personality development and reduce the harmful effects of delayed maturation to a minimum," it also creates considerable maladjustment for special groups of adolescents. Thus,

> while the inadequate personality gets along better in a military environment involving both little need for initiative and [much] direct subjugation to strong

authority, the introverted individual suffers greatly by being thrown headlong into a group situation where introspection and shyness are given scant respect. Some adolescents feel completely crushed and humiliated if they are rejected for military service. [Others] . . . become apprehensive over the forced interruption of education or vocational training. Girls suffer from the loss of male companionship, and, concerned that sweethearts will not return or will outgrow them, rush into hasty marriages. . . . Sex delinquency rises among the younger adolescent girls who resent being "left out" of the new and awesome world of adult status precipitately opened up for their somewhat older contemporaries.[34] On top of all this, there is great social dislocation: Families migrate, parents separate to find work,[46] and what little is left of home life often disintegrates.[2]

Effects of Prolongation

Negative. The general adverse consequences of prolonged status deprivation on adolescent personality development (retardation of maturation, emancipation, and psychosexual development; delay of marriage and of social and economic independence; depreciation of extrinsic self-esteem; increase in level of anxiety) have been discussed in Chapter 7 (see pp. 205–208). We have also called attention to the role of status deprivation in bringing about emotional instability (see p. 146), and have described the characteristics of this condition (see pp. 145–146). Typical fluctuations in the level of emotional instability throughout adolescence have been related to changes in the total load of deprivation, to adjustments in the expectations of adolescents, and to the availability of substitutive sources of status (see pp. 70–71). It has been suggested that the motivation underlying the adolescent's participation in new, status-oriented activities is independently derived from the ego needs of his biosocial position and from intrinsic interest in these activities rather than "sublimated" from frustrated sex drives (see pp. 28–29, and 70).

> Nevertheless, the development of new sources of status—even if autonomously derived rather than sublimated—tends to counterbalance the effects of deprivations in other spheres, making for a more favorable net balance of gratifications (or for a reduction in the net total of frustrations).[2]

In evaluating the general effects of status deprivation on personality development and emotional instability, it is important to bear in mind that

> the behavior of an individual is conditioned not by the environment alone, but by the ways the individual looks at the environment. Each individual is

different in his understanding of the environment and the enhancement he receives from it. . . . Through this process, each individual reacts differently to the same environment.[33]

Thus, there is extreme variability in reaction to status deprivation as a result of marked individual differences in level of ego aspiration, need for status and independence, frustration tolerance, availability of adaptive resources, and habitual modes of adjustment.

Aggression is the most direct and least sophisticated outcome of the adolescent's state of increased behavioral reactivity. Since it is apt to be diffuse, to contribute little toward goal attainment, and to provoke retaliation and counteraggression, it is usually used only when no other adjustive technique is available or when the need for immediate relief from tension is overwhelming. It is not directed against an indiscriminate object but generally relates to an important ego-involved area in the individual's psychological field. Due consideration is also given to the likelihood of and kind of retaliation. An extreme example of organized group aggression is found in the activities of the predatory adolescent gang. Such gangs arise in "disorganized" urban areas where transitory participation in delinquent behavior is considered a normal part of growing up. They are characterized by

fanatical intra-group loyalty, and by strict adherence to the proposition that their predatory activities are justified by society's indifferent or repressive attitude toward their aspirations for status. Such feelings are more commonly expressed by gang members from racial and ethnic minority groups who come to believe that the organized power of society is arrayed against them, that legitimate endeavor is hopelessly futile, and that organized aggression against society is the only path left open to them.[2]

More usually, however, aggressive responses to status deprivation take the form of

exaggerated demands for independence, rejection of the goals of adult maturation, and generalized contempt for established values and for adults; conceit, arrogance, and defiance of authority; a stereotyped hostile attitude toward parents and elders. Not infrequently such aggression finds a pseudo-philosophical outlet [1] in the more introverted youth, expressing itself as a distorted and cynical materialism which denies any possibility of virtue or altruism; as a crass Epicureanism, as nihilism, or (as most recently) in the so-called philosophy of existentialism.[2]

Withdrawal is also a very familiar adolescent response to deprivation. Milder forms are characterized by exaggerated introspectiveness, reserve, secretiveness, and stubborn disinclination to discuss personal problems. More serious manifestations of withdrawal are persistent retreat from social intercourse, asceticism, excessive intellectualization, running away from home, truancy, and suicide. "Many early marriages among adolescents [34] are merely desperate attempts to escape from conflicts and frustrations regarded as insoluble and unbearable." [2]

Other common adjustive techniques of adolescents include: (a) displacement of affect from a genuine source of anxiety to a "trivial, vastly exaggerated or even imaginary somatic defect" (see pp. 155–156); (b) blustering denial of the existence of any problems, or an "attempt to pass them off lightly by a disarming third-person reference to same, or by an air of swaggering indifference"; [2] (c) excessive indulgence in fantasies of a regressive or "superman" nature; [23] (d) manic attempts to find security in frantic bursts of uncritical enthusiasm and undirected activity; and (e) overindulgence in accessible, hedonistic activity, such as compulsive overeating or sexuality.

Positive. In contrast to these negative or maladaptive (but adjustive) reactions to status deprivation are a number of compensatory responses which provide substitutive status. Chief among these is the peer society, which will be discussed at length in Chapter 12. Another

> very common status-seeking activity of adolescents is the attempt to identify themselves emotionally with the roles of glamorous individuals in public life. Thus, adolescent boys may become completely immersed in the minutest details of the lives and exploits of their heroes in the world of sports; while adolescent girls more frequently preoccupy themselves with the doings of movie and radio personalities. Through this very intense and intimate process of identification, a certain amount of reflected status is achieved. The same mechanism is involved in the "crushes" which adolescents "get" on idolized persons in their immediate environment, such as teachers or highly regarded age-mates, usually of the same sex.
>
> In certain individuals, extreme status deprivation ignites a burning ambition to rise above the limitations imposed by their environment, and sometimes, in exceptional cases, enough drive is generated in this manner to enable the individual to lift himself by his own bootstraps to levels of achievement which would ordinarily be thought impossible under the given handicaps. In contrast to the one who succeeds, however, hundreds make the attempt only to become discouraged and drop out along the way.[2]

During periods of extreme economic distress, unusual degrees of status deprivation may stimulate interest in social reconstruction. "In some instances, this leads to the formation of youth movements avowedly concerned with reforming society for the purpose of increasing economic opportunity." [2]

> In these hopes, expectations and anxieties of the adolescent period, and more specifically, in the image that each individual forms for himself and the aspiration he cherishes for human welfare, may be found a strategic means for social change.[19]

DIFFERENTIATION OF THE SOCIAL CLASS ENVIRONMENT

Social Class Structure in the United States

In our heterogeneous society, there is "no such thing as a uniform social environment determining in the same way the growth possibilities of the transitional period for all adolescents." [2] It seems rather that

> the conditions under which persons have access to fundamental biological and social goals are defined by a system of privilege . . . a system of socially ranked groups with varying degrees of social movement existing between them.[15]
>
> This is a type of hierarchy which ranks people in defined subordinate-superordinate relationships without regard for their age, sex, or kinship roles. Listed in order of increasing degrees of in-marriage, the status groups of this third type include (1) social classes, (2) minority ethnic groups, and (3) castes.[14]
>
> Such status differentiations as these have the effect of defining and limiting the developmental environment of the child. . . . Within each of these participation levels with their cultural environment [he] learns characteristic behavior and values concerning family members, sexual and aggressive acts, work, education and a career.[15]

Social Class Differences. Social class differences are all pervasive in our culture, cutting across lines marking other systems of social rank, such as caste and ethnic origin. Although such differences are by no means vague or indefinite, there is greater flexibility or mobility between social classes than between groups formed on the basis of the other two criteria. For practical purposes we may distinguish between three social classes, upper, middle, and lower.

Members of the upper-class come from old families with a long tradition of wealth, social prominence, and gentility. They place a high value upon family tradition, remain aloof from the community

at large, and indulge expensive and esoteric tastes. Since they constitute a very small minority in any locality, and usually refrain
from direct participation in ordinary civic enterprises, the values
of the middle-class are more likely to constitute the official ideology
of the community.[20]

The members of the middle-class, on the other hand, "set great
store by civic virtue" [20] and assume the lead in community affairs.
"They are great believers in education," in the church, and in
marital fidelity. Their child rearing practices stress "self-reliance,
initiative, loyalty, good manners and responsibility to the community. The vices against which they train their children are stealing and destruction of property, sexual immorality, bad manners,
and carelessness in dress and speech." [20] They usually postpone
marriage until they make a good start in life. Their children are
taught to refrain from direct, physical aggression against others,
and constitute the main supports of the library, the Sunday school,
and the scout movement.

The lower-class contains a much larger percentage of individuals
from minority ethnic groups and non-Caucasian racial stock. They
marry early, have larger families, earn their living through unskilled
labor, and live in depressed and overcrowded urban areas. Their
children are apt to be poorly clothed and badly nourished, and to
receive inadequate medical care. They are partial to gambling,
drinking, extra-marital sex experience, and uninhibited use of curse
words. Family life is less stable; separations and "broken homes"
are frequent. Few taboos are directed against physical assault, free
sex play, or premarital intercourse. Honesty is less of a generalized
trait, and stealing outside the home and immediate neighborhood
is often condoned. There is almost no participation in church or
civic affairs. Children spend more time at home with parents and
siblings, drop out of school as soon as it is lawful to do so, and
contribute to the family income both before and during adolescence.[14, 20, 40]

Caste Differences. Skin color is the chief criterion of caste membership in the United States. Of all the systems of social rank it is
the one most "sharply drawn and rigidly enforced." It is a "lifelong

form of rank" that "one can escape . . . in approved fashion only by death." [14]

Negro children and adolescents face special problems of personality development that

> are closely associated with the peculiar social status that their elders are socially and legally compelled to occupy in this society, and the peculiar evaluations of skin color, hair texture, and other physical features that are imposed upon them by the white majority.[13]

Negro children grow up predominantly under lower-class conditions. Broken homes are even more common than among white families in the same social stratum. Because the father is often absent or unreliable, the mother is the chief source of emotional security and the primary authority figure in the Negro home. "Another related feature of the situation is the preference for girls shown by many Negro mothers and grandmothers" which sometimes leads to an unwitting adjustive effeminism on the part of boys.[13] Perhaps the most unfortunate aspect of the personality development of Negro children is their tendency to accept the negative evaluation that white society places upon their skin color and to exhibit preference for members of their own race who are lighter skinned.[13] *

Negroes manifest several characteristic ways of adjusting to the inferior caste position imposed upon them. These special adjustive techniques are a product of their unique cultural history (previous condition of servitude, fervent religious faith) and of the relative hopelessness of their position in the cultural hierarchy for social mobility and access to economic opportunity. Less insuperable handicaps confronting other unfavored minorities (Jews or Italians), on the other hand, are more likely to inspire increased striving or direct aggression. But the futility of striving and direct aggression for the Negro places a premium on withdrawing, escape, and placatory adjustive devices.

Thus, until relatively recently, direct measures for self-defence or racial advancement by Negroes have been quite rare. Displacement of aggression onto other Negroes is a very common phenome-

* This attention by Negroes to gradations in skin color is becoming less frequent and less important than it used to be. In some Negro communities it is a relatively negligible factor in interpersonal relations.[16]

non, partly because it has been encouraged by the lenient attitude
of white courts.[31] A form of negativism or passive sabotage is one
of the most characteristic adjustive techniques used by Negro school
children, and from the standpoint of covert aggression this is emi-
nently successful since reprisals can usually be avoided. Some
Negroes try to escape the racial problem by crossing the "color line,"
by courting wealth and prestige, or by pretending that discrimination is nonexistent. Others identify with the prestige of their white
employers, rationalize all of their shortcomings on the basis of racial
prejudice, become excessively preoccupied with religion, or adopt
an attitude of resignation, of fitting the stereotype of the lazy, shiftless, happy-go-lucky, and childish figures they are popularly supposed
to be.

Powdermaker [31] has analyzed in some detail the psychological
mechanisms underlying the "behavior of the meek, humble, and
unaggressive Negro who is always deferential to whites no matter
what the provocation may be." Besides its efficacy in avoiding trouble
and winning favors it: (a) serves as expiation for guilt feelings from
only partially repressed hostile impulses toward whites; (b) makes
the Negro feel morally superior, and in his mind insures his eventual
triumph over his oppressors in the other world; and (c) provides
feelings of superiority from the fact that through his outward show
of deference the Negro can successfully mislead whites about his
true feelings toward them.[31] Powdermaker observes, however, that
under the impact of increased education, urbanization, and trade
unionism, the obsequious behavior pattern and the "religious emphasis on rewards in Heaven" are giving way to a more aggressive and
militant approach to the quest for status.[31]

Urban-Rural Differences. The rural adolescent grows up in a
world that demands considerable participation in adult tasks and
concerns, and offers much direct experience, responsibility, and
status on a near-adult level. His socialization is regulated more by
the home than by the peer group, and he acquires most of his
status in family rather than peer culture activities. Although he
generally undergoes personality maturation more quickly than the
urban youth, emancipation from parental control takes place more
slowly, and there is less devaluation of parents and resatellization.
He is less exposed to rapid social change, is able to relate to a more

stable set of values, is more likely to subscribe to orthodox religious beliefs and practices, and usually marries at an earlier age.[26] All of these differences generally make the period of adolescent transition less stressful to him than to his urban contemporary.

Impact of Social Stratification on Adolescent Development

The above differences in caste, class, and subcultural environment have been described in some detail, because by affecting the availability of status and the means of acquiring it, they obviously influence the difficulty, the length, and the mechanisms of adolescent personality development. In this section we shall discuss only the effect of social stratification on degree of status deprivation and motivational pattern. The impact of social class stratification on intelligence, interests, sex behavior, education, vocational choice, and peer group organization is described in the separate chapters devoted to these topics.

Economic necessity may force emancipation relatively early on a working class adolescent; on the other hand, wealth and education may prolong the period of dependency in an upper-class youth. Yet while the former may have to *seek* economic independence earlier, he is in no way sure of attaining his goal; whereas the latter *knows* that even if delayed longer, assured economic success will eventually be his. The position of the middle-class youth is somewhere in-between. Success is not assured in advance. He has to fight and struggle for it; but the greater chances of succeeding give him more incentive to strive than his lower class contemporary. He is, thus, more highly motivated, and his behavior is more persistently oriented than that of either the status levels directly above and below him.[2]

Havighurst and Taba point out that in Prairie City "there is a tendency for upper-middle-class youth to be self-directive persons." [20] This type, who corresponds to our non-satellizer,

has a well-developed sense of self or ego, which seeks gratification through personal attainment. It is as if he gains a sense of self-worth only by demonstrating to himself and to others his ability to achieve. This enables him to be self-assertive, ambitious, and to turn things to his own advantage.[20]

The preponderance of middle-class youths in the "self-directive" personality category follows logically from the fact that the child rearing procedures of this class

seem most likely to produce ambitious, responsible, conscientious individuals with a strong drive for self-achievement. This kind of training in the home, coupled with favorable family economic and social position should produce a maximum number of self-directive persons.[20]

Milner's case-study data also support the proposition that clusters of personality traits typical for a sex group within a given social class can be isolated.[29]

On the other hand,

> the social instigations and goals of the lower-middle-class . . . are funda-mentally unlike those of the lower-class. . . . As the middle class child grows older, the effective rewards in maintaining learning are increasingly those of status; they are associated with the prestige of middle- or upper-class rank and culture. The class goals in education, occupation, and status are made to appear real, valuable, and certain to him because he actually begins to experi-ence in his school, clique, and family life some of the prestige responses. The lower-class child, however, *learns* by *not* being rewarded in these prestige relationships that the middle-class goals and gains are neither likely nor desirable for one in his position. He discovers by trial-and-error-learning that he is not going to be rewarded in terms of these long-range status goals, if he is a "good little boy," if he avoids the sexual and recreational exploration available to him in his lower-class environment, or if he studies his lessons. In this learning, he is often more realistic than his teacher, if one judges by the actual cultural role which the society affords him.[14]
>
> In addition, each class must bear its characteristic time sequence and total load of status deprivation. Total load varies inversely with height of class standing; whereas the order in which periods of low and high load tend to follow each other is more likely to be in ascending order for the lower group and in descending order for the upper group.
>
> There are also differences in the type of goals sought and in the approved manner of competing for them. In one group, direct physical attack is the preferred method; in the other, aggression is more polite and indirect, covered by a veneer of disarming amiability. As is to be expected, there are marked differences in the urgency with which adolescents of different class origin [9] view the importance of preserving the *status quo*.[2]
>
> Because identification with caste, class and sex membership groups first become crucially important as ego supports during adolescence, we must reckon with their negative as well as their positive attributes. The fact that a given adolescent in the United States is white, Protestant, upper-class, and can trace his ancestry back to the Pilgrims is a powerful brace to his marginal develop-mental status. But if he is of Negro, Jewish, or Mexican descent, or lives on the wrong side of the tracks, what then? He must surely suffer an additional defla-tion in ego status, the traumatic potential of which must, as always, be evalu-ated in relation to the strength of extrinsic self-acceptance.[3]

It can be said, in addition, that there is sufficient time to build a quite stable system of intrinsic self-esteem within a familial setting before the impact of caste or class becomes a significant factor in the child's psychological field. Depending on whether or not this is done, the psychological trauma of identification with a stigmatized caste or class can assume either central or peripheral importance to the individual's self-esteem. The wide range of individual differences in reaction to this situation certainly lends support to this interpretation.

Interaction between Social Classes

Although it is obvious that interaction and overlapping between social classes has to occur in a culture such as ours, with its highly developed systems of travel, communication and mass media, the preservation of class identity is dependent upon the maintenance of "restricted learning environments." By "defining the group with which an individual may have *intimate* clique relationships, our social class system narrows his training environment." [14] Interaction is discouraged by "powerful and firmly established taboos upon participation outside of one's status level . . . [by pressures] exerted not only by those above . . . but also by persons below . . . and by those in one's particular class." [15] It is understandable that the greater part of the initiative and pressure in the enforcement of class boundaries is exerted from above downwards; at the lower levels, the taboos are mostly defensive and retaliatory rather than derived from a genuine fear of contamination. As already noted, the enforcement of segregation becomes stricter as children approach adolescence and are required to reflect more closely the *mores* of their particular social class group. And since women enjoy a more sheltered position within the confines of the social class to which they owe allegiance, girls are protected more than boys from inter-class contact.[11, 42]

The upper-class provides a homogeneous social atmosphere for their children through the device of the private boarding school.

> Intermingling of different classes is further discouraged by factors of distance (neighborhood) , clothes, and parental pressure. But even more important are feelings of class loyalty which are strongly developed by the time a child reaches adolescence.[2]

Centers [10, 11] found a close parallelism between the class identification feelings of adolescents and adults in the various social strata, which was somewhat greater for girls than for boys and which tended to increase with advancing age.

It is not surprising, therefore, that the organization of adolescent peer groups parallels the social class stratification of our society, and that stratified peer cultures provide the appropriately restricted learning environments necessary for the perpetuation of the social class structure.

> After years of subtle indoctrination along class lines, the adolescent seldom needs any coaching when it comes to the organization of his peer group. "The basis of the social clique is equality of the members in social status and similarity in culture." [15] Thus, a girl at the Junior League level learns to treat girls of her own class with a certain easy familiarity, while maintaining a discreet distance from girls of lower class levels. This feeling is strong enough sometimes even to be applied to *relatives* of different social status. And not only is membership in a social clique limited to individuals of equivalent social levels, but so are "crushes" and identifications.[34] When this unwritten rule of social intercourse is violated, serious maladjustments almost inevitably arise because of the ensuing family discord.[2]

The two chief socializing agents of adolescence, the school and the peer group, work hand in hand in reinforcing the existing stratification of our society. Teachers are predominantly middle-class in origin and outlook. They are strongly disposed to organize the school and to dispense rewards and punishments so as to favor middle-class and to penalize lower-class children.[15, 20, 21] *

The dominant peer culture of the high school is also middle-class, places a high premium upon scholastic success, and enforces adherence to middle-class values and morals. This further disposes teachers to reward conformity to and punish deviation from middle-class standards.

At the same time, it must be admitted that in recent years there has been an increased downward diffusion of middle-class ideology as a result of widespread military service, extension of government-financed college education to many lower-class youths, and dissemination of middle-class points of view through various mass media.[30] However, it is just as erroneous to argue that these levelling influences have completely eradicated social class distinctions as it is to insist that complete homogeneity of attitude and belief prevails within a given social class.

---

* A vivid account of how such a system of privilege and bias operates in a typical secondary school is given in Hollingshead's *Elmtown's Youth*.[21]

TRANSMISSION OF SOCIAL CLASS VALUES AND ASPIRATIONS

Exposure to an appropriately restricted learning environment obviously facilitates the assimilation of differentially appropriate social class values and aspirations. It does not, however, explain per se the motivational auspices under which such internalization takes place. There is, furthermore, the difficult task of explaining how social class values can be effectively transmitted from adults to adolescents in the face of the serious conflict and discord between the two generations. How is it possible for an adolescent to "repudiate the immediate authority of his parents and still retain their social class values?" [3]

To explain the evolution of differential class aspirations among adolescents it is only necessary to carry one step further than we have the concept of "socially adaptive anxiety" developed by Allison Davis.[15] In Chapter 7 we demonstrated how the culture at large engenders *transitional anxiety* as a means of motivating the personality development of adolescents (see p. 207). The transmission of differential *class* levels of aspiration in our society, on the other hand,

is achieved by the maintenance [in] the individual of a certain level of anxiety with regard to the attainment of the required behavior for *his status*. This socialized anxiety plays a major role in propelling him along that cultural route prescribed by his family, school, and later by adult society at his cultural level. . . . The anxiety which middle-status people learn is effective first because it involves the threat of loss of present status [and the severe social penalties associated therewith], and, second, because it leads as the individual may plainly see in "successful persons" to the rewards of power, of social prestige, and of security for one's children. . . . Anxiety leads to striving because only thus can anxiety be reduced to a tolerable level [15] [pp. 204, 214; quoted by permission of the Society].

Long-range anxiety is an efficient taskmaster only if it is reinforced by more proximate contact with the pressures and threats which give it substance. If these are removed by virtue of a break in communication with [parents and] adult society, another more acceptable source of authority for the enforcement of class norms must be found. The peer society fulfills this function admirably since the adolescent does not feel that liberation from its standards is an essential requirement for emancipation. Quite the contrary, conformity to peer standards is one of his most cherished values. He can therefore assign with equanimity to his peer group the proximate power to enforce class aspirations without relinquishing the rebelliousness he deems essential for his development.[3]

Upon the peer group, therefore, devolves the responsibility of maintaining, reinforcing, and transmitting to adolescents the appropriate motivational patterns that parents and adults favor but are unable to communicate and enforce effectively because of the estrangement that has grown up between them and their children.

> And with the power of social ostracism at its disposal, it sees to it that the values, associations, aspirations and behavior patterns of its members adhere closely to the class reference group to which it owes allegiance.[2]

As Sherif and Cantril point out,

> no matter how serious the youthful rebellion and restlessness may be, adult-youth conflict in most cases will be an intra-family and intra-community affair. . . . An adolescent boy was strongly and at times openly critical of everything his parents did. Nevertheless he shared the major class delineations, political views and social distance norms of his upper-middle-class parents.[34]

The need of this boy was to "reject his elders, and not their class aspirations." When these aspirations were espoused and enforced by his peer group they were quite palatable and acceptable.

IMPACT OF SOCIAL CHANGE ON ADOLESCENT DEVELOPMENT

A condition of rapid social change compounds the difficulties of a person who himself is in a period of developmental transition. For added to the marginality and disorientation induced by the abrupt shift in biosocial status are the ambiguities and confusions of the new social environment to which he is required to make an adjustment. To be catapulted from a secure and charted psychological field into one that is virgin and unexplored is bad enough; but when the new field lacks stable landmarks and points of reference, the transition is even more traumatic. Thus,

> adolescents more than any other segment of the population are bound to suffer from the [contradictions] and anxieties inherent in a period of social transition. In fact, it is precisely these doubts and perplexities springing from the rapidity of social change which are in large measure responsible for the difficulties . . . of adolescence in our society.[2]

Rapid social change generates three special kinds of developmental difficulties. (1) Most obvious is the accentuation of the disparity between generations that is responsible for much of the parent-youth conflict (see pp. 229–230). (2) A second difficulty is a function of the fact that when the social order is in a state of flux there is no stable system of values to which the adolescent can confidently anchor himself. A person who is floundering is desperately in need of values that are certain and tangible rather than permeated with inconstancy, doubt, and decay. (3) The most serious difficulty, however, is an outcome of contradiction, ambiguity, and confusion. More threatening and productive of conflict than the existence of an unstable system of values are the irreconcilable demands and expectations that inevitably follow from contradictory social norms.

Ordinarily, when the rate of social change is not immoderate, there is a fair correlation between the social and economic conditions governing the organization of society and the kinds of values that govern the behavior of persons. But when the rate of social change increases, both the realities of social organization and the personal relationships they necessitate grow away from their ideological substrate. As pointed out by Newton Edwards,[18]

> although there has been little hesitation about accepting and using the new products of technology, there has been no corresponding willingness on the part of society to reorganize social institutions and to reorient value systems in accordance with the changed modes of living resulting from technological advances.[2]

Since the debris of outworn values has not been cleared but coexists with changed forms of social organization, a hiatus has developed between the official *values* of the culture and the actual *practices* that are realistically possible in interpersonal relations. And since the child is taught that the world is constructed in the image of the official ideology, he is in for some disillusionment when he finally emerges from the sheltered orbit of childhood. "Sudden exposure to the realities of life destroys his romantic and idealized conceptions of marriage, industry, and government." [2]

> The greatest developmental problem posed by technology has been the confusion in standards which it has created, standards of proper goals and methods of achieving them . . . and standards relating to appropriate class and sex roles. . . . Cultural lag has [also] resulted in an unusual amount of moral confusion making "progressively less effective . . . the historic carriers of the core values of society—family, church, and community." . . . [The adolescent,

for example], had been taught the virtues of humility, forthrightness and honesty. Yet all around him he sees the worldly triumph of dissimulation and aggressiveness. He had been led to believe that merit and virtue are inevitably rewarded with all of the good things of life; but in the actual struggle for position, he finds little chance of "climbing the ladder of success" except through favoritism, shrewd dealing and inherited wealth and status. Under these circumstances what shall he do? Shall he hunt with the hounds or run with the hares? 2

Shall youth be taught to lower their level of expectation, to abandon the ideal of social mobility for social adjustment? Are they to be encouraged to hold fast to the old ideal of social mobility even though most of them will experience failure in its realization? Or will they be encouraged to set their hands to the long and arduous task of so modifying the economy as to make possible the older ideal of equal opportunity in a mobile society? 18 [p. 193; quoted by permission of the Society]

But again, individual reactions to moral confusion are extremely variable. Many adolescents fail to perceive that any inconsistency exists. Some experience severe psychological conflict, others are hardly troubled. To many the new moral practices are abhorrent and are accepted reluctantly and with reservations—for purposes of survival only. But to others these same practices are a welcome invitation to join in an unprincipled and ruthless quest for power at any price (see pp. 261–262).

REFERENCES AND BIBLIOGRAPHY

1. Amado, G.: Ethique et psychologie d'un groupe d'adolescents inadaptes. Evolut. Psychiat. Paris, No. 1, 3–30, 1951.
2. Ausubel, D. P.: Problems of adolescent adjustment. Bulletin, Natl. Assn. Secondary School Principals, *34*:1–84, 1950.
3. Ausubel, D. P.: *Ego Development and the Personality Disorders.* New York: Grune and Stratton, 1952.
4. Ausubel, D. P., Schiff, H. M., and Gasser, E. B.: A preliminary study of developmental trends in sociempathy: Accuracy of perception of own and others' sociometric status. Child Develpm., *23*:111–128, 1952.
5. Bell, H. M.: *Youth Tell Their Story.* Washington, D. C.: American Council on Education, 1938.
6. Benedict, R.: *Patterns of Culture.* Boston: Houghton Mifflin, 1934.
7. Benedict, R.: Continuities and discontinuities in cultural conditioning. Psychiatry, *1*:161–167, 1938.
8. Blos, P.: *The Adolescent Personality.* New York: Appleton-Century, 1941.
9. Centers, R.: *The Psychology of Social Classes.* Princeton, N. J.: Princeton University Press, 1949.
10. Centers, R.: Children of the New Deal: Social stratification and adolescent attitudes. Int. J. Opin. Attitude Res., *4*:315–335, 1950.

11. Centers, R.: Social class identifications of American youth. J. Personality, *18*:290–302, 1950.

12. Curle, A.: Incentives to work: An anthropological appraisal. Hum. Relat., *2*:41–47, 1949.

13. Dai, B.: "Some Problems of Personality Development among Negro Children," in *Personality in Nature, Society, and Culture* (C. Kluckhohn and H. A. Murray, eds.). New York: Knopf, 1949.

14. Davis, A.: American status systems and the socialization of the child. Amer. Sociol. Rev., *6*:345–354, 1941.

15. Davis, A.: "Socialization and Adolescent Personality," in *Adolescence*, 43rd Yearbook, Natl. Soc. Stud. Educ., Part I. Chicago: University of Chicago Press, 1944.

16. Davis, A. and Dollard J.: *Children of Bondage*. Washington, D. C.: American Council on Education, 1940.

17. Davis, A., Gitelson, M., Henry, W., and Ross, H.: *Adolescents in American Culture*. University of Chicago Round Table, No. 576, 1949.

18. Edwards, N.: "The Adolescent in Technological Society," in *Adolescence*, 43rd Yearbook, Nat. Soc. Stud. Educ., Part I. Chicago: University of Chicago Press, 1944.

19. Frank, L. K.: "Adolescence as a Period of Transition," in *Adolescence*, 43rd Yearbook, Natl. Soc. Stud. Educ., Part I. Chicago: University of Chicago Press.

20. Havighurst, R. J. and Taba, H.: *Adolescent Character and Personality*. New York: Wiley, 1949.

21. Hollingshead, A. B.: *Elmtown's Youth: The Impact of Social Classes on Youth*. New York: Wiley, 1949.

22. Jersild, A. T. et al.: *Child Development and the Curriculum*. New York: Teachers College, Columbia University, 1946.

23. Joffe, N. R.: The prolongation of adolescence in America. Complex, No. 4, 28–33, 1951.

24. Kinsey, A. C. et al.: *Sexual Behavior in the Human Male*. Philadelphia: Saunders, 1948.

25. Leal, M. A.: *Physiological Maturity in Relation to Certain Characteristics of Boys and Girls*. Philadelphia: University of Pennsylvania, 1929.

26. Leevy, J. R.: Contrasts in urban and rural family life. Amer. Sociol. Rev., *5*:948–953, 1940.

27. Lynd, R. S. and Lynd, H. M.: *Middletown in Transition*. New York: Harcourt, Brace, 1937.

28. Mead, M.: *From the South Seas*. New York: Wm. Morrow, 1939.

29. Milner, E.: Effects of Sex Role and Social Status on the Early Adolescent Personality. Genet. Psychol. Monogr., *40*:231–325, 1949.

30. Ogilvie, F.: The problem of adolescence. Practicioner, *162*:261–262, 1949.

31. Powdermaker, H.: The channeling of Negro aggression by the cultural process. Amer. J. Sociol., *48*:750–758, 1943.

32. Radin, P.: *Primitive Religion, Its Nature and Origin*. New York: Viking, 1937.

33. Segel, D.: *Frustration in Adolescent Youth*. Washington, D. C.: Federal Security Agency, 1951.

34. Sherif, M. and Cantril, H.: *The Psychology of Ego-Involvements.* New York: Wiley, 1947.
35. Silverman, H. L.: The philosophy and psychology of existentialism. Psychiat. Quart. Supplement, *21*:10–16, 1947.
36. Stendler, C. B.: *Children of Brasstown.* Urbana, Ill.: University of Illinois Press, 1949.
37. Sutherland, R.: *Color, Class, and Personality.* Washington, D. C.: American Council on Education, 1942.
38. Tryon, C. M.: "The Adolescent Peer Culture," in *Adolescence,* 43rd Yearbook, Natl. Soc. Stud. Educ., Part I. Chicago: University of Chicago Press, 1944.
39. Warden, C. J.: *Emergence of Human Culture.* New York: Macmillan, 1936.
40. Warner, W. L. and Lunt, P. S.: *The Social Life of a Modern Community.* New Haven: Yale University Press, 1941.
41. Warner, W. L. and Lunt, P. S.: *The Status System of a Modern Community.* New Haven: Yale University Press, 1942.
42. West, J.: *Plainville, U. S. A.* New York: Columbia University Press, 1945
43. Williams, F. E.: *Russia, Youth, and the Present Day World.* New York: Farrar and Rinehart, 1934.
44. Wright, R.: *Native Son.* New York: Harper, 1940.
45. Wright, R.: *Black Boy.* New York: Harper, 1945.
46. Zachry, C. B.: "Preparing Youth to Be Adults," in *Adolescence,* 43rd Yearbook, Natl. Soc. Stud. Educ., Part I. Chicago: University of Chicago Press, 1944.

CHAPTER 12

The Adolescent Peer Culture

In CONTRAST TO the various negative effects of status deprivation elaborated in the previous chapter, the adolescent peer culture has a positive, adaptive function. Besides providing compensatory status, it plays a major role in facilitating emancipation from the home, transmitting social class values, and focalizing resistance against adult standards and authority, and serves as the principal training institution of the adolescent period.

For all of these reasons the social experience and groupings of adolescents acquire significance and structural characteristics that set them off qualitatively from analogous social phenomena during childhood. It is certainly safe to say that in our society "wherever children or youth are together for any length of time and free to pursue their own purposes there will be a subculture operating." [82] But it is not unreasonable to expect one type of peer group to develop when the aim is to provide more or less casually a subsidiary form of status, and quite a different type of peer group when the major status needs of a prolonged period of sub-adulthood must be satisfied.

Thus, we can anticipate that group life will become a more serious and crucial matter for the adolescent than for the child. The adolescent is more intensely concerned with his relationship to the group, more conscious of relative hierarchical standing in group structure, and more highly motivated by considerations of status in dealing with his fellows. And since the adolescent peer group is the chief instrumentality of a distinctive and semi-independent subculture that provides primary status for its members, we can also expect greater differentiation, stability, and cohesiveness of structural organization, and more striking manifestations of group solidarity.

IMPORTANCE OF SOCIAL RELATIONSHIPS DURING ADOLESCENCE

Much evidence points to the overwhelming preoccupation of adolescents with social experience. In Chapter 10 (see pp. 295, 296), we noted the marked shift of interest patterns to social-sex activities and concerns. Stolz, Jones, and Chaffey[73] and Meek[55] have concluded from extensive controlled observations of adolescent behavior that more than anything else adolescents are concerned with establishing social relationships with age-mates of both sexes, and accept or reject new activities chiefly on the basis of the possibilities they afford for furthering this paramount consideration.

The prepotency of group interests in the extracurricular whirl of adolescent activities is reflected in the exaggerated attention to nuances of interpersonal relationships in spontaneous conversation and clubhouse news sheets, and in the dearth of references to school subjects or situations.[17] The conversation of young adolescent girls is dominated by talk of parties, dates, jokes, and movies;[44] and as they increase in age, high school boys discuss more frequently girls, sex, dates, and social activities.[28] Dates, sex, fraternities, sororities, and dancing are important subjects in college "bull sessions."[75] The increased frequency, length, and gossipy flavor of telephone conversations during adolescence adds further testimony to the adolescent's passionate absorption with interpersonal relationships.

There is, also, increased interest in parties, dancing, and in the use of the automobile for social purposes. Interest and participation in social dancing coincide with the onset of pubescence for both boys and girls and reaches a peak in late adolescence.[51, 73] It is, without doubt, the favorite recreational activity of the adolescent period.[37, 73, 76] Attendance at parties follows a very similar development.[37, 73, 76]

The reasons for this intense preoccupation with social experience are apparent. It is true, of course, that group activity is facilitated by the adolescent's greater mobility and newly won emancipation from the home. Group activity also provides an opportunity for gratifying newly acquired heterosexual needs and interests. Much more important, however, is the adolescent's increasing concern with acquiring primary status as an independent entity. And since there can be no status apart from a system of relationships to a constituted social unit, adolescent peer groups are

> formed spontaneously to serve the function of a social institution, to secure a status and a social identity for youngsters not genuinely provided with such an identity by society at large.[70]

Denied membership in the adult community that dispenses status roles in the central stratum of social interaction, he must create a substitutive albeit peripheral status-giving instrumentality of his own.

Hence, more out of necessity than out of inclination,

> adolescents progressively turn to the closer company of age-mates in their transition from childhood to adulthood . . . in an adverse adult-made world in which they are marginal in varying degrees. They interact in their own adolescent circles, limited and influenced, of course, by their particular social setting at large. . . . [Their] most intense strivings for status and approval take place within such groups. . . . This gives rise to certain norms of behavior, to fashions and fads of dress and amusement peculiar to various adolescent groups. During these years of transition, adolescents achieve immediate status through conformity to the norms of their age-mate groups. For the time being these peculiar adolescent norms of experience and behavior become the adolescent's own values, determining his personal relationships and attitudes to an important degree.[70]

And since the peer group is almost the exclusive source of the extrinsic adequacy that he so desperately seeks, it is hardly surprising that he immerses himself so intensely in group experience, becomes so conscious of his own and others' status in the group, and seems so willing to undergo personal sacrifices to render it loyalty and preserve its integrity.

THE ADOLESCENT PEER GROUP IN RELATION TO THE WIDER COMMUNITY

Like the child, therefore, the adolescent continues to enjoy a buffered relationship to the culture at large. He is anchored in a peripheral subculture of his own making, which cherishes values and establishes criteria of status distinct from those of the adult community. But here the resemblance ends, and several important distinctions arise. First, although many of the adolescent's characteristic interim goals are discontinuous with those of adults, they more nearly approximate adult standards and level of behavior than do the child's. Also, the adolescent is more aware of their interim and substitutive nature, and is simultaneously making plans for his inclusion in the adult world. Second, although isolated from the main currents of adult society, the adolescent has a more lively interest in and keener insight into its inner workings than does his younger contemporary. And last, the adolescent peer culture conforms more closely to the adult model of socialization: a group of non-relatives outside the home determines and controls the individual's major source of current status.

It is clear that the social goals of adolescents are basically oriented toward the adult world, and that the chief function of the adolescent peer group is to provide a substitutive status, from the fact that it dissolves as soon as adolescents achieve anchorage and status roles in the wider community. This basic orientation can also be inferred from the fact that the social experience of the peer group is hardly discontinuous with the types of social skills and attitudes necessary for adult socialization. In fact, one of the chief functions that both adolescents and their culture attribute to the peer group is the apprenticeship it provides for adult living. During the enforced period of waiting the adolescent develops the social skills he believes will aid him when he enters the adult arena. His elders, are grateful for the opportunity to reassure themselves that he has internalized sufficiently well the appropriate attitudinal pattern of his social class reference group to be entrusted with equal membership in it.

Finally, it is important to realize that the adolescent peer group is related to the wider community in the very important sense that its nature, structure, norms, and purposes are largely conditioned by the characteristics of the particular adult culture or subculture in which it is embedded. As a survey of various types of adolescent peer groups shows (see pp. 376–382), such "group formations" fail "in the larger sense" to enjoy

> any existence independent of the social milieu in which they are formed. For these groups are obviously, in turn, products of economic, ethnic, and other major social situations in the society at large. . . . The very factors which give rise to spontaneous groups are inevitably found as features of the larger social system. [And] by the same token, the particular activities, standards, and the

like which provide individuals with social standing, status, or popularity in the larger society or in a particular stratum or locality of that larger society loom as important in the activities of these more or less well-structured subgroups. . . .

In the last analysis [even] the major established standards of success or failure of the gang or the gangster world are derived from the competitive, individualistic and financially hoarding standards of the society at large. . . . The major patterns of the gang world are derived from the social system in which it functions.[70]

GENERAL CHARACTERISTICS OF ADOLESCENT GROUP LIFE

Greater Emphasis Upon Subjective Experience

In contrast to the essentially more extroverted preadolescent who is typically content to *participate* in group activities, the adolescent is much more interested in the subjective analysis of group experience. He is vitally concerned with subtle overtones and elusive undercurrents in interpersonal relations, and attempts through introspection to conceptualize them more precisely. To be accepted formally as an impersonal social entity is no longer sufficient. He craves intimate acceptance as a person and is much more sensitive to the feelings of acceptance and rejection directed both toward himself and toward his fellow group members.[4]

It is, at first glance, difficult to reconcile this greater emphasis upon subjective experience with the adolescent's more fervent participation in group experience and diminished expression of individuality (see p. 176). Why as a more introspective and introverted personality should he manifest so strikingly the characteristics of extroversion? The most plausible suggestion is that despite his greater procilivities toward introversion he is *obliged* to surrender himself more completely to group interests and to forego his individuality because the group and not the home is the major source of his status. The marginality of the adolescent's status, his dependence on peer group acceptance, and the greater structural need of the adolescent peer group for conformity to its standards (see pp. 353–355), all produce an apparent but spurious increase in extroversion. Nevertheless, although the adolescent is required to participate more intensively in group activities and to place greater restraints upon his individuality, there are no restrictions on his introverted tendency to subjectivize experience.

This greater need for more subjective and personal group experience is reflected in the adolescent's disposition to abandon the larger unisexual "gang" for the smaller, heterosexual, and more intimate "crowd" or clique. Except in disorganized urban areas where gangs fulfill a special compensatory function in response to the unique deprivations of boys and girls who live there (see pp. 378, 526), gang interests are more typically representative of the preadolescent era.[45, 89]

More Group Consciousness

In distinguishing the peer groups of childhood from those of adolescence, Goodenough observes that

> in most cases the social groups formed by young children lack the solidarity and the feeling of group-consciousness that characterize the adolescent gang or club.[33]

The factors responsible for this enhancement of group consciousness are threefold. (1) Both structurally and functionally the adolescent peer group is a more definite, cohesive, and more *perceptible* social entity than the group formations of childhood. It is by far a more organized, stable, and distinctive institution than the loosely-knit and casual groupings of children, and serves far more important functions for status needs, training, emancipation and resistance. If only because of the tremendous power it wields over their lives, adolescents have reason to be acutely aware of its existence. (2) Second, group solidarity becomes a more important and meaningful concept during adolescence. The ability of the peer group to gain status and privileges for its members is clearly dependent on the extent to which it can maintain its unity and integrity as a distinctive organization. Every adolescent has a personal stake in enhancing and safeguarding the cohesiveness and influence of the group. Self-interest imposes group-mindedness on him. (3) The greater concern with power and status that adolescents characteristically manifest in and of itself makes them more self-consciously aware of the status-giving and "pressure group" functions of their group formations.

Greater Stratification along Social Class Lines

During adolescence there is much greater selectivity in the organization and composition of peer groups than during childhood. Adolescents are considerably more conscious than children of such factors as social class status, ethnic and racial origin, and religious affiliation, and pay much more attention to these factors in judging the acceptability of their age-mates for peer group member-ship.[22, 43, 73] Supporting evidence for these developmental trends (increasing homogeneity of sociometric choice along racial and ethnic lines, increasing awareness of the symbols of social class status, and increasing conformity of childhood and adolescent racial and ethnic attitudes to adult prejudices) has been presented in Chapter 9.

During adolescence, caste and class lines are drawn much more sharply, and only rarely is there any serious overlapping of social strata in the organization of the adolescent peer group. As pointed out, the reason for this development is the decreasing tolerance that the adult world shows for deviations from the approved pattern of class values as children advance in age. Once they stand at the threshhold of the wider community, "playing is for keeps" and sentimental notions of equality can no longer be indulged. This is not to say that individual differences in personality are no longer important in determining relative status among a heterogenous group of adolescents. Such differences continue to operate, but only *intra*-clique wise, *after* differential factors of social class origin have selectively organized individuals into relatively homogeneous sub-groups. With his and their increasing age it becomes decreasingly possible for a child with a winning personality to gain acceptance from his economically more favored contemporaries if he happens to come from the "wrong side of the tracks."

Heterosexual Basis of Organization

The organization of the adolescent peer group differs strikingly from that of its preadolescent precursor. It is predicated upon hetero-sexual attraction and joint participation in activities suitable for both boys and girls rather than upon antagonism between and segregation of the sexes. Sociometric studies uniformly indicate a fair amount of cross sex choices in the primary grades, an almost complete dearth of such choices during preadolescence, and a rapidly increasing choice of members of the opposite sex during the junior high school and high school periods.[15, 50, 56.] One of the important implicit functions of the adolescent peer group is to provide suitable opportunities for gratifying new interests in persons of the opposite sex.

Their earlier sexual maturation directs girls' interests to such heterosexual social activities as dancing and parties before boys'.[37, 51, 73, 76] During the junior high school period girls take the initiative in converting disinterested and somewhat reluctant boys into dancing partners, and in "dragging" them to parties of their own contrivance. Were it not for this pressure from girls the difference for the sexes in the emergence of these interests would undoubtedly be even greater than it is.[73]

Changes during the Course of Adolescence

In addition to the above trends in adolescent socialization, several characteristic developments take place from early to late adolescence. Structurally, adolescent groups undergo increasing differentiation into more selective and intimate subgroups,[13, 44, 55, 90] and choices of "best friends" become more stable.[39, 78] Dating and "going steady" increase in frequency,[63] and social activities generally show greater formality and sophistication.[13, 55] Toward the close of adolescence the standards and values of the peer group exercise less influence on the behavior and strivings of adolescents. This is shown by their liberation from slavish conformity to peer group practices and by their growing tolerance for deviancy in others.[55, 80, 82] Closer identification with adult patterns of values develops (see p. 249). The outward behavior of adolescents becomes more sedate, restrained, and dignified.[55, 80, 82] Marriage and family life are contemplated as more imminent possibilities,[55, 62] and heterosexual attachments are more commonly perceived as related to problems of long-term affectional needs and mating.[48] Finally, increasingly serious concern is given to vocational choice and preparation.[52, 55]

STRUCTURAL CHARACTERISTICS OF ADOLESCENT PEER GROUPS

Adolescent peer groups use most of the organizational principles of adult societies. These groups resemble adult formations more closely than childhood groupings in formality, stability, complexity and differentiation of roles, and self-consciousness of hierarchical distinctions and interpersonal attitudes. Like adult groups,

> they have group purposes, standards or values, and rules of behavior. . . . Such groups also have methods of securing conformity. . . . [Although] the individuals in any such group may remain constant over a long period of time, many changes [occur] in its objectives . . . its values . . . and its relation to the adult society.[82]

But despite its general similarity to adult groupings,

> the structural properties of the adolescent peer culture are to a certain extent uniquely derived from the special needs of the youth group, and are especially influenced "through imitation of and initiation by members of the next older developmental level."[1]

Although various adolescent groups have many functions in common (see pp. 382–384), a fact which makes for generality in such structural characteristics as differentiation into subgroups, conformity requirements, and effectiveness of sanctions, it is clear that the structural properties of different groups will vary according to (a) the specific aspirations of individual group members, (b) their relative feelings of belongingness in the community as a whole, and (c) the particular or specialized goals and functions of a given peer group. These factors, as will be shown (see pp. 376–382), are demonstrably related to social class values, ethnic and regional traditions, degree of social mobility, and specific kinds of deprivations.[70]

Origins of the Adolescent Peer Group

According to psychoanalytic theory, the adolescent peer group (and indeed, the major portion of the adolescent's preoccupation with group experience) are simple derivatives of the mechanism of sublimation. It is assumed that the energy of the culturally frustrated sex drive is directly channelled into group activities and, as a result, sex needs are vicariously satisfied. We have presented evidence that psychophysiological sex drives cannot be successfully repressed or satisfied by indirect means; that lower class males in our culture participate directly in premarital intercourse; and that middle-class males characteristically gratify these drives by petting and masturbation (see pp. 16–22, 141). Origins of the adolescent peer group can be more parsimoniously traced to (a) the practice, established earlier in childhood and preadolescence, of spontaneously forming age-mate groupings for play purposes, (b) the catalytic effect of the urgent need for achieving anchorage and primary status, and (c) the impossibility of realizing these goals in adult society. Peer group activities undeniably reduce the total load of frustration; but they do this not by vicariously gratifying blocked sex impulses, but by improving the adjustment picture in other important areas of ego needs.

Differentiation into Cliques

Of the adolescent's greater need for more intimate and subjective social experience we can say,

> the age-mate reference group . . . defines identification and personal preferences *only* in broad outlines and *only* for standards and fads common to all who relate themselves to these groups.[70]

Further differentiation inevitably and spontaneously gives rise to

> distinct social strata between which there [is] little real intercourse, . . . each of which [building] up its own barriers, defenses, and feelings of solidarity.[13]

The adolescent *clique* is a more or less permanent, closely-knit, selective, and highly intimate small group of individuals who share "common secrets (sexual and otherwise), common desires, common problems, and common interests such as those based on family background, school activities and the like."[70] Shared purposes, interests, and social class values, although prerequisite, are not sufficient for clique formation. More important are personal compatibility, congeniality, and bonds of mutual admiration and affection. A *crowd,* is a larger social aggregation in which interpersonal feelings are less important and more impersonality prevails. A crowd need only be homogeneous in background, goals, interests, and ideals, and does not require unvarying homogeneity of social distance between members. An adolescent *gang* is similar in all these ways to a crowd, but it is usually unisexual, places greater emphasis upon achieving a specific group goal (sexual, athletic, delinquent, aggressive), requires more solidarity and loyalty from its members, maintains a more hostile, rebellious, and conspiratorial attitude toward organized adult society, and resembles the preadolescent gang in its preoccupation with excitement, adventure, and the formal trappings of organizational secrecy.

Gang interests and activities are displaced by "crowds" and cliques during adolescence [45, 73, 89] except when gang formation is specially favored by urban slum conditions. In accordance with their earlier physiological maturation, "such cliques appear earlier in girls than in boys and continue to operate within a more exclusive and secretive atmosphere." [1, 16, 44, 73, 90] This greater proclivity for clique formation in girls may indicate that they have less access than boys to more formal and public criteria of independent status in the adolescent peer culture. It may also reflect the well-established sex difference in favor of girls to be more interested in people and in the subtleties of interpersonal relationships.[43] Such interests can obviously be gratified more easily in cliques than in larger groups. In support of this interpretation is the fact that adolescent girls but not boys use their perceptions of the sociometric attitudes of their age-mates toward themselves in furthering their status in the group.[3]

Clique differentiation follows a well-defined process of progressive selectivity. The first criterion that is invariably applied includes such factors as family background, social status, and ethnic origin. "The basis of the social clique is equality of the members in social status and similarity in culture." [25] Hollingshead found that three-quarters of the high-school boys and girls in a mid-Western town chose as their "best friend" a person of the same social class, and that for such choices to be mutual even more invariably required membership in an equivalent prestige stratum of society.[38] In the relatively few instances of disparity in social class status among members of the same clique, the individual of lower status reflected the value system of his associates more closely than that of persons in his own class group.[38] Even so, limitations in certain social skills and in the economic where-with-all to participate in certain activities, combined with adverse attitudes of persons in both the upper and lower prestige groups imposed almost insuperable obstacles to the continuance of such relationships.[38]

After the criterion of social class compatibility, other more personal criteria are applied. An important factor during early adolescence is degree of social maturity, which is usually a function of pubescent status. Retarded sexual development prevents an individual from being accepted in a clique of normally mature adolescents.[44] Appropriateness of interests is a more important criterion for membership in a crowd than in a clique; in a clique it is a necessary rather than a sufficient condition. At the clique level, the most crucial selective factors are personality characteristics.

Although the personality characteristics that promote compatibility in a given clique vary, obviously, from one clique to the next, it is reasonable to suppose that an individual who enjoys high sociometric status in a particular "crowd" probably possesses the attributes of personality that would make him acceptable to most of its component cliques. The personality factors associated with high sociometric status at various stages of adolescence will be discussed subsequently (see pp. 362–363).

Snobbishness and exclusiveness in adolescent cliques cannot be interpreted as wholly a result of increased need for more intimate and congenial interpersonal relationships. There are at least two other motivations. (a) By derogating other groups of individuals, perceiving them as inferior or undesirable, and treating them with contempt and scorn, it is clearly possible to enhance one's own marginal status relatively without expending the effort or ingenuity required for positive self-enhancement. This mechanism undoubtedly accounts in part for the strong prejudices of college students toward minority group members,[47] for the condescending attitudes of high prestige cliques (Junior League, fraternity and sorority members) toward the non-elite majority, and for some of the general intolerance shown by adolescents for any kind of deviancy or alleged inadequacy. (b) Second, through snobbishness and cliquishness, it is possible to both "corner" and limit the availability of status. By making status a scarcer commodity, one makes its achievement a more signal accomplishment; by creating a deprived and to-be-pitied out-group, the advantages and enjoyment of in-group status are considerably enhanced. Furthermore, by adroit political maneuvering, cliques (fraternities) are able to acquire a monopoly on all important extracurricular posts and offices in high school and college. It is noteworthy that the high school peer culture is almost completely controlled by boys and girls from middle-class families.[35, 38] This fact emerges from intensive observation of the inner workings of the adolescent peer culture in a typical mid-Western community; [35, 38] it is also evident from the higher mean socioeconomic standing of participants in *all* extracurricular activities of a large high school in comparison with that of the school population as a whole.[71]

That girls are more status-conscious and disdainful of out-group members than boys [16] is probably related to the fact that they traditionally enjoy less social mobility and fewer opportunities for acquiring primary status, and seek to protect more jealously whatever status they do have. That is, even as adults, women depend very largely on derived status (the status that accrues from husband, family, or social group) instead of on primary status that results from individual accomplishment and which is capable of transcending the limitations imposed by family and class origins. It is obviously a matter of self-interest for girls and women belonging to high prestige groups to preserve the hierarchical distinctions from which their status is derived.

Conformity Aspects of the Peer Culture

The exaggerated patterns of conformity within the adolescent peer group constitute perhaps its most unique structural characteristic in comparison with the groupings of children and adults. As adolescents become more and more resistive to adult suggestion and increasingly indifferent to adult approval and disapproval,

the approval or disapproval of peers becomes progressively the most influential force motivating adolescent conduct.[7]

For the adolescent there can be no stronger argument for having or doing a thing than the fact that "all the others are doing it." Nothing is likely to awaken so great an emotional disturbance or cause so much worry as the feeling that he is in some way different from the others. "Others" in this case means the other members of his own particular group; he is not especially concerned about resembling those belonging to some other clan. A fashion started by the leaders of a group, even though it may happen to be uncomfortable or inconvenient, is faithfully copied by all the lesser members. Opinions, prejudices, beliefs, likes, and dislikes are likewise determined by the group, and the boy or girl who differs is made to feel the force of group ostracism unless he has sufficient force of personality to bring the others around to his point of view.[33]

Why the Peer Group Emphasizes Conformity. Despite the apparent self-evidentness of the proposition, it is still necessary to inquire why such exaggerated emphasis is placed upon conformity in adolescent peer groups. Two different kinds of explanations may be plausibly advanced: (a) those relating to the structural requirements of peer groups and (b) those relating to the characteristics of adolescents.

No institution, especially if it has status-giving functions, can exist for any length of time without due regard by its members for uniform, regular, and predictable adherence to a set of avowed rules and traditions.

> Hence, in its efforts to establish a new and distinctive subculture and to evolve a unique set of criteria for the determination of status and prestige, the peer society must do everything in its power to set itself off as recognizably distinct and separate from the adult society which refuses it membership. . . . If this distinctiveness is to be actually attained in fact, it cannot admit the possibility of [widespread] non-conformity; since obviously if every adolescent were permitted to exercise his newly acquired craving for individuality, an unrecognizable medley of behavior patterns would ensue. Under such conditions, there would be no peer culture, and hence no compensatory source of status.[1]

Conformity is also essential to maintain the group solidarity that is necessary to offer effective and organized resistance to the encroachments of adult authority. Obviously, if an appeal to precedent or to a *prevailing* standard of adolescent behavior is to be the basis for exacting privileges and concessions from adults, a solid and united front with a minimum of deviancy must be presented to the world. Once a precedent is established as the result of widespread and uniform acceptance of a given practice, each individual stands to profit from it. Johnny can now say, "I want to stay out until midnight on Saturdays; all the other boys do."

> The principle of group conformity, therefore, is a self-protective device which arises from the need of the peer culture to establish and maintain its identity as the chief adolescent status-giving institution in our society; and he who dares to defy its authority and, thereby, expose the group to possible extinction, becomes an arch criminal, an enemy of peer society, worthy of receiving the supreme penalty in its arsenal of retribution—complete and unequivocal ostracism.[1]

Apart from the structural needs of the peer group, various developmental characteristics of adolescents make them prone to overvalue the importance of conformity. First, any person with marginal status is excessively sensitive to the threat of forfeiting what little status he enjoys as a result of incurring the disapproval of those on whom he is dependent. To allay the anxiety from the threat of disapproval he conforms more than is objectively necessary to retain group acceptance or to avoid censure and reprisal. Thus, many perfectly *safe* opportunities for the expression of individuality are lost.

Second, as pointed out, adolescents are partly *motivated* to perceive age-mates as deviants, non-conformists, and out-groupers because by so doing they can enhance the value of their own conformity and in-group status. The larger the number of persons who can be perceived as *outside* the charmed circle, the more individuals they can perceive as inferior to themselves, the greater their own self-esteem becomes by comparison, and the more status value their in-group membership acquires. These ends can be most expeditiously effected by (a) elevating by fiat certain esoteric practices or characteristics into unique virtues, values, and symbols of status, (b) imposing these standards upon others by having them accept them at face value, and (c) acquiring a very low threshold for the perception of deviancy from these standards so that very few individuals can qualify for admission to the select circle of the originators and only "true" exemplifiers of the hallowed norms.

Why the Peer Group Can Compel Conformity. Pressures for conformity to peer group standards originate both from the group and from within the individual. The group implicitly and explicitly makes clear to the individual that it expects and demands conformity for the moral support, the feeling of belongingness, the anchorage, the derived status, and the opportunities for primary status that it extends to him. These pressures become evident when

the young adolescent finds that he is not automatically taken into the group but must win a place for himself. He does this largely by conforming to *their* standards and subscribing to *their* value patterns, by submerging himself in *their* interests and activities.[65]

Conformity becomes the acknowledged price of acceptance, and full membership is carefully withheld until the group feels reasonably assured of the candidate's willingness to assume the obligations he incurs in return for the patent advantages he gains.

The adolescent has little choice but to accept the proposition that is offered him. He is completely and desperately dependent on the peer group for whatever status, security, and anchorage he is able to achieve during these hectic years of transition. Sherif and Cantril [70] hypothesize that "the degree of influence . . . of age-mate membership groups varies directly with the degree of psychological weaning from grown-ups and the intensity of adult-youth conflict"; and that the need for conformity to peer group standards is in direct proportion to the increasing marginality of the adolescent's status. In his desperate need to gain group approval, "the adolescent [therefore] usually does his best to conform to its standards even at considerable cost to himself." [90] To make certain, he is disposed even to overconform.

After he wins an assured place for himself in the group, still other factors reinforce conforming tendencies. He learns that group approval brings a welcome "reprieve" from his transitional anxiety, uncertainty, and disorientation. If his group approves, he can feel absolutely certain of the correctness of his position. No longer need he be tortured by ambiguity or conflicting standards. With experience he also gains insight into the group's structural need for conformity if it is to survive and maintain its identity. It becomes easier for him to accept the burden of conformity when he perceives that his status and his privileges depend on it.

Last, the adolescent comes to render conformity automatically as a voluntarily assumed obligation growing out of the feelings of loyalty, belongingness, gratitude, and indebtedness generated "in the very process of interaction."

> Group norms may become so well incorporated as personal ego attitudes that individual group members will observe them at the cost of personal punishment and hardship.[70]

In closely-knit groups individuals will undergo much personal self-sacrifice to render each other mutual help or to prosecute group goals. For the sake of the group an adolescent may incur risks and face dangers that he would never dream of undertaking for his own benefit.

> Allegiance to group norms may under certain circumstances . . . be carried

to the point of participation in . . . delinquent activities of which an individual adolescent might personally disapprove.[1]

If the implicit pressures of the group and the internalized restraints and endogenously derived dispositions of the individual are insufficient to keep him in line, explicit sanctions are imposed. Depending on the seriousness of the offense and the nature and functions of the group, the punishment may vary from ridicule, censure, and rebuff to complete ostracism and even death. Shaming and ridicule are the most frequent and widespread forms of penalty used by peer groups. In addition to the privately-felt self-depreciation before the group experienced in any feeling of shame (including the shame of guilt), such shaming practices involve pointed *public* attention to the infraction, publicly administered scorn or rebuke, and the exposure of the culprit to general ridicule, humiliation, and "loss of face." The mere fact that public shaming is resorted to does not necessarily eliminate the possibility that the offender experiences guilt feelings either before and subsequent to his offense or with and following his public humiliation (see pp. 254–255).

Individual Differences in the Need to Conform. The prevalence and strength of conforming tendencies during adolescence does not mean that there are no individual differences in the extent and quality of this trait. The highly self-assertive person, for example, can only restrain his individuality to a point, and the extreme introvert inevitably draws a line beyond which he refuses to participate in boisterous and exhibitionistic activities. The adolescent who has a highly developed set of moral or religious convictions may refuse to condone the practices of his group. Other individuals may have overwhelming interests that are regarded with scorn by their age-mates. Finally, the non-satellizer's need for ego aggrandizement and his lack of loyalty and "we-feeling" may cause him to betray group interests for personal advantage. If any of these personality traits are unusually strong they may lead to a sufficient deviancy either to (a) make the individual unacceptable for peer group membership or to (b) induce him to reject the desirability of identifying himself with his age-mates.

Even apart from these deviancy-prone individuals, the majority of adolescents display a "concomitant urge to be unique, to achieve individuality or 'separateness'." [82]

> After the young adolescent has submerged himself in the group to the point where he cannot be criticized for non-conformity, he must then proceed to gain recognition for himself as an individual.[65]

To avoid group disapproval, such attempts are always kept "within the very narrow frame of the group's pattern. The girl tries, for example, to excel in achieving the ideal appearance." [82]

Some evidence points to the conclusion that the adolescent who manifests the least outward concern with group approval tends to rank highest in sociometric standing.[57]

> But he owes this acceptance to the emotional strength and the self-sufficiency which the refusal to curry favor implies, and not to an attitude of independence in flouting group standards. Self-sufficiency, independence, competence, and initiative are not outlawed by adolescents, [but] . . . have high prestige value among these highly status-conscious individuals as long as . . . the urge to be unique or creative [is] kept within the narrow framework of acceptability recognized by the group.[2]

Impact of Group Structural Needs on Adolescent Values

It is hardly surprising that some of these unique structural characteristics of adolescent peer groups inevitably influence the value systems of adolescents. The need for conformity places a premium on loyalty and moral expediency, encourages snobbishness and intolerance, and de-emphasizes the importance of moral courage and consistency. All of these properties of adolescent moral beliefs have been found typical of the youth of Prairie City [35, 38] (see pp. 267–268).

That adolescents evolve extreme, unique, and esoteric values largely reflects the structural need to establish a distinctive subculture, recognizably different from those of adults and children. Respect for this structural need confines competition between groups and between individuals within a group to a struggle to outdo others in esotericism. From this arises a bewildering array of fads [5] which change swiftly and capriciously; but while each is in vogue, woe unto him who dares to challenge the axiomatic superiority over all other possible alternatives with which it is invested.

Last, the undercurrent of stereotyped hostility and resistiveness to adults, which accounts for much of the peer group's solidarity, gives rise to an emphasis upon norms of behavior that are deliberately perverse and shocking to adult standards. One manifestation of this rebellious attitude is an insistence on exemplifying, both prematurely and in extreme fashion all of the external symbols of adult privilege and sophistication that under ordinary circumstances would be perceived as immoderate and in poor taste.

INTERPERSONAL RELATIONSHIPS WITHIN THE PEER GROUP

Up to this point, we have focused on the general characteristics of group experience during adolescence, and on the structural properties of the adolescent peer group. But what about interpersonal relations among *individual* adolescents? Why do some individuals achieve high status and others low status within the group? Why are some rejected whereas others become leaders? Why do certain individuals choose each other as friends?

All of these are questions about the relationship between individual differences in personality, ability, and intelligence on the one hand, and the "relative standing of the individual [group] member," on the other.[70] Also crucial to this relationship are differences between individuals in their approach to group experience and in their relative needs for status and prestige. Nor should we overlook the fact that as a result of interaction between individual differences in personality or between conflicting needs for superior standing in the group, there are tensions generated that exert a "disruptive influence on intra-group [cohesion], the very factor which accounts for the social effectiveness of the peer group."[1] Because the adolescent has no other alternative but to measure

his success against that of those whose status is similar to his, the greater success of some of them in one aspect or another of development . . . [may] threaten to impair the solidarity of those on whom he depends. Also it may appear to him a direct challenge to his adequacy.[90]

Individual Approaches to Group Experience

Although it is true that in general adolescents have greater need than children to acquire primary status (see pp. 197–198), the

relative magnitude and urgency of this need are inversely proportional to the strength of the residual intrinsic self-esteem that a
given adolescent brings with him from childhood (see p. 184).
The relative urgency of the need for primary status also varies
inversely with the degree of *current* derived status that an adolescent is able to extract from his relationships with others. It follows
that individual differences in the need for status in the adolescent
peer group will depend, at least in part, on the extent to which
satellization takes place during childhood. To the individual with
a normal history of satellization, peer group membership

> provides derived status and constitutes an intrinsic ego support. He experiences
> a certain spontaneous joy and enthusiasm in group activity which follows from
> the "we-feeling" associated with group relatedness. To the non-satellizer, on
> the other hand, the field of interpersonal relations is just another arena in
> which [he] contends for extrinsic status and additional ego aggrandizement.
> There is no identification with or self-subordination to group interests, and no
> possibility of deriving spontaneous satisfaction out of gregarious activity. Every
> social move is carefully deliberated for the possible advantages that may accrue
> from it, and the currency of social interchange is supplied by the synthetic
> manufacture of attitudes, remarks, and behavior which can be construed as
> conventionally appropriate for the specifications of a given situation.[2]

It is also reasonable to anticipate that an individual's approach
to adolescent peer group experience will reflect the impact of the
type of child rearing attitudes to which he has been exposed, the
type of relationships he enjoyed with his first socializers (his parents), and the pattern of his earlier peer relations (popularity, leadership, conformity, cooperation, competition).

Deep-seated personality defects rooted in the parent-child relationship influence many individuals to *avoid* interpersonal relations
to varying degrees in preference to competing for status in the
peer group. Rejected, overdominated, overprotected, underdominated, and overvalued children are heir to personality and behavioral traits that make their incorporation into the peer group
difficult indeed. The peer group is ill-prepared to gratify the special
social needs of one or another of these personalities, needs for
special protection, for continuous direction, or for invariable deference. "Under the circumstances, group life must prove, distasteful
and unsatisfying, inviting retreat to the home."[2]

The failure of rejected, overdominated, and overprotected children "to learn adequate social techniques of self-defense and self-assertion because of the habit of deference to the will of others"[2] also disposes them to avoid the vicissitudes and pitfalls of group experience.

> Furthermore, the overprotected child is oversensitized to the possibility of physical mishandling and unfair treatment at the hands of his age-mates . . . and the overdominated child (who has never learned to protect his rights) is continually fearful of being duped and exploited. . . . The rejected child is especially fearful of a repetition of the rejection he experiences at home. . . . [Hence, they] find it more agreeable and less hazardous (in terms of possible exploitation by others) to curtail their interpersonal relations to a minimum. The social isolation resulting from this withdrawal further limits the possibility of learning realistic social roles. . . . And in the process of utilizing withdrawal as an adjustive technique they usually acquire an habitual introversion which further restricts the scope of their social proclivities.[2]

The prognosis for the eventual assimilation of underdominated and overvalued individuals into the adolescent peer group is somewhat more hopeful. Although they are disheartened by failure to receive the deference to which they are accustomed at home, and although they antagonize their associates by their excessively overbearing and obnoxiously aggressive self-assertion, they frequently learn by adolescence how "to express their aggressiveness in more socially acceptable forms."[2]

Surprising changes in introversion-extroversion and in general approach to group experience may occur at adolescence, when the individual is largely released from the influence of the home and enters the "more autonomous, demanding and status conscious" adolescent peer culture. The essentially "tender-skinned" individual, protected by a benevolent home, who had hitherto impressed others as extroverted, may now show greater introversion when his fate is more completely in the hands of less solicitous age-mates. Contrariwise, an intrinsically "thick-skinned" child, who appeared to recoil from interpersonal relations as a result of rejection or overdomination in the home, may become much more outgoing when his relatively more benevolent peer group plays the major role in his socialization.

Bases for Relative Status and Prestige in the Group

The Evaluation of Peer Group Status. The preceding analysis of individual differences in the need for primary status and in approach to group experience has important implications for the evaluation of a given individual's measured status in the group. First, the adolescent's satisfaction or dissatisfaction with the status he enjoys is a function not only of its absolute magnitude but also of his aspirations for status. Second, this status can lead to feelings of success or failure, of adequacy or inadequacy, only to the extent that he is ego-involved in the group. If the status that the group can bestow lies completely beyond the sphere of his ego interests, it matters little to him whether it is low or high.

Equally important for evaluating an individual's status in the group is the methodological problem of determining it. Traditionally, sociometric techniques measure such status in terms of the weighted frequency with which an individual is chosen as first, second, or third choice by his age-mates for the roles of seat-mate, friend, work-mate, fellow-committee member. However, when the sociometric status scores of an adolescent group obtained in this way were correlated against corresponding scores derived by averaging the ratings of acceptance-rejection given an individual by *all* of the group members, the resulting correlation was only .46.[4] Hence, it means one thing to achieve a relatively high level of popularity with most members of a group, and something quite different to be wanted frequently as a *best* friend. Which type of status is more meaningful can be determined only in reference to the needs and desires of a particular individual. An ostensibly popular adolescent in a "formed group" of casual friends may, in terms of his deep needs for intimate personal relationships, be no more than a "successful isolate" or "stranger in his group" who is compensating for rejection at the hands of the clique he truly wishes to join by participating vigorously in socially acceptable activities.[88] On the other hand, it is also possible for "some individuals with little status in the group [to survive] fairly well because of one or two close friends."[82]

Factors Associated with High Peer Group Status. In general,

high status [is] the resultant at any particular stage of the needs and purposes of the group and the particular readiness of some individuals to clarify, to represent, to give concrete expression to these group needs, purposes and objectives.[82]

Since different groups have different goals and values, since changes occur in the needs, purposes, and personnel of a single group, and since an individual enjoys membership in many different groups and is even valued for different qualities by special subgroups (boys and girls) within a group, the factors associated with high peer group status are extremely variable. Research findings on this question can have reference only to the *mean* prestige value of various characteristics among different representative or special groups of adolescents, and not to the factors that actually account for high or low status in a *particular* group.

Numerous factors of personal background in different areas of adjustment have been found significantly related to sociometric status at three contrasting economic levels "and for adolescents generally." Of great significance is the fact that "a basic commonness" was discovered "in the background experiences predictive of social acceptability among the economic levels." [27] This indicates widespread agreement within the culture about desirable traits of personality. Thus, in both such widely divergent environments as a training school for delinquent girls [42] and a summer camp for boys,[26] the personality traits most socially acceptable were coöperativeness, helpfulness, unselfishness, courtesy, considerateness, self-control, even-temperedness, initiative, resourcefulness, and dependability. Although decorum, poise, good manners, and such social skills as dancing, swimming, and skating are approved by adolescent boys and girls,[18, 61, 77] they do not rank as high in importance as the personality traits listed above.[26, 54, 77]

The pattern of personality characteristics admired in persons of the opposite sex also shows considerable sex agreement during adolescence. Ranking high in the esteem of both sex groups are: intelligence, considerateness, good conversational ability, good sense of humor, and politeness.[54, 77] Boys dislike excessive sophistication, "gold-digging," giggling, "showing-off," and aggressiveness in girls, and girls disapprove of untidiness, unmannerliness, conceit, bragging, and egocentricity in boys.[61] These preferences and dislikes are consistent with the stereotyped pattern of virtues and failings claiming widespread acceptance in the American culture.

Age Trends in the Prestige Value of Different Traits. Despite the general correspondence of preadolescent and adolescent evaluations of personality traits to those of adults, several noteworthy changes occur with increasing age. Between the sixth and twelfth grades, talkativeness, bossiness, and restlessness are increasingly associated with higher social acceptability, whereas the reverse is true of sophistication.[50] At the age of twelve, the demure, sedate, docile, prim, ladylike, and nonaggressive girl who conforms to adult expectations enjoys highest status in the group; but by the age of fifteen, "many of the criteria for the idealized boy such as extroversion, activity, and good sportsmanship are highly acceptable for the girl."[80] Among other admired traits are competence and poise in heterosexual social activities and "the quality of being fascinating or glamorous to the other sex." [80] Among boys there is more continuity from ages twelve to fifteen in the pattern of traits associated with social prestige. Physical skill, aggressiveness, and daring are still important, but overt defiance of adult standards is regarded as immature. Superimposed on the preadolescent pattern is a new emphasis on tidiness, personal acceptability, and social poise in heterosexual situations.[80]

During the same age range, boys and girls both place less emphasis on bravery, quickness, and the ability to be amusing, and value more highly the more mature and adult qualities of broadmindedness, cooperativeness, and dependability.[61] From high school to college there is a similar trend for the traits admired in the opposite sex.[54]

Sex Differences in the Basis of Peer Status. The chief differences in the qualities admired in the opposite sex by adolescent boys and girls lie in the greater emphasis girls place upon family social standing and in the greater emphasis boys place upon "good looks." [54] More important, however, is the greater continuity from preadolescence to adolescence in the quailties that make for high peer status among boys. Unlike boys, girls

have no core value—such as athletic prowess—which persists in the peer culture as a significant determinant of status. Heterosexual effectiveness becomes for adolescent boys just another component of a previously defined masculinity; but in the case of girls it becomes an entirely new and [almost] solitary criterion for femininity and for feminine prestige in the [adolescent] peer society.]

But if boys enjoy an advantage in this respect, girls are more fortunate in another. For a boy to be popular with girls he must first achieve popularity with his own sex "on the basis of superior masculine attributes." But "girls who [are] most attractive to boys [can] be liked or disliked or even regarded almost with indifference by their own sex." [82] If a girl is not accepted by her own sex, another source of acceptance is open to her; whereas rejection by the peer group is more complete and devastating for boys.

Continuity of Peer Status during Adolescence. Because of the continuity in (a) the personality traits that are valued in the culture and in a particular subculture, (b) the personnel of a given peer group, and (c) the personality structure of individuals (see pp. 183–185), it would seem reasonable to expect that relative status in the peer group maintains considerable stability over the adolescent years. Such stability is present even in the three year period between ages seven to ten when peer relations are much more fluid.[9] Between junior and senior high school, there is also considerable continuity in the individuals who provide leadership to the group.[53] However, apart from such indirect and inferential evidence, there are no direct research findings on this problem, except for long-term observations on the structure of street-corner gangs.[86]

On the other hand, changes in the membership and purposes of the peer group and in the pattern of personality traits that are admired at different stages of adolescence * lead to inevitable fluctuations in the relative status of individuals. Even in the highly structured street-corner gang, where positions in the group are relatively well defined and stable,

> they should not be conceived in static terms. To have a position means that the individual has a customary way of interacting with other members of the group. When the pattern of interactions changes, the positions change.[86]

And as a result of such changes in relative status in the group, "some individuals have to cope with the problem of status deflation,

* A relatively frequent cause of loss in status lies in the fact that a particular role (clowning) successfully played at an earlier age may become inappropriate to the changing standards of the group. If an individual who excels in a role fails to perceive the diminished esteem in which it is held, he may continue to play or overplay it and thereby progressively undermine his status in the group.[24]

while others must learn to handle successfully the new power that comes with higher status." [1, 82]

Perception of Status in the Group

Realistic interpersonal relations and the smooth functioning of the group in terms of the differentiated status roles of its component members necessarily depend on the ability (sociempathy) of individuals to perceive to what extent they and others are accepted or rejected by the group. We have noted that this ability improves with increasing age and accounts in part for the greater complexity and differentiation of older peer groups. At the adolescent level girls are significantly superior to boys in predicting the ratings of acceptance-rejection given them by their own but not by the opposite sex group. The sociometric attitudes (acceptance-rejection) of girls are also more accurately *perceived* by both sexes than those of boys. In perceiving the sociometric status of *others,* boys are more accurate for members of their own sex, whereas "girls [are] equally well aware of the status hierarchies within either sex group"; [3] their superiority to boys in this inheres in their ability to perceive more accurately the status of members of the *opposite* sex group.

The chief factor accounting for the relative accuracy of either an adolescent's perception of another's acceptance or rejection of him, or of the other's status in the group is his own degree of acceptance of that other person. [3] Acceptance of another results both in a more accurate perception and in an overestimate; rejection leads to precisely the opposite consequences. Surprisingly enough, there is no relationship whatsoever between ability to perceive own and others' status in the group. But in accordance with the popular notion that women are more sensitive than men in perceiving interpersonal attitudes and thereby "to further their social effectiveness in group situations," adolescent girls (but not boys) who have superior sociempathic ability enjoy higher status in the group. [3]

Adolescent Friendships with Age-Mates of the Same Sex

Adolescent friendships are the ultimate conclusion of the progressive selectivity and differentiation of interpersonal relations along a social distance scale that begins with crowd and clique formation. Although this final step generally occurs within the framework of crowd or clique membership, it may sometimes (as with deviants) be the sole form of positive social intercourse with age-mates.

The purpose of adolescent friendships is not, as in preadolescence, merely to satisfy the need for a congenial but relatively impersonal playmate or companion in the prosecution of mutual interests, but to obtain intimate interpersonal experience and mutual understanding and sympathy. With increasing age, children and adolescents turn more and more to their age-mates in sharing confidences and seeking advice about problems that trouble them.[81] Unlike preadolescents, who are intensely eager for a large number of friends,[37] adolescents desire to form fewer but deeper, more intimate friendships.[55] For similar reasons, "best friends" are almost invariably of the same sex, since it is practically impossible to overcome traditional barriers between the sexes in speaking freely about intimate personal problems, especially those concerning sex. Also, if a cross-sex relationship happens to become highly confidential, it is more than likely to lead eventually to affectional, or marital ties.

Bases for the Selection of Friends. The selective factors in the determination of adolescent friendships can be inferred from two related lines of evidence: (a) from the ways in which pairs of friends are similar, as well as from the extent of this similarity*; and (b) from the verbal statements of adolescents about the qualities they seek or desire in friends. Unfortunately, however, the measuring devices currently available for ascertaining the resemblances between friends are too gross to give adequate insight into the subtle factors that obviously must be operative in generating mutual attraction between individuals. At any rate the evidence we have indicates that friends are more similar than dissimilar to each other[8, 29, 57] and that degree of similarity in various traits differs widely.

First, as one might reasonably anticipate, friends are similar in those items that are necessary for adequate and equitable communication and interaction between persons: in chronological age,[32, 41, 46, 83, 85] mental age,[41, 59] IQ,[10, 26, 46, 85] school grade,[41] and

---

* Degree of similarity is customarily expressed as a coefficient of correlation between the paired scores of a sizeable number of mutual friends on a measure of a given trait.

socioeconomic status.[26, 41, 46] Propinquity is initially an important factor [32, 57] but becomes progressively less important as the increased physical mobility and expanding social horizon of children make it less a limiting condition in the exercise of actual preferences. Similarity in certain kinds of interests,[10, 46] and in total number of interests [26] is frequent, but is not a particularly significant factor since considerable dissimilarity in hobbies and personal interests and activities is compatible with strong ties of mutual friendship.[8, 10]

More important to adolescent friendships is similarity in orientation toward and competence in social relationships as judged by measures of social adjustment,[10] social maturity,[32] social intelligence,[84] and sociality.[83] However, between mutual friends agreement on specific social attitudes does not usually exist.[84, 87] Some similarity has been found in such personality factors as moral knowledge,[26] moral conduct,[34] emotional and behavioral adjustment,[10, 26] dominance,[83] and neuroticism.[84] But in addition to the fact that the grossness of the measures makes interpretation of similarity difficult, the degree of relationship is so low as to be valueless for prediction in individual instances.

Verbal statements by junior high school students,[37, 41] of the qualities desired in friends, stress similarity of skills and interests, but college students place more emphasis on sincerity, kindliness, congeniality, good character, and sense of humor.[8] Other outstanding changes with increasing age in the bases for selecting friends are the diminished importance of propinquity and the increased importance of socioeconomic status (especially for girls), and degree of physical maturity.[46]

The Stability of Adolescent Friendships. The more serious and stable nature of adolescent interpersonal relations generally is reflected in friendships, which also exhibit increasing stability over the age range from eleven to eighteen.[39, 78] When the percentage of correspondence between the choices of best friend made on two occasions separated by a two-week interval is used as the criterion of stability, girls' friendships appear to be more stable than boys' after the age of fifteen.[78] Long-term observation of relationships within an adolescent group, however, leads to the conclusion that the friendships of boys last longer.[46]

Adolescent friendships break up for several reasons, the most self-evident of which is tension generated by disparity in age, ability, physical maturity, and socioeconomic status.[46] But commonly, even when such differences do not exist, individuals simply "grow away from each other" in interests, ideals, goals, and social maturity. Other causes for disaffection include rivalry, group politics, and the innumerable factors that make for friction in interpersonal relationships at any age level. Somewhat more specific to the adolescent period, perhaps, is the disintegration of " 'extension of the self' friendships . . . when dissatisfaction with the self-image is acute." [46]

Sex Differences. The basic differences between the friendships of adolescent boys and girls are related to the tendency for girls to be more snobbish, cliquish, and conscious of social class distinctions. Girls establish more intimate and confidential relationships with each other, whereas boys are traditionally more reserved in revealing confidences and in exhibiting overt affection. These differences are strikingly apparent to anyone who has observed adolescent behavior for any length of time; but they can also be inferred from the greater frequency of clique formation among girls,[15] the greater amount of time they spend with their friends,[8] the more pronounced tendency for girls' friendships to be reciprocal,[29] and the greater frequency with which girls give and expect from each other similar sociometric ratings.[3] In choosing friends, girls pay more attention than boys to social class standing. The conflicting evidence on the relative stability of boys' and girls' friendships has been discussed in the preceding section.

Leadership in Adolescence

In contrast to friendship and popularity, which represent the outcome of the feelings (like-dislike, acceptance-rejection) that group members develop toward each other, leadership is more closely related to the *functional* properties of groups. This does not mean that the leader's personality and the group members' feelings toward him are irrelevant to the achievement and maintenance of leadership. It means rather that those aspects of the leader's personality that affect the functional effectiveness of the group and those particular feelings of group members toward the leader that are related to his functional efficacy are *most* relevant to these problems.

The leader may be best described as the person who "moves the group to action" [24] or as the person around whom the group crystallizes.[64] Leadership, therefore, will be bestowed by the group on that individual who in its judgment has the personality attributes, the experience, and the skills to organize, mobilize, and represent the group best in achieving its paramount needs and goals at a given stage of its development. It is highly significant that

> leaders of a group are significantly superior to non-leaders and isolates in their ability to judge group opinion on familiar and relevant issues. . . . This differential ability on the part of leaders . . . is, however, not evident in unfamiliar, or less familiar or less relevant issues.[19]

In friendship and popularity, however, affectional attitudes toward others operate more as ends in themselves. It is highly possible for a very ineffectual person to be very popular; in fact, many easygoing individuals are popular for this very reason. But although popularity does not necessarily guarantee leadership, leaders, by the very nature of things, can seldom be unpopular for any length of time and retain their status. Although a leader is not obliged to form close friendships within the group, if he does he is more apt to "weather declining status" more satisfactorily.[82]

How Leadership is Achieved and Maintained. In accordance with its functional nature,

> leadership is conferred by the group. . . . [It] is not a mystic, innate quality of the individual, but is status given by the group to the individual who demonstrates power given by the group. . . . To the extent that group goals are permanent, these individuals will tend to maintain their leadership over a period of time. Thus, leadership becomes personified. But it is subject to change whenever the group goals shift.[24]

The popularly held belief that gangs are creatures of dynamic leaders is seldom true. Quite the contrary, "the gang forms and the leader emerges as the result of interaction." [79]

The "group-given" nature of adolescent leadership is apparent from the fact that the leader cannot successfully disregard the established traditions of the group or the common purposes that he is chosen to advance.[79] He cannot wield his power capriciously or abusively;[79] and more than any other member of the group, he is required to honor his obligations scrupulously.[86] Nor can adult authorities impose a leader on the group by choosing a promising candidate and "training" him for leadership. If this is done, actual leadership power is withdrawn by the group, and the adult-imposed individual retains at best a nominal status out of deference to his sponsors.[24]

The group-given nature of leadership can also be inferred from its situational character. The personality attributes or competencies that make for successful leadership in one culture, subculture, peer group, or even in one temporal phase or activity of a single peer group may lead to failure in another. To a certain extent, of course, the prestige of leadership ability in one area carries over without any objective justification to an entirely unrelated area ("halo effect"). Human beings in general feel more secure if they assume that a leader personifies the virtues his office requires. But the more experienced and sophisticated individuals become in group activities, the more they choose leaders on the basis of situational requirements, and the less they confuse the criteria for leadership with popularity or personal loyalty to friends.[24]

Once attained, leadership in adolescence is maintained in various ways. Control through fear of physical prowess is much less important than in preadolescence, but it remains a significant factor in most lower-class gangs.[79, 86] More important in adolescent "crowds" is the leader's ability to give or withdraw belongingness, to help the group achieve its aims by his special skills or general cleverness, to influence the group to place high value upon the activities in which he excels, and to manipulate situations to gratify the special needs and allay the anxieties of insecure persons in the group.[24] If he can succeed with these insecure persons he earns their loyalty and support; but first he must be perceptive enough to sense their difficulties and skillful enough to extend sympathy without incurring the wrath of the group for befriending deviants.

The skillful leader also exercises control and influences his constituency through his lieutenants.[86] And when leadership changes, it generally passes on to one of these rather than to a peripheral member of the group.[86] One of the surest signs of the impending elevation of a person to leadership is his increasing degree of association with individuals of high status in the group.[82]

Characteristics of Adolescent Leaders. Although the characteristics of effective leaders vary depending on the requirements of the specific subculture, peer group, and situation, certain traits obviously have more leadership value than others in the majority of adolescent peer group situations within the general framework of the American culture. Research findings agree that the adolescent leader surpasses the nonleader in five broad areas of personality that are self-evidently related to leadership functions: (a) *physical appearance:* height,[6, 14] weight,[6] strength,[79] and athletic prowess; [14, 79] (b) *intelligence;* [14, 30, 40] (c) *decision-making ability:* discriminating judgment,[12, 40] firmness of decision,[18, 79] low suggestibility,[40] self-confidence,[21] and imagination; [79] (d) *interests:* maturity [40] and breadth [21] of interests, and participation in social [72] and leisure-time activities; [72] (e) *socially relevant aspects of temperament:* extroversion,[12] dominance,[12, 40] liveliness,[30] and good sportsmanship.[30]

Stability of Leadership. Leadership fluctuates with changes in the needs of the group as determined both by social maturation and by various situational factors. Nevertheless, the basic pattern of personality traits associated with leadership ability must remain fairly constant beginning with adolescence. This is shown by the fact that although there is little continuity of leadership from elementary to junior high school,[53] there is considerable continuity from junior to senior high school [53] and from senior high school to college.[20] Furthermore, high school leaders of both sexes are more successful in life after school than nonleaders.[23, 66]

The Socially Rejected or Deviant Adolescent

In the adolescent peer group, deviancy and social rejection are functionally synonymous. Whether the basis for the deviancy is active or passive and whether the deviant role is voluntarily assumed by the individual or forcibly thrust upon him by the group does not alter the fact of social rejection, but it does have important implications for its interpretation, seriousness, and eventual outcome. At any rate, whatever the cause of the deviancy, because of the crucial role played by the peer group during adolescence, the deviant is "placed at a terrible disadvantage in the struggle to emerge mature and adjusted at the conclusion" of this period of

·development.[1] By their own admission at least seven per cent of adolescent boys experience serious difficulty in making friends, and fifteen per cent are seriously concerned by bashfulness.[28]

Socially rejected or deviant adolescents may be conveniently grouped into three main categories: * (a) individuals who by virtue of group-inappropriate personality traits, physical characteristics, or interests are rejected by the group; (b) individuals who reject group experience because they find it traumatic or unrewarding as a result of their personality make-up or social incompetence; and (c) individuals who neither reject nor are rejected by the group because of socially inappropriate or inadequate aspects of personality, but who are willing to accept ostracism from the group, if need be, to pursue other needs and interests. In the third category are opportunists who are willing to flaunt group standards to gain adult approval, highly self-assertive adolescents who are too individualistic to conform to group expectations, individuals with strong moral convictions who spurn any form of moral compromise or expediency, and adolescents with all-consuming interests in esoteric activities that enjoy low status in the crowd.

Characteristics of Socially Rejected Adolescents. The second and third categories of deviants have been discussed elsewhere (see pp. 360–361). In this section we shall confine our attention to the characteristics of individuals who are socially unacceptable to their agemates. Many such individuals (persons rejected or overdominated by parents) concomitantly reject the group because of asocial personality trends, social incompetence, strong nonsocial interests, or fear of rebuff. Others in this group also adjust to their outcast status by adopting a "sour grapes" attitude, by pretending that it is *they* who reject the group, that the group is beneath their notice, and that their isolation is voluntary, admirable, and indicative of special virtue.

Three main clusters of socially unacceptable personality traits

---

* In many instances, of course, all three factors operate in the *same* individual. The overprotected child, for example, is rejected by the group because of negative personality traits, withdraws from group experience because of social incompetence, and may develop strong nonsocial interests as a compensation for his social isolation.

have been found in adolescents who are rejected by their peer group. (a) First are traits associated with the obnoxiously overbearing, aggressive, and egocentric individual who frequently gives a history of being underdominated or overvalued by his parents. Such adolescents are described by their associates as domineering,[26] interfering,[42] bullying,[26] conceited,[58] exhibitionistic,[26] attention-seeking and demanding,[42] resentful of criticism,[42] querulous, and irritable.[42] (b) Another group of socially unacceptable personality traits characterize the adolescent who failed as a child to learn the give-and-take techniques of peer group play, who failed to develop social poise, skills, and effective methods of self-assertion and self-defense. This type of socialization history is typical of the overdominated, overprotected, or rejected child. Others regard him as excessively overdependent,[26] fearful of being misunderstood, abused, or taken advantage of,[26] and given to whining, nagging, and complaining.[42] (c) The third cluster of seriously unacceptable personality traits reflects a degree of introversion sufficiently disabling to interfere with spontaneous and uninhibited participation in group activities and social events. Included in this group are such characteristics as timidity, shyness, withdrawing behavior,[26] preoccupation with introspective experience and intellectual interests, preference for social isolation,[26] a "wet blanket" approach to group activities, lack of social poise and skills,[49] and an apparent apathy and listlessness,[58] which may indicate relative disinterest in the more immediate data of sensory and emotional experience.

Apart from these major personality configurations associated with social rejection in the peer group, individuals characterized as "nervous," "jumpy," [26, 42] noisy,[58] or prone to fabricate alibis and carry grudges [26] enjoy low sociometric status. Adolescents who are overly interested in art, literature, or other esoteric fields are frequently regarded as " 'queers,' fit only for the company of other outcasts and deviants." [1] The merciless law of group conformity is also applied to the unfortunate somatic deviants—the short, the fat, the ugly, the puny, the awkward, the oversized, and the late-maturer.[44, 74]

Evaluation of Social Rejection. In evaluating a given instance of social rejection during adolescence, many factors must be taken into consideration. First, it should be realized that seldom indeed is either acceptance or rejection completely unanimous in any sizeable group. Second, rejection is not as self-evidently obvious as it may seem. Frequently adolescents who perceive themselves as rejected are seriously in error. Teachers also are apt to be mistaken about the group's acceptance or rejection of an individual. The ability of teachers to perceive the sociometric status of their pupils diminishes rapidly with the increasing age of the pupils [3, 56] and is quite low by the time pupils are of high school age.[11] Sometimes, adolescents who are actually rejected are as unaware as their teachers of their status in the group.

Further appraisal of the seriousness of an individual case of rejection requires knowledge of (a) how widely shared the attitude of rejection is in the group, (b) whether it reflects active dislike of or passive indifference toward the person involved, (c) the modifiability of the factors on which the rejection is based, and (d) the availability of other compensatory attachments or interests. Finally, it is important to know whether the individual desires to be accepted by the group, and, if he does not, whether his expressed disdain for acceptance is genuine or the product of rationalization. Although unconcern with status in the group may, in rejection, be associated with relatively little immediate deflation of self-esteem, it may also be symptomatic of much graver defects in personality structure than the rejection of a deviant adolescent who craves acceptance by his age-mates.

Helping the Socially Rejected Individual. Teachers, counselors, and group leaders can do much to help certain types of socially rejected adolescents. With the aid of group members (nondeviants) who reject such individuals least, they can assist the rejected in gaining insight into the reasons for their rejection and in acquiring the skills that enhance status in the group. Smaller classroom subgroups and social gatherings of small groups can provide a social identity for persons who are unable to establish themselves in larger social units. Classroom and extra-curricular situations can be manipulated to increase the social visibility of those particular competencies of the rejected individual that are compatible with the values of the group.

Prognosis of Deviancy. During adolescence deviants and socially rejected individuals are not in an enviable position.

> In varying degrees . . . [they] all face social ridicule, abuse and isolation. . . . The fortunate ones achieve some measure of status and security by forming warm attachments to age-mates of their own kind. Rarely, a sympathetic adult friend or teacher will offer them affection, direction, and encouragement. But more often they are left to flounder uncertainly, to drift farther and farther away from group living, to develop feelings of anxiety and inferiority, to withdraw deeper and deeper into themselves or into a compensatory world of unreality. The more seriously maladjusted may be claimed by suicide or schizophrenia.[1]

With the coming of adulthood, the peer group begins to dissolve and adolescents are absorbed into the wider social community. And concomitantly,

> release comes for the majority of deviants. The recession of the demands for slavish conformity is one of the surest signs of approaching adulthood.[82] Variability is then not only legalized, but, to a certain extent, also becomes desirable. Adolescents suddenly begin to notice the personal qualities of people.[44] They evolve personal goals, personal tastes, personal interests, and personal preferences. The "hideous" deviant is then, for the first time, seen for what he really is—as just *another* different human being. And after years of harrowing isolation, he dares again to lift his head and take his rightful place among his peers.[1]

ADOLESCENT GANGS

Varieties of Deviant Peer Groups

Thus far in our discussion of the structural and functional properties of adolescent peer groups, we have been concerned only with the developmental characteristics that distinguish the group formations of adolescents *generally* from those of children and adults in the American culture. But we are also committed to the proposition that peer group behavior, like all other significant and value-laden activity of adolescence in our own or any culture, must inevitably reflect the distinctive influences of the subculture in which it is rooted (see p. 344). To avoid needless repetition, the preceding analysis of the adolescent peer culture has used as a model the peer groups sharing the typical middle-class values that dominate the school and the official ideology of the community. Requiring further consideration of specific subcultural differences are only those peer groups that deviate markedly from this pattern, those originating from upper- and lower-class strata in our society. And since detailed studies of upper-class peer formations (for example, the Junior League) are not presently available, this section will deal primarily with lower-class adolescent gangs found in disorganized urban areas.

For the purposes of this discussion, we can divide all adolescent peer groups into two main categories, deviant and nondeviant. Nondeviant groups (a) originate from and subscribe to the dominant middle-class ideology of the school and the community, and (b) conform to the basic core of peer group values that characterize the adolescent segment of the middle class. On an informal basis, nondeviant groups function as cliques or crowds. More formally they are organized into unisexual societies (scouts, fraternities, sororities) or into bisexual extra-curricular interest clubs.

Membership in a deviant group is predicated upon (a) lower-class origin, (b) nonconformity to the special values of the dominant (middle-class) peer group, or (c) upon both of these two factors. Except in certain relatively rare instances of extreme parent-youth conflict, the unisexual and highly structured adolescent gang includes only individuals who are "deviant" in both respects. The middle-class youth who does not conform to the standards of his peer group remains a free-lance outcast, teams up informally with other out-groupers, or joins a more formal organization with highly specialized interests (art) or idealistic (religious, social reform) aims. The lower-class adolescent who subscribes to the social class ideology as well as to the adolescent values of the middle-class peer group remains on the fringe of acceptance in nondeviant groups. Usually denied full membership in nondeviant cliques, he settles for a respectable position in an acceptable but more formal interest group.

Street-Corner Gangs

Unlike other adolescent group formations, the street-corner gang is more continuous with and resembles more closely preadolescent peer groups. It differs from the high school "crowd" in having a more aggressive, predatory base, attributable to the need to compensate for deprivations other than those normally associated with adolescence in our culture. It is more of an action group functionally oriented toward the achievement of more concrete goals; as such it requires a more structured organization and greater group solidarity. Similarly because of its special functions, it us usually unisexual, demands a higher standard of loyalty from its members, places greater emphasis upon secrecy and physical prowess, comes into conflict with the law, and imposes more drastic penalties for disloyalty upon its members.

The special deprivations confronting these adolescents consist of (a) material inadequacies associated with low socioeconomic status— lower standards of housing, food, clothing, recreation, economic security, and educational opportunity; (b) restricted social mobility —limited access to the more desirable vocational pursuits; (c) exclusion from the dominant peer groups of school and church, which provide other adolescents with a social identity and interim status; [70] and (d) exposure to the snobbishness and patronizing attitudes of respectable society. In the gang, an organization of his own kind, the street-corner boy not only gains all of the status and security advantages of peer group membership, but also finds escape from the condescension of his "betters," a sense of brotherhood and power, and a measure of aggressive revenge against the society that rejects him.

Origins and Outcomes. Socioeconomic deprivation in itself is not sufficient for adolescent gang formation. An additional indispensable condition seems to be the existence of a more or less segregated, and deteriorating urban slum area providing (a) sufficient isolation from the rest of the community for a separate subculture, (b) adequate protection from the prying eyes of the law, and (c) sufficiently close physical contact for the daily operations of the gang and the emergence of a communal sense of group solidarity.[79, 86] The presence of unassimilated ethnic and racial groups in these areas further stimulates the formation of gangs since "generation conflict" is maximized in families of such groups. In addition to being excluded from nondeviant peer groups, these "second generation" adolescents are unable to identify with their parents and community, and commonly seek to disassociate themselves from the social stigma connected with their family background. The necessity for creating an entirely new social organization as the *only* means of attaining status is even more urgent.[91] And under the protracted stress of such extreme status deprivation, adolescent gangs evolve quite spontaneously from the less structured play groups of preadolescents.[70, 79]

Adolescent gangs disintegrate as their members approach adulthood and attain status in more conventional ways, through marriage, raising a family, earning a livelihood.[70] In proportion to his gradually increasing involvement in the new status-giving functions, the adolescent's participation in gang activities and loyalty to gang standards diminishes. The tapering-off process may take several years. In the meantime, the street-corner boy continues to "hang out" on the corner with the boys, but not with the same single-mindedness as previously.[86] Eventually, the vast number of such adolescents become incorporated into the folds of conventional society and observe the norms of the community at large.[79, 86] Were it not for this shift in values, the typical slum boy's participation in delinquent gang activities would not merely constitute a characteristic transitory phenomenon of adolescent development in disorganized urban areas, but would lead to a permanent career in crime. Fortunately however, this outcome is relatively rare.

Under certain conditions, however, the delinquent adolescent gang member fails to be assimilated by conventional society, and is inducted into the ranks of the adult criminal gang. Whether or not this happens depends on many individual personality factors associated with moral development (see pp. 255–259). Two sociological factors, however, have an important bearing on the eventual outcome. (1) If, by virtue of frequent residence in correctional institutions an adolescent fails to establish rapport with the law-abiding elements of the community or is denied opportunity to engage in legitimate status-giving activities because of his "record," reorientation of his value system understandably fails to occur. (2) A similar lack of reorientation may occur if status deprivation is based not only on age and socioeconomic status, but, is also

associated with discrimination based on such *permanent* factors as racial or national origin. The predatory attitude tends to become fixed since the gang then views the problem of acquiring status as not being limited to adolescence —as in the case of *other* youth—but as a *permanent* struggle against overwhelming odds.[1]

Organization. The special organizational features of the gang related to its unique functions have already been mentioned (see p. 377). The superficial appearance of aimlessness and disorganization that strikes a casual observer is completely misleading.[79] It is probably the gang's appearance of informality that is erroneously equated with planlessness and lack of structure. Actually there are few existing groups that can rival it in degree of differentiation of relationships between members, in stability of roles and status hierarchy, and in the group solidarity that permeates the membership. Years of extremely close association and comradeship in dangerous exploits and in fights with adult authorities, police, and other gangs weld an amazingly cohesive in-group incorporating a complex system of mutually recognized obligations and loyalties.[79, 86]

For the most part, criteria determining gang leadership conform to those outlined for adolescent leaders generally. To some extent, leadership in gangs is more despotically wielded and depends more on such factors as physical prowess, toughness, and fighting ability.[79] However, these factors are more implicit than explicit in the leader's actual exercise of control. In daily operations, ingenuity and cleverness are more important assets.[86] The leader seldom has to resort to force; it usually suffices that he has earned a reputation for being able to take care of himself.

To some extent, also (probably because of the gang's functional orientation), the gang leader occupies a more central position in the group than most other adolescent leaders. Group members relate more to him than to each other, and no decisions of any consequence are ever made in his absence.[86] The leader assumes full initiative and responsibility for carrying out group actions, but legislative decisions are reached through group consensus; formal voting during meetings is a rarity.[86] Negotiations with other gangs and with adults and officials are also conducted by the leader, who thereby gets to be more widely known than the ordinary gang member.[86]

However great his power, the leader cannot abuse or use it capriciously.[79] Power comes solely from the group, and the leader dares not ride roughshod over its acknowledged traditions, goals, and mores.[79] In accordance with his higher status he is required to face hazards from which others shrink, and to be more scrupulous in meeting his obligations than less exalted group members.[86] To a greater extent also, he must be loyal, fairminded, and generous. He is expected to rise above personal vindictiveness, to settle amicably disputes between members.[86]

Norms and Activities. The norms, in such matters as honesty, aggression, and sexual gratification, in adolescent gangs reflect in part the value system of the lower socioeconomic groups from which they originate. But, in addition, as befits a more rebellious group enjoying no status whatever in the adult community, the norms of such youth are more extreme, unconventional, and closer to those of the adult criminal world than to the values professed by their parents. Through contact with the school, the church, the courts, and various social agencies, adolescent gang members have ample opportunity to learn that their way of life is not sanctioned by conventional society. But "mere knowledge of the norms of society" is a much less "potent determinant of behavior" than the status and other needs satisfied by the peer group.[70] At this point in their development, the norms of the gang easily hold the field against the conflicting standards of the world. Identification with gang norms is also facilitated by the fact that home and family loyalties are a minor matter to the street corner boy. Furthermore, not too far below the surface of their official ideology, his parents are in substantial agreement with the norms of his gang.

Being aware of the outlawed status of their value system, leads gang members to formulate justifications for their predatory activities. They evolve an ethical code

> based on the premise that *any* behavior is justifiable as long as it is intended to retaliate for unjust and repressive treatment received at the hands of adult society. In this case, the entire body of criminal law is identified with the status denying adult, and by lashing out at the former they are squaring accounts with the latter.[1]

Despite the availability of such justifications, the gang boy frequently has serious doubt about the moral legitimacy of much of his behavior. This doubt added to his fear of the consequences of apprehension would be strong enough to inhibit delinquent acts were he committing these *alone*. For this reason the overwhelming majority of juvenile offenses are committed by *groups* of boys.[68] The tangible presence of others reinforces identification with group norms, sets aside moral reservations, strengthens feelings of loyalty to the group, and allays fear of personal consequences. All of these factors create potentialities for aggressive, daring, and delinquent group behavior that do not exist when the gang member is operating as an individual.

We do not wish to imply that all adolescents who live in an urban slum area necessarily belong to gangs or subscribe to gang norms. As a result of identification with family, church, school, or settlement house values, or as a consequence of friendships with members of other socioeconomic groups, of reading, or of strong personal convictions, *most* adolescent slum-dwellers do *not* choose to incorporate the norms of their associates or to participate in their activities (see p. 379). In some instances, individuals with unacceptable personality traits (see pp. 373–374) are denied membership in adolescent gangs [36], [68] and as compensation seek identification with more conventional peer groups. They may be more successful in these efforts despite their personal shortcomings (and their social class origin, which bars admittance to exclusive cliques), simply because they can be condescendingly regarded as "better sorts" of lower-class persons who have "seen the light" and "know their place."

The activities of adolescent gangs are extremely variable, running the gamut from nondelinquent athletic competition to various specialized forms of delinquent behavior.[79] Within a given gang, a characteristic type of activity predominates, with a more or less fixed routine.[79, 86] Geographically, also, to avoid conflicting interests, the operations of a gang are restricted to a carefully defined "sphere of influence," the violation of which leads to open warfare.[79] Girls are customarily excluded from active membership in boys' gangs, but in late adolescence may acquire auxiliary status as lovers.[86] Unfortunately, no studies of adolescent girl gangs are presently available. Our knowledge of delinquent behavior in adolescent girls is almost completely limited to sex delinquency (see p. 520).

SUMMARY: FUNCTIONS OF ADOLESCENT PEER GROUPS

The significance of the peer group for adolescent development can be summarized most adequately by listing briefly the various functions it performs:

1. The most significant personality change during adolescence is a diminution in the importance of the status that an individual derives from a dependent relationship to parents, and a corresponding increase in the importance of primary status which he earns in his own right. Since the modern urban community is unable to provide the adolescent with primary status, peer groups are constituted to meet this crucial need.

2. The peer group is also the major source of derived status during adolescence. By achieving acceptance in the group, by subordinating himself to group interests, and by making himself dependent on group approval, the adolescent gains a measure of intrinsic self-esteem that is independent of his achievements or relative status in the group. This "we-feeling" provides security and belongingness, and is a powerful ego support and source of loyalty to group norms.

3. The peer group provides a new frame of reference to relieve the disorientation and loss of anchorage from the abandonment of the childhood frame of reference when childhood biosocial status is surrendered. This disorientation is especially severe in early adolescence because of the adolescent's marginal position in the culture and his rejection by the adult community. The creation of peer group norms rescues him from his "no-man's-land" of orientation and provides relief from uncertainty, indecision, guilt, and anxiety about proper ways of thinking, feeling, and behaving.

4. "In switching his primary allegiances" to the peer group and "in seeking a source of values outside the home," the adolescent makes great strides toward emancipation. He finds a "new source of basic security to supplant the emotional anchorage to parents that had heretofore kept him confined within the dependent walls of childhood." [1] By vesting in his peers the authority to set standards, he affirms his *own* right to self-determination, since he is patently no different from them.[1, 90] No longer need he implicitly subscribe to the belief that only parents and adults can determine what is right. "As a result of the emotional support he derives from his peer group, he gains the courage to break the bonds of parental domination." [1]

5. The peer group also serves as "a bulwark of strength in combatting authority. . . . By pooling their resistance in groups and throwing up barriers of one kind and another against adult author-

ity and interference," adolescents manage to "exclude adults and protect themselves from . . . the coercions that [the latter] are prone to use." [82] By creating precedents and operating as a pressure group, the peer group gains important privileges for its members and emancipates itself from adult and institutional controls. [38]

Adolescents also use the peer group as an organized means of "rejecting completely the accepted standards of adult society" [82] and of "repudiating the necessity for growing up. . . . Even apart from delinquency, practically all resistance to acculturation in our society [82] comes not from individual adolescents but from peer groups." [1]

6. The peer group is *the* major training institution for adolescents in our society. The school's influence on adolescent development inheres largely in its capacity for providing "many of the occasions for adolescent boys and girls to receive the inculcation of adolescent culture—that body of attitudes, beliefs, and practices which is transmitted not by parents and teachers to children but by older to younger adolescents." [31] It is in the peer group that "by *doing* they learn about the social processes of our culture. They clarify their sex roles by acting and being responded to, they learn competition, cooperation, social skills, values and purposes by sharing the common life." [82] All of this is accomplished in an integrated way without self-conscious or self-important pomposity; "for unlike the adult-controlled training institutions and agencies in our society, the peer group does not regard itself as a training agency." [82] And in its role as a training institution the peer group transmits and enforces social class goals and values, since parents no longer enjoy sufficient control or rapport to carry out this function.

7. The peer group provides regularized media and occasions for adolescents to gratify their newly acquired desires for increased heterosexual contacts, as well as a set of norms governing adolescent sex behavior.

8. "As the chief source of adolescent interim status," the effect of the peer group "is to reduce the total load of frustration and to stabilize the entire transitional period." [1] It can offer compensations not only for the deprivations associated with adolescence *per se,* but also for the special deprivations that confront certain adolescents by virtue of their class, ethnic, racial, or religious affiliations.

REFERENCES AND BIBLIOGRAPHY

1. Ausubel, D. P.: Problems of adolescent adjustment. Bulletin, Natl. Assn. Secondary School Principals, *34*:1–84, 1950.
2. Ausubel, D. P.: *Ego Development and the Personality Disorders*. New York: Grune and Stratton, 1952.
3. Ausubel, D. P. and Schiff, H. M.: Intra-Personal and Inter-Personal Determinants of Individual Differences in Sociempathic Ability. J. Soc. Psychol. In Press.
4. Ausubel, D. P., Schiff, H. M., and Gasser, E. B.: A preliminary study of developmental trends in sociempathy: Accuracy of perception of own and others' sociometric status. Child. Develpm., *23*:111–128, 1952.
5. Averill, L. A.: *A Study in the Teen Years*. Boston: Houghton Mifflin, 1936.
6. Bellingrath, G. C.: *Qualities Associated with Leadership in the Extra-Curricular Activities of the High School*. New York: Teachers College, Columbia University, 1930.
7. Blos, P.: *The Adolescent Personality*. New York: Appleton-Century, 1941.
8. Bogardus, R. and Otto, P.: Social psychology of chums. Sociol., and Soc. Res., *20*:260–270, 1936.
9. Bonney, M. E.: The relative stability of social, intellectual, and academic status in grades II to IV, and the inter-relationships between these various forms of growth. J. Educ. Psychol., *34*:88–102, 1943.
10. Bonney, M. E.: A sociometric study of the relationship of some factors to mutual friendships in the elementary, secondary, and college levels. Sociometry, *9*:21–47, 1946.
11. Bonney, M. E.: Sociometric study of agreement between teachers' judgments and student choices. Sociometry: *10*:133–146, 1947.
12. Bowden, A. O.: A study of the personality of student leaders in colleges in the United States. J. Abnorm. Soc. Psychol., *21*:149–160, 1926.
13. Burks, F. W.: *The Tugwell High School Clubhouse (1936–37)*. Berkeley, California: University of California. Unpublished.
14. Caldwell, O. W. and Wellman, B.: Characteristics of school leaders. J. Educ. Res., *14*:1–15, 1926.
15. Campbell, E. H.: The Social-Sex Development of Children. Genet. Psychol. Monogr., *21*:461–552, 1939.
16. Campbell, H. M.: Sex Differences Obtained by the "Guess Who" Technique in Reputation Assessments Given and Received by Adolescent Boys and Girls. Unpublished Ph.D. Dissertation, University of California Library.
17. Cameron, W. J.: *A Study of Social Development in Adolescence*. Berkeley, Calif.: University of California. Unpublished.
18. Carter, T. M.: Comparison of the attitudes of college men with the attitudes of college women in regard to fellowship behavior. J. Soc. Psychol., *14*:145–158, 1941.
19. Chowdry, K., and Newcomb, T. M.: The relative abilities of leaders and non-leaders to estimate opinions of their own groups. J. Abnorm. Soc. Psychol., *47*:51–57, 1952.

20. Courtenay, M. E.: The persistence of leadership. Sch. Rev., *46*:97–107, 1938.
21. Cowley, W. H.: The traits of face to face leaders. J. Abnorm. Soc. Psychol., *26*:304–313, 1931.
22. Criswell, J. H.: *A Sociometric Study of Race Cleavage in the Classroom.* New York: Archives of Psychology (Columbia University), 1939.
23. Crowley, J. J.: High-school backgrounds of successful men and women graduates. Sch. Rev., *48*:205–209, 1940.
24. Cunningham, R. et al.: *Understanding Group Behavior of Boys and Girls.* New York: Teachers College, Columbia University, 1951.
25. Davis, A.: "Socialization and Adolescent Personality," in *Adolescence,* 43rd Yearbook, Natl. Soc. Stud. Educ., Part I. Chicago: University of Chicago Press, 1944.
26. Dimock, H. S.: *Rediscovering the Adolescent.* New York: Association Press, 1937.
27. Feinberg, M. R. and Fryer, D. H.: An investigation of the background experiences of socially accepted and rejected adolescents at three economic levels. Amer. Psychologist, *5*:355, 1950. (Abstract)
28. Fleege, U. H.: *Self-Revelation of the Adolescent Boy.* Milwaukee: Bruce, 1945.
29. Flemming, E. G.: Best Friends. J. Soc. Psychol., *3*:385–390, 1932.
30. Flemming, E. G.: A factor analysis of the personality of high-school leaders. J. Appl. Psychol., *19*:596–605, 1935.
31. Frank, L. K.: "The Adolescent and the Family," in *Adolescence,* 43rd Yearbook, Natl. Soc. Stud. Educ., Part I. Chicago: University of Chicago Press, 1944.
32. Furfey, P. H.: Some factors influencing the selection of boys' chums. J. Appl. Psychol., *11*:47–53, 1927.
33. Goodenough, F. L.: *Developmental Psychology.* New York: Appleton-Century, 1945.
34. Hartshorne, H. and May, M. A.: *Studies in the Nature of Character.* New York: Macmillan, 1930.
35. Havighurst, R. J. and Taba, H.: *Adolescent Character and Personality.* New York: Wiley, 1949.
36. Healey, W. and Bronner, A. F.: *New Light on Delinquency and its Treatment.* New Haven: Yale University Press, 1936.
37. Hicks, J. A. and Hayes, M.: Study of the characteristics of 250 junior-high school children. Child Develpm., *9*:219–242, 1938.
38. Hollingshead, A. B.: *Elmtown's Youth: The Impact of Social Classes on Youth.* New York: Wiley, 1949.
39. Horrocks, J. E. and Thompson, G. G.: A study of the friendship fluctuations of rural boys and girls. J. Genet. Psychol., *69*:189–198, 1946.
40. Hunter, E. C. and Jordan, A. M.: An analysis of qualities associated with leadership among college students. J. Educ. Psychol., *30*:497–509, 1939.
41. Jenkins, G. G.: Factors involved in children's friendships. J. Educ. Psychol., *22*:440–448, 1931.
42. Jennings, H. H.: *Leadership and Isolation.* New York: Longmans, 1943.

43. Jersild, A. T. et al.: *Child Development and the Curriculum.* New York: Teachers College, Columbia University, 1946.
44. Jones, H. E.: *Development in Adolescence.* New York: Appleton-Century, 1943.
45. Jones, M. C.: *ICW Interest Record: Revised Form for Presentation of the Cumulative Record of an Individual, with Group Norms by Items for a Seven Year Period.* Berkeley, Calif.: Institute of Child Welfare, University of California, 1944.
46. Jones, M. C.: Adolescent friendships. Amer. Psychologist, *3:*352, 1948. (Abstract)
47. Katz, D. and Allport, F. H.: *Students' Attitudes.* Syracuse: Craftsman Press, 1931.
48. Kirkpatrick, C. and Caplow, T.: Courtship in a group of Minnesota students. Amer. J. Sociol., *51:*114–125, 1945.
49. Kuhlen, R. G. and Bretsch, H. S.: Sociometric status and personal problems of adolescents. Sociometry: *10:*122–132, 1947.
50. Kuhlen, R. G. and Lee, B. J.: Personality characteristics and social acceptability in adolescence. J. Educ. Psychol., *34:*321–340, 1943.
51. Lehman, H. C.: The play activities of persons of different ages. J. Genet. Psychol., *33:*273–288, 1926.
52. Lehman, H. C. and Witty, P. A.: One more study of permanence of interests. J. Educ. Psychol., *22:*481–492, 1931.
53. Levi, I. J.: Student leadership in elementary and junior high school and its transfer into senior high school. J. Educ. Res., *22:*135–139, 1930.
54. Mather, W. G.: The courtship ideals of high-school youth. Sociol. and Soc. Res., *19:*166–172, 1934.
55. Meek, L. H. *The Personal-Social Development of Boys and Girls with Implications for Secondary Education.* New York: Progressive Education Association, 1940.
56. Moreno, J. L.: *Who Shall Survive?* Washington, D. C.: Nervous and Mental Disease Publishing Co., 1934.
57. Newstetter, W. I., Feldstein, M. J., and Newcomb, T. M.: Group Adjustment: *A Study in Experimental Sociology.* Cleveland: Western Reserve Univ., 1938.
58. Northway, M. L.: Outsiders: A study of the personality pattern of children least acceptable to their age mates. Sociometry, 7:10–25, 1944.
59. Partridge, E. D.: A study of friendships among adolescent boys. J. Genet. Psychol., *43:*472–477, 1933.
60. Partridge, E. D.: *Leadership among Adolescent Boys.* New York: Teachers College, Columbia University, 1934.
61. Pressey, S. L. and Robinson, F. P.: *Psychology and the New Education.* New York: Harper, 1944.
62. Punke, H. H.: Attitudes and ideas of high school youth in regard to marriage. Sch. & Soc., *56:*221–224, 1942.
63. Punke, H. H.: Dating practices of high school youth. Bulletin, Natl. Assn. Secondary School Principals, *28:*47–54, 1944.
64. Redl, F.: Group emotion and leadership. Psychiatry, *5:*573–596, 1942.

388THEORY AND PROBLEMS OF ADOLESCENT DEVELOPMENT

65. Segel, D.: *Frustration in Adolescent Youth.* Washington, D. C.: Federal Security Agency, 1951.
66. Shannon, J. R.: The post-school careers of high-school leaders and high-school scholars. Sch. Rev., *37:*656–665, 1929.
67. Shaw, C. R.: *The Jack-Roller.* Chicago: University of Chicago Press, 1930.
68. Shaw, C. R.: *The Natural History of a Delinquent Career.* Chicago: University of Chicago Press, 1931.
69. Shaw, C. R. et al.: *Brothers in Crime.* Chicago: University of Chicago Press, 1938.
70. Sherif, M. and Cantril, H.: *The Psychology of Ego-Involvements.* New York: Wiley, 1947.
71. Smith, H. P.: A study in the selective character of American secondary education: Participation in school activities as conditioned by socio-economic status and other factors. J. Educ. Psychol., *36:*229–246, 1945.
72. Smith, M. and Nystrom, W. C.: A study of social participation and of leisure time of leaders and non-leaders. J. Appl. Psychol., *21:*251–259, 1937.
73. Stolz, H. R., Jones, M. C., and Chaffey, J.: The junior high school age. Univ. High School J., *15:*63–72, 1937.
74. Stolz, H. R. and Stolz, L. M.: "Adolescent Problems Related to Somatic Variations," in *Adolescence,* 43rd Yearbook, Natl. Soc. Stud. Educ., Part I. Chicago: University of Chicago Press, 1944.
75. Stoke, S. M. and West, E. D.: The conversational interests of college students. Sch. & Soc., *32:*567–570, 1930.
76. Sullenger, T. E.: Extracurricular leisure time activities. Recreation, *32:*509–510, 1938.
77. Taylor, K. W.: *Do Adolescents Need Parents?* New York: Appleton-Century, 1938.
78. Thompson, G. G. and Horrocks, J. E.: A study of the friendship fluctuations of urban boys and girls. J. Genet. Psychol., *70:*53–63, 1947.
79. Thrasher, F. M.: *The Gang.* Chicago: University of Chicago Press, 1927.
80. Tryon, C. M.: *Evaluations of Adolescent Personality by Adolescents.* Monogr. Soc. Res. Child Develpm., 4, No. 4, 1939.
81. Tryon, C. M.: *UC Inventory I, Social and Emotional Adjustment.* Berkeley, Calif.: Institute of Child Welfare, University of California, 1939.
82. Tryon, C. M.: "The Adolescent Peer Culture," in *Adolescence,* 43rd Yearbook, Natl. Soc. Stud. Educ., Part I. Chicago: University of Chicago Press, 1944.
83. Van Dyne, E. V.: Personality traits and friendship formation in adolescent girls. J. Soc. Psychol., *12:*291–303, 1940.
84. Vreeland, F. M. and Corey, S. M.: A study of college friendships. J. Abnorm. Soc. Psychol., *30:*229–236, 1935.
85. Wellman, B.: The school child's choice of companions. J. Educ. Res., *14:*126–132, 1926.
86. Whyte, W. F.: *Street Corner Society.* Chicago: University of Chicago Press, 1943.

THE ADOLESCENT PEER CULTURE

87. Winslow, C. N.: A study of the extent of agreement between friends' opinions and their ability to estimate the opinions of each other. J. Soc. Psychol., *8*:433–442, 1937.

88. Wittenberg, R. M. and Berg, J.: The Stranger in the Group. Am. J. Orthopsychiat., *22*:89–97, 1952.

89. Wolman, B.: Spontaneous groups of children and adolescents in Israel. J. Soc. Psychol., *34*:171–182, 1951.

90. Zachry, C. B. and Lighty, M.: *Emotion and Conduct in Adolescence.* New York: Appleton-Century, 1940.

91. Zorbaugh, H. W.: *The Gold Coast and the Slum.* Chicago: University of Chicago Press, 1929.

CHAPTER 13

Sexual Behavior in Adolescence

IN PREVIOUS CHAPTERS we have discused the endocrine changes of pubescence and their more *general psychological* consequences in sex awareness, drive, and interests. We have also pointed to the existence of various psychobiological problems associated with gonadal maturation: the universal need to adjust to the perplexity and uneasiness generated by a strange and potent new drive; the necessity of subjecting for the first time since early childhood an emergent drive of organic origin to *initial* control and direction in accordance with social expectations; the cultural pressures exerted upon adolescent individuals to assume an appropriate biological sex role; and the general developmental trend for modes of sexual gratification to become increasingly more specific and differentiated with the progress of adolescence.

Our task in this chapter is four-fold: (1) to consider the extent to which the psychological consequences of gonadal maturation are culturally modifiable; (2) to assay the importance of sexuality in adolescent personality development and adjustment; (3) to examine various psychosocial aspects of adolescent sexuality; and (4) to formulate some principles of sex education and guidance appropriate for our culture.

PSYCHOSOCIAL ASPECTS OF SEXUALITY

In contrast to the psychobiological problems of adolescent sexuality that enjoy universal cultural distribution, psychosocial sex problems are culture-bound, reflecting the influence of the particular values, regulatory devices, and social conditions within a given culture. We shall be concerned here with five main categories of psychosocial sex problems: (a) peculiarities in psychosexual maturation that follow from the general cultural (or subcultural) orientation to sexuality: attitudes of acceptance or deprecation; of shame, guilt, and avoidance, or of naturalness and enjoyment; emphasis upon psychophysiological or psychoaffectional * aspects of sexuality; degree of sameness or difference in conceptions of male and female biological sex roles; (b) differences in patterns of socially provided opportunities for and restrictions upon adolescent sexual gratification, and in the degree to which social sanctions are internalized by the adolescent; (c) differences in specific practices and varieties of sexual expression, in the frequency and types of sexual outlets available to adolescent boys and girls growing up in different social environments; (d) different ways of regulating and formalizing the social and interpersonal aspects of erotic relationships between the sexes, for example, courting behavior, heterosexual activities in the peer group; and (e) differences in social sex role, in the personality attributes and socioeconomic functions customarily associated with masculinity and femininity.

In this section we shall consider the first two of these problems. It will be more profitable to reserve consideration of the remaining three problems until some attention is given to the modifiability of hormonally conditioned sex behavior and to the general importance of sexuality in adolescent development.

Different Cultural Orientations Toward Sexuality

Some idea of the tremendous variability in cultural orientation toward sexuality can be gained by comparing the sex attitudes of four primitive cultures in the South Seas [44] with those of our own culture.

Adolescent sex practices in Samoa reflect an elaboration of the physiological and sensuous aspects of sexuality, which are culturally emphasized, in contradistinction to the affectional components, which are relatively ignored. For both men and women, physiological sex urges are regarded as natural and pleasurable, although requiring more stimulation and having slower maturation in women. No unfavorable moral judgments are applied to sexual gratification on a physiological level, the only strictures being aesthetic, and directed against overt "unseemliness." No importance is attached to deep or permanent emotional attachments; the stability of mar-

* See page 141 for a discussion of the distinction between psychophysiological and psychoaffectional sex urges.

riage depends upon social and economic factors. Adolescent pre-marital sex adventures mirror the general promiscuity and lack of deep emotion or ego-involvement in sex relationships. No attempt is made to synthesize seriously the physiological and affectional components of sex. Whereas in our society comparable sexual behavior is regarded as more typical of adolescent emotional imma-turity, in Samoa, adolescent sex conduct is not considered to be unrepresentative of the adult approach to sexuality. The Samoan attitude toward virginity and fidelity is typical of their whole philosophy of sex: desirable in theory, intriguing in practice, but hardly credible considering the "sexual nature of man"—except where it is demanded by considerations of social status.

The Samoan orientation toward sexuality comes closest to that of adolescents in the underprivileged segment of our own society, except that among the latter it meets with more formal taboos, which, however, are tacitly ignored. Also in this latter instance, it is less typical of adults in the same socioeconomic environment.

The Mundugumor attitude toward sexuality, like the Samoan, seems to reflect the characteristic personality constellation of the culture. Just as the easy-going Samoan expresses his casual style of life in the carefree and superficial emotional expression that char-acterizes his promiscuous sex activity, so the hard, aggressive, indi-vidualistic Mundugumor reveals his personality in the type of sex relationship that he establishes. Rigorous social taboos against prom-iscuity satisfy his passion for "keeping up appearances"; but these are in no sense internalized sufficiently to prevent the adolescent's vigorous, aggressive individuality from breaking through the frus-trating barriers of adult-made social standards to gratify passionate physiological needs by skillful clandestine efforts. Like the Samoan, the Mundugumor accepts the desirability of the physiological aspects of sexual expression which also supersede the affectional components; the Mundugumor, however, is characteristically more vigorous, pas-sionate, aggressive, and possessive in his attitudes and overt behavior. Also unlike their Samoan contemporaries, Mundugumor girls are more aggressive, and take more initiative in arranging the clan-destine liaisons. As one might imagine the Mundugumor places more value on virginity than the Samoan, but this is not sufficient to discourage premarital sexual ardor.

Among the Arapesh, psychosexual development follows an entirely different pattern from that of either of the two cultures described. Because of long years,

> during which husband and wife live together like brother and sister . . . actual sex intercourse does not spring from a different order of feeling from the affection that one has for one's daughter or one's sister. It is simply a more final and complete expression of the same kind of feeling. And it is not regarded as a spontaneous response of the human being to an internal sexual stimulus. The Arapesh have no fear that children left to themselves will copulate, or that young people going about in adolescent groups will experiment with sex. The only young people who are believed likely to indulge in any overt sex expression are "husband and wife," the betrothed pair who have been reared in the knowledge that they are to be mates.[44]

Both men and women find complete satisfaction of their sex needs in monogamous marriage. There is, however, this difference from monogamous marriage in our society: the physical component is not regarded as something inherently ugly and shameful (made tolerable by the marriage tie), but rather as a natural and acceptable accompaniment of an adult affectional relationship. Although sex is desirable affectional play in the mature relationship between man and wife, it is regarded as dangerous and antithetical to growth in those who have not yet attained their maturity.

If the Victorians had a felt need for a model of sexual behavior, it is a pity that they did not know of the existence of Manus society. Of all these four peoples, the Manus has approximated most closely the Victorian and dual standard of sex morality still current in our culture. Only they carry their Puritanism one step further. They recognize, as we do, the strength and naturalness of the male physiological sex drive, and just as inconsistently as we apply strict taboos that aim at seriously outlawing its expression; but secretly, rape remains the ideal goal of sexual behavior. Women are not supposed to experience physiological sex drives; but whereas our Victorian morality concedes the right of women to enjoy marital sex relations on an affectional basis, so much shame and repugnance is attached to sex in Manus society that even in the legalized marriage relationship it is distasteful. This difference might partly be a result of the fact that the Manus marriage is from start to finish a pure business proposition with no affectional elements. In a very literal sense it corresponds to legalized prostitution. Men do not deny their strong physiological urges; but because they fear the wrath of the spirits, they confine their overt activities to enforced marital intercourse, enjoying rape mainly in fantasy.

Doctrinally and traditionally our own cultural orientation toward sexuality parallels the Manus.

> The sexual urge is regarded as an inherently evil and reprehensible drive which is tolerated only because it is necessary for the reproduction of the species. In the case of the male, a concession is made to the acknowledged strength of the sexual urge in that its existence is given a certain recognized status; but, nevertheless, it is formally expected that repression will be practised until marriage. In the case of the female, physiological sex drive is presumed to be non-existent, and sexual expression is regarded as permissable only as part of her affectional duties as a wife. Since [so many] parents take the view that sex must be denied, and not even discussed, it is hardly surprising that children and adolescents have such distorted attitudes toward sexuality—attitudes that combine all the elements of shame, disgust, fear, guilt, mystery, and anxiety.[1]

But the status of sexuality in our own culture is much more complicated and confusing than that among the Manus. For coexisting with our repressive doctrinal approach are lower-class norms that are comparable to the Samoan; scientific notions of the "naturalness" of sex expression; romantic ideals and affectional standards that are also applied to male sex behavior; and some acknowledgment of the legitimacy of psychophysiological sex behavior among women. When to this cultural repression, distortion, and confusion is added the abnormally slow pace of emotional and social development in adolescence, it is no wonder that psychosexual maturation proceeds so slowly, especially in girls. "Thus, boys and girls are generally incapable at sixteen or eighteen of the deep emotional involvement" that our culture regards as necessary and desirable for successful marital love relationships. "Both sexes reveal extreme flightiness, superficiality and indiscriminateness in their heterosexual activities." [1]

Cultural Patterns of Regulating Adolescent Sex Activity

From this brief ethnological survey of sex behavior, it is evident that the social regulation of adolescent sex activity is closely related to the broader constellation of attitudes and values that the culture applies to sexuality in general. These regulatory practices can be classified on the basis of (a) the degree of tolerance or repressiveness toward adolescent sex expression, (b) the relative degree of emphasis placed upon psychophysiological or psychoaffectional sex behavior, and (c) the extent to which different standards are set for boys and girls.

At one extreme of cultural permissiveness (Samoa), no restrictions whatsoever are placed on adolescent sex activity. At the other extreme (Manus girls, Puritanically-raised girls in our culture), the prohibitions on sex activity are so severe that no sex drive at all, not even psychoaffectional, is developed. Between these extremes, in increasing order of repressiveness are: (a) formal prohibitions against sexual intercourse that are not seriously enforced and are not internalized by the adolescent (lower-class boys in our culture); (b) social taboos against premarital intercourse that are not internalized but are enforced seriously and rigorously enough to require clandestine gratification of sex (Mundugumor boys and girls); (c) social recognition of the existence of physiological sex drives accompanied by serious cultural expectations of sexual abstinence until marriage that *are* effectively internalized by adolescents (Manus boys, middle-class boys in our culture); and (d) social denial of psychophysiological sex drives modified by tolerance for psychoaffectional sex activity during marriage (middle-class girls in our culture). Among the Arapesh, the dimension of cultural permissiveness is somewhat irrelevant. It is true that no overt restrictions are imposed; but at the same time it is implicitly expected that adolescents will develop only psychoaffectional sex urges restricted to betrothed marital partners.

Regarding the relative emphasis placed upon the psychophysiological and psychoaffectional aspects of sex, the Arapesh recognize only psychoaffectional sexuality, whereas the Samoan, Manus, and Mundugumor cultures primarily emphasize the psychophysiological. In our own culture both components are prominent and vary in importance with sex and class membership. The same type of sexual urges are attributed to both males and females in the Samoan, Arapesh, and Mundugumor cultures, whereas the Manus and our cultures make sharp qualitative distinctions between male and female sex drives.

From even the limited ethnological data reviewed above and in other parts of this volume,[41, 43, 63] it is apparent that primitive cultures cannot be contrasted to our own as having nonrepressive, matter-of-fact, and "simple" attitudes toward sexuality. Restrictions of varying degrees of severity against adolescent sex activity have been described for the Kwoma, Mundugumor, Navaho, and Manus cultures; and in the Manus culture, the rigorousness of the repression, and the aura of shame, ugliness, prudery, and sinfulness surrounding sex exceeds by far anything known in our own culture. Neither are we alone in adhering to a "double standard" of sex morality, nor the furthest advanced in psychoaffectional standards of sex behavior. Furthermore, the tolerance for adolescent sex expression shown by lower socioeconomic groups in our society places them near the permissive end of a cross-cultural continuum of this aspect of sexuality. All we can say with definiteness is that in our own culture marriage is delayed longer and attitudes toward sex are more heterogeneous and more confused than in most other cultures.

THE NATURE AND CULTURAL MODIFIABILITY OF SEX BEHAVIOR

True (adult or postpubescent) sexuality can only be conceptualized "as a form of self-expression . . . which is related to the individual's experience of himself in a biological sex role." [2] The adoption of a biological sex role is dependent upon: (a) the individual's ability to experience the unique feeling-tones and psychological content that is either functionally or historically related to hormonal stimulation; and (b) cultural sanction of such experience, and recognition of the individual as a sexually mature adult. It follows that although biological sex role may be largely or (in certain instances of postpubescent castration) completely maintained by psychological stimulation, some degree of contact with functional quantities of gonadal sex hormones is necessary at some point in development.*

It is also apparent that gonadal stimulation can be regarded only as a necessary, not as a sufficient condition for the development of biological sex role. The mere presence of gonadal hormones does not guarantee the emergence of sex drives if the culture decrees that these are not to develop or that the individual is not yet

---

* Prepubescent castrates do not develop sex drives (see p. 140).

sexually mature. Sex hormones *never* arouse sex drives in Manus girls, and several years elapse between Samoan girl's pubescence and the onset of her sexual activity.[44] There is a similar lag for many girls in our own culture.[18, 57] And among the Arapesh, gonadal hormones do not result in sex impulses without an affectional content.

Once the basis of biological sex role is laid, further differentiation inevitably occurs. One type of differentiation is in the distinction between psychophysiological and psychoaffectional sex drives. Other aspects of differentiation include the sex object desired, the type of activity or erogenous zone implicated, the degree of passivity or initiative displayed, and the appropriateness of the sex role adopted. The factors that facilitate or retard the adoption of an appropriate (heterosexual) sex role and the various inappropriate outcomes have already been discussed (see pp. 143–144). That the differentiation of appropriate biological sex roles depends upon psychological factors over and above the hormonal substrate of sexual behavior is shown by the fact that injection of appropriate male or female sex hormones does not intensify heterosexual behavior, but merely reinforces the pre-existing sex role, whichever it may be.[19]

Preadolescent versus Adolescent Sexuality

Since the enactment of a biological sex role implies the existence of feelings and impulses in the individual that are dependent upon gonadal stimulation and upon social recognition of him as a sexually mature individual, it follows that there must be a qualitative difference between preadolescent and adolescent sexuality. There is considerable evidence of sensuous sex activity, sexual curiosity and exploration, and experimentation with and imitation of adult sex roles in prepubescent children (see pp. 136–138); and although the extent of such activity varies from culture to culture, there is no evidence of a "latency period" during the years of middle childhood and preadolescence. [19, 31, 38, 51] But it is

an assumption of quite another order to equate these activities with adult sexuality . . . even if . . . similar organs are involved in both instances. A child and biologist may both peer through a microscope, but one would hesitate to refer to the former as a scientist on this basis.[2]

Data of Kinsey and others, already cited, indicate that after pubescence, there is always a complete break in the qualitative meaning and significance of sex activity, and frequently considerable temporal discontinuity as well (see pp. 137–138).

Such discontinuity, in no way incompatible with general principles of child or adolescent development, is certainly to be expected following the introduction of any new potent variable (functional levels of gonadal hormones). And since this discontinuity in *experience* is biologically inevitable, the culture can at best avoid discontinuity in *training* by refraining from inculcating in the child *attitudes* about sexuality that he must perforce unlearn before he can function effectively as an adult.[7]

The Repressibility of Sex Urges

Strictly speaking, sex urges can only be repressed in the sense that as a result of extreme cultural denial they are never actualized from their hormonal substrate (see pp. 136–140). Hence, *agenesis* would be a more precise designation for this phenomenon than repression. It occurs, as we have seen, among Manus girls and among Puritanically-reared girls in our culture. Among the Arapesh agenesis is restricted solely to the psychophysiological sex drive. The advocates of the sex repression theory of adolescent emotional stability have committed the double error (a) of minimizing in a general way the power of the culture to suppress or modify successfully the development of even basic potential drives, and (b) of assuming that sex drives are either performed entities stored in the "unconscious," or inevitable consequences of gonadal stimulation rather than potential derivatives of sex hormones dependent upon favorable experience for eventual consummation.

Once sex drives have been actualized from their physiological substrate they become much too urgent and insistent to be repressed in the majority of individuals. Several investigators have reported that in our own culture only rarely do postpubescent males have extremely low sexual outlets; [31, 32, 59] and usually when this occurs special reasons (general apathy and incapacity to respond to sexual stimuli) exist for this anomaly.[31] When social sanctions or moral scruples prevent sexual gratification through premarital intercourse, some direct substitutive outlet such as masturbation or petting is the general practice.[31, 32, 59]

The psychoanalytic doctrine of sublimation, which proposes that the energy of frustrated sex drives provides the motivation for all of the constructive pursuits of adolescents and others and that through such pursuits vicarious sexual satisfaction is achieved, is hardly credible. Obviously there can be no sublimation if sex drives are not repressed but are gratified through premarital intercourse by lower-class males and through direct substitutive sex activity by middle-class males. Second, there is no reputable evidence to indicate that the *same* "blocked" energy of frustrated sex urges powers other activities, or that any of these activities yield vicarious sexual satisfaction. It is true that any constructive, self-enhancing activity provides compensation for frustration; but this does not necessarily mean that the compensatory activity is energized by the frustration or that the compensation makes up *in kind* for the *specific* deprivation.

It is more reasonable to conceive of motives as continually and independently generated in the course of reacting to new experiences and expectations rather than as derivatives of a single fountain-head of drive; and although frustration admittedly is a powerful spur to compensatory activity, positive impulses to explore the environment, independent of frustration, can also motivate purposeful activity. During adolescence the individual is confronted by numerous status problems (apart from sexual frustration) that are sufficiently insistent to instigate adjustive efforts such as peer group activity; and the functional origins of these efforts are either freshly generated or are rooted in adjustments found successful in the past (preadolescent group formations).

Detrimental Effects of Sex Repression

Mead's Manus data,[44] as well as psychiatric experience with Puritanically-reared women in our own culture, indicate that suppression of sex drive to the point of agenesis does not produce psychological stress. And the suppression of non-affectional sexuality (Arapesh) or the imposition of either rigorous (Mundugumor) or merely formal (lower-class American) prohibitions on premarital intercourse are not attended by psychological stress. As long as the adolescent does not *internalize* moral obligations to abide by these taboos, and as long as opportunities for clandestine gratification are available, no more mental conflict is generated than under conditions of unrestricted freedom as in Samoa.

Serious psychological stress from sex develops in middle-class boys because of (a) the ideological confusion that results in attempts to rationalize the logically incompatible cultural position (which the culture refuses to acknowledge as illogical) that psychophysiological sex urges are "natural" but at the same time must be repressed on ethico-religious grounds until marriage; and (b) the psychological impossibility of repressing a drive that they are morally obligated to repress. They are placed in the unenviable forced choice situation in which self-denial leads to unbearable psychophysiological tension, and self-indulgence gives rise to strong guilt feelings. The only realistic solution to this dilemma is to relieve the psychophysiological tension through autoeroticism and petting, and to find moral comfort in the fact that by refraining from intravaginal intercourse, they preserve technical virginity. But they still cannot avoid guilt feelings resulting from the substitutive equivalence of these activities with the interdicted goal of complete sexual intercourse; and the chronic existence of such guilt necessarily plays havoc with self-esteem.

The frustration of acknowledged sexual goals has other deleterious effects on self-esteem. Incomplete self-expression sexually comes to symbolize the adolescent's sub-adult status in society and causes pervasive and gnawing feelings of deprivation, inferiority, and demoralization. He becomes preoccupied with this frustration, overvalues its importance and lets it distract him from other activities. Some adolescents find in masturbation a preferred escape from rather than a substitute for normal heterosexual reality; and others become fixed at the level of sexual satisfaction that can be derived from petting and regard intercourse as an anti-climax.

> Not to be ignored either are the exaggerated defenses which some adolescents erect against their sexual impulses. This may result in asceticism or in an over-intellectualization of all the emotional problems of living. It is possible to explain in such a fashion *some* cases of adolescent preoccupation with philosophical, social, and political problems.[1]

Middle-class girls reared in traditionally Victorian or orthodox religious environments are spared most of these consequences.

> Theirs is not the difficult task of reconciling the idea of moral guilt . . . with the seemingly overpowering strength of a natural biological impulse. They don't face the temptation that if they transgress only occasionally—especially if they are not caught—they can probably get away with it. Instead the matter is settled very simply for them; they are told, and usually accept the fact, that they simply do not have these urges. . . .
>
> But times are changing for girls. As a result of recent trends in sex education, girls are beginning to wonder if they too are endowed with physiological sex urges. And as they wonder they are forced to wrestle with the moral problem of repression. In any case, there is considerable overlapping. The late-maturing boy suffers less than the early-maturing boy since he has less need for sexual outlet. The girl with irrepressible physiological needs must face considerable conflict because of society's harsh views regarding aggressive sex behavior in females.[1]

For the adolescent girl, however, sex repression creates marital problems that usually do not arise for boys. To effect a successful marital adjustment, "she will have to harmonize her own feelings and attitudes with their less inhibited correlates in her husband." [1] Total repression results in frigidity; and even for those girls who eventually accept a psychoaffectional sex role, "the idea of sex may be associated with such odium and repugnance that even in connection with affectional purposes there are strong inhibitions" that are only gradually overcome.[1] According to Kinsey's data, one of the two most important

> sexual factors which most often cause difficulty in the upper-level marriage . . . is the failure of the female to participate with the abandon which is necessary for the successful consummation of any sexual relation.[31]

The other factor listed by Kinsey—"the failure of the male to show skill on sexual approach and technique"—may also be attributed in part to the effects of extreme sex repression.[31]

THE IMPORTANCE OF SEXUALITY IN ADOLESCENT DEVELOPMENT AND ADJUSTMENT

Relationships between Sexuality and Adolescent Personality Maturation

The hormonal changes, the alterations in body form, and the psychological correlates of both naturally play a major role in adolescent personality development. We have referred to these characteristics of pubescence as the consummatory factors in precipitating the transitional personality phase of adolescence (see pp. 192–194). They accomplish this not only through their effect on cultural expectations, but also endogenously by their impact on the individual. The adolescent reacts to his adult body form, his newly acquired reproductive capacity, and his mature sexual drives by raising his aspirations for volitional independence and primary status. However, just because pubescence is the crucial catalytic agent that initiates the adolescent period of development, sexuality cannot be regarded as the central problem of adolescence.

Newly acquired sexual urges pose a significant obstacle to personality maturation also since they are the chief source of hedonistic need during adolescence. The control and regulation of a new organic drive creates an emergent problem of adaptation that has not arisen since early childhood. It is true that the individual is now older, more experienced in self-control, more responsive to moral obligations, and more highly motivated by status considerations to postpone the need for immediate hedonistic gratification. But by the same token he is also more self-assertive and resistive to adult standards and direction.

Insistent sex needs not only threaten other long-range goals, but also, as the Rankians point out, threaten the individual's newly acquired volitional independence.[25] Genuine affectional relationships imply considerable self-surrender and limitation of personal autonomy. These can be avoided either by asceticism, or by entering into numerous and superficial psychophysiological sex relations (promiscuity).

Sexuality and Adolescent Adjustment

Sexuality is an important area of adolescent adjustment. Whether existing sex needs are gratified or denied affects the total balance between frustration and satisfaction and, hence, the over-all stressfulness of adolescence. Stressfulness is also influenced by conflict or guilt feelings about sex, and impinges upon the individual's behavioral reactivity or emotional stability. Frustrations of sex needs may result in preoccupation with and overvaluation of sexuality, bothersome distractions, and compensatory attempts at self-enhancement in other directions. By symbolizing his sub-adult status or by instigating guilt-producing substitutive sex outlets, these frustrations may impair self-esteem.

Because of the intense psychological conflict about sex in middle-class boys in our society and because of the unrealistic cultural "avoidance and deprecation of the subject of sex in the face of . . . [their] positive knowledge of its actual importance," these adolescents subjectively overvalue the relative importance of sexuality in the total scheme of things. But regardless of its actual intrinsic importance, there is no gainsaying the phenomenological reality of this overvaluation to these adolescents. In a much different category is the social scientists' interpretative overvaluation of the importance of sexuality in adolescent adjustment.

Much of this interpretative overvaluation can be attributed to deficiencies in the type and sources of information about sex behavior that have in part only recently been remedied. Before Kinsey's [31] monumental study * of the sexual expression of the American male, most available conceptions of adolescent sex activity were conjectural.† Previous studies were superficial and did not sample large or representative enough segments of the population. And in keeping with their psychoanalytic orientation, many psychologists and psychiatrists were too liable to over-generalize from case histories drawn from middle-class patients and from their own middle-class backgrounds.

Among those who are concerned with interpreting adolescent psychology in our culture, the point of view has been steadily gaining ground that the American adolescent owes the greater part of his characteristic emotional instability to the inordinate amount of sex frustration he experiences. This opinion is customarily bolstered by citing Mead's Samoan data, which are overgeneralized to support the hypothesis than an invariable, one-to-one, causal

* "Kinsey's data have been subjected to statistical attack on the grounds that they are not adequately representative of the lower educational levels. It has also been suggested that the median rather than the mean would be a more valid measure of sexual outlet, . . . [since it would be less distorted by] the inclusion in the data of high outlets conceivably due to compulsive sexuality. Nevertheless this study remains the most representative and exhaustive performed to date." [1]

† Kinsey's differential findings by social class were foreshadowed in various studies of social stratification.[16, 42]

relationship prevails between the stressfulness of adolescence and the degree of cultural repression of adolescent sex activity.

When we consider *all* of the evidence, however, it becomes apparent that sex frustration is only one of *many* factors in adolescent status deprivation, and one of the *less* crucial factors leading to a stressful adolescence. First, there is no simple relationship between the severity of cultural restrictions on sexual expression and the degree of psychological conflict from sex (see pp. 399–401). Such conflict develops only when simultaneously sex drives are generated and moral prohibitions against their expression are internalized. In our society, therefore, psychological conflict about sex is hardly characteristic of adolescents generally since (a) eighty-five per cent of American male adolescents accept premarital intercourse as natural and desirable and, despite the existence of formal expectations to the contrary, exercise this conviction almost as freely as Samoan adolescents; [31] and (b) many girls either develop no sex urges at all or only psychoaffectional sex drives. Psychological stress from sex is impressive only in middle-class adolescent males, and not because of psychophysiological tensions produced by repression *per se* (since such tensions are relieved by masturbation and petting) but because of the psychological ambiguity of the situation, the guilt feelings engendered, and the invidious reflections on self-esteem.

Second, there is very little relationship between experienced degree of conflict about sex and the *total* stressfulness of adolescence because other nonsexual factors are more crucial in determining that stressfulness. Depending on the operation of these other factors, absence of sex repression and lack of psychological conflict about sex can coexist with either a relatively unstressful adolescence (as in Samoa), or with an extremely stressful adolescence (as among lower socioeconomic groups in our own culture). Whenever adolescence is simultaneously nonstressful and unaccompanied by little mental conflict about sex, other more compelling reasons unrelated to sexuality can usually be found for the idyllic nature of adolescent development. Samoans, for example, adopt an extremely casual approach to life and do not engage in any frantic struggle for status; and Arapesh adolescents are warmly accepted and eagerly integrated into a benevolent noncompetitive culture.

On the other hand, in primitive cultures in which a stressful adolescence coexists with considerable conflict about sex, there are also other reasons for the experienced difficulty of adolescence. In the Mundugumor, Manus, and Kwoma cultures, greater emphasis is placed on status, the culture as a whole is more competitive and aggressive, the adolescent has a more marginal position in society, and status is more persistently withheld from him (see pp. 18–19, 20). Hence, although sexual problems undoubtedly add to the stressfulness of adolescence in the Manus [44] and other primitive cultures,[43] greater weight must be given to the traumatic potential of these nonsexual factors.

If this proposition holds true for primitive cultures, it can be applied with even greater validity to our own culture; for the differences among primitive cultures in nonsexual determinants of adolescent stress are relatively minor in comparison with the corresponding difference between primitive and complex cultures (see pp. 321–324). When so many important variables contributing to a stressful adolescence are simultaneously operative, the presence or absence of sexual conflict is a relatively negligible factor. Thus, although the lower-class adolescent male in our society is spared the trauma of psychological conflict about sex, his adolescence on the whole is no less stressful than that of his middle-class contemporary.

VARIETIES OF ADOLESCENT SEXUAL EXPRESSION IN OUR CULTURE

Frequency and Types of Sex Outlets in Boys

By the age of fifteen, ninety-two per cent of all males have their first orgasm, two-thirds of them through masturbation, one-eighth through heterosexual coitus, and five per cent through homosexual contact (the remainder through miscellaneous outlets).

> After the initial experience in ejaculation, practically all males become regular in their sexual activity. This involves monthly, weekly, or even daily ejaculation. . . . Ninety-nine per cent of the boys begin regular sex lives *immediately* after the first ejaculation.[31]

Pointing perhaps to innate constitutional differences in sexual capacity is the fact that boys who mature earlier not only experience twice as much total outlet per week as late-maturing boys during the early years of adolescence, but also maintain this difference in rate for the remainder of their active sex lives.[31]

The age of maximal sexual outlet occurs between sixteen and seventeen, the mean frequency of outlet reaching 3.4 per week. This peak is maintained with only slight diminution until the age of thirty, after which it tapers off gradually.[31]

> The identification of the sexually most active period at late adolescence will come as a surprise to most persons. . . . By law, society provides a source of regular sexual outlet in marriage, in part because it recognizes the sexual need of the older male; but it fails to recognize that teen-age boys are potentially more capable and often more active than their thirty-five-year-old fathers. . . . The problem of sexual adjustment for the younger male is one which became especially aggravated during the last one hundred years, and then primarily in England and in America under an increasing moral suppression which has coincided with an increasing delay in age of marriage. This has resulted in an intensification of the struggle between the boy's biological capacity and the sanctions imposed by the older male. . . . The fact that the unmarried male still manages to find an outlet of 3.4 per week demonstrates the failure of the attempt to impose complete abstinence upon him.[31]

Types of Sexual Outlet. Although restrictions on adolescent sexual expression may have increased in comparison to those of one hundred years ago, there are reasons for believing that the trend has been reversed over the past thirty years.[42] In middle-class circles, there is a much more liberal, matter-of-fact attitude today toward adolescent sex activity. Largely as a result of the popularization of biological and psychological knowledge, psychophysiological sex activity of adolescent males is regarded with increasing tolerance. Masturbation and petting, having acquired a certain measure of respectability at the upper socioeconomic levels, are no longer in disrepute; and although it is still officially banned, this general liberalization of cultural attitude has to some extent affected even practice of premarital intercourse. More important, perhaps, for premarital intercourse are the decreasing severity of chaperonage and the widespread availability of contraceptives, which allay the twin fears of pregnancy and venereal disease. If these empirically unsubstantiated impressions of social trend are correct, an increasing proportion of middle-class adolescent sex outlet is being diverted from masturbation and nocturnal emissions to petting and premarital intercourse. This trend, at any rate, is evident from early to late adolescence as adolescents become more experienced in discovering "socio-sexual" outlets.[31]

Masturbation is the chief sexual outlet of early adolescence and shows a marked increase in incidence with the onset of puberty.[31, 51] Heterosexual petting, which increases in frequency and in intimacy of contact with increasing age,[31, 51] eventually involves as many as eighty-eight per cent of all boys.[31] Thirty per cent of Kinsey's adolescent male population reported petting to orgasm.[31] Premarital intercourse constitutes twenty-five per cent of the total male sex outlet before the age of sixteen, and forty per cent of total outlet between the ages of sixteen to twenty. Among lower-class boys it is almost universally a regular form of sexual outlet in late adolescence; in middle-class boys its occurrence is typically sporadic.[31] Transitory, "social" homosexuality—as a manifestation of sexual deprivation rather than as a preferred sexual outlet—is much more widespread than is commonly believed. During early adolescence it involves approximately one-third of all males at the high-school educational level [31, 51] and constitutes as high as seven per cent of the total sexual outlet.[31]

Social Class Differences

One of the most significant contributions of the Kinsey study is its empirical verification of earlier sociological impressions [16, 42] that sex attitudes and behavior differ widely but consistently among the various socioeconomic strata of our population. More frequently among lower-level than among upper-level boys, adolescent sex activity is a continuation of preadolescent sex play; and more frequently, also, heterosexual intercourse is the source of initial ejaculation.

> Masturbation is a more frequent outlet among the upper social level males where during the last two or three decades it has been allowed as a not too immoral substitute for premarital intercourse, but most of the less-educated eighty-five per cent of the population consider masturbation neither normal nor moral.[31]

Intercourse is the primary sexual outlet for the greater majority of lower-class boys. "By the age of fifteen, the active incidence (of premarital coitus) includes nearly half of the lower educational groups but only ten per cent of the boys who will ultimately go to college." [31] The upper educational groups more usually practice intercourse only after a prolonged petting relationship, if they do so at all, and commonly restrict participation to a prospective spouse.[31] The lower-level group, on the contrary, are more apt to have intercourse only with girls for whom they lack both respect and affection.

In his general orientation to sexuality,

> the lower-level male differentiates [more] sharply between psychophysiological and psychoaffectional sex needs, and prior to marriage openly admits that at times he satisfies each independently of the other. The upper-level male acknowledges that his psychophysiological sex desires exist, but feels that they ought to be repressed for moral reasons. The latter being too difficult, he compromises by first restricting himself to auto-erotic practices. But then, finding even this outlet insufficient, he discovers in petting a "socio-sexual" outlet that still enables him to keep intact his own virginity and that of his female partner. He [convinces] himself . . . that as long as he refrains from intra-vaginal intercourse, he is repressing the major portion of his psychophysiological immorality.[1]

Lower-level boys are unable to grasp the logic of this position.

> They have nothing like this strong taboo against pre-marital intercourse, and, on the contrary, accept it as natural and inevitable and as a desirable thing. Lower-level taboos are more often turned against an avoidance of intercourse and against any substitution for simple and direct coitus.[31]

How are these social class norms of sex behavior enforced during the rebellious period of parent-youth estrangement?

> On first thought one might imagine that the upper-level adolescent would just relish the opportunity of defying the rigid sex mores advocated by his parents. Wouldn't this be the precise area in which he could shock [them] most effectively? But actually, although he does revolt partly against the sex deprivations to which he is subjected, he nevertheless incorporates so many of the standards of his class that he is still closer by far to the sex norms of his repressive parents than to those of his contemporary comrades in rebellion among the lower-level groups.[1]

The coercive and punitive aspects of this enforcement are undertaken by the peer group, which

> by providing a new and more acceptable source of authority . . . insures the continuity [of class norms] without interfering with the task of self-assertion and liberation from parental domination.[1]

The more crucial aspect of enforcement, however, lies within, in the powerful inhibitions associated with the internalization of the class and family moral edicts that sexual intercourse apart from marriage is unethical. And once petting becomes established as a substitute for intercourse, canalization adds to its attractiveness.

All heterosexual orgasm experience becomes conditioned upon prior petting. It is, therefore, not surprising that [even] when . . . the opportunity for intercourse is no longer restricted, petting still persists as pre-coital play.[31] On the other hand, the inhibitions in relation to non-marital intercourse perpetuate themselves by creating through continued lack of experience an actual incapacity for finding opportunities for same. In direct contrast, the lower-level male who has no inhibitions about premarital intercourse is amazingly successful in finding opportunities for it among girls of his own age group. And never having any substitutive need for petting, he looks down upon it as a pervertedly indirect means of obtaining sexual gratification, indulging infrequently in it both before and after marriage.[1]

Sex Expression in Adolescent Girls

Much less definitive information about sexual behavior is available for adolescent girls than for boys. According to preliminary data from Kinsey's study, fewer than a quarter of all females, as compared to ninety-two per cent of males, experience orgasm by the age of fifteen. "The female population is twenty-nine years old before it includes as high a percentage of experienced individuals as is to be found in the male curve at fifteen." [31] In striking contrast to the regularity of male sexual activity, "there are women who go for periods of time ranging from a year to ten or twenty years between their earlier experiences and the subsequent adoption of regularity." [31] With respect to total outlet,

the average adolescent girl gets along well enough with a fifth as much sexual activity as the adolescent boy; and the frequency of outlet in the female in her twenties and early thirties is still below that of the average male adolescent.[31]

All of the evidence for the comparative incidence of specific sexual outlets indicates a lower frequency among girls than among boys. Masturbation is at least twice as common in boys as in girls.[64] Ninety-two per cent of college girls in one study admitted to petting;[57] but "most of the action in a petting relationship originates with the male. Most of it is designed to stimulate the female." [31] At the upper educational levels, about half as many girls as boys participate in premarital intercourse.[10, 23, 38, 51, 60]

Psychosexual maturation is slower and more gradual in girls than in boys. This is hardly surprising when we consider that

> girls in our culture tend more to grow up with a single (psychoaffectional) goal of sex activity, whereas boys, depending on class affiliation, adhere in varying degrees to a double standard. In the first place, [the former] requires greater emotional maturity, growing gradually with depth of affectional involvement. . . . Secondly, in many women, the idea of sex may be associated with such odium and repugnance that even in connection with affectional purposes there are strong inhibitions which may or may not be overcome slowly in the course of a happy marital relationship. [Hence] it is not uncommon that many women reach an ascending peak of sexual interest and activity in their late thirties [31] at a time when the sex drive of their husbands is flagging.[1]

Although psychophysiological sex urges are certainly not absent among girls—as many as twenty-five per cent of unmarried young women in one study admitted to frequent masturbation [38]—there are good reasons for believing that these urges are more highly subordinated to psychoaffectional sex impulses than among boys. The relative frequency of masturbation [64] is a good indication of this major difference in sex behavior between boys and girls. More girls than boys believe that sexual immorality is more deserving of condemnation in girls than in boys.[53] In heterosexual peer relationships, an adolescent girl is primarily concerned with the social prestige to be derived from "going steady" with a boy, and for this reason may "tolerate" his sexual attentions, which she might otherwise regard with indifference or resentment. "To the [boy], however, the matter of sexual gratification is by no means incidental, but is just as important as the prestige value of the conquest." [1]

The participation of girls in petting relationships is frequently predicated upon such factors as fear of unpopularity, desire to please their partners, and insufficient courage to act contrary to group norms and expectations.[54, 57] Girls approve less of necking and petting than boys do,[53, 56] and prefer greater conservatism in petting.[53] "Overdemanding in intimate relationships" is one of the six main criticisms that high school girls make of their dates.[53] Boys, on the other hand, include among their chief peeves about girls the complaints that they are "emotionally cold and unresponsive," and "easily offended and disgusted." [53] Consistent with these differences is the fact that girls are more disapproving than boys of premarital intercourse.[54, 56]

Interpretation of Sex Differences. Much more data about the sex behavior of women will be needed before the above differences in sexual expression can be properly evaluated.

> We will want to know how the total outlet of adult women compares with that of adult men; whether class differences prevail in the sexual activities of females as they do in the case of males; whether adult women have more psychophysiological sex drive than adolescent girls. However, on the basis of what [comparative] ethnological data we do have, it seems reasonable to conclude that existing differences in psychosexual development between men and women in our culture are [largely culturally conditioned rather than] . . . biologically determined.[1]

The development of psychophysiological sex urges can be repressed more easily in girls than in boys because girls

> are subjected to greater family and social pressures in this respect, and are, therefore, more or less able to accept . . . at face value the polite social implication that sexual gratification may be important—but to men only.[1]

Once this proposition is accepted, it seems only natural and proper that it should be the female rather than the male "who needs to be stimulated to sexual activity; . . . that a girl should reject the sexual advances of boys for whom she has no affection," but if a boy does likewise he should be "dubbed a dolt and a fool." [1]

The same logic underlies the prevailing "double standard" of sexual morality. As long as psychophysiological sex drives are presumed to be normally absent in girls, a girl who acts as if this were not so is by definition abnormally and perversely licentious. College students believe that it is more immoral for women than for men to tell obscene stories or to engage in illicit sex relations.[30] The girl is considered more solely responsible for the control of petting [54] and for the preservation of her virginity; and the boy is free to try to "get away with" as much as her vigilance and his own conscience permit him.

> Hence, her sexual indiscretions cannot be forgiven, whereas [in] boys, the legitimacy of premarital intercourse, although formally interdicted, is almost taken for granted at the lower educational level, and forgivable if it occurs at the upper level.[1]

In comparison with the situation in our own culture, among the Manus the divergence between male and female biological sex roles is even greater. Women develop neither psychophysiological nor psychoaffectional sex drives, and men develop only the latter. Manus women loathe intercourse and welcome "children because it gives their husbands a new interest and diverts their unwelcome attention from themselves; . . . [whereas] rape, the swift and sudden capture of an unwilling victim, is still the men's ideal." [44]

Among the Arapesh, Mundugumor, and Navaho, the reverse is true: men and women are presumed to have more or less identical sex urges. Arapesh men and women both adopt a purely psycho-affectional approach to sex. In Mundugumor society, men and women share an equally intense psychophysiological orientation to sexuality. Girls are positively and aggressively sexed and usually take the initiative in the bush liaison. "The love affairs of the young married couple are sudden and highly charged, characterized by passion rather than by tenderness or romance." [44] Finally among the Navaho there is no suggestion of the Anglo-Saxon conception that

> women are, or ought to be, too "pure" to be interested in sex, that they merely submit to intercourse as part of their marital duties and in order to have children. . . . Indeed many women have a local reputation for being desirous, active, or initiatory in sex matters.[41]

Evaluation of the Major Sex Outlets *

Masturbation. In recent years there has been a violent swing in the direction of informed professional opinion about the detrimental consequences of masturbation. Most investigators today agree that the chief damage caused by masturbation comes from experiencing (a) related feelings of guilt and impaired self-esteem, and (b) anxiety about incurring the manifold forms of physical, mental, and moral deterioration popularly associated with the practice. Although this position is essentially sounder than the earlier one, since no physical or psychological damage has ever

---

* This evaluation of sex outlets is based only on psychological criteria. Complete evaluation must also take into account the relevant moral issues. These are discussed on pages 430–433.

been traced to the effects of masturbation *per se,** the implications of the practice as an escape from heterosexual reality must be considered. From what we know about canalization, the danger always exists that "through conditioning it may become more than a substitute for heterosexual activity and evolve as an end in itself." [1]

On the positive side,

> as an outlet for accumulated psychophysiological sexual tension which might otherwise interfere with the satisfactory performance of the adolescent's school and other responsibilities, it fulfills a useful function, [especially] in the case of those individuals who have compunctions about sexual contact with the opposite sex on any other but a psychoaffectional basis.[1]

Petting. The same dangers—guilt feelings, anxiety, and canalization—exist for petting. However, "since it is closer to the goal of heterosexual activity, and, under any circumstances, is a more meaningful and emotional sexual experience," it must be regarded as preferable to masturbation.[1] An exception to this statement applies when, on idealistic grounds, an adolescent feels obliged to refrain from interpersonal sexual outlets unless he entertains feelings of genuine affection for the person involved.

In addition to involving less moral conflict for middle-class adolescents, petting also offers certain

> practical advantages to [individuals] who are either ignorant about prophylactic measures regarding birth control and venereal disease, or who are very alarmed about these possibilities. . . . It [also] probably serves a desirable function by reducing autoeroticism, and . . . by releasing some of the unnatural inhibitions about sexual expression, especially in the female. . . . The nervous tension presumably aroused by petting has been grossly exaggerated.[31] If orgasm results there is no residual tension. If orgasm does not occur, any tension which does not subside spontaneously is frequently relieved by masturbation, the event which would otherwise have [transpired] in the first place.[1]

Premarital Intercourse. Provided it is not productive of moral conflict, premarital intercourse is undoubtedly the most satisfactory sexual outlet of the three. The precise outcome depends upon the type of partner, the degree of acceptability without conflict, the

---

* Kinsey points with justice to the fact that most medical writers help to perpetuate such anxieties by virtue of their unwillingness to make this statement unequivocally.[31]

conditions under which it occurs, and the worries about pregnancy and venereal disease that are generated.[31] Kinsey reports that few males ever regret premarital intercourse,[31] "but this is probably less true of females, as most psychiatrists can testify from clinical experience."[1]

DIFFERENTIATION OF SOCIAL SEX ROLES

Components of Social Sex Role

In contrast to biological sex role, which refers to feeling tones, behavior, and impulses functionally or historically dependent upon gonadal stimulation, social sex role refers to the differential functions, status, and personality traits that each culture traditionally assumes to inhere in the very fact of sex membership. Social sex roles in a given culture are generally regarded as self-evident reflections of the essential nature of man and woman. That men and women perform social and economic functions that vary widely from culture to culture in degree of similarity is an anthropological commonplace; and to a greater or lesser extent, different cultures provide differential training for boys and girls that will equip them for the distinctive tasks they will perform as men and women. Such differential training takes place in our own culture [42, 62] as well as in more primitive cultures [41, 45] (see p. 188), but it is less thorough-going as a result of the greater discontinuity between the status worlds of children and adults (see pp. 189–191). In our own culture, as Parsons [47] points out, girls suffer less than boys from this discontinuity in training, since as children both are reared primarily by the mother who can provide a visible model of behavior as well as concrete experience with appropriate tasks only for the female sex role.

Another important aspect of social sex role is the hierarchical ordering of relations between the sexes in terms of (a) the relative values placed by the culture upon maleness and femaleness respectively, and (b) the degree of access each sex has to positions of social power and privilege. In most familial, vocational, and institutional situations in our culture,

the male is trained for the superordinate roles while the female is restricted largely to subordinate positions. As in other types of inferior social rankings, however, the female position allows a certain degree of chronic aggression, sabotage, and cleverness against the superior rank.[15]

From an early age boys learn to be contemptuous of the female sex role; and although girls resent and complain about the disrespect shown their sex,[53] they generally accept at face value the prevailing view of their inferiority.[37] Whereas boys express scorn for girls' tasks, games, and future role in life, and seldom if ever desire to change sex, girls not infrequently are envious of and wish they were boys.[62] The male equivalent of a "tomboy," who reads girls' books and relishes housework and sewing, is indeed a rarity (see p. 297).

The third important component of social sex role is the prevailing cultural conception of masculinity and femininity. This consists of a

stereotyped, composite personality portrait of man and woman, defining the emotions, interests, moral attitudes, and character traits thought proper and desirable for each sex.[1]

Our culture, for example, claims that men and women

are different kinds of people. Men are stronger, bolder, less pure, less refined, more logical, more reasonable. . . . Women are more delicate, stronger in sympathy, understanding, and insight, less mechanically adept, more immersed in petty detail and in personalities, and given to "getting emotional over things."[42]

These notions of masculinity and femininity have deep and often obscure roots in the culture. In general, however, they are derived from the respective socioeconomic functions and statuses of men and women, and from the culturally determined characteristics of appropriate male and female body types and biological sex roles.

The Impact of Pubescence on Social Sex Role

It is during adolescence that the youth in our culture first acquires clear-cut and unambiguous conceptions of adult masculinity and femininity. Both girls and boys earn their highest femininity and masculinity scores, respectively, on the Goodenough M-F test when they reach the age corresponding to the usual time of sexual maturation in either sex.[22] The facilitating effect of adolescence on the emergence of social sex roles can be attributed in part to (a) greater perceptual sensitivity to social situations and interpersonal relationships (see p. 366), and to (b) the greater importance of social sex role at this stage of development.

> During childhood [social] sex role is primarily differentiated for purposes of play. But in adolescence the aim of differentiation is more serious by far, involving a more or less permanent assignment of social, vocational, and family tasks and aspirations together with their appropriate personality traits.[1]

But pubescence *per se* must be an important factor in the development of social sex role in view of the fact that pubescent individuals make higher scores on the M-F test than nonpubescent individuals of equivalent chronological age.[61] This does not mean that sex hormones exert a *direct* influence on the individual's development of the appropriate masculine or feminine personality attributes. The immediate effects of sex hormones under favorable conditions are merely to increase sex consciousness and awareness of sex differences, and to develop distinctive characteristics of male and female body type. But as a result of increased sensitivity to sex differences, the individual becomes more aware of "the social expectations and values attached to the male or female body." As a result of reacting to his own changed body form, of reacting to the sexuality of others, and of being reacted to as a sexual object, he comes to identify with a given adult sex clan and to incorporate the personality characteristics compatible with the social expectations of membership in that clan. He thus acquires the complete constellation of differential personality traits associated with male and female socioeconomic functions, with the physical criteria of masculine and feminine attractiveness, and with the properties of male and female biological sex role.

The mere development of the body-type characteristics that follows from the sex-appropriate pattern of endocrine stimulation does not of itself result either in cultural norms of masculine or feminine attractiveness or in individual identification with and incorporation of the appropriate physical criteria of masculinity or femininity. The physical values that are culturally chosen as criteria of masculine or feminine physical attractiveness are not implicit in the sex differences themselves; they are arbitrarily selected from a large number of secondary sex characteristics and at arbitrarily designated points on a continuum of male and female body types.

The same holds true for biological sex role: neither its original emergence nor subsequent differentiation are implicit in pubescence (see pp. 142–144). In cultures in which a sharp distinction is made between male and female biological sex roles (Manus, American), there is a correspondingly greater polarization of the concepts of masculinity and femininity; and when this distinction is not made (Mundugumor, Arapesh), the essential natures of man and woman are conceived as more alike.

Once learned, the concept of social sex role is continually reinforced by the availability of vivid perceptual cues, i.e., objective and culturally determined differences in the appearance, behavior, and presumed personality traits of the two sexes. Thus, not only the cultural existence of polarized concepts of masculinity and femininity, but also the adolescent's identification with these concepts is facilitated by the presence of culturally defined differences in sex appropriate physical traits, biological role, and socioeconomic functions. Biological and social sex roles are simultaneously differentiated in our culture, and each mutually reinforces the other.

The Transitional Social Sex Role of Adolescence

Since the adolescent is not admitted to membership in society at large, he can play a social sex role only in his own peer group. It is inevitable that this role will be transitional and discontinuous with both its childhood and adult counterparts. The appropriate constellations of masculine and feminine traits associated with high peer group status have been discussed in detail (see pp. 362–363). They are related, at least in part, to the unique interim goals and values of the peer group.

In relation to preadolescence, the social sex role of adolescence requires a break with the derived status inherent in the role of emotionally dependent son or daughter. Boys must primarily aspire to an extrinsic status based upon their own performance abilities; and girls must aspire both to a derived status based upon their husbands' careers, and to a primary status related to their own home-making abilities. In relation to the adult social sex role, a similar degree of discontinuity prevails.

> By contrast with the emphasis on responsibility in this role, the orientation of the youth culture is more or less specifically irresponsible. One of its dominant notes is having a good time.[47]

In choosing its leaders the youth culture places great emphasis upon the importance of being an "all-round" personality, and relatively little weight on competence in a narrow field of specialization.[47] Male athletic prowess carries little prestige value in the adult culture; and sexual attractiveness or glamourousness in the female is a relatively minor component of the social sex role of adult women.[47]

Nevertheless, despite this evidence of discontinuity, (just as in the transmission of major social class goals, values, and attitudes) the essential differential aspects of social sex role filter down into and are transmitted by the peer culture. It is true, of course, that in the middle- and upper middle-classes, there is "up through college . . . no sex differentiation in the process of formal education"; [47] such differentiation takes place first at the post-graduate level where there is a "direct connection with future occupational careers." [47] But despite the presumption of sex equality in future vocational roles that is initially engendered by this nondiscriminatory preparatory (high school and college) education, neither boys nor girls seriously doubt that eventually considerable differentiation of occupational status will take place on the basis of sex membership. Girls adopt a more ambivalent and less ego-involved attitude than boys toward expressed vocational choice; if they contemplate marriage, they look upon a career as essentially a temporary, stop-gap expedient.* Whereas the middle-class boy fully anticipates that he will be expected to create through his own vocational efforts and achievements the social status of his future family, few girls in the same social class expect as married women to compete with men in their own fields or at occupational levels of equivalent social prestige.[47] They expect to fall heir to a derived status dependent upon their husbands' station in life, and to acquire primary status in the roles of mother and housewife, supplemented perhaps by participation in cultural and community welfare activities.[47]

Sex Differences in the Acquisition of Social Sex Role

In some ways the acquisition of social sex role is more difficult for boys, but in other ways it is more difficult for girls. Boys are required to undergo greater personality change.

* Based upon unpublished data of the writer.

The implications of emancipation—independence, self-reliance, striving for [primary status]—are applied more thoroughly in their case; whereas to a very large degree, women [as wives] can retain many of the dependent and docile attributes of childhood personality status.[1]

For boys there is also less continuity from the adolescent to the adult social sex roles. Athletic ability and heterosexual effectiveness are less related to the adult male role than glamourousness is to the adult female role.

Girls, on the other hand, experience more difficulty in the transition between preadolescent and adolescent social sex roles since they lack a core value, such as athletic prowess, which persists from one stage to the next as a significant determinant of peer group status (see p. 364). The concepts of femininity and female sex role in our culture are also less stable and less consistent than the corresponding concepts for boys.

Girls today are torn by the desire to realize their earlier image of themselves as women concerned with children, home, and a husband, and by the social and educational pressure to justify themselves in some socially recognized position.[20]

This cultural conflict naturally has its repercussions in the peer group. Not only are girls confused about their own preferences, but they are also in doubt about the preferences of their boy friends (and future husbands) and parents. The attitudes of all three groups toward femininity are highly inconsistent; but boys are more inconsistent than girls, and the disparity between the youth of opposite sex toward femininity exceeds the corresponding difference between the parents.[34] Thus, parents and daughter, daughter and her fiancee, and the two parents themselves may all be at odds on this issue.

It is highly improbable that very many girls develop serious or long lasting illusions about the ultimate sex differentiation of occupational roles, despite the apparent equality of educational opportunities. Nevertheless, many of them must be quite confused at times by the ambiguity and inconsistency in this situation; and others are conceivably quite disillusioned when they find their paths to careers blocked by sex discrimination. In other instances, the serious demands of a professional career, when added to the negative attitudes of parents and boy friends, make the combination of marriage and career incompatible and require a choice between the two. Both outcomes are reflected in the fact that relatively few women choose professional careers and that fewer still are able to combine such careers with marriage. In any event there is much more uncertainty, confusion, and conflict about this problem than in previous generations when only a single choice existed.

> Special social conditions also impinge on this question. In the twenties, a wave of feminism swept America, creating a generation of career-minded women. But the protracted economic depression in the thirties contracted job opportunities so sharply that a reversal in orientation took place, this time toward the home. The war then swung the pendulum in the opposite direction. All of these trend reversals are to say the least, most confusing to the modern adolescent girl.[1]

Perhaps, as the Lynds [42] contend, the underlying basis of the cultural confusion is the fact that although technological changes have necessarily produced certain changes in the traditional role of women, these

> modifications have been in the kind of behavior sanctioned by the culture, *not* in the belief that men and women are different in character and temperament. . . . The modifications of the behavior patterns themselves consist in *tolerated exceptions* rather than in the development of any clear alternatives meeting with group approval.[42]

Girls are not *really* driven by the culture as are boys to prove their adequacy and maintain their self-esteem by their accomplishments. And lacking this powerful cultural instigation to achievement, in comparison to her average male counterpart, the career-oriented girl must either be motivated by an unusually high order of intellectual curiosity and creativity or has unusually great needs for ego enhancement that are rooted in her individual personality development.

Biological or Social Determination of Social Sex Role

Since the culture determines the socioeconomic functions, the relative status, the physical criteria of masculinity and femininity, and the biological sex roles of men and women, social sex role is primarily a cultural derivative rather than an inevitable consequence of endocrinological differences. In all cultures social sex roles constitute institutionalized patterns of behavior that are transmitted to boys and girls by differential treatment, training, and expecations;

and it is especially during adolescence, when physical changes in body form make identification with an adult sex clan possible, that these roles are effectively incorporated into ego structure.

All of this becomes much more evident when we look outside our own culture and discover that its concepts of masculinity and femininity are not the only ones natural and possible in human societies. When the difference in the socioeconomic roles of the sexes lies in a direction opposite to that of our own culture, as among the Tchambuli, our notions of masculinity and femininity are precisely reversed; [44] and, on the other hand, when little distinction is made between these roles, as in the Soviet Union, there is correspondingly less of a "dichotomy of personality characteristics [between] man and woman." [55] Similarly, when male and female biological sex roles are presumed to be more identical (Arapesh, Mundugumor), both sexes are expected to conform to similar ideals of character.[44]

In taking this position it is not necessary to assume, as many social psychologists and anthropologists do, that biological factors play no role whatever in conditioning sex differences in personality. We have cited evidence in support of the proposition that gonadal hormones and prolactin can bring about significant changes in such temperamental characteristics as aggressiveness and motherliness (see pp. 147–148). Nevertheless, personality differences that are conditioned by hormonal factors would not prevail unless they were supported by cultural variables operating in the same direction. And since cultural influences are able to negate and even reverse the consequences of biological conditioning, they must be accounted the prepotent factors in determining social sex role.

HETEROSEXUAL PEER GROUP AND COURTING BEHAVIOR

Our culture, like all other cultures, establishes formal and institutionalized practices and regulations governing the interpersonal relationships between the sexes. Invariably, the formality and rigorousness of these regulations increase as children reach adolescence; for beginning with pubescence, heterosexual relationships seriously impinge on such culturally important matters as biological sex role, social class status, and family organization. Whatever the mores that govern the approaches that children of opposite sex can make to each other (physically or socially), they are almost invariably significantly different in relation to adults.[7]

Since, in our culture, the adolescent's social life and opportunities for sexual expression are almost entirely limited to his peer group, he is obliged to devise instrumentalities for formal heterosexual contact within its structural organization. In contrast to preadolescent group formations, adolescent peer groups are generally predicated upon heterosexual membership and activities suitable for both sexes. Heterosexual social and courting interests are undoubtedly stimulated by gonadal maturation, as evidenced by their earlier appearance in girls than in boys (see p. 297). But the facts that an interval of a year occurs between pubescence and the appearance of these interests in girls and that a further interval of time interposes between the initial appearance of the interests and their translation into suitable activities [29, 57] shows that other factors (parental attitudes, identification with peer group activities, the learning of new social techniques) are also involved.

Courting relationships in the peer group serve several important functions. They provide for both sexes the major source of recreational activity during adolescence. For both boys and girls they are the source of most romantic and psychoaffectional sex experience and the basis for locating and choosing a suitable mate. For middle-class boys (and to a lesser extent girls) they provide in petting experience an important source of sexual gratification; and for both sexes, but especially for girls, they are a significant determinant of intra-group status and prestige.

Developmental Changes in Heterosexual Relationships

Preadolescent Segregation. Characteristic of our culture is a voluntary segregation of the sexes during the years of middle childhood and preadolescence. This is manifested by a lack of cross-sex sociometric choices (see p. 347), marked preference for like-sex individuals,[14, 21, 58] avoidance of physical contact with members of the opposite sex,[14] extreme sex-typing of games and activities, and numerous expressions of indifference, dislike, and rivalry.

This state of affairs does not come about accidentally. Boys and girls of this age have no great need for each other, but they do have many reasons for estrangement and mutual antagonism. Different social sex roles place emphasis upon different kinds of activities, which for practical purposes necessitates the formation of unisexual play groups. Boys are imbued with male chauvinism, and girls retaliate in kind by finding reasons for deprecating the male sex. Because girls are more docile, obedient, and conforming to adult direction at home and at school they receive preferential treatment. This provides an endless source of rivalry, discord, resentment, aggression and counter-aggression. All of these factors promote strong feelings of intra-sex solidarity and the utilization of the opposite sex as a convenient object for the displacement of hostile feelings of any origin.

Transitional Heterosexual Patterns. Because of this tradition of segregation and antagonism, and the consequent absence of any recognized channels of communication, early heterosexual interests cannot be manifested frankly and overtly. Hence arises a need for various covert and transitional ways of expressing heterosexual interests. One of the most widely practiced of these utilizes elaborate patterns of pseudo-disapproval and of studied and labored simulated hostility.

> Boys and girls form in clusters of their own furtively eyeing each other while carrying on no organized activity of their own. Again there may be chasing and pushing and tussling reminiscent of the fracases of nursery school children.[29]

Embarrassed and self-conscious about their emergent hormonally instigated interest in the opposite sex,

> a feeling which is disallowed by the childhood social code, children approaching adolescence first reveal this interest in the only socially acceptable way open to them—in antagonism.[1]

Another transitional form of development that does not markedly conflict with recognized preadolescent patterns and requires no new social learnings in relation to peers of the opposite sex is the early adolescent "crush." It involves strong attraction to and admiration of (a) a peer of the same sex, or (b) an older person of the opposite sex. It is a well-suited substitutive outlet for heterosexual interests when adolescent boys and girls are still self-conscious and awkward about approaching each other.

The first type of "crush" is more common in girls than in boys,[28] and, according to one study, involves the overwhelming majority of girls.[38] This sex difference is compatible with the previously noted tendency for girls to be more concerned than boys with intimate interpersonal experience (see p. 369). However, such "crushes" are of relatively short duration and are replaced in almost all instances by normal heterosexual relationships as soon as these can be established with greater ease. Although these frequently involve very close association, some physical affection, and even intense jealousy (especially in girls), sexual connotations are seldom present and homosexuality is only a rare consequence.[38] "Crush" behavior toward an older person of the opposite sex partakes more of romantic idealization and hero worship; and silent adoration is most usually the only feasible way of expressing the felt devotion that is intense but quickly dissipated.

Development of the Romantic Pattern. Once past the initial self-consciousness and bewilderment, when their status as adolescents is clearly enough established to dispense with the earlier norms of segregation, the heterosexual interests of boys and girls come into the open frankly and unabashedly. Initially these overt manifestations are apt to be exaggerated, boisterous, silly, affectedly uninhibited, and randomly directed. Gradually, however, they become more restrained, dignified, patterned, and selective. Giddy interest in all members of the opposite sex gives way to a more concentrated interest in one person or in a favored few. Formal dating displaces diffuse, unorganized activity. With increasing age, "going steady" becomes more common, involving more than a third of high school students and more than half of college students.[46] The college group was also found to be more critical of their dates.

In addition to greater selectivity other factors add to the growing stability of adolescent heterosexual relationships. As they grow older, the relationships of adolescents are more romantic and affectional, with greater depth of emotion.[35] As dating becomes increasingly oriented toward mating needs, these relationships necessarily become less casual. Over ninety per cent of high school seniors contemplate marriage,[48] and the majority regard the ages of nineteen to twenty-one, or twenty-two to twenty-four as "equally appropriate ages for marriage." [53]

The current romantic pattern of courtship involving the notions of voluntary selection of a mate, "special affinity" between the betrothed pair, and idealization of the loved one, is neither typical of most cultures nor of very long standing in our own culture. To a very large extent it is a function of our cultural concept of the feminine sex role, of our official psychoaffectional orientation toward sexuality, of the general aura of mystery surrounding sex, and of the lack of communication between the sexes during pre-adolescence. Psychoaffectional expressions of sexuality, however, need not be based on romantic love. Both among the Arapesh [44] and the Navaho,[41] for example, marriages are "arranged" by parents and families. Also, "the Navaho theory is that one woman will do as well as another so long as she is healthy, industrious, and competent." [41] Nevertheless in neither culture is there an absence of deep emotional content in the relationship between the sexes. It is interesting that despite the great emphasis we place upon psychological compatibility in marriage, marriage partners are much more similar in social background factors than in personality characteristics.[11, 12]

Dating and Courting Beliefs

High school students are about evenly divided in the belief that either thirteen to fourteen, or fifteen to sixteen are the most appropriate ages for first dates.[53] In actual practice, almost half of high school freshmen and more than eighty per cent of high school seniors participate in dating.[49] The majority of high school students agree that girls should not share the expenses of dates.[53] More boys than girls approve of girls asking for dates and of kissing on the first date.[53] The characteristics that each sex admires and dislikes in their dates and the difference between the sexes in these respects have been discussed (see pp. 363, 365).

Of the characteristics thought desirable in a prospective mate, physical and mental fitness, desire for a normal family life with children, dependability and trustworthiness, compatible interests, good personal appearance and manners, and pleasant disposition and sense of humor are chosen most frequently by high school students.[53] Forty-two per cent of the boys want their future mates to know how to cook and keep house, and sixty-two per cent of the girls (especially those from high income groups) are concerned with their mates' prospects for making money and getting ahead.[53] In general boys place more value on physical attractiveness, whereas girls lay greater stress on their parents' approval of their choice and on the traits of dependability and considerateness.[53]

Our ideals of social mobility are reflected in the fact that overwhelming majorities of college students want their mates to have equal or better intelligence and education than themselves,[54] but that only a quarter of a comparable group would not marry into families with a social status inferior to that of their own.[3] As many as twenty per cent of college students expressed the view that Catholics and Protestants could not intermarry successfully, and forty-two per cent believed that marriages between Jews and non-Jews could not be successful.[54] A majority of high school girls prefer their prospective mates to be one to two years older than themselves, whereas the reverse is true of boys.[54] Except for older men and persons in upper socioeconomic groups,[26] residential propinquity is an important limiting factor in the selection of a mate.[9]

Courtship Problems and Heterosexual Adjustment

The courtship problems that bother adolescents most have to do with (a) the legitimacy of premarital sex intimacies—kissing, petting, intercourse; [13] (b) dating practices—"blind," "pick-up," "girl-made" dates; [13] (c) characteristics limiting the suitability of a prospective mate—age, religious and educational differences; [13] and (d) difficulties experienced in love affairs—quarrels, loss of interest, fear of over-involvement,[36] the nature of "true love," "two-timing," long engagements, terminating engagements.[13]

Factors Influencing the Outcome of Heterosexual Adjustment. Whether or not heterosexual adjustment during adolescence will be successful is not a matter of chance. Depending upon the personality characteristics of the individual and upon the favorableness of his environment, he may either fail to adopt an appropriate biological sex role (sex perversion, sex delinquency, asexuality), or he may experience delayed or inadequate heterosexual maturation.[8, 31] The importance of learning experiences in achieving heterosexual adjustment is pointed up by the series of developmental changes in the relationship between the sexes during the course of adolescence (see pp. 421–425), by the relatively large number of love affairs of most individuals before choosing a mate,[24, 38] by the increasing degree of dissatisfaction from high school to college age with numbers of the opposite sex,[46] and by the increasing degree of affectional success in successive love affairs.[35]

Three main categories of unfavorable factors are implicated in heterosexual maladjustment during adolescence: (a) *unfortunate parental attitudes and parent-child relationships:* the example of an unhappy marriage in the home, the parents' deprecation of sex or of the sex of adolescent,[20] parental clinging to the adolescent child or preventing him from making heterosexual contacts with his peers, parental ridicule of early heterosexual ineffectiveness, unwholesome family relationships; [65] (b) *personality traits* associated with asocial tendencies (excessive introversion, timidity, insecurity, anxiety, impaired self-esteem,[65] asceticism, and overintellectualization), and with inappropriate differentiation of biological sex role (narcissism or overidentification with the sex role of the parent of opposite sex) (see p. 144); and (c) *insufficient opportunity for learning experiences,* from extreme physical unattractiveness, isolation from the peer group [65] or members of the opposite sex,[64] and lack of social skills.

The less serious of these influences, such as parental restrictiveness, asocial personality traits, and insufficient opportunity for heterosexual experience, usually only limit the rate and maximum extent of normal heterosexual maturation or lead to transitory aberrations in psychosexual development. In the latter category belongs the situational homosexuality associated with sexual deprivation.[31, 64] On the other hand, defects in personality traits directly influencing the appropriate differentiation of biological sex role may lead to permanent homosexuality; and extreme parental deprecation of sexuality or of a particular (male or female) sex role may lead to asexuality (frigidity, psychic impotence) or to sex delinquency (see p. 144).

SEX EDUCATION AND GUIDANCE

Adolescents' Sources of Sex Information

Until recently all available data indicated that adolescents received the major part of their sex information from age-mates of the same sex. College students in one study listed friends, books, and parents in that order as the three major sources of their sex education.[54] A large survey of youth between sixteen and twenty-four years of age in the middle 1930's revealed that about seventy per cent received their instruction about sex from contemporaries; in this group, however, more girls than boys and more white than Negro youth received sex instruction from their parents.[6] Very similar findings were reported in a study of mid-Western adolescent boys.[50]

The most recent, large-scale, representative survey of high school students [53] indicates a possible reversal of this trend. Parents, friends, and reading (in the order given) were the three most frequently mentioned sources of sex information; and parents were more frequently the main source of sex education for students coming from higher income and higher educational levels. Also, twice as many girls as boys claimed that they received the greater part of their sex instruction at home.[53]

The Need for Sex Education in the Schools

The urgent need for sex education in the schools is evident from the vast amount of misinformation modern youth have about sex, from the frequency and urgency of their sex problems, and from the lack of adequate sources of sex instruction and guidance presently available to adolescent boys and girls. We have referred to one study [13] that indicates that a considerable amount of perplexity exists among adolescents about problems of dating, courting, sex intimacies, and the meaning of love. Another study of sex problems in adolescents showed that boys reported an average of seven worries per individual about various aspects of sex.[33] It is also a fair inference, supported by some evidence,[57] that much adolescent sexual experimentation is undertaken for no better reason than to relieve the curiosity that could be more appropriately satisfied by adequate and reliable information. And an even graver consequence of inadequate sex instruction is the fact that distorted attitudes about sexuality are associated with low levels of marital happiness.[60]

In the face of this unmistakable need for sex information, the percentage of parents who reportedly offer no instruction varies from forty-eight to sixty-two in various studies.[10, 13, 50, 60] Even in the most recent survey, which showed parents to be the chief source of sex instruction, only thirty-five per cent of the students reported that their parents assumed this responsibility.[53] Even if most parents were willing to impart sex instruction to their adolescent children, how many of them would be in sufficiently good rapport and sufficiently skillful and well-informed to do so adequately? In one study of adolescent boys, when parents did attempt sex instruction, only two per cent of their sons felt they did an adequate job, and only twenty-seven per cent thought they did a fair job. A majority of adolescents also believe that the school should take some responsibility for sex education.[6, 53, 54]

A Program of General Sex Education

To be satisfactory and nonoffensive to parents of different moral beliefs and persuasions, the school can attempt to offer only a very general sex education. Such education would be concerned with the physiology and psychology of normal sexual development and with the emotional and ethical goals of sex expression. It would leave to individual guidance specific problems about various sexual practices.

Any effective program of sex education would also have to be geared to developmental "changes in the form of children's concern as they move from the early adolescent into the late adolescent period."[29] L. K. Frank makes the following pertinent comment:

> It is . . . ironic to recall that when boys and girls are most eager to make an approach to each other, to discover what a man and woman mean to each other, and how they should act toward each other, we can only offer them sex education, i.e., teaching about procreation, which is the last thing they are really concerned about. They want to know not about babies, but what you can do with sex, what you can give and receive from the other, what love means. Instead of giving them our best knowledge and wisest counsel and helping them to direct these interests, the cautious parents may instead concentrate upon terrorizing them with the dangers of venereal disease [20] [pp. 243, 244; quoted by permission of the Society].

Thus, whereas instruction about reproduction, conception, the birth process and the anatomy and physiology of sex are developmentally suited to the concerns of preadolescence, young adolescents are understandably more interested in the emotional and moral aspects of sex, in psychosexual development, and in problems of courting. Older adolescents have a more relevant interest in problems of marriage, home-making, and the family.

Much of these materials could undoubtedly be learned with other established courses of study such as biology, hygiene, and home economics. It is extremely doubtful, however, whether the present preparation of teachers equips them to handle these problems properly.

Ethical Orientation. The most vital aspect of the general program of sex education proposed is an insistence that sex education is meaningless unless it can be related to

> the meaning, the role, and the importance of sex in the modern world. To separate these questions from the province of sex [education] is to make of it a meaningless jumble of isolated facts, merely to substitute five-syllable for four-letter words.[1]

The writer, in other words, cannot accept the point of view that sex education must be only factual and descriptive in nature and must not presume to tell an individual how to behave in an activity that is primarily personal rather than social in nature.

What is forgotten in all such arguments is that every culture accepts an implicit set of ethical values for significant behavior and proceeds as a matter of self-preservation to educate the young to accept these values. Does anyone after all object to the "one-sided" advocacy of the virtues of democracy, honesty, truthfulness, and kindliness in our schools?

> Since it is impossible to conceive of any directed behavior which is devoid of either purpose or moral content, how can guidance neglect either aspect? The individual still retains his right of self-determination by being free to accept or reject the goals and standards offered him, providing that his behavior does not infringe upon the rights or interests of others.[1]

One position on the ethical orientation of sex education that could be taken but seldom is (at least explicitly) is that our culture should adopt the Samoan code of sex morality. This would be consistent with the widespread attitude that the stressfulness of adolescence is directly correlated with the severity of social restrictions on sexual expression. But we have already seen that there is no single, inevitable, or universal pattern of psychosexual development and that the suppression of physiological sex urges is not invariably associated with psychological conflict. In the light of this finding it is possible to suggest a more realistic solution, which is also more appropriate to the emotional and aesthetic ideals of our society. And the finding that the Arapesh are able to prevent effectively the development of physiological sex drives merely through passive de-emphasis and to channel all sex urges and consciousness along affectional lines lends credence to the belief that a psychoaffectional goal of sex behavior is neither unrealistic nor impossible (with proper sex education) in our culture.

The argument that "free expression of the psychophysiological component of sex" is more "natural" is psychologically irrelevant since

practically every other "natural" drive in man has been drastically modified and channeled into highly differentiated and limited modes of expression. In advocating a psychoaffectional goal of sexual behavior, however, it need not be given the same negative connotations which it has acquired in our own Anglo-Saxon culture. In other words, our present-day acceptance of psychoaffectional sexuality need not be regarded at the lesser of two evils . . . as [something intrinsically] ugly and reprehensible, as "something to be relegated to the darkness of the night" . . . [but to be] tolerated . . . in relation to marital affectional needs. . . . Instead it can be given an more positive emphasis as in the Arapesh society [44] where it is regarded as an added means of enrichening and beautifying an affectional relationship between man and woman.

Sexual activity, then, could become but a component of the emotional expression of the total personality, instead of a partially repressed emotional outlet in women, and a combination of physiological and affectional behavior in men (each of which is frequently pursued independently of the other). This concept of sexuality [presumes] a high degree of ego-involvement which disallows a casual attitude toward sex activity, such as that which underlies sexual promiscuity, experimentation and flirtation. . . . The goal toward which it strives is the monogamous type of marital relationship which we have already adopted in our society. The difference, however, would be that marriage would be advocated as the best possible medium for enhancing a psychoaffectional sexual partnership rather than as the factor which in itself legitimizes something which is inherently [shameful].[1]

If our culture would adopt and teach this point of view, "psychosexual development would proceed accordingly," and adolescent boys and girls would really feel this way about sex. The problems associated with

> psychophysiological sex needs would for the most part vanish. And if marriage could occur at a reasonably early age, the sexual turmoil which now characterizes adolescent development [in so many individuals] would be a thing of the past.[1]

Sex Guidance

Such a program of sex education is concerned with general problems in sexual development and expression and with a *long-range* attempt to redirect psychosexual development in accordance with certain specified value judgments on the goals of sexuality. Sex guidance, on the other hand, deals with individual problems of sexual adjustment and can only be handled effectively within the framework of a counseling relationship.

This does not mean that guidance must take place in an amoral setting, that the counselor is concerned only with clarifying the sex problems of his client or with helping him adjust his inner sex needs to the limitations imposed by the environment. In the counseling relationship, sexual problems must be placed in an ethical context of meaning and objectives. It is the counselor's right (and duty) to communicate his own moral formulations and judgments to the client. He cannot, of course, insist that the client accept his position, but he can give him the benefit of reacting to a set of mature moral expectations representative of the culture at large. And in so doing he encourages the individual to approach his sex problems from the standpoint of some system of values rather than from the standpoint that one way is as good as another provided it reduces tension or yields satisfaction.

Two persistent ethical problems arise in modern sex guidance: (a) the management of existing psychophysiological sex needs and (b) the management of psychoaffectional sex needs before marriage. Adolescents might very well be able to accept the proposition that society should so regulate psychosexual development in the future that individuals will develop only psychoaffectional sex drives. But what are they to do in the meantime with their *own* psychophysiological drives? The only answer consistent with the philosophy advocated is that the gratification of physiological sex tensions by autoeroticism is more in keeping with the psychoaffectional ideal than the utilization of a "socio-sexual" outlet such as petting or intercourse. If this principle is acceptable, what then are we to tell adolescents who are genuinely in love but unable to marry about the ethics of premarital intercourse? To remain consistent we would have to admit that although premarital sex relations are obviously less satisfactory than marital relations they are nevertheless compatible with a psychoaffectional approach to sexuality.

Realistic sex guidance, however, cannot

ignore the social reality in which adolescents live. By the time they appear for guidance, depending on their social *milieu,* they have already incorporated a vast array of sexual attitudes, urges, inhibitions, taboos, and morally weighted opinions about the desirability and legitimacy of various forms of sexual activity. One can only present certain moral formulations to them and point out how they could be applied in practice. But because of the course which psychosexual development has *already* taken, one cannot expect that these precepts will be either acceptable or realistically applicable in every case. In practice, therefore, after putting the question of sexuality in its proper context of goal and purpose, the best one can do is to equip the boy and girl for intelligent self-determination.[1]

To do this one must supply precise and reliable information about the advantages and disadvantages, the issues and the implications of the various forms of sexual outlet (see pp. 412–414). And to be meaningful and helpful, "answers to such questions must be specific and related to the adolescent's actual problems." [1]

REFERENCES AND BIBLIOGRAPHY

1. Ausubel, D. P.: Problems of adolescent adjustment. Bulletin, Natl. Assn. Secondary School Principals, *34:*1–84, 1950.
2. Ausubel, D. P.: *Ego Development and the Personality Disorders.* New York: Grune and Stratton, 1952.
3. Baber, R. E.: Some mate selection standards of college students and their parents. J. Soc. Hyg., *22:*115–125, 1936.
4. Beach, F. A.: *Hormones and Behavior.* New York: Paul B. Hoeber, 1948.
5. Beach, F. A.: "Body Chemistry and Perception," in *Perception: An Approach to Personality* (R. R. Blake and G. V. Ramsey, eds.). New York: Ronald, 1951.
6. Bell, H. M.: *Youth Tell Their Story.* Washington, D. C.: American Council on Education, 1938.

7. Benedict, R.: Continuities and discontinuities in cultural conditioning. Psychiatry, *1*:161–167, 1938.

8. Blanchard, P.: "Adolescent Experience in Relation to Personality and Behavior," in *Personality and the Behavior Disorders* (J. McV. Hunt, ed.), Vol. II, New York: Ronald, 1944.

9. Bossard, J. H. S.: Residential propinquity as a factor in marriage selection. Am. J. Sociol., *38*:219–224, 1932.

10. Bromley, D. D. and Britten, F. H.: *Youth and Sex: A Study of 1300 College Students.* New York: Harper, 1938.

11. Burgess, E. W. and Wallin, P.: Homogamy in personality characteristics. J. Abnorm. Soc. Psychol., *39*:475–481, 1944.

12. Burgess, E. W. and Wallin, P.: Homogamy in social characteristics. Amer. J. Sociol., *49*:109–124, 1943.

13. Butterfield, O. M.: *Love Problems of Adolescence.* New York: Teachers College, Columbia University, 1939.

14. Campbell, E. H.: The Social-Sex Development of Children. Genet. Psychol. Mongr., *21*:461–552, 1939.

15. Davis, A.: American status systems and the socialization of the child. Amer. Sociol. Rev., *6*:345–354, 1941.

16. Davis, A. and Dollard, J.: *Children of Bondage.* Washington, D. C.: American Council on Education, 1940.

17. Davis, K. B.: *Sex Factors in the Lives of Twenty-Two Hundred Women.* New York: Harper, 1929.

18. Ellis, H.: *Studies in the Psychology of Sex.* New York: Random House, 1936.

19. Ford, C. S. and Beach, F. A.: *Patterns of Sexual Behavior.* New York: Harper and Paul B. Hoeber, 1951.

20. Frank, L. K.: "The Adolescent and the Family," in *Adolescence*, 43rd Yearbook, Natl. Soc. Stud. Educ., Part I. Chicago: University of Chicago Press, 1944.

21. Furfey, P. H.: *The Gang Age: A Study of the Preadolescent Boy and His Recreational Needs.* New York: Macmillan, 1926.

22. Goodenough, F. L.: *Developmental Psychology.* New York: Appleton-Century, 1945.

23. Hamilton, G. V.: *A Research in Marriage.* New York: Boni, 1929.

24. Hamilton, G. V. and MacGowan, K.: *What is Wrong with Marriage?* New York: Boni, 1928.

25. Hankins, D.: The psychology and direct treatment of adolescents. Ment. Hyg., *27*:238–247, 1943.

26. Harris, D.: Age and occupational factors in the residential propinquity of marriage partners. J. Soc. Psychol., *6*:257–261, 1935.

27. Honzik, M. P.: Sex differences in the occurrence of materials in the play constructions of pre-adolescents. Child Develpm., *22*:15–36, 1951.

28. Hurlock, E. B., and Klein, E. R.: Adolescent "crushes". Child Develpm., *5*:63–80, 1934.

29. Jersild, A. T., et al.: *Child Development and the Curriculum*. New York: Teachers College, Columbia Univ., 1946.

30. Katz, D., and Allport, F. H.: *Students' Attitudes*. Syracuse: Craftsman Press, 1931.

31. Kinsey, A. C., et al.: *Sexual Behavior in the Human Male*. Philadelphia: Saunders, 1948.

32. Kirkendall, L. A.: *Sex Adjustments of Young Men*. New York: Harper, 1940.

33. Kirkendall, L. A.: Sex problems of adolescents. Marriage Hygiene, *1*:205–208, 1948.

34. Kirkpatrick, C.: A comparison of generations in regard to attitudes toward feminism. J. Genet. Psychol., *49*:343–361, 1936.

35. Kirkpatrick, C., and Caplow, T.: Courtship in a group of Minnesota Students. Am. J. Sociol., *51*:114–125, 1945.

36. Kirkpatrick, C., and Caplow, T.: Emotional trends in the courtship experiences of college students as expressed by graphs with some observations on methodological implications. Amer. Sociol. Rev., *10*:619–626, 1945.

37. Kitay, P. M.: A comparison of the sexes in their attitudes and beliefs about women: A study of prestige groups. Sociometry, *3*:399–407, 1940.

38. Landis, C., et al.: *Sex in Development*. New York: Paul B. Hoeber, 1940.

39. Landis, C., and Bolles, M. M.: *Personality and Sexuality of Physically Handicapped Women*. New York: Paul B. Hoeber, 1942.

40. Lawton, S. U. and Archer, J.: *Sexual Conduct of the Teen-Ager*. New York: Spectrolux, 1951.

41. Leighton, D. and Kluckhohn, C.: *Children of the People: The Navaho Individual and His Development*. Cambridge: Harvard University Press, 1947.

42. Lynd, R. S. and Lynd, H. M.: *Middletown in Transition*. New York: Harcourt, Brace, 1937.

43. Malinowski, B.: *Sex and Repression in Savage Society*. New York: Harcourt, Brace, 1927.

44. Mead, M.: *From the South Seas*. New York: William Morrow, 1939.

45. Mead, M.: *Male and Female: A Study of the Sexes in a Changing World*. New York: William Morrow, 1949.

46. Mather, W. G.: The courtship ideals of high-school youth. Sociol. & Soc. Res., *19*:166–172, 1934.

47. Parsons, T.: Age and sex in the social structure of the United States. Amer. Sociol. Rev., *7*:604–616, 1942.

48. Punke, H. H.: Attitudes and ideals of high school youth in regard to marriage. Sch. & Soc., *56*:221–224, 1942.

49. Punke, H. H.: Dating practices of high-school youth. Bulletin, Nat. Assn. Secondary School Principals. *28*:47–54, 1944.

50. Ramsey, G. V.: The sex information of younger boys. Amer. J. Orthopsychiat., *13*:347–352, 1943.

51. Ramsey, G. V.: The sexual development of boys. Amer. J. Psychol., *56*:217–233, 1943.

52. Ramsey, G. V.: *Factors in the Sex Life of 291 Boys*. Ann Arbor, Mich.: Edwards, 1950.

53. Remmers, H. H., Drucker, A. J., and Christensen, H. T.: Courtship conduct as viewed by high school youth. Purdue Opin. Panel, X, No. 2 (Report No. 27), 1950.

54. Rockwood, L. D. and Ford, M. E. N.: *Youth, Marriage and Parenthood*. New York: Wiley, 1945.

55. Sherif, M. and Cantril, H.: *The Psychology of Ego-Involvements*. New York: Wiley, 1947.

56. Skaggs, E. B.: Sex differences in moral attitudes. J. Soc. Psychol., *11*:3–10, 1940.

57. Smith, G. V.: Certain aspects of the sex life of the adolescent girl. J. Appl. Psychol., *8*:347–349, 1924.

58. Sullivan, Sister C.: *A Scale for Measuring Developmental Age in Girls*. Stud. Psychol. Psychiat. Cathol. Univ. America, Vol. III, No. 4, 1934.

59. Taylor, W. S.: *A Critique of Sublimation in Males: A Study of Forty Superior Single Men*. Genet. Psychol. Monog., XIII, No. 1, 1933.

60. Terman, L. M.: *Psychological Factors in Marital Happiness*. New York: McGraw-Hill, 1938.

61. Terman, L. M. and Miles, C. C.: *Sex and Personality*. New York: McGraw-Hill, 1936.

62. West, J.: *Plainville, U. S. A.* New York: Columbia University Press, 1945.

63. Whiting, J. W. M.: *Becoming a Kwoma*. New Haven: Yale University Press, 1941.

64. Willoughby, R. R.: *Sexuality in the Second Decade*. Monogr. Soc. Res. Child Developm., Vol. II, No. 3, 1937.

65. Wolford, O. P.: How early background affects dating behavior. J. Home Econ., *40*:505–506, 1948.

CHAPTER 14

Problems of Vocational Choice
in Adolescence

IMPLICIT IN THE FOREGOING treatment of diverse aspects of adolescent development has been the assumption that problems of vocational goals and placement are crucially significant both for personality maturation during adolescence and for the eventual attainment of adult status. We have seen that on the solution of these problems rest the possibilities for full emancipation from the home, for economic self-sufficiency, for social recognition as an equal member of adult society, for complete psychosexual maturation, and for the establishment of an independent family unit. And consistent with the increasing importance of occupational status for current and imminent adjustment, children manifest increasingly greater concern with problems of vocational choice and preparation as they proceed from preadolescence to early and late adolescence.[42, 44] Vocational problems ranked first among the problems checked by high-school students in one study; [45] and in another large-scale survey, the achievement of economic security was regarded by two-thirds of the youth as the most preplexing personal problem confronting them.[6] It is this smoldering concern with vocational problems that offers convincing proof of the fact that, despite his apparent preoccupation with the immediate and often esoteric activities of his interim peer culture, the adolescent's primary goals are really predicated upon inclusion in the adult world.

In all cultures, although varying degrees of emphasis are placed upon the acquisition of superior status or competence, it is the individual's occupation, broadly conceived, through which primary status is attained or expressed. Whenever socioeconomic roles are differentiated by a functional division of labor or a hierarchy of social prestige values, the typical occupation of a man defines and symbolizes his relative position in the stratified social organization that almost inevitably results. In our own culture,

> the most fundamental basis of the family's status is the occupational status of the husband and father. . . . This is a status occupied by an individual by virtue of his individual qualities and achievements. But both directly and indirectly, more than any other single factor, it determines the status of the family in the social structure, directly because of the symbolic significance of the office or occupation as a symbol of prestige, indirectly because as the principal source of family income it determines the standard of living of the family.[47]

We have also observed that adolescents internalize the general level of status aspirations of their particular cultural or subcultural milieu and sustain this level of aspiration by an appropriate degree of "socially adaptive" anxiety about the status they are expected to achieve (see pp. 335–336). And it is as a result of this process of differential internalization of status needs that *mean* differences between cultures or subcultures in the relative importance of acquiring prestige, preeminence, or superordinate position in the social hierarchy are transmitted and maintained. Nevertheless we are obliged to reckon with the universal fact that considerable variability is found in the relative status needs of different individuals *within* a homogeneous cultural setting and that such differences in urgency and magnitude of need are largely a function of the presence or absence of intrinsic feelings of adequacy (see pp. 209–214).

In various other contexts we have touched upon additional *psychobiological* relationships between adolescent development and the acquisition of occupational status. Regardless of the extent to which children may contribute to the economic life of the community before pubescence, the significance of their occupational participation undergoes profound qualitative changes after they mature sexually and achieve recognition as adults (see pp. 193 and 194). Social expectations of the quantity, imminence, initiative, and independence of occupational activity inevitably increase as the individual enters adolescence; and he himself views the problem of vocation with increasing seriousness and concern. But even more important than these changes is the fact that only *after* sexual maturation do the economic contributions of the individual make him eligible for initial consideration as an equal member of the adult community (see p. 68).

In considering the acquisition of adult status we have also been obliged to discuss in previous chapters such *psychosocial* aspects of vocation as (a) the prolongation of adolescence and the period of sub-adulthood because of lack of the availability of work experience (see pp. 205–207 and 321–322); (b) the effects of reduced social mobility, of technological changes in the kinds of available work experience, of war, and of economic depression on the rate of adolescent personality maturation; (c) the differentiation and transmission of social class aspirations for appropriate levels of vocational status (see pp. 335–336); (d) social class differences in earliness of exposure to the vicissitudes of vocational life (see p. 332); and (e) vocational implications of social sex role (see pp. 414–420).

In the present chapter we shall re-examine these general problems related to the acquisition of adult status in the more specific context of vocational choice. We shall attempt (a) to review the major developmental aspects of vocational choice—age of onset, rate of growth, stability, and relationship to pubescence; (b) to assess the influence of various individual and social determinants of vocational choice, such as intelligence, interests, special abilities, prestige needs, work experiences, economic urgency, social sex role, and social class membership; (c) to evaluate the occupational choices of adolescents in terms of compatibility with realistic possibilities, appropriateness of underlying patterns of interests and abilities, degree of factual knowledge about self and job entering into occupational decisions, awareness of underlying motivations, and outcomes of early vocational experience; and (d) to consider some of the issues in vocational guidance and work experience.

DEVELOPMENTAL CHANGES IN VOCATIONAL CHOICE

Since vocational choice reflects the selective operation both of interests and of motivational orientation, orderly developmental changes are inevitable in any cultural environment as the biosocial status of the child undergoes significant alteration from childhood to adolescence. In this sense it is possible to use an individual's pattern of vocational choices and interests as a rough index of his developmental maturity.

The principal impact of adolescence on vocational choices is a change in motivational orientation. As a result of the increased emphasis upon the acquisition of primary status, vocational interests become less important as ends in themselves and more important as vehicles through which extrinsic status may eventually be attained. The child is less concerned with vocational matters as a source of status than as a source of imaginative and exciting play; and in expressing a vocational choice, therefore, he places more weight upon the possibilities for glamor and excitement in a given occupation than on the prestige it carries in the adult world. But with increasing age, there is a steady increase in the percentage of boys and girls who renounce such glamorous occupations as cowboy, detective, and movie actress for the more realistically prestige-giving callings of medicine, law, nursing, teaching, stenography.[34, 40, 42, 43]

The effect of pubescence on vocational choice, is indirect, rather than attributable to the direct influence of gonadal hormones. It is through his own reactions and the reactions of others to his changed bodily appearance that the physiological events of pubescence alter the adolescent's pattern of vocational concerns. And because both the individual and his culture respond to the phenomenon of sexual maturation by expecting much more independence and primary status, the whole problem of vocational adjustment is suddenly pushed into the foreground of the psychological field, acquiring new significance, urgency, and anxiety-tinged imminence.

In accordance with their more precocious sexual maturation, serious vocational choices emerge earlier in girls than in boys.[25, 30] It is also significant that the "vocational interests of brighter children tend to develop earlier than those of duller children." [13, 14] This difference undoubtedly reflects greater sensitivity to changing environmental demands and superior ability in directing adjustive efforts into more appropriate channels.

But although the onset of pubescence does invest the problem of occupational choice with new significance and urgency, there is reason to believe that the changes that do occur are less abrupt than the corresponding physical or emotional consequences of gonadal maturation. Other variables unrelated to the implications of pubescence for personality development must also be considered.

Many preadolescent children, for example, have strong intellectual or mechanical interests that lack practicality or relevance to the world of adult status. Others have made strong emotional commitments to impractical occupational choices which they find difficult to surrender. In many instances, strongly canalized interests will prove highly resistant to the influence of the new motivational orientation of adolescence. Redirection of vocational interest patterns along more appropriate lines may, therefore, be a very slow and gradual process.

In any event, it must be realized that the majority of the determinants of vocational choice, ability, interest, intelligence, personality, sex, family pressures, social class membership, operate before as well as after pubescence. Whatever changes occur in response to the altered social expectations associated with puberty are superimposed upon an existing pattern of vocational preferences which is already highly determined in the possible directions it may take. The contribution of adolescence to vocational choice lies largely in the adaptation of pre-existing occupational dispositions to the changed status needs that emerge at this stage of personality development. There is, therefore, considerable continuity from childhood to adolescence in the content and in the determinants of vocational choice. Discontinuity arises mainly in relation to the new Gestalt of motivational orientation in which occupational problems become embedded at adolescence.

The Stability of Vocational Interests

There is very little definitive data on how stable the vocational choices of adolescents actually are. However, we can make reasonable inferences about their stability from the considerable amount of data available on comparable aspects of vocational *interests*. Earlier work in this area

furnished a basis for a general belief that the vocational interests of young people are unstable and unsubstantial. This view rests in part upon inadequate data obtained by use of a variety of questionnaire techniques, many of which were superficial and unreliable. It rests in part upon emphasis on data from children in earlier adolescence to the neglect of the transitional phase. It rests in part upon the neglect of individual differences in interest development [13] [p. 259; this, and the following quotations in this section with citation of reference *13*, are by permission of the Society].

Most of the marked changes in vocational interest occur in early adolescence as the more naive, glamorous, and impractical preferences of childhood fail to meet the test of reality and the needs of adult status. Oftentimes, earlier occupational choices need not be scrapped in entirety but can be recast along more realistic lines. By middle adolescence, however, inventoried vocational interests are fairly stable. A high score on one scale of an instrument such as the Strong Vocational Interest Blank "indicates a strong probability, not a certainty, that [an adolescent] will have the same interests a year later":

> During the high school years and the years immediately following, there is little evidence of systematic increase or decrease of scores. The pattern of interests undergoes some change, but with fewer systematic changes than might be expected.[13]

The test-retest reliability of vocational interest inventories shows consistent improvement throughout the high school period and into the college years.[11, 14, 59, 64] Rate of change undergoes gradual deceleration until the age of twenty-five, after which time vocational interests usually remain virtually stable.[58, 61]

DETERMINANTS OF VOCATIONAL CHOICE

As already indicated, the factors that determine an individual's eventual vocational choice are operative from the very beginning of his developmental career. Even at the moment of conception initial directional (genetic) influences are brought to bear on such important determinants of occupational choice as intelligence, special abilities, interests, personality, and sex membership. And from the moment of birth he is subjected to differential parental and social class influences associated with his membership in a particular family group. By the close of childhood the cumulative selective impact of these various factors on occupational preference is extremely well established, although their actual influence is often masked by the special imaginative functions that vocational choices serve in the world of play. At adolescence, however, such diversionary influences are no longer operative, and whatever latent vocational predispositions exist come actively to the fore. And it is these predispositions, modified and given new significance in the changed motivational context of adolescence, which to a large extent determine ultimate occupational choice.

Apart from the intrinsic determinants of vocational preference, several other factors operate either to accelerate or retard the crystallization of an expressed occupational choice. "Merely by making a verbal statement of [such] choice, and advertising the fact," the adolescent can gain some prestige or standing in his crowd.

> This is especially true in the case of those who are sensitive to the prestige aspects of occupations, and who have some need for achievement or recognition which can be satisfied by identifying themselves with a given field of work.[13]

The making of a definite choice also confers security and relieves anxiety by structuring the field and dissipating uncertainty, indecision, and ambiguity. It gives the adolescent an early start in his quest for economic security and independence by setting a tangible goal toward which he can immediately direct his efforts and training and thereby acquire appropriate competencies.

On the other hand, there are equally influential reasons for postponing as long as possible the formulation of an ultimate vocational choice. In view of the large number of possible vocations, his lack of first-hand knowledge about the vast majority of them, and the absence of adequate opportunity for comparing his qualifications with those of his fellows, the adolescent may quite understandably wish to await further maturity and trial-and-error experience before committing himself to such an important and often irrevocable decision. Two mutually antagonistic sets of forces impinge upon the advisability of reaching an early occupational choice. And although the ensuing conflict may itself be uncomfortable and produce tension, it probably exercises a beneficial effect by combatting both the anxiety reducing tendency to make an immediate but possibly arbitrary or capricious decision and the natural inclination to avoid coming to grips with a difficult and frequently distressing problem.

Social Sex Role

Even though the vocational interests of girls emerge earlier than those of boys (see p. 440), it is a commonplace observation that at all socioeconomic levels in our society the former are subjected to less social pressure to achieve primary status through vocational success.

It is hardly surprising, therefore, that relatively few girls develop serious and sustained aspirations for a permanent vocational career. This does not mean, of course, that many girls do not have patterns of occupational interests that are highly appropriate for traditionally masculine vocations. In fact, interest inventories show that precisely the opposite is true.[15] However, interests are not likely to be implemented in the absence of suitable motivations. Regardless of the suitability of their interests, it is patently unrealistic to expect girls to be unambivalent about long-term vocational careers when they either contemplate marriage and homemaking within a few years, or know that certain fields are for all practical purposes closed to women.

For these reasons girls are willing to settle for more subordinate occupational careers involving less preparation and little competition with men, for careers that can either be conveniently pursued until marriage or used as supplementary sources of postmarital income. All of these considerations when added to the weight of tradition tend to confine the vocational choices available to women to nursing, teaching, and secretarial work.[14, 43, 61] These limitations are not without certain advantages. For one thing, girls are apt to be better informed than boys about the requirements, duties, job opportunities, and remuneration of their chosen occupations. For another, since they can afford to be more modest in their vocational aspirations, these are less frequently out of line with realistic possibilities.[6]

Family Pressures

The impact of family pressures on vocational choice is so pervasive and often so subtle and indirect that its precise influence is difficult to evaluate. If we examine the evidence for the specific and explicit influence of parents on the occupational decisions of adolescents, we are left with the impression that relatively few wish to pursue the vocations of their fathers[35] and that the majority both deny heeding the advice and suggestion of their elders[1] and set their occupational aspirations at a higher level.[35] This situation, however, is as it should be when we consider the prevailing estrangement between youth and their parents and the widespread acceptance of the tradition of social mobility. But there are several good reasons for believing that the *actual* influence of parents on their offspring's vocational choices is great indeed.

In the first place, parents are in a strategic position to orient the development of the child's interests throughout childhood in a given general or specific direction by the judicious provision of differential rewards and play materials. It is noteworthy, for example, that many young children deliberately select the same specific occupations as their fathers.[39] Other children, especially those who are unassertive or who have overdominating parents, may implicitly accept their parents' plans for their vocational futures without even being aware of it. Second, parent attitudes are largely instrumental in determining the magnitude of the child's individual personality needs for primary status by affecting (a) the extent to which the child can acquire intrinsic feelings of adequacy and (b) the extent to which his potential accomplishments are regarded as a vicarious source of parental ego enhancement.

Third, prior to adolescence, the parents serve as the chief agents of the culture in transmitting to the child differential social class aspirations for a given level of occupational prestige. The cumulative effect of years of subtle indoctrination along these lines reinforced by peer group pressures during adolescence leads to the assimilation of sufficient "socially adaptive" anxiety to insure the maintenance of appropriate levels of striving.

Finally, during adolescence itself, it is the family's socioeconomic status that makes possible or impossible the implementation of various high-level vocational goals through such devices as subsidizing technical education, furnishing capital or contacts necessary for launching a career, and offering a reprieve from the urgency of finding immediate employment. Thus, we can mainly credit the influence of the family for the fact that although adolescents are resistive to the specific vocational suggestions of their parents, in general, they achieve an occupational status commensurate with their family (and social class) background.[20]

Social Class Factors and Socio-Economic Conditions

As the child approaches adolescence, social class pressures toward choosing a vocation commensurate with the occupational status needs and aspirations of his class reference group become more pointed and explicit. No longer can elders indulge expressions of vocational choice that reflect glamorous notions or imaginative fancies. The situation is comparable to the one we have already observed in changing standards of adult tolerance toward children's relative indifference to social class, ethnic, and religious distinctions in organizing their social groups (see p. 266). With the approach of adolescence, as the game begins to be played "for keeps," parents find "democratic" notions no longer amusing, but downright threatening to their equanimity as they contemplate their offspring's futures.

It is in relation to these differential social class pressures that "job prestige" becomes an important factor in the relative acceptability of various occupations to a given adolescent. Widespread agreement exists at all socioeconomic levels about the general hierarchical ranking of different occupations along a gradient of social prestige.[28, 29, 41, 56] The factors accounting for relative rank on this scale are not always clear. Undoubtedly, income, educational level, supervisory control, and level of responsibility are important considerations. For our purposes, it is only necessary to observe that the stratification of occupations is socially determined and "is regarded in much the same manner by persons in various classes."[13]

This fact shows quite clearly that job prestige does not operate directly as a determinant of vocational choice, but only indirectly by defining a range of vocations that confer sufficient occupational status to be compatible with the socially instigated prestige needs of individuals from different social class levels. That is, the perceived hierarchy of occupations does not influence vocational choice as such, since persons at all social levels perceive this hierarchy in much the same way and yet make very different choices. An individual does not necessarily choose one job in preference to another because he perceives it as carrying more prestige. He uses his perceptions of the prestige hierarchy of vocations to select an occupation that is compatible with the needs for vocational status and prestige that he has internalized from his class reference group.

As will be pointed out later, the prestige rating of a job also helps determine its acceptability in terms of individual differences in needs for prestige within a given social class stratum. The stability of a vocational choice, therefore, is largely a function of its relatively stable position in the hierarchy of occupational prestige, which enables it to satisfy enduring and persistent needs for prestige determined both by individual personality development and by social class membership. The fact that the prestige attributes of jobs are seldom acknowledged by adolescents as important determinants of their vocational choices [50] does not belie their actual importance. In a democratic society, which officially denies the existence of any system of rank or privilege in the social organization of its members, it is more comfortable for such considerations to remain unformulated in explicit terms or at least not easily accessible to conscious awareness.

Another socially derived factor that adds to the occupational prestige needs of adolescents and hence to the stability of their occupational choices is our cultural tradition of social mobility.

> Young people wish to climb, to secure higher status, to receive higher rewards. Their hopes are often out of line with reasonable expectations. They are hardly to be censured for this. Their attitudes have been assimilated from the surrounding environment which bristles with expectations of climbing, of beginning at the bottom and working up, etc. There is, however, very little evidence in our contemporary economy, in peace time to justify a belief in any widespread "upward mobility" with regard to occupations [13] [p. 269].

It is largely this vision of social mobility that causes adolescent boys from lower socioeconomic groups to aspire beyond the vocational attainments of their parents.[35]

Social class membership acts in still another way besides its influence on occupational prestige needs to determine vocational choice. The economic urgency of finding immediate employment and of contributing to his family's support may force the adolescent, regardless of his actual inclinations, to adopt the short-range view and aspire to a low level occupation that is immediately available and requires no further preparation. That this is actually the situation is shown by the fact that adolescents from lower economic strata begin work at a younger age and find initial employment at lower occupational levels than their more economically privileged contemporaries.[20] At any date, it should be self-evident that

> under present conditions the desire to enter the professions is much more often realistic when held by privileged persons, than when held by those in the lower social and economic groups.[13]

Last, general socioeconomic conditions, apart from factors of social class membership, affect the character of vocational choice. Such conditions include the general occupational outlook as determined by a war-time economy or by economic depression and prosperity, as well as more specific regional or industry-wide fluctuations in job demand. They affect not only the relative attractiveness of different occupations, but also the degree of social mobility and the disposition of the adolescent to aspire to higher levels of vocational status.

Individual Differences

Just as important as the influence of socioeconomic conditions and of the various groups (sex clan, family, social class) with whom the adolescent identifies himself are numerous important differences between individuals that are significantly related to vocational choice. This variability accounts not only for overlapping between different sex and social class groups in choice of occupational level, but also for differences in the specific choices made within a given level. We shall have to consider differences in intelligence, ability, personality traits, and prestige needs which affect the differentiation of the psychological field with respect to relative degree of ego-involvement in various vocations.

Intelligence. Generally speaking the vocational choices of adolescents are compatible with the intellectual requirements of different occupations.[10, 51] That is, level of intelligence operates as a selective factor in propelling brighter individuals toward vocations that demand more intelligence, and in directing the vocational choices of duller individuals toward less intellectually demanding occupations. This relationship is also apparent in the "significant pattern of correlations" between inventoried interests and intelligence.[11, 12, 13, 14, 64] Although such correlations are generally low, since vocational interest inventories are concerned with measuring areas of interest rather than with ascertaining occupational level within a given area, they are in the expected direction in relation to "the intellectual requirements of occupations."[13]

Intelligence also affects vocational choice in other ways than influencing intellectual level of chosen occupation.

The vocational interests of brighter children tend to develop earlier than those of duller children, and are often better suited to individual circumstances. The bright person is more often well adjusted vocationally and, if undecided, appears characteristically to be troubled by a particular type of problem, namely choice among several well-developed interests. The less-intelligent person much more often experiences indecision based upon the absence of well-developed interests or upon the development of interests which are totally inappropriate to the individual's abilities or opportunities. The bright person has the advantage that the occupations open to him are more satisfying. The less-intelligent person has the advantage that the great majority of occupations suited to his abilities are such as to require little training, and consequently such as to permit extensive use of vocational try-outs as a method of improving vocational orientation [13] [pp. 270, 271].

Special Abilities and Aptitudes. The relative abilities and aptitudes of an individual undoubtedly affect his vocational interests just as they do his interests in general. Superior ability in a given field leads to success, which in turn inspires frequent participation and further development of the ability. The fact that corresponding interest and ability scores are negligibly correlated in a given population [8, 67] does not, as has been so frequently stated, contradict this statement of relationship. Since specialized interests and abilities are each affected by so many *other* hereditary and environmental variables, it is hardly reasonable to expect that there will be very much correspondence from one ranking to the other between the relative positions of different members of a group when ranked in order of interest and aptitude respectively. A much fairer method of testing this hypothesized relationship between vocational interest and ability is to correlate hierarchies of interests and abilities *within* a single individual. Related evidence bearing on this in scholastic interests and aptitudes [66] suggests, for example, that if computational interests were to hold the highest rank on an individual's vocational interest profile, the chances are good that his vocational aptitude profile would show a similar peak. At the same time, it is entirely conceivable that his actual computational ability would only be great enough to earn him median rank in relation to the national norms for his age and sex group.

The relationship between ability and vocational interests is further complicated by the fact that early statements of vocational preference are unrealistic and influenced by many factors extrinsic to the essential functions of a vocation. Furthermore, unlike most other expressions of interest that are based upon some backlog of experience, expressed vocational choice can seldom be tested against any concrete experiences of success or failure in related tasks or activities. Hence, it requires considerable maturity of the adolescent, both in general level of sophistication and in the degree of relevant experience needed to make a satisfactory comparative appraisal of his pattern of aptitudes, before he can even take the factor of ability into account in selecting a suitable vocation. It is, therefore, not at all surprising that scholastic achievement seems to have very little influence on the occupational choices of young adolescents.[31] Significantly enough, however, with increasing age, considerations of ability play a much more important role in choosing an appropriate occupation.[31] Hence, to appreciate truly the influence of special abilities and aptitudes on vocational choice, it is probably necessary (a) to correlate hierarchies of interest and ability within a single person rather than paired interest and aptitude scores among a group of persons, and (b) to wait until vocational interest patterns become relatively stable before undertaking correlational studies of this nature.

Motivational Factors and Prestige Needs. We have shown how the character of vocational choice is influenced by *group* differences in needs for primary status and prestige that are related to sex, pubescent status, and social class background. Such differences primarily influence the level of occupational status to which an individual aspires. In addition, we must consider *individual* differences in needs for prestige and social recognition which play an important role in determining the nature of vocational ambitions. As pointed out in a previous chapter, the magnitude of such needs is a function both of constitutional factors and of the availability of residual feelings of intrinsic self-esteem from the parent-child relationship (see pp. 182 and 211). It influences vocational choice in at least two different ways: (a) in the selection of an occupation that is perceived as having a personally satisfying level of job prestige; and (b) in the differential selection of one of several vocations at the same level of prestige which differ in the degree of social visibility or administrative power they offer the individual. Together with their socially instigated counterparts these personality derived needs for occupational status and prestige are responsible for much of the stability and persistence of vocational choices, even in the face of highly adverse environmental conditions or of completely inappropriate abilities.

It is quite apparent that underlying motivations are not self-evidently given in the mere existence of vocational interests or preferences. Many different motivations can account for the same general kinds or levels of interests. We are not obliged to conclude, for example, that all individuals who have high vocational ambitions are necessarily motivated by prepotent prestige needs. In certain instances, such ambitions are mainly powered by unusually strong urges to explore challenging problems, by intellectual curiosity, by a high order of talent or ability, by devotion to ideals of social service. Only by careful motivational analysis, aided by complete knowledge of the life history of an individual and by certain objective measures of motivation,[3, 38] can we hope to appraise the relative influence of prestige needs in determining vocational choice.

Other Personality Traits. Since it is commonly accepted in our culture that different occupations require different constellations of personality traits, adolescents undoubtedly give some attention to temperamental compatibility in selecting their life work. It is in this sense that personality structure acts as an important determinant of vocational choice.

One of the chief ways in which personality exerts this selective influence is by affecting the types of interests an individual develops. When adolescents are queried about the factors that enter into their selection of particular vocations, they place greatest emphasis upon interest.[31] And it would seem that no other judgment of relative influence could possibly be made, since it is in this area of decision that most opportunity apparently exists for the exercise of volitional choice and individuality. Most adolescents are either overtly bludgeoned or subtly coerced by socioeconomic pressures and conditions into striving for a given *level* of occupational status; and when influenced by the more individual aspects of prestige needs, they are very rarely aware of their precise nature. It is mostly in the weighing of specific interests in the types of activities associated with different vocations that the opportunity for deliberate decision-making arises.

One aspect of the task of matching job requirements with suitable personality characteristics, therefore, can be resolved by ascertaining to what extent an individual's pattern of vocational interests conforms to that of successful persons in his occupation of choice.[36, 61] The validity of this approach is confirmed by the fact that the typical vocational interest profiles of different occupational groups, as determined by standardized inventories, differ systematically among each other and in logically predictable ways.[36, 61]

That interest profiles should reflect those aspects of personality that have relevance for vocational choice is hardly surprising. The differentiation of an individual's psychological field into areas of relative ego-involvement (interest) is, after all, determined in much the same way as is his personality structure itself, by the interaction of the unique pattern of experiences, rewards, and values to which he has been exposed with his equally unique pattern of genetically acquired predispositions to develop in certain designated directions. The types of interests that a person manifests are excellent indicators of his underlying personality traits; and it is only to be expected that if personality factors are to influence vocational choice, they would largely do so through the medium of differential interest patterns.

Because of their organic relationship to personality organization, vocational interests

> are not dependent upon specific occupational experiences for their develop-
> ment. They are undoubtedly based upon some aspects of experience, but are
> often found to be strongly developed and stable prior to entrance into any
> occupation.[13]

In some instances they can be related to attitudes arising from significant personal experiences.

> The choice of teaching, for example, has been shown to be related more closely
> to a favorable attitude towards school or to admiration for a particular teacher
> than to the socio-economic level of the home, the intelligence or achievement
> of the pupil or the fact that other members of the family are already members
> of the teaching profession.[26]

Other aspects of personality besides interests and motivation also influence vocational choice. Such products of personality maturation as an individual's needs for volitional independence and freedom from control, his frustration tolerance, his ability to postpone hedonistic gratification, his sense of responsibility, and his degree of executive independence are self-evidently related to the types of occupations he considers personally acceptable. For example, an inordinately strong need for emancipation from the home coupled with low frustration tolerance and inability to postpone hedonistic satisfactions may influence an adolescent to settle for a low level job requiring little preparation. Other outstanding personality traits that obviously qualify or disqualify certain individuals for particular occupations are introversion-extroversion, anxiety level, egocentricity-sociocentricity, level of energy, and psychological sensitivity.

AN EVALUATION OF THE VOCATIONAL CHOICES OF ADOLESCENTS

Realistic or Unrealistic?

How realistic are the vocational choices of adolescents in terms of available job opportunities? All investigations of the occupational ambitions of youth both in *and* out of high school [6, 33, 35, 52, 70] agree that the expressed vocational choices of adolescents are out of line with actual economic needs as measured by census reports of the distribution of the working population in different occupations. The discrepancy between desire and availability is in all instances caused (a) by too few adolescents wanting to enter the lower level occupations in which the need for manpower is greatest and in which the larger number of them must eventually find employment, and (b) by too many adolescents aspiring to prepare for professional and technical fields that cannot possibly accommodate all of the eager candidates for admission. For example, not one of the ten vocations most preferred by adolescent boys actually appears on the list of ten occupations they most frequently enter.[6] We must conclude that the vocational ambitions of adolescents are unrealistic and overly sanguine in terms of the statistical probabilities of their ever gaining entrance into their occupations of choice. Under these circumstances, a large number of individuals are inevitably doomed to chronic frustration, job disillusionment, and general dissatisfaction with what life has to offer them.

Many writers are inclined to deny that the occupational choices of adolescents are truly unrealistic, or if they do admit this, are disposed to discount its significance. It is pointed out that although the vocational preferences of adolescents are excessively ambitious, their actual *expectations* of entering their occupations of choice are not greatly out of line with realistic probabilities.[33] In considering whether this fact seriously qualifies the significance of the conclusion reached above, we must realize that the *functional* goal toward which an individual strives in his daily operations is more nearly reflected by his expressed occupational choice than by his level of expectation. Few persons actually aspire to a goal that is no higher than that which they probably expect to achieve or would be willing to accept if they had to. It is the individual's expressed statement of choice, not his prediction of ultimate outcome, that constitutes his functional level of aspiration and determines whether or not he will experience feelings of success or failure, of adequacy or inadequacy in actual vocational achievement. This level of aspiration is an "action" goal "allied to practical motives" rather than an "ideal" goal. It already reflects considerable compromise with realistic considerations since it differs markedly from the "ideal" level of aspiration adolescents give when asked what they "would *really* like to do" if they were not required to heed environmental limitations upon vocational choice.*

It is also alleged sometimes that the vocational choices of adolescents are not *really* unrealistic but only reflective (a) of differential social class pressures for achieving high occupational status or (b) of prevailing notions of social mobility. The first factor can adequately explain why the vocational aspirations of upper- and middle-class adolescents are on the average more ambitious than those of lower-class youth.[35] The second factor can likewise explain why young people from all social class backgrounds strive above the occupational levels achieved by their parents, and why this tendency is most pronounced among lower-class youth.[35] † But by finding

---

* These distinctions between functional level of aspiration (expressed vocational choice), level of expectation, and "ideal" level of aspiration are based upon unpublished data of the writer pertaining to the vocational attitudes of junior and senior students attending University High School, Urbana, Illinois.

† Under conditions of upward social mobility, the availability of greater "ceiling" necessarily makes for greater disparity between the occupational levels of fathers and the corresponding aspirations of their children at the lower as opposed

credible reasons for explaining why the vocational choices of adolescents are unrealistic, we are in no sense refuting the fact that they actually are so.

It is perfectly understandable why young people from all social class strata over-aspire in relation to realistic probabilities of achievement, although it is true that in middle- and upper-class youth such aspirations for professional status are more realistically grounded. It is also understandable why

the vocational ambitions of young people and of unemployed people [are] often impractical; ·. . . often relatively independent of the general demand, of local opportunity, and of abilities and other assets.[13]

And we are hardly blaming youth for being influenced by these factors. We are merely pointing out that one inevitable outcome of the operation of such influences is the generation of unrealistic vocational ambitions.

Relationship to Factual Knowledge of Self and Job

To what extent are the vocational choices of adolescents based upon factual knowledge of the requirements and nature of different jobs and of the appropriateness of their own interests and abilities for these? The answer to this question is unfortunately no more encouraging than the answer to the preceding question about the reality or unreality of occupational choice. When adolescents are questioned about the necessary steps in preparing for the vocations they have chosen, about the duties and tasks involved, the remuneration they expect to receive, and the job opportunities available, their replies in general are amazingly vague, naive, and unrelated to the actual job situation.[33, 65] * A substantial percentage of high school students also select occupations for which their interests are either completely inappropriate * or for which their level of intelli-

---

to the upper end of the economic scale. Thus, although the vocational aspirations of lower-class adolescents are less ambitious (on an absolute basis) than those of their more privileged contemporaries, they are relatively higher when compared to the mean occupational status of the respective paternal groups.

* These statements are also supported by unpublished data of the writer's described in the first footnote in this chapter.

gence is not even minimally adequate.[10, 24] Again many reasons can explain why these facts are so discouraging; but unpleasant facts are none the less true after they are explained.

In the first place, vocational choices are poorly grounded on pertinent information because of the pressures exerted on adolescents to reach an early decision about occupational preference. Such pressures emanate from the inescapable necessity of choosing between alternative curricula in high school and college, from the economic urgency of finding a job in the near future, or simply from the need to gain the security and reprieve from anxiety that are associated with the resolution of any uncertainty or ambiguity (see p. 443). Thus pressured into making a premature decision, it is hardly surprising that adolescents will frequently make arbitrary or capricious choices.

Second, the prospects of reaching a sound and well-informed decision are not enhanced by the existence of countless numbers of jobs the requirements and relative attractiveness of which are constantly changing. Third, it is rarely possible for an adolescent to acquire any first-hand work experience in the occupation of his choice. Child labor laws, trade union practices, parental objections to early employment, and the complex forms of preparatory training required for modern specialized occupations make extensive sampling of different vocations highly impractical. Thus,

> when the time comes for a vocational tryout, he discovers that . . . he is ignorant of the fundamental facts about most occupations, doesn't know which one he is best fitted for and doesn't know the essential facts about his own talents and weaknesses in comparison with those of other persons.[13]

To compensate for this deficiency in direct experience, greater maturity of judgment is needed, as well as more time to acquire related and vicarious experience that will provide more valid knowledge of jobs and of vocational aspects of self. But this extension of time is not available *before* decisions have to be made. When it finally does become available, it is frequently too late to scrap the investment already made in several years of training and to start anew in search of a more appropriate vocation.

Finally, accurate perception of the requirements and characteristics of jobs and of the personal qualifications that are necessary is frequently impeded by potent prestige needs—even when all of the necessary information for making a sound decision is at hand. Perceptions are notoriously selective. If the need is great enough, obvious environmental obstacles and hazards may be ignored or minimized, distasteful aspects of prestige-giving occupations may be overlooked, and glaring deficiencies in ability and temperamental suitability may be blithely disregarded.

It is therefore pertinent to inquire how much real "freedom of choice" exists in the selection of a vocation. The modern adolescent has a tremendously wider range of vocations to choose from than his grandfather had, but lacking access to the type of experience necessary for making a valid decision between alternatives, the greater number of choices only increases his bewilderment instead of genuinely adding to his sense of volitional freedom. But even if a sounder factual basis existed for reaching vocational decisions, true deliberative judgment could not be exercised without greater awareness of the underlying motivations entering into occupational choice. In the present climate of vocational decision-making, adolescents seem highly reluctant to acknowledge and come to grips with the factors influencing the types of occupations they select. Despite all of the presumptive evidence to the contrary, they consider such factors as "job prestige" and occupational status as relatively negligible when asked to rank in order of importance the factors that influenced their choice.* Such conventionally acceptable reasons as "interest" and "ability" invariably receive top mention.

It is this unwillingness among adolescents to acknowledge consciously what it is they really want from a vocation, plus unrealistically high vocational aspirations and the absence of sufficiently sound knowledge of self and jobs that leads to such widespread vocational dissatisfaction among adults. The fact that nearly half of a large group of adults expressed the desire to start afresh in a new occupation if that were only possible [49] indicates that vocational choices are being made too early, with inadequate knowledge and experience, and without enough awareness of the underlying issues and motivations to permit the exercise of rational and mature deliberation.

* Based upon unpublished data of the writer described in the first footnote in this chapter and upon reference 50.

VOCATIONAL GUIDANCE

The Need for Vocational Guidance

The foregoing evaluation of the occupational choices of adolescents convincingly demonstrates that modern youth is confronted by extremely complex and baffling problems in the quest for suitable vocational placement. It leads inescapably to the conclusion that for a substantial percentage of youth the goal of vocational adjustment cannot be attained without some form of vocational education or guidance. Regardless of which criterion we use to appraise the occupational choices of adolescents, we find them all too frequently portentous of eventual vocational maladjustment; and unfortunately, this dismal prognosis is borne out by evidence of widespread job dissatisfaction among the present generation of young adults.[49]

If vocational adjustment were a less crucial factor for personality maturation and the attainment of adult status (see p. 437), we would have less cause for concern. But since such maladjustment not only retards so many other important aspects of development but also spills over into every conceivable component of current life adjustment, we cannot afford to ignore the mental hygiene possibilities inherent in the field of vocational guidance. There is much common sense in the view that

an adolescent who has a vocational goal before him, . . . one in which he has confidence and a reasonable degree of assurance that he can succeed, will almost certainly have fewer problems than one who does not have such a plan. . . . Many of the troubles of young people grow out of the fact that they have no large purpose motivating their daily behavior. The human animal is [so constituted] that, with a given accepted purpose luring him on, he will organize his whole behavior pattern around it. In this sense, competent vocational guidance can help to reduce the number and seriousness of the problems in the other areas of life.[48]

To an increasingly greater extent

schools . . . are becoming aware of the importance of preparing adolescents for the difficulties of business or commercial life. . . . Assistance in the choice of suitable employment is now in many countries coming to be recognized as an essential activity of the secondary school.[26]

Such assistance is being provided in the form of (a) vocationally oriented courses such as typing and industrial arts, (b) courses dealing with occupational information, (c) vocational counseling, and (d) various types of work experience programs.

All of these are steps in the right direction. They need in no way interfere with the unique responsibility of the school in transmitting our cultural heritage or in imparting a core body of knowledge and intellectual skills. In a broader sense the school is also one of the important agencies concerned with preparing young people for life. It cannot turn its back on the serious problems of vocational adjustment that its graduates will inevitably encounter. It cannot pretend that the transition from school boy to working man is easy, natural, or fraught with only ordinary hazards. And, as will be pointed out later, the school is in a strategic position to foster certain aspects of vocational guidance, such as work experience, which no other cultural agency could conveniently attempt to handle.

Vocational Guidance versus Psychotherapy

Since the typical adjustment problems of adolescence are developmental or situational in nature, i.e., products of the difficulties and uncertainties involved in acquiring adult status,

> many of the anxieties of adolescents and young adults would disappear entirely, or be considerably alleviated if they could achieve the proper type of job placement. Hence in the more *usual* type of adolescent maladjustment, the psychotherapeutic possibilities inherent in vocational guidance, greatly exceed those present in extended exploration of conflictful emotional material.[2]

Even when adolescents suffer from serious personality disturbances, it is extremely important to focus attention on current problems of vocational adjustment while probing more deeply into etiological factors.

> Only too frequently, [however], does the latter goal become the main preoccupation of the psychotherapeutic session, while the immediate urgency for vocational adaptation is deemphasized so effectively that by implication it is regarded as almost irrelevant to the patient's psychological disturbance. It is hardly surprising then that, if in the course of extensive psychotherapy, substantial progress toward vocational progress is not simultaneously made (rather than postponed to await the solution of emotional conflicts), all the potential benefits of ventilation, catharsis, insight, and transference might be largely nullified by the patient's failure to possess the one practical instrument he needs to effect his maturation. And thus after completing several years of the treat-

ment on which he had pinned his highest hopes, he emerges more crushed and forlorn than before; because not only does he still have his original emotional conflicts, but now he is also several years older, still a child in his father's house, and the prospect of vocational adjustment is still but a vague and intangible dream.[2]

Vocational counseling does not imply that the counselor makes decisions for his client. Neither does it imply, however, that he must merely assist the client in clarifying his goals and attitudes without expressing any judgment reactions regardless of how unrealistic or defeatist the client's approach may be. As we have emphasized so often before, maturation in no area of personality occurs spontaneously, but largely in response to perceived social expectations. The vocational counselor cannot afford to play only the role of neutral catalyst in helping the adolescent perceive and reorganize his vocational attitudes. He is also charged with the responsibility of representing the expectations of the culture about the direction in which mature occupational adjustment is perceived to lie. Hence,

it is the counselor's constant duty to emphasize and to have the adolescent accept the imperative need for vocational adjustment as the core problem of adult maturation. . . . In the event that an unsatisfying compromise must be accepted, it should be pointed out that vocational stabilization at any level of aspiration, if tangible and realistic, is preferable by far to grandiose but vaguer expectations, or to a complete absence of any adjustment. This proposition is not as self-evident as it seems, since the number of individuals with hypertrophied ego demands is legion who, on being denied their whole-loaf ambitions, seem to prefer no loaf at all to taking many proffered varieties of half-loaf solutions.[2]

Foci of Concern in Vocational Guidance

Vocational guidance is concerned with such tasks as providing factual information about jobs, clarifying and making more accessible to consciousness the motivations underlying occupational choice, ascertaining the occupational status or level to which an individual can realistically aspire, and appraising the kinds of jobs to which he is suited by his particular pattern of interests and abilities.

Clarification of Goals. The first task of vocational guidance is not concerned so much with narrowing down the field of suitable occupations as in *widening* the relevant field from which appropriate choices may be made, and in making the processes of choice more conscious and deliberate. The net result of these two operations is to increase the range, the freedom, and the rational and factual basis of vocational choice. Until these two steps are taken, there is no possibility of satisfactorily clarifying occupational goals and of proceeding to the next steps of choosing appropriate occupational levels and areas of activity.

The provision of relevant occupational information has a real place in a program of vocational guidance. When an adolescent knows such things as the requirements, duties, job opportunities, and remuneration of as many different kinds of occupations as possible, his range of choice has been tremendously extended, and a sound, factual basis for decision-making actually exists. The effectiveness of an informational approach, *per se,* is both variable and limited. It is more apt to be effective when the basic difficulty in occupational choice stems from lack of knowledge and experience rather than from unrealistic motivational pressures. The duller individual is more likely to benefit from the first stages of such a program since it supplies him with information that he would have difficulty in ferreting out for himself. The brighter person is more quick to perceive the relevancy of general information to his own situation.

Although the over-all effect of vocational information programs is to make occupational choices more realistic,[5, 53] experience has shown that their beneficial influence can be greatly enhanced when the information is made personally relevant and meaningful, taken out of a general academic context and applied specifically to the vocational problems of a given individual.[9, 57] It is at this point that vocational education becomes vocational counseling. Counseling, however, does more than individualize the meaning and applicability of information. It also clarifies and brings to the surface an individual's vague and unverbalized attitudes and motivations about occupations and occupational role.

Why is this process necessary and beneficial? In the first place, attitudes and goals that are private and unverbalized are not subject to the corrective influences of a shared social reality. Inevitably, therefore, they fail to measure up to social expectations or to reasonable standards of realistic planning. Second, such unformulated

and often distorted attitudes unknowingly influence vocational decisions, and thus interfere to an undeterminable extent with the
processes of deliberate choice. Genuine freedom of choice can only
exist when there is substantial awareness of the underlying pressures
and motivations, of the relative contributions of interest, ability,
family and social class influences, individual prestige needs, desire
for job security or high financial returns to the eventual decision.
But awareness of the existence of certain motivations does not necessarily guarantee insight into their effect on vocational choice;
this relationship must be explicitly worked out before insight can
be assumed. Neither does awareness of a motive necessarily negate
its influence. It merely makes the latter more modifiable and brings
it into the field of *conscious* determinants impinging upon volitional
choice.

Occupational Status. One of the first problems awaiting consideration after preliminary exploration and clarification of the field of
occupations and occupational goals is the determination of an
appropriate level of occupational status. The needs for vocational
prestige that are engendered in the course of personality development, whether reflective of general social class pressures or of more
intimate interpersonal relationships, are real and insistent. They
cannot be ignored or lightly brushed aside. When clearly formulated
and brought out into the open, however, they can be dealt with more
rationally and related to realistic limitations.

It is a fairly safe asumption that, all other things being equal,
vocational satisfaction will be maximal when an individual attains
an occupational status that is conmmensurate with the magnitude
of his prestige aspirations. Depending on this factor, and assuming
again that other things are equal, a level of occupational status
that is deemed appropriate for one person may be either too high
or too low for another. Once the absolute level of occupational
prestige needs is ascertained in the course of skillful interviewing,*

---

* A special instrument has also been designed to measure occupational prestige
needs.[38] The subject is presented with a list of ninety occupational activities
arranged in groups of three which are relatively homogeneous with respect to
kind of activity but which differ in degree of job prestige. In each group he indicates his preference. His total score, computed on the basis of differential weights
assigned to different degrees of job prestige, is reflective of his mean level of
prestige aspiration over the entire range of occupations presented.

it has to be brought into line with such realistic considerations as occupational demand, financial backing for education, capacity for sustained motivation, intelligence, and ability. If these factors do not support the existing level of vocational aspiration, a forthright attempt at lowering that level is indicated; and until the client can emotionally accept the desirability of taking this step it is exceedingly doubtful whether counseling can effect any further progress.

Although each case has to be considered on an individual basis, we have noted that in general the occupational aspirations of adolescents are unrealistically high; and "in view of the persistent trend toward reduced social mobility, a general devaluation of vocational ambitions would seem to be indicated." [2] Whenever possible, some degree of compensation can be effected within a given level of occupational status by giving preference to those vocations that offer greater possibilities of attaining supervisory control or public recognition.

Determining Specific Occupational Choice. The second major problem in selecting a vocation is deciding upon an appropriate *area* of occupational activity. This involves the choice of a general field of work or job family and the choice of a level of complexity within that job family. For example, both machinist and mechanical engineer belong in the same job family (machine trades) but at different levels of complexity. To a very large extent, of course, level of complexity coincides with occupational status. Counseling about choice of occupational field involves such considerations as interests, intelligence, aptitude and job availability.

Used judiciously in counseling situations,[14, 19, 60, 68, 69] vocational interest inventories are valuable aids in selecting an appropriate field of work. Since they are reflective both of personality traits and of differential ego-involvement relevant for occupational compatibility (see p. 452), they are useful for predicting educational choice [68, 69] and entrance into different occupations.[60] For similar reasons they are predictive of occupational contentment and so of vocational stability,[23, 60] and of educational [21, 22] and vocational [61] success. It stands to reason that individuals who are contented in a given work will over the long pull be successful in it, even though they may originally show less aptitude than other persons who manifest no particular interest. Also, as indicated above (see p. 298), an individual is usually able to do best what he is most interested in doing although this does not necessarily mean that he will show more initial aptitude than a disinterested individual (see p. 449).

For determining level of job complexity within a given field of work, intelligence quotient is a very useful indicator. Although it is true that general intelligence is highly differentiated by the time of adolescence (see p. 284), differentiation occurs along the lines of major interest patterns. It is a fair assumption that intelligence will be differentially concentrated in areas related to high vocational interest and can, therefore, be used as a measure of the complexity of the problems an individual is equipped to handle in those areas.

Aptitude tests are sometimes useful in reinforcing impressions derived from interview and other materials, but, generally speaking, are not very helpful in the selection of a particular field of work. Only when indicative of gross ineptitude are they likely to have much prognostic significance in individual cases.

The reasons for this unsatisfactory state of affairs are many. In the first place, most aptitude tests, particularly those in the psycho-motor field, have very low validity coefficients.[18, 26, 63] A number of instruments usually have to be combined in a differentially weighted battery to approach even a respectable multiple coefficient of correlation with an independent criterion of occupational success; but such batteries are time-consuming, difficult to administer, and even then rarely yield validity coefficients high enough to be useful for individual prediction.[26] Second, because mechanical skills are highly specific[7, 18] (see pp. 123–124), it is practically impossible to construct a mechanical aptitude test that will predict success in a large variety of jobs involving different kinds of mechanical operations. To be even relatively efficient for guidance purposes, a mechanical abilities test would have to almost duplicate the specific tasks of a given job; but then, by definition, its predictive value would be highly restricted. Third, psychomotor aptitude tests, as usually administered, measure initial ability to adjust to a new task rather than ultimate capacity after practice has rendered the task familiar;[18, 26] and it is the ultimate capacity that is naturally more important for production and job success.

Finally,

there is reason to believe that later skilled performance is related as much to interest, ambition, and general competence of methods of working as to anything which can fairly be described as initial mechanical aptitude. . . . Improvements in the kind of tuition given and in the attitude of the trainees as well as increases in the amount of practice appear, therefore, to be of greater practical usefulness in determining the final skill of a group of employees than excessive attention to refinements in the techniques of selection on the lines of any of the analytic aptitude tests of special abilities.[26]

Because "the predictive value of achievement tests applied after actual trial of [an occupation] is higher than that of most skilled single testing of so-called aptitudes," [26] vocational try-outs are extremely useful for occupational guidance. But such try-outs are not feasible for occupations involving long years of preparation. Work experience has other values for guidance apart from providing an index of relative ability; but since it also involves issues transcending vocational guidance, we shall consider it under a separate heading.

WORK EXPERIENCE DURING ADOLESCENCE *

Usefulness for Vocational Planning

One of the more important uses to which adolescent job experience can be put is in making occupational choices more realistic. Sustained firsthand experience with actual working conditions takes the glamor out of jobs. It also tests the genuineness of expressed interests, reveals to what extent contentment can be derived from a given field of work, and is a more significant indicator than aptitude tests of relative ability to succeed in a given job family. Diversified work experience, therefore, can be of great assistance in narrowing down the field from which eventual vocational choice will be made.

For work experience to serve this function, it must be approached explicitly from the standpoint of finding out useful information about self in relation to the vocational world.[16] Merely working long hours or earning money as an end in itself without adopting this exploratory orientation only results in a set of specific learnings that cannot be applied to the more general problems involved in vocational choice.

* Much of this discussion is based on T. E. Christensen's, "Getting Job Experience." [16]

Other Values of Work Experience

Work experience can do a great deal to cushion the transition between school and work.[37, 46] School life obviously offers little indication of what lies ahead in the vocational world.[32]

> Many adolescents nowadays leave school with the hopeful anticipation that they will find in the business world a kindliness and cooperativeness similar to those which they have met in the more or less child-centered school society of which they have formed a part. Disappointment often follows and the transition to adult status is consequently, in many cases, unnecessarily difficult. . . .
>
> New skills have to be learnt and insight into new situations has to be achieved. . . . The adolescent is a novice. . . . He is an outsider in a new group. . . . All the others know what is expected of them. The adolescent makes mistakes and experiences teasing as to clumsiness in work or inexperience in social relations. For all such reasons there is in the years of apprenticeship an element of insecurity and distress which is greater or less in proportion to the wisdom and the kindliness of all the members of the working community.[26]

Job experience also provides a "down to earth" opportunity for learning to get along with people—peers, superiors, and subordinates—in situations that are very much different from any adjustive problem the adolescent has ever been confronted with before. It also makes possible for the first time the learning of work habits and attitudes that can only be acquired in an actual job. It is understandable why most employers demand such experience before they are willing even to consider an applicant for a position and why they are so reluctant to let him acquire it on *their* time. And in addition to these patent advantages that work experience confers, it enables the adolescent to perceive more clearly the value and relevancy of many school subjects and provides invaluable practice in the management of earnings.[16]

The Role of the School

If job experience is to become systematically available to a majority of adolescents and if it is to be optimally useful for guidance purposes, it seems that the secondary school will have to take the initiative in establishing suitable programs.* In the first place,

* It is not implied here that the responsibility for inaugurating work experience programs is solely the school's. Industry and various community agencies obviously have to cooperate if such programs are to be successful. However, it is

under ordinary peace-time conditions, it is becoming increasingly more difficult for young people to obtain entry jobs requiring no previous training or experience. "In addition, opportunities for work experience in the home are becoming more and more restricted."[16] Without some aid in getting job experience, it is hardly likely that many adolescents, except those who are driven by economic necessity or who display uncommon initiative, will be fortunate enough to obtain it on their own resources. Second, only the school is in a position to integrate satisfactorily work experience with a program of vocational guidance and to prevent it from making excessive demands on the time needed for academic and extracurricular activities. And last, the type of supervision that an agency such as the school can exercise is necessary to safeguard adolescents from exploitation and from exposure to hazardous or unhealthful occupations.

REFERENCES AND BIBLIOGRAPHY

1. Anderson, W. A.: Some social factors associated with the vocational choices of college men. J. Educ. Sociol., 6:100–113, 1932.
2. Ausubel, D. P.: Problems of adolescent adjustment. Bulletin, Natl. Assn. Secondary School Principals, 34:1–84, 1950.
3. Ausubel, D. P.: Prestige Motivation of Gifted Children. Genet. Psychol. Monogr., 43:53–117, 1951.
4. Ausubel, D. P.: Ego Development and the Personality Disorders. New York: Grune and Stratton, 1952.
5. Bateman, R. M. and Remmers, H. H.: Attitudes of high-school freshmen toward occupations of their choice before and after studying the occupations by means of a career book. J. Educ. Psychol., 30:657–666, 1939.
6. Bell, H. M.: Youth Tell Their Story. Washington, D. C.: American Council on Education, 1938.
7. Bennett, G. K. and Cruikshank, R. M.: A Summary of Manual and Mechanical Ability Tests. New York: Psychological Corporation, 1942.
8. Berdie, R. F.: Factors related to vocational interests. Psychol. Bull., 41:137–157, 1944.
9. Bunting, J. R.: Counselling alters pupils' choice. Occupations, 18:174–176, 1939.
10. Byrns, R.: Relation of vocational choice to mental ability and occupational opportunity. Sch. Rev., 47:101–109, 1939.

---

not realistic to expect that any agency apart from the school will be sufficiently motivated to take the initiatory steps or to adopt a primarily educational orientation toward job experience.

11. Canning, L., Taylor, K. V., and Carter, H. D.: Permanence of vocational interests of high-school boys. J. Educ. Psychol., *32*:481–494, 1941.
12. Carter, H. D.: Twin similarities in occupational interests. J. Educ. Psychol., *23*:641–655, 1932.
13. Carter, H. D.: "The Development of Interest in Vocations," in *Adolescence*, 43rd Yearbook, Natl. Soc. Stud. Educ., Part I. Chicago: University of Chicago Press, 1944.
14. Carter, H. D. and Jones, M. C.: Vocational attitude patterns in high-school students. J. Educ. Psychol., *29*:321–334, 1938.
15. Carter, H. D. and Strong, E. K.: Sex differences in occupational interests of high-school students. Personnel Journal, *12*:166–175, 1933.
16. Christensen, T. E.: *Getting Job Experience.* Chicago: Science Research Associates, 1949.
17. Clark, C. D. and Gist, N. P.: Intelligence as a factor in occupational choice. Amer. Sociol. Rev., *3*:683–694, 1938.
18. Cronbach, L. J.: *Essentials of Psychological Testing.* New York: Harper, 1949.
19. Darley, J. G.: Counseling on the basis of interest measurement. Educ. & Psychol. Measurement, *1*:35–42, 1941.
20. Davidson, P. E. and Anderson, H. D.: *Occupational Mobility in an American Community.* Stanford, Calif.: Stanford University Press, 1937.
21. Duffy, E. and Crissy, W. J. E.: Evaluative attitudes as related to vocational interests and academic achievement. J. Abnorm. Soc. Psychol., *35*:226–245, 1940.
22. Dunlap, J. W.: Preferences as indicators of specific academic achievement. J. Educ. Psychol., *26*:411–415, 1935.
23. Dyer, D. T.: The relation between vocational interests of men in college and their subsequent occupational histories for ten years. J. Appl. Psychol., *23*:280–288, 1939.
24. Feingold, G. A.: The relation between intelligence and vocational choices of high school pupils. J. Appl. Psychol., *7*:143–153, 1923.
25. Finch, F. H. and Odoroff, M. E.: Sex differences in vocational interests. J. Educ. Psychol., *30*:151–156, 1939.
26. Fleming, C. M.: *Adolescence: Its Social Psychology.* New York: International Universities Press, 1949.
27. Fryer, D.: Occupational intelligence standards. Sch. & Soc., *16*:273–277, 1933.
28. Hartmann, G. W.: The occupational prestige of representative professions in American society. Psychol. Bull., *31*:695–696, 1934.
29. Hartmann, G. W.: The prestige of occupations. Personnel Journal, *13*:144–152, 1934.
30. Hicks, J. A. and Hayes, M.: Study of the characteristics of 250 junior-high school children. Child Develpm., *9*:219–242, 1938.
31. Hurlock, E. B. and Jansing, C.: The vocational attitudes of boys and girls of high-school age. J. Genet. Psychol., *44*:175–191, 1934.
32. Jahoda, G.: Adolescent attitudes to starting work. Occup. Psychol. Lond., *23*:184–188, 1949.

33. Jones, E. S.: Relation of ability to preferred and probable occupation. Educ. Admn. & Superv., *26:*220–226, 1940.

34. Jones, H. E.: *Development in Adolescence.* New York: Appleton-Century, 1943.

35. Kroger, R. and Louttit, C. M.: The influence of father's occupation on the vocational choices of high-school boys. J. Appl. Psychol., *19:*203–212, 1935.

36. Kuder, G. F.: *Revised Manual for the Kuder Preference Record.* Chicago: Science Research Associates, 1946.

37. Lane, R. E. and Logan, R. F. L.: The adolescent at work. Practitioner, *162:* 287–298, 1949.

38. Lee, E. A. and Thorpe, L. P.: *Occupational Interest Inventory, Intermediate Form A.* Los Angeles: California Test Bureau, 1944.

39. Lehman, H. C. and Witty, P. A.: Some factors which influence the child's choice of vocations. Elem. Sch. Journal, *31:*285–291, 1930.

40. Lehman, H. C. and Witty, P. A.: A study of vocational attitudes in relation to pubescence. Amer. J. Psychol., *43:*93–101, 1931.

41. Lehman, H. C. and Witty, P. A.: Further study of the social status of occupations. J. Educ. Sociol., *5:*101–112, 1931.

42. Lehman, H. C. and Witty, P. A.: One more study of permanence of interests. J. Educ. Psychol., *22:*481–492, 1931.

43. Lehman, H. C. and Witty, P. A.: Sex differences in vocational attitudes. J. Appl. Psychol., *20:*576–585, 1936.

44. Meek, L. H.: *The Personal—Social Development of Boys and Girls with Implications for Secondary Education.* New York: Progressive Education Association, 1940.

45. Mooney, R.: Surveying high school students' problems by means of a problem check list. Educ. Res. Bull., *21:*57–69, 1942.

46. Moss, R. M.: From school to work. Child, *16:*25–27, 1951.

47. Parsons, T.: Age and sex in the social structure of the United States. Amer. Sociol. Rev., *7:*604–616, 1942.

48. Partridge, E. D.: "Guidance of the Adolescent," in *Handbook of Child Guidance* (E. Harms, ed.). New York: Child Care Publications, 1947.

49. Paterson, D. G. and Stone, C. H.: Dissatisfactions with work among adult workers. Occupations, *21:*219–221, 1942.

50. Peters, E. F.: Factors which contribute to youth's vocational choice. J. Appl. Psychol., *25:*428–430, 1941.

51. Proctor, W. M.: A 13 year follow-up of high school pupils. Occupations, *15:* 306–310, 1937.

52. Rainey, H. P. et al.: *How Fare American Youth?* New York: Appleton-Century, 1937.

53. Remmers, H. H. and Whisler, L. D.: The effects of a guidance program on vocational attitudes. Purdue University Stud. Higher Educ., *34:*68–82, 1938.

54. Roper, E.: Occupational contentment. Fortune Survey No. 5. Fortune, *17:* 86–88, 1938.

55. Sisson, E. D.: Vocational choices of students from cities, towns, and farms. Sch. & Soc., *54:*94–96, 1941.

56. Smith, M.: An empirical scale of prestige status of occupations. Amer. Sociol. Rev., 8:185–192, 1943.
57. Stone, C. H.: Evaluation Program in Vocational Orientation. Univ. Minnesota Stud. Higher Educ., 1941.
58. Strong, E. K.: *Change in Interests with Age*. Stanford, Calif.: Stanford University Press, 1931.
59. Strong, E. K.: Permanence of vocational interests. J. Educ. Psychol., 25:336–344, 1934.
60. Strong, E. K.: Predictive value of the vocational interest test. J. Educ. Psychol., 26:331–349, 1935.
61. Strong, E. K.: *Vocational Interests of Men and Women*. Stanford, Calif.: Stanford University Press, 1943.
62. Super, D. E.: *Dynamics of Vocational Adjustment*. New York: Harper, 1942.
63. Super, D. E.: *Appraising Vocational Fitness by Means of Psychological Tests*. New York: Harper, 1949.
64. Taylor, K. V. and Carter, H. D.: Retest consistency of vocational interest patterns of high-school girls. J. Consult. Psychol., 6:95–101, 1942.
65. Thomsen, A.: Expectation in relation to achievement and happiness. J. Abnorm. Soc. Psychol., 38:58–73, 1943.
66. Thorndike, E. L.: Early interests: Their permanence and relation to abilities. Sch. & Soc., 5:178–179, 1917.
67. Triggs, F. O.: A study of the relation of the Kuder Preference Record scores to other various measures. Educ. and Psychol. Measurement, 6:3–16, 1946.
68. Van Tuyl, K. and Eurich, A. C.: Measuring the interests of college students with different major subjects. J. Appl. Psychol., 18:27–44, 1934.
69. Walters, A. and Eurich, A. C.: A quantitative study of the major interests of college students. J. Educ. Psychol., 27:561–571, 1936.
70. Witty, P. A., Garfield, S., and Brink, W. G.: A comparison of the vocational interests of Negro and white high-school students. J. Educ. Psychol., 32:124–132, 1941.

CHAPTER 15

Adolescents and the School

IN COMMON WITH all other institutions and the problems (and people) to which they relate, the channels of influence between school and adolescents invariably run in both directions. One direction is obvious. As a formally constituted agency dedicated to the task of training adolescents, the school in very deliberate fashion profoundly influences intellectual and moral growth. Less deliberately, but no less definitely, the interpersonal environment of the school impinges upon many of the developmental tasks of adolescence—emancipation from the home, the acquisition of primary status, and the achievement of greater volitional independence in dealings with adults. Even more informally the school contributes to the growing social stratification that characterizes adolescent group life and provides opportunity for furthering peer culture activities and heterosexual adjustment.

The influence of adolescence on the school is considerably less obvious. As a result of the personality changes and intellectual development during adolescence, important modifications occur in the cognitive, interpersonal, and motivational aspects of learning. But although these changes in the learning process *actually* influence what goes on in school by affecting what is learned and how learning takes place, appropriate adjustments in teaching methods, curricular organization, and in the social climate of the school have not necessarily taken place. In the light of institutional inertia and resistance to change, this discrepancy between existing knowledge of psychological processes and prevailing training practices is hardly surprising. We have encountered the same phenomenon ("cultural lag") before in noting how official ideological values remain constant despite changes in their socioeconomic substrate that necessarily induce profound modifications in the actual moral behavior of individuals (see p. 337).

GENERAL FUNCTIONS OF THE SCHOOL DURING ADOLESCENCE

As a training institution, the school is primarily an instrument of cultural survival designed to perpetuate and improve a given way of life. Every culture implicitly accepts a set of values for significant aspects of behavior, interpersonal relations, and social organization. And if a culture is to survive, much of education must be concerned with inculcating these values in the young of all ages before they can be invested with adult status. This function of education has won so much explicit recognition and unqualified acceptance in such areas as aesthetics, character traits, and government that it is difficult to appreciate the position of those who contend that values are purely personal and that the sole business of schools is to "teach facts" (see p. 430).

A second training function of the school, the value of which has only recently been challenged, is the development of various intellectual skills and the attainment of increased understanding in such cultural areas as art, science, literature, mathematics. The value and importance of knowledge as an end in itself have been unduly de-emphasized by certain educators who have been oversold on the virtues of "applied education," of gearing the curriculum to expressed interests, current concerns, and problems of "life adjustment." A very extreme statement of this point of view would be that only intellectually superior or college-bound students should be exposed to academic subjects and that for all other adolescents the main purpose of secondary education should be preparation for vocational, family, and other forms of "life adjustment."

The third training function of the secondary school is to facilitate personality maturation in adolescents. As pointed out, whether by design or otherwise, the school cannot help but play a role in the personality changes of adolescence. Merely by providing an arena in which young people interact with each other and with adults, the school influences important aspects of personality structure at a time when these are undergoing significant change. And since the school *has* to play *some* role in this development it might just as well be as constructive as possible. For to the extent that the developmental tasks of adolescents are or are not fulfilled, we acquire or fail to acquire mature citizens who are capable of carrying on and improving the culture.

It can also be convincingly argued that since the culture sets the standards by which adult maturity is judged and has so much to gain by the realization of these standards, it acquires the associated training responsibilities. From the standpoint of educational philosophy it is not difficult to defend the proposition that "education [in the broader sense] is also concerned with the development of personality, with the problems of individual adjustment."[18] There is no *a priori* reason for believing that the chief social institution charged with responsibility for training the young must necessarily be concerned with one exclusive aspect of development (the intellectual) rather than with the individual's total potentiality for growth. If pupils are to be equipped with symbolical tools to solve intellectual problems, there is no reason why they cannot also be prepared to meet other problems of adjustment. If the school does not assume this responsibility who else can and will? Nevertheless, there are probably as many educators who adopt the extreme subject matter approach to education as there are proponents of the extreme "life adjustment" orientation.

IMPACT OF THE SCHOOL ON THE DEVELOPMENTAL TASKS OF ADOLESCENCE

Emancipation from Parents

The school facilitates in several important ways the adolescent's emancipation from home and parents. By providing other parent-like adults (teachers) with whom he can satellize, it makes the relinquishment of emotional dependence on parents less abrupt and less traumatic. The home source of derived status seems more expendable when it can be replaced by another that is also more socially acceptable during the adolescent period. In addition, the school progressively displaces the home as the major adult source from which the adolescent derives his normative values. It thereby devalues the parent's omniscience, infallibility, and monopoly on truth, and hence, his capacity for conferring derived status by fiat. Finally, by being able to offer the adolescent an important current source of primary status utterly beyond the resources of the urban home, the school enjoys an overwhelming advantage in competing for his loyalty.

The school is also in a strategic position as a respected neutral bystander to ease the tensions between parents and their adolescent children that are incident to the struggle for emancipation. Merely by re-establishing broken lines of communication and interpreting one to the other, much of the conflict that follows from misunderstanding can be alleviated.

The Acquisition of Primary Status

During adolescence the importance of the school as a source of primary status naturally increases as this status assumes a central rather than a subsidiary role in the individual's personality structure. This does not necessarily mean that the adolescent likes school any better; in fact, evidence points to just the opposite conclusion.[31] What it means is that the motivational orientation underlying the adolescent's approach to learning subject matter and assimilating goals and values becomes progressively more dominated by the need for self-enhancement as a person in his own right.

The school offers two different but related kinds of primary status. The more current variety is merely a reflection of relative competence in mastering the curriculum and the relative class standing that accrues from this accomplishment. School achievement not only is related to character reputation on a community-wide basis,[26] but also is significantly related to sociometric status * (more so in girls than in boys). The second variety of primary status that the school offers has less current than "stepping stone" value. For example, certain courses of study and levels of graded school performance are prerequisite for college or vocational entrance. Similarly, vocational education and guidance and work experience programs have important implications for the *future* acquisition of primary status.

It is important to realize that the primary status that the adolescent can acquire in school has the same interim quality as the

---

* Based on unpublished data of the writer on junior and senior high school students attending University High School, Urbana, Illinois.

status available to him in the peer group. It relates to peripheral activities far removed from the main stream of status-giving operations in the adult world. But rarely is achievement in these activities regarded as an intrinsically worthwhile goal in its own right as are, for example, many of the activities of the peer group. It has mainly "stop-gap" or substitutive value in lieu of real adult status; and in relation to future status aspirations it is largely perceived as part of an arbitrary sequence than as organically and logically related to the ultimate operations on which these aspirations are based. High school or college achievement can in no sense match the status that a full-time job can confer in terms of ego enhancement or maturational value (see p. 320).

Acquiring Greater Volitional Independence in Dealing with Adults

One of the primary maturational tasks of adolescents is to acquire the volitional independence, the self-assertion, and the self-determination characteristic of adult status. In large measure this means adopting an entirely new orientation to adults and adult authority, learning how to resist adult domination, and learning how to react to adults as peers rather than as awesome beings with a qualitatively superior status. To be sure, all of these changes are only commensurate with the new biosocial status to which adolescents are aspiring, and their realization is motivated by the various pressures precipitating this transitional stage of personality development (see pp. 186–194). Resistance to authoritarianism is also increased by the growing need for reciprocity in moral obligations (see p. 251) and by diminished tolerance for nonfunctional moral absolutism (see p. 250). But the pressure of insistent needs is not alone sufficient to result in the acquisition of a difficult new behavioral role at variance with the cumulative impact of all previous experience.

> Youth can learn to be adults only through living and working with adults. ... The nature of their social behavior depends on the kinds of relationships which they experience.[36]

Since the school provides the larger number and the more important occasions and opportunities for adolescents to interact with adults, the types of adult-youth relationships established in the secondary school have a crucial bearing on the outcome of this basic developmental task. It will be necessary to examine the reactions that pupils make to teachers as persons, the perceptions that adolescents and teachers have of each other, and the varieties of social climates that exist in the school and their impact on the attainment of volitional independence.

How Teachers Perceive Pupils. How accurate are teachers' perceptions of the attitudes, motivations, interests, personality traits, and sociometric feelings of their pupils? The evidence on this question is not very encouraging. Teachers are unable to predict with any degree of accuracy high school pupils' responses to questions on their interests, hobbies, and personality characteristics.[6] Even in elementary school, the correspondence between pupils' and teachers' explanations of the motivations of pupils' behavior and academic strivings is negligible.[4] Teachers' perceptions of the sociometric status of their pupils become increasingly more inaccurate as they progress through the grades [5, 37] and are especially poor in the high school period.[10]

It is not difficult to find explanations for this unfortunate state of affairs. Teachers are simply not aware of the distinctive standards and values that operate in the lives of adolescents.[36] By the age of adolescence, the estrangement between children and their elders has made considerable progress and is compounded by the outright hostility and anti-adult attitudes manifested by youth. Channels of communication break down, and teachers are obliged to interpret pupils' behavior at face value [36] or by their own standards and frames of reference. They fall back upon interpretive biases from recollections of their own adolescence [9] and from norms of behavior that pertain exclusively to their own middle-class backgrounds.[15] In evaluating other aspects of the adolescent's personality or adjustment they are not unnaturally influenced by his conformity to the requirements of the school situation. There is a moderately high correlation between high school pupils' school achievement and teachers' ratings of *personal* adjustment.* Teachers tend to over-

---

* In the writer's study of junior and senior high school students in University High School, Urbana, Illinois, cumulative grade point average correlated .60 with teachers' current ratings of personal adjustment.

rate the popularity of children with whom they have satisfactory relationships, and vice versa.[10, 23]

The implications of these findings are obvious. If teachers cannot perceive the interests, the attitudes, the goals, and the aspirations of their pupils, they will naturally be unable to counsel them intelligently or to adapt effectively the interpersonal climate of the school to their developmental needs. Lacking adequate understanding of adolescent behavior, they will be unable to interpret misbehavior, to respond adequately to it, or to institute appropriate preventative and disciplinary measures. And unfortunately, although general knowledge of adolescent development facilitates the understanding of *particular* adolescents, it is no substitute when psychological perceptiveness or sufficient interpersonal contact is lacking.

Ability to empathize with adolescents does not necessarily obligate teachers to adopt their values nor does it guarantee effectiveness in dealing with them. Understanding is necessary but not sufficient for skilled interpersonal relationships, since many other abilities and personality traits that are probably uncorrelated with psychological sensitivity (poise, self-assurance, sociocentrism, firmness, leadership qualities) are necessary for translating accurate perceptions into appropriate behavior.

How Pupils Perceive Teachers. The different ways in which pupils perceive the behavior and roles of teachers define and limit in much the same way as teachers' perceptions of pupils the kinds of interpersonal relationships that can be established in the school and their impact on personality development. The evidence is clear that pupils respond to teachers as persons and not only as dispensers of knowledge. Their affective reactions to teachers, for example, seem to depend as much on the personality characteristics of teachers as on their teaching skill, although there is considerable overlap between teachers liked best and teachers thought most effective.[24] Whereas pupils admire teaching skill, clarity, task-orientation, and good classroom control, they are equally appreciative of fairness, impartiality, friendliness, patience, cheerfulness, and sympathetic understanding.[24] They like teachers who are interested in pupils, who are helpful, kindly, and considerate of their feelings.[24]

Another study of pupils' perceptions of teachers shows that teachers are seen as playing three major kinds of roles, as friends, opponents, and manipulators of status in learning situations.[14] As friends, they are "older and wiser" persons, helpful counselors, heroes, givers of security, and occasionally "pals." As opponents they are cast as "kill-joys" who arbitrarily interfere with legitimate pleasures, as "enemies" to be "fought" and "outwitted," and as demons of power to be feared, respected, and placated. Much of this role obviously represents a displacement of hostile feelings from original parental targets. Teachers also share much of the brunt of adolescents' general anti-adult orientation. In the learning aspects of the school situation they are perceived as "necessary evils" in the acquisition of knowledge, efficient organizers in the direction of work projects, "steppingstones" to future status rewards, dispensers of approval and disapproval, and as moral arbiters who can absolve from guilt as well as point the acusing finger.[14]

These pupil perceptions of teachers' roles naturally mirror the less desirable existing authoritarian practices as well as many commendable exceptions to these practices. What is more important, however, is their demonstration that pupils undoubtedly operate on the conviction that teachers are important interpersonal influences in their lives. Both their perceptions and their affective reactions indicate that they think it possible for teachers to play a more constructive role in helping them attain a peer relationship with adults. But before this change can ever be effected, teachers must not only become more accurately aware of the needs and aspirations of particular adolescents, but they must also become aware of the current roles their pupils assign to them.

Implications of Authoritarianism for Adult-Youth Relationships. In most secondary schools adolescents experience little change in ascendance-submission relationships from the "adult rule-child obedience" pattern of the elementary school.[9, 14]

> From nursery school to the university, from early childhood to adult life, the prevailing educational milieu at home and in school is authoritarian and paternalistic. The opportunities for exercising initiative, independence and responsibility are always far behind the actual capacity for same at any stage of development.[2]

In general, overt compliance is the most common response that adolescents make to this situation, especially if they come from middle-class homes that place a great premium upon academic achievement.[14] Other adolescents may react with open aggression and hostility to teachers, with negativism or passive sabotage. Still others may drop out of school as soon as it is legal to do so. Because of the drastic consequences of outright rebellion, there is little opportunity for experimentation or alternation of behavior. Those who intend to remain in school and profit vocationally from school attendance must become reconciled to a continuation of the same subordinate childhood role.

Because of culturally and hormonally instigated pressures for attaining greater volitional independence and self-assertion, there is good reason for believing that the authority of the school is not *really* accepted by many adolescents, but gives rise to suppressed resentment and various negatively toned emotional attitudes and reactions. Forced to play a role out of keeping with their new, semi-adult self-concept and its associated expectations of a higher order of self-determination, they must inevitably suffer a loss in self-esteem. Contemplation of any other course of action, however, arouses anxiety about internalized aspirations for vocational status that are thereby threatened. The school situation, therefore, generates ambivalent, conflictful attitudes in adolescents, attitudes that can only add to their existing emotional instability. Furthermore, fear-inhibited self-expression obviously does not permit the degree of spontaneity and reality testing that is necessary for acquiring the volitional attributes of adult role behavior. It is no wonder that only "a very small proportion of students leaving the secondary school can meet adults with poise and ease." [36]

Experimental studies of the impact of authoritarian leadership on childrens' groups also point to various undesirable effects on group morale and solidarity.[35] In comparison with children in democratically governed groups, pupils who are subjected to autocratic control are more aggressive, direct their aggression against scapegoat group members rather than against the group leader, and adopt more submissive, placatory, and attention-demanding attitudes in dealing with the leader. They also manifest less "we-feeling," show less capacity for mobilizing constructive group effort in overcoming frustrating conditions, and are less capable of self-disciplined work and behavior when direct supervision is removed. It seems reasonable to expect that these outcomes would be even more negative in adolescents whose needs for self-determination are much greater than those of children, but who receive approximately the same type of authoritarian treatment in the school environment.

Partly as a reaction against traditional authoritarian practices, a small minority of schools under the influence of ultra-permissive doctrines of child rearing have instituted a *laissez-faire* social climate in the classroom. This approach allows children to do as they please, emphasizes freedom from restraint and discipline as an end in itself, strives for lack of structure and organization in school activities, and conceives of frustration as an unqualified evil to be avoided at any cost. Under such "catch-as-catch-can" conditions, aggressive pupils become ruthless, whereas retiring children become even more withdrawn. Observation of groups in which this pattern exists shows that it leads "inevitably to . . . confusion, insecurity, and keen competition for power among group members." [14] Pupils fail to learn the normative demands of society and how to operate within the limits these set, do not succeed in learning how to deal effectively with adults, and develop unrealistic expectations of the social structure of vocational life. Other unfavorable effects of excessive permissiveness on personality maturation have been discussed elsewhere (see pp. 202 and 240).

Democratic Discipline in the School Setting. In contrast to the authoritarian and *laissez-faire* patterns of control, some schools have managed to create a democratic climate of adult-youth interaction that is more compatible with the developmental needs of adolescents. This kind of atmosphere has been achieved in part through various devices that enable young people to share in the planning and management of the curriculum and in the regulation of student activities and discipline. When properly paced and geared to actual capacities for self-determination, such attempts have been uniformly successful in improving group morale and in facilitating the development of mature, responsible, and realistically grounded volitional independence.[14]

These procedures are in no way based upon the assumption that individuals mature spontaneously without being confronted with the normative demands of society (see p. 201). Although the goal toward which they aim is the achievement of self-discipline, the need for external controls and for the explicit definition of the limits of socially acceptable behavior is not denied (see p. 202). They also take into account the cumulative impact of prior conditioning to anxiety reduction and other extrinsic motivations (examinations, grades, promotions) in the learning situation, and do not seek unrealistically to predicate *all* learning activity upon intrinsic needs for knowledge.

More important perhaps than effective administrative machinery in achieving a wholesome democratic atmosphere in the school is teachers' adoption of certain kinds of attitudes toward pupils. In essence these consist of respect for the dignity and feelings of students as persons, and care in avoiding techniques of condescension, sarcasm, or abuse of superior knowledge and position. They presuppose that hierarchical distinctions between students and teachers will be based upon objective differences in knowledge and maturity rather than upon such formal and arbitrary props as titles, degrees, and academic status.

Appropriate discipline in the secondary school is impersonal and matter-of-fact. It avoids recrimination and punitive implications. Whenever possible it is enforced by lateral (peer) sanctions rather than imposed from above. It respects the adolescent's greater need for rational and functional rules based upon reciprocal obligation, and appeals more to logic than to loyalty or to the need for adult approval. And since more sophisticated social awareness enables youth to perceive more easily than children discrepancies between precept and practice, the moral principles upon which discipline is based will only be genuinely internalized if verbal exhortations are reinforced by personal example.[24]

Other Developmental Tasks of Adolescence

In addition to its impact on the basic maturational tasks of adolescence described above (emancipation from parents, acquisition of primary status and volitional independence), the school also influences growth and adjustment in two other areas of personality that are crucially significant during this period of development—peer group and heterosexual relationships. As already pointed out, the peer group is for many reasons the chief training and socializing institution of adolescence (see p. 384). By bringing adolescent boys and girls together for so many hours a day, the school necessarily serves as the primary locus in which the peer culture operates. It is in an unusually strategic position to facilitate the social development of adolescents by providing a diversified and constructive framework of social and extra-curricular activities in which boys and girls can socialize each other by practicing their biological and social sex roles in a peer setting.

Adolescents can also profit from more "direct instruction . . . in the basic skills required for every day social activity." [36] They need training, for example, in "how to meet people, how to introduce friends to other friends and to parents, how to order food," in social dancing and ballroom etiquette, in personal grooming. The need for school instruction in sex and courting problems and in boy-girl relationships has already been discussed (see pp. 428–429).

IMPLICATIONS OF ADOLESCENT PERSONALITY DEVELOPMENT FOR SCHOOL LEARNING

Adolescent personality development is especially relevant to the motivational aspects of learning. It not only influences the way in which the individual assimilates goals and values but also his reasons for learning academic subject matter. Such motivations obviously do not operate in a social vacuum but in relation to other persons both as individuals and as representatives of the culture. In assimilating values and implementing his learning orientation in the school environment, the adolescent reacts especially to the personality of the teacher. Depending on his particular motivational orientation he responds in different ways to the type of person she is and to the different roles she plays—with acceptance or rejection, self-assertion or submission, feelings of dependent identification or of emulatory self-enhancement.

The teacher's behavior, therefore—her objectivity or subjectivity, her personal relatedness or detachment, the extent to which her practices are authoritarian or democratic—is an important variable affecting the motivational aspect of the learning process. Its appropriateness to a given adolescent's learning orientation can either facilitate or hinder the learning of values, goals, and subject matter. It can affect the development and differentiation of interests and ability and even the motivational basis of learning itself. The personality of the teacher induces different affective reactions to subject matter [13] and influences the adolescent's decision to either continue or terminate his schooling.[16, 33] The motivational climate (praise, reproof, social recognition, competition) engendered by the teacher also influences learning outcomes [29, 30] and work output [4] in an academic setting.

Considering the importance of interpersonal factors in school learning, they have received "only passing recognition [from] learning theorists and sparse application to educational practice." [2] L. K. Frank explains this anomaly as follows:

> Educational programs shrink from any frank acceptance of the underlying personality make-up and emotional reactions of students as entering into the educational situation—because to do so would bring about a widespread collapse of the whole educational philosophy and undermining of approved pedagogy.[22]

Hence, we shall consider first the impact on school learning of personality changes that are characteristic of adolescents generally as an age group. Following this it will be necessary to relate individual differences in personality development to differences in learning orientation and appropriate teaching practices.

Impact of General Personality Changes on Learning Orientation

As a direct consequence of the increased importance of primary status during the adolescent period, the incorporative orientation (see p. 199) assumes a more centrally significant position in the individual's motivational approach to learning experience. In accepting the need for learning various skills, subject matter content, values and goals, such considerations as self-enhancement, increased competence, social recognition, and status in the group become more relevant and important; and correspondingly, need for parental and adult approval or blind loyalty to persons become less important motivational criteria since they are less effective in advancing primary status goals.

At the same time it is also possible for the adolescent to make greater use of the exploratory orientation in learning situations.

THEORY AND PROBLEMS OF ADOLESCENT DEVELOPMENT

This is a more task-oriented, objective, problem-solving approach to learning, in which the individual disregards considerations of status (primary or derived) enhancement in setting his level of aspiration. Instead he places more weight on such intrinsic motivations as intellectual curiosity and pays more heed to such criteria as objective evidence and logical validity in determining the acceptability of values and beliefs. The adoption of the exploratory orientation is tremendously facilitated by the opportunity to carry the examination of controversial issues to their logical conclusion without fear of endangering the derived status from parental approval. It is also favored by the adolescent's greater need for volitional independence, his greater resistance to authoritarian indoctrination, and his greater capacity for approaching specific moral problems from a more self-consistent set of general propositions (see p. 249). On the other hand, full exploitation of this learning orientation is limited by the very marginality of his status, which disposes him to conform to the norms and expectations of those agencies (peer group and school) that control the source of his status.

The satellizing orientation to learning (see p. 172) is by no means completely abandoned during adolescence. In general, however, it plays a less prominent role in the total motivational picture and is related to more socially acceptable sources of derived status than parents, that is, to teachers, youth leaders, and peer group. In some cases, deep attachments to authoritarian adult figures during adolescence may represent attempts by strong satellizers to compensate for the loss of satellizing ideological direction from parents; in other cases such attachments reduce guilt feelings from repudiation of parental values. And although the need for parental approval may cease to be an important factor in academic striving, scholastic achievement is still a significant determinant of an adolescent's character reputation and sociometric status (see p. 474).

These changes in learning orientation, with a generalized anti-adult attitude, make adolescents less disposed to accept the prestige authority of teachers in assimilating value judgments or in perceiving as meaningful and important learning tasks which impress them as trivial and pointless. They are more inclined to reject such subject matter content and to reject alien values that are forcibly imposed upon them as soon as this is expedient, that is, after passing examinations and courses.[11, 39] In general they are less resistive to activity plans and administrative regulations if they are permitted to share in their development and in the processes of decision-making.

Importance of Current Concerns

The problems of adjustment that adolescents face—emancipation from parents, somatic deviations, relationships with peers, adults, and members of the opposite sex—are very real and important to them. Their importance is magnified by the limited time perspective of adolescence, which extends situational difficulties interminably into the future. When adolescents are actually queried about the types of subject matter they would like to include in the secondary school curriculum, these practical and immediate concerns figure very prominently in their replies.[17, 28] But

> the traditional high school too often is concerned with teaching things which the student may have use for some time in the future with little attempt made to relate them to present pupil needs and interests. . . . [Hence] the curriculum is by many pupils felt to be alien to their interests and removed from their environment.[39]

Regardless of the compartmentalized approach that the school may adopt toward education, the adolescent relates the goals of academic learning to his current developmental tasks. Psychologically, these tasks are too urgent to be ignored. Hence, education must perforce be concerned with problems youth consider to be important. If young people perceive the school as uninterested in these problems, they react either by losing interest in the academic materials the school values or by feeling guilty for being preoccupied with supposedly trivial matters. If current concerns are not relieved, they inevitably serve as distractions from other constituted responsibilities.

To be related to present needs and purposes, learning tasks need not necessarily deal with problems of adolescent adjustment. Academic knowledge can have current experience value, if its acquisition becomes a goal in its own right. It is unrealistic to expect that all school subjects will have, even remotely, practical implications. The value of much of school learning can be defended only because it improves an individual's understanding of important ideas in his

culture. And if adolescents could be motivated to perceive knowledge in this light, it could conceivably constitute an important and
exciting part of their current psychological field.

Nevertheless, many academic subjects do have actual relevance for
future vocational goals. The difficulty is that these goals cannot be
given vivid representation in current reality unless success in preparatory learning activities can be perceived as organically related
to their attainment. As long as such activities constitute only formal
and arbitrary hurdles barring access to distant goals, they have no
current reference other than as stop-gap devices, as stepping stones
to future status. A course in biology, for example, can only be
made *very* relevant to the present purposes of students aspiring to
careers in the medical sciences if the relationship between medicine
and biology is made explicitly clear.

School marks can serve as immediate sources of primary status,
as indicators that progress is being made toward an ultimate vocational goal or as indices of success in mastering certain skills and
understandings. All three purposes are useful in increasing the
current relevance of school experience provided marks do not
displace the achievement they symbolize as the actual goals of academic striving. This situation inevitably develops when school learnings are not accepted as intrinsically important or as organically
related to vocational goals. Under such conditions,

> marks become ends in themselves . . . and pupils are likely to drop considera-
> tion of the area subject matter the moment they know the marks they will
> receive.[39]

Although it is fashionable to condemn the use of school marks as
an unqualified evil it seems illogical to discard potentially useful
devices merely because they are sometimes abused.

We have repeatedly emphasized that adolescents are also vitally
concerned with their future admittance into adult status as well as
with the concerns of their interim peer culture (see pp. 318 and 344).
Such concerns can be alleviated in part if some portion of school
activity can be perceived as organically related to progress toward
the goal of economic independence. The need for vocational guidance and work experience is quite apparent when we consider that
a large percentage of college graduates at the age of twenty-two
"are less prepared to earn a living and actually have less earning

capacity without further training than a commercial-school graduate." [3]

Individual Differences

Adolescents as a group display a different motivational orientation toward learning situations from that of preadolescents. In all probability, however, there are greater differences among individual adolescents than between adolescents and other age groups. Depending upon individual differences in personality development, different motivational orientations toward learning (satellizing, incorporative, exploratory) receive varying emphasis over and above the influence exerted by general developmental trends. We must reckon with individual patterns of learning orientations, which affect not only the mode of assimilating goals and values but also the motivations underlying the effort and activity of acquiring academic skills and knowledge.

Although incorporative and exploratory orientations generally become more important for adolescents, individuals who satellize as children continue in part to use the satellizing orientation in the secondary school. Non-satellizers rely chiefly on the former two learning orientations. In varying degrees all three motivational components are usually present in most individuals. Not infrequently, as a result of continued successful experience, motivations that are originally absent in a given learning activity are developed retroactively. A socially rejected adolescent may seek originally to achieve superior competence in some academic field solely for compensatory ego enhancement. Eventually, however, he may develop genuine task-oriented interests that are functionally autonomous of his original motivation.

As the difficulty of school work increases progressively, and as developmental changes in motivation occur, there may be marked shifts in the academic standings of certain individuals. A highly motivated child of only average ability finds it much more difficult to lead his class in high school and college than in elementary school. And conversely, a bright but poorly motivated child may improve his academic standing as a result of the increased developmental pressures for acquiring primary status.

The Satellizing Learning Orientation. In acquiring knowledge the motivation underlying the satellizing orientation is to gain the approval and acceptance of the person with whom the satellizing relationship is established. The assimilation of goals and values is, similarly, an expression of personal loyalty; dependent identification with another person is primary, and uncritical acceptance of his values regardless of their content is a secondary outcome. When satellizing relationships are strong, the learner is predisposed to perceive the world using the values and expectations of his preceptor since his derived status is dependent thereon. Prestige suggestion is

> accepted because of the need of the individual to agree with the person making the suggestion. In such cases, the individual first accepts the suggestion, and then the perceptual qualities of the object are changed.[34]

This perceptual set is reinforced by personal loyalty and by the need to avoid the guilt that would follow from beliefs contrary to those of the person whose prestige authority is unconditionally accepted on a satellizing basis. The object of hero worship under such conditions is not to displace the hero or to emulate his attainments, but to identify in a subservient capacity and thereby to share vicariously in his status.

When values are accepted on a satellizing basis, resistance to new learning proceeds largely from conflicting ideological trends in the new set of values, which can only be accepted at the cost of repudiating prior loyalties and assuming the associated burden of guilt. Nevertheless, this must take place for resatellization to occur.

> Learning . . . proceeds by a process of forming successive personal identifications each of which involves overcoming the resistance inherent in the necessity of repudiating a prior identification.[2]

The learner feels secure in his derived status only as long as approval is forthcoming. He finds disapproval threatening and when incurred through disloyalty productive of guilt feelings.

The Incorporative Learning Orientation. The motivation underlying the incorporative orientation toward the learning of skills and subject matter is enhancement of primary status through improving competence and achieving social recognition. Values and goal are assimilated on a comparable basis when they are perceived as contributing to the primary status of the individual.

> This learning process is strictly an act of independence requiring no subservience of self to others. . . . New values [are] incorporated, that is, taken bodily into his own value system, and regarded as his own without any implication of a [dependent] emotional bond arising between him and his preceptor. . . . The voluntary expression of dependence is inconceivable in such persons—since to them dependence is tantamount to admission of the inferiority against which all their strivings are directed.[2]

Prestige suggestion is not accepted blindly because of a need to agree with the person making the suggestion, but because the authority of the suggester is respected as relevantly influencing the outcome of the quest for primary status. The object of hero worship is to emulate and displace the hero, to use him as a guide and stepping stone to comparable achievements.

Since non-satellizers

> do not learn primarily by forming personal identifications, and, hence, in their system of values have no deep primary allegiances, the possibility of experiencing guilt by virtue of repudiating these loyalties is not present.[2]

New values are resisted because they constitute a potential threat to self-esteem by challenging (a) the existing system of values organized on an ego prestige basis and (b) various presumptions of independence, originality, infallibility and omniscience. Because the non-satellizer lacks

> sufficient confidence in the ultimate outcome of the learning process, he is naturally reluctant to undertake new learning which could end in failure, or at any rate constitute a threat to his security while still incomplete and tentative.[2]

Resistance is eventually overcome when the "possibility of future ego aggrandizement by incorporation of the new value" is perceived.[2]

Since non-satellizers are more likely to suffer from impaired self-esteem and from anxiety (see p. 211), they are more likely to feel inadequate in new learning situations, to over-respond with fear, and to avoid improvisation (see p. 292). Initial failure in new learning tasks induces disproportionate lowering of self-esteem, panic, and impairment of performance ability. Disapproval does not threaten a relationship from which vicarious status is derived or provoke feelings of guilt; it serves as an objective index of failure with attendant consequences to self-esteem. The motivation for learning is generally higher than in non-satellizers because self-esteem is dependent solely upon extrinsic considerations and is largely a function of superior accomplishment.

Implications of Learning Orientations for Teaching Practices. If different pupils have different motivational orientations toward learning, teaching practices must necessarily be directed toward pupils as individuals rather than as members of an age group. Although it is apparent that pupils must be taught in a group, some opportunity always exists for individualization of the teacher's interpersonal role.

All three learning orientations are affected by what the teacher does as a person. But for the teacher to take the personality of the learner into account, he must necessarily be subjective in handling pupils and relate himself as a person to them. This type of interpersonal relationship is more important than the formal mode of communication between pupils and teacher (lecture, discussion, group process). The appropriateness of one or another of the formal methods largely depends on the teacher's own personality.

The teacher can not ignore the fact that to learners who adopt the satellizing orientation he is

> more than an impersonal vehicle for the transmission of knowledge, [that] students . . . look to him as a sympathetic human being with whom they can identify emotionally.[3]

He must appreciate the basis of resistance to new ideas. And because of the obvious disadvantages of the student's tendency to accept ideas passively and uncritically, he should try to

> tone down the dependent aspects of satellization. . . . In the classroom this can be done by (a) objectifying discussion as much as possible, and by refusing to accept "blind" identification with the instructor's opinions; (b) by avoiding the use of praise when the student agrees with the instructor's point of view and the use of disapproval when the student's reaction is critical; (c) by avoiding the use of paternalistic teaching despite the satellizer's responsiveness to same; and (d) by refraining from making agreement with the instructor the price of the personal emotional acceptance which he so eagerly seeks.[2]

In relation to adolescents who learn more through the incorporative and exploratory orientations, "the role of the teacher should be that of a human catalyst—serving to objectify and clarify the data that are to be incorporated."[2] It is more important for the teacher to use his subjectively derived insights in minimizing the resistance that non-satellizers show to new learning materials (see p. 489). He can help do this by de-emphasizing status differences between himself and the pupil,

> by objectifying discussion as much as possible and divorcing it from all connotations of a personal struggle between wills;[11] by avoiding paternalistic teaching techniques; by bestowing as much approval as possible, and by avoiding disapproval, especially at the beginning, thereby bolstering self-esteem in the face of initial difficulties when it is apt to suffer unduly from deflation. [He] should recognize the panic which ensues upon confrontation with new situations and upon experiencing early defeat, and should allow the student to withdraw as gracefully as possible without taking advantage of this panic to drive home a point.[2]

IMPLICATIONS OF ADOLESCENT INTELLECTUAL DEVELOPMENT FOR SCHOOL PRACTICES

The Problem of Meaningfulness

Learning is not entirely a matter of personality interaction between pupil and teacher. Many objective properties of ideas and the form in which they are presented influence the meaningfulness of subject matter and the outcome of school learning.

> The process of learning may also be described *objectively* in . . . terms . . . of those inner structural and organizational changes which occur in ideas while they acquire individual meaningfulness. . . . At any given time when an individual is exposed to a new idea . . . a certain equilibrium prevails between that idea and the totality of his prevailing organization of concepts. . . . The process by which such new ideas are "imbedded"[1] in the existing structure involves the mechanisms of leveling, sharpening, and assimilation.[2]

During adolescence, developmental changes in the cognitive aspects of intellectual maturation require recognition from the school. As a result of these changes, the acquisition of meaningfulness depends more than ever on conceptual understanding, integration of knowledge, relevancy to perceived needs and active learning.

Resistance to rote learning—the parroting of memorized phrases

without any real conceptual understanding or perception of meaningful relationships—increases during adolescence. Many adolescents
continue to

> memorize [their] way through the theorems of geometry without having any
> real grasp of their meaning, or to repeat dutifully in a literature class that a
> certain writer was a romanticist, another a realist, another full of "whimsy"
> without having a clear notion of why these labels are applied.[32]

But they probably learn less, forget more, and acquire more negative
attitudes toward school as a result than they did under comparable
circumstances as children. For one thing, this mouthing of meaningless phrases is more of an affront to minds that have a greater
capacity to perceive and conceptualize symbolical relationships. For
another, there is less disposition to accept at face value the prestige
suggestion of teachers when they assert that such learnings are
necessary and important.

An important factor in generating clear and stable meanings is
achieving a proper balance between concepts and their supporting
data. Concepts that cannot be related to illustrative experience or
relevant examples soon become meaningless words. This is true of
much teaching in the social sciences. On the other hand, most high
school and college courses in mathematics and the sciences place
undue emphasis on solving problems and performing laboratory
exercises; and instructors seldom realize that students can solve
complex problems in differential calculus or molar solutions without
having the faintest notion of what calculus is about or what a
molar solution is, simply by memorizing a series of procedural steps
grouped under "type problems." Generally speaking, learning i
more meaningful when it proceeds from lower to higher degrees o
differentiation, when a student starts with a general conceptua
overview that furnishes orientation and direction and then work
"backwards" filling in details, specifics, and supporting evidence.

Because cognitive growth during adolescence results in thinkin
at a higher level of abstraction and self-consistency (see pp. 249 an
285), a more integrated and less fragmented approach to knowledg
is necessary for meaningful learning. Students are more concerne
with obtaining an interrelated view of the various subjects withi
the school curriculum and with reconciling the content of schoc

knowledge with life goals and perceptions of reality from other sources. Various kinds of "core" curricula have been devised to break down artificial subject matter boundaries and to correct the situation in which students take countless courses but succeed only

> in acquiring fragments of information, without any substantial competence in the narrow subject matter area, let alone an increase in their general understanding of things.[32]

The Role of Needs in Meaningful Learning. For meaningful learning to occur, subject matter must be related to felt needs. Inability to see any need for a subject is the reason students mention most frequently for losing interest in high school studies.[42] Doing, without being interested in what one is doing results in little learning [12]—since only that material can be meaningfully assimilated which is relevant to areas of concern and disturbance in the psychological field of the individual. It is unrealistic to expect that school subjects can be effectively learned until adolescents develop a felt need to acquire knowledge and understanding as ends in themselves "rather than simply as tools for solving emotional problems or for meeting the ulterior demands of everyday life." [32] Once such a need is developed, learning naturally becomes more meaningful; but it is difficult to stimulate the development of such needs until subject matter can be presented meaningfully in the first place.

We have already referred to the mistaken notion in some educational circles of regarding expressed needs as the only possible basis on which to organize a curriculum, as endogenously derived, and as axiomatically reflective of what is "truly best" for the individual (see p. 289). One of the primary functions of education is, in fact, to stimulate the development of potentially worthwhile needs. The choices that individuals make themselves are not invariably as appropriate or beneficial as teleological theorists would have us believe. Sometimes they are adaptive, but at other times they are destructive. The moth, for example, "self-selects" to perish in the flames. Recognition of the role of needs in learning means that teachers should try to develop needs in students for the subject matter they want to present as well as take cognizance of existing concerns. It does not mean that the curriculum should be restricted to the specific interests that happen to be present in a group of children growing up under particular conditions of intellectual and socioeconomic stimulation.

The Importance of Active Learning. Since meaningfulness is largely a *personal* phenomenon, it can be achieved only if the individual is willing to expend the active effort required to integrate new conceptual material into his unique frame of reference. This means translating and rephrasing new ideas into his own terms and relating them to his own experience, personal history, and system of values.[11]

If learning is to be active, ultimate responsibility for its accomplishment must lie with the student.[11] Students, not teachers, need to ask more of the questions and to be more concerned with formulating perceived problems than with learning answers to questions where problems are not perceived.[12] The teacher cannot learn for the student nor navigate intellectually for him. He can only present ideas as meaningfully as possible—and more from a psychological than from a logical criterion of meaningfulness. The actual job of articulating new ideas into a personal frame of reference can only be performed by the learner. It follows that ideas that are forcibly imposed upon students or passively and uncritically accepted by them cannot possibly be meaningful.

> It is far too late to start making students responsible for the direction of their education when they reach the graduate level of instruction; it should be recognized from the start that real learning [11] occurs only when there is active participation, when students have actual experience with the reality to which concepts refer instead of merely mouthing what is spoon-fed to them.[3]

The Extension of Schooling

Since intellectual growth continues longer than was previously thought—especially in the more complex mental functions (see pp. 277 and 282)—all adolescents could benefit from the extension of schooling beyond the teen years. Duller pupils could probably master many subjects that are too difficult in early adolescence several years later. However, the increasing differentiation of mental ability in late adolescence requires a corresponding diversification of subject matter if all pupils are to have optimal opportunities for further intellectual development and academic success.

The complexity of modern culture necessarily extends the period of adolescent training and indoctrination as well as the span of intellectual development. More time is needed to transmit the cultural values and the core of skills and knowledge that adolescents require to function optimally as adults in our society. But this development and training do not necessarily have to be completed before youth can win a respected place in the adult vocational world. Many young people can more profitably complete their education in the initial phases of their vocational careers. Ways of telescoping the educational preparation of youth "destined for the professions" should be considered to correct the disproportionate number of years spent in training in comparison with the actual time left for professional accomplishment.[38]

Grouping versus Individualization

The problem of effective teaching is tremendously complicated by the wide range of variabiilty in knowledge, ability, interest, motivation, and social maturity typical of high school classes. To make possible greater homogeneity of teaching methods, rate of progress, and level of difficulty appropriate for the majority of pupils in a given class, and hence greater economy and efficiency of teaching and learning efforts, homogeneous grouping of pupils has been attempted by many school systems. Apart from such issues as the stigma attached to membership in a duller group and the beneficial effect of exposing duller to brighter pupils, inherent difficulties in the grouping approach have prevented the reduction of sufficient variability to justify the effort involved.

Because any one of a large number of relevant criteria could be legitimately chosen as the basis for grouping, the selection of a single criterion fails to control variability along other dimensions and may even increase it. If, for example, adolescents were grouped on the basis of physiological or social maturity, intellectual heterogeneity would be increased. Grouping on the basis of intelligence fails to eliminate the wide range of variability in academic achievement that is found within a narrow range of IQ scores; and grouping on the basis of achievement creates the same difficulty with respect to intelligence, and should, besides, be done separately for each subject matter field. In addition, neither of these two methods reduces the heterogeneity caused by differences in social maturity, intellectual curiosity, and other variables relevant to learning and peer relationships in the classroom.

But even if homogeneous grouping were feasible in the more identifiable and measurable of these variables, there is such wide variability in personality, experience, life goals, and motivational orientation to learning that the teacher would still have to treat pupils as individuals. Thus

> it is wiser to attempt a progressive adaptation of tuition to individual differences (and to encourage children by individualized activities to proceed as swiftly as they can) than it is to spend time first upon classifying according to ability and then upon mass teaching of supposedly homogeneous groups.[21]

Individualization of instruction also has an advantage over grouping practices that include demotion and acceleration of students (a) in keeping pupils together with their chronological age mates and (b) in preventing the social dislocation and sense of failure in school that inevitably follow from the repetition of grades.[39] The achievement of this goal

> requires more than increasing the number of teachers. It means finding teachers who are inspired with the ideal of imparting learning factors for growth, who regard teaching as a challenging assignment in personality development rather than as the fulfillment of a chore by means of which they earn their bread.[3]

SOCIAL STRATIFICATION IN THE SCHOOL

The American secondary school quite naturally reflects the existing social stratification in the culture and in the adolescent peer group. It also reflects differential social class attitudes toward the school and motivations for academic success. Just as important is the fact that the school contributes to this stratification and helps perpetuate it by the type of curriculum it offers, the kinds of demands it makes on boys and girls, and by the differential treatment it accords pupils from different socioeconomic backgrounds.

Middle-Class Domination of the High School Peer Group

The increasing degree of social class stratification of adolescent group formations (see p. 347) is faithfully mirrored in the organization of the high school peer group. The moral values of this group are predominantly based upon middle-class norms and standards, chief of which is acceptance of the importance of high academic achievement. Adolescents who accept and achieve this goal enjoy good character reputations regardless of their social class membership.[26] Middle-class adolescents participate more in extra-curricular activities [40] and occupy the choice elective and activity positions.[26, 27] More important, perhaps, are the subtle and intangible barriers to participation in the more intimate crowds and cliques. As pointed out, there is little crossing of class lines in clique organization (see p. 351). Boys and girls from lower social class strata bitterly resent the patronizing and condescending attitudes of their more fortunate contemporaries. They feel snubbed, unwanted, and left out of things.[26, 27] When this situation becomes too intolerable it undoubtedly influences their decision to drop out of school.[26, 27, 33]

Favoritism by Teachers

Since most teachers have middle-class backgrounds, they find it difficult to understand the goals, values, and behavior of pupils from other social class backgrounds. Normal ethnocentric bias predisposes them to believe that their own class values are self-evidently true and proper and that deviations therefrom necessarily reflect waywardness. On the other hand, since middle-class boys and girls behave in accordance with their expectations and accept and enforce the standards of the school, teachers are usually as prejudiced in their favor as they are prejudiced against children from other social strata.

In addition to these natural inclinations to reward conformity to middle-class ideology, teachers are influenced by other pressures, both explicit and implicit, in giving preferential treatment to pupils whose families enjoy higher social status. Middle- and upper-class parents are active in civic and school affairs, members of school boards, and leaders in parent-teacher asociations. Even if no explicit pressures are exerted, teachers and school administrators, knowing on what side their bread is buttered, are disposed to see things their way. Teachers are also intimidated somewhat from taking action against refractory but popular members of leading cliques, who when supported by their clique mates may be surprisingly rebellious.[27] Under such circumstances many teachers are reluctant to force a showdown that will incite the enmity of pupils who are influential in their own right as well as through the position of their parents.

Differential Social Class Motivation in the School Setting

As already pointed out, members of the middle-class are "great believers in education" and in the possibility of attaining superior vocational status and furthering social mobility through education. This attitude is transmitted to their children and is sustained and enforced by peer group sanctions and by appropriate levels of transitional anxiety. It also seems plausible that motivations and attitudes such as these selectively influence the differentiation of general intelligence along verbal lines (see p. 281) and effect greater actualization of genetically determined endowment in verbal intelligence (see p. 288). In large part they determine the middle-class pupil's greater tendency to perceive the teacher as a "necessary evil" and a "stepping stone" rather than as a friend.[14]

In the light of these motivations and of the actual probabilities of entering college and acquiring professional status, passing courses and achieving good grades are real rewards with current as well as stepping stone status value. To lower-class adolescents, on the other hand, who place no great value on education and who gradually learn that professional status is beyond their grasp, these rewards are unreal and valueless.[15] Why bother to remain in school and learn meaningless lessons?

"Drop-Outs" as a Function of Social Class Status

Viewed from the standpoint of the foregoing data, it is no wonder that there is practically a linear relationship between social class status and survival in school.* To begin with, it costs money to attend school (lunches, transportation, clothes, laboratory and activity fees) and to keep up with the adolescent crowd in appropriate clothes and amusements.[16, 33] Second, youth from lower-class homes are more urgently required to contribute to the family

---

* Only one child out of thirteen among professional and technical workers fails to go beyond the eighth grade. Among skilled workers the comparable ratio is one out of three, and among unskilled workers it is two out of three.[7]

income.[16, 33] No less important are the reasons alluded to above—discriminatory attitudes of teachers and peers, lack of social class tradition recognizing the importance and desirability of education, and the absence of real rewards, current or future, for studying hard and conforming to middle-class standards. Low verbal intelligence to the extent that it is correlated with low socioeconomic status is also a minor contributing factor.

THE ADOLESCENT'S EVALUATION OF THE SCHOOL

From first grade through high school the child experiences an increasing degree of dissatisfaction with his school environment. The evidence unfortunately points to a gradual deterioration of his school morale as he climbs the educational ladder.[31] The first-grader is usually enthusiastic about school, about his teacher, and about academic achievement. With increasing age, however, his enthusiasm wanes and gives way to boredom, indifference, and complaint. School becomes a chore and a burden, fortunately punctuated by recess, sports, and holidays [31]—something to be endured rather than relished. When an adolescent refers to a high school "activity" he generally means an extra-curricular activity, not a school subject. In the spontaneous conversation of adolescents one hears little mention of the academic pursuits that fill the greater part of their working day (see p. 342).

When adolescents survey the high school curriculum, they express greater interest in courses of study related to current personal concerns and problems of adjustment than in the traditional academic subject matter.[17, 28] A particular lack of interest is expressed in social studies.[31] And in accounting for their loss of interest in high school subjects, students emphasize such factors as inadequacy of teaching methods, dissatisfaction with teachers, and inappropriateness of content and difficulty level of subject matter.[42]

These very same reasons are prominent in the explanations that pupils give for dropping out of school.[16, 33] Thus, although most adolescents today enter high school, only slightly more than half are graduated.[8] Economic and social class factors are related to survival in high school, but they tell only part of the story. Low intelligence, inferior school achievement, and poor academic aptitude leading to school failure account for an additional part of the mortality.[16, 39] The rest can be attributed to the fact that many adolescents are disinterested in what the school has to offer them and are disgruntled because the school refuses to provide help with problems that disturb and concern them.

> In countries in which free participation in continued schooling is encouraged, the age of leaving school has been shown to be more directly related to school experiences of success than to the occupation of the parents, to socio-economic level, or to initial performance [in] an entrance examination.[21]

What Can Be Done?

The reactions of adolescents to the secondary school curriculum hardly present an encouraging picture of the current educational scene. Yet they could scarcely be much different if we consider to what extent the implications of adolescent development for educational practice have been ignored. Nevertheless they do not in the least imply

> that secondary education should abandon the more strictly intellectual and cultural areas. To do so would be a denial of the adolescent's continuing capacity for intellectual growth, his ability . . . to expand his intellectual horizons, to find new outlets for his curiosity, to add to his general information.[32]

Since interest in ideas can with suitable stimulation be developed at all levels of intellectual ability,

> it is not necessary to suppose that there are groups whose potentialities are so one-sided that they must be left to the quite illiterate repetition of relatively simple mechanical manipulations.[21]

At least four major kinds of changes will have to be effected in the management of the secondary school before the goal of transmitting the ideas and ideology of our culture can ever be realized.

1. More use will have to be made of a psychological approach to cognitive learning that is developmentally appropriate for adolescents. In essence this involves the methodology of maximizing meaningfulness—developing felt needs for acquiring knowledge in various subject matter areas, emphasizing conceptual understanding as against rote memorization, increasing the interrelatedness of school subjects, and requiring adolescents to adopt a more active role in the learning process. In addition to making the acquisition of knowledge an end in itself, school can be given more current experi-

ence value by making more explicit whatever relevance courses of study have for future vocational goals.

2. Subjective and interpersonal factors in the learning process require greater recognition. Teachers cannot ignore individual differences in motivational orientation to learning. A more democratic social climate in the classroom is necessary to reduce resistance to learning, to foster more active and creative learning, and to help adolescents acquire greater volitional independence in dealing with adults.

3. Current problems of adjustment and future vocational concerns cannot be ignored without instigating negative attitudes toward school and creating distractions from academic pursuits. These problems are related in an important way to the outcome of personality maturation for which the school as a training institution has an undeniable responsibility.

4. Since the secondary school no longer caters to a highly selected social class group, it must be made more attractive to adolescents from all social class backgrounds. This means ending middle-class domination of the high school peer culture, eliminating discriminatory practices by teachers and pupils, and making the academic rewards the school has to offer more real to lower-class adolescents by increasing the accessibility of college education and professional status to families of limited means.

REFERENCES AND BIBLIOGRAPHY

1. Allport, G. W. and Postman, L. J.: The basic psychology of rumor. Trans. N. Y. Acad. Sci., Series II, 8:61–81, 1945.
2. Ausubel, D. P.: Ego development and the learning process. Child Develpm., 20:173–190, 1949.
3. Ausubel, D. P.: Problems of adolescent adjustment. Bulletin, Natl. Assn. Secondary School Principals, 34:1–84, 1950.
4. Ausubel, D. P.: Prestige Motivation of Gifted Children. Genet. Psychol. Monogr., 43:53–117, 1951.
5. Ausubel, D. P., Schiff, H. M., and Gasser, E. B.: A preliminary study of developmental trends in sociempathy: Accuracy of perception of own and others' sociometric status. Child. Develpm., 23:111–128, 1952.
6. Baker, H. L.: High-school teachers' knowledge of their pupils. Sch. Rev., 46:175–190, 1938.
7. Bell, H. M.: Youth Tell Their Story. Washington, D. C.: American Council on Education, 1938.

8. *Biennial Survey of Education in the United States, 1946–48.* Washington, D. C.: Government Printing Office.

9. Blos, P.: *The Adolescent Personality.* New York: Appleton-Century, 1941.

10. Bonney, M. E.: Sociometric study of agreement between teacher judgments and student choices. Sociometry, *10:*133–146, 1947.

11. Cantor, N.: *The Dynamics of Learning.* Buffalo: Foster and Stewart, 1946.

12. Cantor, N.: *The Teaching-Learning Process: A Study in Interpersonal Relations.* New York: Dryden, 1953.

13. Corey, S. M. and Beary, G. S.: The effect of teacher popularity upon attitudes toward school subjects. J. Educ. Psychol., *29:*665–670, 1938.

14. Cunningham, R. et al.: *Understanding Group Behavior of Boys and Girls.* New York: Teachers College, Columbia University, 1951.

15. Davis, A.: American status systems and the socialization of the child. Amer. Sociol. Rev., *6:*345–354, 1941.

16. Dillon, H. J.: *Early School Leavers.* New York: National Child Labor Committee, 1949.

17. Doane, D. C.: *The Needs of Youth: An Evaluation for Curriculum Purposes.* New York: Teachers College, Columbia University, 1942.

18. Edwards, N.: "The Adolescent in Technological Society," in *Adolescence,* 43rd Yearbook, Natl. Soc. Stud. Educ., Part I. Chicago: University of Chicago Press, 1944.

19. Fehlman, C.: *Parents and Teachers View the Child.* New York: Teachers College, Columbia University, 1949.

20. Finch, F. H.: *Enrollment Increases and Changes in the Mental Level of the High-School Population.* Appl. Psychol. Monogr. No. 10, 1946.

21. Fleming, C. M.: *Adolescence: Its Social Psychology.* New York: International Universities Press, 1949.

22. Frank, L. K.: Dilemma of leadership. Psychiatry, *2:*343–361, 1939.

23. Gronlund, N. E.: The accuracy of teachers' judgments concerning the sociometric status of sixth-grade pupils. Sociometry, *13:*197–225, 329–357, 1950.

24. Hart, F. W.: *Teachers and Teaching.* New York: Macmillan, 1934.

25. Havighurst, R. J., Robinson, M. Z., and Dorr, M.: The development of the ideal self in childhood and adolescence. J. Educ. Res., *40:*241–257, 1946.

26. Havighurst, R. J. and Taba, H.: *Adolescent Character and Personality.* New York: Wiley, 1949.

27. Hollingshead, A. B.: *Elmtown's Youth.* New York: Wiley, 1949.

28. Hopkins, L. T.: Seniors survey the high school. Teachers Col. Rec., *42:*116–122, 1940.

29. Hurlock, E. B.: *Value of Praise and Reproof as Incentives for Children.* New York: Archives of Psychology (Columbia University), 1925.

30. Hurlock, E. B.: The use of group rivalry as an incentive. J. Abnorm. Soc. Psychol., *22:*278–290, 1927.

31. Jersild, A. T. and Tasch, R. J.: *Children's Interests and What They Suggest for Education.* New York: Teachers College, Columbia University, 1949.

32. Jersild, A. T. et al.: *Child Development and the Curriculum.* New York: Teachers College, Columbia University, 1946.

33. Johnson, E. S. and Legg, C. E.: Why young people leave school. Bulletin, Natl. Assn. Secondary School Principals, *28*:3–28, 1944.
34. Krech, D. and Crutchfield, R. S.: *Theory and Problems of Social Psychology.* New York: McGraw-Hill, 1948.
35. Lippitt, R.: An Experimental Study of the Effect of Democratic and Authoritarian Group Atmospheres. Univ. Iowa Stud. Child Welfare, XVI, No. 3. Iowa City: University of Iowa Press, 1940.
36. Mackenzie, G. N.: "Implications for Teachers and Counselors," in *Adolescence,* 43rd Yearbook, Natl. Soc. Stud. Educ., Part I. Chicago: University of Chicago Press, 1944.
37. Moreno, J. L.: *Who Shall Survive?* Washington, D. C.: Nervous and Mental Disease Publishing Co., 1934.
38. Segel, D.: *Intellectual Abilities in the Adolescent Period.* Washington, D. C.: Federal Security Agency, 1948.
39. Segel, D.: *Frustration in Adolescent Youth.* Washington, D. C.: Federal Security Agency, 1951.
40. Smith, H. P.: A study in the selective character of American secondary education: Participation in school activities as conditioned by socio-economic status and other factors. J. Educ. Psychol., *36*:229–246, 1945.
41. Warner, W. L., Havighrust, R. J., and Loeb, M. B.: *Who Shall Be Educated?* New York: Harper, 1944.
42. Young, F. M.: Causes for loss of interest in high-school subjects as reported by 631 college students. J. Educ. Res., *25*:110–115, 1932.

PART FOUR

Maladjustment and
Mental Hygiene

Behavior Disorders and Delinquency in Adolescence

THE EVALUATION OF BEHAVIOR DISORDER IN ADOLESCENCE

BEHAVIOR DISTURBANCES in adolescence are exceedingly common and often appear extreme in nature, serious, and alarming. On the other hand, in evaluating the seriousness of behavioral deviations during adolescence we cannot apply the same yardstick that we would use at other stages of the life span. If the adjustments that adolescents achieve seem extreme and bizarre by adult standards, we should not forget that the developmental pressures to which they are subjected in our culture can hardly be regarded as mild or ordinary.[8] As Blos [8] points out, even relatively severe deviations from acceptable behavioral standards are not necessarily ominous in their prognostic implications. Adolescent behavior can only be meaningfully appraised in terms of adolescent norms.

The chief problem in diagnosing the behavior disorders of adolescence is deciding whether the "abnormal" behavior of a particular adolescent is merely an exaggerated expression of the self-limited emotional instability characteristic of a transitional phase of development, or whether it is reflective of a more fundamental personality defect rooted in childhood experience. Before such a decision can be reached, careful and thorough appraisal of an individual's complete developmental history is necessary. The observer who merely pays attention to the grossness of overt manifestations (symptoms) will almost certainly be misled. It is reassuring to appreciate at the outset that the greater part

of the so-called problems of adolescents have to do with normal reactions or normal phases through which the adolescent passes in his journey toward adulthood.[14]

No other conclusion is possible "because certainly ninety per cent of adolescents do get through this stage of development without any serious emotional scars." [14]

The Role of Emotional Instability

We have already considered emotional instability as a generalized state of altered behavioral reactivity characterized by a well-defined syndrome of response tendencies and subjective reactions (see p. 145). This condition, which can be induced in animals and man by a large variety of physiological and psychological stimuli, is typical of adolescent adjustment because of the many psychobiological and psychosocial determinants of stress that are operative during this period of growth (see p. 146). That adolescent development should be stressful and productive of emotional instability is a logical deduction that could defensibly be reached merely from consideration of the numerous and difficult developmental tasks and problems of adolescence presented in the preceding chapters. This logical impression, however, is also confirmed by observations of research and clinical workers,* by results from projective tests and other indirect measures, and by some studies using adjustment inventories.†

Many of the more nonspecific characteristics of adolescent emotional instability merely reflect a lowered threshold of behavioral reactivity, a tendency to respond intensely, diffusely, and in an undirected and unadaptive fashion to stimuli that would otherwise be too weak or too general to provoke any response whatever. Much of the exaggerated, flighty, labile, irritable, and apparently random behavior of adolescents belongs in this category. On the other hand, part of it can certainly be attributed to the undifferentiated state of their new biosocial status. Before habitual techniques of adjustment to new problems are evolved, before canalized modes of satisfying new needs are established, and before the requirements of new roles are learned, behavior must necessarily be fluid, exploratory, and experimental. [8]

Whenever emotional instability is induced in part or in whole by frustration of goal-directed behavior, by deprivation of need or

---

* See the summary of findings given in pages 146–147 and also reference 23.

† See reference 29 and conflicting evidence summarized on p. 147.

status, or by threat to physical integrity, the lowered threshold of behavioral reactivity is invariably accompanied by such subjective responses as rage, insecurity, inadequacy, and anxiety. These emotionally charged feelings occur in response to the threat to self-esteem, security, and ability to cope with the environment that is inherent in such situations. They provide additional incentive to the individual to remove or overcome the threat confronting him since they are uncomfortable, tension producing affects; and the lowered threshold of behavioral reactivity facilitates the setting up of various adjustive mechanisms, the most direct and immediate of which is aggression. But because direct aggression is not very adjustive—since fear of retaliation and guilt feelings generate fresh threat —it is generally displaced by more devious, compensatory, or escape adjustive mechanisms (see pp. 325–326).

If feelings of inadequacy or anxiety become overwhelming (panic), disruptive behavior such as blocking or paralysis of activity, agitation, perseveration of unadaptive responses, apathy, or depression may occur, interfering with work and school responsibilities and interpersonal relations. Such reactions, which are in no sense adjustive, are too severe to be attributed to the transitional pressures of adolescence alone and are generally referable to neurotic anxiety rooted in a non-satellizing history of personality development (see pp. 208–214).

The majority of behavior disorders during adolescence, therefore, are merely exaggerated manifestations of different aspects of the syndrome of emotional instability. They can be related to instances in which greater than ordinary developmental pressures that are situational in nature are operative over a period of years. In such cases a history of maladjustment is not usually present, either before or subsequent to adolescence. Improvement occurs over the course of adolescence as boys and girls become reconciled to an extended period of sub-adulthood, evolve anxiety reducing adjustive mechanisms, and create compensatory interim status for themselves. Because of more severe conflicts associated with emancipation from parental domination and with acquisition of social sex role, girls consistently show evidence of greater emotional instability than boys (see p. 227). Last, the intensity, the course, the sources, and the manifestations of emotional instability vary in accordance with social class membership (see p. 331). Thus, before deciding whether any individual's behavior is normal or abnormal, it must first be related to his *social reality* . . . Failure to take such considerations into account and generalizing on the basis of clinical experience derived mainly from upper- and middle-class sources have resulted in some of the original misconceptions of psychoanalysis, particularly those relating to psychosexual development and to sexual repression.[2]

The Importance of Childhood Experience

One can only feel relatively sure that adolescent behavior disorder reflects transitory emotional instability instigated by developmental pressures, provided there is no childhood history of personality defect or maladjustment. If, on the other hand, behavior disorder or the predisposing conditions existed in childhood, the difficulties of adolescence can be blamed only for exacerbating not for generating the pathological trends a particular adolescent manifests.

Investigation of persistently serious or lasting behavior pathology in adolescents (neurosis, psychosis, delinquency) shows that the origin of such disorder is almost invariably conditioned by constitutional or developmental factors in the home before the onset of adolescence.[42, 50, 51] Wittman and Huffman [51] in comparing the developmental, adjustment, and personality characteristics of psychotic, psychoneurotic, delinquent, and normal adolescents, found that the parent-child relationship was of crucial significance in determining the particular type of adolescent behavior disturbance that resulted. Schizophrenic youths were extremely introverted and gave evidence of poor disciplinary, social, and emotional adjustment during childhood.

> Psychotic patients [rated] their mothers as definitely below average in emotional stability, and definitely over-solicitous and over-protective. They [described] themselves on the average as dependent and with very strong emotional relationships [to] their mothers.[51]

Our analysis of personality development in Chapter 7 supports the same conclusion about the childhood origin of serious behavior disorder. The personality defects of *non-satellizers* (see pp. 208–214) —lack of intrinsic self-esteem, susceptibility to neurotic anxiety and its complications, difficulties in peer group socialization, vulnerability of moral obligations in the face of ego enhancement needs —are all products of parent attitudes of rejection or extrinsic valuation that are especially damaging in the preschool years. Similarly, the maturational deficiencies to which satellizers are predisposed as a consequence of exposure to overprotective, underdominating and overdominating parent attitudes, begin in middle childhood and preadolescence, when these attitudes interfere with the implementation of maturational tasks such as acquiring independent sources of status, frustration tolerance, self-critical ability, capacity for postponing hedonistic gratification (see pp. 239–241). Even "reactive" maturational failure in non-satellizers is generally attributable to a change in parent attitude that occurs before adolescence (see pp. 241–243). And when the development of behavior disorder is conditioned by such potent constitutional factors as extreme introversion or hedonistic needs that interfere with socialization and reality adjustment, on the one hand, and adult maturation on the other, there is evidence of their detrimental operation quite early in an individual's developmental history.

The Role of Adolescence

The incidence of behavior disorder and delinquency increases markedly during adolescence. Mental hospital admissions in the second half of the second decade of life show a ten-fold increase over the first decade,[33] and there is a corresponding increase in the frequency of delinquency,[46] "nervous breakdowns," suicidal attempts, alcoholism, and drug addiction.[12] But except for delinquency, and notwithstanding the fact that these rates would undoubtedly be much higher were there less stigma attached to the occurrence of mental disease, the incidence of serious behavior disorder requiring institutionalization is relatively low in comparison with subsequent decades of life.[33] It would seem, therefore, that adolescence serves mostly as a rigorous testing and proving ground of the adequacy of personality structure laid down in the childhood years. Existing defects are more glaring, but in most instances are not basic enough to lead to more than transitory disturbances. Even when personality defects are more basic, adolescent experience acts mostly as an aggravating condition. The actual terminal point for the appearance of most serious personality disorder is after, rather than during adolescence.

The combination of psychobiological and psychosocial sources of emotional instability makes adolescence a difficult period of adjustment even for individuals with very normal personalities. The satellizer in addition has to "learn a new, independent way of life," and must contend with guilt feelings from the repudiation of primary loyalties to parents.

> His needs for primary status are not adequately met, thereby depressing his extrinsic self-esteem. . . . But unlike the non-satellizer he has a basic fund of intrinsic adequacy to fall back upon. The anxiety he experiences is transitional in nature and referable to environmental stress.[3]

The very same deprivations are much more threatening to the non-satellizer, who, possessing no intrinsic adequacy, reacts with more anxiety and sometimes with catastrophic impairment of self-esteem.

> His ego adequacy is wholly a creature of the environmental vicissitudes which deny or gratify the hypertophied ego demands on which he has staked his value as a human being.[3]

For prognostic purposes, therefore, it is important to differentiate ordinary transitional anxiety in adolescence from the actual or latent neurotic anxiety of non-satellizers (see pp. 209–213).

If non-satellizers are more subject than satellizers to neurotic anxiety during adolescence, satellizers are more strongly predisposed to undergo maturational failure. Since they are required to effect a greater total change in personality structure and "are less motivated by the need for extrinsic status" to do so, maturation is more drastically retarded by such unfavorable parent attitudes as overprotection and underdomination. As a result of maturational failure, adolescents fail to acquire the goal structure of adults. They do not aspire to primary status, to long-range goals, to volitional and executive independence. They lack adequate frustration tolerance, self-critical ability, and feelings of responsibility. Their adjustment to an adult world of reality is not very successful. Extreme introverts find it possible under such conditions to withdraw from social reality and find gratification of hedonistic needs in fantasy. More extroverted individuals try to satisfy childish, pleasure-seeking goals in reality, and at the same time hide their failure as adults from themselves by developing an adjustive impairment of the self-critical faculty. From the ranks of such persons "are recruited vagrants, hobos, drug addicts . . . pool-room-hangers-on . . . confidence men, etc." [3] Narcotic addiction is especially adjustive since it both gives rise to effortless and voluptuous sensations of pleasure and inhibits the self-critical faculty

> to the point where the addict becomes easily contented with his inadequate hedonistic adjustment to life, and is more easily able to evade and overlook responsibilities; and where in the complete absence of any actual accomplishment he feels supremely satisfied with himself and his future.[1]

How then can we summarize the role of adolescent experience in relation to the behavior disorders of adolescence? Developmental pressures increase emotional instability leading to transitory behavioral disturbances in many adolescents who have quite normal personalities. But in the absence of intrinsic self-esteem, these same pressures may instigate neurotic anxiety and its complications; and because of increased social expectations of mature motivational behavior, maturational defects also become more glaring in adolescence, sometimes resulting in such extreme consequences as schizophrenia, drug addiction, and vagrancy. More commonly, however, the stressfulness of adolescence merely compounds existing predispositions to these disorders by exposing serious defects in personality structure. These defects make adjustment to adult social reality seem either difficult and unlikely because of inadequate goal structure or unduly threatening to self-esteem because of lack of intrinsic adequacy. The actual onset of serious behavior disorder necessitating institutionalization is more usually postponed until adulthood. In either case the basic personality defects that are the primary etiological factors are essentially products of unfavorable childhood experience.

The Meaning of Frustration

Frustration is the common psychological denominator underlying the conditions that instigate emotional instability, precipitate more serious behavior disorder, and induce various adjustive mechanisms. Frequently, it is not appreciated that by definition frustration is purely a subjective phenomenon, not coextensive with the objective barriers or deprivations that most commonly bring it about. To be sure, magnitude of deprivation is not unrelated to the seriousness of the frustration that results. Everything else being equal, the longer and more completely adolescents are deprived of adult status, acceptance in the peer group, gratification of sex needs, success in school, the more frustrated they are apt to become. But to ascertain how much actual frustration this situation produces in a given adolescent, several subjectively oriented questions must first be asked.

(1) To begin with, how ego-involved is the adolescent in the particular goal, achievement of which has ostensibly been frustrated? We have already seen that ego-involvement is a highly selective process and that success and failure occur only in areas in which there is ego-involvement. (2) How high is the adolescent's level of aspiration and how resistive to lowering in the face of initial failure? If aspirational levels are not high or if they can be realistically adjusted to correspond to the difficulty of a task, the degree of frustration is not nearly as severe as when the reverse is true. (3) To what extent are goals overlapping, conflicting, or mutually exclusive? Low achievement could conceivably be quite gratifying when success would preclude achievement of other more desirable goals, and vice versa. When conflicting goals are equally desirable, indecision could easily result in frustration of both goals, whereas choice of one goal would inevitably generate frustration of the other. (4) What resources does the adolescent have for coping with the problem? Whether or not a situation of given difficulty will result in frustration obviously depends on the availability of appropriate skills and resources. Depending on the nature of the problem, such factors as high or low levels of intelligence, health, energy, physical or social skills, and the availability of counseling assistance or financial backing may be very important in determining whether deprivation occurs and if it does occur how effectively it can be overcome or compensated for. (5) How much self-critical ability does the adolescent have? To experience failure, he must be able to perceive the shortcomings and inadequacies of his performance. As already noted, adjustive impairment of self-critical ability frequently occurs in immature and inadequate persons. (6) Finally how much frustration tolerance does he possess? More important than whether frustration does or does not occur is the impact it has on behavior, which in turn is a function of various aspects of degree of tolerance to frustration. Operationally, this refers to how much frustration an individual can withstand without manifesting undue anxiety, loss of self-estem, or unadaptive rage, without showing disorganization and impairment of performance or self-critical ability, without abandoning realistic goals, and without resorting to distortive adjustive techniques.

Answers to these questions will be determined by differential factors of constitution, personality development, and resources available for adaptation.

In interpreting the meaning of frustration, it is necessary also to discount the widespread teleological notion that all behavior is motivated, goal directed, or adjustive in function. Frustration does not necessarily induce adjustive behavior. Most of the subjective responses accompanying frustration (feelings of inadequacy, anxiety, insecurity) as well as many of the behavioral consequences of the lowered threshold of reactivity (flightiness, irritability, emotional lability) are merely manifestations of apprehensive awareness of threat or of negative self-reactions, occasioned by such awareness, that have no adjustive value whatever. Furthermore, when these subjective responses become extreme, as in states of panic, behavior becomes disorganized and is characterized by blocking, blind aggression, rigidity, compulsiveness, unadaptive perseveration, and aimless agitation. Contrary to Maier's [31] hypothesis, however, such reactions to frustration are not necessarily typical; they are only precipitated by catastrophic or unusually threatening stiuations. Under more ordinary circumstances, frustration gives rise to adjustive behavior in addition to milder nonadjustive responses indicating awareness of threat. The adjustive behavior may or may not be adaptive or constructive. Oftentimes, in fact, it leads to serious distortions of personality.

A CLASSIFICATION OF ADOLESCENT BEHAVIOR DISORDERS

The foregoing considerations lead to the following three-fold classification of behavior disorders during adolescence. (1) In the first group are disturbances, essentially unrelated to the tasks of adolescent development that are merely residual from the childhood era. They consist of

> maladjustments which primarily represent a continuation of difficulties arising from failure to solve some of the the developmental tasks of childhood . . . which adolescence only aggravates further.[2]

These include the anxiety and delinquency disorders of non-satellizers and the disturbances in peer group socialization attributable to unfavorable parent attitudes and constitutional factors.

(2) In the second group are disturbances that are more specifically relevant to the maturational tasks and adjustment problems of adolescence per se. It is convenient to divide this group into two separate categories: (a) transitory behavior disorders reflecting increased emotional instability and (b) serious maturational failure largely conditioned by undesirable child rearing practices. Typical of the transitory disorders are the exaggerated adjustive responses to status deprivation catalogued in Chapter 11 (see pp. 324–326), sporadic delinquency, "experimental" drug addiction (see p. 517), and occasional repudiation of the goals of maturation. Maturational failure, on the other hand, refers to the more permanent and serious disorders of personality maturation,* which predispose the affected individual to schizophrenia, "adjustive" drug addiction, and vagrancy.

Both the "residual" and the "maturational failure" disorders, in contrast to the "transitory" group, are rooted in childhood experience, are resistive to treatment, do not materially improve with the termination of adolescence, and have an unfavorable or guarded prognosis. Further discussion of the "residual" disorders of childhood is beyond the scope of this volume and can be properly found in textbooks of psychopathology. It should be mentioned, however, that overt pathological manifestations cannot always be found when childhood developmental history is reviewed.

> Since adolescence is such a rigorous test of the soundness of the foundations of personality laid in childhood, many earlier disturbances scarcely noted before, or thought to be benign, may suddenly flare up and become alarming during adolescence. . . . Once removed from the protected environment of the home and required to compete on an equal footing with other boys and girls, once subjected to the multifarious stresses and strains associated with adolescent adjustment in our society, once mercilessly exposed under the dissection microscope of the peer society in its efforts to make him conform as closely to every other adolescent as one new penny to another, it is inconceivable that any boy or girl who has a basic personality defect [could] continue successfully to mask its presence.[2]

Problems of differential diagnosis between the transitory and the two more serious categories of adolescent behavior disorder have already been discussed in relation to parent-youth conflict (see pp.

---

* See the discussion of "developmental" and "reactive" maturational failure, pp. 239–243.

233–235) and maturational disturbances (see pp. 238–239). Failure to differentiate between transitory and serious behavior disorders leads to much unnecessary pessimism in evaluating the adjustment status of youth. In 1951, for example, an outbreak of narcotic drug addiction among teen-agers led to unfounded fears that a large percentage of adolescents once initiated into this practice would remain life-long victims because of a "physiological dependence" on the drug. Totally ignored in all of this speculation was the fact that only adolescents who fail to undergo normal maturation are in any danger of becoming permanent addicts, since only for such persons do the opiates have lasting adjustive value and that it is this psychological adjustive value of opiates rather than "physiological dependence" that is the essential cause of addiction. Most adolescents who sample drugs do so out of reckless bravado or because of exposure to addicts and dope peddlers in slum areas of large cities. When

> the rebellious, venturesome, "try anything" adolescent boy who otherwise has a normal personality structure . . . tries drugs, he finds that they have little adjustive value for him because he is really concerned with mature achievement in a real world.[4]

For him it is sufficient that by having "his fling . . . he has served his purpose of asserting himself and defying adult authority." [4] The main reasons for the teen-age epidemic of drug addiction in 1951 were (a) an intensification of normal adolescent thrill-seeking by the fatalism associated with prolonged international crisis and (b) an increase in the supply of illicit narcotic drugs coupled with a decline in the number of confirmed drug addicts.[4]

DELINQUENCY IN ADOLESCENCE

Incidence

Criminal behavior is "characteristically a youthful occupation." [11] The incidence of delinquency rises slowly during the first half of the second decade, then climbs precipitously until age 19.[46] During the early twenties, the rate of delinquency continues to increase, but less steeply, reaches a peak before age twenty-five, and declines rapidly thereafter.

Why does delinquency differ from other serious behavior disorders, which do not typically reach their peak incidence until later in life? One suggestion is that aggression is the most direct and primitive response made to frustration and is displaced as more efficacious and need-satisfying adjustive techniques are learned with increasing age.[11] This phenomenon is especially evident in disorganized urban areas where, in addition, conditions favor the temporary alienation of the moral values of adolescents from those of conventional society (see p. 381). Another factor apparently inheres in the delayed or retarded personality maturation of certain individuals who, for this reason, reach at a more advanced age the same degree of moral development that most other persons attain in adolescence. Delinquency in satellizers attributable to overdominating, underdominating, and overprotecting parent attitudes frequently follows this pattern.

To view the problem of adolescent delinquency in perspective, we must realize that only a small percentage (perhaps ten per cent) of all adolescents ever become legally delinquent. This is true even though the vast majority of college males retrospectively admit to sporadic offenses against the law.[40] Actually, very few delinquent acts result in apprehension, formal arrest, and prosecution, especially when the offender enjoys high socioeconomic status or lives on the right side of the tracks. In addition, many moral crimes and forms of anti-social behavior violate no existing statute. In interpreting statistics on delinquency, we have to bear in mind that the term refers only to *habitual* unlawful activity that is apprehended and results in judicial action.* It should be clear, therefore, that official incidence rates are always *minimal* estimates of the actual prevalence of delinquency during adolescence.

Compared to Preadolescence. The probability of delinquency during adolescence is very much greater if there is a childhood history of anti-social behavior.[7, 15, 22] In fact, approximately two-thirds of adolescent delinquents begin their delinquent careers in preadolescence.[15, 22] Nevertheless, in addition to implicating a larger number

---

* The distinction between delinquency and crime rests solely on the age of the offender which determines whether he comes under the jurisdiction of a juvenile court. The age jurisdiction of such courts varies considerably from one state to another.

of individuals, the adolescent period is characteristically associated with a more regular, serious, and organized kind of delinquency. One obvious explanation for this difference is the fact that

> in adolescence the child often strikes back for the first time just because he is now strong enough or well enough integrated against a problem that has actually been quite as pressing for a number of years.[39]

Greater freedom of movement and less adult supervision during adolescence also make it more possible to implement delinquent behavior.

More important perhaps than greater opportunity and capacity for executing delinquent acts are the transitional pressures, the anti-adult and aggressive attitudes, and the peer group sanctions that exist during adolescence. Prolonged status deprivation super-imposed upon many other psychosocial and psychobiological problems increases emotional instability and lowers the threshold for aggressive response against the perceived frustrating agents or their symbolical equivalents. This reaction is bolstered by supportive peer group attitudes and sanctions.

Pubescence per se exerts no direct influence on the incidence of delinquency, which starts to increase at this time simply because the causal factors listed do not commonly become operative before a child attains sexual maturity. Furthermore, as already pointed out, delinquency generally has historical antecedents in childhood and reaches peak incidence in the late teens and early twenties rather than at the age of pubescence.

Sex Differences. Important differences exist between boys and girls in the incidence, age of onset, etiology, and kind of delinquency practiced. Four [49] to seven [32] times as many boys as girls become delinquent, but the ratio of boys to girls has shown a steady decline over the past fifty years. Boys also become involved in delinquency at an earlier age than girls. This difference is partly a function of the greater supervision to which younger adolescent girls are subjected, and partly a function of the fact that sex offenses constitute a more frequent category of delinquency among girls.* However, if these differences are culturally determined and reflect cultural

---

* Sex delinquency generally presupposes anatomical sexual maturity, occurring rarely in prepubescent girls.

attitudes toward male and female social sex roles, we can expect them to become increasingly less pronounced in the future.

Sex differences in the kinds of offenses committed are even more striking. Stealing, mischief, traffic violations, truancy, and running away from home are the major misdemeanors of adolescent boys.[32, 49] Delinquent girls, on the other hand, are most frequently charged with ungovernability, sex offenses, and leaving home.[49]

Female sex delinquents "are not commonly driven by sex urges per se." [22] Girls who fail to receive adequate affection and acceptance at home may resort to promiscuous sex experience as a way of obtaining warmth and acceptance from men * or

> for the secondary gains of attention, the pleasure of being taken to restaurants and amusement places, or the excitement of having other new experiences.[22]

In other similar cases, sex delinquency may be practiced in peer groups expressly organized for this purpose. L. K. Frank suggests that sex delinquency occurs in girls whose fathers adopt a hostile and deprecating attitude toward the female sex, and who then utilize their sexuality as a means of "exercising power over men" and in this way gaining "revenge for the years of humiliation they suffered as girls." [13]

The greater frequency of sex delinquency among girls can be explained by several factors. First, because of prevailing cultural notions about sex differences in biological sex role, it requires less actual misconduct by girls to be charged with sex offenses. Second, since the social, emotional, and academic adjustment of delinquent girls is much superior to that of delinquent boys,[51] there is reason to suppose that sex delinquency involves less pathological involvement of total personality structure than other forms of delinquency. Wittman and Huffman thus believe that the maladjustment of delinquent girls "is primarily related not to personality difficulties within themselves, but to difficulties of adjustment within the family group and to their general environment."[51] Third, the use of heterosexual attractiveness as a means of obtaining primary or adult status is more widely accepted as an appropriate technique for women than for men. Adolescent girls, especially those who are sexually attractive or over-developed,† are thus more prone than boys to utilize their

---

* See L. W. Sontag.[26]

† Early or prominent sexual development occurs more frequently in delinquent than in nondelinquent girls.[10]

sexuality as a short-cut device for rapidly acquiring adult status. During World War II, this factor was probably responsible for the rise in sex delinquency among younger adolescent girls who were "left out" of the new world of more legitimate adult status that suddenly opened up for their somewhat older contemporaries.[45]

The Problem of Culpability

Complicating the psychological assessment of delinquency are various moral and legal issues that do not arise in other forms of behavior disorder. And to make matters more complex, the various disciplines and professions that deal with delinquency adopt widely divergent approaches to these issues.

The legal point of view is closest to that of "the man in the street." Since

> the law is primarily concerned with protecting the interests and safety of individuals, groups, and society, the most practical assumption to make is that in the absence of evidence to the contrary, unlawful acts are willfully committed and render the offender liable to punishment. The strict legal test for responsibility only requires that the accused person know right from wrong and be able to appreciate the nature and quality of his act.[3]

Psychologists and sociologists, on the other hand, deny that the issue of moral accountability is relevant in delinquency. In line with the prevailing deterministic philosophy dominating the social sciences, the concept of moral accountability is held to be based on the discredited notion of "free will."

> The moral character of an individual is presumed to be shaped by forces beyond his control and, therefore, immune from any judgmental process with ethical implications. Immoral behavior is [regarded as] . . . no different from any other kind of undesirable behavior.[3]

The sociologist places greatest weight upon social disorganization and conditions of socioeconomic deprivation in accounting for delinquent behavior. Psychologists and psychiatrists believe that

> delinquency is primarily a problem of disordered personality development arising from unfortunate relationships between the child and significant persons in his psychological field rather than a manifestation of disturbance in grosser patterns of social organization.[3]

Sociologists and psychologists both agree, however, that since the causes of delinquency lie beyond the control of the individual, the

prevailing judicial insistence on moral accountability is both inconsistent and based on archaic and unscientific notions of behavior.
Typical of this approach is Zachry's statement that

> to isolate certain forms of emotional disturbance and to label them with a
> term of opprobrium is both scientifically inaccurate and inimical to the inter-
> ests of youth. It presupposes an attitude of sitting in moral judgment, of
> attaching blame for behavior which should be considered a symptom of dis-
> turbance.[52]

In this dispute between the jurist and the social scientist the
writer is inclined to side with the jurist. Just because social and
psychological causes can be identified as contributing to an individual's delinquency does not mean that he must forthwith be
absolved from all moral accountability.

> There has been too great a tendency in modern psychological thinking about
> criminality toward divorcing all behavior of its ethical content. . . . It seems
> just as one-sided to ascribe all anti-social behavior to underlying psychological
> disturbances as to see in it only a manifestation of basic immorality. From the
> standpoint of individual behavior, there is a moral aspect to most purposeful
> human activity, the psychological reality of which cannot be ignored. And
> while this aspect is so closely interwoven with the aspect of psychological dis-
> turbance that the two can hardly be separated, the relative significance of each
> in a given case of delinquency is usually clear enough to allow some judgment
> as to the individual's moral and legal accountability.[2]

Acceptance of behavioral determinism does not necessarily imply
repudiation of the notion of moral accountability. Because we can
satisfactorily explain the dynamics and the developmental history
of anti-social attitudes we are not obliged to regard the offender
as free from blame.

> Regardless of events beyond his control that once transpired, if he can
> *presently* recognize a moral obligation and is physically and psychologically
> capable of exercising inhibitory control, he is accountable for his misdeeds. . . .
> The vast majority of immoral and delinquent acts are committed under con-
> ditions where there is clear awareness of a moral issue and reasonable opportu-
> nity for exercising inhibitory control in conformity with the perceived direction
> of moral duty.[3]

This concept of culpability goes beyond the formal legal definition. It refers also to "acts of cruelty, injustice and treachery" which
violate no statute or legal precedent. It does not preclude the application of rehabilitative, preventive, or therapeutic measures, or

presuppose a spirit of vindictiveness. "The notion of liability to punishment following misbehavior" is an essential component of the concept of moral obligation which cannot be abandoned without jeopardizing the very basis of conscience formation. "If therapy alone were instituted culpable immoral behavior would not be distinguishable in any way from other behavior disorders." [3] And in addition, it (punishment) serves the very necessary function of protecting society from its predatory members.[3]

Differential Diagnosis of Delinquency

The operation of multiple causality in the development of behavior disorders is nowhere more striking than in delinquency. Seldom if ever is any single factor alone sufficiently prepotent to induce sustained or habitual anti-social behavior.[18] Delinquency is in no sense a homogeneous category of behavioral disturbance. Underlying the least common denominator of overt unlawful activity are many different kinds of etiological factors that often bear little or no relationship to each other.

This does not mean that classification is not possible. Causal factors can be grouped into major categories; and even if several factors are simultaneously operative, experienced observers are usually able to agree upon the one that is etiologically most crucial after careful study of the case history.

As in other adolescent behavior disorders, classification is not merely a matter of academic interest but is extremely important for prognostic purposes. The three-fold classification used above can also be used here. On the one hand, there is the prognostically hopeful variety of delinquency that involves no serious abnormality in character development but reflects, for the most part, the transitory pressures of adolescent emotional instability and exposure to the delinquent or ambivalent moral values of neighborhood peer group and general subcultural milieu. Such delinquency is facilitated by the presence of certain temperamental traits (see pp. 531–532) but seldom becomes permanent unless sustained by such factors as frequent institutionalization in "reform schools," inability to obtain legitimate employment, minority group membership, and strong identification with delinquent parents or siblings. On the other hand, two other categories of prognostically less favorable delinquency reflect (a) residual childhood defects in character development (in non-satellizers) or (b) maturational defects in character referable to the developmental tasks of adolescence (especially in satellizers). These types of delinquency are more frequently associated with a childhood history of anti-social conduct and are also facilitated by the possession of certain personality traits relating to the presence and channelling of aggressive responses and by the transitional pressures described above. But under ordinary circumstances neither of these by themselves will lead to permanent delinquency.

Many lines of evidence support the validity of distinguishing between the less serious, transitory form of environmentally and situationally-conditioned adolescent delinquency and the more serious, character-conditioned delinquency that is also aggravated by adolescence. In general, such evidence points to the inability of social factors to produce either transitory delinquency in the majority of adolescents growing up under unfavorable environmental conditions or permanent delinquency in more than a small percentage of such individuals.[30] Even in the worst slum districts, only a small minority of adolescents become habitually delinquent.[18, 22, 44] More young people choose to identify with the sanctioned value system of conventional society, which is transmitted by the home, school, church, organized youth groups, than with the values of the delinquent gang. It is important to bear in mind that although the prevailing ideology of lower socioeconomic groups may differ in many important respects from those of middle- and upper-class groups, it is in no sense essentially or predominantly at odds with the law. Even the majority of the members of adolescent delinquent gangs eventually break their connection with unlawful activities and settle down to a more conventional existence (see p. 379). And finally, it should be pointed out that some adolescents from optimal social environments—many more than are ever officially charged with delinquency—become habitually wayward.

Etiological Factors

Transitional Pressures of Adolescence. Several factors peculiar to the nature of adolescent development in our culture contribute to the greater incidence of delinquency during this period. In the first place, delinquency is an aggressive response, and adolescents have a larger fund of aggression than members of other age groups. This situation is both a direct product of the prolonged status deprivation to which they are subjected and a manifestation of the reduced threshold for aggression characteristic of states of emotional instability. As suggested earlier, aggression is the simplest and most direct response to frustration, and accordingly is displaced as other more adjustive techniques are learned. Nevertheless, it is sustained over a period of several years by the general anti-adult orientation that crystallizes from the identification of adults as the agents responsible for the thwarting of their bid for independence and primary status.

"Moreover, an act of aggression sometimes results from the feeling that the world is hostile toward the aggressor." [52] Thus the adoption of a vindictive attitude toward young delinquents may also instigate counter-aggression.

> To place the badge "delinquent" upon them at the age when they are most sensitive, most easily wounded only confirms them in their belief and consequently tends to intensify the impulse toward aggression.[52]

All that passes as aggression, however, does not conform to the behavioral definition. Much of the restlessness, thrill-seeking, and recklessness of adolescents that takes an unlawful turn (truancy, traffic violations, disorderly conduct, sampling of narcotics) is only a manifestation of generalized lowering of the threshold of reactivity and does not reflect any deliberately aggressive or anti-social intent. Also, much of the rebellious self-assertiveness of adolescents that appears to be a reactive form of aggression is instead a more positive expression of the developmental need for greater volitional independence. Finally, in assessing the significance of aggression in relation to delinquent behavior, it is important to realize

> that there are class standards regulating the overt expression of direct physical aggression; and, hence, what might almost be regarded as normal for one class might be viewed with alarm if occurring in another social setting.[2]

The expression of aggressive behavior is facilitated in adolescence by the normative and coercive power of the peer group. Adolescents find aggressive group action much more efficacious in advancing their interests than individual acts of rebellion. Bolstered by group suggestion and moral sanction the individual adolescent will often participate in aggressive, anti-social behavior that he would never think of undertaking by himself. In participating in such activity he also responds to implied coercive threats of ostracism and to genuine feelings of loyalty to the group. Hence, most delinquent activity is committed by groups rather than by individuals.[22, 32, 39]

Some delinquency must also be attributed to the difficulty that the adolescent experiences in trying to anchor himself to a stable set of moral values. At this time he is seeking to divorce concepts of moral obligation from slavish dependence on parental loyalties and to locate "emulatory models for a rational and reciprocal ethical code" predicated on a societal basis.[3] But because of the prevailing moral confusion, the weakening of traditional core values in our society, the widespread existence of corruption and lax morality in high places, and the cynical emphasis upon expediency and material success that he sees all around him, identification with an upright way of life is not a self-evident alternative. He is tempted to experiment with various norms of ethical conduct, some of which are patently delinquent. Because of his marginal status and his vulnerability to group pressure, he is especially prone to swim with the tide and pursue a policy of moral expediency (see p. 252). Under such circumstances—when exposed to the influence of a delinquent peer group—the decision to cast his lot with crime can unfortunately be made more readily than we prefer to believe.

Disorganized Urban Areas. The existence of special socioeconomic deprivations and of disorganized urban areas provide suitable conditions for the emergence of delinquent juvenile gangs.[32, 44] Such gangs make possible a more organized and sustained channeling of aggressive impulses into delinquent activities based upon a predatory set of values. But although their anti-social values are continually reinforced by alienation from conventional society and by close association with their fellows over a period of years in a cohesive action group, permanent delinquency is a relatively rare outcome (see p. 524).

Adolescent residents of urban slum areas naturally face all of the deprivations and developmental changes productive of increased aggression among youth in general. In addition, many other factors engender further hostility and anti-social attitudes. Such areas are characterized by overcrowding, substandard housing, large families, poverty, inadequate nutrition and medical care, high rates of tuberculosis and mental disease, unemployment, absence of suitable recreational facilities.[32, 44] They are populated by newly arrived and, hence, economically poorly established immigrants and minority groups (Negroes, Puerto Ricans, Mexicans) who are also harassed by racial and ethnic discrimination.[39] * In school, the children of these minority and lower socioeconomic groups are exposed to condescending and patronizing attitudes, to slurs, taunts, and discriminatory practices of age-mates and teachers (see p. 497). They soon learn that their educational and vocational opportunities are highly circumscribed. In their immediate environment they are daily witnesses of crime, vice, and violence. Protected by the geographical isolation of the slum and the protection it offers from police and adult supervision, delinquent gangs can flourish with immeasurably greater ease than in homogeneous rural communities.[20]

Psychological conditions within the home are equally conducive to the development of anti-social impulses. Parents quarrel more openly. Beatings, drunkenness, marital infidelity, separations, and desertions are relatively common in this environment. The frequency of irresponsible, shiftless, incompetent, harassed, and overburdened parents incapable of providing adequate supervision for their children is also greater.[22] Parents often fail to provide suitable ethical training, sometimes furnish an example of delinquency by their own conduct,[18, 22] and not infrequently condone or show little concern over wayward behavior.[16, 20] Less emphasis is placed on school achievement, church affiliation, and participation in community organizations.[20, 39]

Once organized the delinquent gang perpetuates itself through its closely knit, highly differentiated social structure, its system of mutual obligations and loyalties, and through the adherence of its members to a delinquent code of ethics that is consciously chosen in preference to the sanctioned values of society.[21, 45] Delinquents are generally very social individuals with a highly developed sense of comradeship and personal loyalty to their fellows.[21, 22, 45] They justify their predatory activity against society on the grounds that it is retaliatory for unjust and repressive treatment and that it is

---

* Delinquency rates for Negroes, for example, are substantially higher than those for whites.[32, 48]

the only possible way of obtaining status and gratifying their needs (see pp. 325 and 381).

Residual Defects in Moral Development. In contrast to the transitional and situational causal factors described above are residual defects in moral development. Such defects help explain why youths from even optimal social environments become ensnared in delinquency. They also account in part for the selective occurrence of delinquency in only a small minority of exposed slum dwellers and for the small number of cases that terminate in permanent delinquency. The moral development of non-satellizing children and the defects in conscience to which they are predisposed have already been elaborated in considerable detail (see pp. 256–258).

It is not at all surprising that the incidence of delinquency is so much greater under conditions of child rearing that lead to an absence of satellization, when parents are rejecting and neglectful and make children feel unloved, unwanted, and insecure in affectional relationships.[18, 21, 27] The delinquent pattern may first originate when such children discover that the only way they can obtain some attention is by participating in disapproved behavior.[24] Delinquents more frequently judge their parents as lacking in solicitude, affection, and concern for their futures, and as harsh, unjust disciplinarians who abuse their power and authority.[18, 22, 51] Their family life is marked by conflict, hostility, and disharmony.[21] They lack close emotional ties with parents, feel little regard for them, and tend to disavow the values the parents prize most highly.[53] They resent parental authority and training measures since they do not feel that their parents truly have their welfare at heart. But since aggression at home leads to swift reprisals, they transfer their rebelliousness and hatred of authority to other adults, turning on society for the revenge they seek against parents.[18, 22] In some instances the desired revenge is obtained merely by participating in disapproved activities. Not infrequently, however, rejecting, narcissistic parents are not at all concerned over the anti-social behavior of their offspring as long as they themselves are not put to any trouble by it.[16, 18]

More basic to the delinquency of rejected children than the need for revenge is the unstable basis of moral obligation, the failure to abandon completely infantile notions of irresponsibility, and the failure to accept implicitly in early childhood parental values and personal responsibility to abide by parental dicta; the precarious dependability of a system of ethical controls that relies so heavily on external pressures and reaction formation when urgent considerations of ego enhancement are at stake; and the tendency to suffer selective impairment of the self-critical faculty with respect to moral lapses and to claim exemption from the moral code that applies to "ordinary" people (see pp. 256–257). These same factors, especially the latter one, are also operative in the overvalued child who is rejected in later childhood.

The aggressive, anti-social psychopath is an extreme and relatively rare example of this type of moral agenesis. For him harsh parental rejection is combined with an extremely self-assertive personality whose

> needs for counter aggression and vengeance are so great that considerations of expediency are cast aside, and complete and overt rebellion against parental standards takes place. Not only does a sense of personal moral obligation fail to develop, but also any internalization of ethical values whatsoever. The same hostile, rebellious attitude is later carried over in relation to social norms which the individual identifies with the hateful figures of his parents. Thus, there is no possibiltiy of developing a sense of justice or obligation on rational grounds. Even the interests of self-aggrandizement are subordinated to the need for wanton destructiveness and aggressive retaliation against moral or legal authority.[3]

From an early age this type of individual manifests ruthless, calculating, cruel, unfeeling, and remorseless behavior which appears to be incorrigible. In the underworld he is the conscienceless and unscrupulous criminal, the cold-blooded, egocentric murderer who shows affection and loyalty for no one.

Maturational Defects in Moral Development. Some instances of delinquency can be attributed to unfortunate parental practices (underdomination, overdomination, overprotection) which interfere with normal maturational changes in the conscience development of satellizers during preadolescence and adolescence. Overdominated and overprotected children experience difficulty in establishing moral obligations on a societal basis, in becoming responsible to the moral authority of society as against the moral authority of parents, in independently formulating generalized principles of conduct based on abstract principles of equity rather than on feelings of personal loyalty. If the parents themselves are wayward, this blind and personal identification with their specific code of values inevitably leads to delinquency. Death or physical removal of the parent may also favor the development of delinquency by creating a moral vacuum. In certain instances, originally acceptable authoritarian discipline may become less palatable with increasing age, resulting in overt rebellion or passive sabotage against parental standards.

The underdominated child develops more serious defects in moral structure. Because of lax discipline he fails to learn to curb aggressive impulses and to postpone immediate gratification of hedonistic needs. As a result, he may develop strong guilt feelings and an expiatory need for punishment, which he tries to provoke through flagrantly unacceptable behavior.[6, 21, 24] In addition, inadequate external supports are available for the internalization of moral standards. Last, overindulgent parental behavior confirms his belief that he is a specially privileged person exempt from the moral obligations that apply to others, and interferes with the normal development of self-critical ability.

The writer takes issue with the often expressed view that identification with parents (on the basis of their willingness to satisfy dependency needs) is both necessary and sufficient for children to acquire control over hedonistic impulses.[6] In the first place, such control can be achieved on other bases than satellization. Nonsatellizers, for example, appreciate that self-denial is necessary to avoid punishment and gain ego enhancement. It is true that they may resent the restrictions imposed by parents, but unless the need for revenge is unusually great, their inordinately high ego aspirations ordinarily suffice to curb the desire for immediate gratification of pleasure-seeking goals. More commonly the failure to learn self-control is an outcome of excessive permissiveness in the home environment (see p. 240).

The prognosis of delinquency conditioned by these maturational defects is fortunately better than that of the non-satellizing variety discussed above. Attenuation of infantile irresponsibility and implicit acceptance of parental values in early childhood provide a more stable foundation for conscience. Delinquent behavior is less apt to be serious, ruthless, and vindictive since it is oriented more toward hedonistic self-indulgence than toward self-aggrandizement or obtaining revenge. Last, beginning with adolescence, the child comes less under the control of parents and is more exposed to influences (school, peer group, employer) that exert a less detrimental effect upon moral development. Subsequent improvement of delinquent behavior in late adolescence and early adulthood substantiates the view that maturation in such cases is retarded rather than arrested.[17]

Other Psychological Factors. Other temperamental traits and psychological variables unrelated to moral development as such may also play a role in the genesis of delinquency. These factors likewise help explain the selective incidence of delinquent behavior in only a minority of adolescents who suffer from moral defects or live in disorganized urban areas.

Organic brain injuries (post-encephalitic Parkinsonism, postconcussion syndrome) are only rarely related to delinquency.[9] Mental deficiency occurs more frequently among delinquents; [22] their mean IQ is also somewhat lower than that of nondelinquents.[38] The significance of both facts must be qualified by the skewed distribution of IQ's in slum areas. Delinquents do not compare unfavorably with their nondelinquent siblings on tests of mental ability.[22] Low IQ *per se* cannot be an important etiological factor in delinquency but may constitute part of the larger constellation of variables associated with depressed socioeconomic conditions that contributes to the development of delinquent behavior. Intellectual deficit, for example, increases suggestibility, the tendency to take unwise chances, and the probability of apprehension. The school achievement of delinquents is also not commensurate with their verbal intelligence,[18] thereby increasing the incidence of school failure and the inclination for truancy which is one of the earliest and most frequent of juvenile offenses.

Apart from causes rooted in unsatisfactory parent-child relationships, delinquents may be more prone for other temperamental reasons to utilize aggression as a defense or status-gaining mechanism.[21, 39] In contrast to nondelinquents they have been described as more restless and active,[21] self-assertive, defiant, impulsive, suspicious, stubborn, crowd-minded, danger-loving, and destructive.[18] All other things being equal, individuals possessing such personality traits are more likely to learn and habitually practice unacceptably aggressive ways of satisfying needs and reducing anxiety. It may also be that as a result of experiencing higher levels of frustration associated with physical, intellectual, and educational handicaps,[21, 39] they are more unhappy, discontented, and insecure than other adolescents, thereby having greater cause for aggression.[21, 22]

Preventive Measures

It is universally agreed among authorities on juvenile delinquency that prevention is a much more feasible goal than treatment.[16, 18, 21] To be effective, preventive measures must understandably be aimed at the etiological factors discussed above.

One of the more significant aspects of a preventive program involves measures to reduce the emotional instability of adolescence. Since psychobiological determinants of emotional instability cannot readily be influenced, attention must be directed toward minimizing the factors that prolong status deprivation, providing more work experience and earlier job opportunities, making earlier marriage possible, increasing social mobility (see pp. 541–542). Much could be done merely by making school experience a more effective source of interim status and by reducing the amount of frustration that adolescents, especially those from lower socioeconomic backgrounds, meet in the school situation[22] (see p. 501).

The elimination of disorganized urban areas and of such associated conditions as the segregation of minority groups is an obvious aspect of any preventive program but is necessarily a long-range objective. Nevertheless, it seems highly unlikely that much progress can be made toward reducing the transitory, situationally-conditioned delinquency of the slums until the underlying socioeconomic picture is improved.[44] In the interim, "programs of community action initiated and carried on by the concerted efforts of citizens and local residents interested in improvement of the community life in all its aspects" can do much to improve the morale of the inhabitants. The use of local talent in delinquency areas for constructive purposes and the assumption of responsibility for and control of a community betterment program by the local residents constitute the basic features of the Chicago Area Projects.[44] The participants in such a program

> achieve a sense of self-reliance, preserve their self-respect, and enhance their status among their neighbors by contributing time and energy to the creation of better opportunities for children.[44]

Not only is such self-initiated effort more likely to result in constructive change, but also by avoiding the condescending attitudes of non-indigenous philanthropic institutions and by meeting potential delinquents on their own ground, it neutralizes the natural diffidence with which most crusaders and reformers have been greeted by disturbed and aggressive-minded boys and girls.[44]

Last, a preventive program must be directed at reducing the incidence of deviant moral development. Essentially this involves the mental hygiene of parent-youth relationships during adolescence (see pp. 539–541), the extension of parent education in child-rearing, the establishment of more child guidance clinics, earlier identification and guidance of potential delinquents, and closer collaboration between teachers and parents. In instances of particularly undesirable parent-child relationships, teachers can play a constructive role in moral development as parent substitutes by providing a more appropriate emulatory model and pattern of disciplinary control. Considerable improvement in moral development could also be anticipated were there a restoration of greater uprightness and consistency of ethical standards in civic, business, and professional life.[22]

REFERENCES AND BIBLIOGRAPHY

1. Ausubel, D. P.: The Psychopathology and treatment of drug addiction in relation to the mental hygiene movement. Psychiat. Quart. Supplement, *22:* Part II, 219–250, 1948.
2. Ausubel, D. P.: Problems of adolescent adjustment. Bulletin, Natl. Assn. Secondary School Principals, *34:*1–84, 1950.
3. Ausubel, D. P.: *Ego Development and the Personality Disorders.* New York: Grune & Stratton, 1952.
4. Ausubel, D. P.: An evaluation of recent adolescent drug addiction. Ment. Hyg., *36:*373–382, 1952.
5. Bennett, C. C.: Problem children, delinquency, and treatment. Rev. Educ. Res., *10:*440–449, 1940.

6. Bettelheim, B.: "The Special School for Emotionally Disturbed Children," in *Juvenile Delinquency and the Schools* 47th Yearbook, Natl. Soc. Stud. Educ., Part I. Chicago: University of Chicago Press, 1948.

7. Blanchard, P.: "Adolescent Experience in Relation to Personality and Behavior," in *Personality and the Behavior Disorders* (J. McV. Hunt, ed.), Vol. II. New York: Ronald, 1944.

8. Blos, P.: *The Adolescent Personality: A Study of Individual Behavior.* New York: Appleton-Century, 1941.

9. Bovet, L.: *Psychiatric Aspects of Juvenile Delinquency.* Geneva: World Health Organization, 1951.

10. Burt, C.: *The Young Delinquent.* New York: Appleton, 1925.

11. Dollard, J. et al.: *Frustration and Aggression.* New Haven: Yale University Press, 1939.

12. Frank, L. K.: "Adolescence as a Period of Transition," in *Adolescence*, 43rd Yearbook, Natl. Soc. Stud. Educ., Part I. Chicago: University of Chicago Press, 1944.

13. Frank, L. K.: "The Adolescent and the Family," in *Adolescence*, 43rd Yearbook, Natl. Soc. Stud. Educ., Part I. Chicago: University of Chicago Press, 1944.

14. Gardner, G. E.: The mental health of normal adolescents. Ment. Hyg., *31:*529–540, 1947.

15. Glueck, S. and Glueck, E. T.: *Five Hundred Criminal Careers.* New York: Knopf, 1933.

16. Glueck, S. and Glueck, E. T.: *One Thousand Juvenile Delinquents.* Cambridge: Harvard University Press, 1934.

17. Glueck, S. and Glueck, E. T.: *Later Criminal Carers.* New York: Commonwealth Fund, 1937.

18. Glueck, S. and Glueck, E. T.: *Unraveling Juvenile Delinquency.* New York: Commonwealth Fund, 1950.

19. Harris, D. B.: Relationships among play interests and delinquency in boys. Am. J. Orthopsychiat., *13:*631–637, 1943.

20. Havighurst, R. J. and Taba, H.: *Adolescent Character and Personality.* New York: Wiley, 1949.

21. Healey, W. and Bronner, A. F.: *New Light on Delinquency and its Treatment.* New Haven: Yale University Press, 1936.

22. Healey, W. and Bronner, A. F.: "What Makes a Child Delinquent?" in *Juvenile Delinquency and the Schools*, 47th Yearbook, Natl. Soc. Stud. Educ., Part I. Chicago: University of Chicago Press, 1948.

23. Ivins, W. H., Fox, W. H., and Segel, D.: A study of a secondary school program in the light of characteristics and needs of youth. Bulletin, School Educ. Indiana University, Vol. XXV, No. 6, 1949.

24. Jackson, L.: A study of sado-masochistic attitudes in a group of delinquent girls by means of a specially designed projection test. Brit. M. J. Psychol., *22:*53–65, 1949.

25. Jameson, A. T.: Psychological factors contributing to the delinquency of girls. J. Juv. Res., *22*:25–32, 1938.

26. Karpman, B. (Ch.), Chess, S., Lurie, L. A., Sontag, L. W., and Schmideberg, M.: Psychodynamics of Child Delinquency (Round Table, 1952), Am. J. Orthopsychiat., *23*:1–69, 1953.

27. Lander, J.: Traumatic factors in the background of 116 delinquent boys. Am. J. Orthopsychiat., *11*:150–156, 1941.

28. Langdon, G. and Stout, I. W.: *These Well Adjusted Children.* New York: John Day, 1950.

29. Lucena, J. et al.: O test de Rorschach en um gruppo de adolescentes. Neurobiologia, Pernambuco, *11*:275–344, 1948.

30. Lurie, L. A. et al.: Environmental influence. Am. J. Orthopsychiat., *13*:150–162, 1943.

31. Maier, N. R. F.: *Frustration: The Study of Behavior without a Goal.* New York: McGraw-Hill, 1949.

32. Maller, J. B.: Juvenile delinquency in New York City: A summary of a comprehensive report. J. Psychol., *3*:1–25, 1937.

33. Malzberg, B.: A statistical study of the prevalence and types of mental disease among children and adolescents. Psychiat. Quart., *5*:511–537, 1931.

34. Markey, O. B.: A study of aggressive sex misbehavior in adolescents brought to juvenile court. Am. J. Orthopsychiat., *20*:719–731, 1950.

35. Mohr, G. J.: Psychiatric problems of adolescence. J. A. M. A., *137*:1589–1592, 1948.

36. Neubauer, P. B. and Steinert, J.: Schizophrenia in adolescence. Nervous Child, *10*:129–134, 1952.

37. Ojemann, R. H.: "How to Work with Parents in Preventing Delinquency," in *Juvenile Delinquency and the Schools,* 47th Yearbook, Natl. Soc. Stud. Educ., Part I. Chicago: University of Chicago Press, 1948.

38. Owen, M. B.: The intelligence of institutionalized juvenile delinquents. J. Juv. Res., *21*:199–204, 1937.

39. Plant, J. S.: "Who is the Delinquent?" in *Juvenile Delinquency and the Schools,* 47th Yearbook, Natl. Soc. Stud. Educ., Part I. Chicago: University of Chicago Press, 1948.

40. Porterfield, A. L.: Delinquency and its outcome in court and college. Am. J. Sociol., *49*:199–208, 1943.

41. Redl, F. and Wineman, D.: *Children Who Hate.* Glencoe, Ill.: Free Press, 1951.

42. Reichard, S. and Tillman, C.: Patterns of parent-child relationships in schizophrenia. Psychiatry, *13*:247–257, 1950.

43. Segel, D.: *Frustration in Adolescent Youth.* Washington, D. C.: Federal Security Agency, 1951.

44. Shaw, C. R. and McKay, H. D.: *Juvenile Delinquency and Urban Areas.* Chicago: University of Chicago Press, 1942.

45. Sherif, M. and Cantril, H.: *The Psychology of Ego-Involvements.* New York: Wiley, 1947.

46. Shuttleworth, F. K.: *The Adolescent Period: A Graphic Atlas.* Monogr. Soc. Res. Child Develpm., XIV, No. 1, 1949.

47. Stevens, G. C.: Autobiographical material concerning the childhood environments and the effects on the after-adjustments of 100 recidivists and 100 college freshmen. Am. J. Orthopsychiat., 2:279–303, 1932.

48. U. S. Children's Bureau: Juvenile-Court Statistics. Washington, D. C.: U. S. Dept. of Labor, 1934.

49. U. S. Children's Bureau: Juvenile-Court Statistics, 1944 and 1945. Washington, D. C.: Federal Security Agency, 1946.

50. Warren, W.: Abnormal behavior and mental breakdown in adolescence. J. Ment. Sc., 95:589–624, 1949.

51. Wittman, M. P. and Huffman, A. V.: A comparative study of developmental, adjustment, and personality characteristics of psychotic, psychoneurotic, delinquent, and normally-adjusted teen-age youth. J. Genet. Psychol., 66:167–182, 1945.

52. Zachry, C. B.: "Preparing Youth to be Adults," in *Adolescence,* 43rd Yearbook, Natl. Soc. Stud. Educ., Part I. Chicago: University of Chicago Press, 1944.

53. Zucker, H. J.: *Affectional Identification and Delinquency.* New York: Archives of Psychology (Columbia University), 1943.

CHAPTER 17

Mental Hygiene and Guidance

MANY SPECIFIC ASPECTS of mental hygiene and guidance in adolescence have been considered in the chapters on sexual behavior (see pp. 432–433), vocational choice (see pp. 458–465), and the school (see pp. 500–501). In this chapter we shall consider only some very general principles relevant to the mental health and guidance of adolescent boys and girls.

THE IMPORTANCE OF PARENT-CHILD RELATIONSHIPS IN PREADOLESCENCE

The crucial significance of parent-child relationships during childhood and preadolescence for normal personality maturation has been elaborated in great detail (see pp. 200–205). The role of unfortunate child rearing practices in predisposing the individual toward both maturational failure (see pp. 238–243) and various defects in personality structure associated with non-satellization (see pp. 208–214) has also been considered, as well as the relationship of each of these conditions to adolescent behavior disorders and delinquency (see Chapter 16). It follows that the most important aspect of the mental hygiene of adolescence is to minimize the incidence of undesirable parent attitudes and practices *before* the onset of this stage of personality development. And if such practices and their detrimental consequences on children's personalities do occur, it is unrealistic to hope for any substantial improvement following psychotherapy with children "without some change in parental attitude or in the home situation." [16] No other outcome is conceivable in view of the fact that children

are largely under the immediate control of powerful adults who in most cases are responsible for the adjustive difficulties involved, and without whose cooperation, improvement in the interpersonal environment and implementation of insight would be impossible.[2]

537

The Difficulty of Changing Parent Attitudes

The difficulties inherent in the task of modifying unfavorable parent attitudes certainly furnish little basis for rampant optimism in this direction. The "sources of a parent's inadequacies as a parent are found in his own childhood" [12] and are, therefore, highly resistive to change. The personality trends that make a parent narcissistic, preoccupied, and hostile (rejecting) or over- or under-dominating are quite stable by the time an individual reaches adulthood. If child rearing practices gratify important needs in the parent, if they provide compensatory ego enhancement (overdomination, overvaluation), or reduce anxiety (overprotection), they are especially resistive to modification. But even when these deep-seated personality factors are not operative, for the parent "just to admit the need for drastic revision is tantamount to indicting himself as a parent." [1] Mere awareness of attitudes

> that put him in an unfavorable light . . . is [often] far less traumatic than directly pleading guilty to these failings by open admission, or indirectly by modification of his practices.[2]

The difficulty of change is further compounded by the parent's subscription to a "formal philosophy of child rearing." Sometimes this philosophy is merely an "out-and-out" rationalization of underlying attitudes, providing a supportive cognitive facade. Othertimes "it may have the status of an objective conviction relatively unrelated to attitudinal considerations." [2] In such instances modification can be effected more easily since it is necessary only to convince the parent intellectually. The existence of an underlying attitudinal substrate, on the other hand, constitutes a more formidable challenge, which if not met often results in "an unbridgable gap between theoretical understanding and practical application." [1] But even without fundamental change in the underlying personality basis for parental practices, genuine intellectual convictions *can* considerably influence the parent-child relationship for the better. They

> may do this just by opposing contrary personality trends and mitigating their severity without necessarily being potent enough to reverse them entirely. One should, therefore, never underestimate the potentialities of intellectual convictions for effecting personality change despite present-day psychological emphasis on the irrelevancy of all except emotional factors.[2]

It is true, of course, that such superficial changes in parental practices have limited value since they are unspontaneous and are often betrayed "in the smaller and less deliberate aspects of behavior." [2] More can be expected from parent education and therapy "in cases where detrimental parent attitudes stem from more ignorance and misinformation rather than from severe distortions in personality structure." [2] In either case one must reckon with the

> particular fads and fashions in child rearing which are in current vogue. Presently, this statement is just as applicable to excessive permissiveness as twenty years ago it was to an overly impersonal and highly controlled child rearing regimen.[2]

Social pressure can also have a positive effect in overcoming undesirable parent attitudes (for example, overdomination). But although

> the rejecting parent tends to be socially frowned upon nowadays, the same narcissistic preoccupation with himself that causes him to neglect his child provides him with a thick skin in the face of public or private criticism. The overvaluing parent, on the other hand, poses as a model of devotion.[1]

IMPROVING PARENT-YOUTH RELATIONS

Although many aspects of parent-youth relationships are almost inevitably bound to be conflictful during adolescence, this does not necessarily preclude the simultaneous operation of more positive factors. "Intimate and confidential relationships with parents" are not only possible but are also "definitely connected with good adjustment *during* adolescence." [14]

> The importance of this confidential relationship is that it furnishes a natural basis for the child's seeking of guidance from the parent when he feels that he needs it. The ambivalence of the adolescent's attitude toward emancipation is such that "beneath the indifference and devaluation there is a strong inner need for parental aid and parental guidance." [6] But parent-youth hostility has been stereotyped to such a degree that the child is generally too ill at ease to approach his parents even when he'd like to most. This is truly unfortunate since it adds to the abruptness of the adolescent transitional period which, if made more gradual at the onset (while shortened throughout), might help to cushion some of the stresses and strains of adolescence. If parents, on the other hand, could accept the fact that emancipation does not necessarily imply cutting the child adrift emotionally as soon as he matures sexually, the painfulness of the adolescent's emotional marginality might be considerably reduced.[1]

Measures aimed at minimizing parent-youth conflict—improving the balance between increased demands and responsibilities, on the one hand, and greater privileges on the other (see p. 223), recognizing the adolescent's greater needs for volitional independence, especially in girls (see pp. 226–227), and utilizing changed methods of discipline and control (see pp. 235–237)—have already been considered. In addition it has been suggested that

> giving the adolescent a place at the family councils would be a most constructive way both of showing respect for his developing adulthood and of adding dignity to his precarious status. . . .[21]
> Parent-youth conflict would also be alleviated if parents could refrain from responding in kind to the aggressive provocations of adolescents since this only sets up a vicious cycle based on the "*either-or* proposition from which unfortunately neither the adolescent nor the parent can withdraw without serious loss of face." [6] The former at least has the justification of emotional instabilty to excuse his behavior.[1]

It has become fashionable to make parents assume the entire responsibility for strained parent-youth relationships. Actually the blame is only partially theirs. Much of the discord can be attributed to "generation" differences in temperament, outlook, and values. Some of it is a function of the adolescent's exaggerated, unrealistic, and often unreasonable demands for independence, the anti-adult orientation of his peer group, his ambivalence about the process of maturation, his tendency to hold his parents responsible for the burden of status deprivation he bears, and his frequent failure to perceive actual changes in parent attitude (perceptual constancy). Furthermore, the difficulty of the parent's position should be appreciated. It is not easy (even with the best of intentions) to relinquish control over children because of the heavy emotional investment involved in parenthood and the long-standing habit of interference. And if the parent interprets his adolescent children in the light of his own adolescence or resents the idea of eventual displacement, he certainly cannot be judged too harshly for these very human failings.

When parent-youth conflict is largely a function of transitional adolescent pressures and is superimposed upon basically wholesome interpersonal relationships, simple mediation can be very effective.[13]

> The improvement in adolescent behavior which often follows from merely interpreting the adolescent to his parents and teachers is truly astounding.

While there are many basic reasons for parent-youth conflict, there is no doubt but that the presence or absence of tolerance and understanding is the differential factor which makes a given relationship either tolerable and confidential or continuously explosive and acrimonious.[1]

THE SOCIAL HYGIENE OF ADOLESCENCE

The premise underlying the suggestions in this section is that it is the responsibility of adult society to provide the proper conditions under which youth can develop and attain maturity. No help can be given

> our restless and disturbed young people until we recognize our own responsibility in regard to them and accept the fact that it is we who have failed them and not they who have failed us. Then and only then can we take measures to meet their needs.[21]

The difficulties caused by the abrupt onset of adolescence could be considerably minimized by purposeful reduction of the present discontinuity in the value, interest, and status systems of children and adolescents (see pp. 189–192). Unfortunately, because of the complexities of modern industrial civilization, more than token participation by children in the activities of adults would not be very feasible. Much more realistic is the possibility of *shortening* the period of status deprivation necessitated by present socioeconomic arrangements.

> Since . . . the social order is being constantly altered under the impact of highly motivated pressure groups, there is no reason to resign ourselves passively to the immutability of this social situation insofar as it affects adolescents. It is possible for society to *create* conditions under which adolescents can achieve a large measure of status, responsibility, and importance in community projects and organization. In our own times, we have seen the establishment of such projects as the National Youth Administration and the C.C.C. camps. We have also seen what youth has been able to accomplish for the war effort. There is no reason why adolescents cannot be assigned definite responsibilities in relation to community welfare projects and receive commensurate rewards and recognition. The Veterans Administration is presently revolutionizing the social basis of late adolescence. By subsidizing education and vocational training, it is accelerating the achievement of adult status by making possible early marriage and emancipation from parental economic support. Sooner or later, society will realize that the economic investment in such projects is trifling compared to the potential return in making constructive use of youthful energies, in facilitating adult maturation, and in reducing the harmful effects of emotional instability.[1]

Unnecessarily severe transitional anxiety can be lessened by giving adolescents greater assurance of eventually attaining adult status. In essence this means increasing social mobility. Nothing is

more discouraging to the ambitions of youth [than] . . . the fact that, as a result of the tremendous concentration and centralization of economic power which characterizes our industrial society today, social mobility is decreasing, "and in the struggle for status, inherited wealth and position are beginning to count for more than energy and capacity." [1]

Although the problem of social mobility is more directly relevant to the *existing* aspirations of middle-class youths, it also affects the possibility of modifying the goals and value systems of lower-class adolescents.

In order . . . to make low-status children anxious to work hard, study hard, save their money, and accept stricter sex mores, our society must convince them of the reality of the rewards at the end of the anxiety-laden climb. . . . Our society cannot hope, therefore, to educate the greater mass of lower-class people in any really effective way until it has real rewards to offer them for learning the necessary anxiety [4] [p. 214; quoted by permission of the Society].

As already pointed out (see p. 173n), this anxiety need not necessarily "be directed toward achieving money, power, and competitive position," but could be oriented more toward the goals of self-realization and social usefulness.

Because the peer group is undoubtedly fated to remain the major training institution of adolescence,

society must do everything in its power both to further the establishment of a constructive peer culture and to see to it that every boy and girl makes some satisfactory emotional adjustment to it. The latter point is obvious since we can see all around us the unhappy position of the deviant who is ostracized for so many years from the company of his fellows. The former point is becoming increasingly more important due to the "unprecedented amount of leisure time that [has become] available to the adolescent as a result of the diminution of farm chores and the postponement of gainful employment." [14] The need for guidance in leisure becomes apparent when we witness the growth of spectator sports which "at best represent a shallow participation and little or no real development, either physical or mental for those who participate." [14] . . . The failure of society to prepare youth adequately for enjoying the constructive use of leisure time is revealed even in a great city like New York where a startling number of adolescents not only do not participate in any athletic activity, but also belong to no organized social-recreational group and cultivate no personal hobby. [1]

COUNSELING IN ADOLESCENCE

Because adolescence is a period of increased self-assertion and volitional independence, successful guidance must necessarily be as non-authoritarian as possible.* Maximum emphasis must be placed on "self-determination and free acceptance in the choice of goals" [1] rather than upon forceful "imposition of an alien set of values." [3]

Nondirective therapists [15] have made two very significant contributions to the counseling of adolescents. (1) They have emphasized the importance of a nonauthoritarian therapeutic relationship for the acquisition and emotional acceptance of insight and the minimization of resistance to change. Corollary principles stress the value (a) of the client's self-discovery of his underlying attitudes and motivations, (b) of endogenous stimulation of behavioral reorganization, and (c) of empathic ability and emotional relatedness of the counselor. (2) They have focused attention upon the importance of effecting adjustment to current, situational problems and have pointed out the disastrous consequences of ignoring such problems for several years while waiting for the client to acquire "depth" insight (see p. 459).

Both of these major nondirective principles constitute significant advances over previously accepted notions of counseling and psychotherapy. Unfortunately, they have been over-generalized and have failed to take into account realistic limitations. For reasons that will be elaborated below, we cannot accept the gratuitous assumptions that (a) neither developmental aspects of maladjustment nor diagnostic considerations are relevant to the counseling situation; (b) that counselors may only reflect or clarify the client's productions but should not presume to express any expectations (moral or otherwise) or judgments; (c) that *all* insight must necessarily represent the product of self-discovery; (d) that *all* behavioral change must be endogenously induced; (e) that interpretation, supportive measures, and manipulation of the environment have no place in counseling; and (f) that the counselor must have no authority and must not assume the initiative in or attempt to structure the counseling relationship.

---

* As will be pointed out later (see p. 545), it is impossible to avoid certain inevitably authoritarian aspects of the counselor's role.

The fact that "in the final analysis it is only the individual himself who can actually effect reorganization of his own personality structure" does not in any sense rule out the propriety or the relevance of external sources of insight or stimulation for behavioral change. In counseling, as well as in all life situations, perceptual and motivational reorientation occur partly "under the impact of mature social expectations and within a realistic framework of interpersonal relations which does not ignore relevant moral problems." [2] The expression of expectations and judgmental reactions by the counselor in no way violates the principles that the individual is primarily responsible for himself or that change cannot be imposed from without.

> To the patient, the therapist represents the expectations of the social reality to which he has not yet succeeded in adjusting adequately. Much of the stimulus for change in motivation, attitude, and adjustive behavior during the period of treatment will come from the expectations of the therapist in his role of social reality surrogate. However, if the latter takes the position that it is the patient's prerogative to structure the framework of expectancy and set the limits in the relationship, the patient not only feels under no pressure to abandon his unrealistic, autistic, or immature framework of reference, but also feels justifiably encouraged to seek adjustment within such a framework with the tacit approval, support and sanction of the therapist. . . . [Similarly], if the therapist articulates no moral expectations and fails to express ethical judgments, the patient is justified in assuming that the former either approves of his immoral behavior or else considers that *any* type of ethical solution he (the patient) is satisfied with is also satisfactory to the therapist. In the latter case, therapy takes place in an amoral setting. . . . Proper timing, good rapport, and tact on the part of the therapist are necessary as well as a constructive approach rather than an attitude of condemnation. However, if in spite of skillful handling the patient discontinues therapy because of the therapist's expression of moral judgment, it is doubtful whether he could have benefited from it in the first place. [2]

The degree of initiative, responsibility, and self-direction that a given client can assume in a counseling relationship cannot be dogmatically fixed at the start of therapy but must be adapted to the requirements of his personality, the severity of his problem and to fluctuations in his condition. [2] An adolescent who is "disorganized, panic-stricken, or hopelessly caught between the vicious cycle of anxiety and the fixed, perseverative, and maladaptive responses which it tends to engender" obviously cannot be expected to take the initiative and rely on his own innate capacities for therapeutic change.[2] At this stage he needs support, reassurance, interpretation, suggestion, practical advice, and whatever benefit can be derived from sedatives and environmental manipulation.[2]

Even after the client is past the stage of panic, there is no reason that he cannot avail himself of the insights and re-educative assistance of the counselor in modifying his perceptual and motivational patterns and his adjustive techniques. Not only is self-discovery not an indispensable condition for the acceptance of insight or the initiation of change, but also it is frequently an impossible and unrealistic goal.

> Directed guidance . . . in restructuring [the client's] environment and response repertory . . . is also necessary in chronic maladjustments such as anxiety disorders if progress is to be made in solving current problems of adjustment, and if fixed and rigid defensive mechanisms which prevent efficient learning and working are to be overcome. The anxiety neurotic who has acquired maladaptive ways of learning, perceiving, and setting goals is not free to independently select and utilize beneficial insights . . . because of potent reaction sensitivities which predispose his behavior along rigidly channelized lines of a defensive nature.[2]

The therapist is also obliged to take the initiative in those counseling relationships in which the client is withdrawn, hostile, or suspicious. Under such circumstances the therapist cannot passively allow the client to explore the situation by himself to ascertain whether or not it is threatening to him, since it is precisely in this area that his social maturity is most glaringly deficient.[18] "Warmth and love" is also no magic formula that will automatically dissolve the aggressiveness of hostile adolescents. Such might be true in instances of reactive aggression induced by situational variables, but not where "character-conditioned hostility" is deeply ingrained as a fixed defence against anxiety.[18]

> It is equally unrealistic to deny the inherent authority residing in the role of the therapist and to set up the dictum that therapeutic benefit is limited in instances where the therapist is in a position of authority in relation to the patient. In the first place, the very fact that one individual appeals for help on the basis of another's expert knowledge inevitably injects an authoritarian aspect into the relationship. Secondly, if the therapist plays his necessary role of representing cultural expectations and defining limits for the therapeutic relationship, he automatically becomes invested with authority. . . . Lastly,

the therapist's effectiveness depends upon his being perceived by the patient as an individual of strength, someone to be respected rather than pushed around like an ineffective, underdominating parent. Without authority he can set no realistic limits; and in the absence of such limits, therapy can only compound existing ego damage.[2]

Finally, it should be pointed out that although attention to current concerns and therapy need not be postponed until a definitive diagnosis is made, permanent therapeutic change cannot be effected in the absence of developmental diagnosis.

Meaningful insight into the present adjustive situation cannot be gained by patient or therapist by examining only the end product of development. Neither sequence nor process of growth is deducible from eventual outcome although the latter necessarily reflects their operation. The practical clinical significance of this consideration enters into one of the first decisions that the therapist is obliged to make in every case he undertakes: Are the adjustive difficulties of the patient an outcome of current transitional or situational pressures, or are they reflective of serious abnormalities in ego devaluation or maturation? Until this question can be answered, no intelligent decision with respect to prognosis, length, depth, urgency, and type of therapy indicated can be made.[2]

To treat adolescents successfully, the counselor must have a good theoretical understanding of adolescent development and must have considerable first-hand experience with adolescent behavior at different social class levels. The difficulties associated with the latter requirements have already been considered (see p. 476). In addition, he should be a sensitive, empathic individual capable of relating emotionally to others. These traits plus a constructive personality are much more important than formal adherence to permissive counseling techniques, which not infrequently are superimposed upon an authoritarian and destructive orientation to human beings.

SOME GENERAL PRINCIPLES IN GUIDING ADOLESCENTS

In concluding this section on the guidance of adolescents, four general principles not previously considered under more specific headings may be mentioned.

(1) There is a certain urgency about solving problems of matura-

tion as they arise and about making definite progress in social and emotional growth from year to year.

> Developmental tasks which are not accomplished successfully leave the boy or girl with a lack of readiness for further development and for the tasks which the school imposes. Those who are retarded are branded as out of step and queer.[10]

(2) "The ideals of youth [are influenced] as much or more through the presence and behavior of teachers, clergy, and youth group leaders as through their verbal teachings." [9]

(3) The adolescent should be encouraged to

> adjust satisfactorily to a current reality, even if it is inconsistent, and far from what it could or might be. Even while endeavoring to change them, it is necessary to recognize established laws and customs, irrational or otherwise. The adolescent must be prepared "for the kind of world he is apt to face, not the kind adults wish existed but as yet have been unable to create. . . . [To do otherwise] is to invite him to choose a life of continual unadjustment." [14] This does not imply that the *status quo* must be accepted for what it is, but rather that a mature attitude toward social change be adopted, an attitude that does not "encourage the adolescent to batter his head against the wall of custom simply because these customs are inconsistent." [14] However, this certain minimal and desirable degree of conformity to social custom is still a far cry from advocating a policy of "hunting with the hounds." Adolescents must be taught to express and courageously defend their moral principles.[1]

(4) Finally, nothing is more important in the guidance of adolescents than maintaining that proper sense of perspective which is notoriously lacking in youth. As a transitional period in personality development, adolescence presents "certain specific, transitory, and self-limited problems in adjustment." [1]

> It is only that the new demands for final adult status lend to the trial-and-error aspects and to the many varied but none the less normal phases of adolescent behavior—its bizarre, unpredictable, and . . . worrisome characteristics. My main therapeutic approach to the parents of adolescents—my main treatment, advice and prescription to them in the face of such behavior—is the tried-and-true phrase of the men of the ancient church who, when beset by the unpredictable and seemingly uncontrollable, comforted themselves and one another with the words, "It will pass. It will pass." [6] *

---

* From *Mental Hygiene,* a quarterly journal, published by the National Association for Mental Health, Inc., New York City.

REFERENCES AND BIBLIOGRAPHY

1. Ausubel, D. P.: Problems of adolescent adjustment. Bulletin, Natl. Assn. Secondary School Principals, *34*:1–84, 1950.
2. Ausubel, D. P.: *Ego Development and the Personality Disorders.* New York: Grune & Stratton, 1952.
3. Cantor, N.: *The Dynamics of Learning.* Buffalo: Foster & Stewart, 1946.
4. Davis, A.: "Socialization and Adolescent Personality," in *Adolescence,* 43rd Yearbook, Natl. Soc. Stud. Educ., Part I. Chicago: University of Chicago Press, 1944.
5. Edwards, N.: "The Adolescent in Technological Society," in *Adolescence,* 43rd Yearbook, Natl. Soc. Stud. Educ., Part I. Chicago: University of Chicago Press, 1944.
6. Gardner, G. E.: The Mental health of normal adolescents. Ment. Hyg., *31:* 529–540, 1947.
7. Hacker, F. J. and Geleerd, E. R.: Freedom and authority in adolescence. Am. J. Orthopsychiat., *15*:621–630.
8. Harms, E.: Ego-inflation and ego-deflation, a fundamental concept of analytic psychology of childhood. Nerv. Child. *6*:284–300, 1947.
9. Havighurst, R. J., Robinson, M. Z., and Dorr, M.: The development of the ideal self in childhood and adolescence. J. Educ. Res., *40*:241–257, 1946.
10. Mackenzie, G. N.: "Implications for Teachers and Counselors," in *Adolescence,* 43rd Yearbook, Natl. Soc. Stud. Educ., Part I. Chicago: University of Chicago Press, 1944.
11. Mead, M.: *From the South Seas.* New York: William Morrow, 1939.
12. Meyers, C. E.: Emancipation of adolescents from parental control. Nerv. Child, *5*:251–262, 1946.
13. Mittelmann, B.: Briefer psychotherapy in psychosomatic disorders of children and adolescents. Nerv. Child, *8*:291–300, 1949.
14. Partridge, E. D.: "Guidance of the Adolescent," in *Handbook of Child Guidance* (E. Harms, ed.). New York: Child Care Publications, 1947.
15. Rogers, C. R.: *Client-Centered Therapy.* Boston: Houghton Mifflin, 1951.
16. Rotenberg, G.: Need for case work with parents in treatment of adolescents. Smith College. Stud. Social Work, *17*:127–128, 1946. Abstract of thesis.
17. Segel, D.: *Frustration in Adolescent Youth.* Washington, D. C.: Federal Security Agency, 1951.
18. Sobel, R.: Treatment of character-conditioned hostility in adolescents. Nerv. Child. *8*:301–310, 1949.
19. Williamson, E. G.: *Counseling Adolescents.* New York: McGraw-Hill, 1950.
20. Wittman, M. P. and Huffman, A. V.: A comparative study of developmental, adjustment, and personality characteristics of psychotic, psychoneurotic, delinquent, and normally adjusted teen-age youths. J. Genet. Psychol., *66*:167–182, 1945.
21. Zachry, C. B.: "Preparing Youth to be Adults," in *Adolescence,* 43rd Yearbook, Natl. Soc. Stud. Educ., Part I. Chicago: University of Chicago Press, 1944.

Author Index

ABBOTT, M. A., 301
Abernathy, E. M., 301
Abt, L. E., 31n, 37
Ackerson, L., 307
Adorno, T. W., 272, 301
Allen, L., 303
Allport, F. H., 274, 387, 435
Allport, G. W., 72, 180, 214, 501
Altman, I., 105
Amado, G., 338
Anderson, H. D., 468
Anderson, J. E., 31n, 37, 301
Anderson, W. A., 467
Archer, J., 435
Arnold, M., 274
Asher, E. J., 301
Ashley - Montagu, M. F., 105
Ausubel, D. P., 27n, 37, 50, 72, 129, 164, 176n, 214, 243, 272, 302, 338, 385, 433, 467, 501, 533, 548
Averill, L. A., 385

BABER, R. E., 433
Baker, E., 215
Baker, H. L., 501
Baldwin, B. T., 105, 129
Barker, R. G., 31n, 38, 105, 129, 151, 166, 216, 222, 224, 243, 245, 255, 275, 306
Bartlett, E. R., 272
Bateman, R. M., 467
Bayer, L. M., 86, 87, 105
Bayley, N., 86, 87, 105, 114, 129, 150, 164
Beach, F. A., 164, 433, 434
Beary, G. S., 502
Beck, S. J., 166, 216, 275, 306
Beebe, G. W., 106
Beekman, E., 275
Bell, H. M., 50, 273, 302, 338, 433, 467, 501
Bellak, L., 31n, 37
Bellingrath, G. C., 385

Benedict, R., 13n, 37, 68n, 72, 190, 214, 273, 317, 338, 434
Bennett, E. M., 275
Bennett, C. C., 533
Bennett, G. K., 467
Berdie, R. F., 467
Berg, J., 389
Bernreuter, R. G., 164
Best, C. H., 105
Bettelheim, B., 534
Biber, B., 214, 302
Blanchard, P., 37, 434, 534
Blatz, W. E., 164
Block, V. L., 226n, 244
Blos, P., 72, 164, 244, 338, 385, 502, 534
Boas, F., 105, 129
Bogardus, R., 385
Bolles, M. M., 165, 435
Bonney, M. E., 385, 502
Bossard, J. H. S., 434
Bovet, L., 534
Bowden, A. O., 385
Bower, P. A., 127
Bowles, G. T., 129
Boyd, W. A., 105
Boynton, P. L., 302
Bretsch, H. S., 387
Briggs, E. S., 302
Brink, W. G., 302, 470
Britten, F. H., 434
Bromley, D. D., 434
Bronner, A. F., 386, 534
Brown, F. J., 273, 302
Brown, M., 214
Brown, T. G., 106
Bruner, J. S., 180, 214
Bryan, A. I., 303
Bühler, C., 244
Bunting, J. R., 467
Burgess, E. W., 434
Burks, F. W., 385
Burt, C., 534
Busby, L. M., 129
Butterfield, O. M., 434
Byrns, R., 467

CALDWELL, O. W., 273, 274, 385
Cameron, N., 214

Cameron, W. J., 385
Campbell, A. A., 273
Campbell, E. H., 385, 434
Campbell, H. M., 385
Canning, L., 468
Cantor, N., 502, 548
Cantril, H., xiii, xiiin, xvi, 22, 38, 50, 72, 166, 275, 291n, 305, 336, 340, 356, 388, 436, 535
Caplow, T., 387, 435
Carey, T. F., 302
Carpenter, H. S., 303
Carter, H. D., 214, 468, 470
Carter, T. M., 385
Cattell, R. B., 302
Centers, R., 273, 333, 338, 339
Chaffey, J., 342, 388
Chant, S. N. F., 164
Chess, S., 535
Childers, A. T., 164
Chawdry, K., 385
Christensen, H. T., 436
Christensen, T. E., 465n, 468
Ciocco, A., 105
Clark, C. D., 468
Clark, E. T., 273
Clark, T., 130
Clark, W. R., 302
Cole, L., 50, 70, 72
Collins, S. D., 105, 130
Conrad, H. S., 72, 282, 302, 304
Corey, S. M., 49, 50, 388, 502
Cornell, E. L., 302
Courtenay, M. E., 386
Cowley, W. H., 386
Crampton, C. W., 105, 112, 116, 130
Crissy, W. J. E., 468
Criswell, J. H., 386
Cronbach, L. J., 31n, 37, 468
Crowley, J. J., 386
Cruikshank, R. M., 467
Crutchfield, R. S., xvi, xvin, 503

Cunningham, R., 244, 386, 502
Curle, A., 189n, 214, 339

DAI, B., 339
Dale, E., 244, 302
Darley, J. G., 468
Davenport, C. B., 130
Davidson, P. E., 468
Davis, A., 13n, 37, 72, 214, 281, 339, 386, 434, 502, 548
Davis, K. B., 164, 434
Davis, R. M., 307
Davis, W. A., 302
Dearborn, W. F., 302
Dennis, W., 5, 6, 37, 126, 130, 164
Despert, J. L., 279, 302
Dillon, H. J., 502
Dimock, H. S., 105, 118, 130, 164, 219, 244, 250n, 255, 273, 303, 386
Doane, D. C., 502
Dolger, H., 105
Dollard, J., 13n, 15, 37, 71, 72, 339, 434, 534
Dorr, M., 219, 244, 273, 502, 548
Drucker, A. J., 436
Dudycha, G. J., 273
Duffy, E., 468
Dunbar, H. F., 164
Dunlap, J. W., 468
Durost, W. N., 303
Durwald, V., 165
Duwald, V. F., 245
Dyer, D. T., 468
Dysinger, W. S., 148n, 303

EAGLESON, O. W., 214
Eberhart, J. C., 273
Eberhart, W., 303
Edwards, N. 337, 339, 502, 548
Elder, V., 303
Ellis, H., 164, 434
Engle, E. T., 105
English, O. S., 226n, 244
Espenschade, A., 130
Eurich, A. C., 470

FALK, E. A., 131
Fehlman, C., 502
Feinberg, M. R., 386
Feingold, G. A., 468
Feldstein, M. J., 387

Finch, F. H., 303, 468, 502
Fleege, U. H., 386
Fleming, C. M., 303, 468, 502
Flemming, E. G., 386
Flory, C. D., 130, 303
Ford, C. S., 164, 434
Ford, M. E. N., 436
Forman, H. J., 214
Fox, W. H., 534
Frank, L. K., 130, 144, 164, 195, 214, 244, 339, 386, 429, 434, 502, 520, 534
Franzblau, A. N., 273, 303
Freeman, F. N., 282, 302, 303, 305
Frankel-Brunswik, E., 273
Freud, A., 37
Freud, S., 37
Fryer, D. H., 386, 468
Furfey, P. H., 164, 294, 303, 386, 434

GABRIEL, A., 244
Gaier, E. L., 303
Gardner, G. E., 229, 244, 534, 548
Garfield, S., 470
Garrett, H. E., 303
Garside, H. V., 129
Gasser, E. B., 214, 338, 385, 501
Geleerd, E. R., 37, 548
Gesell, A., 186
Gilbert, H. H., 303
Gilliand, A. R., 273
Gist, N. P., 468
Gitelson, M., 339
Glueck, E. T., 273, 534
Glueck, S., 273, 534
Goldman, M., 302
Gonick, M. R., 105, 222, 243
Goodenough, F. L., 386, 434
Gould, H. N., 105
Gould, M. R., 105
Greulich, W. W., 31n, 37, 105, 107, 115, 130
Gronlund, N. E., 502
Grote, P., 131

HABBE, S., 164
Hacker, F. J., 37, 548
Hackett, C. G., 244
Haeckel, E., 11, 12

Hall, G. S., xii, 10, 11, 12, 13, 24, 37
Hamilton, G. V., 145, 164, 165, 434
Hankins, D., 29, 37, 434
Harms, E., 548
Harris, D. B., 272, 434, 534
Harris, J. A., 72, 105, 130
Harris, R. E., 303
Harrower, M. R., 273
Hart, F. W., 502
Hartman, C. G., 106
Hartmann, G. W., 468
Hartshorne, H., 249, 273, 386
Hartson, L., 303
Havighurst, R. J., 31n, 37, 219, 244, 252, 258, 262, 265, 267, 273, 303, 304, 305, 331, 339, 386, 502, 503, 534, 548
Hayes, M., 386, 468
Healey, W., 386, 534
Hendrickson, G., 303
Henry, W., 339
Hertz, M. R., 215
Hertzman, M., 215
Hicks, J. A., 386, 468
Hill, D. S., 273
Hillery, M. P., 270n
Hinton, R. Jr., 305
Hollingshead, A. B., 274, 334n, 339, 351, 386, 502
Hollingworth, L. S., 215, 270, 273, 289n, 303
Holzinger, K. J., 305
Honzik, M. P., 303, 434
Hopkins, L. T., 502
Horrocks, J. E., 37, 386, 388
Howard, F. E., 130
Howells, T. H., 274, 303
Hsaio, H. H., 302
Huffman, A. V., 245, 520, 536, 548
Hughes, B. O., 72
Hunter, E. C., 386
Hurlock, E. B., 146, 165, 434, 468, 502

IVINS, W. H., 534

JACK, L. M., 128, 130
Jackson, C. M., 72, 105, 130
Jackson, L., 534
Jahoda, G., 468

Jameson, A. T., 535
Jandorf, E. M., 180, 214
Janke, L. L., 303, 304
Janney, J. E., 305
Jansing, C., 468
Jenkins, G. G., 386
Jennings, H. H., 386
Jersild, A. T., 50, 119, 124, 130, 150, 165, 215, 244, 274, 299, 304, 339, 387, 435, 502
Joffe, N. R., 339
Johnson, B. L., 304
Johnson, E. S., 503
Johnston, J. A., 106
Jones, E. S., 274, 469
Jones, H. E., 31n, 37, 72, 106, 122n, 123, 127, 128, 130, 165, 215, 282, 302, 304, 387, 469
Jones, M. C., 131, 304, 342, 387, 388, 468
Jones, V., 274
Jordan, A. M., 304, 386
Joseph, A., 215
Josselyn, I. M., 106

KAGAN, H. E., 274
Kanner, L., 27n, 37
Kardiner, A., 274
Karpman, B., 535
Katz, D., 274, 387, 435
Keene, C. N., 304
Kepler, M. O., 166
Kinsey, A. C., 37, 72, 106, 138, 165, 274, 339, 398, 401, 403, 403n, 407, 413n, 414, 435
Kirkendall, L. A., 37, 165, 435
Kirkpatrick, C., 387, 435
Kitay, P. M., 435
Klein, E. R., 434
Klineberg, O., 37
Kluckhohn, C. K. M., 168n, 171n, 181, 181n, 188n, 190n, 198n, 215, 231n, 233n, 237n, 244, 253, 274, 435
Koch, H. L., 274
Komarovsky, M., 244
Koskas, R., 244
Krech, D., xvi, xvin, 503
Kroger, R., 469
Krogman, W. M., 117, 131
Krout, M. H., 244
Kuder, G. F., 469

Kuhlen, R. G., 50, 68n, 72, 126, 131, 145, 165, 215, 274, 304, 305, 387

LANDER, J., 535
Landis, C., 165, 435
Lane, R. E., 469
Langdon, G., 535
Lawton, S. U., 435
Lazar, M., 304
Leal, M. A., 339
Lee, B. J., 387
Lee, E. A., 469
Leery, J. R., 339
Legg, C. E., 503
Lehman, H. C., 304, 307, 387, 469
Leighton, D. C., 168n, 171n, 181, 181n, 188n, 190n, 198n, 215, 231n, 233n, 237n, 244, 253, 274, 435
Leonard, E. A., 244
Levi, I. J., 387
Levinson, D. J., 273
Levy, D. M., 148, 165, 244
Levy, J., 304
Lewin, K., 54, 72, 244
Lewis, W. D., 304
Lima, M., 306
Linton, R., 274
Lippitt, R., 244, 503
Locke, J., 25
Loeb, M. B., 503
Logan, R. F. L., 469
Lorge, I., 304
Louttit, C. M., 469
Lowrey, G. H., 106
Lucena, J., 304, 535
Lucht, K. G., 244
Lundeen, G. E., 273, 274
Lunt, P. S., 307, 340
Lurie, L. A., 535
Lurie, M. B., 106
Lynd, H. M., 13n, 38, 244, 339, 435
Lynd, R. S., 13n, 38, 244, 339, 435
Lyness, P. I., 305

MACCOBY, E. E., 305
MacFarlane, J. W., 303
MacGowan, K., 434
Mackenzie, G. N., 244, 503, 548
Maier, N. R. F., 145, 165, 515, 535

Maller, J. B., 274, 535
Malinowski, B., 138, 165, 435
Malzberg, B., 535
Manwell, E. M., 130
Marchetti, A. A., 106
Maresh, M. M., 106, 131
Margulies, H., 215
Markey, F. V., 215
Markey, O. B., 535
Martin, V., 214
Masserman, J. H., 145, 165
Mather, W. G., 305, 387, 435
Mathews, E., 165
May, M. A., 249, 273, 386
McCloy, C. H., 131
McGehee, W. A., 304
McKay, H. D., 535
McNemar, Q., 305
Mead, M., 13, 13n, 38, 72, 196, 215, 254, 272, 274, 339, 399, 403, 435, 548
Meek, L. H., 342, 387, 469
Meltzer, H., 274
Menaker, J., 106
Mengert, I. G., 130
Merrill, M. A., 277, 306
Messerschmidt, R., 245
Meyers, C. E., 215, 245, 548
Michaud, S., 305
Miles, C. C., 134, 166, 306, 436
Mills, C. A., 106
Milner, E., 332, 339
Minard, R. D., 274
Mitchell, A. M., 305
Mitchell, C., 305
Mittelmann, B., 548
Mohr, G. J., 535
Molish, H. B., 166, 216, 275, 306
Mooney, R., 50, 469
Moreno, J. J., 274, 387, 503
Moss, R. M., 469
Mullahy, P., 191n
Murphy, G., 27n, 38, 215
Murray, V. F., 215
Myers, M. S., 275

NEILON, P., 215
Nelson, E., 274
Nestrick, W. V., 131
Neubauer, P. B., 535

Newcomb, T. M., 274, 385, 387
Newman, H. H., 305
Newstetter, W. I., 387
Nichols, C. A., 274
Northway, M. L., 387
Nunberg, H., 38
Nystrom, W. C., 388

OAKES, M. E., 275, 305
Oden, M. H., 291, 306
Odoroff, M. E., 468
Ogilvie, F., 339
Ogle, C., 106
Ojemann, R. H., 245, 535
Oleson, R., 106
Olson, W. C., 72
Orlansky, H., 27n, 38
Otto, P., 385
Owen, M. B., 535

PAPANICOLAOU, G. N., 131
Parsons, T., 435, 469
Parten, M. B., 215
Partridge, E. D., 387, 469, 548
Patrick, J. R., 275
Paterson, D. G., 72, 105, 130, 469
Pavlov, I. P., 145, 165
Perl, R. E., 303
Perrin, F. A., 165
Peters, E. F., 469
Piaget, J., 250, 251, 275
Pierce, H. O., 279, 302
Pixley, E., 275
Plant, J. S., 535
Pope, C., 50
Porterfield, A. L., 535
Postman, L. J., 501
Powdermaker, H., 330, 339
Pressey, S. L., 275, 305, 387
Proctor, W. M., 469
Punke, H. H., 275, 387, 435
Purvis, A. W., 305

RADIN, P., 13n, 38, 339
Rainey, H. P., 469
Ramsey, G. V., 106, 165, 435, 436
Rank, O., 29, 38
Redl, F., 387, 535
Regensburg, J., 305

Reichard, S., 535
Remmers, H. H., 165, 245, 249, 275, 436, 467, 469
Reymert, M., 305
Reynolds, E. L., 106, 131
Richardson, C. A., 305
Richey, H. G., 106, 131
Robinson, F. P., 275, 305, 387
Robinson, M. Z., 219, 244, 273, 502, 548
Rockwood, L. D., 436
Rogers, A. L., 305
Rogers, C. R., 548
Rommetveit, R., 275
Roper, E., 469
Rosander, A. C., 275
Ross, C. C., 305
Ross, H., 339
Rotenberg, G., 548
Rothney, J. W. M., 302
Ruckmick, C. A., 148n, 303

SALTER, M. D., 164
Sanford, R. N., 273
Scammon, R. E., 72, 105, 130
Schiff, H. M., 214, 302, 338, 385, 501
Schilder, P., 165
Schmideberg, M., 535
Schonfeld, W. A., 106, 131, 165
Schulman, M. J., 305
Sears, P. S., 305
Sears, R. R., 27n, 38
Seashore, R. H., 122n, 123, 131
Segel, D., 305, 339, 388, 503, 534, 535, 548
Sender, S., 146, 165
Shaffer, L. F., 165, 215
Shannon, J. R., 388
Sharp, D. L., 165
Shaw, C. R., 388, 535
Shelesnyak, M. C., 105
Sherif, M., xiii, xiiin, xvi, 22, 38, 50, 72, 166, 275, 291, 305, 336, 340, 356, 388, 436, 535
Sherman, A. W., 223, 245
Shirley, M. M., 215
Shock, N. W., 96, 106, 166
Shuey, A. M., 306
Shuttleworth, F. K., 93, 107, 131, 306, 536
Silverman, H. L., 245, 340

Silverman, S. S., 166, 215
Simmons, K., 107, 131
Sims, V. M., 275
Sisson, E. D., 469
Skaggs, E. B., 436
Smith, G. V., 436
Smith, H. P., 166, 388, 503
Smith, M., 388, 470
Snyder, T. A., 306
Sobel, R., 548
Sollenberger, R. T., 134, 166, 306
Sontag, L. W., 520n, 535
Spitz, R. A., 215
Stagner, R., 244, 245
Steinert, J., 535
Stendler, C. B., 215, 275, 340
Stevens, G. C., 245, 536
Stockard, C. R., 131
Stoke, S. M., 388
Stokes, C. W., 305
Stolz, H. R., 72, 107, 118, 131, 162, 166, 215, 342, 388
Stolz, L. M., 72, 107, 118, 131, 162, 166, 215, 388
Stone, C. H., 469, 470
Stone, C. P., 129, 151, 166, 216, 224, 245, 255, 275, 304, 306
Stott, L. H., 226, 226n, 245
Stout, I. W., 535
Strang, R., 275
Strong, E. K., 306, 468, 470
Sullenger, T. E., 388
Sullivan, Sister C., 294, 306, 436
Super, D. E., 470
Sutherland, R., 340
Svehla, G., 274
Symonds, P. M., 50, 166, 216, 245, 306

TABA, H., 31n, 37, 252, 258, 262, 265, 267, 273, 331, 339, 386, 502, 534
Tasch, R. J., 502
Taylor, K. V., 468, 470
Taylor, K. W., 388
Taylor, N. B., 105
Taylor, W. S., 38, 166, 436
Ter Keurst, A. J., 275
Terman, L. M., 134, 166, 245, 277, 291, 305, 306, 436

Thetford, W. N., 166, 216, 275, 306
Thompson, C. W., 303
Thompson, G. G., 166, 275, 386, 388
Thomsen, A., 470
Thorndike, E. L., 306, 470
Thorndike, R. L., 306
Thorpe, L. P., 469
Thrasher, F. M., 388
Thurstone, L. L., 227n, 307
Tillman, C., 535
Todd, T. W., 131
Triggs, F. O., 307, 470
Tryon, C. M., 146, 166, 226n, 245, 340, 388
Tuddenham, R. D., 114, 129, 150, 164
Tudor-Hart, B. E., 275
Tyler, I. K., 307

VALENTINE, W. L., 275
Van Dalen, D. B., 131
Van Dyne, E. V., 388
Van Tuyl, K., 470
Viteles, M. S., 132
Vreeland, F. M., 388

WALLIN, P., 434
Walters, A., 470
Warden, C. J., 340
Warner, W. L., 307, 340, 503
Warren, W., 536
Washburn, R. W., 216
Washburne, J. N., 216
Wechsler, D., 166, 307
Wellman, B., 385, 388
Weltman, N., 249, 275
West, E. D., 388
West, J., 340, 436
Wetzel, N. C., 132
Wheeler, L. R., 307
Whisler, L. D., 165, 245, 469
White, R. K., 244
Whiting, J. W. M., 13n, 38, 436
Whitley, M. T., 307
Whyte, W. F., 388
Wile, I. S., 307
Willgoose, C. E., 132
Williams, F. E., 13n, 38, 340

Williamson, E. G., 548
Willoughby, R. R., 166, 436
Wineman, D., 535
Winslow, C. N., 389
Wissler, C., 132
Wittels, R., 38
Wittenberg, R. M., 389
Wittman, M. P., 245, 520, 536, 548
Witty, P. A., 304, 307, 387, 469, 470
Wolford, O. P., 436
Wolman, B., 389
Wright, B. A., 105, 222, 243
Wright, H. F., 31n, 38
Wright, R., 340

YOUNG, F. M., 503

ZACHRY, C. B., 216, 245, 340, 389, 522, 536, 548
Zacker, H. J., 245, 536
Zorbaugh, H. W., 389

Subject Index

ABILITY, and interests, 449–450
and vocational choice, 449
Acceptance (parental), and satellization, 171
Accidents in adolescence, 100–104
causes of, 104
sex differences in, 104
types of, 104
Accident-proneness, 100
Acne, 91, 96, 97
and androgens, 103n
cause of, 91
and gonadal imbalance, 103
incidence of, 100
psychological significance of, 103, 152–153, 162
sex differences in, 153
treatment of, 103
Acquired characteristics, inheritance of, 12, 24

Addison's disease, 81, 101
thymus gland in, 96
Adequacy, feelings of, in childhood, 172
in infancy, 170
in non-satellizers, 211
and personality adequacy, 183–184
sources of, 201
Adjustment (adolescent), in bright and dull, 289–290
constitutional basis of, 43
difficulty of, 512, 513
and intelligence, 289–291
in non-satellizers, 512–513
in satellizers, 512–513
techniques of, 42–43
psychobiological aspects, 42
psychosocial aspects, 42–43
Adolescence
abrupt onset of, 57–59
and anxiety, 59
and disorientation, 59

Adolescence—*Cont'd*
abrupt onset of—*Cont'd*
  and insecurity, 59
  among Manus, 59
as an age period, 5–6
approaches to
  biogenetic, xii, 10
  biological, 10–13, 311
  Dennis', 5–7, 12
  eclectic, 12
  empirical, xii, 9
  ethnocentric bias in, 13
  ethnological, 13–14, 13n
  G. Stanley Hall's, 10, 24
  impressionistic, 9
  measurement, 9
  psychoanalytic, xii, 24–29
  Rankian, 29–30
  social, xii–xiii, 10, 12–15, 311
biological factors in, 14–15
biosocial shifts in status in, 22
definition of, 73
developmental homogeneity in, 6
difficulty of
  among Arapesh, 16–21
  in complex cultures, 20–21
  ethnological survey of, 15–22
  among Kwama, 20
  among lower class, 21–22
  among Manus, 19–20
  among middle-class, 21–22
  among Mundugumors, 20–21
  in primitive cultures, 20–21
duration of, 59–61
  vs. abruptness, 59–60
  defined, 60
  importance, 60
  and need for interim status, 60–61
field of, 3–4
as field of specialization, xii
  justification for, 4–7
genetic determination of, 11
and human behavior, 7
individual differences in, 7
in infra-humans, 11, 40
among Manus, 11
onset of, 21
in other cultures, 13
personality reorganization in, 23
as a phylogenetic phenomenon, 11
preparation for in childhood, 57–59
prolongation of
  causes, 319–324
  and economic depression, 439
  effects, 61, 324–327
  and social class, 331
  and social mobility, 439

  and unavailability of jobs, 439
vs. pubescence, 73
rate of psychological change in, 6
ritual demarcation of, 21
in Samoa, 19
shifts in biosocial status in, 24
social regulation of, 45
as stage of personality development,
  xii, 7, 22–24, 48–49
stages of, 70–72
  chronological, 70
  as function of stress, 70
  initial, 70
status changes in, 43–44
"storm and stress" in, 13
theories of, 12
  biogenetic, xii
  and cultural anthropology, xii
  psychoanalytic, xii
  social, xii–xiii
as a transitional stage, 41
Adolescent growth spurt, 111–116
age of, 112
  and age of pubescence, 112, 113–114
  in boys, 112
  determinants, 112
  in girls, 112
  and hormonal stimulation, 112
in delayed puberty, 114
endocrine aspects of, 114–116
initiation of, 114–115
  and gonadal hormones, 115
  and growth hormone, 114
  patterns of, 112
in precocious puberty, 114
termination of, 114–116
  and gonadal hormones, 115–116
  and growth hormone, 114
Adolescent problems
classification of, 39–46
  descriptive, 39
  in terms of origins, 39
  value of, 39
definition of, 40–41, 44
nature of, 40–41, 44
psychobiological, 40–44
psychosocial, 40, 44–46
sources of, 41–44, 44–46
Adolescents
socioeconomic status of, 43–44
and wider community, 313–319
  discontinuity in status, 317
  discontinuity in values, 316–318
  estrangement between, 316–319
Adornment, interest in, 150–151
  effect of menarche on, 151
  in preadolescence, 150–151

underlying motivations, 151
Adrenal cortex, 63, 77
  and bone growth, 115
  growth curve of, 78
  and growth in strength, 115
  hypertrophic tumors of, 79, 101
  in prepubescence, 79, 80
  role in pubescence, 79, 80
  and secondary sex characteristics, 86
  secretion of sex hormones by, 79
Adult roles, 44–45
  kinds of, 44
Adult stature
  and age of pubescence, 108–109, 113–
    114, 116
  and anterior pituitary gland, 109
  determinants of, 108–109
  in early and late puberty, 113
  effect of heredity on, 109
  in late puberty, 113
  effect of nutrition, 109
  and precocious puberty, 113
  prediction of, 109
  and prepubescent height, 109, 113
  racial differences in, 109n
Adulthood, abrupt onset of, 59
Aggression, 42
  and androgens, 147
  and castration, 147
  and delinquency, 518, 524–525
  and estrus, 147
  and peer group, 525–526
  social class norms of, 525
Alcoholism, incidence in adolescence, 511
Alorese culture, preadolescent sex play in,
  136
Androgens, 79, 80
  and aggressive behavior, 147
  and bone growth, 115
  effect on glans penis, 140
  and growth in strength, 119
  and ossification, 115, 116
Androgen-estrogen ratio, 79, 80
Androgyny, scale of, 86
Anterior pituitary gland, 76
  hypertrophic tumors of, 79, 101
Anti-social psychopath, moral agenesis in,
  529
  characteristics of, 529
Anxiety
  and abruptness of adolescence, 59
  and emotional instability, 145, 509
  Freud's views on, 26
  and guilt, 247
  and learning, 292

neurotic, 211n, 509
  in non-satellizers, 211, 489–491, 512
  in overvalued child, 213, 213n
  in rejected child, 212
  physiological symptoms of, 156
  and self-esteem, 509
  and sex repression, 15, 26
  "socialized," see Anxiety, transitional
  transitional, 55, 56
    in adolescence, 55–56
    causes of, 55–56
    consequences of, 56
    cultural generation of, 56
    and developmental regression, 70
    and personality maturation, 207
    reduction of, 56
    and self-esteem, 55
    "socially adaptive" nature of, 56
    sources of, 56
    and stages of adolescence, 71
    and transmission of values, 335
    and vocational choice, 445, 453
Aptitude, and vocational choice, 449
Arapesh culture
  adolescent stress in, 404
  biological sex role in, 417
  courting behavior in, 425
  psychosexual development in, 15
  repression of sex drives in, 398
  sex drive in, 141, 142, 397
  sex orientation in, 431
  sexuality in, 393, 396
  sex differences, 412
  social sex role in, 417, 431
Asceticism, 26, 30, 402, 427
  and prolongation of adolescence, 326
Asexuality, 144, 427
Aspirations for self-enhancement, 23
"Asynchrony of development," 118
  psychological reactions to, 151–152
Atheism, in college students, 269
Attitudes, disorientation in, 54
Authoritarianism, in schools, 478–480
  effects of, 478–480
  pupils' acceptance of, 479
Autoeroticism, see Masturbation
Automobile driving, interest in, 342
Awkwardness (adolescent), 120
  and abruptness of growth, 126–127
  causes of, 126–127
    biological, 126
    social, 126
  consequences of, 120
  and unevenness of growth, 126

BASAL metabolic rate, definition of, 97
  during pubescence, 97

Basal metabolic rate—*Cont'd*
  sex differences in, 97
  and thyroid gland, 97
Behavior disorders
  classification of, 515–517
    "maturational failure," 516
    residual, 516
    serious, 516
    transitory, 516
  and constitutional factors, 511
  differential diagnosis of, 516–517
  evaluation of, 507–513
  importance of childhood experience for,
    510–511
  incidence of, 511–513
  in non-satellizers, 515
  onset of, 513
  and parent attitudes, 511
  and parent-child relationships, 510
  prognosis of, 516
  psychoanalytic misconceptions of, 509
  relative seriousness of, 507–508
  role of adolescence in, 511–513
  role of emotional instability in, 508–
    510
Betsileo culture, moral confusion in, 261
Biological sex role, xiii, 22, 27, 49, 67,
  396
  American, 417
  Arapesh, 417
  differentiation of, 397
  effect of pubescence on, 143
  facilitation of, 143–144
  formation of, 144–145
  influence of sex hormones on, 143
  Manus, 417
  Mundugumor, 417
  outcome of, 144
  polarization of, 417
  in preadolescence, 142–143
  precipitation of, 142
  prerequisites for, 142–143
  and pubescence, 416–417
  relation to sex drive, 142
  retarding factors, 144
Biosocial dependency, in childhood, 193
Biosocial status
  in adolescence, 178
  in childhood, 178
  in infancy, 178
  shifts in, 15, 53
Bisexuality, 144
"Blackheads," 91
Blood pressure (in adolescence)
  diastolic, 97–98
  and exercise, 98
  sex differences in, 98
  systolic, 97–98

Body build, 87–88
  changes during pubescence, 87–88
  kinds of variations in, 87
  psychological reactions to, 159–160
  salient features of, 88
  standards of, 87
Body changes, perceptual reactions to, 134
  social reactions to, 134
Body image, 135–136
  adolescent changes in, 135–136
  components of, 135–136
  definition of, 135
  in preadolescence, 135
Body odor, 152
Body proportions (adolescent), 117–118
  chronology of changes in, 117
  in early maturers, 118
  face, 117
  in late maturers, 118
  nose, 117
  sex differences in, 117
  trunk-leg ratio, 117
Bone changes, in adolescence, 110–111
Bone growth
  and adrenal cortex, 115
  and androgens, 115, 116
  in childhood, 110
  and estrogens, 115, 116
  and gonadal hormones, 115–116
  and growth hormone, 114–116
Bone structure, in adolescence, 110–111
Brace test, effect of pubescence on, 127
Breasts, areola of, 87
  in childhood, 87
  development of, 77, 86, 87
  hormonal stimulation of, 87
  in infants, 87
  in males, 87
  nipple of, 87
  pathological conditions of, 87
  psychological significance of, 86–87
  during pubescence, 87

CANALIZATION, and personality continuity, 184
Cardiovascular changes (pubescent), 77,
  97–98
  and adrenal cortex, 98
  blood pressure, 97–98
  cardiac capacity, 97
  and exercise tolerance, 98
  minute volume, 98
  pulse pressure, 98
  sex differences in, 98
  stroke volume, 98
Case history method, 35–36, 37
  misuse of, xv
  value of, xv

Caste
    basis of, 328–329
    and skin color, 328, 329, 329n
Castration, 81
    and aggressive behavior, 147
    effect on sex drive, 139, 140n
    and voice changes, 92
Chamorros, parent attitudes of, 167
Cheyenne Indians, child-adult dichotomy
    among, 190
Chicago Area Projects, 533
Child-adult dichotomy, see Parent-child
    estrangement
Childhood experience, as psychobiological
    factor, 42
Circulatory adjustment, 98
    and exercise tolerance, 98
    sex differences, 98
Climate, effect of on pubescence, 81
Cliques (adolescent), 346
    basis of, 351–352
    definition of, 350
    formation of, 350–353
    and interests, 352
    and personal acceptability, 352
    and pubescent status, 351–352
    snobbishness in, 352–353
        in schools, 353
    and social class status, 351
Conscience, components of, 246–247
    definition of, 246
    and guilt, 247
    and inhibitory control, 247
    and intellectual growth, 247
    and moral obligation, 246
    and self-critical faculty, 247
Constitution, and personality constancy,
    182
Continuity, developmental, 40, 48
    in adolescence, 46–48
    reasons for, 47
"Core curriculum," 493
Corticotropic hormone, 76
    in childhood, 78
    influence on adrenal cortex, 77
    in prepubescence, 79, 80
    in pubescence, 78, 80
Counseling (adolescent), 543–547
    directive, 545
    need for diagnosis in, 546
    non-authoritarian, 543
    non-directive, 543–546
Counselors, characteristics of, 547
Courting behavior, 421–427
    functions of, 422
    and pubescence, 422
    romantic pattern of, 424–425
        and affection, 425

    among Arapesh, 425
    concepts of, 425
    cultural differences in, 425
    among Navaho Indians, 425
Courting beliefs, 425–426
Courting problems, 426
"Cross-sectional" methods, 32–36
"Crowds" (adolescent), 346–350
"Crushes," 326
    outcome of, 424
    sex differences in, 423–424
    as transitional behavior, 423
    types of, 423–424
Culpability, in delinquency, 521–522
"Cultural lag," 337–338
Curriculum organization, 493–494
Cushing's syndrome, 101
    and obesity, 104

DANCING, interest in, 342
Data, developmental
    case study, 35–36
    "cross-sectional," 31–34, 36
    longitudinal, 32–36
    representative, xv, xvi, xvin, 31, 36
    and theoretical framework, 36
Dating, 348, 424
Dating beliefs, 425
    sex differences in, 425
Day dreaming, and pubescence, 176–177
Delayed puberty, 78, 82, 83
    adolescent growth spurt in, 114
    and adult stature, 113
    causes of, 101–102
    sequence in, 95
Delinquency (adolescent)
    age trends in, 517–518
    and aggression, 518, 524–525
    and authoritarian discipline, 236
    classification of, 523–524
    compared to preadolescent, 518–519
    definition of, 518
    differential diagnosis of, 523–524
    distinction from crime, 518n
    etiological factors in, 524–532
        aggression, 524–525
        frustration, 532
        gang formation, 526
        home conditions, 527
        intellectual deficit, 531
        moral confusion, 526
        moral defects, 527–531
        organic brain injuries, 531
        parent attitudes, 528–529
        peer group pressures, 525–526
        personality traits, 531–532
        post-concussion syndrome, 531
        post-encephalitic Parkinsonism, 531

Delinquency (adolescent)—*Cont'd*
  etiological factors in—*Cont'd*
    racial and ethnic discrimination, 527
    slum areas, 526–528
    transitional pressures, 524–526
  group nature of, 381–382
  impact of pubescence on, 519
  incidence of, 511, 517–518
  multiple causality of, 523
  and parent-youth conflict, 232
  preventive measures against, 532–533
  problem of culpability in, 521–523
  prognosis of, 523–524, 530–531
  and prolongation of adolescence, 325
  sex differences in, 519–521
  sporadic, 516
  transitory, 523, 524
Delinquents (adolescent)
  gregarious nature of, 527–528
  loyalties of, 527–528
Demagogy, 196
Dependence, executive, in childhood, 171,
    172
  in infancy, 168
  perception of, 169
  and volitional dependence, 171
  and volitional omnipotence, 169
Dependence-independence, issue of, 178
Dependence, volitional, in childhood, 174
  and executive dependence, 171
Dependency, biosocial, 185
  in childhood, 167–175
  determinants of, 167–170
  and parent attitudes, 167
  perception of, 169
  qualifying factors in, 167–170
Depression, economic
  and prolongation of adolescence, 322–
    323, 439
  as a psychosocial problem, 45
  and vocational choice, 448
Desatellization, and primary status, 197–
    199
  in childhood, 173
  difficulties of, 205
  and exploratory orientation, 199–200
  and "extended family," 203
  facilitation of, 203
  mechanisms of, 194–200
  and resatellization, 194–197
  and unconditional acceptance, 202
Developmental age, 294
  Furfey's test of, 294
  Sullivan's test of, 294
Developmental regression
  factors involved in, 70
  prevention of, 69–70

Developmental tasks, of adolescence, 46,
    48–50
  completed, 47
  kinds of, 49
  and personality maturation, 49–50
  unfinished, 47
Deviant adolescents, *see* Socially rejected
    adolescent
Diabetes, in adolescence, 102
Diaries, 176
Diphtheria, in adolescence, 101
Discipline (in adolescence), 235–238
  authoritarian, 235–236
  changed methods of, 235–237
  democratic, 480–481
  externalized, 238
  impersonal, 236
  internalized, 238
  by lateral sanctions, 237
  lax, 237
  among Navaho Indians, 235–236, 237
  need for, 237–238
  non-vindictive, 236
  and personality maturation, 237
  in schools, 480–481
  through shaming, 237
  use of punishment in, 237–238
  use of reward in, 237–238
Disease
  during adolescence, 99–104
  age patterns in, 99
  crippling, 181
  importance of, 99–100
  infections, 99
Disorientation, and abruptness of adoles-
    cence, 59
Displacement of affect, 156
"Disuse atrophy," of heart muscle, 125
Dobu culture, moral confusion in, 261
"Double standard," 262, 396, 410, 411
Drives, acquired, 138
  definition of, 139n
  direction of, 41, 76
  emergent, 42, 76
  patterning of, 45
  primary, 138
  psychoanalytic conception of, 138
  secondary, 138
  socialization of, 41, 42, 45, 76
"Drop-outs" (school), 498–500
Drug addiction, adjustive, 516, 517
  differential diagnosis of, 517
  frequency of in adolescence, 511
  outbreak of in 1951, 517
  predispositions to, 512–513
  prognosis of, 517
  transitory, 516, 517

ECONOMIC SECURITY, as an adolescent problem, 437
youth's concern about, 320
Ego aspirations, in non-satellizers, 208, 209, 211
Ego devaluation, in infancy, 170–171
and negativism, 172
in non-satellizers, 208–209
and satellization, 172
Ego development, during adolescence, 24
and frustration, 514
and personality reorganization, 23
Ego revaluation, 177
Egocentricity, infantile, 250
and moral obligations, 251
and vocational choice, 453
"Elmtown's Youth," 334
Emancipation (from home) in adolescence, 49
and adult personality status, 217, 218, 224
and age-mate socialization, 219–220
age trends in, 218–219
and attitude toward authority, 222
correlation with pubescent status, 219
criteria of, 219
definition of, 217
delay of, 65
determinants of, 218–219
developmental tasks of, 218
Dimock's scale for, 219
and ego revaluation, 177
facilitating factors, 222–223
goals of, 233
in infra-humans, 217
and introversion-extroversion, 222
meaning of, 217–218
mechanisms of, 219–221
and parent devaluation, 221
and parent rivalry, 204
and parent socialization, 219
partial, 65, 224
and peer group, 220, **341**
and personality maturation, 218
and physical maturity, 222
and physical mobility, 220
preconditions for, 221
and primary status, 221
in primitive cultures, 21, 223
and prolongation of adolescence, 224, 324
and pubescence, 217, 221
and religious activity, 272
and resatellization, 220–221
retarding factors, 203–204, 220–221
in rural cultures, 223
and school, 471, 473

sex differences in, 222–223
social class differences, 223
social determinants, 223
and social horizon, 220
and socioeconomic dependence, 218
stages of, 218–219
unevenness in, 64, 217–218, 223–224
in urban cultures, 223
and withdrawal of derived status, 221
Emotion, social regulation of, 45
Emotional changes (adolescent), 145–148
lack of evidence about, 145
measurement of, 145
non-specific, 145–147
specific, 147–148
Emotional instability (adolescent)
causes of, 145, 146
characteristics of, 146
confusion as cause, 145
developmental sources of, 146
effect on IQ, 278–279
evidence for, 146–147
and frustration, 145
and hormonal imbalance, 145
and hyperinsulinism, 145
manifestations of, 509
and menopause, 145
non-specific aspects of, 508
and prolongation of adolescence, 324
psychobiological sources of, 146
psychological sources of, 145, 146
psychosocial sources of, 146
role of in behavior disorders, 508–510
sex differences in, 147, 509
and sex repression, 26, 398, 403–404
sex repression, theory of, 15–22
social class differences in, 509
subjective symptoms of, 509
symptoms of, 145–146
and thyroid dysfunction, 145
Emotional lability, 146
Endocrine disorders, in adolescence, 101–103
Endocrine glands
changes with age, 78–79
extirpation of, 78
growth of, 78–79
surgical removal of, 78
Endocrinology, of pubescence, 79
Epicureanism, 232
Epiphysial cartilage, in adolescence, 110–111
Erotic stimuli, 140–141
Estrogens, 79, 80
and bone growth, 115
in menstruation, 84
and ossification, 115, 116

Ethnic origin, and peer group, 347
Eunuchoidism, and voice changes, 92
Evidence (developmental), difficulties of obtaining, 31
  problems of, 30–37
Exercise tolerance (adolescent), 98
Exhibitionism, in preadolescence, 136
Existentialism, and parent-youth conflict, 232
Exploratory orientation, 201
  and age-mate socialization, 200
  in childhood, 199
  and desatellization, 199–200
  and intellectual maturation, 250
  limitations of, 200
  and moral development, 247–248
  nature of, 199
  and religious beliefs, 271
  in school learning, 483–484, 487
Extrinsically valued child, see Overvalued child

FALLOPIAN TUBES, 80
Fat, deposition of in pubescence, 88
  distribution of, 117
Fear, adolescent changes in, 148
Femininity, 88
  cultural concepts of, 415
  effect of pubescence on 415–416
Feminism, 420
Fixation, in psychosexual development, 27
Flightiness, 146
Friendliness, concepts of during adolescence, 267–268
Friendships (adolescent), 366–369
  bases for selection, 367–368
  "best," 367
  disruption of, 369
  function of, 367
  nature of, 367
  sex differences in, 369
  stability of, 368–369
Fröhlich's syndrome, 83, 86, 101
  and obesity, 104
Frustration, adjustive responses to, 514
  and behavioral resources, 514
  disorganizing responses to, 514
  and ego-involvement, 514
  and frustration tolerance, 514
  and level of aspiration, 514
  Maier's concept of, 515
  meaning of, 513–515
  objective aspects of, 513–514
  and personality maturation, 201–202
  and self-critical ability, 514
  subjective nature of, 513–514

Frustration-aggression hypothesis, and emotional instability, 515
Frustration tolerance, 24, 201–202
  and frustration, 514
  in non-satellizers, 210
  in overvalued child, 213–214
  and vocational choice, 452

GANGS (adolescent), 350–351, 376–382
  adolescent vs. preadolescent, 346
  characteristics of, 350–351
  girl, 382
  predatory, 325
  "street-corner," 377–382
    activities of, 382
    conditions for formation of, 378
    vs. "crowds," 377
    deterioration of, 379
    and "generation conflict," 378
    girls in, 382
    nature of, 377–378
    norms of, 381–387
    organization of, 378, 380–381
    origins of, 378
    perpetuation of, 379
    solidarity of, 380
    special deprivations experienced by, 378
    unisexual nature of, 382
Gangster, values of, 345
General intelligence (in adolescence), 276–277
  differential aspects of, 280–285
    among brightness groups, 282–283
    impact of schooling on, 282
    occupational differences, 280–281
    sex differences, 280
    socioeconomic differences, 280–281
    among sub-abilities, 282–283
  differentiation of, 277n, 281, 283–284
    in brightness groups, 284
    causes of, 284
    for different sub-abilities, 284
    effect of environment on, 281
    evidence of, 284
    implications for curriculum, 284
    relative to schooling, 282, 284
    relative to sex, 280, 284
    in social class groups, 281, 284
  distribution of, 279–280
    historical trends in, 280
    sex differences in, 280
  effect of emotional instability on, 278
  effect of environment on, 281
  effect of pubescence on, 277–279
  growth curve of, 276–277

horizontal growth in, 277
influence of heredity on, 280
among Kentucky mountain children, 281
measurement of, 281
  test bias in, 281
in precocious puberty, 278
and socioeconomic deprivation, 281
terminal point of, 277
for brightness groups, 277
validity of concept of, 277n
variability in, 280
  sex differences, 280
vertical growth in, 277
"Generation conflict," 229, 230
and "street-corner" gangs, 378
Genitalia
  female, 82, 83
  growth of, 81
  hormonal stimulation of, 81
  male, 81-83
    norms of, 82-83
    psychological significance of, 81-82
    variability in size, 82-83
  in neonate, 81
  underdevelopment of, 83
    genetic causes of, 82, 83
    hormonal causes of, 83
    treatment of, 83
"Going-steady," 347
Goiter, in adolescence, 102-103
Gonadal hormones, 77
  and bone growth, 115
  in prepubescence, 80
Gonadal imbalance, in adolescence, 95, 96, 102, 103
Gonadotropic hormones, 76, 78
  influence on gonads, 77
  and production of ova, 81
  and production of sperm, 81
  during pubescence, 80
  in urine, 80
Gonads
  growth during prepubescence, 80
  growth during pubescence, 80
  and mumps, 81
  tuberculosis of, 81
Goodenough M-F test, 415-416
  effect of pubescence on, 415-416
Grooming, interest in, 150-151, 177
  effect of menarche on, 151
  in preadolescence, 150-151
  underlying motivations, 151
Group experience (adolescent), 342
  age trends in, 348
  extrovertiveness of, 345

general characteristics of, 345-348
goals of, 344
heterosexual basis of, 347-348
and heterosexual relationships, 342
individual approaches to, 359-361
  and childhood experience, 360
  and need for primary status, 360
  in overdominated child, 360-361
  in overprotected child, 360-361
  in overvalued child, 360-361
  and parent-child relationship, 360
  in rejected child, 360-361
  and satellization, 360
preoccupation with, 342
and social identity, 343
solidarity of, 346-347
as source of primary status, 342-343
stratification of, 346-347
subjectivity of, 345-346
Group life, see Group experience
Grouping (in school)
  difficulties of, 495-496
  disadvantages of, 495-496
  vs. individualization, 495-496
Growth hormone (pituitary), 78, 81, 114
  and skeletal growth, 78
Growth spurt, see Adolescent growth spurt
Guidance (in adolescence)
  general principles of, 546-547
  perspective in, 547
Guilt feelings, in adolescence, 253-255
  components of, 247
  conditions for development of, 253
  and conscience, 247
  definition of, 247
  and external sanctions, 253-254
  and internal sanctions, 253-254
  Margaret Mead's views of, 253-254
  among Navaho Indians, 250
  psychoanalytic view of, 253-254
  and shame, 247, 253-255
Gynecomastia, 87

HAIR, 88-90
  axillary, 88, 89
  causes of variability in, 88
  changes during pubescence, 88-90
  facial, 88-90
    as criterion of male pubescence, 89
    psychological reactions to, 152
    sequence of growth, 90
    sex differences, 89
  of head, 88
  medullation of, 88
  pigmentation of, 88

Hair—*Cont'd*
  pubic, 88, 89
    in boys, 89
    as criterion of pubescence, 89, 92
    in girls, 89
    pigmentation of, 89
    during pubescence, 88
  sex differences in, 88–90
  sex inappropriateness in, 88
  terminal, 88
Health, general
  during adolescence, 99–104
  and age of pubescence, 81
  effect on pubescence, 75
Heart disease, in adolescence, 100
Hedonistic needs, 49
  in adolescence, 180
    attenuation of, 185, 193
    in overvalued child, 214
    postponement of in childhood, 172
    and vocational choice, 452–453
Height, maximum yearly increment in
  as criterion of pubescence, 93
  mean age of, 92–93
Heredity, and age of pubescence, 81
  phylogenetic, 73–75
  and pubescence, 73–75
Heresy (adolescent), and parent-youth conflict, 271
Hermaphroditism, 83
Hero worship
  in non-satellizers, 487
  in satellizers, 488
Heterosexual activities, and school, 471
Heterosexual adjustment
  determinants of, 426–427
  prognostic factors in, 427
Heterosexual interests, sex differences in, 348
Heterosexual relationships (adolescent)
  vs. childhood, 421–422
  developmental changes in, 422–425
    preadolescent segregation, 422–423
    romantic pattern, 424–425
    transitional patterns, 424–425
  functions of, 422
  institutionalization of, 421–422
  interests in, 422
    and pubescence, 422
  and peer group, 422
  and school, 482
  stability of, 424–425
Heterosexuality, establishment of, 26, 27
Hips, rounding of, 88
  widening of, 117
Hirsutism, 89

Hobbies (adolescent), 301
Homosexual outlets, frequency of in boys, 405, 407
Homosexuality, 26
  causes of, 144
  determinants of, 427
  effect of sex hormones on, 140
  transitory, 407–427
Honesty, concepts of in adolescence, 268
Hopi culture, preadolescent sex play in, 136
Hormonal imbalance
  and behavioral reactivity, 133, 154
  and emotional instability, 145
  and emotional response, 133
Hormones, determination of in urine, 78

"ID" DRIVES, 24–25
Ideas, inheritance of, 24–25
Identification
  with glamorous figures, 326
  with social class, 332, 333, 334
Ifugao culture, preadolescent sex play in, 136
Immaturity, perceptual, 168–169
  and feelings of omnipotence, 169
  and negativism, 169
  and personality development, 168–169
  and volitional independence, 169
Inadequacy feelings, and emotional insecurity, 145
Incorporative orientation, 199, 201
  and hero worship, 489
  and intellectual maturation, 250
  and moral development, 247–248
  and religious belief, 271
  in school learning, 483, 487, 488–490
Independence, executive
  in adolescence, 179
  in childhood, 172, 185
  in non-satellizers, 210
Independence, volitional, 178, 186
  acquisition of in childhood, 173
  in adolescence, 177
  attributes of, 201
  determinants of, 201
  and ego revaluation, 171
  in non-satellizers, 209–210
  perception of, 168, 169
  and perceptual immaturity, 169
  practice in, 201
  and school, 471, 475–476
Independence-dependence needs, 24, 49
  in Rankian psychology, 29–30
Infantile sexuality, 27
Infectious diseases, in adolescence, 101

Insecurity, feelings of, 54, 56n
    and abrupt onset of adolescence, 59
    and emotional instability, 145
    in infancy, 169–170
Instinct theory, 25
Intellect, effect of pubescence on, 278
Intellectual deficit, and delinquency, 531
Intellectual growth, see Intellectual maturation
Intellectual maturation (adolescent)
    absence of spurt in, 276
    and causal thinking, 286
    continuity of, 276
    and exploratory orientation, 250
    growth curve of, 276
    impact of pubescence on, 276, 277–279
    and incorporative orientation, 250
    increased abstraction in, 285
    increased symbolization in, 285
    and meaningfulness, 491–493
    and moral development, 249–250
    nature of, 285–286
    pattern of, 276
    and personality development, 286–292
    and religious beliefs, 271
    and Rorschach's test, 285
    and school practices, 471, 491–496
    and self-critical ability, 250
    and superstitious beliefs, 286
Intellectualization, 26, 427
    and prolongation of adolescence, 326
Intelligence, see also General intelligence
        and Intellectual maturation
    and academic success, 291
    and adjustment, 289–291, 289n
    and conduct, 265–266
    deficiencies in, 289
        adjustment to, 289
    and honesty, 265–266
    and interest patterns, 288–289
    and moral beliefs, 265
    and moral knowledge, 265
    and motivational habits, 289
    and occupational choice, 291, 448–449,
        455–456
    and occupational success, 291
    and personality traits, 287–288, 288n
    as source of problems, 290
    valuation of by adolescence, 289
    and vocational interests, 448–449
Interests (adolescent)
    and abilities, 288–289, 298–299, 449
    changes in, 134–135, 294
        abruptness of, 294
        influence of pubescence on, 134

    measurement of, 134
        and urinary androgens, 134
    complexity of, 294
    continuity of, 294
    and curriculum organization, 299
    determinants of, 295–296
        ability, 298
        individual proclivities, 298
        intellectual maturation, 295–296
        personality differences, 298–299
        psychobiological, 295
        psychosocial, 295
        pubescence, 295–297
        race, 298
        sex, 296–297
        social class, 298
        social environment, 297–298
        urban-rural residence, 297–298
    and developmental age, 294
    and ego-involvement, 293
    fads in, 295
    general characteristics of, 294–295
    in heterosexual activities, 295
    hobbies, 301
    importance of, 292–294
    as indices of maturity, 293–294
    as indices of personality, 294
    mass media, 300–301
        magazines, 300
        movies, 300–301
        newspapers, 300
        radio, 300–301
        television, 300
    maturity of, 134
        effect of pubescence on, 134
    meaning of, 292–294
    as motives, 292–293
    motives underlying, 293
    nature of in adolescence, 292–301
    and needs, 299
    number of, 295
    as organizers, 293
    patterns of, among bright and dull, 288
        and intelligence, 288–289
    in physical activities, 124–125
    play, 297
    rate of change in, 294
    reading, 300
    in social activities, 295
    in spectator activities, 295
    time for, 295
Intermarriage, adolescent beliefs about,
    426
Introversion-extroversion, 176–177
    changes in adolescence, 361
    and emancipation, 222

Introversion-extroversion—*Cont'd*
modifiability of, 181–182
and social rejection, 374
and vocational choice, 453
Involution, abruptness of onset in, 59
IQ, awareness of, 289
in vocational guidance, 464
Italians, adjustive mechanisms in, 329

JEWS, adjustive mechanisms in, 329
"Job families," 463
"Job prestige," 446–447
agreement about, 446
perception of, 446
social determination of, 446
stability of, 447
and vocational choice, 446–447
Judgment (adolescent)
of causality, 286
effect of emotional instability on, 286
effect of pubescence on, 279, 286
egocentricity in, 285
objectivity of, 285
of relevance, 286
and schooling, 286
and self-critical faculty, 285

KWOMA, adolescent stress among, 405
sexuality among, 396

"LAISSEZ-FAIRE" PRACTICES, in
schools, 480
"Latency" period, 25–27
critique of, 27
Leaders (adolescent), characteristics of,
372
Leadership (adolescent), 369–372
achievement of, 370–371
bases for, 370
compared to friendship, 369
compared to popularity, 369
continuity of, 372
definition of, 370
generality of, 372
"halo-effect" in, 371
maintenance of, 370–371
nature of, 369–370
obligations of, 371
situational aspects of, 371
Leadership (gang)
characteristics of, 380
determinants of, 380
functions of, 380
obligations of, 380
role of leader in, 380

Learning orientation, 202
in childhood, 172
effect of personality maturation on, 483–485
exploratory, 199–200
and guilt feelings, 172
incorporative, 175, 199
individual differences in, 487–491
non-satellizers, 209, 487
satellizers, 487
implications for teaching, 490–491
and personality constancy, 183
in school, 482–483, 483–485
satellizing, 175, 199
Lepacha culture, preadolescent sex play in,
136
Level of aspiration, and frustration, 514
Liberality, in moral values, 248
"Longitudinal" method, 32–37
advantages of, 32–35
definition of, 32
disadvantages of, 34–35
in measuring effects of pubescence, 33–35
Lower-class, adolescent stress in, 404
members of, 328
and premarital intercourse, 409
sex repression in, 399
sexuality in, 392
Loyalty, concepts of during adolescence,
268

MAGAZINE INTERESTS, changes in
adolescence, 300
Manus culture
abruptness of adolescence in, 59
adolescent stress in, 405
biological sex role in, 417
difficulty of adolescence in, 20
marriage in, 19
moral confusion in, 261
psychosexual deevlopment in, 16
sex drives in, 141, 142, 397
sex frustration of girls in, 20
sex repression in, 398, 399
sexuality in, 393–396
sex differences in, 412
social sex role in, 417
Marital difficulties, and sex repression,
401
Masculinity, 88
cultural concepts of, 415
effect of pubescence on, 134–135, 415–416
Masculinity-femininity test, 297

Mass media, 300–301
Masturbation, 18, 399–400
  advantages of, 413
  disadvantages of, 412–413
  evaluation of, 412–413
  fixation of, 400
  frequency of in boys, 405, 407
  frequency of in girls, 409, 410
  in middle-class boys, 400, 404
  in preadolescence, 136
  social class differences in, 407–408
  social tolerance for, 406
Maternal behavior, and menstruation, 148
  and prolactin, 148
Maturation (pubescent), see also Pubescence
  early, advantages of, 149
    disadvantages of, 149–150
    problems of, 148–150
    sex differences in, 150
  late, consequences of, 149–150
    problems of, 148–150
    sex differences in, 150
  rate of, 148–149
Maturation, personality, see Personality maturation
Maturation, spontaneous, 186
Maturational defects, 238–239
Maturational failure, 238–240
  and adjustive drug addiction, 516
  and child rearing practices, 238–243
  classification of, 239
  "developmental", 239–241
  "reactive", 241–243
  and schizophrenia, 516
Maturational retardation, 239
Maturity, meaning of, 238
Meaningfulness, and active learning, 494
  importance for learning, 491
  and intellectual maturation, 491–493
  maximization of, 500–501
  problem of, 491–493
  and responsibility for learning, 494
  role of needs in, 493–494
Measles, in adolescence, 101
Mechanical abilities (in adolescence), 122–124
  compared to gross motor skills, 122–123
  general factor in, 123
  group factors in, 123
  growth of, 122–123
  influence of pubescence on, 122
  intercorrelations among, 123
  nature of, 122

sex differences in, 123–124
  specificity of, 123
  tests of, 123
Medical problems (adolescent), 101–104
Menarche, see also Menstruation and Pubescence
  age of, 74
  compared to first ejaculation, 84
  as criterion of pubescence, 83–84, 92
  as criterion of reproductive capacity, 84
  delayed, 101
  genetic factors in, 74
  psychological significance of, 84
Menopause, effect on sex drive, 137
Menstrual cycle, 84
Menstruation, disorders of, 102
  duration of, 148
    and motherliness, 148
  and estrogens, 84
  irregularity of, 84, 102
  and ovulation, 84
  physical symptoms of, 84
  physiology of, 84
  and progesterone, 84
  psychological reactions to, 152
Mental hospital admissions, in adolescence, 511
Middle-class
  sexuality in, 394–395
  values of, 328
Middle-class boys
  masturbation in, 404
  petting in, 404, 409
  premarital intercourse in, 409
  sex repression in, 400
Middle-class girls, sex repression in, 401
Moral absolutism, 250–251
Moral accountability, see Moral responsibility
Moral agenesis, 529
Moral behavior, growth in consistency of, 249
Moral beliefs (adolescent), 263–268
  acquisition of, 264
  actual, 263–264, 265–266
  changes in, 264
  and cognitive limitations, 266
  community influence on, 264
  conformity of, 264
  expediency of, 265–266, 268
  expressed, 263, 265
  family influence on, 264
  general characteristics of, 264–265
  inconsistency of, 264

Moral beliefs (adolescent)—*Cont'd*
  and intelligence, 265
  and moral knowledge, 265
  and moral reputation, 262
  school influence on, 264
  specificity of, 266–268
Moral conduct, and religious belief, 272
Moral confusion
  among Betsileo, 261
  and delinquency, 526
  among Dobu, 261
  effects of, 261–262
  individual reactions to, 261–262, 338
    in non-satellizers, 262
    in satellizers, 262
  among Manus, 261
  prevalence of, 261
  in primitive cultures, 21
Moral courage (in adolescence), 268
Moral development (adolescent), 246–255
  aberrations in, 256–259
  in adaptive persons, 259
  in defiant persons, 259
  effective of environment on, 259
  and exploratory orientation, 247–248
  and incorporative orientation, 247–248
  homogeneity of, 260
  individual differences in, 255–262
    personality determinants of, 255–259
    and pubescence, 255
    and social class factors, 259–262
    socioeconomic factors, 259–263
    and intellectual maturation, 249–250
  in non-satellizers, 256
  in overdominated child, 258
  in overprotected child, 258
  in overvalued child, 257, 258
  in rejected child, 257
  and school, 471
  in self-directive person, 259
  in submissive person, 258–259
  in underdominated child, 258
Moral knowledge, 265
Moral obligation, 246, 246n, 247
  reciprocity of, 250, 251
  repudiation of, 256–257
  unilaterality of, 250
Moral perfectionism (adolescent), 252
Moral reputation, 262–263
  and character, 262–263
  definition of, 262
  determinants of, 262
  and middle-class values, 262
  and moral beliefs, 262
  and religious observance, 263

  and school achievement, 263, 474
  significance of, 262–263
  and social class status, 263
Moral responsibility, 24
  in adolescence, 179–180
  in childhood, 185
  in non-satellizers, 210
Moral standards (adolescent), 252
Moral values
  age trends in, 249
  changed basis of, 248
  continuity in, 248
  correspondence with parents', 249
  expediency in, 252
  independence of assimilation, 247–248
    and liberal views, 248
    and tolerance, 248
  stereotypy of, 252
  wider social base of, 249
Morbidity, rate of
  during adolescence, 100
  during preadolescence, 100
Mortality, rate of
  in adolescence, 100
  in childhood, 100
  in infancy, 100
  in preadolescence, 100
Motor development, importance, 119–120
  and personality development, 119–120
  and primary status, 120
  and self-esteem, 120
  and skeletal changes, 119
  and social adjustment, 120
  and vocational adjustment, 120
Motor skills, gross
  and coaching, 128–129
  components of, 121
  guidance in, 128–129
  influence of practice on, 121
  and personal-social adjustment, 127–129
  and popularity, 127–128
  and pubescent status, 121
  sex differences in, 121–122, 127
  and strength, 121
Movie interests, adolescent changes in, 300–301
Mumps, 81, 101
Mundugumor culture
  adolescent stress in, 405
  biological sex role in, 417
  psychosexual development in, 17
  sex repression in, 399
  sexuality in, 392, 395, 396
    sex differences in, 412
  social sex role in, 417, 421
Muscle mass, 63

Muscle strength, 63
Muscular development (adolescent), 88
    and androgens, 109–110
    sex differences in, 109–110

NARCISSISM, 427
Navaho culture
    child-adult dichotomy in, 190
    courting behavior in, 425
    discipline in, 235–237
    displacement of conflict in, 231
    guilt feelings in, 253–254
    modifiability of personality in, 181
    obedience in, 202–203, 235
    parent attitudes in, 167–168
    parent-youth conflict in, 233
    personality maturation in, 188
    primary status in, 173, 178, 205
    sanctions for behavior in, 188
    sexuality in, 396
        sex differences in, 412
    shame in, 253–254
    weaning in, 170–171
Negativism
    in adolescence, 179
    and ego devaluation, 172, 179
    in four-year-old, 169
    infant vs. adolescent, 179
    in Negroes, 330
    and perceptual immaturity, 169
    and permissiveness, 186
Negroes
    adjustive mechanisms in, 329–330
    delinquency in, 527n
    negativism in, 330
    personality development in, 329
    submissive behavior in, 330
Neurotic adolescents, parent-child relation-
        ships in, 510
Newspaper interests, in adolescence, 300
Nicknames, and somatic defects, 157
Nihilism, and parent-youth conflict, 232
Non-satellization
    causes of, 208
    consequences of, 208
    and delinquent trends, 528–529
    and ego devaluation, 208
    and personality maturation, 209–211
    and primary status, 210
Non-satellizers, see also Non-satellization
    adequacy feelings in, 208, 211
    adjustive difficulties of, 512, 513
    anxiety in, 489
    behavior disorders in, 515
    conformity in, 357
    ego aspirations in, 208, 209, 211

    ego devaluation in, 208
    executive independence in, 210
    frustration tolerance in, 210
    hero worship in, 489
    learning orientation in, 209, 211n
    moral confusion in, 262
    moral development in, 256–258
    moral responsibility in, 210
    neurotic anxiety in, 211, 513
        and peer group, 211
    personality defects in, 510
    personality maturation in, 208–214
    and prestige authority, 489
    primary status in, 210
    rejected vs. overvalued, 209
    resistance to learning in, 489–491
    school learning in, 487
    security feelings in, 208
    self-critical ability in, 210
    self-esteem in, 211
    teaching practices for, 490–491
    volitional independence in, 209–210
Nutrition (in adolescence)
    and age of pubescence, 75, 81
    disturbances of, 103–104
    requirements of, 103–104
        calcium, 103
        iodine, 102–103
        iron, 103
        protein, 103
        vitamin D, 103

OBEDIENCE
    authoritarian, 235–236
    authority for, 203
    impersonal, 202–203
    among Navaho Indians, 202–203, 235
    and shame, 203
    unconditional, 202
Obesity (in adolescence)
    causes of, 104
    circularity of, 157
    consequences of, 104
    and Cushing's syndrome, 104
    and Fröhlich's syndrome, 104
    psychological consequences of, 159–160
    psychosomatic aspects, 157
    social consequences of, 160
Occupation, and primary status, 437
    and hierarchical status, 437–438
Occupational choice, see Vocational choice
Occupational outlook, and vocational
        choice, 448
Oedipal situation, 25–26
    critique of, 27, 27n

Ojibwa, Canadian, child-adult dichotomy among, 190–191
Omnipotence, and executive dependence, 169
   perception of, 168
   and perceptual immaturity, 169
Omniscience, parental, 192
Ossification (in adolescence), and Vitamin D, 110
Ovaries, 79
Overdominated child
   approach to group experience in, 360–361
   maturational failure in, 241, 243
   moral development of, 258
   social rejection of, 374
Overdomination (parental), 42
   and moral defects, 529–530
   and delinquent trends, 529–530
Overpermissiveness, in schools, 480
Overprotected child
   approach to group experience in, 360–361
   maturational failure in, 240
   moral development in, 258
   social rejection of, 373n, 374
Overprotection (parental), 42
   and moral defects, 529–530
   and personality maturation, 201
Overvalued child, 209
   in adolescence, 213
   approach to group experience in, 360–361
   frustration tolerance in, 213–214
   hedonistic motivation in, 214
   maturational failure in, 241–242
   moral development in, 257–258
   nature of, 213
   neurotic anxiety in, 213, 213n
   reaction to aggression in, 213
   vs. rejected child, 213
   self-critical ability in, 214
   social rejection of, 374
Ovulation, 77, 81, 94
   and menstruation, 84

PARENT ATTITUDES
   and biosocial realities, 167
   among Chamorros, 167
   and child rearing fads, 539
   and delinquent trends, 528–529
   difficulty of changing, 538–539
   and heterosexual adjustment, 427
   ideological basis of, 538
   in infancy, 167

   intercultural differences in, 208
   intracultural differences in, 208
   among Navaho Indians, 167
   and parent-youth conflict, 226–227, 234
   and personality constancy, 182–183
   and primary status needs, 445
   as a psychobiological factor, 42
   psychosocial aspects of, 42
   underlying basis of, 538
   value of changing, 538–539
Parent-child estrangement, 189–192, 198
   among Cheyenne Indians, 190
   consequences of, 192
   and desatellization, 192
   and ego maturation, 192
   and "generation conflict", 195
   among Navaho Indians, 190
   among Ojibwa Indians, 190–191
   in primitive cultures, 189–190
   and rate of social change, 195
   and resatellization, 195
   in rural cultures, 189
   in urban cultures, 189–192
Parent-child relationships
   and approach to group experience, 360
   in delinquent youths, 510
   and heterosexual adjustment, 427
   importance of, 537–539
     for adolescent adjustment, 537–539
     for adolescent guidance, 537–539
   in neurotic youth, 510
   in normal youth, 510
   in psychotic youth, 510
   in schizophrenic youth, 510
Parent-youth conflict
   after adolescence, 224–225
   during adolescence, 224–235
   amelioration of, 539–541
   antecedents of, 224–225
   in boys, 224–225, 227
   caused by adolescent, 228–229
   caused by parent attitudes, 226–227
   caused by restrictive practices, 226–227
   in childhood, 224
   classification of, 234
   consequences of, 234
   due to displacement, 228
   displacement of, 231–232
     and epicureanism, 232
     and existentialism, 232
     intellectual, 231–232
     and international attitudes, 232
     and juvenile delinquency, 232
     among Navaho Indians, 231
     and nihilism, 232

and radicalism, 231–232
and religious heresy, 232, 271
and economic depression, 230
effect of pubescence on, 224
effect of war economy on, 323
father in, 227
and "generation conflict", 229–230
in girls, 224–225, 227
inevitability of, 233
mother in, 227
among Navaho Indians, 233
normality of, 232
outcome of, 235
overt issues of, 225
and parent attitudes, 234
and parent projection, 228
and peer group, 229
prognosis of, 232–235
prognostically favorable, 234
prognostically unfavorable, 234
and rapid social change, 336–337
and ridicule, 227–228
and school, 474
sex differences in, 224–227
and social factors, 230
transitory nature of, 233
underlying causes of, 226–230
and value differences, 229–230
Parent-youth relations, improvement of, 539–541
importance of, 539
Parties, interest in, 342
Pediatrics, field of, 5
Peeking, preadolescent, 136
Peer culture, see Peer group
Peer group (adolescent)
adolescent vs. childhood, 343–344
and aggressive activity, 525
as apprenticeship, 344
in childhood, 191
clique formation in, 350–353
conformity aspects of, 348, 353–358
conformity in, 353–358
and adolescent values, 358–359
advantages of, 354–356
exaggeration of, 354–355
functions of, 354
and group solidarity, 354
nature of, 353
need for, 354–355
reasons for, 353–355, 356
and status marginality, 354–355, 356
and status needs, 354–355
conformity to standards of, 355–358
enforcement of, 355–357

individual differences in, 357–358
and need for uniqueness, 358
as price of acceptance, 355
reinforcing factors, 356
deviant, 376–382
source of membership, 377
varieties of, 376–377
and emancipation, 220, 341
and enforcement of sex norms, 409
functions of, 382–384
and heterosexual relationships, 422
impact on adolescent values, 358–359
and interim status, 206
interpersonal relations in, 359–376
and moral absolutism, 250
non-deviant, 377
and non-satellizers, 211
origins of, 349–350
psychoanalytic theory of, 349
and parent-youth conflict, 229
and prolongation of adolescence, 326
and racial origin, 347
relative status and prestige in, 362–366
basis for, 362–365
continuity of, 365–366
determinants of, 362–363
evaluation of, 362
fluctuations in, 365, 366
measurement of, 362
perception of, 186, 314, 366
and religious affiliation, 347
in school, 471, 482, 496–497
middle-class domination of, 496–497
and social class, 334, 341
and social sex role, 418
and socioeconomic factors, 344–345
as source of interim status, 344
as source of primary status, 191, 221
as source of status, 71–72, 341
structural characteristics of, 341, 348–359
as sublimation, 28, 71
training functions of, 344
and wider community, 343–345
Peer group norms, allegiance to, 356–357
and delinquency, 357
Penis, 77, 80
circumference, 82, 83
diameter, 82
length, 82, 83
measurement of, 82
Perception, of vocational requirements, 456–457
"Perceptual constancy", and personality continuity, 182

Personality, adolescent
  compared with childhood, 177–180
  compared with infancy, 177–180
  continuity with childhood, 179–180
  developmental tasks of, 177–180
  Rank's views of, 178
Personality development
  among anti-Nazi refugees, 181
  in children, 181
Personality development (adolescent)
  and cognitive organization, 291–292
  continuity in, 180–185
    and canalization, 184
    and constitutional factors, 182
    determinants of, 180
    and ego structure, 183
    evidence for, 180–181
    examples of, 180–181
    and feelings of adequacy, 183–184
    and feelings of security, 184
    and genetic factors, 182
    and learning orientation, 183
    and parent attitudes, 182–183
    and "perceptual constancy", 182
    psychological basis of, 182–185
    and "reaction-sensitivity", 184–185
    Rorschach evidence of, 181
  and learning orientation, 287
  modifiability of, 181–182
Personality maturation (adolescent)
  and adult experience, 207
  and attitudinal lag, 204
  and availability of status, 206–207
  and child's ambivalence, 205
  childhood vs. adolescent, 193
  childhood vs. adult, 193
  consummatory factor in, 192–194
  course of, 43
  and cultural factors, 205–208
  cultural regulation of, 189
  cultural uniformities in, 174
  determinants of, 193–194
  and discipline, 237
  effect of war on, 323–324
  and emancipation, 193, 218
  facilitating factors, 200–208
  and familial factors, 189, 200–205
  and frustration, 201–202
  general direction of, 189
  goals of, 174–175
  in home environment, 195
  and learning orientation, 482–485
  in non-satellizers, 208–214
    outcome of, 209–210
  and obedience, 203

  in overvalued children, 213–214
  and parent ambivalence, 204
  and parent attitudes, 200–201
  and parent overprotection, 201
  and parent rivalry, 204
  and parent underdomination, 201–202
  and "perceptual constancy", 204
  preparatory aspects of, 185–192, 193
    determinants of, 186–189
    economic pressures for, 187
    and motor growth, 186
    and parental demands, 187
    and perceptual growth, 186
    and satellization, 185
    social pressures for, 187
  process of, 174–175
  psychobiological uniformities in, 42–43
  and pubescence, 192–194
  in rejected child, 211–213
    outcome of, 211–212
  retarding factors, 200–208
  in rural cultures, 195
  and school, 471
  and school learning, 482–491
  and social expectations, 206–207
  and socioeconomic conditions, 206
  specific cultural aspects of, 189
  tasks of, 176
  and unconditional acceptance, 202
Personality status, adult, 61
  adolescent's misconceptions of, 316
  attainment of, 66, 70, 315–316
    role of pubescence in, 67–68, 69
    unevenness in, 64
  children's misconceptions of, 316
  criteria of, 315
  vs. emancipation, 217–218
  initiation of, 66, 70
  misconceptions concerning, 151
  nature of, 315
  in primitive cultures, 315
  and pubescence, 174
  and "rites of passage," 317
  withholding of, 316
Personality status, childhood, termination
    of, 58–59
Personality status, and emancipation, 224
Personality structure, reorganization of
    174–175
  need for in adolescence, 174–175
Petting, 18, 400
  advantages of, 413
  attitudes of girls toward, 410
  and canalization, 409
  evaluation of, 413

fixation of, 400
frequency of, 407
  in girls, 409–410
  in middle-class boys, 400, 404
  increased tolerance toward, 406
  persistence of in marriage, 409
  social class differences in, 407–408
Physical activities, interest in, 124–126
  during adolescence, 124
  age changes in, 124
  and aging, 125
  causes of loss, 124–125
  consequences of loss, 125
  and motor skills, 124
  sex differences, 124
Physical education program in schools, 125
Placenta, formation of, 84
Pneumonia, in adolescence, 100
Poliomyelitis, in adolescence, 100
Political movements, adolescent participation in, 315, 315n
Population of subjects, representative, xv, xvi, xvin
Post-concussion syndrome, and delinquency, 531
Post-encephalitic Parkinsonism, and delinquency, 532
Prayer, beliefs about in adolescence, 269
Preadolescence, sex activity in, 27
Precocious puberty, 78, 79, 115n
  adolescent growth spurt in, 114
  and adult stature, 113
  causes of, 101–102
  growth in strength in, 118
  intellectual maturation in, 278
  pathological causes of, 79
  sequence in, 95
Pregnancy, in adolescence, 102
  cesarean section in, 102
  toxemia in, 102
Prejudices
  in adolescence, 266–267
    ethnic, 266
    racial, 266–267
    religious, 267
  in childhood, 266
  and education, 267
  and rationality, 267
Premarital intercourse, 18
  attitudes of girls toward, 411
  evaluation of, 413–414
  frequency in boys, 405
  frequency in girls, 410
  increased frequency of, 406
  increased tolerance toward, 406

among Kwama, 20
  in lower-class adolescents, 17
  in middle-class adolescents, 17–18
  among Mundugumors, 17, 20
  in Samoa, 17
  social class differences in, 407–408
Prepubescence
  adrenal cortex in, 79
  corticotropic hormones in, 79
  endocrinological picture in, 79–80
  boys vs. girls, 79–80
  gonadal hormones in, 79
Prepubescent height, and age of pubescence, 81
Prepubescent weight, and age of pubescence, 81
Pressey Interest-Attitude test, 134
Prestige authority
  in non-satellizers, 489
  in satellizers, 489
  in school learning, 484–485, 488
Prestige needs, determinants of, 450
  and vocational choice, 450–451, 456–457
Prestige suggestion, see Prestige authority
Primary sex characteristics, 77, 81–85
  definition of, 81
  deviations in, 158, 161
    counseling about, 159
    importance of, 158
    treatment of, 159
  and masculinity, 158–159
  psychological reactions to, 152
  and sex drive, 158–159
Progesterone, and menstruation, 84
Projection, 42
Prolactin, and maternal behavior, 148, 421
Promiscuity, sexual, 402
Psychobiological problems
  definition of, xiii
  nature of, 311–312
Psychological change, rate of in adolescence, 6
Psychological transition
  abruptness of onset, 41, 57–59
  absolute, 53
  anxiety in, 41
  and attitudinal change, 54
  cultural differences in, 45
  difficulty of, 45, 57, 59
  and disorientation, 41, 54
  duration of, 57
  and marginality, 53–54, 55
  nature of, 41, 55
  precipitating factors, 65–69
  in childhood, 68–69

Psychological transition—*Cont'd*
  precipitating factors—*Cont'd*
    consummatory, 66
    individual, 66
    physiological, 66, 67
    preparatory, 66, 67
    in Samoa, 68
    social, 66–67
  preparation for, 57–59
  prolongation of, 45
  properties of, 41
  and pubescence, 67–68
  quantitative differences in, 45
  relative, 53
  resistance to, 54
  temporal dimensions of, 57–59
  unevenness of, 41
"Psychology of Ego-Involvements", xiii
Psychosexual development
  among Arapesh, 16
  boys vs. girls, 410
  comparative, 15–22
  fixation in, 27
  in lower-class, 17
  among Manus, 16
  in middle class, 17
  among Mundugumors, 17
  psychoanalytic theory of, 25–29
  puritanical, 16
  rate of, 394
  among Samoans, 17
Psychosocial problems
  of American adolescents, 313
  categories of, 312
  definition of, xiv
  nature of, 311–313
Psychosomatic disorders, 156–157
  circularity of, 157
  frequency of in adolescence, 153–154
Psychosomatic relationships, 153
Psychotherapy, vocational aspects of, 459–460
Psychotic adolescents, 510
Puberty rites, 316
  sex differences in, 316
Pubescence
  vs. adolescence, 73
  and adult sexuality, 396
  as in age interval, 93
  age of onset, 74, 93
    and adult stature, 113–114, 116
    effect of climate on, 75
    effect of general health on, 75
    effect of nutrition on, 75
    influence of environment on, 73–75
    factors associated with, 81

age range of, in boys, 92–93
  in girls, 92–93
and biological sex role, 416–417
as catalytic agent, 193
chronology of, 74, 75, 92
and clique membership, 351–352
constancy in, 73–75
as constellation of changes, 93
and courting behavior, 422
criteria of, 92, 93–94
definition of, 73, 93
and delinquency rates, 518
effect on intellect, 278
effect on interests, 296–297
effect on judgment, 278
and emancipation, 217, 219, 221
environmental influence on, 74–75
evaluation of, 94
genetics of, 73–75
and heterosexual interests, 296, 296n, 422
and hormonal disequilibrium, 96
impact on social sex role, 415–417
in infra-humans, 75
initiation of, 78–81
  role of endocrines in, 78–81
and initiation of personality change, 42
and intellectual maturation, 276, 277–279
measurement of effects of, 33–34
and moral development, 256
nature of, 73–78
and occupational status, 438
onset of, 92–93
and personality maturation, 192–194
phylogenetic nature of, 73–75
physiological changes in, 95–99
precocious, *see* Precocious puberty
in primitive cultures, 75–76
as a psychobiological problem, 75–76
psychological correlates of, 133–134
and religious awakening, 270
sequence in, 73, 92, 94–95
  phylogenetic invariability of, 94
  and tissue responsiveness, 95
temporal aspects of, 92–95
variability in, 73–75
and vocational choice, 440
Pubescent changes, levels of, 76–78
Pulse pressure, during adolescence, 98
Pulse rate during adolescence, 98
  and exercise, 98
  sex difference in, 98
Pupils
  perception of by teachers, 476–477
  perceptions of teachers, 477–478

RACIAL DISCRIMINATION, and delinquency, 527
and "street-corner" gangs, 378–379
"Racial unconscious", theory of, 24
Radicalism, and parent-youth conflict, 231–
232
Radio interests, adolescent changes in,
300–301
Rate of growth
discrepancies in, 57, 61–65
causes of in adolescence, 62–63, 64
consequences of, 64–65
emotional, 62
genetic determinants of, 62
genital, 63
hormonal determinants of, 62–63
intellectual, 62, 63
interrelatedness of, 63
lymphoid, 63
parallelism in, 63
physical, 62
physiological, 62
social, 62
unevenness in, 63–64
Rationalization, 146
Reaction-formation, 257
"Reaction-sensitivity", and personality continuity, 185
Reading interests (adolescent), 300
Recapitulation, biological, Haeckel's theory
of, 11–12
Recapitulation, psychological
G. S. Hall's theory of, xii, 10–13, 24
Rousseau's theory of, 11
Regression, 146
Rejected child
in adolescence, 209, 211–213
approach to group experience, 360–361
delinquent trends in, 528–529
maturational failure in, 243
moral development in, 257–258
neurotic anxiety in, 212
vs. overvalued child, 213
in peer group, 212
reaction to aggression, 212
satellizing trends in, 212
socialization of, 212
social rejection of, 374
withdrawal in, 212–213
Rejection (parental), 42
and satellization, 171
Religion, status of in adolescence, 268–272
impact of adolescence on, 270–272
and intellectual maturation, 271
and personality, 271–272
Religious activity, as displacement, 272
Religious affiliation, and peer group, 347

Religious awakening
age of, 270
and pubescence, 270
nature of, 270–271
Religious beliefs (adolescent), 268–270
and college attendance, 269
denominational differences in, 270
and emancipation, 271–272
and exploratory orientation, 271
and incorporative orientation, 271
and intellectual maturation, 271
and intelligence, 270
and moral conduct, 272
and personality structure, 272
radical, 270
and resatellization, 272
and satellizing orientation, 271
sex differences in, 268, 270
social class differences in, 269
urban-rural differences in, 268
Religious conflicts, in adolescence, 270
Religious conversion, see Religious awakening
Religious heresy, and parent-youth conflict, 232
Religious observance (adolescent), 269
denominational differences in, 269
and moral reputation, 263, 272
sex differences in, 269
Religious orthodoxy, and mode of thinking, 272
and value assimilation, 272
Repression, 42
Resatellization, 194–197
and emancipation, 220–221
and parent-child estrangement, 195
and religious activity, 272
in rural cultures, 195
in Samoa, 195
in urban cultures, 195
Respiratory changes (adolescent), 77, 99
in rate, 99
sex differences, 99
in volume, 99
Responsibility, concepts of in adolescence,
268
Retarded puberty, see Delayed puberty
Rheumatic fever, in adolescence, 101
Rickets, 99
"Rites of passage," 317
Rituals, adolescent, 414
Rivalry, parental, 204
Romantic behavior, 424–425
Rorschach's test
and adolescent emotionality, 146
and conformity trends, 249
and intellectual maturation, 285

Rorschach's test—*Cont'd*
 and personality continuity, 181
 and personality development, 177
Rote learning, in adolescence, 491–492
Rural residence, *see* Urban-rural residence

SAMOAN CULTURE
 adolescent stress in, 404
 boy-girl relations in, 19
 initiation of adolescence in, 68, 68n
 personality maturation in, 195
 postponement of sex activity in, 19
 psychosexual development in, 17
 sex activity in, 400
 sex drive in, 397
 sex morality in, 431
 sexuality in, 391, 394–396
Sanctions, behavioral, 188
Satellization
 and attitudes, 172
 consequences of, 172
 and ego devaluation, 172
 extreme, 203
 and extrinsic valuation, 171
 and learning, 172
 origin of, 171
 and parental acceptance, 171
 and parental rejection, 171
 prerequisites for, 171
 undermining of, 173
 and value assimilation, 172
Satellizers
 adjustive difficulties of, 512–513
 approach to group experience in, 360
 delinquent trends in, 529–530
 and drug addiction, 512–513
 hero worship in, 488
 maturational failure in, 512–513
 and moral confusion, 262
 moral development in, 258
 personality defects in, 511
 and prestige authority, 488
 resistance to learning in, 482, 490
 teaching practices for, 490–491
Satellizing orientation, 119
 nature of, 488
 and religious belief, 271
 and school learning, 484, 487
Scaling (test), 276n
Schizophrenic adolescents, 510
School
 adolescent's evaluation of, 499–500
 authoritarianism in, 478–480
  impact on adolescent development,
   478–480
  effect on group morale, 479–480
  pupil's reaction to, 479
 and "cultural lag," 471

democratic discipline in, 480–481
 and derived status, 473
 and desatellization, 192
 desirable changes in, 500–501
 dissatisfaction with, 499
  age trends in, 499
  reasons for, 499–500
 and emancipation, 192, 471
 general functions of in adolescence,
  472–473
 and heterosexual relationships, 471, 482
 influence of adolescence on, 471
 and intellectual maturation, 471
 "laissez faire" practices in, 480
 and moral growth, 471
 and parent-youth conflict, 474
 and peer group, 471, 482
 and personality maturation, 471
 and primary status, 191, 471–475
 and social class, 334, 471, 496–499
 as source of derived status, 191
 survival in, 499
 ultrapermissiveness in, 480
 and volitional independence, 471, 475–
  476
School achievement
 and moral reputation, 263, 474
 and pupil adjustment, 476, 476n
 and sociometric status, 474
School grouping, and pubescence, 278
School learning
 and current adolescent concerns, 485–48[?]
 current value of, 485–486
 and exploratory orientation, 483–484
 and incorporative orientation, 483
 and individual differences, 487–491
 and prestige authority, 484–485
 resistance to learning, 488–491
 and satellizing orientation, 485
 and social class, 498
School marks
 abuse of, 486
 functions of, 486
 as indices of academic success, 486
 as indices of vocational progress, 486
 as sources of primary status, 486
Schooling, extended, 494–495
 effects of, 320
 need for, 494–495
 and occupational security, 320
Sebaceous glands, 90–91
 and acne, 91
 functions of, 91
 pathology of, 91
Secondary sex characteristics, 77, 85–92
 and adrenal cortex, 86
 anatomic basis of, 86
 continuous distribution of, 85

definition of, 85
importance of, 85
inappropriate, 486
overlapping between sexes in, 85–86
pathology of, 86
physiological basis of, 86
vs. primary sex characteristics, 85
psychological reactions to, 152
Secretiveness, 326
Security, feelings of, 24
in childhood, 172
and personality continuity, 183–184
sources of, 201
Segregation of sexes, 422–423
"Selective morality," 261
Self, centrality of in adolescence, 176–177
Self-critical ability, 201n
and conscience, 247
and frustration, 514
inhibition of, 257
and intellectual maturation, 247, 250
in non-satellizers, 210
in overvalued child, 214
Self-critical faculty, see Self-critical ability
Self-discipline, 238
Self-esteem, 24, 201
and aspirations for status, 55
definition of, 55
determinants of, 55
and prolongation of adolescence, 324
in satellizers, 211
threats to, 55
and transitional anxiety, 55
Senescence, abruptness of onset, 59
Sex activity (adolescent), 136–137
cultural variability in, 136–137
cultural regulation of, 394–396
in infra-humans, 136
postponement of, 64, 65
vs. preadolescent, 27, 136–138
premature, 64, 65
Rankian interpretation of, 29–30
sex differences in, 395
social class differences in, 27
substitutive, 65
Sex awareness, 136–142
Sex behavior, cultural variability of, 396–401
Sex conflict, and adolescent stress, 404
among Arapesh, 404
among Kwama, 405
in lower-class, 404
among Manus, 405
among Mundugumors, 405
in Samoa, 404
Sex delinquency, 427, 519–520
and biological sex role, 144
causes of, 520–521

interpretation of, 520–521
and pubescence, 520n
sex differences in, 520–521
in World War II, 521
Sex drives
actualization of, 140
agenesis vs. repression, 141, 398
among Arapesh, 141, 397
differentiated from sex hormones, 138
effect of castration on, 139–140
effect of menopause on, 139
emergent, 136, 178
in eunuchs, 140
insistence of, 402
and personality maturation, 402
in Manus girls, 141, 397
mechanism of hormonal action on, 140
in middle-class males, 141
nature of, 138–139
patterning of, 15
and postpuberal castration, 137
in prepubescent castrates, 396
psychoaffectional, 141–142
psychophysiological, 81, 141–142
repressibility of, 141
repression of, see Sex repression
in Samoan girls, 397
and sex hormones, 133–134, 138–141,
    396–397
in subprimates, 139
in women, 139
socialization of, 178
Sex education, 428–432
general program of, 429–432
characteristics of, 429–432
developmental aspects of, 429–430
ethical aspects of, 430–432
methods of, 430
need for in schools, 428–429
outcome of, 432
Sex experimentation, 428
in preadolescence, 27
Sex expression (adolescent), varieties of,
405–414
Sex guidance, 432–433
Sex hormones, 133–134, 138–141, 396–397
see also Gonadal hormones
actualization of into drives, 140
and adult sexuality, 396
and affectional responses, 148
and anxiety, 148
and biological sex role, 143
and fear behavior, 148
effects on behavior, 15
relation to sex drives, 133–134, 138–
141, 396–397
Sex information, 428–429

Sex interests, in adolescence, 137
  adolescent vs. preadolescent, 136–137
  in infra-humans, 136
Sex needs
  psychoaffectional, management of, 432–433
  psychophysiological, management of, 432–433
Sex outlets
  and age of pubescence, 405–406
  evaluation of, 412–414
  female
    compared to male, 409
    frequency of, 409
    regularity of, 409
    types of, 409–410
  male
    age of maximal, 406
    frequency of, 405–406
    low, 398
    regularity of, 405
    social class differences in, 407
    types of, 406–407
  substitutive, 65
Sex play, adult vs. childhood, 137–138
  preadolescent, 136–137
Sex problems, frequency of, 428
Sex repression, 71, 141
  and anxiety, 26
  effects of, 399–401
    among Arapesh, 398–399
    and asceticism, 400
    in lower-class, 399
    among Manus girls, 398, 399
    in middle class boys, 400, 404
    in middle class girls, 401, 404
    among Mundugumors, 399
    and overintellectualization, 400
    and preoccupation with sex, 400
    on self-esteem, 400
    and emotional instability, 15–22, 26, 398, 403–404
    and fixation of masturbation, 400
    and fixation of petting, 400
    and marital difficulties, 401
Sexual intercourse, in preadolescents, 136
Sexual maturation, early, 101
  late, 101
Sexual promiscuity, 30
Sexuality
  adult, 137, 396
    definition of, 396
    determinants of, 396
  adolescent, importance of, 402–405
    overvaluation of, 405
    Rank's views of, 402
  in childhood, 137–138

  control of, 402
  cultural orientation toward, 390–396
    among Arapesh, 393, 396
    among Kwama, 396
    in lower-class, 392, 408
    among Manus, 393–394, 395, 396
    in middle-class, 394, 395, 408
    among Mundugumors, 392, 395, 396
    among Navaho Indians, 396
    in Samoa, 391, 394, 395, 396
    Victorian, 393
  "double standard" of, 396
  infantile, 27
  postpubescent, 137, 396
    vs. prepubescent, 137–138, 397–398
  psychoaffectional, 391, 391n, 392, 393, 394, 395, 397, 410, 416
  psychophysiological, 391, 391n, 392, 393, 394, 395, 397, 410, 411
  psychosocial aspects of, 396
  sex differences in, 411–412
Shame
  as a behavioral sanction, 188
  as discipline, 237
  and guilt, 253–255
  guiltless, 255
  among Navaho Indians, 253–254
  and obedience, 203
Shoulders, broadening of, 88, 117
"Skeletal age," and adult stature, 110
  and age of pubescence, 110
  as index of sex maturity, 110
  sex differences in, 110
Skeletal growth
  in adolescence, determinants of, 108
    and hormonal stimulation, 81, 108
    importance of, 108
    kinds of changes, 108
    and pubescent cycle, 108
    qualitative changes, 109–110
    sex differences, 108
    tissues involved, 108
  in childhood, 112
  duration of, 111
  in infancy, 112
  in preadolescent, 112
  unevenness of, 111–112
Skin color, and caste, 328, 329, 329n
Slum areas
  and delinquency, 526–528
  socioeconomic deprivation in, 526–527
  and "street-corner" gangs, 378
Slum-dwellers (adolescent)
  delinquency in, 382
  gang membership in, 382
  values of, 382
Snobbishness, 352–353

Social change
  and "cultural lag," 337
  impact of on adolescence, 336–338
  and parent-child estrangement, 195
  and parent-youth conflict, 336–337
  as a psychosocial problem, 45
  rate of, 195
  in primitive cultures, 21
Social class, and adolescent development, 331–333
  and adjustive techniques, 332
  and clique formation, 351
  definition of, 327–328
  effect on IQ, 280–281, 284
  effect on moral development, 260–261
  and emotional instability, 509
  and interest patterns, 291
  and motivation, 332, 498
  negative aspects of, 332–333
  and norms of aggression, 525
  and peer group, 347
  and personality type, 331–332
  and reputation, 263
  and school, 334, 334n, 471, 496–499
  and school "drop-outs," 498–499
  and social sex role, 418
  and status deprivation, 332
  and vocational choice, 445–447
Social classes
  barriers between, 333
  identification with, 332–334
  interaction between, 333–335
  overlapping between, 333
  and peer group, 334
  segregation of, 333
    sex differences in, 333–334
  teacher membership in, 334
Social class status, perception of, 169, 186, 314, 317
Social class structure and adolescent development, 327–331
Social class values, 327–328
  diffusion of, 334–335
  internalization of, 335
  and transitional anxiety, 335
  transmission of, 335–336
    role of peer group in, 335–336
Social experience, see Group experience
Social hygiene, of adolescence, 541–542
Socialization, by age-mates
  consequences of, 196
  and demagogy, 196
  and desatellization, 196
  effect on self-evaluation, 196
  effect on social change, 196
  and emancipation, 219–220
  and exploratory orientation, 200

  and guilt feelings, 253–255
  and parent devaluation, 196
  and resatellization, 194–195
  in rural cultures, 195
  in urban cultures, 194–195
Socialization, by parent, 195–196
  and emancipation, 219
Socially rejected adolescents
  characteristics of, 373–374
  classification of, 373
  completeness of, 375
  and deviancy, 372–373
  evaluation of, 374–375
  frequency of, 373
  management of, 375–376
  perception of, 375
  prognosis of, 376
Social mobility, 338
  and courting beliefs, 426
  and occupational status needs, 463
  and prolongation of adolescence, 439
  and vocational choice, 447, 454, 454n
Social movements, 315, 315n
Social order (the), awareness of in adolescence, 313–315
  contact with in adolescence, 313–315
Social sex role, 22
  adolescent vs. adult, 417–418
  American, 417
  Arapesh, 417, 421
  and biological sex role, 417
  biological or social determination of, 415, 420–421
  components of, 414, 415
  definition of, 414
  differentiation of, 414–421
  difficulty of, 418–419
    sex differences in, 418–420
  female, conflict in, 419–420
    cultural confusion in, 419–420
  hierarchical aspects of, 414–415
  identification with, 416
  impact of pubescence on, 415–417
  among Manus, 417
  among Mundugumors, 417
  nature of, 414
  overlapping of, 414
  polarization of, 417
  sex differences in 418–420
  in Soviet Union, 421
  among Tchambuli, 421
  training for, 414
  transitional, 417–418
  transmission of, 418, 420–421
    by peer group, 418
  and vocational choice, 443
Social skills, and peer group status, 363

Social stratification, *see* Social class
Sociempathy, 169, 177, 366
    definition of, 366
    determinants of, 366
    sex differences in, 366
    and sociometric status, 186, 314, 366
    of teachers, 476
Sociometric cleavage
    on ethnic, racial lines, 266, 347
    on sex lines, 347–348
    on social class lines, 266, 347
Sociometric status, awareness of, 169, 177
    and school achievement, 474
Sociometric techniques, 362
Somatic changes
    adjustment to, 150–153
    embarrassment about, 150
    perceptual reactions to, 150–151
    personality reactions to, 151–152
Somatic defects
    auditory, 154
    cardiac, 154
    and ego damage, 155
    orthopedic, 154
    peer group reaction to, 154–155
    psychological concomitants of, 154–156
    self-reaction to, 155
    sensory, 154–155
    social consequences of, 154–155
    and social immaturity, 155–156
    and threshold of reactivity, 154
    visual, 154
Somatic deviations
    adjustment to, 153–164
    vs. defects, 157
    differential reactions to, 162
    effect on personality, 153
    effect on self-concept, 153
    exaggeration of importance of, 163
    frequency of, 157–159
    guidance concerning, 163–164
    and heterosexual effectiveness, 161
        sex differences in, 161
    importance of in adolescence, 160–162
    and peer group status, 161
    seriousness of outcome, 162–164
    types of, 157–159
Soviet Union, social sex roles in, 421
Spectator activities, 124
Spermatazoa, production of, 77, 81
Standards, internalization of, 187
Stanford-Binet test, 277
Stature, short, consequences of, 159
    tall, 159
Status, adult, *see* Personality Status, adult
Status, derived, 55–58, 211n
    definition of, 58n
    displacement of, 197

and emancipation, 227
origin of, 171
and peer group, 191
peripheral or central, 193
and school, 191, 473
sex differences in, 418
subsidiary sources of, 183–184
withdrawal of, 221
Status, hierarchical, 437–438
Status, interim, 197, 206, 315
    and duration of adolescence, 60–61
    instability of, 61
    limitations of, 61
    nature of, 60, 61
    and peer group, 206, 315, 344
    purposes of, 61
    in schools, 315
Status, marginality of, 53–55, 61
Status, occupational, needs for, 462, 462n
    psychobiological aspects of, 438
    psychosocial aspects of, 439
    and pubescence, 438
    and social mobility, 447
    and vocational guidance, 462–463
    and vocational satisfaction, 462
Status, primary, 184, 186, 211n
    in adolescence, 177, 180
    availability of, 205
        in primitive cultures, 205
        in rural cultures, 205
        in Western civilization, 205
    in childhood, 58, 69, 173, 173n
    childhood vs. adult, 58
    cultural differences in, 198
    definition of, 58n
    and desatellization, 197–199
    and ego revaluation, 177
    and group activity, 342–343
    in the home, 197
    and motor development, 120
    nature of, 198
    among Navaho Indians, 198
    needs for, 198, 359–360
    in non-satellizer, 210
    and occupation, 437
    and parent attitudes, 445
    and peer group, 191
    peripheral or central, 193
    and school, 471, 473–475
    and school achievement, 191
    sex differences in, 418
    societal norms of, 198
    sources of in childhood, 191
    and vocational choice, 440
    and vocational interest, 440
    and volitional independence, 179
Status, transitional, 198–199

Strength (adolescent)
  and adrenal cortex, 119
  and androgens, 119
  causes of changes in, 118, 119
  and cultural conditioning, 119
  growth in, 118–119
  and hormonal stimulation, 118
  and motor development, 118
  and pubescent status, 118, 121
  in precocious puberty, 118
  sex differences in, 118, 119
  and thymus gland, 119
Sterility, in adolescence, 84
Stress (psychological) in adolescence
  Dollard's views on, 71
  initial, 71
  reasons for, 71–72
  and sex conflict, 404–405
  somatic concomitants of, 156–157
  stages of, 71–72
  and transitional anxiety, 71
Strong Vocational Interest blank, 442
Subadulthood, prolongation of, 205–206
Sublimation, 25, 26, 28, 71
  and artistic efforts, 28–29
  critique of theory of, 28–29, 71–72, 399
  in middle-class youths, 28–29
Suicide, incidence of in adolescence, 511
"Superego," formation of, 25
Superstitions
  age trends in, 267
  historical trends in, 267
  and school instruction, 267
Sweat glands (in pubescence), 90, 91

TCHAMBULI CULTURE, sex role in, 421
Teacher behavior
  effect on learning, 483
  and pupils' learning orientation, 482–483
  pupils' reaction to, 482–483
  and school achievement, 483
Teachers
  favoritism by, 497–498
  perceived role of, 478
  perceptions of pupils, 476–477
  perceptions of by pupils, 476–477
  social class values of, 334
Teaching, as a profession, 452
Television, adolescent interest in, 300
Testes, 77, 79
  volume of, 82, 83
Thymus gland, 63
  in adolescence, 96–97
  in childhood, 97
  functions of, 96–97
  and growth in strength, 118
  and lymphatic growth, 97

  and muscular strength, 97
  relation to adrenal cortex, 96–97
  and sexual maturation, 96
  and skeletal growth, 96
Thyroid gland, in adolescence, 97
  and basal metabolic rate, 97
Time perspective, in adolescence, 162
Tissue growth, in adolescence, 117
Tissue responsiveness, 80
Tolerance, in moral values, 248
Toxemia of pregnancy, in adolescence, 102
Trobriand culture, preadolescent sex play in, 136, 138
Truancy, 326
Tuberculosis, in adolescence, 99, 100, 101

UNDERDOMINATED CHILD
  approach to group experience, 360–361
  maturational failure in, 240
  moral development in, 258
  social rejection of, 374
Underdomination (parental), 42
  and delinquent trends, 529–530
  and personality maturation, 201
Underprotection (parental), 42
Unemployment, as a psychosocial problem, 45
Upper-class, values of, 327–328
Urban-rural residence
  and adolescent development, 330–331
  and age of marriage, 331
  and emancipation, 330
  and rate of social change, 330
  and religious beliefs, 331
  and resatellization, 330
  and socialization, 330
  and source of status, 330
Uterus, 77, 80

VALUATION, extrinsic (parental), and satellization, 171
Values
  assimilation of, 24, 247–248
  conflicts in, 45
  consistency in, 260–261
  impact on peer group, 358–359
  "official," 260
  as a psychosocial problem, 45
  and religious orthodoxy, 272
Vellus, 88
Visceral growth, 81
Vocational adjustment, 458, 460
Vocational aptitude tests
  generality of, 464
  limitations of, 464–465
  validity of, 464
  and vocational guidance, 464–465

Vocational choice
  compared to paternal occupation, 454, 454n
  deliberation in, 457
  determinants of, 442–453
    family pressures, 444–445
    individual differences, 448–453
    job prestige, 446–447
    before pubescence, 442
    social class factors, 445–447
    social mobility, 447
    social sex role, 443–444
    socioeconomic, 448
    urgency of employment, 447
  developmental changes in, 439–442
    abruptness of, 440–441
    bright vs. dull, 440
    continuity in, 441
    discontinuity in, 441
    motivational orientation, 440
    nature of, 441
    before pubescence, 441
    reasons for, 439
    sex differences, 440
  and developmental maturity, 439
  evaluation of, 453–458
    reality level, 453–455
    relation to factual knowledge, 455–457
  "expressed," 454, 454n
  expression of, 443
  freedom of, 457, 461, 462
  "ideal," 454, 454n
  influence of pubescence on, 440
  informational basis of, 455–456
  and intelligence, 456
  interest in, 437
    age trends, 437
  and interests, 455
  parental influence on, 444–445
  and perception, 457
  postponement of, 443
  pressures for early decision, 456
  and primary status, 440
  in primitive cultures, 21
  and scholastic achievement, 450
  similarity to parents', 444
  and social sex role, 443–444
  stability of, 441
  and transitional anxiety, 445
Vocational counseling, 460
Vocational expectations, 454, 454n
Vocational goals, reality of, 177
Vocational guidance
  clarification of goals in, 460–462
  foci of concern in, 460–465
    determination of specific choice, 463–465

    occupational status needs, 462–463
    need for, 458–459
    vs. psychotherapy, 459–460
    role of school in, 458–459
Vocational information, and vocational choice, 455–456
Vocational information programs
  effectiveness of, 461
  function of, 461
  improvement of, 461
  individualization of, 461
Vocational interests
  and abilities, 449–450
  canalization of, 441
  developmental changes, in, 440
  as indices of personality, 452
  and intelligence, 449–450
  origin of, 452
  and personality structure, 451–452
  and primary status, 440
  rate of change in, 442
  stability of, 441–442
  underlying motivations of, 451
  and vocational choice, 451–452
Vocational interest inventories
  rationale of, 451
  reliability of, 442
  use in vocational guidance, 463–464
  and vocational satisfaction, 463
  and vocational success, 463–464
Vocational problems, importance of, 437
Vocational roles, sex differences in, 418
Vocational satisfaction, 457
  and occupational status needs, 462
  and vocational interests, 464
Vocational status, see Status, occupational
Vocational success, and vocational interests, 463–464
Vocational try-outs, 465
Voice changes (adolescent), 77, 91–92

WAR, as a psychosocial problem, 45
War economy
  effect on adolescents, 323–324
  effect on parent-youth conflict, 323
  and vocational choice, 448
Weaning
  among Navaho Indians, 170–171
  among Chamorros, 170–171
Wetzel grid technique, 117
Withdrawal, 42, 325–326
  and emotional instability, 146
Work, distinction from play, 189, 189n
Work experience programs, 465–467
  role of school in, 466–467, 466n
  values of, 465–466

YOUTH MOVEMENTS, 327